International and EU Aviation Law

International and EU Aviation Law

Selected Issues

Edited by

Elmar M. Giemulla
and
Ludwig Weber

Wolters Kluwer
Law & Business

Published by:
Kluwer Law International
PO Box 316
2400 AH Alphen aan den Rijn
The Netherlands
Website: www.kluwerlaw.com

Sold and distributed in North, Central and South America by:
Aspen Publishers, Inc.
7201 McKinney Circle
Frederick, MD 21704
United States of America
Email: customer.service@aspenpublishers.com

Sold and distributed in all other countries by:
Turpin Distribution Services Ltd.
Stratton Business Park
Pegasus Drive, Biggleswade
Bedfordshire SG18 8TQ
United Kingdom
Email: kluwerlaw@turpin-distribution.com

Printed on acid-free paper.

ISBN 978-90-411-2645-0

Printed and Bound by CPI Group (UK) Ltd, Croydon, CR0 4YY.

Summary of Contents

Table of Contents

Chapter 6
Liability in International Law (Private Air Law) **223**
Elmar M. Giemulla and Heiko van Schyndel

Preface

In presenting selected issues of international and EU aviation law, this book covers the subject matter primarily in terms of aviation law subjects while making references to aspects of aviation policy where appropriate. It is intended to serve not only as a reference tool, but also as source of more detailed information on key subjects of interest for legal practitioners, the academic community and in particular students of aviation law. We hope that this book will contribute to familiarizing a larger number of readers, not only specialists, with international and EU aviation law and related policy and regulatory issues.

The subject matter is presented in two parts. Part I is entitled 'Issues of Worldwide Aviation Law' and deals with those subjects which are legally regulated on a worldwide basis, including the Chicago Convention system, the Warsaw Convention system and other important subjects. The chapter describing the transition from regulation to deregulation (Chapter 4) is also presented in this part, since deregulation policies and Open Skies Agreements are no longer considered regional in nature, but have been adopted in many parts of the world. Part II, Issues of EU Aviation Law', covers most relevant aspects of EU Aviation Law.

The authors who have contributed to this book are recognized experts in their respective fields. While the book as a whole is the result of a cooperative effort, each author is responsible for his part. The list of authors and their respective contributions is to be found at page ii.

The various chapters reflect the fact that aviation law is in a state of rapid change. Several tendencies can be observed in relation to contemporary international and national aviation law. Firstly, the sustained efforts of governments, airlines and private industry to improve aviation safety and security has resulted in an increasing number of national regulations and international rules related to safety and security seeking to implement best practices. In the field of aviation safety, they are to the extent possible based on consensus. In the fields of aviation security, air transport regulation, and bilateral air transport agreements, such consensual rulemaking is mostly not feasible and more classical procedures are used. Secondly, in the field of economic regulation, the divide between deregulation – liberalization policies at the one hand and protectionist policies on the other hand is giving way to innovative thinking and new forms of cooperation, which take account of the specific interests of the players involved. The 'horizontal agreements' between the European Union and numerous non-European countries are examples in this regard. Thirdly, at the national level, governments are increasingly willing to adapt their national aviation legislation and regulations to regional and sub-regional requirements and policies, in pursuit of regional and sub-regional harmonization for the benefit of an improved air transport system in the region.

The contributors attempt to present these and other contemporary developments against the background of classical aviation law and regulation. They do not lay claim to reflect the subject in an exhaustive manner, since it was necessary to set priorities and focus on certain issues while leaving aside others.

The contributors have taken into account developments until spring 2011 as far as possible.

The Editors

Part I

Fundamentals of International Aviation Law: Selected Issues

Chapter 1

Chicago System: Genesis and Main Characteristics

Elmar M. Giemulla

I. GENERAL

Aviation is a transnational, border-crossing phenomenon. Without aviation, the globalization of the flow of people and goods, and of the mixing of cultures would have been impossible. Without aviation, the global awareness that we all live together on one planet could not have developed.

The contrast between this modern awareness and the virtually archaic organizational principle of humans – the principle of national sovereignty – could hardly be starkly. A limited number of people (a nation) live on a limited part of Earth's surface (the national territory) and not only claim this area exclusively to themselves, but also claim that it provides the only legitimation to be entitled to exercise legal power (government) on this limited area. This archaic principle is generally known as 'Sovereignty of Nations' or 'Self-Determination of the Peoples' and is based on the assumption that humans are still organized into 'tribes' that have settled, but that such settlement is the exact reason why they claim exclusiveness of all powers for themselves on the part of Earth's surface that they have occupied.

It is no contradiction to this principle that there are countries that unite, or at least try to unite, several such tribes under the umbrella of one (sometimes artificial) nation ('nation building'). Quite the opposite is true: it is a confirmation and

Elmar M. Giemulla & Ludwig Weber, *International and EU Aviation Law: Selected Issues*, pp. 3–62.

reinforcement of the principle of self-determination of the peoples and the peacemaking nature of this principle when the attempt is made to create organizational units that are better prepared to face the modern economic, social, and political challenges in a way that takes the right of self-determination of the individual tribes into account. These examples are mainly found in Africa, Asia, and the Middle East, but Europe can also be mentioned in this context.

The consequences of this archaic organization principle are obvious: although there are so-called areas of international sovereignty in the world, that is, areas that are not claimed by anyone (especially the high seas), there are no areas that are considered 'mutual property for all of mankind', even though this is sometimes suggested for obvious political reasons.[1] Accordingly, airspace is not such 'mutual property for all humans' either, although this would be a basis that would make many things easier in terms of the legal organization of aviation. However, it would also create a number of problems. Humans would, for example, have mutual sovereignty over the airspace, but this would mean that humans would also have to create the relevant organizational structures to effectively exercise this mutual sovereignty.

Considering the airspace as international sovereign territory – similar to the high seas – would, on the one hand, lead to freedoms of air not having to be explicitly granted (the global airspace would then be a global open sky). On the other hand, this would create the problem of which sovereign power would be entitled to define and implement the regulations that would have to be followed when using the airspace.

This discussion was held at the beginning of the last century, based on the two opposing notions of the 'principle of freedom of the air' and the 'principle of sovereignty of the air'. Fauchille (1901)[2] and the *Institut de droit international* (1911) were of the opinion that – in accordance with the principle of the freedom of the seas – the global air is the common property of humans. However, one must weigh against this notion that the high seas border the surface of a sovereign territory, while the airspace is above the surface of a sovereign territory. This, of course, affects interests of safety and security of the nations below such airspace.

The Paris Convention of 1919[3] (CINA – *Commission internationale de navigation aérienne*), on the other hand, supported the principle of (national) sovereignty of the air.[4] The fact that a 'legislative authority' was to be established on the basis of this convention (Article 34) was, in a way, a contradiction to the notion of the convention. Every authority with legislative functions can derive its powers only from the principle of sovereignty. Since this principle is closely connected to the term of 'nation', it is impossible to imagine how an international organization could exercise such powers or whose sovereign powers this should be. This would

1. See the Resolution of the Council on Environmental Education of 24 May 1988 (88/C 177/03): *The environment as the common heritage of mankind.*
2. Fauchille, 'Le domaine aérien et le regime juridique des aérostats', *Revue générale de Droit international publique,* Vol. 8 (1901), 414.
3. 11 *LNTS* 173.
4. For details see s. III.B.2.1.ii.

only be possible if the Member States would explicitly grant such organization sovereignty powers. However, it would then no longer be simply an 'international', but instead, a 'supranational' organization (such as the European Union (EU)). Creating an appropriate balance in the various bodies of such an organization would be an insurmountable task in light of the global mission of such an organization and the economic, social, and political differences among the nations of this planet.

Therefore, the following basic factors need to be considered when establishing a global legal framework for aviation.

Aviation is basically a border-crossing enterprise. Consequently, this would make necessary a global legislature (for rule making) and a global administrator (for rule enforcing). However, there is neither a 'world state' nor a 'world legislature' (parliament) nor a 'world government' (administration). Despite all progress that humans have made over the last sixty years, the term 'sovereignty' still rests with the principle of national States, organized by self-determined peoples, living in their own territories.

Although sovereignty powers can in theory be conferred to supranational organizations (as is the case with EU and the North Atlantic Treaty Organization [NATO]), this has not happened in the case of the International Civil Aviation Organization (ICAO) for obvious reasons. The ICAO is simply an 'international' organization without its own or conferred sovereignty powers.[5] Legal globalization of aviation is only possible under the principle of 'internationalism' (as opposed to 'supranationalism') through the following:

- a convention in which the members pledge to comply with or implement decisions reached together (by majority). In aviation, this is of course the Chicago Convention;[6]
- an organization that can reach such decisions. In aviation, this is of course the ICAO;[7]

The legal framework, within which such an organization has to act, is defined and limited by the principle of national sovereignty described above: the fact that the power over a defined piece of land (including territorial waters and the air above a State's territory) is claimed by a group of people living there especially means that any other State power is excluded and that the entrance of others not belonging to that group is subject to permission.

Therefore, executing global air traffic requires at least

- the allocation of an air operator to a specific country (registration);
- rights to operate in countries other than the state of registration;
- common standards for technical issues in aviation (certification and licensing);

5. For details see Ch. 3 I.
6. 15 *UNTS* 295, *ICAO Doc.* 7300.
7. For details see Ch. 3 I.

- an organization responsible for the definition and issuance of common standards;
- a convention in which the Member States have pledged to implement standards issued by the stated organization into national law, that is, to issue them as binding norms and to enforce them on the basis of their sovereign rights.

II. THE WAY TO CHICAGO

This option has been chosen by the so-called Chicago system.[8] However, the way to Chicago was 'a long and winding road'.

A. Beginnings

Obviously, conditions for the permission to operate aircraft were initially the most important aspect of aviation law. In the beginning, operating aircraft was often subject to the general provisions of public law, that is, practically of police law. 'In France, for instance, a police directive was issued on 23 April 1784, aimed directly and exclusively at the balloons of the Montgolfier Brothers: flights were not to take place without prior authorization.'[9]

Actual development of an independent public aviation and air traffic law only started in the beginning of the twentieth century. For example, French law expert Fauchille suggested establishing a convention on international air traffic around 1900.[10]

The first aviation agreement[11] regulating international air traffic was the German-Austrian Agreement on crossing national borders on both sides with military balloons. This agreement is dated 6 August/2 November 1898[12] and was concluded through the diplomatic exchange of notes.

The first international multilateral contractual agreement relating to air traffic was the 1899 Hague Declaration, which prohibited 'launching of projectiles and explosives from balloons, and other methods of similar nature'. However, the declaration only remained in force until 1904. The prohibition was renewed by the 1907 XIV Hague Convention; however, it did not come into force again as a result of insufficient ratification.[13]

8. See below s. III.
9. I. H. Ph. Diederiks-Verschoor, *An Introduction to Air Law*, 7th rev. edn (2001), 2.
10. Fauchille, 'Le domaine aérien et le regime juridique des aérostats', *Revue générale de Droit international publique,* Vol. 8 (1901), 414.
11. See Meyer, *Freiheit der Luft als Rechtsproblem* (Freedom of the Air as a legal problem) (Zürich, 1944), 24; Bentzien, in Benkö/Kröll, *Luft- und Weltraumrecht im 21. Jahrhundert* (Aviation and space law in the 21st century) (2001), 1.
12. Bentzien, in: Benkö/Kröll, *ibid.*
13. *Ibid.*

B. Air Navigation Conference, Paris (1910)

Since German balloonists often crossed the border and entered France because of the nature of their non-steerable aircraft (i.e., completed international air traffic in today's sense of the word), France initially pushed for the conclusion of a bilateral agreement on air traffic with Germany, but was not averse to conclude a multilateral agreement either. Delegates from nineteen European countries attended the first diplomatic aviation conference, which was held in Paris in 1910. At the end of the conference, Germany, Denmark, Italy, Romania, Switzerland, Austria-Hungary, Spain, Monaco, Russia, Turkey, France, the Netherlands, Serbia, Belgium, Bulgaria, England, Portugal, and Sweden adopted a draft for an international convention on aviation entitled '*Projet d'une convention internationale relative à la navigation aérienne*'.[14] The convention was to include seven chapters and fifty-five articles. The following chapters were planned:

- (I) Nationality of Aircraft and Registration Requirements
- (II) Approval and Airworthiness Certificates
- (III) Authorization of Air Traffic within the Borders and above a National Territory
- (IV) Regulations on Takeoff, Landing and Flight
- (V) Customs and Freight
- (VI) Public Aircraft
- (VII) Final Provisions.

Because of opposing opinions of the States concerning the application of the theory of air sovereignty, air zones, or air freedom, the conference did not have any results. International traffic of civil aircraft meant that the States had to decide whether to tolerate run-in or whether authorization would be required.

The 'theory of freedom of the air' says that aircraft of any kind may fly through the airspace of countries at any height without being disturbed. This theory was criticized because it does not appropriately take into account the fundamental needs for protection of countries.

The goal of the 'theory of air zones' was to achieve a division of the airspace (in terms of height) into three categories, similar to maritime law. The same way in which territorial waters of a country are subject to the territorial sovereignty of the riparian state, such territorial sovereignty was also assumed up to a certain height above the national territory of a country. Similar to a contiguous zone on the water, a zone was also to be defined in the airspace in which the countries were still granted certain control rights. Furthermore, the 'atmospheric Open Sea' of the airspace was an imitation of the high seas.

The 'theory of air sovereignty', on the other hand, aims to grant a State absolute power over the airspace over that State. Pursuant to this theory, the

---

14. Bethkenhagen, *Die Entwicklung des Luftrechts bis zum Luftverkehrsgesetz von 1922* (The development of aviation law until the air traffic law of 1922) (Peter Lang, Frankfurt, 2004), 84.

airspace above the high seas and above non-occupied areas shall not be subject to any sovereign power. The main argument against the theory of air sovereignty was that the sovereignty of a State could not extend indefinitely into space.

The Verona 1910 International Conference on Aviation Law and the 1913 International Law Association both confirmed the principle of air sovereignty. The Pan-American Aeronautic Federation in Santiago in 1916, the Inter-Alliance Conference in Budapest in 1918, and the first Nordic Aviation Conference in Stockholm in 1918 also voted for this principle.[15]

It is not really surprising that the States finally rejected the theory of freedom of the air and claimed national sovereignty of the airspace above their sovereign territories and the corresponding territorial waters. This meant that all international traffic was now subject to authorization. The theory of air sovereignty has remained fixed in national laws and international aviation agreements up to this day.

Because of the failure to reach a multilateral regulation, the First Bilateral Air Services Agreement was concluded between Germany and France in 1913 through correspondence between the French Ambassador and the Secretary of State for Foreign Affairs in Berlin.[16]

C. National Regulations until World War I

Failure to adopt an international regulation speeded up the development of national aviation legislation.

As early as 29 July 1910, the Police Ordinance for the province of Brandenburg and the state police district of Berlin came into force, which exclusively included regulations for aircraft.[17] Pilots of aircraft in the Berlin-Brandenburg region were thereby required to hold a certificate in accordance with the provisions of the *Fédération Aéronautique Internationale.* Pursuant to the regulation on international flights and participation in air displays,[18] only pilots who held such a certificate were authorized to fly aircraft. However, overflight of built-up areas was prohibited under threat of legal punishment.[19] Almost three months later, the Prussian ordinance of 22 October 1910 relating to government measures against air navigation and aviation[20] was adopted, which was the first to define provisions on air traffic for all of Prussia. Two accidents with aircraft claiming five lives in June and July of 1910[21] were the reason for the ordinance to be adopted. It included a general obligation for pilots to be authorized by a pilot's license, which

15. Meyer, *ibid.*, 72.
16. *RGBl.* 1913, 601, see Bentzien, in Benkö/Kröll, *Luft- und Weltraumrecht im 21. Jahrhundert* (Aviation and space law in the 21st century), 1.
17. See Bethkenhagen, *ibid.*, 303 et seq. w.r.t. the 1910 special edition of the Gazette of the Royal Government of Potsdam and the City of Berlin, 365.
18. Bethkenhagen, *ibid.*, 54.
19. Bethkenhagen, *ibid.*, 61.
20. 1910 Official gazette of the Prussian Ministry of the Interior, 317 et seq.; Printed in *ibid.*, 306 et seq.
21. Bethkenhagen, *ibid.*, 65.

had to be issued by the German Pilot's Association.[22] Furthermore, all issued permits and international flights were based on types. Flights over congested areas were then generally permitted, provided that they did not pose a risk to public safety.[23] Except for three German states, all governments of the German Reich had adopted legal provisions similar to the 1910 Prussian ordinance by 1912.[24] Furthermore, Germany was making increased efforts to establish standardized aviation law, and the first draft bill was presented in August 1912.[25]

In France, the *Aéro Club de France* had developed air traffic regulations that also prohibited overflight of cities[26] so as to protect urban areas from the danger of crashing airplanes. In its 1911 Aerial Navigation Act, England prohibited the entering of English airspace without prior authorization. Russia also prohibited non-permitted entry into Russian airspace in 1912.[27]

D. World War I and Aviation Law

During World War I, aviation was exclusively dominated by the military, as civil aviation was prohibited (at least in Germany).[28] World War I brought advancements at least with regards to the question of national air sovereignty, as both the nations involved in the war as well as the neutral countries were of the opinion that the airspace above their national territories was unrestrictedly subject to their national sovereignty both with regards to space and matter. Thus, they undoubtedly manifested the principle of air sovereignty.[29] Thereby, World War I contributed to solving the dispute among the theory of freedom of the air, the theory of air sovereignty, and the theory of air zones, with the theory of air sovereignty clearly winning.

In the beginning of World War I, Switzerland's position was that Swiss airspace had to be neutral.[30] As a consequence, the airspace above the other neutral territories was also considered neutral airspace.

The London Ultimatum of 5 May 1921[31] banned Germany from both civil aviation and production of airplanes.[32]

---

22. Bethkenhagen, *ibid.*, 78, 306.
23. Bethkenhagen, *ibid.*, 79, 306.
24. Bethkenhagen, *ibid.*, 82.
25. Printed in Bethkenhagen, *ibid.*, 308 et seq.
26. Bethkenhagen, *ibid.*, 61.
27. Riese, *Luftrecht* (Air Law) (Koehler, 1949), 75.
28. Bethkenhagen, *ibid.*, 39.
29. Meyer, *ibid.*, 74.
30. Riese, *ibid.*, 75.
31. On 5 May 1921, the British Prime Minister David Lloyd George delivered a six-day ultimatum of the Allied Forces of World War I to the German Ambassador in London. Germany was to accept the payment plan adopted by the Entente powers one month before, which had set the total reparation payments at 132 billion gold marks. Furthermore, the German Reich was summoned to complete demilitarization and 'extradite a number of German war criminals' as had been determined by the Treaty of Versailles. In case of non-compliance, the Allied Forces threatened to occupy the Ruhr area.
32. Venzke, *Pioniere des Himmels* (Pioneers of the Skies) (Artemis & Winkler, 2002), 42.

E. 1919 Paris Convention

Shortly after the end of World War I, scheduled flights started operating between Paris and London on 8 February 1919. In that year, trans-oceanic flight became a reality with two crossings of the Atlantic Ocean. Aviation had finally become truly international.

The idea of an international regulation of air navigation was again discussed at the peace conference held after World War I. This time, there was complete agreement among the ex-Allied States, as the respective governments realized that aviation, which had made great advances during the war, would develop rapidly as a means of international transport. It was therefore agreed to hold an international conference to lay down the principles of rules for air traffic that would serve as the basis for uniform international regulations. This Convention (the Paris Convention) was signed by the representative of each participating country on 13 October 1919.

The Paris Convention Relating to the Regulation of Aerial Navigation[33] entered the history books as the first multilateral regulation of international air traffic. The provisions of the Convention basically cover the nationality of the aircraft, acceptance of airworthiness certificates, and authorizations, as well as obligations relating to run-in. The Convention was supplemented by technical Annexes regulating additional details.

With regards to its content, in addition to recognizing air sovereignty, the Convention granted the contracting States the right to conclude special agreements with non-contracting countries. This regulation had become necessary to enable non-contracting States to enter and fly over the contractual area. The remaining chapters (a total of nine) dealt with nationality and registration of aircraft (Chapter 2), certificates of airworthiness and competency of the flight crew and mutual recognition of the contracting States (Chapter 3), air navigation above contractual territory (Chapter 4), rules on behaviour during the flight and during landing and departure (Chapter 5), the prohibited transport of explosives and other dangerous material (Chapter 6), state aircraft (Chapter 7), the International Commission for Air Navigation (CINA) (Chapter 8) and the final provisions (Chapter 9). Technical specifications are included in eight Annexes to the Convention.[34]

The Convention established CINA. Apart from functions as an administrative organ, arbitrator, and panel of experts, CINA was also granted limited lawmaking rights. On the one hand, changes to the text of the contract had to be presented to CINA before being put to the vote. On the other hand, the annexes could be changed through a qualified majority, meaning that the Convention made them binding for all contracting States, including those that had voted against such change. This had the great advantage of a high level of standardization of technical provisions of aviation, but it also had the significant disadvantage that the United

33. 11 *LNTS* 173.
34. Riese, *ibid.*, 82 et seq.

States (US) was not willing or able to submit to binding provisions of an international body, among other reasons, because of constitutional concerns.[35]

Even States that were not part of the Paris Convention recognized the theory of air sovereignty in bilateral air services agreements (BASAs).[36] On a national level, this time also saw the adoption of a great number of aviation laws, such as the Decision by the Federal Council of Switzerland, the German Aviation Law[37] of 1922, and the French *Loi réglementant la navigation aérienne* of 1924.[38]

F. The CIANA and the Havana Convention

As multilateral regulations, the Ibero-American Convention on Air Navigation of 1 November 1926 (CIANA) and the Pan-American Convention on Commercial Aviation of 20 February 1928 (Havana Convention) are the counterpart of the Paris Convention Relating to the Regulation of Aerial Navigation for the American Continents.

The Ibero-American Convention on Air Navigation (*Convencion Ibero-americano de Navegación Aérea*),[39] also called CIANA, was concluded at the initiative of Spain among Spain, Portugal, and the South American states who were not part of CINA. It was signed at Madrid on 1 November 1926.[40]

Some aspects of CIANA were a contrast to CINA, on the one hand because it aimed to treat all nations equally in aviation, and on the other hand because the aviation commission envisioned by the convention was not to be governed by the League of Nations. However, it imitated CINA in many aspects, and many articles were even literally copied. When Spain and Argentina joined CINA and many South American states joined the Pan-American Convention, CIANA lost some of its significance.[41]

The Pan-American Convention on Commercial Aviation[42] was signed in Havana on 20 February 1928 and was supplemented by the *Convention sur le transit d'avions,* which was signed in Buenos Aires on 19 June 1935. In the Convention, the contracting States pledged not to introduce charges for transit flight through their territories and to limit control measures to those absolutely necessary.[43] The Havana Convention did not include any annexes and did not establish any aviation commission.[44]

35. Riese, *ibid.*, 84 et seq.
36. Riese, *ibid.*, 76.
37. See Bethkenhagen, *ibid.*
38. Riese, *ibid.*, 10.
39. 3 *Hudson* 2019 (1926); Meyer, *ibid.*, 25.
40. See Diederiks-Verschoor, *ibid.*, 6; Meyer, *ibid.*, 57 et seq.; Riese, *ibid.*, 85 et seq.
41. Riese, *ibid.*, 86.
42. 128 *British and Foreign State Papers*, 505 USTS, 840; 4 *Hudson* 2354 (1931); Meyer, *ibid.*, 25; Riese, *ibid.*, 86.
43. See Meyer, *ibid.*, 58 et seq.
44. Riese, *ibid.*, 87.

The Paris Convention, the Ibero-American Convention, and the Pan-American Convention all manifested the principle of air sovereignty.[45] Therefore, the following has applied since then: 'The sovereign territory of a state includes the airspace above its surface insofar as human activity can develop there with the current state of technology'.[46]

G. Establishment of an Aviation Regulation for the Post-War Period

In the following twenty years, international air traffic expanded rapidly, first in Europe, whose short international distances were within the range of aircraft of the 1920s.

Although the Paris and Havana Conventions served a useful purpose, they were seen to be no longer adequate for the years after World War II because of the immense wartime development of aerial transport. There was some readiness to concede that commercial air rights as well as technical and navigational regulations should be governed by an international agreement.

Detailed discussion of matters of how to organize global aviation after World War II were mainly held in the Anglo-Saxon legal environments; the US had already established a global military air transport system during World War II, which could easily have been transformed into a civil traffic system after the end of the war.[47] In 1943, US Vice President Wallace presented a seven-point programme for post-war aviation, which included regulations in the following areas:[48]

(1) The banning of Germany and Japan from building airplanes and from any form of air traffic.
(2) The establishment of an international aviation authority.
(3) Internationalization of the main global airports.
(4) The creation of an international air police (United Nations Peace Air Force).
(5) Internationalization of aviation.

In 1943, US President Roosevelt joined the discussion on the question of freedom of the air by making a declaration. In his opinion, free airspace meant free use of airports irrespective of their owners. Furthermore, he pleaded for air traffic on a private economic basis that was only to be nationally organized or subsidized in exceptional cases.[49] He also established a commission that was to work on aviation questions of the future. This commission made the following recommendations:[50]

45. Meyer, *ibid.*, 75; Riese, *ibid.*, 76.
46. Meyer, *ibid.*, 93.
47. Meyer, *ibid.*, 16; Riese, *ibid.* 97.
48. Meyer, *ibid.*, 19.
49. Meyer, *ibid.* 20.
50. Meyer, *ibid.* 20 et seq.

(1) Establishment of an international body that was to correspond to and replace the prewar European institutions IATA (International Air Traffic Association) and CINA in terms of their organization and their responsibilities.
(2) Establishment of a special airport authority by the United Nations (UN) that is responsible for financing and administration of certain internationally significant airports as a trustee.
(3) Admission of all large American air carriers to overseas air traffic.
(4) Operation on airways towards the US and the UN based on reciprocity. Opponents of war of the UN are excluded.
(5) When lubricants are to be taken over or such takeover is necessary for technical reasons, run-in and overflight of sovereign territories, except for exclusion zones, is effectuated based on bilateral agreements, takeover of passengers or freight remains prohibited.

The commission also pleaded to call an international conference on aviation as quickly as possible to clarify all these issues. Subsequently, more and more claims for a new aviation convention were raised that should provide regulations on air safety and monitoring of the global airways and replace the conventions that were in force.[51] It was to regulate a number of issues that were thus far variously regulated or not solved on an international level. Until 1944, international aviation law did not include such specific regulations applicable to air traffic in free airspace above the high seas and Stateless areas, as maritime law did. It was undisputed that the provisions of BASAs, the Paris Convention, the Ibero-American Convention, and the Pan-American Convention on Air Navigation were also to apply to the airspace above the open seas and Stateless areas.[52] In any case, the provisions of the country of registration[53] did already in particular apply to criminal incidents on board an aircraft if the aircraft was travelling beyond a sovereign national territory in free airspace. On the other hand, although the Hague Legal Commission had already developed a draft for air war rules in 1923, which also followed the theory of air sovereignty,[54] no air war rules had been established by the end of World War II yet that could have been used as a guideline in the future in the event of a war. However, there was general consent that the recognized regulations of national laws and air services agreements would have to apply in times of war as a result of the unwritten behavioural rules in the air, since these laws and agreements did not only apply to times of peace, but would also have to be applied in the event of a war as a result of a lack of contrasting provisions.[55]

---

51. Meyer, *ibid.*, 22.
52. Meyer, *ibid.*, 66.
53. The state in which the aircraft is listed in a public register.
54. Meyer, *ibid.* 76.
55. Meyer, *ibid.* 67.

III. THE CHICAGO SYSTEM

A. MULTILATERALISM VERSUS BILATERALISM

The Convention on International Civil Aviation (Chicago Convention)[56] was adopted and signed on the final day of the International Civil Aviation Conference, which was held from 1 November to 7 December 1944 at Chicago, Illinois, United States. The Conference, which was attended by fifty-two States, was called by the US government with the objective of establishing a legal framework for the development of international civil aviation after World War II. This action was taken even prior to the Conference of San Francisco in the spring of 1945, which adopted the UN Charter. On the basis of the Chicago Convention, the ICAO was established.[57]

The ICAO replaced all other existing commissions and was to be the main point of contact for all aviation matters. Accordingly, the CINA, for example, completed its liquidation, which had been decided upon in 1946, in 1948.[58]

The so-called Chicago system includes the following conventions and agreements:

- the Convention on International Civil Aviation (Chicago Convention), in which the Member States grant each other the right of departure and landing for non-commercial purposes (Articles 5 and 6 of the Convention) and on the basis of which the ICAO was established;
- the International Air Transit Agreement[59] (adopted together with the Chicago Convention) in which the Member States grant each other the right of departure and landing for technical purposes (first and second freedom, for details see below);
- the International Air Transport Agreement[60] (which never entered into force), in which three commercial freedoms are formulated. Since this agreement was simply a 'dead paper', these commercial freedoms together with some other so-called commercial freedoms that developed later must be granted by means of a BASA between two States;[61]
- the Interim Agreement on International Civil Aviation,[62] which formed the basis for setting up the provisional ICAO (PICAO), pending the entry into force of the Convention on 4 April 1947.

---

56. 15 *UNTS* 295, *ICAO Doc.* 7300.
57. For details see Ch. 3 I.
58. Riese, *ibid.* 34 n. 1a.
59. 84 *UNTS* 389; *ICAO Doc.* 7500.
60. 171 *UNTS* 387; *ICAO Doc.* App. IV-2187.
61. For details see s. III.B.2.i.
62. 15 *UNTS* 295.

The following overview shows the current situation of the Chicago System:[63]

Convention on International Civil Aviation

ICAO Doc. No.	*Title and Date*	*Short-Title Description*
7300	Convention on International Civil Aviation[64] Signed at Chicago, 7 December 1944.	Chicago Convention: constitution of ICAO
7500	International Air Services Transit Agreement[65] Signed at Chicago on 7 December 1944.	Transit Agreement: two freedoms of the air
8970	Protocol Relating to an Amendment to the Convention on International Civil Aviation [Article 50(a)][66] Signed at New York on 12 March 1971.	Article 50(a) (1971): increase of Council to thirty members
8971	Protocol Relating to an Amendment to the Convention on International Civil Aviation [Article 56][67] Signed at Vienna on 7 July 1971.	Article 56 (1971): increase of Air Navigation Commission (ANC) to fifteen members
9123	Protocol Relating to an Amendment to the Convention on International Civil Aviation [Article 50(a)][68] Signed at Montreal on 16 October 1974.	Article 50(a) (1974): increase of Council to thirty-three members
9208	Protocol Relating to an Amendment to the Convention on International Civil Aviation [Final Paragraph, Russian Text][69] Signed at Montreal on 30 September 1977.	Final Paragraph (1977): referring to the authentic Russian text

63. <www.icao.int/eSHOP/conventions_list.htm>.
64. 15 *UNTS* 295.
65. 84 *UNTS* 389.
66. 893 *UNTS* 117.
67. 958 *UNTS* 217.
68. 1175 *UNTS* 297.
69. 2133 *UNTS* 43.

ICAO Doc. No.	Title and Date	Short-Title Description
9217	Protocol on the Authentic Quadrilingual Text of the Convention on International Civil Aviation (Chicago, 1944) Signed at Montreal on 30 September 1977.	Protocol on Authentic Quadrilingual Text (1977)
9318	Protocol Relating to an Amendment to the Convention on International Civil Aviation [Article 83*bis*][70] Signed at Montreal on 6 October 1980.	Article 83*bis:* lease, charter, or interchange The subject of this Protocol is the transfer of certain safety-related functions and duties from the states of registry to the state of the operator in case of lease, charter, or interchange of aircraft.
9436	Protocol Relating to an Amendment to the Convention on International Civil Aviation [Article 3*bis*][71] Signed at Montreal on 10 May 1984.	Article 3*bis:* Non-use of weapons against civil aircraft in flight The subject of this protocol is the non-use of weapons against civil aircraft in flight.
9544	Protocol Relating to an Amendment to the Convention on International Civil Aviation [Article 56][72] Signed at Montreal on 6 October 1989.	Article 56 (1989): increase of ANC to nineteen members This Protocol provides for the increase of the Air Navigation Commission to nineteen members.
9561	Protocol Relating to an Amendment to the Convention on International Civil Aviation [Article 50(a)][73] Signed at Montreal on 26 October 1990.	Article 50(a) (1990): increase of Council to thirty-six members This Protocol provides for the increase of the ICAO Council to thirty-six members.

70. 2122 *UNTS* 321.
71. 2122 *UNTS* 337.
72. 2320 *UNTS* 79.
73. 2216 *UNTS* 483.

ICAO Doc. No.	*Title and Date*	*Short-Title Description*
9663	Protocol on the Authentic Quinquelingual Text of the Convention on International Civil Aviation (Chicago, 1944)[74] Signed at Montreal on 29 September 1995.	Protocol on Authentic Quinquelingual Text (1995)
9664	Protocol Relating to an Amendment to the Convention on International Civil Aviation [Final Paragraph, Arabic Text][75] Signed at Montreal on 29 September 1995.	Final Paragraph (1995): referring to the authentic Arabic text
9721	Protocol on the Authentic Six-Language Text of the Convention on International Civil Aviation (Chicago, 1944)[76] Signed at Montreal on 1 October 1998.	Protocol on authentic six-language text (1998)
9722	Protocol Relating to an Amendment to the Convention on International Civil Aviation [Final Paragraph, Chinese Text][77] Signed at Montreal on 1 October 1998.	Final Paragraph (1998): referring to the authentic Chinese text

After the Chicago Convention came into force, thousands of BASAs were concluded, in which the affected States, under certain conditions, granted each other the freedoms that were not included in the Transit Agreement, that is, commercial freedoms. The Bermuda I[78] Agreement served as a kind of blueprint. It was concluded in 1946 between Great Britain and the US. At the insistence of the British negotiators, it was highly restrictive because they feared that 'giving in' to US demands for a 'free for all' would lead to the then financially and operationally superior US air carriers' total domination of the global air transport industry.[79] The following freedoms of the air were generally granted in the BASAs.

74. Not yet in force.
75. Not yet in force.
76. Not yet in force.
77. Not yet in force.
78. Agreement between the United Kingdom and United States, 11 February 1946, 60 Stat. 1499, 3 *UNTS* 253.
79. For details on the development see s. 2.a.i.

1. Freedoms of the Air

The rights or privileges, in respect of scheduled international air services, granted by one State to another State or States:[80]

- First Freedom of the Air: the right to fly across its territory without landing.
- Second Freedom of the Air: the right to land in its territory for non-traffic purposes.
- Third Freedom of the Air: the right to put down, in the territory of the first State, traffic coming from the home State of the carrier.
- Fourth Freedom of the Air: the right to take on, in the territory of the first State, traffic destined for the home State of the carrier.
- Fifth Freedom of the Air: the right to put down and to take on, in the territory of the first State, traffic coming from or destined to a third State.

ICAO characterizes all freedoms beyond the fifth as 'so-called' because only the first five freedoms have been officially recognized as such by international treaty:

- Sixth Freedom of the Air: the right of transporting, via the home State of the carrier, traffic moving between two other States.
- Seventh Freedom of the Air: the right of transporting traffic between the territory of the granting State and any third State with no requirement to include on such operation any point in the territory of the recipient State.
- Eighth Freedom of the Air: the right of transporting cabotage traffic between two points in the territory of the granting State on a service that originates or terminates in the home country of the foreign carrier or (in connection with the so-called Seventh Freedom of the Air) outside the territory of the granting State (also known as 'consecutive' cabotage).
- Ninth Freedom of the Air: the right of transporting cabotage traffic of the granting State on a service performed entirely within the territory of the granting State (also known as 'stand alone' cabotage).

B. The Chicago Convention

1. Structure of the Convention

The Chicago Convention[81] is structured the following way:

- Part I: Air Navigation:
  - General Principles and Application of the Convention
  - Flight over Territory of Contracting States
  - Nationality of Aircraft

80. *Manual on the Regulation of International Air Transport* (*ICAO Doc.* 9626, Part 4).
81. 15 *UNTS* 295, *ICAO Doc.* 7300.

  - Measures to Facilitate Air Navigation
  - Conditions to be Fulfilled with Respect to Aircraft
  - International Standards and Recommended Practices (SARPs)
- Part II: The ICAO:
  - The Organization
  - The Assembly
  - The Council
  - The Air Navigation Committee
  - Personnel
  - Finance
  - Other International Arrangements
- Part III: International Air Transport:
  - Information and Reports
  - Airports and Other Air Navigation Facilities
  - Joint Operating Organizations and Pooled Services
- Part IV: Final Provisions:
  - Other Aeronautical Agreements and Arrangements
  - Disputes and Default
  - War
  - Ratifications, Adherences, Amendments and Denunciations

2. Some Relevant Legal Issues

a. The Airspace: Sovereignty of the Air (Article 1) and the Granting of Traffic Rights: Bilateral Air Services Agreements

Pursuant to the above considerations prior to negotiations of the Chicago Convention, Article 1 of the Convention states that 'the contracting States recognize that every state has complete and exclusive sovereignty over the airspace above its territory'. This means that the Convention is generally based on the principle of sovereignty of the air. At the same time, it also means that every freedom of being in the airspace of another State, for whichever reason, is subject to the explicit authorization of such State. On the basis of the international principle of reciprocity, this means that such freedoms can only be granted when the other contracting State does the same at the same time, that is, grants the first contracting State the same freedoms. Such mutual – or reciprocal – granting of freedoms generally happens on the basis of international, multilateral, or bilateral agreements. However, individual authorizations granted by the respective government for special political or economic reasons are also possible.

Pursuant to Article 6 of the Convention, commercial traffic rights are granted in so-called air services agreements, which are usually bilateral agreements. The globe is covered by a network of approximately 5,000 BASAs. They form the basis for operating scheduled air services between the individual contracting States. Such agreements have to be deposited at the ICAO in Montreal (Article 83 of the Convention). The ICAO has a database of the World's Air Services

Agreements.[82] This database contains codified summaries of the main provisions of BASAs filed with ICAO.

The market organization created by bilateral agreements is based on three main principles:

- Bilateralism: Traffic rights are part of the State sovereignty and are granted to selected partner States in bilateral agreements.
- Reciprocity: Any limitation of air sovereignty can only be achieved in international negotiations based on the principle of reciprocity.
- Fair and equal opportunity: The air carriers of both contracting States must have the fair and equal opportunity to operate on the designated routes; free spaces are again subject to the principle of reciprocity.

i. System

BASAs generally have the following structure. The order of the individual clauses can, however, vary in the different agreements:

- Definitions.
- Granting of traffic rights and route schedule.
- Designation and operating authorization (ownership clause and obligation to comply with national aviation laws).
- Revocation or limitation of operating authorization.
- Equal treatment with regard to fees (airport and air-traffic control fees).
- Exemption from customs duties and other fees.
- Transfer of revenue (from sale of air transport services in the other contracting State).
- Principles on the operation of the agreed scheduled service (equal competition and determination of offered air transport).
- Provision of company details and statistics (notification of route schedules and transport statistics).
- Tariffs (tariff establishment and approval).
- Commercial activities (authorization to establish sales offices and handling organization in the territory of the other contracting State, except traffic handling of aircraft).
- Aviation security (obligation to protect the security of civil aviation against acts of unlawful interferences).
- Entry and control of travel documents (of transported flight passengers).
- Exchange of ideas (between the aviation authorities of both contracting States about application, interpretation, and change of the agreement).
- Consultations (between both contracting States on application, interpretation, and change of the agreement).
- Settlement of disputes (arbitration clause).
- Multilateral agreements (priority).

82. *ICAO Doc.* 9511 <www.icao.int/icao/en/cd_pub_list.htm>.

- Registration at the ICAO.
- Former agreements.
- Ratification, entry into force, and duration.
- Termination.

The mutually granted routes are defined in special route schedules that are usually not a formal part of the air services agreements, but are rather adopted through a corresponding authorization in the agreements through special exchange of diplomatic notes between the governments of the contracting States. The route schedule includes a more detailed definition of the service routes of the air carrier(s) designated by each party through a definition of the points in accordance with the following system:

Departure points from the country of origin of the air carrier	Intermediate points	Points in the other contracting State	Points beyond the other contracting State

Furthermore, the route schedule includes special provisions on whether individual points can be omitted and on which sections of the route commercial freedoms may be executed. Often, additional agreements include essential aviation law regulations that are the result of aviation negotiations between the involved governments. Supplementary to the air services agreement and the route schedules, these additional agreements define the extent and use of commercial freedoms in a more or less liberal, but mostly restrictive, manner, and the coordination of the mutually designated air carriers in terms of execution of scheduled services between the two countries or on specific sections of the route are possibly also defined. These additional agreements are usually confidential and are, therefore, not notified to the ICAO.

ii. BASA-Types

Several basic types of air services agreements have been developed and became models of others, and they are, therefore, used as standard blueprints.

(1) Chicago-Type

A model contract for a BASA authorized in accordance with Article 83 of the Convention was already developed at the Chicago conference.[83] This model contract basically included the following regulations:

- Designation of air carriers of the contracting parties and issuance and revocation of operating authorizations (Article 2).

83. *Final Act to the Convention of 7 Dec. 1944*, s. VIII.

- Equal treatment to national air carriers with regard to charging airport usage fees (Article 4a).
- Mutual recognition of certificates of airworthiness and flight licenses (Article 5).
- Obligation to comply with national laws on entry and departure from the territory of the other contracting State and on air traffic within its territory as well as entry and departure of passengers, flight crew, and cargo (Article 6a and b).
- Settlement of disputes (Article 9).
- Termination of the agreement (Article 10).
- Route schedule as annex defining points of departure, intermediate points, and destinations of the planned route.

This model contract was initially the basis for a great number of BASAs (until October 1947 as declared by the ICAO legal committee pursuant to Article 64 of the Convention). However, it did not include any regulations on the extent of traffic rights, especially of the fifth freedom, questions of capacity and tariffs, which had to be regulated separately.

(2) Bermuda-Type (Bermuda I)

The most important bilateral air services agreement since the Chicago conference was the Bermuda Agreement that was concluded in Bermuda on 11 February 1946 between Great Britain and the US.[84] It was a compromise between the absolute freedom of traffic sought by the US and the strict economic organization and allocation of scheduled air traffic requested by Great Britain. It basically included the following regulations:

- General principles to be followed by air carriers of both nations in scheduled air traffic (Final Act).
- Air traffic at the lowest economically acceptable prices (paragraph 1).
- Provision of air services adapted to the traffic volume between the two States as well as the demand (paragraphs 3 and 6) with *ex-post-facto* control by the contracting States during regular consultations (Annex I, Article 9, paragraph 9).
- Equal opportunities (paragraph 4), mutual considerateness, and no disadvantaged and discriminating treatment (paragraph 5).
- Granting of traffic rights on the designated routes defined in a route schedule with the individual flight sections and points of arrival and departure and intermediate points (Annex I, Article 1, and Appendix 3) in addition to proceedings in the case of route changes (Appendix 4) and change of gauge (Appendix 5).

84. Agreement between the United Kingdom and United States, 11 February 1946, 60 Stat. 1499, *TAIS* 1507, 3 *UNTS* 253.

- Multiple designation and operating authorization of the air carriers authorized to exercise the traffic rights (Annex I, Article 2) plus ownership clause (Annex I, Article 6).
- Price setting processes through the IATA to prevent mutual price cutting (Appendix 2).

These regulations also met the interests of other States that were in the process of establishing their own air carriers with which they were seeking access to global air traffic – an important factor for the development of their economies – while protecting such national air carriers from the risks of absolute competition. The Bermuda Agreement is based on a rather liberal understanding by granting the air carriers mostly free room for organization; however, it requires a balance of technical and economic achievement potential of the air carriers of both contracting States. This precondition is in particular not met when granted opposing rights cannot be exercised because of the absence of a national air carrier or when a national air carrier is only in the process of being established (e.g., in developing countries). In these cases, attempts were and are often made to restrict the Bermuda Agreement through additional agreements or through one-sided provisions in the operating authorization of the air carrier of the other contracting State. This usually happens through the following provisions:

- Single designation.
- Requirement to conclude a prior agreement between the air carriers of both nations on profit share (pool convention) as a precondition for granting traffic rights in bilateral scheduled air services.
- Definition of the number of frequencies and capacity (predetermination).
- Refusal, restriction, or quotation of the fifth freedom.
- Price setting by the aviation authorities of both States.

Only States outside the European economic area and the North Atlantic with main air traffic destinations or States that have a key position as peripheral areas can still get away with such restrictive agreements.

(3) Bermuda II-Type

However, the Bermuda I Agreement also does not work any more when overcapacity, declining traffic development and so on lead to an extensive use of formally authorized options that end up damaging both parties and can later only be brought back into balance with considerable difficulty. Such a situation occurred when the situation of aviation deteriorated significantly in the 1970s because of the oil crisis and the general economic recession. This lead to Great Britain terminating the Bermuda Agreement in 1975 to return to a more restrictive practice. On 23 June 1977, after more than one year of fierce negotiation, Great Britain and the US signed a new air services agreement, again in Bermuda.[85] This Bermuda

85. Agreement between the Government of the United States of America and the Government of the United Kingdom of Great Britain and Northern Ireland concerning Air Service, 23 July 1997, 1079 *UNTS* 21 (No. 16509) and *UKTS* (1977) 76.

II Agreement restricts some liberal regulations of the first Bermuda Convention while loosening others:

- Exceptions from the principle of multiple designation of air carriers for two main routes of North Atlantic traffic (London – New York, London – Los Angeles), for which each contracting State may only designate one air carrier.
- Removal of the fifth freedom behind London for American air carriers except for services to four German airports and transit rights without taking up new traffic (so-called blind-sector rights) to points in Europe.
- Introduction of stricter prior control of planned frequencies and capacities of air service demand by defining a maximum number of frequencies and a consultation process to prevent overcapacities (Article 11).
- Retention of the IATA price-setting system while also authorizing individual price requests of the air carriers and double approval requirements of prices with possible consultation processes and, in the case of no agreement being reached, continuing application of current prices; establishment of a constant tariff working group to fight illegal discounts and to prevent disputes.

This agreement, specifically tailored to the market between the US and Great Britain with its partially restrictive designation and capacity regulations, has not reached the same role of serving as a model for other agreements as its predecessor. It was a contrast to the liberal aviation policies of the US that had begun under the Carter Administration and had in fact had the desired effects for the EC, whose efforts to apply the competition provisions of the EC Treaty to European aviation and to liberalize the inner-Community aviation market were confirmed.

(4) Liberal Type

Given the strong and continuous increase of global air traffic, the increased share of charter air traffic, the abandoned price fixing of the IATA price agreements for traffic to and from the US and within the EC, and the increased competition between mostly privatized air carriers, it is most likely that the trend towards further liberalization of international scheduled air services will continue. If no liberal international transport agreement can be developed in this changed situation within the ICAO again, the content of future BASAs will be much more liberal. Apart from the definition of technical and flight operational conditions and mutual acceptance of according certificates, the following general regulations would be possible:

- multiple designations of private air carriers of both contracting States;
- loosening of the ownership clause;
- access to all international airports in the respective contracting States, possibly with the option of restriction in the case of congestion for environmental reasons;
- unlimited traffic rights of the third, fourth, and fifth freedoms and of cabotage;

- free use of foreign equipment;
- cooperative operation of scheduled air services in all cooperation forms and combinations;
- free decision on frequencies and applied capacity;
- free price organization, possibly with right of rejection for departing traffic;
- consultation processes concerning joint definitions of limitations in emergency situations.

Many governments now aim to achieve further liberalization of their relationships with third countries wherever markets are expected to provide the conditions for fair competition, because guaranteed fair competition at equal and fair conditions and a balance of economic advantages for both States are the basis of such liberal air services agreements, and because any contracting State naturally aims to secure an appropriate share in the aviation markets that reflects its achievement potential. German aviation policies also aim at increasing its traffic rights and the possibilities for using them in the interest of German air carriers.

iii. Main Aspects

The following is a short description of the most important clauses of BASAs:

(1) General Principles

The agreements contain the principle that 'air carriers of any contracting State must have the fair and equal opportunity to operate on any of the routes defined in the route schedule' (fair and equal opportunity). In the Bermuda II Agreement, this principle refers to the possibilities of competition with the designated air carriers of the other contracting party (Preamble, third clause, Article 11, paragraph 1). The same applies to the German-American Protocol Agreement of 1 November 1978 (Article 5, paragraph a).

It is further provided that 'when operating international air services on the routes defined in the route schedule, each designated air carrier of a contracting party is to take the interests of the other contracting party into consideration so that air services operated by such air carriers on the same routes or on the same parts of a route is not unduly affected.'

(2) Designation and Operating Authorizations of Air Carriers

According to the air services agreements, the contracting States designate the air carrier(s) that is/are to operate air services on the agreed routes and grant the designated air carrier(s) operating authorizations. A designated air carrier can be replaced by another air carrier at any time, in which case such new air carrier has the same rights and is subject to the same obligations as the air carrier it replaces.

Generally, each contracting State only designates one air carrier for each route, so that there are always two air carriers servicing one route (single designation). This allows the State to control directly market access of an air carrier, which also influences the share of the market between the two air carriers servicing the route. Multiple designations, on the other hand, allow each contracting State to designate several air carriers to use the traffic rights granted to such State on the routes defined in the route schedule. States that do not have a national air carrier, but rather several, usually privately owned air carriers, therefore aim for multiple designations in the agreements.

(3) Ownership clause

Almost all air services agreements include an ownership clause, which allows a contracting State to reject issuance of the operating authorization for air services to the air carrier designated by the other contracting State when such air carrier, upon request, fails to provide proof that the majority of ownership in the air carrier and its actual control belong to nationals or incorporations of the other contracting State or such State itself. According to the principle of bilateralism of granting of traffic rights between the two contracting States, this is to prevent the granted rights from being misused by the air carrier of a third country. Operating activities of such an air carrier are subject to an air services agreement concluded with its country of origin.

Compliance with this clause will become more difficult in the future for scheduled air service with third States outside the EC because EC Member States are obligated by EC law to define air carriers as authorized air carriers for exercising traffic rights on the agreed routes that are located in their sovereign territory, but largely owned by nationals or incorporations of another EC Member State and that are actually subject to control of such State and its citizens or incorporations.[86] In its decision from 5 November 2002, the European Court of Justice (ECJ) ruled that the clause on ownership and control in the air services agreements is in breach of ex-Article 52 EC Treaty (now 43) (right of establishment).

(4) Exchange of Traffic Rights

The exchange of traffic rights regulates the mutual granting of overflight, technical landing, and traffic rights on the routes defined in the route schedule. These air traffic rights constitute very valuable economic advantages for both the involved air carriers and for the States granting these rights. One simple example of these advantages is the overflight right (first freedom) which can be of particular importance for certain routes (e.g., over Siberia or Alaska to Japan, over Indonesia to Australia, over Brazil to Chile and Argentina etc.).

The right of non-commercial landings (second freedom) is also an important precondition for scheduled long-distance flights, not only because of the necessity to refuel determined by the range of the aircraft, but it is also of real economic significance with regard to saving fuel costs by refuelling at inexpensive intermediate points, especially in times of energy becoming more and more scarce and fuel becoming more and more expensive.

86. For details see Ch. 10 I.

Traffic rights of the third and fourth freedom are basic preconditions for taking up air services between both contracting States. Their value is determined by the traffic volume between these States. In case of only one-way traffic, the traffic economic interest of the country of origin is opposed by the tourist and foreign exchange interests of the receiving country. When one contracting State does not have its own national air carrier that is able to exercise the granted traffic rights of the third and fourth freedom, it usually claims shares in the economic profit of the air services provided by the air carrier of the other contracting party, for example, by concluding a pool agreement.

Traffic of the fifth right especially gains economic significance for commercial use of routes that connect intermediate points with points in the other contracting State or for routes going beyond points in the other contracting State with points beyond in third States. However, granting such traffic rights also affects the interests of the third States involved, in which the intermediate points or the points beyond the other contracting State are located. Every contracting State will, therefore, have to consider its relationship to these third States when deciding to grant traffic rights of the fifth freedom. On the other hand, granted rights can only be exercised when they have also been granted by the third States. If using aircraft with greater range and high traffic volume of the third and fourth freedom allowed for economic direct connections, traffic of the fifth freedom becomes less significant on such routes. When fifth freedoms are not granted for a particular section of the route, it can still be important to be allowed to fly this section of the route to discharge traffic from the country of origin of the aircraft to a final destination located in a third State or to take up traffic on board destined for the country of origin at such a point. Through combined servicing of two destination points without traffic rights between these points (blind sectors), the air carrier saves having to operate separate services to the other contracting State and to the third State. If it is permitted to take traffic on such a route that the air carrier has transported to the other contracting State itself for such traffic to travel on to the third State after a stopover (so-called stopover traffic), this significantly simplifies the prohibition of execution of traffic rights of the fifth freedom.

However, third-State traffic can also be developed in a different way in the case of absence of the fifth freedom rights by using the so-called sixth freedom. An air carrier does this by first transporting its traffic designated for a third State from the other State to its country of origin, exercising the fourth freedom, and then, exercising the third freedom, on to the third State. These options are of particularly great economic significance for States for which their own traffic volume is insufficient for sustaining their air carriers (e.g., European neighbour States).

The obligation of States to grant cabotage rights (eighth freedom) to other air carriers once they have been granted (included in Article 7 of the ICAO-Convention) has led to air carriers, considering this consequence, generally not granting access to domestic services to foreign air carriers, but reserving these services to their own air carriers. This is being used on a regular basis. Foreign air carriers have only been granted cabotage rights on selected routes in the case of true reciprocity or to make up for advantages of equal value. Up until the German

Reunification, air traffic to Berlin, which was reserved to the three occupying powers, was a special case of cabotage traffic that was based on special legal principles and, therefore, was an exception to the prohibition of Article 7 clause 2 of the ICAO Convention.

The States negotiate the traffic rights of the various freedoms in accordance with the *do-ut-des* principle (principle of reciprocity). It depends on the negotiating power of the States involved, which depends on their industrial power and power with regard to aviation politics, as well as their geographic location, their own traffic volume, and their tourist appeal. The situation is already difficult when trying to obtain overflight rights for States that have not signed the transit agreement and that can use their geographic advantage as an argument (e.g., Russia, Indonesia, and Brazil). Obtaining traffic rights of the third and fourth freedom is often difficult for States that are not yet able to use according opposing rights for their own air carriers (e.g., States in the so-called Third World). However, States of very different geographic size and location and with a different number and size of their own air carriers face each other with very different negotiating powers (e.g., US or Canada towards Germany). In the case of the fifth freedom, States in peripheral geographic locations (US, Australia, and Japan) often take up key positions, which they can easily take advantage of when dealing with a small State surrounded by several neighbouring States. Large States in terms of size (e.g., US and Canada) that do not grant access to their domestic transport (eighth freedom), offer no comparable balancing advantages for intercontinental traffic rights of the fifth freedom (e.g., in Europe). Furthermore, granting traffic rights of the fifth freedom also affects the interests of the third States involved, in which the intermediate points or the points behind the other contracting State are located. Such a State then has to take its relationship to such third States into consideration when making a decision (e.g., Australia's relationship to the Association of Southeast Asian Nations [ASEAN]). On the other hand, possibly granted rights can only be exercised when they have also been granted by the third States.

(5) Capacity

A service offer (capacity) is determined by:

- the size (seat, room, and weight capacity) of the servicing aircraft;
- the number of services per week or per day;
- the distribution of flights in terms of time on certain days of the week and times of the day.

The capacity clauses of the air services agreements include the principles that are to be used to determine the service capacity of the designated air carriers of the contracting States. Several models need to be distinguished.

(a) Bermuda Clause

Most bilateral agreements are based on the capacity provisions of the Bermuda I Agreement, which assumes a liberal basic position and states that the service offer to be provided on the designated routes must in particular correspond to the expected service demand between the two contracting States (third and fourth freedoms). When air carriers have also been granted rights of the fifth freedom, these are, 'in the interest of an orderly development of international air traffic', to be executed in a way that the service offer is adapted to:

- the traffic demand from and to the sovereign territory of the contracting party that has designated the air carriers;
- the existing traffic demand in the areas of transit while taking local and regional air services into consideration; and
- the requirements of an economic operation of the transit air carriers.

The Bermuda clause allows air carriers of both contracting States to be very flexible when determining the respective shares in the entire transport service volume. However, there is one restriction: in the case of one party signing the bilateral agreement being unsatisfied with the extent or the share that one air carrier has in transport services, a consultation mechanism can be started. States thus have the option of *ex-post-facto*-control with regard to capacities, which is one of the main elements of the Bermuda Agreement.

Such control is effectuated using statistics that the designated air carriers have to provide to the contracting parties. This Bermuda clause is also included in the new Bermuda II Agreement, which includes the additional obligation of both contracting States to prevent both overcapacities and undercapacities.

(b) Predetermination-Clause

This clause stipulates predetermination of the offered capacity. It is often used when States with air carriers that differ in terms of economic strength conclude an air services agreement, since the State with the economically weaker air carrier (e.g., a State of the so-called Third World) is interested to ensure such air carrier a certain share in the total service offer. This clause assumes that the air carriers of two countries are entitled exclusively and equally to operate air services between these two countries and that such air carriers themselves reach agreements on distribution of the services that have to be offered to meet the demand, which then again have to be authorized by the governments of the States involved. As opposed to the Bermuda clause, the predetermination rule does not require later control, but rather predetermination of capacities.

The advantages of the predetermination clause are ensuring equal shares and mutual benefit when operating the agreed services, preventing overcapacity through close adaptation of the service offer to the demand and guaranteeing high profitability of operated services. However, it is also clear that this rule, on the other hand, significantly restricts the planning and development opportunities of air carriers, which strive for expansion to increase productivity, which is prevented through being dependent on the authorization of the air carrier of the other contracting State.

(c) Free-Determination-Clause
In the Second ICAO Aviation Conference in spring 1980, the US proposed a Free-Determination Clause to counteract the development towards even more restrictions in scheduled air traffic and to strengthen the liberalization of global air traffic that they were envisioning. This clause is based on the principle of fair and equal competition opportunities of the designated air carriers of both contracting States, but also aims to give each of these air carriers the responsibility of free determination of the capacity that such air carrier deems appropriate for meeting the expected demand without being subject to restrictions by the government. Each of the designated air carriers can, therefore, operate any number of flights with aircraft of any capacity on the designated routes without later option of control of revocation. The governments of both contracting States shall also pledge to stop any form of discrimination or unfair competition at the disadvantage of a designated air carrier of the other contracting State and to refrain from any one-sided limitation of traffic volume, flight frequency, and other regulations of operation, as well as the type of aircraft used by the designated air carrier of the other contracting State, as long as it is not required for customs processing, technical, operational, or environmental reasons under uniform conditions pursuant to Article 15 of the ICAO Convention. Furthermore, no contracting State shall impose any first refusal requirements, uplift ratios, non-objection fees, or any other claims contradictory to the purposes of the agreement on the designated air carriers of the other contracting States with regard to capacity, frequency, or traffic.

This far-reaching deregulation of market access has prevailed on the racecourse of global air traffic: the North Atlantic. It can be found in many bilateral agreements between the US and European countries and has now also been included in agreements of the US with the EC.[87] However, it requires potent air carriers and a similar traffic volume on both sides. Since such conditions do not yet exist in other traffic areas than traffic between the US and several European or Asian states, predetermination and Bermuda clauses are still very prevalent in these agreements.

(d) Change of equipment
The Bermuda I Agreement already included the permission to change flight equipment, for example, after a stopover, if meaningful for economic reasons, for example, because only a small number of passengers continued their travel without changing capacity (change of gauge). Service beyond the point of change of equipment may be continued with one or two aircraft to the same or different destinations under the same or different flight numbers whose capacity for departing services is overall not bigger, for arriving services overall not smaller than that of the arriving aircraft. Furthermore, operation of such aircraft for such services must be planned together with operation of

87. For details see Ch. 8 II.

the arriving or departing aircraft, meaning it must be designated as a connecting service in the route schedule (e.g., paragraph D of the newly formulated route schedule of the German-American Air Services Agreement concluded through Article 1 of the Interim Agreement of 24 May 1994). Such options are only profitable for air carriers that provide air services between two contracting States over large distances and, therefore, let passengers that were transported with large-scale equipment over long distances continue their travels with smaller aircraft to their final destinations. It has, therefore, become of particular significance for transatlantic traffic.

(e) Combination of services
Normally, the traffic rights granted in a bilateral air services agreement are exercised on the routes defined in the route schedule in a way that the designated air carrier provides regular – daily or weekly – services with an aircraft for a designated route for the duration of a route schedule period from points in the country of origin through intermediate points to points in the other contracting States and points under a certain flight number. Liberal agreements now provide the possibility to combine various flight numbers on one operation of an aircraft. This means that different aircraft with different flight numbers arriving from third States can continue to intermediate points, points in the other contracting State, or points beyond in one aircraft keeping their flight numbers after having changed equipment. After changing equipment at these points, they can then again continue their own services under their respective flight numbers to their final destinations in the other contracting State or points in third countries. This combination of air services requires the involved air carriers also having obtained the appropriate authorization by the involved third States.

Such combination options are especially interesting for air carriers that collect traffic from routes with low traffic volumes at hubs, then transport it from these hubs in larger airplanes to other hubs and from there distribute passengers again. This allows for a more efficient use of the capacity of the operating aircraft. For flight passengers or traffic users, this has the advantage that they are offered services with good connections and therefore often inexpensive scheduled services directly to the desired destination by only one air carrier without having to change to another air carrier, which sometimes has unpleasant consequences that mostly involve losing time.

(f) Joint operation of air services (code-sharing)
Globalization of the economy naturally also affects internationally operating air carriers to a great extent. Company mergers or takeovers are, however, opposed by the nationality clauses in the individual aviation laws as well as in the bilateral agreements: Air carriers that operate scheduled services from a particular country not only have to be registered in that country, but also have to be largely owned and controlled by citizens of that country. This also applies to the EC as a unified economic area. This is why a type of cooperation between air carriers has developed in recent time that opens up markets and

connections to each other and thereby is in some way similar to a corporate merger. So-called code-sharing means that one air carrier also uses the flight service of another air carrier in a way that it books its own transport volume – passengers and freight – under its own flight number on the flight service of the other air carrier, which remains solely responsible for operation of the flight. This usually works in both directions. The underlying contracts between these two air carriers can be of various natures. What is important is the fact that code-sharing allows the flight operated on the service of the other air carrier to appear as a direct service by the first air carrier under its flight number, possibly with two flight numbers, and therefore as its 'on-line' connection in the computer reservation systems. Code-sharing requires both involved air carriers to have traffic rights including the agreed frequencies or capacities on the same serviced routes and to have been authorized to perform code-sharing.[88]

This right not only enables the two air carriers involved to exercise the traffic rights made available to both air carriers by the route schedule to a greater extent, but also to use the operating capacity in a more rational way. Furthermore, code-sharing partners receive access to the market of the other air carrier. It is only through code-sharing that aviation alliances become possible and meaningful. It is of great significance that the code-sharing service is represented as on-line-connection and not as a connection requiring changing to the services of another air carrier in the computer reservation systems. However, the passenger has to be informed that it is a code-sharing service when purchasing the ticket. Simply using a double flight number would not be sufficient since it is not stated on the flight passenger's ticket. The flight passenger would then only learn about the double flight number during processing at the airport without any prior information, which would surprise or even upset him, especially because the selection of one particular air carrier is often a very conscious decision.

Pursuant to Article 15 of Council Regulation (EEC) No. 1008/2008[89] (formerly: Article 7 of Council Regulation (EEC) No. 2408/92[90]), the Member States grant inner-Community air carriers permission to operationally connect air services and use the same flight number. Code-sharing is also an important element in the newly concluded Air Services Agreements between the US and European countries (also Article 5 of the Interim Agreement with the Federal Republic of Germany of 24 May 1994 or Article 9, paragraph 6 of the Agreement USA/Germany). It allows close cooperation between the involved air carriers in the form of close market relationship and coordination of products and route schedules. It is a type of interline agreement. This is what makes it different from so-called blocked space agreements, where a certain contingent

88. VG Köln, Beschluss vom 1. Oktober 1993 (4 L 1236/93), *ZLW* (German Journal of Air and Space Law) (1994), 363.
89. *OJ* No. L 293 of 31 Oct. 2008, 3.
90. *OJ* No. L 240 of 24 Aug. 1992, 8.

of seats is fixed on the flight service of the other air carrier under whose number the service operates. Code-sharing, on the other hand, is a market instrument in accordance with the interline rules.[91]

Code-sharing only becomes problematic when it is effectuated by air carriers from third States, because these air carriers then participate in the market between the partners of the bilateral air services agreement. Therefore, code-sharing with third-State air carriers generally only grants access to the respective domestic air service on the condition that the domestic services are operated by the domestic air carriers (also Article 5 Sections C (2) and (3) of the German-American Interim Agreement of 24 May 1994).

Thus, code-sharing is not a legal term, but a colloquial term that designates a complex economic phenomenon. As such, it has to be integrated into the area of public and private aviation law. Especially, restrictions to traffic rights, capacities, or frequencies defined in bilateral agreements must not be bypassed by code-sharing. Furthermore, the air carrier must not dispose of its liability towards its contracting partner (the passenger) by transporting the passenger though another air carrier and possibly trying to eliminate liability *inter partes*.[92]

(6) Tariffs

The tariff provisions in BASAs generally do not provide for governments of the involved States to determine the tariffs, but leave the structure of tariffs up to the air carriers, which then have to present them to the aviation authorities for authorization:

(a) Tariff determination criteria

BASAs based on the Bermuda I Agreement provide that the tariffs for the routes defined in the route schedule 'are determined with consideration of all factors such as operating costs, a reasonable profit, the special conditions of various routes and tariffs of other air carriers servicing the same route or parts of the same route'. Adjusting to the more liberal agreements that have been concluded in the meantime as well as to the EC regulations, the revised German model agreement now only requires that the tariffs applied on the designated routes take the following aspects into consideration: operating costs, a reasonable profit, existing competitive and market conditions, and the interests of the user.

The cost/profit situation of the air carriers that forms the basis for calculating the tariffs is based on the assumption that only an economically healthy air carrier can guarantee safe, reliable, and effective scheduled air services. This requires cost-effective tariffs according to performance. The cost/profit structure of the respective air carrier is, therefore, the main economic basis of tariffs, more specifically the cost/profit situation of scheduled air service as one particular

91. See De Groot, Code-Sharing, United States' policies and the lessons for Europe, *Air & Space Law* (1994), 62.
92. Giemulla/van Schyndel, 'Rechtsprobleme des Codesharing' (Code-sharing: Legal problems), Vol. 7–8, 1997 *TranspR* (Transport Law) (1997), 257.

branch of the air carrier. However, sufficient liquidation of the investment capital including reasonable interest of the invested equity has to be guaranteed (e.g., Article 6, paragraph 1a of the former Regulation (EEC) No. 2409/92[93]).

The requirement included in the tariff articles of the agreements that tariffs shall refer to the route determined in the route schedule and are to take the special conditions of the various routes into consideration, does not, however, take the network character of air services into account, which makes dividing costs and profits for the individual routes or parts of a route of a connected network more difficult. Air services that touch several points or also have feeder or distribution functions to other services in addition to point-to-point services, hardly allow for the network to be divided into route specific annual accounts, especially performance reports and attribution of common, fixed, and related costs. Therefore, a cost/profit calculation for the entire network, or at least a cost/profit calculation with internal balance of cost for certain traffic areas, must be accepted as being sufficient.

Apart from protection against overpriced tariffs, traffic users have a right of equal treatment with regard to location and tariff system. Equal treatment in location means guaranteeing the same tariffs for the same air services in any location and preventing location-specific special charges. From a German point of view, this can only be applied to the area of the Federal Republic of Germany and means that location disadvantages of individual airports must not be strengthened by differentiating tariffs in both domestic and international scheduled air service, but that it has to be based on a standard – for example, distance related – tariff calculation system. The principle of personal equal treatment of traffic users within a tariff system, which can also be expressed with the term 'non-discriminatory',[94] only allows differentiations in the tariff system of an air carrier following criteria applying to everybody in the same way. Tariff reductions must be justified towards the passenger paying the full price by conditions of participation that appropriately and sufficiently limit the travellers' flexibility.

(b) Tariff determination

Since very few air carriers exclusively affect service between two countries, but mostly include intermediate points and continuing service, the tariff articles of almost all air services agreements that follow the model of the Bermuda I Agreement provide that both air carriers, when determining tariffs, should comply with decisions that can be applied due to the tariff determination process of the International Air Transport Association (IATA). IATA was assigned an important organizational function for air services when taking on the responsibility for tariff coordination. The goal was to create the conditions necessary for a functional air traffic system with globally

93. *OJ* No. L 240 of 24 Aug. 1992, 1. Now repealed by Art. 27 of Regulation (EC) No. 1008/2008 of the European Parliament and of the Council of 24 Sep. 2008 on common rules for the operation of air services in the Community, *OJ* No. L 293 of 31 Oct. 2008, 3.
94. Cf. Art. 23 of EC-Regulation 1008/2008.

interchangeable licenses, cooperation of air carriers in booking, processing of passengers, freight, and luggage.

However, this task became much more difficult for IATA through the economic development in international air traffic, especially above the North Atlantic, through increasing competition from casual air carriers, through conclusion of liberal air services agreements, but especially through the show cause process of the American Civil Aeronautics Board, which questioned the indemnity of IATA tariff determination from US antitrust law.

(c) Tariff approval

Pursuant to the tariff clauses of the traditional air services agreements of the Bermuda I Type, the designated air carriers have to present the tariffs that they want to apply on the routes determined in the route schedule to the aviation authorities of both contracting States for approval not later than one month before the planned first day of application. The tariffs may only be applied when they have been approved by both aviation authorities, the so-called double approval rule. In the case of the aviation authority of one contracting State not being prepared to accept the tariffs or parts of the tariffs, the aviation authorities first have to discuss the matter. The new tariffs can only be introduced when the authorities reach an agreement in the course of such discussions or when, in the case of non-agreement, the matter is decided by arbitration.

When the US, in the course of its deregulation policies, no longer permitted its air carriers operating in the North Atlantic air traffic to participate in multilateral tariff determination within the IATA or in bilateral tariff agreements, conflicts arose concerning the responsibility of tariff determination that was now with the governments. The extremely liberal American aviation policies were shared by very few States (and especially not by States of the so-called Third World), and even States that were open for revision of the agreements were not willing to completely give up tariff control. To prevent conflict situations, the US offered such States the 'country of origin disapproval rule'. According to this rule, the country of origin of the service can make the final decision on which tariffs are to be applied for the traffic starting in its country in the case of disagreement. This meant that the State retained the possibility to influence strongly at least departing air services. However, contrary to the traditional double approval rule this clause entails a limitation because a government's own ideas on competition, tariff determination, and market behaviour can only be implemented for air services originating in its own territory.

Where the US had managed to implement its liberal model agreement, the double disapproval or mutual disagreement rule included in this agreement applies. According to this rule, the tariffs of the air carriers are only submitted at the aviation authorities of both contracting States and automatically come into force when they are not specifically suspended by the aviation authorities of both contracting States. However, this is only possible when both aviation authorities agree that the tariffs are of a predatory price nature or have discriminating effects. This includes tariffs that are either set below the cost level to push competitors from the market or that are overpriced, taking advantage of market dominance. It is also prohibited to keep tariffs artificially low through direct or indirect government subsidies. In the case of differing ideas on competition and market conditions, it will be difficult for both aviation authorities to reach an agreement. There is no provision for arbitration. Therefore, the air carriers can determine their tariffs basically as they wish, and the tariffs can be completely fixed as a result of the conditions of free competition. This clause is the complete opposite of the double approval rule included in the Bermuda I Agreement and even goes far beyond the 'country of origin disapproval rule'. Its fundamental idea was also the basis of the EEC regulation on fares and rates for air services (Regulation EEC No. 2409/92[95]) applied to inner-Community air services from 1993 to 2008.

While tariffs for domestic and inner-Community air services were initially subject to Regulation EEC No. 2409/92 and where now Article 22 of Regulation EC No. 1008/2008 applies, the tariffs of the bilateral agreements as a general rule remain applicable for international air services between domestic airports and airports located outside the EU.

(d) Tariff control

The Bermuda I Type Agreements are based on the assumption of an organized aviation market, whose profitability has to be ensured by achieving high occupancy rates through capacities closely adapted to traffic demand and by making appropriate profit through a fixed tariff system. This also caused guarantee of complying with the fixed tariffs. Since, pursuant to these agreements, it was mainly up to the designated air carriers to determine the tariffs to be applied globally together with other air carriers within the limits of the IATA, the governments had also appointed the task of monitoring of these tariffs to the IATA by authorizing the self-monitoring system of the IATA.

However, it was also in the interest of the IATA to keep the existing market organization of international air services functional and to protect air carriers bound to the tariffs determined at the traffic conferences by their membership in the IATA against ruinous competition through tariff dumping.

Therefore, the IATA had developed its own tariff monitoring system. A Compliance Office subordinate to the IATA General Director identified tariff breaches, which were given a warning, punished by a fine of up to USD 50,000, and, in the worst cases, exclusion of the respective member from the IATA upon lawsuit by the General Director of the Breaches Commission.

Reorganization of the IATA, the absence of concluded tariff agreements in their own traffic areas (especially the North Atlantic), and fares of many outsiders that are not members of the IATA as well as the liberalization within the EC have made it much more difficult for the IATA to monitor compliance

95. *OJ* No. L 240 of 24 Aug. 1992, 1.

with tariffs. This was true for both the area of passengers and the area of freight. The IATA thought it was no longer justified to disadvantage its members by encouraging them to stick to the tariffs when outsiders were able to stay below the IATA tariffs as they pleased. In the course of its reorientation in 1979, the liberalization of the markets in air services with the US and in inner-Community air traffic in particular caused the IATA to shift the focus of its tariff monitoring function in an attempt to prevent tariff irregularities. For this purpose, it introduced the Fair Deal Monitoring Programme, which replaced the stricter Compliance Programme, established a Fair Deal Monitoring Group, and significantly reduced the number of controllers. It limited its sanctions to warnings and reprimands of small violations in summary proceedings, suing only severe violations at the Federation Court and temporary cancellation of tariff monitoring for a traffic area. The IATA thought that it had met the concerns of its changed significance in international aviation through this change of its tariff monitoring policies.

However, tariff monitoring of the IATA is of virtually no significance any longer under the liberal air services agreements.

b. The Airspace: Responsibility (Article 1)

i. General

The Principle of Sovereignty of the Air does not only serve the purpose of excluding any other State power from the airspace of a State. It also bears consequences on the responsibility of a State over its airspace. To name some examples set forth in the Convention: Every aircraft must be registered in some State and bear its nationality (Articles 17 and 18). States must also ensure that their aircraft will comply with the rules and regulations in force wherever the aircraft may be (Article 12). States are also required to issue certificates of airworthiness for their aircraft and to provide licenses for the crews of those aircraft (Articles 31 and 32). Last but not least, the state of registry has jurisdiction over offences committed on board its aircraft.[96]

ii. Standards and Recommended Practices and Procedures for Air Navigation Services: Compliances and Departures (Articles 37 and 38)

An important tool of organizing and guaranteeing safety on a worldwide-standardized level is set forth in Articles 37 and 38 of the Convention. These two articles define the mechanism for the goal described as follows in the Preamble of the Convention: 'It is desirable to avoid friction and to promote that cooperation between nations and peoples upon which the peace of the world depends . . . '

The choice of the word 'desirable' shows that the authors of the Convention were in an unavoidable conflict of goals: on the one hand, creating the highest

96. Convention on Offenses and Certain Other Acts Committed on Board Aircraft, Art. 3, 14 Sep. 1963, 704 UNTS 219, 20 U.S.T. 2941.

possible rate of standardization of aviation requirements and procedures worldwide, while on the other hand, not setting such high requirements that it becomes impossible for the majority of less-developed countries to meet these requirements and at the same time not setting them so low that they stay below the standards that have already been achieved in the more-developed economies.

This 'on the one hand and on the other hand' has become obvious in the mechanism of Articles 37 and 38 of the Convention, while a distinction is made between standards and recommended practices and procedures. Pursuant to Article 37 (adoption of international standards and procedures) '(e)ach contracting State undertakes to collaborate in securing the highest practicable degree of uniformity in regulations, standards, procedures, and organization in relation to aircraft, personnel, airways and auxiliary services in all matters in which such uniformity will facilitate and improve air navigation. To this end the International Civil Aviation Organization shall adopt and amend from time to time, as may be necessary, international standards and recommended practices and procedures dealing with . . . ' a number of issues listed there.

Article 38 allows 'departures from international standards and procedures' under certain conditions: 'Any state which finds it impracticable to comply in all respects with any such international standard or procedure, or to bring its own regulations or practices into full accord with any international standard or procedure after amendment of the latter, or which deems it necessary to adopt regulations or practices differing in any particular respect from those established by an international standard, shall give immediate notification to the International Civil Aviation Organization of the differences between its own practice and that established by the international standard.' (first Sentence).

While the Member States are generally only obligated to adopt standards and procedures (see headline above Article 37), complying with recommendations is not binding (also see Sentence 1 of Article 37). Accordingly, there is no reason to make it binding for Member States to give notification when deviating from a recommendation. Such a notification is only compulsory in the case of non-compliance with a standard or a procedure (provided by Article 38).

An 'international standard' in the sense of Articles 37, 38, and 54 is defined as 'any specification for characteristics, configuration, material, performance, personnel or procedure, the uniform application of *which is recognized as necessary* for the safety or regularity of international air navigation and to which contracting States will conform in accordance with the Convention; in the event of impossibility of compliance, notification to the Council is compulsory under Article 38 of the Convention'[97] (emphasis added). The differences to SARPs notified by States are published in Supplements to Annexes.

A 'recommended practice' in the sense of Articles 37 and 54 is defined as 'any specification for physical characteristics, configuration, material, performance, personnel or procedure, the uniform application of *which is recognized as desirable* in the interest of safety, regularity or efficiency of international air

97. ICAO Assembly Resolution A35-14.

navigation and to which contracting States will endeavour to conform in accordance with the Convention'[98] (emphasis added). Although not obligatory, States are invited to inform the Council of non-compliance.

Finally, international procedures have been laid down specifically for air navigation services (PANS).[99] They comprise operating practices and material too detailed for Standards or Recommended Practices – they often amplify the basic principles in the corresponding SARPs. To qualify for PANS status, the material should be suitable for application on a worldwide basis. The Council invites contracting States to publish any differences in their aeronautical information publications when knowledge of the differences is important to the safety of air navigation. In practice, they are treated on the same footing as standards in most respects.[100]

SARPs are formulated in broad terms and restricted to essential requirements. For complex systems such as communications equipment, SARPs material is constructed in two sections: core SARPs – material of a fundamental regulatory nature contained within the main body of the Annexes, and detailed technical specifications placed either in Appendices to Annexes or in manuals. In 2006, ICAO (presented by the Secretariat) issued guidelines for the development of SARPs material for complex systems.[101]

International SARPs are adopted by the Council and its subsidiary bodies and incorporated as Annexes to the Convention. Under Article 54 Lit. l) of the Convention, the Council shall 'adopt, in accordance with the provisions of Chapter VI of this Convention, international SARPs; for convenience, designate them as Annexes to this Convention; and notify all contracting States of the action taken' (see also Article 90 of the Convention). Meanwhile, there are eighteen Annexes to the Chicago Convention that cover all aspects of international civil aviation:

- Annex 1 Personnel Licensing (1948).
- Annex 2 Rules of the Air (1948).
- Annex 3 Meteorological Service for International Air Navigation (1948).
- Annex 4 Aeronautical Charts (1948).
- Annex 5 Units of Measurement to Be Used in Air and Ground Operations (1948).
- Annex 6 Operation of Aircraft (1948).
- Annex 7 Aircraft Nationality and Registration Marks (1949).
- Annex 8 Airworthiness of Aircraft (1949).
- Annex 9 Facilitation (1949).
- Annex 10 Aeronautical Telecommunications (1949).
- Annex 11 Air Traffic Services (1950).
- Annex 12 Search and Rescue (1950).

98. *Ibid.*
99. See in particular the PANS-OPS, *ICAO Doc.* 8168; PANS/ATM, ICAO Doc. 4444; PANS/ABC, *ICAO Doc.* 8400; and the SUPPS, *ICAO Doc.* 7030.
100. *Ibid.*
101. *Ibid.*

- Annex 13 Aircraft Accident and Incident Investigation (1951).
- Annex 14 Aerodromes (1951).
- Annex 15 Aeronautical Information Services (1953).
- Annex 16 Environmental Protection (1971).
- Annex 17 Security – Safeguarding International Civil Aviation against Acts of Unlawful Interference (1974).
- Annex 18 The Safe Transport of Dangerous Goods by Air (1984).

The following organs of ICAO are in charge of setting and issuing:[102]

- Procedures for Air Navigation Services (PANS), approved by the Council (Air Navigation Commission).
- Regional Supplementary Procedures – referred to as SUPPs and approved by the Council, SUPPs have applications in the respective ICAO regions. Although the material in SUPPs is similar to that in PANS, SUPPs do not have the worldwide applicability of PANS.
- Guidance material in several formats, published by the Secretary General. Guidance material is produced to supplement the SARPs and PANS and to facilitate their implementation. Guidance material is issued as Attachments to Annexes or in separate documents such as manuals, circulars, and lists of addresses. Usually it is approved at the same time as the related SARPs are adopted.
- Manuals provide information to supplement and/or amplify SARPs and PANS. They are specifically designed to facilitate implementation and are amended periodically to ensure that their contents reflect current practices and procedures.
- Circulars make available specialized information of interest to contracting States. Unlike manuals, circulars are not normally updated.

iii. Airport and Similar Charges/Russian Overflight Charges (Article 15)

Under Article 15 (last Sentence) of the Convention '(n)o fees, dues or other charges shall be imposed by any contracting State in respect solely of the right of transit over or entry into or exit from its territory of any aircraft of a contracting State or persons or property thereon'.

Against the background of the overall contents of Article 15, this means also that no charges shall be raised from which the proceeds are not used as remuneration for the use of an airport or air navigation facilities.

(a) ICAO Resolution on Taxation in International Air Transport

Each contracting State shall reduce to the fullest practicable extent and make plans to eliminate as soon as its economic conditions permit all forms of taxation on the sale or use of international transport by air, including taxes on gross receipts of operators and taxes levied directly on passengers or shippers.[103]

102. <www.icao.int/icao/en/anb/mais/>.

103. ICAO's Policies on Taxation in the Field of International Air Transport, *ICAO Doc.* 8632, <www.icao.int/icaonet/dcs/8632/8632_cons_en.pdf>.

(b) ICAO Policies on Charges for Airports and Air Navigation
The Chicago Convention permits the imposition of charges specifically to recover the costs of providing facilities and services to international civil aviation.[104] User charges are the basic source of income for an airport. Airport charges can represent a significant portion of the overall costs of air carriers, amounting for instance, from 10% to 20% of the total operating costs of a typical one-to-two-hour regional flight. The level of investment at an airport necessarily needs to be reflected in the level and structure of charges. Article 15 of the Chicago Convention (1944) set forth the following:

> Any charges that may be imposed or permitted to be imposed by a contracting State for the use of such airports and air navigation facilities by the aircraft of any other contracting State shall not be higher:
>
> (a) As to aircraft not engaged in scheduled international air services, than those that would be paid by its national aircraft of the same class engaged in similar operations, and
> (b) As to aircraft engaged in scheduled international air services, than those that would be paid by its national aircraft engaged in similar international air services.

Non-discrimination, uniformity, covering the cost of the facilities and services, are the main issues in this regard.
Charge differentials affect entry and exit, but they may also influence the nature of competition in the international aviation market. It could represent a disadvantage to operate in high-cost airports rather than in markets where the costs are lower.

The ICAO has a set of manuals that specifically address issues at airports and facilities in relation to the political and economic fields, such as the ICAO's *Policies on Charges for Airports and Air Navigation Services*,[105] which sets forth recommendations and conclusions on these subjects, the *Manual on Air Navigation Services Economics*,[106] which provides guidance material to assist those responsible for the management of air navigation services, and the *Airport Economics Manual*,[107] which provides guidance to those responsible for airport management. A new document prepared by the ICAO Secretary, *Performance Management and Measurement for Air Navigation Services Providers,* was presented in Spain in 2007 and focused on safety, as well as quality of service issues such as capacity, delay and flight efficiency, productivity, and cost-effectiveness.

(c) Russian Overflight Charges
This provision of Article 15, last Sentence, prohibits imposing a charge for simply granting the right (of transit) as such. Consequently, overflight charges would be

104. ICAO's Policies on Charges for Airports and Air Navigation Services, *ICAO Doc.* 9082, <www.icao.int/icaonet/dcs/9082/9082_7ed_en.pdf>.
105. *ICAO Doc.* 9082.
106. *ICAO Doc.* 9161.
107. *ICAO Doc.* 9562.

illegal, since the Russian Federation as the legal successor of the Union of Soviet Socialist Republics (USSR) is a Member State of the Convention and since such charges would not be in return of a service (air traffic control /ATC/ services), but would be imposed for the 'overflight right' as such. The Russian side recognized this and chose an obviously legally less vulnerable way when negotiating air service agreements. European carriers had to conclude commercial agreements with Aeroflot to pay 'royalties' for the use of the Siberian air routes to Asia (app. EUR 300 million p. a.).

The nature of 'royalties' are not charges (imposed by a State), but (commercial) fees for one air carrier granting another one a commercial chance.

The (legal) option to charge a fee for granting this chance requires that having this chance was initially of monetary value. Therefore, the question arises whether the traffic rights exercised by a designated air carrier are part of the assets of such air carrier.

The reasons for traffic rights to be established are usually the bilateral agreements between the respective States, which define capacities, frequencies, and destination points. The involved States grant each other the same chances in the non-liberalized agreements at least, which mainly not happens for (commercial) protection of the respective domestic air carrier from those of the contracting State, but which is rather a reflection of the international principle of reciprocity. When the designated carrier(s) is/are not able to fully exercise these rights and when such carrier(s) grant(s) the carrier of the contracting State the right to exercise traffic rights granted to the first carrier, then this happens in the interest of both contracting States (using the entire capacity in the interest of complete servicing of traffic between the two contracting States). Thus, traffic rights are legal positions subject to public law that were not, at least not mainly, established in the interest of the involved carriers and therefore do not constitute any subjective legal position of such carriers. Therefore, they cannot be commercialized from a legal perspective either. Requiring a commercial agreement to be concluded as a precondition for granting traffic rights to foreign air carriers is therefore illegal as well.

This legal concept is becoming more and more prevalent in Russia as well (also as a result of the pressure of the World Trade Organization (WTO), which demanded 'royalties' to be suspended before allowing the Russian Federation into the WTO. Negotiations between the European Union and Russia in the end of November 2006 led to a political agreement on the draft for a decision on signing and temporarily applying the agreement with Russia on agreed principles of modernization of the existing system for using Trans-Siberian routes. This agreement – if it is ratified by the Russian Parliament – will put an end to a twenty-year conflict. Existing payments are to be gradually decreased from 2010–2013. From 2014, there are to be transparent fees for Siberia overflights. The usual navigation fees as per the Chicago Convention, which cover the costs of ATC and are used for its development would be the only fees that would still apply. Trade commissioner Peter Mandelson commented that '(t)his matter has long been a disturbing factor in the trade relationship between the EU and Russia.' The agreement showed 'that the

EU and Russia are capable of solving trade conflicts by negotiation if they want to.'[108]

iv. Air Traffic Control Services (Article 28)

Under Article 28 subsection (a) '(e)ach contracting State undertakes . . . to provide, in its territory, airports, radio services, meteorological services and other air navigation facilities to facilitate international air navigation, in accordance with standards and practices recommended or established from time to time, pursuant to this Convention . . . '. The background of this provision is that each State is responsible for provision and functioning of the mentioned air navigation facilities in its airspace. It must be derived from this provision that the State not only has to provide ATC for its airspace, but that it is also responsible for the according ATC organization. The 'ideal type' behind this provision is certainly the notion that a State either operates ATC through its own administrative unit or through a company that such State can influence at any time and with any regard, that is by holding the majority of voting shares.

Navigation of aircraft, ATC and advisory services provided to aircraft, is facilitated by electronic and other navigation aids, by data acquisition and data processing systems, by radar systems, communications networks, and automated flight data processing and display systems.

Let us not forget the latest innovation: the Communications, Navigation, and Surveillance Systems for Air Traffic Management (CNS/ATM). Undoubtedly, the concept represents a revolution in ATM systems, which involves elements such as communications, navigation, and surveillance.

The communications element encompasses the complementary use of satellite- and ground-based technology to provide global coverage in the exchange of aeronautical data and voice communication between users and automated systems.

In navigation, it provides accurate, reliable, and seamless position determination capability for the benefit of the pilot.

For surveillance, it provides the air controller the position of the aircraft.

The use of satellite systems in air navigation was initiated during the fifteenth Period of the Assembly of the ICAO and was the point of departure of the subsequent studies. Those were times of the first space explorations and the first participations of the UN to preserve neutrality in this type of activity.

Resolution A15-1 refers to the ICAO's participation in the exploration and development of the space programmes. This resolution was the basis of the establishment of the ASTRAP (Application of Space Techniques Relating to Aviation Panel) on 26 March 1968.

Later, in October 1977, during the twenty-second Period of the Assembly, these elements were launched in Resolution A22-20,[109] which assigned to the

108. <http://europa.eu/rapid/pressReleasesAction.do?reference=IP/06/1626&format=HTML&aged=1&language= DE&guiLanguage=en>.
109. <www.icao.int/icao/en/assembl/a22/docs/a22_res01.djvu>.

ICAO the responsibility of representing international civil aviation in all the issues concerning outer space, requiring the Council to continue the studies so as to indicate the operational and technical requirements necessary for the establishment of an international air navigation system with the use of satellites.

On this date, the commitment of the ICAO as a leader in the field was born. Later, the resolution was replaced by Resolution A29-11,[110] which contains a list of criteria on the special programme calling for the use of space technology in air navigation.

This resolution also reinforces the proactive functions of the ICAO to introduce the concept of CNS/ATM with an appropriate balance between safety and economic aspects.

This concept was elaborated step-by-step during the Air Navigation Conferences, and was originally known as the Future Air Navigation System (FANS).

In April 1972, during the seventh Conference in Montreal, the use of the satellite technologies in air navigation was debated, and the need to create an international programme to research, develop, and evaluate the new system was recognized.

A few years later, during the tenth Air Navigation Conference in September 1991, the participants strongly supported the concept, adopting Recommendation 9/1.

Meanwhile, the FANS Committee developed the studies finished in 1988, with guideline, documents, and model cases to facilitate the contracting States' preparation, execution, and provision of air navigation services based on the new system.

However, the crucial point was made at the tenth Air Navigation Conference, with twenty-three recommendations, among others, regarding the need to consider institutional arrangements on a global level.

In July 1989, the Council of the ICAO established the FANS II Committee with the objective of coordinating and planning the transition period during which it should implement the CNS/ATM concept.

The result of the participation of the FANS II Committee was the identification of certain legal aspects for each scenario, with the following elements:

- relationship with the providers;
- uniformity in the contractual element;
- its mandatory nature;
- relationship with the Chicago Convention 1944; and
- liability system.

The last consideration brings us to the role of the Legal Committee of the ICAO in the development of CNS/ATM.

During the twenty-seventh Period (March-April 1990), the Legal Committee emphasized the need to coordinate the legal studies with the work agenda of the FANS II Committee.

---

110. <www.icao.int/icao/en/assembl/a29/docs/a29_res01.djvu>.

During the twenty-eighth Period (May 1992), the Legal Committee worked on the bases prepared by the aforementioned technical group. At the twenty-ninth Session of the Legal Committee, in accordance with the work prepared by Dr Kenneth Rattray (Jamaica), the Rapporteur on the matter, a draft Memorandum of Understanding (MOU) was presented as a starting point for the draft of an international legal instrument. Such a document should have the form of an international convention or agreement, in the opinion of the Rapporteur, based on several principles, such as universal accessibility, duration of services and absence of charges, compliance with the ICAO's SARPs, responsibility and liability for services, provision of information and monitoring by the ICAO, and preservation of sovereignty and the rights of States to control aircraft operations and enforce safety regulations within their own territories.

In July 1994, the need to prepare an international legal framework to put the concept in force was recognized.

Two groups worked on the conditions of the transition from the traditional elements to the new concept. The CNS/ATM Systems Implementation Task Force (CASITAF) was created in 1994, integrated by twenty-three members, representatives of fifteen contracting States and international entities, and a Group of Experts in Economic Aspects of the Air Navigation Services (ANSEP), established in the same year.

During the thirty-first Period of the Assembly, the participants underlined again the need to create a legal framework to cover all of the aspects presented by the CNC/ATM.

On 9 March 1994, the Council of the ICAO adopted a policy statement outlining the fundamental principles to be adhered to in the implementation and operation of the CNS/ATM systems.

Among others, they include the following:

- universal accessibility;
- sovereignty, authority, and responsibility of States;
- responsibility and role of the ICAO for the adoption and amendment of SARPs;
- technical cooperation;
- use of existing organizational structure and institutional arrangements;
- evolutionary implementation of the Global Navigation Satellite System (GNSS);
- efficient airspace organization and utilization;
- continuity and quality of services; and
- reasonable cost allocation to users.

In October 1994, the US sent a letter to the Council of the ICAO formalizing its offer of a Global Positioning System (GPS) for use by the international community. A similar offer was made by the Russian Federation of the provision for a standard Global Orbiting Navigation Satellite System (GLONASS) to the world aeronautic community, on 4 February 1996. Both offers of free signals from space were accepted by the Council, and despite comments about their legal validity, among other issues, neither the President nor the Council had the faculty to accept on behalf of the international air community, a commitment regarding the arrangements of GNSS, in line with Article 65 of the Chicago Convention (1944). Nevertheless, the documents represent a moral commitment by the US as well as by the Russian Federation.

The Worldwide CNS/ATM Systems Implementation Conference was called by the ICAO in Rio de Janeiro, Brazil, in May 1998. Civil aviation authorities and industry representatives participated, and the primary objective of the conference was to convince service providers and financial institutions that implementation of the systems would generate a significant positive return on investment, which could be recovered through user charges.

The conference finally adopted a Declaration on Global Air Navigation Systems for the Twenty First Century, declaring, *inter alia*, that:

> Increasing levels of cooperation at the national, sub regional and global levels, will be necessary to ensure transparency and interoperability between system elements,
>
> The operation of air navigation services by autonomous authorities may contribute to significant economies, increased efficiency and transparency,
>
> Financing and operations of CNS/ATM systems can be of common benefit to lenders, borrowers and users,
>
> Sound financial management is critical to securing financing for CNS/ATM projects,
>
> Planning and implementation of the systems should be on the basis of homogenous air traffic management areas and major international traffic flows, taking into account the diversity of technology.

Whatever administrative mechanism is chosen by the contracting States, it is recommended that the cost of implementing and operating the CNS/ATM be recovered through user charges in accordance with the services cost recovery policy. Article 15 of the Chicago Convention establishes the following principles:

- Uniform conditions shall apply to the use, by aircraft of all contracting States, of airport and air navigation facilities provided in the territory of a contracting State.
- Any charge imposed for the use of such airports and air navigation facilities by the aircraft of other contracting State shall not be higher than those that would be paid by its national aircraft engaged in similar operations.
- No fees, dues, or other charges shall be imposed by any contracting State in respect solely of the right of transit over or entry into or exit from its territory of any aircraft of a contracting State.

Finally, it is extremely important that every State takes into account the previsions contained in Article 28 of the Chicago Convention; each contracting State has undertaken, so far as it may find practicable, to provide in its territory air navigation facilities in accordance with the ICAO's SARPs.

The implementation of CNS/ATM on a global basis will be completed in a few years. The deadline was fixed for 2010, but there are still many concerns over how it will be performed. Many developing countries expressed that there should be an international legal framework to ensure the principles of transparency, continuity, and consequent responsibility in case of eventual damages caused by negligence in the provision of the signal.

Today, air navigation services are suffering from a State-induced fragmentation that is driven by different policy goals and objectives, different national legislation, different standards, different procedures, and different systems in each contracting State. Undoubtedly, the institutional fragmentation impacts safety, efficiency, and capacity, and has an adverse effect on performance. To overcome the fragmentation, the CNS-ATM must be applied throughout the entire civil aeronautics community.

One important tool is the Performance Based Navigation (PBN) that represents the transference from conventional ground based navigation aids and procedures to satellite-based navigation aids and area navigation procedures. The concept needs a coordinated action plan to assist States in the implementation of PBN according to ICAO guidelines.

At present, the major players of the air transport industry support the implementation of PBN. Clear benefits of the PNB are amongst others more efficient take-offs and landings, reduction of fuel burn, airport and airspace congestion. Such an approach is in line with the decision adopted by the 36th Session of the ICAO Assembly in 2007 that urged all Member States of the ICAO to have PBN implementation plans ready by 2009.

Given a number of new technological and organizational developments, the question arises whether Article 28 is still appropriate in modern times or whether and how the requirements of this provision can be further developed in a modern manner. This affects at least the following two developments:

(a) Denationalization of ATC Providers
Over the past years, governments have privatized ATC providers more and more, that is, the governments gradually withdrew from their ATC companies and therefore naturally lost their influence on these organizations. In the European Union, the 'single European sky concept'[111] leads to an ATC organization becoming active in the 'Functional Airspace Blocs' (FABs) to be established. Such organization is either a multinational organization or belongs to another State which belongs to a FAB. In both cases, it is only natural that the decisive influence of the government decreases to a minority share in all involved States (multinational organization) or is completely lost in most of the involved States. In the first case, it is no longer the respective State that is responsible for its own airspace, but the involved States. In the second case, the responsibility is even with the ATC provider of a foreign State that operates services in another State. Finally, neither one's own nor another State has the majority influence in the case of

111. For details see Ch. 19 I. F.

privatization, which would ensure that the obligations provided in Article 28 are met. In any case, this development means a loss of influence of the respective government on its airspace and reduces the possibility of the government to assume its responsibility conferred by Article 28 of the Convention.

When considering Article 28 of the Convention, such constructions are therefore only acceptable when the law of the affected State grants the governments the right to influence ATC activities in its State at any given time.

(b) GNSS Systems, not Controlled by States – Implications of Article 28
ICAO took the following position on this: 'A state may delegate the provision function to another entity, including a commercial or private operator . . . The State nevertheless remains responsible for setting and maintaining the standards of the services provided and for the quality of services provided . . . Under those circumstances . . . the relevant states continue to be responsible under Article 28 of the Chicago Convention, regardless of such delegation . . . The implementation of Global Navigation Satellite System (GNSS) leaves unaffected the responsibility of states under Article 28, . . . a state using these signals for providing Air Navigation Services remained responsible under Article 28 despite the fact that it did not control such signals'.[112]

The US's view is the following: 'The United States believe that the legal framework does offer continued serviceability and urges the Conference to recognize this fact accordingly. During the implementation of Communications, Navigation, and Surveillance Systems for Air Traffic Management (CNS/ATM), we have discovered no gaps in the legal framework; that is, we have found no problem that cannot be solved because of defects in the legal or institutional tools available to apply to it. Constraints have proved primarily to be of a technical nature or a matter of the lack of resources and political will, not due to a lack of law . . . Work on legal issues must not be permitted to delay technical implementation of CNS/ATM. This conference should declare the same proviso'.[113]

However, the European view is different and somewhat more problem oriented:

'. . . most States will not be directly involved in the operation of GNSS systems . . . Air navigation within their sovereign airspace will consequently rely heavily on facilities beyond their direct control . . . States will have to ensure in particular that they are able to meet their commitments under Article 28 of the Chicago Convention.

States need to be satisfied that the GNSS signals and services offered within their airspace meet the appropriate performance requirements in terms of integrity, reliability, accuracy, and continuity and that their liability is clearly defined. Presently, no comprehensive framework exists that can provide the equal certainty

112. ICAO, Air Navigation Services Economic Panel, Report on financial and related Organizational and Managerial Aspects of Global Navigation Satellite System (GNSS). Provision and Operation, *ICAO Doc.* 9660 (May 1996), § 2.6 and *ICAO Secretariat Report*, § 3.8.1.
113. AN-Conf/11-WP/160 presented by the US.

required for states or for industry. In a global environment, reliance on national laws and procedures is not sufficient to deal effectively with the challenge of technological advances'.[114]

c. *The Airspace: Definition and Extension (Article 2)*

i. Definition

The question of how the sovereign airspace of a nation is defined is essential as a basis and, at the same time, as a limitation of the principle of sovereignty of the air. Article 1 of the Convention bases the lateral borders of airspace on the respective sovereign territory, but this leaves two questions unanswered, namely:

- Which areas are part of the territory of a State?
- Which criteria apply for the vertical border of the airspace?

Article 2 of the Convention provides the following answer to the first question: 'For the purposes of this Convention the territory of a State shall be deemed to be the land areas and territorial waters thereto under the sovereignty, suzerainty, protection or mandate of such State'. The vertical border is traditionally set at about 80 to 120 km above the ground surface. The criteria for this is equally simple and plausible: since an aircraft is defined by the fact that it 'can derive support in the atmosphere from the reactions of the air . . . ',[115] *their* operating area not only depends on the airspace, but also the other way around: airspace depends on whether aircraft can still move in it as aircraft (as opposed to as rockets).

The so-called Kármán line lies at an altitude of 100 km (62.1 miles) above Earth's sea level, and it is commonly used to define the boundary between Earth's atmosphere and outer space. This definition is accepted by the *Fédération Aéronautique Internationale* (FAI), which is an international standard-setting and record-keeping body for aeronautics and astronautics. The line was named after Theodore von Kármán, a Hungarian-American engineer and physicist who was active primarily in the fields of aeronautics. He first calculated that around this altitude Earth's atmosphere becomes too thin for aeronautical purposes (because any vehicle at this altitude would have to travel faster than orbital velocity to derive sufficient aerodynamic lift from the atmosphere to support itself). Also, there is an abrupt increase in atmospheric temperature and interaction with solar radiation.[116]

Another approach for drawing a line between airspace and outer space is that the airspace ends shortly before a satellite can be operated (cir. 90 km). Some national space acts set the border at 100 up to 120 km.

---

114. AN-Conf/11-WP/153 presented by the European Organization for the Safety of Air Navigation EUROCONTROL, on behalf of its Member States and those of ECAC.
115. See the original text of Annexes 6 and 7 and the amended text of Annex 7 to the Chicago Convention. See also the ICAO Lexicon, 5th edn 1980, *ICAO Doc.* 9294, Vol. 11.
116. Dr S. Sanz Fernández de Córdoba, *100 km altitude boundary for astronautics*, <www.fai.org/astronautics/100km.asp>.

Defining the sovereign airspace is not only important to exclude other States and their citizens from using it or to base such use on an explicit authorization, but it also entails the obligation for the State to take responsibility for the safety of air traffic in its airspace. This responsibility is particularly reflected in Article 26 (investigation of accidents), Article 28 (air navigation facilities and standard systems), and in Article 37 (adoption of international standards and procedures).

There are obviously a number of situations for which this assumption of responsibility limited to a restricted airspace does not offer an adequate solution. For example, ATC is also necessary over the high seas – in an airspace for which there is no national responsibility. Furthermore, it is sometimes necessary to extend ATC into the neighbouring airspace for operational reasons. Finally, the question arises of which national sovereignty is the basis for the Rules of the Air over the high seas being put into force.

ii. Extension

(a) Air Traffic Control over the High Seas

For operational reasons, some ATC providers need to extend their services to parts of the high seas adjacent to their territories. As an example, Germany offers such services over parts of the Atlantic so as to make approaches to some of its airports possible. Other examples are Denmark and Iceland, which render ATC services over the North Atlantic under the Joint Support Agreements of 1956.[117] However, this is not an extension of the airspace of the involved States, but rather an extension of their ATC services to non-sovereign areas. The legal basis in the cases of Denmark and Iceland is the Joint Support Agreement; in cases such as the German example, it is the factual service of the respective ATC providers, which is accepted by the users by means of factual action.

(b) Air Traffic Control in Foreign Airspace

The situation is similar in cases in which the services of an ATC provider are extended to a neighbouring sovereign territory for operational reasons as well. However, one decisive difference from the cases mentioned above is the fact that foreign sovereign power is touched upon here, that is, two sovereign powers come into conflict with each other. There are two possible solutions in such cases:

- The sovereign power of one State is extended to the neighbouring sovereign territory. However, this would require a bilateral convention (with the agreement of both involved parliaments), since extension of one's own sovereign power to a foreign territory or tolerating execution of foreign sovereign power on one's own territory is related to the essential matters of principle of the nature of a nation.

---

117. Agreement on the Joint Financing of Certain Air Navigation Services in Iceland (334 *UNTS* 13; [1959] *ATS* 8) as amended by the Montreal Protocol of 1982 (*ICAO Doc.* 9586-*JS/682*) and the Agreement on the Joint Financing of Certain Air Navigation Services in Greenland (334 *UNTS* 89; [1959] *ATS* 7) as amended by the Montreal Protocol of 1982 (*ICAO Doc.* 9586-*JS/682*).

- One's own sovereign rights are transferred to a foreign ATC. This view is the basis for the European Single European Sky (SES)-Conception.[118] According to this conception, FABs are to be established that cover the airspace of several States. ATC providers are to provide services in these FABs that either come from one of the involved States or are organized in a multinational manner. In each of these cases, the ATC provider of its own country will not exclusively exercise the sovereign powers of such country, but will also operate in other airspaces. This is not only equivalent to abandoning sovereign powers, but it is also a contradiction to Article 28 of the Convention.[119]

(c) Rules of the Air over the High Seas
Finally, the question arises on which basis the Rules of the Air apply in the airspace above the high seas, since there is no sovereign power that could determine or even enforce these rules there. The Convention solves the issue with a legal fiction with Article 12, Sentence 3, stating, 'Over the high seas, the rules in force shall be those established under this Convention', that is, the standards that are formulated in Annex 2 of the Convention. This is one of the rare examples for the immediate applicability of the Annexes (international rather than national law).

d. Civil and State Aircraft

The basis of the Convention, the principle of sovereignty of the air, is not only an agreed basis for the legal structure of the Convention, but it also simply repeats an international principle that would also apply without specifically being mentioned in the Convention. This also becomes clear from the words of Article 1, after which the contracting States do not 'grant', but 'recognize' this principle. The 'complete and exclusive sovereignty over the airspace above its territory' is thus not set by the Convention, but also exists without it and is simply specifically and generally recognized.

This fact is especially important for the areas that are not subject to the Convention, namely, the area of state aircraft. Article 3 (on civil and state aircraft) states in Subsection (a): 'This Convention shall be applicable only to civil aircraft, and shall not be applicable to state aircraft'. This means that operation of State aircraft is not subject to the Convention, but to general international regulations. Considering this, it is essential whether the principle of sovereignty of the air is only a randomly set basis for the application area of the Convention or whether it applies as a whole – that is, also for State aircraft – and therefore only is quoted in the Convention. The general understanding is that the aforementioned principle

118. Single European Sky, for details see Ch. 10 I. F.
119. For details see s. III.B.2.c.iv.

applies universally and therefore also is applicable to State aircraft. This means that foreign sovereignty is touched upon when operating State aircraft in foreign territories, and such operation requires an explicit authorization. It does not enjoy the privileges that apply to civil aviation as per the Chicago system, that is, neither the first two (technical) freedoms pursuant to the Transit Agreement nor the privileges of non-commercial traffic under Article 5 of the Convention.

i. Applicability of the Convention: Civil Aircraft (Article 3)

Article 3, Subsection (a) describes the area of applicability of the Convention: 'This Convention shall be applicable only to civil aircraft, and shall not be applicable to state aircraft'. This statement has to be understood in the context that Article 1 of the Convention emphasizes the general international principle of sovereignty of the air as a principle that claims universal application and therefore also – but not exclusively – is a basic precondition for the Convention and its interpretation. Placing it in front of the description of the area of application of the Convention thus not only is an editorial question, but also serves to show that this principle shall apply to all possible cases, that is not only for civil aircraft and thereby for the application area of the Convention, but also for State aircraft.[120]

The description of the area of applicability in Article 3, Subsection (a) thus initially has two consequences in this context:

- The principle of sovereignty of the air also – and particularly – applies to State aircraft, which means that every entry of a State aircraft into foreign airspace requires the explicit authorization of the respective State. Such authorization can – as always – be granted either on a multilateral basis (as done for example by the North Atlantic Treaty Organization or the NATO Status of Forces Agreement [NATO SOFA][121]) or on a bilateral basis. This principle is again specifically emphasized in Article 3, Subsection (c): 'No state aircraft of a contracting State shall fly over the territory of another state or land thereon without authorization by special agreement or otherwise, and in accordance with the terms thereof'. Since this type of air traffic was specifically excluded from the area of applicability of the Convention as per Article 3, Subsections (a) and (b), the Convention does not constitute a 'special agreement' in the sense of Article 3, Subsection (c).
- However, the principle of sovereignty of the air also applies to civil aircraft, while the Chicago System concretizes and limits it in several regards (on a multinational basis). Additional limitations and granting are typically effectuated through BASAs.[122]

120. For a definition of this term see details under s. ii.
121. 199 *UNTS* 1953.
122. For details see s. III.B.2.i.

ii. Distinction between Civil and State Aircraft

Therefore, the question of making a distinction between civil and State aircraft is of special significance.[123] Article 3, Subsection (b) of the Convention reads as follows: 'Aircraft used in military, customs and police services shall be deemed to be state aircraft'. The fact that aircraft that are registered for one State and operate under national service are State aircraft is certainly undisputed. Since the Chicago Convention does not cover them, their entry into foreign territory requires a specific authorization. However, Article 3, Subsection (b) is not a definition of State aircraft because of the word 'deemed'.[124] As Andrew S. Williams[125] rightly points out, it merely provides a rebuttable presumption that an aircraft used in certain activities at a particular time will be deemed to be a State aircraft. Accordingly, the presumption applies to the nature of the flight and not to the aircraft itself. It is not based on the aircraft's design or technical characteristics, call sign, registration, or markings – all of which fall within the competence of its state of nationality. The Convention thus adopts a functional approach for the determination of its character as a State aircraft. If an aircraft is used in any of three activities – military, customs, or police services – it will be deemed to be a State aircraft. No more precise definition of military aircraft is provided.

Thus, in the sense of the Chicago Convention, police or military operations from the air are always executed with a 'state aircraft', even if the aircraft has a civil registration. This functional view already becomes apparent from the words chosen in the Chicago Convention. As mentioned above, Article 3, Lit. (b) of the Convention defines State aircraft as 'aircraft used in military, customs and police services'. Thereby, an aircraft can also be a State aircraft when it is not registered for one of the aforementioned State organizations, but is used for their purposes.

However, the question arises of whether other uses than the ones listed in Article 3, Lit. (b) can qualify an aircraft as a State aircraft or whether the aforementioned examples are the only ones. In the recent years, this question especially needed to be considered with regard to flights of foreign secret services in the airspaces of foreign States for which no authorization had been obtained. There is no unanimous opinion on the nature of Article 3, Lit. (b). It is only known that the president of the negotiation commission of the Chicago Convention, several years after the Convention came into force, held that Article 3, Lit. (b) was exclusive.[126] The systematic structure of Article 3 seems to be an argument against this opinion. Pursuant to Lit. (a), the Convention 'shall not be applicable to state aircraft'.

---

123. See e.g. Michael Milde, 'Interception of Civil Aircraft v. Misuse of Civil Aviation (Background of Amendment 27 to Annex 2)', *Annals of Air & Space Law* 11 (1986): 105, 106.
124. Chester D. Taylor, *International Flight of Military Aircraft in Peacetime: A Legal Analysis* (1968), 28 FED. B.J., Federal bar journal (Washington, D.C.) 36, 48.
125. Andrew S. Williams, 'The interception of civil aircraft over the high seas in the global war on terror', *Air Force Law Review, Vol. 59* (Spring 2007), 73 – 151, <http://findarticles.com/p/articles/mi_m6007/is_59/ai_n24960885/pg_1?tag=artBody;col1>.
126. Secretariat Study on 'Civil/State Aircraft', *Document C-WP/9835* of 22 Sep. 1993, 9.

Lit. (b) only justifies fiction for part of the State aircraft listed in Lit. (a).[127] Otherwise, the two-part structure of the regulation would not make any sense. This is especially true because there are also regulations with a one-part structure in international agreements that do not specifically exclude State aircraft in general from the area of application, but only aircraft in the service of the military, customs, or the police.[128] Regulation EC No. 549/2004 (on Single European Sky)[129] also assumes that the term *state aircraft* is not exclusively defined: '*General air traffic* means . . . all movements of state aircraft (including military, customs and police aircraft) when these movements are carried out in conformity with the procedures of the ICAO.'[130] Considering that the authorization obligation included in Article 3 of the Chicago Convention shall ensure sovereignty of a State over its sovereign territory, it is not clear why service flights of a secret service should be less 'state' than those of police or customs. Because of the non-application of the Chicago Convention, service flights of a foreign secret service with civil registered aircraft are also subject to authorization.

iii. Misuse of Civil Aviation (Article 4)

The question arises of whether aircraft with civil registration that are used for secret service purposes belong to non-commercial casual services or whether they have to be considered State aircraft. Pursuant to Article 5 of the Chicago Convention, entry of all aircraft of non-commercial casual services[131] does not require prior authorization. Authorization is not required when a secret service only uses an aircraft with civil registration for transporting staff or material without preparing or pursuing sovereign action in the foreign airspace, such as violence against people (especially prisoner transport) or intelligence service observations. Such a flight cannot be distinguished from 'group travel' – which does not require permission – of secret service staff in a scheduled service aircraft. While their secret entry might violate other aspects of the territorial sovereignty of the foreign State,[132] it does not violate any aviation laws for a scheduled service.

---

127. Schwenk/Giemulla, *Handbuch des Luftverkehrsrechts* (Handbook on Aviation Law), 3rd edn (Köln, 2005) 266; Center for Human Rights and Global Justice, Enabling Torture (2006), 5, <www.chrgj.org/docs/BriefingPaperEnablingTorture.pdf>; contrary opinion: Bourbonniere/ Haeck *ibid.*, 897; open: Hakimi, The Council of Europe Addresses CIA Rendition and Detention Program, *Am. J. Int. Law* 101, No. 2 (2007): 442 - 452.
128. See e.g. Art. 13 of the Convention on the International Recognition of Rights in Aircraft of 19 Jun. 1948, *BGBl.* 1959 II 129; Art. 26 of the Convention on damage caused by foreign aircraft, Rome, of 7 Oct. 1952, Art. 1 No. 4 of the Convention on Offences committed on board Aircraft from 14 Sep. 1963, *BGBl.* 1969 II 121; Convention for the Suppression of Unlawful Acts Against the Safety of Civil Aviation of 23 Sep. 1971, *BGBl.* 1977 II 1230.
129. *OJ* No. L 96 of 31 Mar. 2004, 1.
130. *OJ* No. L 96 of 31 Mar. 2004, 1.
131. See Schwenk/Giemulla, *Handbuch des Luftverkehrsrechts* (Handbook on Aviation Law), 3rd edn (2005), 752.
132. See Federal Constitutional Court, *NJW* (German specialist legal magazine) (2004), 141, 143; Geiger, *Grundgesetz und Völkerrecht* (Constitutional Law and International Law) 3rd edn (2002), § 60 II 2 c.

At the same time, this means that flights of secret services, even when they are carried out with aircraft with civil registration, require permission when sovereign action is prepared or carried out in the foreign airspace. Concealing this fact, that is conscious use of civil registered aircraft without informing the involved State, also is a violation of the Chicago Convention.[133] Under Article 4 of the Convention (on misuse of civil aviation) '(e)ach contracting State agrees not to use civil aviation for any purpose inconsistent with the aims of this Convention.'

iv. Use of Weapons against Civil Aircraft (Article 3*bis*)

The distinction between civil and State aircraft determined by Article 3 of the Convention should in fact make it evident to only use weapons against State aircraft in the event of unauthorized entry or other prohibited action of such aircraft. However, the question arises of whether this also applies when a civil aircraft is misused or suspected to be misused for State purposes. Article 3*bis* (on the refrain from resorting to the use of weapons) states in Subsection (a): 'The contracting States recognize that every State must refrain from resorting to the use of weapons against civil aircraft in flight and that, in case of interception, the lives of persons on board and the safety of aircraft must not be endangered. This provision shall not be interpreted as modifying in any way the rights and obligations of States set forth in the Charter of the United Nations'.

As is well known, Article 3*bis* is a reaction to the shooting down of KE 007. The ICAO Assembly voted in 1984 to amend the Chicago Convention by adopting Article 3*bis*, which came into force on 1 October 1998, for the States that ratified the new article. The vote came in response to the destruction of Korean Air carrier Flight 007 by Soviet fighters on 31 August 1983, resulting in the deaths of 269 passengers and its crew. The Korean air carrier had innocently strayed into Soviet airspace – probably as a result of faulty computer programming[134] – and was mistaken for a US military reconnaissance aircraft spotted earlier in the region. The investigation disclosed that the Korean air carrier had its navigation lights on and its strobe lights on. However, the Soviet fighter did not make any effort to identify the aircraft, to communicate with it, or to request it to land.[135]

There are many reasons to question the effectiveness of Article 3*bis*. In particular, the events of 'September 11' have shown that aircraft can be turned into weapons and misused as a means of attack against a State or a society. The last Sentence of Article 3*bis*, Subsection (a) offers the option for neutralization of the provision ('This provision shall not be interpreted as modifying in any way the rights and obligations of States set forth in the Charter of the United Nations'), especially with the help of Article 51 of the Charter of the UN, which reads as

133. See also Michael Milde, 'Interception of Civil Aircraft v. Misuse of Civil Aviation (Background of Amendment 27 to Annex 2)', *Annals Of Air & Space Law* 11 (1998): 105, 106.

134. See Bin Cheng, The destruction of KAL flight KE007, and Art. 3*bis* of the Chicago Convention, in *Air Worthy*, 47–74.

135. Michael Milde, KE 007 – 'final' truth and consequences, *Essays* 357, 358; Bin Cheng, *ibid.*, 49, 54.

follows: 'Nothing in the present Charter shall impair the inherent right of individual or collective self-defence if an armed attack occurs against a Member of the United Nations, until the Security Council has taken measures necessary to maintain international peace and security . . . '.

For Article 3*bis* of the Convention to keep any sense at all, it is necessary to interpret the exception with the help of Article 51 of the Charter of the UN as closely as possible. The main question in this regard is that of designation, with the key words being *armed attack* and *self-defence*. There is some concern with the term *attack,* which traditionally has had to stem from so-called combatants, that is, from armed military forces that are deployed by one State against another. The latter is the main issue because of the fact that it has to be an attack against a member of the UN, that is, an attack against a State against which this State can use measures of self-defence. The model that forms the basis for Article 51 of the Charter of the UN, therefore, is the attack of a State against another State and its reactions of self-defence. Considering this main model, the consequence is that the attacking State must carry out this attack with an army organized by this State and accordingly is fought back against by the army of the attacked State. This situation is usually described with the term *war.*

Cases such as 'September 11' are considerably different from this scheme in many regards, except if it is presumed that an 'armed attack' can also stem from criminals. However, in this case, not only the boundaries of threats of war and criminal threats become quite obscure, but also the boundaries for the reactions to such threats. Should the army continue to be limited to fighting back against military attacks, or should it also be permitted to be used for fighting criminals? There are many complex consequences. This is also, but not only, about the question of whether criminals should then be treated as prisoners of war as well. Finally, this leads to the fact that boundaries between war and peace become quite obscure. For the time being, the full extent of the consequences this obliteration would have on the civil society remains anybody's guess.

At the moment, there are legal bases for shooting down civil aircraft that have been turned into weapons by terrorists, for example, in Russia, France, Austria, Switzerland, and the US. In Germany, however, such laws have been suspended by the Constitutional Court, which reasoned that the killing of innocent humans – no matter what the reasons are – is a violation of dignity of mankind.

e. Airports in Aviation Regulation

According to Article 68 of the Chicago Convention each contracting State may, subject to the provisions of the Convention, designate the airports which any international air service may use. The principles contained in the Chicago Convention of 1944 regarding airports are:

- Every contracting State must open its airports to public use under uniform conditions, subject to reciprocity.

- The ICAO has the faculty to provide technical assistance to a State in enhancing the safety and obtaining uniformity of the airport system in case of shortcomings.

Also, Article 28 requires, *inter alia*, that:

> (e) Each contracting State undertakes, so far as it may find practicable, to: provide, in its territory, airports, . . . to facilitate international air navigation, in accordance with the standards and practices recommended or established from time to time, pursuant to this convention.

Article 28 makes the State responsible for making available airports within their territory as a public service for air transport users.

An airport or aerodrome is a defined area on land or water that is used for the arrival, departure, and surface movement of aircraft. The airport is more than a simple landing place for aircraft, and is also more than an aerodrome – this last term is used almost synonymously, though in a more generic sense. An airport is an aerodrome with facilities – consequently, we can say that all airports are aerodromes, but that not all aerodromes are airports. From a legal point of view, an airport can be considered a private object of the State, because its utilization is not open to all citizens: it has legal restrictions and principles that differentiate it from objects of public nature.

The airport is an *universitas rerum,* meaning a set of universal objects, with one purpose and with links among each element. The airport can be considered a centre of legal relationships, which brings together important economic, political, commercial, and technical interests, and has to serve not only the country where it is located, for, due to the links with the areas that it covers, it is an important factor of integration in the economic and political field of a region.

Annex 14: Aerodrome of the ICAO, defines an aerodrome as an 'area of earth or water, including all the facilities, installations, and equipment, destined wholly or partially to the arrival, departure, and movement of aircraft.'

Due to the great importance of infrastructure for air navigation, the ICAO covers the topic of airports and aerodromes in many different documents and guidelines.

Alongside their technical and political influence, airports have a significant economic importance, due to the possibilities of revenue resulting from the movement of air traffic (passengers and goods).

The ICAO types airports in accordance with their size. They are Class A, with runways with a length of 2,150 meters or more; Class B, with runways of 1,500 meters or more; and Class C, with runways of 1,050 meters or more.

Airports can also be differentiated by the type of aircraft they serve:

(a) a *heliport* is an aerodrome or a defined area on a structure used for the landing, takeoff or surface movement of helicopters;
(b) a *stolport* is an airport specifically designed for STOL aircraft separate from conventional airport facilities.

Airports can also be characterized by their type of activity:

(a) a *commercial airport* is an airport used by the general public that includes facilities for processing passengers, handling cargo, and servicing commercial aircraft; and
(b) a *private airport* serves primarily small, privately owned aircraft, flying, clubs, and so on.

Also, there are:

(a) a *domestic airport*, an airport used for domestic air services only;
(b) a *regional airport,* which generally refers to an airport of a medium or small city that is mainly served by short-haul regional services;
(c) an *international airport,* a designated airport of entry and departure for international air services, where formalities such as customs, immigration, public health, animal and plant quarantine, and similar procedures are carried out; and
(d) a *gateway airport*, an international airport that is the first point of arrival or last point of departure in a State for international air services.

Airports can also be civil or military, depending on their use in civil operations or military activity.

From another point of view, airports can be:

(a) *regular*, contemplated in the flight plan for the ordinary activity of air carriers, or
(b) *alternative*, in accordance with the SARPs of Annex 2: Rules of the Air of the ICAO.

Subject to their legal nature, airports can be property of the State, communal, or private.

Annex 9 contains the definition of an international airport as an airport designated by the contracting State in its territory allocated as a point of arrival and departure of international air traffic, where the customs, migration, public health (sanitary provisions concerning persons, animals, and plants), and similar procedures are performed.

An international airport will be considered an airport, the finance or management of which is the responsibility of two or more States, based on special arrangements signed by the States concerned. An example is the airport of Basel-Mulhouse, built on French territory. France and Switzerland signed an agreement to operate the airport in 1949.[136]

The Chicago Convention contains three basic principles regarding the regulation of international airports.

136. Convention franco-suisse du 4 juillet 1949 relative à la construction et à l'exploitation de l'aéroport de Bâle-Mulhouse, à Blotzheim, *Suisse Recueil officiel du droit fédéral* (1950),1334.

- Every contracting State shall open its airport to international air traffic under reciprocal conditions.
- Every contracting State shall offer the other States facilities and airport services, in conformity with the traffic requirements.
- The ICAO has the faculty to intervene and provide assistance with the purpose of improving and standardizing the airport system of each State, allowing States the freedom to establish, plan, and manage their airport systems (Articles 15, 22, 28, 37, 69, and 76 of the Chicago Convention, 1944).

The importance of airports in the field of air transportation is reflected in the national Air Regulations or Aeronautical Codes, with several articles on definitions, classifications, limitations to private property to facilitate their establishment and development, the prevention of obstacles to air navigation, and the possibility of expropriation in some cases required by the modification or enlargement of the installations.

There is a certain amount of uniformity in the concepts and systems in the majority of the regulations. Airdromes shall be deemed public when they are open to public use – all the others shall be deemed private.

The need for certification to operate as an airdrome is the competence of the authority that will establish the conditions of its operation.

Aircraft must take off from and land on public or private airdromes. This obligation need not apply in cases of 'acts of God', or in cases involving public aircraft carrying out their duties or in the cases of aid or rescue work, or aircraft in health service work.

Other previsions regulate the landing of aircraft on private property: special requirements based on safety and security reasons establish the duty of the owner of the private aerodromes to oversee the operations.

The private property necessary for the installation of aerodromes and their improvements, and for airports already established and their supporting facilities, is thereby declared to be of public use and subject to expropriation, under administrative measures adopted by the competent national authorities. Also, equipment such as beacons, signal systems, radio communications, and meteorological aids and such others being necessary or useful for air navigation are considered support facilities.

If at the time at which the establishment or operation of an aerodrome is authorized, there are near it buildings, structures, or other works of whatever nature that might render difficult the arrival or departure of aircraft, the competent authority shall be empowered to order them demolished or removed completely or partially, provided the property has been expropriated or purchased.

The national authority may order the demolition or removal of buildings, structures, or works erected in violation of the air navigation regulations, and, if necessary, resort to judicial intervention, and no right of compensation shall arise.

Safety reasons indicate the need to mark by appropriate markings or lights all the obstacles, which, in the opinion of the competent authority, constitute a danger to aviation. The costs of installing and maintaining such devices fall upon the owner of the structure involved. Such warning devices shall be set up in accordance with the regulations established by the competent authority.

Annex 9: Facilitation refers to the 'free airport' as an international airport where the passenger, baggage, mail, goods, and supplies may embark, disembark, and remain, without being subject to any taxes, customs charges, and (with exceptions in exceptional circumstances) any examination.

Annex 9 of the Convention embodies the SARPs and guidance material pertaining specifically to facilitation of landside formalities for clearance of aircraft and commercial traffic through the requirements of customs, immigration, public health, and agriculture authorities. It also provides a framework for planners and managers of international airport operations, describing maximum limits on obligations of industry and minimum facilities to be provided by governments. In addition, Annex 9 specifies methods and procedures for carrying out clearance operations, in such a manner as to meet the twin objectives of effective compliance with the laws of States and productivity for the operators, airports, and government inspection entities.

Interestingly, Annex 9 is periodically updated by the FAL Panel or the Facilitation Division, whose last meeting was held in El Cairo, Egypt, in 2006. After a review by contracting States and adoption by the Council of the ICAO, the SARPs were incorporated in the Eleventh Edition of Annex 9.

The functions of FAL are based on the following ten articles of the Chicago Convention:

- Article 10 – Landing at customs airport.
- Article 13 – Entry and clearance regulations.
- Article 14 – Prevention of spread of diseases.
- Article 22 – Facilitation of formalities.
- Article 23 – Customs and immigration procedures.
- Article 24 – Customs duty.
- Article 29 – Documents carried in aircraft.
- Article 35 – Cargo restrictions.
- Article 37 – Adoption of international standards and procedures.
- Article 38 – Departures from international standards and procedures.

Airports are interested in facilitation so as to reduce congestion in passenger terminals and in cargo sheds. Annex 9 introduced a number of SARPs concerning access to air services and airport facilities by elderly and disabled persons, such as the opportunity for wheelchair users to use their own wheelchairs to move to and from the aircraft, uniformity of criteria for accessibility of air transport by persons with reduced mobility, the establishment and coordination of training programmes for personnel handling elderly and disabled persons, practices relating to special equipment in aircraft, allocation of seats, type of lighting in aircraft, the use of wheelchairs on board, and accessibility of all the elements of the chain of a journey by persons with reduced mobility.

Two major strategic objectives of the ICAO in the field of airport enhancement are safety and security.

To ensure an appropriate level of safety and efficiency of all airport operations, the SARPs contained in Annex 14 set forth that aerodromes must be fully implemented and enforced. Through the ICAO Universal Safety Oversight Audit Programme (USOAP) (which is mandatory), since 2005, all Annexes were expanded with safety-related provisions, including Annex 14, which covers aerodrome design and operations.

During the last, thirty-sixth Session of the ICAO Assembly in September 2007, a report prepared by the Secretary of the international organization was presented that provides indications for enhancing not only the runways themselves but also the systemic context in which such improvements must be defined and carried out.

One of the most critical areas is the shortcoming in the effective implementation of various components of legislation in compliance with the Chicago Convention. In approximately 75% of the contracting States audited, almost the totality of 190 have approved primary aviation legislation through air law codes or minor regulations.

Many contracting States have not developed an effective system for amending their regulations pursuant to receiving ICAO Annex amendments. Worse, the majority does not possess a quick system for identification and notification of differences of the Annex with respect to their legislation.

A large number of States have not established an organizational structure responsible for the certification and surveillance of aerodromes, and have not defined the functions and responsibilities of the aerodrome regulatory technical staff.

They do not have sufficient human resources with the technical skill required for the certification and surveillance of aerodromes, particularly in the areas of airport operations and certification.

In the security field, Annex17: Security to the Convention on International Civil Aviation, 8th Edition, must be implemented, particularly the quality control programme, which ensures the validity of the procedures and measures adopted by all the participants of the aviation business.

States are responsible for ensuring the implementation of adequate security measures at airports pursuant to the provisions of the aforementioned Annex.

They may delegate the task of providing individual security functions to agencies such as airport entities, air carriers, and local police.

The costs of the adoption of the appropriate measures, equipment, and training personnel are covered through charges. Furthermore, guidance on security costs and charges is included in the ICAO's Airport Economics Manual.[137]

After September 2001, many costly measures were implemented that increased the required number of tasks in the screening process at airports, both

137. *ICAO Doc.* 9562.

for the passenger and the screening personnel. Passenger volumes have continued to grow, and airports have had to respond by building and equipping additional screening channels. Airports have also had to employ, on average 10% more screening staff to manage the additional workload and to prepare passengers for screening, with the resulting operational and financial effects.

The general position sustained by airports as well as by air carriers is that this situation represents an unfair burden, as the responsibility for protecting citizens from terrorist attacks must primarily rest with the State.

Chapter 2

The Sources and the Structure of International Aviation Law

Elmar M. Giemulla

The transnational nature of aviation means that its regulations cannot exclusively be dealt with on a national level. Therefore, the greatest part of aviation law is international law. The term *international law* means that this field of law – as opposed to national or supranational law as European law – is applicable in another country or in several other countries or between countries in addition to one's own country beyond national or European law because of bilateral or multilateral international agreements. In most cases, national laws on ratification of international agreements ensure that international law is also national law in the respective contracting States. As in any other field of law, there are two main categories of aviation agreements to be distinguished in international aviation law: those of public and those of private law.

I. PUBLIC INTERNATIONAL AVIATION LAW

A. Multilateral Agreements

The Vienna Convention on the Law of Treaties[1] defined the Multilateral Agreement as:

1. 1155 *UNTS* 331; 8 *ILM* 679.

Elmar M. Giemulla & Ludwig Weber, *International and EU Aviation Law: Selected Issues*, pp. 63–74.

> an international agreement concluded between states in written form and governed by international law, whether embodied in a single instrument or in two or more related instruments and whatever its particular designation.

The international community has concluded a number of multilateral agreements that are part of public law and that essentially deal with air traffic issues.

The most important historical conventions are the Convention on the Regulation of Air Navigation (Paris, 1919),[2] the Ibero-American Convention on Air Navigation (Madrid, 1926),[3] and the Pan-American Convention on Commercial Aviation (Havana, 1928).[4]

The Paris Convention (1919) contains forty-two Articles and eight technical Annexes (A to H). The Convention established the principle of complete and exclusive sovereignty of the contracting States over the airspace above their territory (Article 1), but at the same time, recognized the right of innocent passage in times of peace time of aircraft of the other contracting States, provided the contracting State reserves the right to indicate itineraries to aircraft without landing in its territory (Article 15). Each contracting State may also, for reasons of military necessity or public safety, uniformly restrict or prohibit the aircraft of other States from flying over certain areas of its territory, without distinction between national aircraft and the aircraft of other contracting States (Article 3). In accordance with the Convention, an aircraft has the nationality of the State in which it is registered (Article 6). No scheduled international air service with or without stopover may be operated over or into the territory of a contracting State, except with special permission or other authorization of that State (Article 15). The Paris Convention established that each aircraft of a contracting State shall carry documents on board (Article 19), with mandatory safekeeping of the journey logbook for two years after the last registration (Article 20). In addition, the Convention established the right to search aircraft of the other contracting States on landing or departures, and to inspect their certificates and other documents (Article 21). In Article 34, the Convention created the International Air Navigation Commission (IANC-CINA) with a special mandate to adjust and update the standards of the technical Annexes of the Convention. The Paris Convention (1919) was in force until 1947, when the Chicago Convention was ratified.

The Ibero-American Air Navigation Convention (Madrid, 1926), was signed by Spain, Portugal, and nineteen Latin America states, and followed the provisions of the Paris Convention (1919) only with amendments to Articles 5 and 34. It was ratified by a few States (Spain, Costa Rica, Mexico, Paraguay, and the Dominican Republic) and never entered into force.

The Pan-American Commercial Aviation Convention (Havana, 1928), was modelled after the Paris Convention (1919) with differences such as disallowing the operation of scheduled air transport services without previous permission or

2. 11 *LNTS* 173, see <www.aviation.go.th/airtrans/airlaw/1914.html>.
3. Convenio Ibero-americano de Navegación Aérea, or CIANA, 3 *Hudson* 2019 (1926).
4. 128 *British and Foreign State Papers*, 505 *USTS*, 840; 4 *Hudson* 2354 (1931).

other authorization (Article 21). Until 1944, the Pan-American Convention was ratified by eleven countries.

The overview below refers to the list of recent multilateral agreements published by the International Civil Aviation Organization (ICAO).

International Conventions – Public Law

ICAO Doc. No.	*Title and Date*	*Short-Title Description*
8364	Convention on Offences and Certain Other Acts Committed on Board Aircraft[5] Signed at Tokyo on 14 September 1963.	Tokyo Convention (1963): Offences and other acts committed on board aircraft.
8920	Convention for the Suppression of Unlawful Seizure of Aircraft[6] Signed at The Hague on 16 December 1970.	Hague Convention (1970): Unlawful seizure of aircraft.
8966	Convention for the Suppression of Unlawful Acts Against the Safety of Civil Aviation[7] Signed at Montreal on 23 September 1971.	Montreal Convention: Unlawful acts against the safety of civil aviation.
9571	Convention on the Marking of Plastic Explosives for the Purpose of Detection[8] Done at Montreal on 1 March 1991.	Convention on the Marking of Plastic Explosives (1991)
-[9]	Convention on the Suppression of Unlawful Acts Relating to International Civil Aviation[10]	Beijing Convention (2010)

5. 704 *UNTS* 219; 20 *UST* 2941; 2 *ILM* 1042 (1963).
6. 860 *UNTS* 105; 22 *UST* 1641; 10 *ILM* 133 (1971).
7. 974 *UNTS* 177; 24 *UST* 564; 10 *ILM* 1151 (1971).
8. 30 *ILM* 721 (1991).
9. <www.icao.int/DCAS2010/restr/docs/beijing_convention_multi.pdf>.
10. Not yet in force.

Protocols

Doc. No.	*Title and Date*	*Short-Title Description*
9518	Protocol for the Suppression of Unlawful Acts of Violence at Airports Serving International Civil Aviation, Supplementary to the Convention for the Suppression of Unlawful Acts Against the Safety of Civil Aviation.[11] Done at Montreal on 23 September 1971. Signed at Montreal on 24 February 1988.	Montreal Supplementary Protocol (1988): Acts of violence at airports.
-[12]	Protocol Supplementary to the Convention for the Suppression of Unlawful Seizure of Aircraft[13]	Beijing Protocol (2010)

B. BILATERAL AGREEMENTS

In addition to the multilateral aviation agreements, States have concluded a great number of bilateral agreements in the area of public aviation law between each other. In accordance with Article 83 of the Chicago Convention (1944),[14] any contracting State may make arrangements not inconsistent with the provisions of this Convention.[15] To maintain transparency, this article indicates that such arrangements shall be forthwith registered with the Council, which shall make them public as soon as possible. Both in terms of number and in terms of significance, the Bilateral Air Service Agreements (BASAs) on scheduled air transport are predominant. These agreements grant traffic rights of their designated carriers to the respective contracting parties on the principle of reciprocity. Agreements that have not yet come into force, but have been signed or initialled and partially only have been declared applicable temporarily, also need to be considered in this context. These include frequencies and capacity: 50 to 50 (and possibly, pool agreements), restriction of the fifth freedom, tariffs (negotiated by the International Air Transport Association [IATA]): double approval or double disapproval, agreed landing points ('gateway cities'), and designated carriers (single, double, or multiple designation).

11. 1589 *UNTS* 474.
12. <www.icao.int/DCAS2010/restr/docs/beijing_protocol_multi.pdf>.
13. Not yet in force.
14. 15 *UNTS* 295, *ICAO Doc*. 7300.
15. For more details see Chapter 6 Section 2.

In general, regardless of the specific type of bilateral agreement negotiated, most agreements have a general structure, as follows:

- an initial Preamble, which identifies the contracting parties, and declares that they have agreed to different clauses that integrate the document, such as a designation and authorization to one or more air carriers to operate the agreed services;
- a capacity article, with a methodology for regulation of the quantity of services offered under the agreement;
- a tariff clause;
- a commercial operations or commercial opportunities clause, specifying the rights to do business;
- soft rights, such as the use of computer reservation systems;
- hard rights: route, traffic, operational, and capacity rights, and the aviation security article, which sets forth procedures for cooperation between the parties to avoid or deal with situations involving acts of unlawful interference with the security of civil aviation;
- a safety clause referring to airworthiness, for the mutual recognition by the parties of each other's certificates of airworthiness and competency; and finally,
- a protocol clause to facilitate settlement of disputes, termination, or revocation of the agreement, and so on.

From 1992 onwards, the United States (US) concluded separate liberal bilaterals with a number of European Community (EC) members. In 1994, the EC Commission claimed external competence; in 2002, the European Court of Justice (ECJ)[16] held that:

- the bilaterals are only illegal insofar as they provide fifth freedom rights to US carriers and to other EC members with conditions contrary to EC law;
- the EC Treaty grants the Commission external competence in air transport only if expressly mandated by the Council.

In 2003, the Council gave the Commission the mandate for negotiations with the US. The new 'bilateral' agreement entered into force (provisionally) on 30 March 2008.[17] Its main contents were the following:

- Removal of restrictions on route rights:
  - Any EC airline will be able to fly from any European city to any American city and from there onwards to third destinations (outside the US). Conversely, any US airline will be allowed to fly into any European Union (EU) airport and from there to third destinations (also inside the EU).

16. Judgments of the Court of 5 Nov. 2002, C-466/98 – C-469/98, C-471/98, C-472/98, C-475/98, C-476/98, *ECR* (2002) I-9427, I-9519, I-9575, I-9627, I-9681, I-9741, I-9797, and I-9855.
17. *OJ* No. L 134 of 25 May 2007, 1.

  - This will mainly affect London Heathrow (more than 40% of all flights from Europe to America), and where, up to recently, only four carriers (British Airways, Virgin Atlantic, American Airlines, and United) had authorization to fly the transatlantic route.
- Cabotage:
  - While US airlines can fly within Europe (except for cabotage), it does not allow European airlines to fly domestic US routes.
  - However, European carriers have the right to establish subsidiaries in the US, which can carry domestic traffic.
- Foreign ownership:
  - European companies can buy up to 100% of non-voting shares in US airlines, but not more than 25% of voting rights.
  - As a new rule, vice versa.
- Suspension clause:
  - The EU obtained a 'suspension clause' that commits the US to opening up its domestic market and loosening its rules on foreign investment and ownership by mid-2010.
  - Negotiations have already been resumed.

II. PRIVATE INTERNATIONAL AVIATION LAW

The multilateral agreements that belong to private law naturally mainly deal with liability issues between air carriers and their contracting partners on the one hand (Warsaw or Montreal Conventions) or between operators of aircraft and third parties on the other hand (Rome).[18]

The overview below refers to the list of multilateral agreements published by the ICAO.

International Conventions – Private Law

ICAO Doc. No.	*Title and Date*	*Short-Title Description*
–	Convention for the Unification of Certain Rules relating to International Carriage by Air[19] Signed at Warsaw on 12 October 1929.	Warsaw Convention (1929): Rules for international carriage by air.

18. For details see Ch. 7 on these two liability complexes.
19. Authentic French Text: *II Conférence Internationale de Droit Privé Aerién*, 4–12 Octobre 1929, Varsovie 1930, 220 et seq.; for British translation, see *Schedule to the United Kingdom Carriage by Air Act*, 1932; 22 & 23 Geo.5, ch. 36); for American translation, see [49 Stat. 3000; T.S 876].

ICAO Doc. No.	*Title and Date*	*Short-Title Description*
7620	Convention on the International Recognition of Rights in Aircraft[20] Signed at Geneva on 19 June 1948.	Geneva Convention (1944): Recognition of rights in aircraft.
7364	Convention on Damage Caused by Foreign Aircraft to Third Parties on the Surface[21] Signed at Rome on 7 October 1952.	Rome Convention (1952): Damage to third parties on surface.
8181	Convention, Supplementary to the Warsaw Convention, for the Unification of Certain Rules Relating to International Carriage by Air Performed by a Person Other than the Contracting Carrier[22] Signed at Guadalajara on 18 September 1961.	Guadalajara Convention (1961): Supplementing Warsaw Convention 1929.
9740	Convention for the Unification of Certain Rules for International Carriage by Air[23] Done at Montreal on 28 May 1999.	Montreal Convention (1999): Rules for international carriage by air.
9793	Convention on International Interests in Mobile Equipment.[24] Signed at Cape Town on 16 November 2001.	Cape Town Convention (2001): International Interests in Mobile Equipment.
9919	Convention on Compensation for Damage Caused by Aircraft to Third Parties[25]	General Risks Convention (2009)
9920	Convention on Compensation for Damage to Third Parties, Resulting from Acts of Unlawful Interference Involving Aircraft[26]	Unlawful Interference Compensation Convention (2009)

20. 310 *UNTS* 151.
21. 310 *UNTS* 181.
22. 500 *UNTS* 32.
23. 2242 *UNTS* 350.
24. *OJ* No. L 121 of 15 May 2009, 8.
25. Not yet in force.
26. Not yet in force.

Protocols

Doc. No.	*Title and Date*	*Short-Title Description*
7632	Protocol to Amend the Convention for the Unification of Certain Rules Relating to International Carriage by Air[27] Signed at Warsaw on 12 October 1929 Signed at The Hague on 28 September 1955.	Hague Protocol (1955): Amending Warsaw Convention of 1929.
8932	Protocol to Amend the Convention for the Unification of Certain Rules Relating to International Carriage by Air[28] Signed at Warsaw on 12 October 1929 as Amended by the Protocol done at The Hague on 28 September 1955 Signed at Guatemala City on 8 March 1971. Second edition, incorporating the authentic text of the Protocol in the Russian language as approved by the Council of ICAO, signed on 9 October 1975.	Guatemala City Protocol (1971): Amending Warsaw Convention of 1929 as amended by The Hague Protocol of 1955.
9145	Additional Protocol No. 1 to Amend the Convention for the Unification of Certain Rules Relating to International Carriage by Air[29] Signed at Warsaw on 12 October 1929 Signed at Montreal on 25 September 1975.	Additional Protocol No. 1 (1975): Amending Warsaw Convention of 1929.
9146	Additional Protocol No. 2 to Amend the Convention for the Unification of Certain Rules Relating to International Carriage by Air[30] Signed at Warsaw on 12 October 1929 as Amended by the Protocol done at The Hague on 28 September 1955 Signed at Montreal on 25 September 1975.	Additional Protocol No. 2 (1975): Amending Warsaw Convention of 1929 as amended by The Hague Protocol of 1955.
9147	Additional Protocol No. 3 to Amend the Convention for the Unification of Certain Rules Relating to International Carriage by Air[31]	Additional Protocol No. 3 (1975): Amending Warsaw Convention of 1929 as

27. 478 *UNTS* 371; 10 *ILM* 613.
28. 10 *ILM* 613 (1971).
29. 2097 *UNTS* 28.
30. 2097 *UNTS* 69.
31. Not in force.

Doc. No.	*Title and Date*	*Short-Title Description*
	Signed at Warsaw on 12 October 1929 as Amended by the Protocol done at The Hague on 28 September 1955 and at Guatemala City on 8 March 1971 Signed at Montreal on 25 September 1975.	amended by The Hague Protocol of 1955 and Guatemala City Protocol of 1971.
9148	Montreal Protocol No. 4 to Amend the Convention for the Unification of Certain Rules Relating to International Carriage by Air[32] Signed at Warsaw on 12 October 1929 as Amended by the Protocol Done at The Hague on 28 September 1955 Signed at Montreal on 25 September 1975.	Montreal Protocol No. 4 (1975): amending Warsaw Convention of 1929 as amended by The Hague Protocol of 1955.
9257	Protocol to Amend the Convention on Damage Caused by Foreign Aircraft to Third Parties on the Surface[33] Signed at Rome on 7 October 1952 Signed at Montreal on 23 September 1978.	Montreal Protocol (1978): Amending Rome Convention of 1952.
9794	Protocol to the Convention on International Interests in Mobile Equipment on Matters Specific to Aircraft Equipment[34] Signed at Cape Town on 16 November 2001.	Cape Town Aircraft Protocol (2001): Protocol to the Cape Town Convention on Matters Specific to Aircraft Equipment.
9795	Consolidated Text of the Convention on International Interests in Mobile Equipment and the Protocol to the Convention on International Interests in Mobile Equipment on Matters Specific to Aircraft Equipment[35] Signed at Cape Town on 16 November 2001.	Consolidated Text of the Cape Town Convention and Aircraft Protocol (2001): International Interests in Mobile Equipment specific to Aircraft Equipment.

32. 2145 *UNTS* 36.
33. 2195 *UNTS* 372.
34. *OJ* No. L 121 of 15 May 2009, 25.
35. See <www.aviation.go.th/airtrans/airlaw/consolidate.html>.

In 2008, the ICAO Council considered a working paper that provided a report of the sixth meeting of the Special Group on the Modernization of the Rome Convention of 1952.[36] The Council was informed that the Special Group had developed the texts of two draft conventions:

- Convention on Compensation for Damage Caused by Aircraft to Third Parties, in case of unlawful interference (commonly referred to as 'the Unlawful Interference Compensation Convention');[37] and
- Convention on Compensation for Damage Caused by Aircraft to Third Parties (commonly called 'the General Risks Convention').[38]

The Committee decided that both drafts are final drafts ready for transmittal to the Council and for presentation to the Member States and ultimately to a diplomatic conference.[39]

The two conventions setting out international compensation and liability rules for damage caused by aircraft to third parties were adopted by the diplomatic conference hosted by the International Civil Aviation Organization (ICAO), from 20 April to 2 May 2009.

One legal instrument adopted by the Conference is the Convention on Compensation for Damage to Third Parties, Resulting from Acts of Unlawful Interference Involving Aircraft.[40] It has the objective of providing compensation for damage to third parties as a result of acts of unlawful interference involving aircraft. At the heart of this new instrument is the creation of an International Civil Aviation Compensation Fund which may potentially provide victims of an event compensation in addition to that paid by the aircraft operator, up to an amount of 3 billion Special Drawing Rights (approximately USD 4.5 billion).

The other instrument, the Convention on Compensation for Damage Caused by Aircraft to Third Parties,[41] modernizes the current legal framework provided for under the 1952 Rome Convention and related Protocol of 1978. It covers cases of damage caused by aircraft as a result of safety related matters and not involving an act of unlawful interference and provides for full compensation of victims.[42]

III. THE GENERAL PRINCIPLES OF AVIATION LAW

In addition to the (written) public and private law general principles play a significant role in international air law. The general principles of the legal discipline are the basic notions and guidelines that address the legal solution of the many

36. 310 *UNTS* 181.
37. *DCCD Doc. No. 3*, <www.icao.int/DCCD2009/docs/DCCD_doc_3_en.pdf>
38. *DCCD Doc. No. 4*, <www.icao.int/DCCD2009/docs/DCCD_doc_4_en.pdf>
39. For more details see <www.icao.int/DCCD2009/>.
40. *DCCD Doc. No. 43* <www.icao.int/DCCD2009/docs/DCCD_doc_43_en.pdf>.
41. *DCCD Doc. No. 42* <www.icao.int/DCCD2009/docs/DCCD_doc_42_en.pdf>.
42. See *ICAO News Release* PIO 05/09 <www.icao.int/icao/en/nr/2009/pio200905_e.pdf>.

different problems that derive from air navigation. Among others, the most important basic principles are the following:

- States have the exclusive and absolutely sovereignty over the airspace that covers their territories. This principle justifies the power of the State to punish airspace violations, and to grant previous authorization to foreign airlines to operate scheduled air transport services over its territory.
- Certain rights of the third persons as landowners yield in favour of the general interest in air navigation activity. This basic element is the basis for building height restrictions in the vicinity of airports, the duty to mark aeronautical obstacles that represent a potential risk for air traffic, and so on.
- Aircraft cannot remain inactive, as their activities serve the general interest, among others, to ensure communication with distant locations. This is why the seizure of aircraft does not produce the immobility of the aircraft, except in exceptional cases. The Rome Convention of 1933,[43] on the preventive seizure of aircraft, Article 3, contains the exemptions of the seizure of the following:
  (a) aircraft exclusively appropriated to a State service, including the postal service, but excluding commercial service;
  (b) aircraft actually in service on a regular line of public transport, together with the indispensable reserve aircraft;
  (c) every other aircraft appropriated to the carriage of persons or goods for reward, when such aircraft is ready to start on such carriage, unless the arrest is in respect to a contract debt incurred for the purposes of the journey that the aircraft is about to make, or of a claim that has arisen in the course of the journey.
- The air trip must be completed. This principle justifies that without the need for special authorization, the air commander shall be empowered to make purchases and incur expenses necessary for the trip and to protect baggage, goods, and mail that are being transported. Also in the event that he considers it unavoidable for the safety of the aircraft and subject to special requirements, the commander of aircraft may jettison goods and baggage during the flight. If a choice is possible, he shall jettison things of lesser value. The air commander shall be under a duty to assure himself of the proper operation of the aircraft before departure and of weather conditions en route, and it shall be his responsibility to decide whether the flight should be suspended.
- Compensation of liability is limited. This general principle is opposed to the principle of unlimited compensation contemplated in civil law.

43. 192 *LNTS* 289.

IV. LEGAL TRADITIONS AND ANALOGICAL LAWS

Legal traditions of aeronautical activity are a source of aviation law and consist of certain long-established behaviours, ways, and customs, related to aeronautical activity.

Ways are long-accepted practices in the celebration of legal negotiations. Customs are traditions imposed in a community, usually of mandatory observation. Both have in common the fact that they consist of the repetition of a behaviour during a long time, but the custom has the additional element of the obligation to observe it.

In a situation in which a specific legal solution to a certain problem does not exist, referred to in continental law as 'the absence of law', ways and customs are the formal source of aviation law.

Many authors indicate as example of ways and customs the General Conditions of the Air Transport adopted by the IATA, incorporated as clauses in the air transport documents, such as the ticket and the airway bill, before the electronic emission thereof.

Other sources of aviation law are analogical laws, when faced with the absence of a specific legal solution. Through the deductive mechanism of interpretation, it is possible to arrive at an appropriate legal solution. Such is the case with commercial law or maritime law, because in the end, all the branches of law integrate the general legal order.

Chapter 3
International Organizations

Ludwig Weber

I. INTERNATIONAL CIVIL AVIATION ORGANIZATION

A. Historical Background

The International Civil Aviation Organization (ICAO) came into being on 4 April 1947 upon entry into force of the Convention on International Civil Aviation.[1] Part II of the Convention sets out the constitutive provisions regarding ICAO, including its objectives, organs and institutional structure and status as an international intergovernmental organization.

The Convention on International Civil Aviation was adopted and signed on the final day of the International Civil Aviation Conference, which was held from 1 November 1994 to 7 December 1944 at Chicago, Illinois, US.[2] The Conference, which was attended by fifty-two States, was called by the United States Government with the objective of establishing a legal framework for the development of international civil aviation after the Second World War.[3] This action was taken

1. ICAO Doc. 7300/8.
2. *Proceedings of the International Civil Aviation Conference*, Chicago, Illinois, 1 Nov. 1944-7 Dec. 1944 (Washington: US Department of State Printing Office, 1948), 2 Vols.
3. See Invitation of the United States of America to the Conference, in: *Proceedings of the International Civil Aviation Conference,* 11

Elmar M. Giemulla & Ludwig Weber, *International and EU Aviation Law: Selected Issues*, pp. 75–128.

even prior to the Conference of San Francisco in the spring of 1945, which adopted the United Nations Charter.[4]

During the Chicago Conference, four main proposals were submitted. Australia and New Zealand advocated the internationalization of all civil aviation (except on domestic routes), including the setting up of a single international global airline and an international air authority to regulate and supervise it.[5] The United Kingdom's proposal provided for the establishment of an 'International Air Authority' with extensive regulatory powers in economic as well as technical matters.[6] The proposal of the United States emphasized freedom of the air and a pro-competitive environment, in which free enterprise airlines would operate in a competitive international market, with free exchange of landing rights between States.[7] It envisaged the creation of an 'International Aviation Assembly', with functions in the field of setting technical standards. Finally, the Canadian proposal envisaged an 'International Air Authority', with powers in the field *of economic regulation,* in which regional councils would issue certificates for, and would regulate, international air services.[8]

As a result of its deliberations, the Conference adopted a compromise under which a new international body called the International Civil Aeronautics Organization (ICAO) would be set up with mainly technical standard-setting responsibilities and general overall supervisory functions.[9] Economic regulation was to be left to bilateral regulation between States, except regulation of fares, rates and tariffs, which was left to multilateral self-regulation by industry conferences subject to governmental approval. This compromise was embodied in the Convention on International Civil Aviation, which was the main instrument adopted by the Conference and which also sets forth the constitution of ICAO; the 'International Air Service Transit Agreement',[10] which provides for the mutual exchange of transit rights; the 'Five Freedoms Agreement',[11] which provides for

4. *Guide to the Charter of the United Nations* (New York: United Nations Publication Office, 1962).
5. Conference Doc. 49: International Ownership and Operation of Air Services on Prescribed International Trunk Routes, Resolution to be moved by Hon. D.G. Sullivan, Chairman, New Zealand Delegation, in: *Proceedings of the International Civil Aviation Conference,* 549; see also: Verbatim Minutes of Plenary Session, November 8, in: *Proceedings of the International Civil Aviation Conference*, 539–543.
6. Conference Doc. 48: United Kingdom Proposal on International Air Transport, in: *Proceedings of the International Civil Aviation Conference*, 566.
7. Conference Doc. 16: United States Proposal of a Convention on Air Navigation, in: *Proceedings of the International Civil Aviation Conference*, 554.
8. Conference Doc. 50: Canadian Revised Preliminary Draft of an International Air Convention, in: *Proceedings of the International Civil Aviation Conference*, Vol. I, 570 et seq.
9. See L. Weber, 'Chicago Convention', in *Encyclopedia of Public International Law,* ed. R. Bernhardt Vol. I (Amsterdam/London/New York/Tokyo: North Holland/Elsevier, 1992), 571 et seq. with further references.
10. 84 *UNTS* 389.
11. 171 *UNTS* 387. The UK refrained from adhering. The United States signed the Agreement, but withdrew on 25 Jul. 1947, after it became sufficiently clear that the Agreement would not receive the necessary international support. For the notice of withdrawal, see 22 Avi.728.

the mutual exchange of traffic rights, but which has remained a dead letter; and the 'Interim Agreement on International Civil Aviation',[12] which provided for the setting up of the *'Provisional International Civil Aviation Organization'* (PICAO), pending the entry into force of the main Convention, which occurred on 4 April 1947.

The Interim Agreement on International Civil Aviation entered into force barely six months after its adoption, on the day of the twenty-sixth acceptance, that is, 6 June 1945.[13] Pursuant to its Articles I to VII, the PICAO was established with an interim Assembly, an interim Council, a Secretary General, and headquarters in Montreal, Canada.[14] Three committees were created, namely, a Committee on Air Transport, a Committee on Air Navigation (which was later transformed to become the Air Navigation Commission of ICAO), and a Committee on International Conventions on Civil Aviation.[15] Article VII provided that at the time of coming into force of the Convention on International Civil Aviation, the records and property of PICAO shall be transferred to the permanent organization ICAO, and PICAO functions shall cease. Hence, after twenty months of operation of PICAO, on 4 April 1947, ICAO came into being and succeeded PICAO.[16]

B. Structure

1. Objectives

The objectives of the Organization are set out in Article 44 of the Convention on International Civil Aviation, which provides as follows:

> The aims and objectives of the Organization are to develop the principles and techniques of international air navigation and to foster the planning and development of international air transport so as to:
>
> (a) Insure the safe and orderly growth of international civil aviation throughout the world;

12. 171 *UNTS* 345.
13. Article XVII of the Agreement provided for entry into force upon acceptance by twenty-six States, specifying that acceptance may be expressed by informing the United States Government as depositary 'whether signature on its behalf shall constitute an acceptance of the Agreement by that Government and an obligation binding upon it'.
14. Pursuant to Art. III s. 3, Dr. Edward Warner, member of the US Civil Aeronautics Board, was elected President of the PICAO Interim Council. Pursuant to Art. III s. 5 para. 4, Dr Albert Roper (France), who had been Secretary General of the International Commission for Air Navigation (ICAN) since 1922, was appointed Secretary General of PICAO on 17 Aug. 1945.
15. See Art. III, ss 5 and 6 of the Interim Agreement.
16. See B. Cheng, *The Law of International Air Transport* (London: Stevens, 1962), 64; J.C. Cooper, 'Air Transport and World Organization', *Yale Law Journal* 55 (1946): 1191 et seq., 1205; M. Le Goff, *The Present State of Air Law* (The Hague: Nijhoff, 1956), 8. In accordance with Art. 91 (b) of the *Convention on International Civil Aviation,* the Convention came into force thirty days after deposit of the twenty-sixth instrument of ratification.

(b) Encourage the arts of aircraft design and operation for peaceful purposes;
(c) Encourage the development of airways, airports, and air navigation facilities for international civil aviation;
(d) Meet the needs of the peoples of the world for safe, regular, efficient and economical air transport;
(e) Prevent economic waste caused by unreasonable competition;
(f) Insure that the rights of contracting States are fully respected and that every contracting State has a fair opportunity to operate international airlines;
(g) Avoid discrimination between contracting States;
(h) Promote safety of flight in international air navigation;
(i) Promote generally the development of all aspects of international civil aeronautics.

These aims and objectives are to be seen in the context of the Preamble of the Convention, which, in its essential parts, reads as follows:

> Whereas the future development of international civil aviation can greatly help to create and preserve friendship and understanding among the nations and peoples of the world, yet its abuse can become a threat to the general security; and
>
> Whereas it is desirable to avoid friction and to promote that cooperation between nations and peoples upon which the peace of the world depends;
>
> Therefore, the undersigned governments having agreed on certain principles and arrangements in order that international civil aviation may be developed in a safe and orderly manner and that international air transport services may be established on the basis of equality of opportunity and operated soundly and economically.

The reference in the chapeau clause of Article 44 to the development of 'the principles and techniques of international air navigation' and to the fostering of 'the planning and development of international air transport' emphasizes the predominantly technical nature of the mandate of the Organization,[17] while planning and development functions in relation to air transport are also part of the broad overall mandate of ICAO. The term *air navigation* relates principally to the technical and operational aspects of aircraft movement, whereas *air transport* relates to the transportation by air of passengers, baggage, cargo, and mail. The overall mandate of ICAO comprised, from a historical perspective, first and foremost the rebuilding of international civil aviation, since the Second World War had

17. See K. Hailbronner, 'International Civil Aviation Organization' in *Encyclopedia of Public International Law,* ed. R. Bernhardt Vol. II (Max Planck Institute for Comparative Public Law and International Law, Oxford University Press, Heidelberg,1995), 1070 et seq.; W. Binaghi, 'The Role of ICAO', in: *The Freedom of the Air* (n. 21), 17 et seq.

brought it largely to a standstill.[18] In doing so, the promotion of aviation safety and later the promotion of aviation security became a central element. While the term *aviation safety* relates to technical and operational safety of flight, the term *aviation security* relates to safeguarding civil aviation against acts of unlawful interference. The objective of safety is mentioned in paragraphs (a), (d) and (h) of Article 44, as well as in the Preamble, third paragraph, and thus figures prominently among the specifically enumerated objectives. In the course of more than sixty years of operation of the Organization, the objective of safety has clearly been recognized as the objective with the highest overall priority.[19] Safety of flight is the basis, the *conditio sine qua non*, for all aviation activities, be they commercial, non-commercial, general aviation, or other flying activities.[20]

The promotion of safety has mainly been carried out through development and continuous updating of a comprehensive set of 'Technical Standards and Recommended Practices' (so-called SARPs) set out in the Annexes to the Convention. In recent years, the standard-setting activities of the Organization have been supplemented by a system to monitor implementation of the technical safety standards by ICAO Member States (Universal Safety Oversight Audit Programme)[21] as well as an integrated Global Aviation Safety Plan.[22]

Because of the increasing number of hijackings, acts of sabotage, and terrorist attacks on civil aircraft since the 1960s,[23] the objective of ensuring and promoting aviation security has similarly gained high priority. Although not expressly mentioned in Article 44 of the Convention, since this phenomenon did not exist at the time of its adoption, Article 4 prohibits misuse of civil aviation, namely, the 'use [of] civil aviation for any purpose inconsistent with the aims of this Convention'. Aviation safety and aviation security have in practice come to be regarded as two

---

18. A.D. Groenewege, *Compendium of International Civil Aviation*, 2nd edn (Montreal: IADC, 1998/99), 18 et seq.
19. See Assembly Resolution A37-5: *The Universal Safety Oversight Audit Programme (USOAP) Continuous Monitoring Approach,* first Whereas clause; A32-11: *Establishment of an ICAO universal safety oversight audit programme,* first Whereas clause, *ICAO Doc.* 9790 (Assembly Resolutions in Force), I-53; see also Assembly Resolution A37-4: *ICAO Global Planning for Safety,* and previous resolutions A32-15 and A33-16:*ICAO Global Aviation Safety Plan (GASP),* first Whereas clause.
20. Assembly Resolutions A37-2 and A37-3, first Whereas clause, and A33-16, *ibid.*; see also: Global Aviation Safety Plan (GASP), ed. ICAO (2001); D. Olson, 'Striving for aviation safety', in *100 Years of Civil Aviation,* ed. ICAO (Montreal and London: ICAO and ICS Ltd, 2003), 114 et seq.
21. ICAO Assembly Resolution A37-5, and previously A36-4, A35-6, A32-11, A33-8, and A33-9; see also the *Report of the DGCA Conference on a Global Strategy for Safety Oversight, ICAO Doc.* 9707; *ICAO Oversight Audit Manual, ICAO Doc. 9735*; *ICAO Safety Oversight Manual, Doc. 9734.*
22. See below n. 28.
23. B. Cheng, 'Crimes on Board Aircraft', *Current Legal Problems* 12 (1959): 177 et seq.; E. McWhinney, *The Illegal Diversion of Aircraft and International Law* (Dordrecht/Boston/Lancaster: Nijhoff, 1987); D.D. Joyner, *A Contemporary Concept of Piracy in International Law: The Status of Aerial Hijacking as an International Crime* (Dobbs Ferry/Leiden: Oceana/Sijthoff, 1974).

sides of the same coin.[24] Therefore, the objective of promoting and ensuring aviation security has been recognized as being of equal priority as that of promoting aviation safety. As a consequence, standard-setting activities in this area have been supplemented by a system to monitor implementation of the aviation security standards by ICAO Member States (Universal Security Audit Programme)[25] as well as an Aviation Security Action Plan.[26]

Among the other numerous objectives of the Organization, the planning and development of a new system to facilitate and improve communications, air navigation, surveillance, and air traffic management should be mentioned. The use of satellite technology and advanced communications systems have been combined for the development of an integrated, global, satellite-based system to support communications, navigation, surveillance, and air-traffic management for the needs of commercial and non-commercial aviation (the so-called CNS/ATM System).[27] This system is in a stage of gradual implementation.

2. Status

ICAO has the status of a 'specialized agency of the United Nations' in the sense of *Article 7 of the United Nations Charter*, by virtue of the *Agreement between the United Nations and ICAO* of 1947, which came into force on 13 May 1947,[28] and by virtue of the Convention on the Privileges and Immunities of the Specialized Agencies of 21 November 1947.[29] It possesses legal personality, both at the level of international law (Article II of the 1947 Convention) as well as at the level of national law (Article 47 of the Convention on International Civil Aviation). Under the latter provision, ICAO shall enjoy full juridical personality wherever compatible with the constitution and laws of the State concerned.

ICAO enjoys the privileges and immunities spelled out in the 1947 Convention, including its Annex III.[30] As regards the headquarters of the Organization in

24. G.D. Kyriakopoulos, *La sécurité de l'aviation civile en droit international public* (Athens/Brussels: A.N. Sakkoulas/Bruylant, 1999).
25. The ICAO USAP was launched in November 2002 as part of the Aviation Security Action Plan. See the Report in *ICAO Doc.* 9826 – Supplement, 18 et seq.
26. The ICAO Aviation Security Action Plan was adopted by the Council of ICAO during its 166th Session (June 2002). See Assembly Resolution A35-9, Appendix E and more recently Assembly Resolution A37-17, Appendix A, 6th and 7th Whereas clauses.
27. *Report of the World-wide CNS/ATM Systems Implementation Conference*, *ICAO Doc.* 9719; Global Air Navigation Plan for CNS/TM Systems, *ICAO Doc.* 9750.
28. *Agreement between the United Nations and the International Civil Aviation Organization*, dated 13 May 1947, *ICAO Doc.* 7970; *UNTS* Vol. 8 (1947), 324 et seq.
29. 33 *UNTS* 242-261 (1948). See C.W. Jenks, *International Immunities* (London: Stevens and Sons, 1961); D. B. Michaels, *International Privileges and Immunities, A case for a Universal Statute* (The Hague: Nijhoff, 1971). The final text of the Annexes to the 1947 Convention, which includes 'Annex III: International Civil Aviation Organization' was approved on 29 Dec. 1951.
30. Annex III was approved by the ICAO Assembly in Assembly Resolution A2-26 and transmitted to the UN Secretary General on 11 Aug. 1948. For the text of Annex III, see *ibid.* (n. 60).

Montreal, Canada, ICAO enjoys the privileges and immunities set out in the Headquarters Agreement between ICAO and Canada signed on 4 and 9 October 1990,[31] and the Agreement supplementary thereto dated 28 May 1999.[32] The privileges and immunities under the Headquarters Agreement are in line with those enjoyed by other UN specialized agencies, and include in particular immunity of the Organization's property and assets, inviolability of its headquarters premises, and recognition of the Organization's juridical personality.

The constitution of ICAO is set out in Part II of the Convention on International Civil Aviation. When the Convention was adopted in 1944, its drafters may have envisaged ICAO as a global, all-encompassing international intergovernmental agency for civil aviation, as can be deduced from Article 44, Subparagraphs (d) and (i) and Article 55 Subparagraph (a). Under the latter provision, ICAO may set up subordinate air transport commissions on a regional basis, so as to respond to regional needs.[33] So far, however, Article 55 Subparagraph (a) has never been used. Instead, several regional intergovernmental bodies for civil aviation have been set up outside of Article 55 (a), namely the European Civil Aviation Conference (ECAC), the African Civil Aviation Commission (AFCAC), the Latin American Civil Aviation Commission (LACAC) and the Arab Civil Aviation Commission (ACAC).[34] Three of these, namely, ECAC, AFCAC, and LACAC, are neither part of ICAO nor completely independent from it, but enjoy an intermediate status.[35] They operate their headquarters from the premises of the respective Regional Office of ICAO, administer their staff under the ICAO umbrella, and coordinate their work programme, as appropriate, with ICAO.[36] ACAC operates without such institutional links, but de facto cooperates with ICAO.[37]

The setting up of such bodies with 'intermediate' status has, to some extent, been controversial, in view of Article 55 (a) of the Convention.[38] However, these bodies should be seen as in line with the Convention as long as they do not overlap,

31. *ICAO Doc.* 9541.
32. *Supplementary Agreement between the International Civil Aviation Organization and the Government of Canada Regarding the Headquarters of the International Civil Aviation Organization, ICAO Doc.* 9591– Supplementary Agreement.
33. See on Art. 55 (a): *Repertory-Guide to the Convention on International Civil Aviation*, 2nd edn (1977), *ICAO Doc.* 8900/2, Art. 55.
34. See for more details below, Assembly Resolutions A10-5: *Relationship of ICAO with the European Civil Aviation Conference,* superseded by A27-17 and A18-21: *Air Transport Work in the Regions – General Policy*, also superseded by A27-17. For the latter Resolution, see *ICAO Doc.* 9790.
35. L. Weber, 'European Civil Aviation Conference', in: *Encyclopaedia*, ed. R. Bernhardt (n. 9), Vol. II (1995), 137 et seq., with further references; Assembly Resolution A27-17: *Relationship between ICAO and Regional Civil Aviation Bodies, ICAO Doc.* 9790.
36. Assembly Resolution A27-17, Resolving clause 2.a).
37. ACAC participated in the recent ICAO Assemblies and invited, in turn, ICAO representatives to certain of its meetings; ACAC also receives certain documentation from ICAO related to its activities.
38. L. Weber, *'Les éléments de la coopération dans le cadre de la Commission européenne de l'aviation civile (CEAC)'*, 31 *RFDA* (1977), 388 et seq., at 408–409, with further references.

duplicate, or impede the work carried out by ICAO. In fact, Article 83, first sentence of the Convention provides that subject to Article 82, any Contracting State may make arrangements not inconsistent with the provisions of the Convention.[39]

3. Organs

a. The Assembly

The Assembly is the main policy-setting body of ICAO. Each of the 190 members of ICAO has a seat in the Assembly and one vote.[40] It meets in ordinary session once every three years, and may meet in extraordinary sessions at any time upon call of the Council, or at the request of at least one-fifth of the membership.[41]

A majority of the Contracting States constitute a quorum for the meetings of the Assembly. Decisions require a simple majority of votes cast;[42] in practice, however, virtually all decisions of the Assembly are taken by *consensus*. The taking of formal votes is rare. Most decisions on substantive matters are taken in the form of a resolution.

Many Assembly resolutions are detailed policy-setting documents not only for the Council, the Secretariat, and other organs of the Organization, but also for the Member States.[43] While they may contain instructions to the Council, the Secretariat or other ICAO bodies, they may also contain principles, policies, or guidance to be followed by the Member States.[44]

Whether or not such resolutions have any legally binding effect on Member States is controversial, in particular with reference to the notion of 'soft law'.[45] However, the persuasive nature of the material used in such resolutions, the high degree of expertise on which it is usually based, and the universal acceptance at the time of adoption usually have the effect of ensuring their implementation.[46]

39. L. Weber, *ibid.*, 137 et seq.
40. Article 48 b) of the Convention; Rule 3 of the *Standing Rules of Procedure of the Assembly of the International Civil Aviation Organization*, 5th edn (1990), *Doc. 7600/5.*
41. Article 48 a) of the Convention; Rules 1 and 2 of the Standing Rules of Procedure of the Assembly, *ibid.* (n. 31).
42. Article 48 c) of the Convention; Rule 28 of the Standing Rules of Procedure of the Assembly, *ibid.* (n. 31).
43. See, e.g. Assembly Resolution A37-18: *Consolidated statement of continuing ICAO policies and practices related to environmental protection – general provisions, noise and local air quality*; Assembly Resolution A37-17: *Consolidated statement of continuing ICAO policies related to the safeguarding of international civil aviation against acts of unlawful interference*, Resolutions adopted by the Assembly, 37th session, Provisional edition (November 2010).
44. See e.g. A37-18, Appendices C to F; A37-17, Appendices C to G.
45. The term 'soft law' has been coined with particular reference to the declarations and resolutions of the UN General Assembly, as well as with regard to similar acts of the Assemblies of Parties of the UN Specialized Agencies. See on this matter D. Thürer, 'Soft Law', in *Encyclopaedia of Public International Law,* ed. Bernhardt Vol. IV (2000), 452 et seq., with further references.
46. See T. Buergenthal, *Law-Making in the International Civil Aviation organization*, Syracuse Press, N.Y. (1969), 226 et seq., 229–230.

The Assembly's powers and duties are laid down in Article 49 of the Convention, in particular to the following:[47]

- elect the Members States of the Council for three years;[48]
- vote on annual budgets and determine the financial arrangements of the Organization (in practice, a package of three annual budgets, referred to as triennial budget, is voted upon);[49]
- review expenditures and approve the accounts of the Organization;[50]
- delegate to the Council the powers and authority necessary or desirable;[51]
- consider proposals for amendments to the Convention;[52] deal with any matter within the sphere of action of the Organization not specifically assigned to the Council.[53]

For the discharge of these responsibilities, the Assembly usually establishes the following subsidiary bodies for the duration of its ordinary triennial session, in accordance with Rules 14 to 22 of the Standing Rules of Procedure for the Assembly:[54]

- the Executive Committee,[55] which has the task of coordinating the work of all other subsidiary bodies of the Assembly and of preparing the main policy decisions in the Plenary (Article 15 of the Standing Rules of Procedure);
- the Technical Commission, which has responsibility in air navigation matters and related subjects;[56]
- the Economic Commission, which has responsibility in air transport matters;
- the Legal Commission, which has responsibility in legal matters;[57]
- the Administrative Commission,[58] which has responsibility in budgetary, financial, and related matters; regarding the triennial budget, the Administrative Commission is usually assisted by a Budget Working Group,[59] which reports to the Administrative Commission.

47. On decision-making of the Assembly under Art. 49 of the Convention, see *Repertory-Guide to the Convention on International Civil Aviation*, 2nd edn (1977), *ICAO Doc.* 8900/2, Art. 49.
48. Article 49 b); Rules 55-63 Standing Rules of Procedure of the Assembly, *ibid.* (n. 31).
49. Article 49 e); Rules 24 et seq. Standing Rules of Procedure, *ibid.*
50. Article 49 f); Rules 24 et seq. Standing Rules of Procedure, *ibid.*
51. Article 49 h); Rules 24 et seq. Standing Rules of Procedure, *ibid.*
52. Article 49 j); Rules 24 et seq. Standing Rules of Procedure, *ibid.*
53. Article 49 k) of the Convention; Arts 24 et seq. Standing Rules of Procedure, *ibid.*
54. Standing Rules of Procedure, *ibid.*
55. Rules 14 a) and 15 Standing Rules of Procedure, *ibid.*
56. This Commission, which is not specifically mentioned in the Standing Rules of Procedure of the Assembly, is established under Rules 14 and 18, and has the composition as set out in Rule 21.
57. See n. 47above.
58. This Commission is foreseen in Rule 14 c) of the Standing Rules of Procedure. It has the composition as set out in Rule 21.
59. Under Rule 19 of the Standing Rules of Procedure, any Commission may create Working Groups. A Working Group shall consist of a limited number of members appointed by the

All four Commissions report to the Plenary of the Assembly, either directly, or if coordination is required, through the Executive Committee,[60] or if established, the Coordination Committee.[61]

The decisions of the Assembly in the form of assembly resolutions are published after each session and disseminated to all Member States; this publication contains the new resolutions adopted, along with all previous assembly resolutions which continue to be in force.[62]

b. The Council and Its Committees

The Council is a 'permanent body responsible to the Assembly', Article 50 (a) of the Convention. It is composed of thirty-six Contracting States elected by the Assembly,[63] which have each one seat and one vote. The Council is the executive governing body of the Organization.

In electing the members of the Council, the Assembly shall, in accordance with Article 50 (b) of the Convention, give adequate representation to the following:[64]

(1) the States of chief importance in air transport (so-called Part 1, eleven States);[65]
(2) the States which make the largest contribution to the provision of international air navigation facilities (so-called Part 2, twelve States);[66]
(3) the States whose designation will ensure that all the major geographic areas of the world are represented on the Council (so-called Part 3, thirteen States).[67]

Decisions of the Council require approval by a majority of all its members (Article 52 of the Convention). However, when adopting Annexes to the Convention, or amendments to such Annexes,[68] action by the Council requires a two-thirds majority (twenty-five votes), in accordance with Articles 90 and 54 paragraph (l) of the Convention. Under its Rules of Procedure, the Council may also take certain

---

Chairman of the Commission, not more than one member being appointed from any one delegation; see Rule 21.

60. See Rules 14 a) and 15 of the Standing Rules of Procedure.
61. See Rules 14 b) and 16 of the Standing Rules of Procedure.
62. See e.g. Assembly Resolutions in Force (as of 8 Oct. 2004), *ICAO Doc*. 9848.
63. The Council was enlarged in 2003 from 33 to 36 States when the Protocol of Amendment signed on 26 Oct. 1990 entered into force; 34th Session (Extraordinary) of the Assembly, 31 Mar. 2003-1 Apr. 2003.
64. See Rule 56 of the Standing Rules of Procedure of the Assembly.
65. Rule 56 i) of the Standing Rules of Procedure; the number of States elected in Part 1 is subject to the decision of the Assembly.
66. Rule 56 ii) of the Standing Rules of Procedure; the number of States elected in Part 2 is subject to the decision of the Assembly.
67. Rule 56 iii) of the Standing Rules of Procedure; the number of States elected in Part 3 is subject to the decision of the Assembly.
68. Articles 54 e) and m) and 90 of the Convention.

decisions of procedural nature by simple majority of votes cast (Articles 37, second Sentence, and 42 paragraph (b) of the Rules of Procedure for the Council), although the statutory majority for decisions is an absolute majority under Article 52 of the Convention.[69]

In accordance with Articles 54 and 55 of the Convention, the Council has a multitude of legislative, administrative, and judicial functions. These are divided up in mandatory functions (Article 54) and permissive functions (Article 55).

Among the legislative functions are, in particular, the following:[70]

- the adoption of international standards and recommended practices (SARPs) in the form of Annexes to the Convention, and amendments thereto (Articles 90, 54 (l)); the Council has up to now adopted eighteen Annexes and one of its major functions in practice is to keep these eighteen Annexes up-to-date by adopting appropriate amendments.[71]

Administrative functions of the Council are the following:[72]

- the administration of the finances of the Organization in accordance with Chapters XII and XV;
- the appointment of the Secretary General and making provision for other personnel of the Secretariat, as required (Article 55 (h));
- the collection and dissemination of information on air navigation and air transport services;
- the reporting of infractions of the Convention (Article 54 (j) and (k));
- the submission of annual reports to the Assembly and the carrying out of directions of the Assembly (Article 54 (a) and (b)).

Regarding the last point, the Council fulfils the important function of administering and supervising the Universal Safety Oversight Audit Programme (USOAP)[73] as well as the Universal Security Audit Programme (USAP).[74] The gradual

69. Article 52 of the Convention provides that 'decisions of the Council shall require approval by a majority of its members.' In light of this provision, the question may arise whether the Rules of Procedure, which are permitting simple majority voting (see Rule 63 of the Rules of Procedure for the Council, *Doc.* 7559/5), are 'constitutional'. It has been argued in this respect that the Council, when adopting its Rules of Procedure, decided with absolute majority under Art. 52, and that the requirement of Art. 52 was therefore satisfied. It has also been pointed out that the decisions of the Council falling under the simple majority rule in the Rules of Procedure are mainly of procedural nature and not substantive. In practice, the Council applies the *consensus* principle on virtually all issues (except adoption of Annexes and amendments thereto). Therefore, this issue has more theoretical than any practical significance.
70. See on this matter T. Buergenthal, *ibid.* (n. 1).
71. Articles 54 m) and 90 of the Convention.
72. *Repertory-Guide to the Convention on International Civil Aviation*, Second Edition, *ICAO Doc.* 8900/2, Articles 54 a), b), f), h)-k).
73. H. Belai, 'Expanding programme to adopt systems approach to future audits', *ICAO Journa*l 58 no. 9 (2003): 4 et seq.; L. Weber, *ibid.* (n. 18), 301 et seq. with further references.
74. ICAO Secretariat, 'Historic Conference agrees on strategy for strengthening aviation security', I*CAO Journal* 57 no. 2 (2002): 5 et seq.; A. Kotaite, 'Civil aviation security is an integral part of

introduction of these programmes as mandatory programmes since 2001 has taken up an important part of the Council's time and efforts, and can be regarded as successful.[75]

Judicial functions of the Council are the following:[76]

- the adjudication of disputes between Contracting States relating to the interpretation or application of the Convention or its Annexes (Articles 84 and 54(b));
- the adjudication of disputes between Contracting States relating to the interpretation or application of the International Air Services Transit Agreement (Article 66 of the Convention, Article II Transit Agreement, and Article 1 of the Rules for the Settlement of Differences).

In practice, and in accordance with the ICAO Rules for the Settlement of Differences,[77] the Council has, to the extent possible, acted as a mediator between the parties which have brought complaints before the Council.[78] Therefore, in virtually all cases brought before the Council, it was possible to arrive at a settlement agreed between the parties.[79] Where necessary, the Council has not shied away from taking clear procedural decisions in adversarial situations.[80] However, the Council's policy of favouring negotiated settlements has been predicated on the consideration that disputes between Contracting States, even if clothed in a legal agreement, are usually predominantly political in nature and should therefore be settled by political means, that is, negotiation whenever possible, instead of adjudication.[81]

---

our global security', *ICAO Journal* 57 no. 5 (2002): 4 et seq.; D. Antonini, 'Annex 17 Standards will be primary focus of forthcoming security system audits', *ICAO Journal* 57 no. 5 (2002): 11 et seq. On the USAP as it evolved since 2002, see L. Weber, *ibid.* (n. 18), 307 et seq.; Assembly Working Paper A37-WP/32 EX/12: Implementation and Evolution of the ICAO Universal Security Audit Programme (26/07/10); Assembly Resolution A37-5, Whereas clauses.

75. See Assembly Resolution A37-5, 8th Whereas clause; A35-6, operating clause 1; Assembly Resolution A35-9, Appendix E, 9th whereas clause, *ICAO Doc.* 9848.
76. On the judicial functions of the Council, see J. Erler, *Rechtsfragen der ICAO: Die Internationale Zivilluftfahrtorganisation und ihre Mitgliedstaaten* (1967), 185–196; B. Cheng, *The Law of International Air Transport* (1962), 100–105; R. Mankiewicz, *Organisation internationale de l'aviation Civile, Annuaire Français de droit international* (1957), 383 et seq.; T. Buergenthal, *ibid.* (n. 1), 123 et seq.; *Repertory-Guide to the Convention on International Civil Aviation*, Arts 84 et seq.
77. *ICAO Doc.* 7782/2.
78. For the cases submitted to the Council, see below.
79. See below.
80. See e.g. the decision of the Council to reject the Preliminary Objections of the fifteen Member States of the EU in: *United States and 15 European States* (2000) ('Hushkits'), C-DEC 161/6; see also C-WP 11380, Memorandum SG 1670/00 and SG 1674/00, and C-DEC 161/4 and 5.
81. Buergenthal, *ibid.* (n. 1), 161 remarks with regard to the complaint procedure under the Transit and Transport Agreements that it 'is designed primarily to provide machinery for the adjustment of frictions of an economic or political type that might otherwise disrupt the orderly operation of the system established by the Transit and Transport Agreements'. A similar remark could also be made with regard to the procedures under Ch. XVIII (Arts 84 et seq.) of the Convention.

Under Article 54 (n), the Council 'shall consider any matter relating to the Convention that any Contracting State refers to it'. In practice, the majority of cases brought before the Council under this provision involved complaints about other Contracting States allegedly not complying with the provisions of the Convention.[82]

As a matter of standing practice, these cases under Article 54 (n) have not been treated as cases of formal adjudication, so that the Rules for the Settlement of Differences do not apply.[83] Instead, the parties complaining and complained of are invited by the Council to attend as invited observers under Article 53 of the Convention[84] (unless they are members of the Council), and are given an opportunity to state their case before the Council. The Rules of Procedure for the Council apply in these cases.[85] The Council will usually favour negotiations between the parties and, if necessary, will make recommendations or suggestions to the parties. If appropriate, the Council may proceed to make a decision on the matter.[86] The proceedings under Article 54 (n) can be regarded as quasi-judiciary.

In accordance with Article 51, the President of the Council is an official elected for a term of three years, subject to re-election. He shall serve as representative of the Council and carry out the functions that the Council assigns to him. In practice, a large number of functions are delegated to the President of the Council, in particular during those periods when the Council is not in session.[87] In accordance with Articles 59 and 60, the President of the Council has the status of an international civil servant of ICAO, who receives emoluments from ICAO and who must not be under employment with any Contracting State.[88]

In accordance with Article 54 (d), the Council has established an Air Transport Committee.[89] Similarly, under Article 54 (c) and its Rules of Procedure, the Council has established a number of other Committees, namely,

---

82. See below.
83. This fact renders the procedure under Art. 54 (n) more flexible in relation to the needs of the particular dispute. From a formal viewpoint, Art. 54 (n) is an entirely open-ended provision as regards the subject-matter which a Contracting State may refer to the Council, and does not presuppose an adversarial procedure. In all cases of Art. 54 (n), the *Rules of Procedure for the Council*, Doc. 7559/5, apply.
84. Article 53 of the Convention requires that the party invited to participate, without a vote, in the discussions of the Council be especially affected in its interests by the question considered by the Council.
85. *ICAO Doc.* 7559/5.
86. See e.g. C-DEC 164/5 regarding an 'Amendment to the Common Nadi/Auckland Oceanic FIR boundary'.
87. Delegation of functions is done on the basis of Art. 51 c) of the Convention and Arts 19-23, 63, of the *Rules of Procedure for the Council, Doc.* 7559/5.
88. Both Arts 59 and 60 of the Convention mention the President of the Council expressly for the avoidance of doubt about his status. See *Repertory-Guide to the Convention of International Civil Aviation,* 2nd edn, *ICAO Doc.* 8900/2, Arts 59 and 60.
89. The Air Transport Committee is the only Committee of the Council expressly mentioned in the Convention, and under Art. 54 (d) it is a mandatory committee; the other committees have been set up under the Council's Rules of Procedure, Rule 17 (formerly Rule 14).

– the Finance Committee;[90]
– the Technical Cooperation Committee;[91]
– the Joint Support Committee;[92]and
– the Committee on Unlawful Interference.[93]

These committees are composed of representatives of the Council, or their alternates, and they have between eleven and fifteen members. The committees usually meet during the first phase of each Council session (so-called Committee Phase) to prepare the discussion in full Council during the second phase (so-called Council Phase).[94] Their work is subject to the Rules of Procedure for the Standing Committees of the Council.[95] All committees report to the Council through the respective committee chairman, who is usually an experienced representative of the Council.

To prepare the Council's decisions on the Edward Warner Award, the Council has also established the Edward Warner Committee, whose work is governed by the Rules of Procedure of the Edward Warner Fund. It is the object of the Edward Warner Fund to award every three years the Edward Warner Award, consisting of a gold medal and an Award Certificate, to a person having made an outstanding contribution to the advancement of International Civil Aviation.

c. The Air Navigation Commission

The Air Navigation Commission, established by the Council under Article 54 (e) and Chapter X of the Convention, is the main technical body of the Organization.[96] In accordance with Article 57 (a) of the Convention, its principal function is to consider amendments or modifications to the Annexes to the Convention and to recommend them to the Council. It shall also advise the Council on the collection and dissemination of information it considers necessary and useful for the advancement of air navigation (Article 57 (c) of the Convention).[97]

The Air Navigation Commission is now composed of nineteen members appointed by the Council in their personal capacity as experts (not as representatives) from among persons nominated by Contracting States.[98] An amendment to

90. See Rule 17 of the *Rules of Procedure for the Council, ICAO Doc.* 7559/8; Rule 1 a) of the *Rules of Procedure for Standing Committees of the Council, ICAO Doc.* 8146 – *(5th edition 2007).*
91. *Rules of Procedure for Standing Committees of the Council, ibid.* (n. 90), Rule 1 b).
92. *Rules of Procedure for Standing Committees of the Council, ibid.* (n. 90), Rule 1 a).
93. Rule 1 b) of the *Rules of Procedure for Standing Committees of the Council, ibid.*, 2 and the *Special Provisions applicable to other Standing Committees of the Council,* Committee on Unlawful Interference, *ibid.* (n. 90).
94. Rule 20 of the *Rules of Procedure for the Council, Doc.* 7559/8.
95. *Ibid.* (n. 90).
96. See *Rules of Procedure for the Air Navigation Commission, Doc.* 8229, Arts 1-3; T. Buergenthal, *ibid.* (n. 1), 9 et seq.
97. See also the *Rules of Procedure for the Air Navigation Commission, ICAO Doc.* 8229.
98. Article 56, first Sentence, of the Convention; Rule 16 (a) of the *Rules of Procedure of the Council, ibid.* (n. 90).

Article 56 providing for an increase of the members of the Commission from fifteen to nineteen members came into force on 18 April 2005.[99]

The President of the Air Navigation Commission is appointed by the Council, usually for a term of office of one year, subject to re-appointment.[100] The members are appointed by the Council from among persons nominated by Contracting States, and their term of office extends from the time of their appointment until their nomination is withdrawn by the State having nominated them.

It is the practice of the Air Navigation Commission to develop and prepare recommendations for Amendments to the Annexes to the Convention through a detailed and elaborate procedure, which ensures *consensus* and support among Contracting States for the amendment.[101] This will be the basis for, and will facilitate, implementation of an amendment setting forth new SARPs by Contracting States, once the amendment is formally adopted by the Council.

The Air Navigation Commission reports in all matters to the Council.[102] The Council may, under Article 55 (b), delegate to the Air Navigation Commission duties additional to those set out in the Convention; however, it has made use of this option only sparingly.

d. *The Legal Committee*

The Legal Committee was set up by the Assembly during its first session in 1947 (Assembly Resolution A1-46).[103] It has the task of advising the Council and the Assembly on legal questions and the important function of preparing drafts for international conventions or protocols in the field of air law.[104] Its membership comprises all 190 Contracting States and each member has one vote.[105] Decisions require a simple majority of votes cast, including decisions in the preparation of drafts for instruments of international air law when adopting a draft for submission to the Council.[106] In practice, most decisions in the Legal Committee are taken by

99. On this date, the *Protocol Relating to an Amendment to the Convention on International Civil Aviation* (Art. 56), signed in Montreal on 6 Oct. 1989, entered into force upon reaching 108 ratifications. See *Doc. 9544*.
100. Rule 15 (a) of the *Rules of Procedure for the Council, Doc. 7559/8.*
101. For the procedure, see Assembly Resolution A37-15: *Consolidated statement of ICAO continuing policies and associated practices related specifically to air navigation*, Appendix A. See previously A36-13, Appendices A and following.
102. Article 57 (a) of the Convention; *Rules of Procedure for the Air Navigation Commission, Doc.* 8229.
103. No longer in force (see *Doc.* 9848 – Assembly Resolutions in force (as of 8 Oct. 2004)), Appendix A; see now A37-22: *Consolidated statement of continuing ICAO policies in the legal field,* Appendices A-E.
104. See *ibid.* (n. 104), Appendix B; *Legal Committee – Constitution – Procedure for Approval of Draft Conventions – Rules of Procedure, Doc. 7669 – LC/139/5.*
105. Legal Committee, *Rules of Procedure, Doc. 7669*;
106. Legal Committee, *Rules of Procedure*, Rule 38, *Doc. 7669 – LC/139/5*. However, a two-thirds majority is required for decisions on adoption of a text at international conferences on air law (Diplomatic Conferences) convened under the auspices of ICAO; the same applies in case the

consensus. The procedure which the Committee applies in the preparation of draft instruments of international air law are laid down in the Procedure for approval of draft conventions on international air law (Assembly Resolution A31-15,[107] Appendix B) and additionally in the Appendix to the Rules of Procedure for the Legal Committee (ICAO Doc. 7669-LC/139/5), entitled Organization and Working Methods of the Legal Committee.

The elaboration of a draft text is first entrusted to the secretariat, or to a subcommittee of the Legal Committee. More recently, this task has also been entrusted in several cases to the secretariat assisted by a secretariat study group.[108] When the subcommittee (or the secretariat study group) has completed its work in drafting a first draft text, it will be submitted to the Legal Committee. The Committee will usually revise the draft, in light of the views of its 189 members. Once the Legal Committee has completed its work on the text, it is adopted by the Committee and submitted to the Council for consideration, together with a report thereon. The Council may take such action as it deems fit including the circulation of the draft to Contracting States and international organizations for comment.[109] The comment period shall not be less than four months if it considers the text is not yet sufficiently mature, or it may refer the text back to the Committee, or to a special group, for further consideration; if it considers that the text is sufficiently mature, it will convene a diplomatic conference for the purpose of formal adoption and signature of the new instrument.[110]

This elaborate procedure has resulted in the widespread acceptance and ratification of most international air law instruments which the ICAO Legal Committee has developed.

e. *Air Navigation Conferences and Divisional Meetings*

Air navigation conferences may be convened by the Council from time to time, as circumstances require.[111] An air navigation conference will usually be called when its task encompasses a substantial number of interrelated subjects of worldwide scope falling within several air navigation fields, so as to discuss and recommend new techniques, new technology, or new procedures for the advancement of air navigation.[112]

Legal Committee does not accept the text prepared by a sub-committee as a basis of discussion.

107. Assembly Resolution A31-15, Appendix B, which suspended Resolutions A7-6 and A27-3.

108. This was the case in the Warsaw Convention modernization process, which led to the adoption of the Montreal Convention of 1999, see *ICAO Doc*. 9775, Vol. III – Preparatory Material; similarly, in the Rome Convention modernization process, a text was elaborated by the Secretariat with the assistance of a secretariat study group.

109. See Assembly Resolution A37-22, Appendix B.

110. *Ibid.* (n. 110).

111. See *Directives to Divisional-type Air Navigation Meetings and Rules of Procedure for their Conduct, ICAO Doc*. 8143 – AN/873/3, Part I, s. 4.

112. See *ibid.* (n. 112), Part I s. 2.2.

All 190 Contracting States are entitled to attend an air navigation conference. While according to the Rules of Procedure,[113] each State has one vote, recommendations and conclusions are usually adopted by *consensus*. An air navigation conference may set up committees and subcommittees, as required by its work. Its work will usually result in recommendations and conclusions taking into account 'advancement of aeronautical science and technology' and resulting in 'improvement of techniques, technology or procedures', which it will address to the Council for decision.[114] For example, the tenth air navigation conference in 1992 recommended the introduction of the new satellite-based CNS/ATM concept for international civil aviation, and the eventual phasing out of terrestrial air navigation services.[115] The eleventh air navigation conference held in 2003 reviewed the implementation of the CNS/ATM system and endorsed the development of the Global Air Traffic Management (ATM) Operational Concept. The conclusions and recommendations of an air navigation conference may have a far-reaching impact on the advancement of air navigation.

Divisional meetings are meetings of worldwide scope dealing with one or a few specific subject matters in the air navigation or air transport fields, for example, aircraft accident investigation, aviation meteorology, or facilitation.[116] Such meetings are convened by the Council for the purpose of progressing the resolution of problems of worldwide importance, including the development of amendments to the Annexes and other basic documents in the air navigation or air transport field.[117]

All Contracting States may participate in such meetings on an equal basis. They shall be convened only when justified by the number and importance of the problem to be dealt with, and when there is the likelihood of constructive action on them.[118] Meetings convened on this basis may be requested to conduct exploratory discussions on matters not yet mature for definite action.

Any recommendations or conclusions of a divisional meeting will be addressed to the Council, which may decide to have them reviewed by the Air Navigation Commission or other relevant bodies, in particular when amendments to Annexes are being considered.

---

113. See *ibid.* (n. 112), Part III, ss 2 & 16.
114. See Directives to Divisional-type Air Navigation Meetings, *ibid.* (n. 112), Part I.
115. *Report of the 10th Air Navigation Conference*, 5 Sep. 1991-20 Sep. 1991, *ICAO Doc.* 9583.
116. See e.g. *Report of the 10th Air Navigation Conference*, 5 Sep. 1991-20 Sep. 1991, *ICAO Doc.* 9583 *Report of the Aeronautical Information Services Aeronautical Charts (AIS/MAP) Divisional Meeting (1998), Doc. 9733*; *Report of the Meteorology (MET) Divisional Meeting (2002), Doc. 9812.*
117. Assembly Resolution A36-13, Appendix B: *Air navigation meetings of worldwide scope*, operating clause 1, now superseded by A37-15 which no longer contains Appendix B. Such meetings may also be called to discuss matters in the air transport field.
118. Appendix B paragraph 2 to Assembly Resolution A36-13: *Consolidated statement of ICAO continuing policies and associated practices related specifically to air navigation,* now superseded by A37-15 which no longer contains Appendix B.

f. Panels and Working Groups

Panels are groups of experts of limited size which may be set up by the Air Navigation Commission[119] or by the Council. Such panels shall be established when it is necessary to advance the solution of special problems requiring expert advice, including technical problems which cannot be solved adequately or expeditiously by the Air Navigation Commission through other established facilities.[120] The experts who are members of a panel sit on the panel in their personal capacity as experts, not as a representative of their State.

In practice, panels have been an important element in the advancement of the work of the Air Navigation Commission as regards the various Annexes (e.g., in recent years, the Operations Panel, the Obstacle Clearance Panel, the Airworthiness Panel, the Aviation Security Panel, etc.).[121]

The advice that panels provide is expert advice. Therefore, their reports are presented as the advice of a group of experts to the Air Navigation Commission or to the body having set up the panel; consequently, they cannot be considered as representing the view of Contracting States.[122]

Panels, as well as many other ICAO subsidiary bodies, may set up working groups in accordance with their Rules of Procedure so as to advance their work. These working groups will usually have a specific task set out in their terms of reference, and limited membership. It is general practice that Member States of the parent body not represented on a working group may participate as an observer if they so wish.

Working groups should be distinguished from *secretariat study groups,* which are set up by the Secretariat and are composed of experts from Contracting States. They are moderated by an officer of the Secretariat. Their task is usually to advance the work of the Secretariat in developing proposals or draft texts, such as draft international air law instruments for the consideration of the Legal Committee or Legal Subcommittee.

g. The Secretariat

The secretariat of the Organization is headed by the Secretary General, who is the chief executive officer of ICAO in accordance with Article 54 (h) of the Convention. The Secretary General is appointed by the Council, which shall also make provision for 'the appointment of such other personnel as may be necessary, in accordance with the provisions of chapter XI.'[123] Chapter XI of the Convention

119. See the *Directives for Panels of the Air Navigation Commission*, *ICAO Doc.* 7984/4, ss 1-3.
120. See Appendix C to Assembly Resolution A36-13, *ibid.*, (n. 118): *Panels of the Air Navigation Commission (ANC)*, para. 1.
121. See *Supplementary Report on Activities of the Organization in the first half of 2004*, Assembly – 35th Session, *Doc. 9826* – Supplement, 3, 5.
122. See Appendix C to Assembly Resolution A36-13 *ibid.*, (n. 118), Associated Practice. Now superseded bu A37-15 which no longer contains Appendix C.
123. Article 54 (h) of the Convention, second half-sentence.

leaves it to the Council to determine 'the method of appointment and termination of appointment, the training, and the salaries, allowances, and conditions of service of the Secretary General and other personnel of the Organization...'.[124] In particular, Article 59 provides for the international character of the personnel of the Organization, and Article 60 sets out the basis for privileges and immunities of such personnel.[125] The Organization's staff enjoys such privileges and immunities in accordance with the 1947 Convention on the Privileges and Immunities of the Specialized Agencies, including its Annex III.

On the basis of Articles 58 and 59, the Council has adopted staff regulations (the ICAO Service Code), which govern the conditions of service of all ICAO staff.[126] These are modelled upon the UN Service Code, since ICAO is part of the UN Common System. In practice, most aspects of the Service Code, in particular as regards appointments, salaries, and conditions of service, are therefore governed by the rules and practices of the UN Common System.[127]

The Secretariat consists of approximately 700 staff, of which ca. 550 are located at headquarters in Montreal and ca. 150 are located at the seven Regional Offices,[128] namely Bangkok, Cairo, Dakar, Lima, Mexico City, Nairobi, and Paris.

Organizationally, the Secretariat is divided into five bureaux, that is, the Air Navigation Bureau, the Air Transport Bureau, the Legal Bureau, the Administrative Bureau, and the Technical Cooperation Bureau.[129] Each of these bureaux is headed by a director who reports to the Secretary General. The Secretary General's Office comprises the External Affairs and Public Relations Office, the Finance Branch, the Internal Audit Office, and the Regional Affairs Office. The Regional Offices report through the Regional Affairs Office to the Secretary General.

C. Law-Making Functions

The Convention does not specifically mention any competences of the Organization for the development and adoption of international conventions or

124. Article 58 of the Convention.
125. Article 60 of the Convention should be read in conjunction with the 1947 *Convention on the Privileges and Immunities of the Specialized Agencies,* adopted by the UN General Assembly on 21 Nov. 1947, *UNTS* Vol. 33 (1948), 242, including its Annex III (International Civil Aviation Organization), approved 29 Dec. 1951.
126. *ICAO Service Code, Doc. 7350.*
127. See Art. XII of the Agreement between the UN and *ICAO, Doc. 7970,* which recognizes that the eventual development of a single unified international civil service is desirable from the standpoint of effective administrative co-ordination. See also Assembly Resolution A21-12: *International Civil Service Commission, ICAO Doc.* 9848.
128. These figures relate to 2011. They obviously fluctuate with the triennial budget. From 2005 onwards, a slight decrease of permanent staff took place due to the triennial budgets 2005–2007 and 2008–2010.
129. This structure is reflected in the Programme Budget of ICAO; see Assembly Resolution A37-26, Part C: Regular Programme, Clause 1., in: *Resolutions adopted by the 37th session of the Assembly (Provisional edition)*, November 2010.

protocols in the field of air law. From a strict legal viewpoint, the adoption of such conventions or protocols by diplomatic conferences are acts of the participating Member States, not of organs of the Organization. The diplomatic conferences, although convened under the auspices of the Organization, are sovereign bodies not forming part of the Organization itself.[130] The conventions and protocols adopted are subsequently signed and ratified by the participating Member States; the role of the Organization is usually limited to the function of 'depositary' of the respective legal instrument, as a result of the final clauses of the instrument specifically entrusting the Organization with this function.[131]

Nevertheless, it has been the long-standing practice of the Organization to be actively involved in the preparation of international air law instruments prior to their submission to a diplomatic conference.

Assembly Resolution A1-46, which was adopted at the first ICAO Assembly in 1947, provided for the creation of the ICAO Legal Committee as a 'permanent body of the Organization constituted by the Assembly'. The constitution of the Legal Committee was annexed to A1-46.[132] The Legal Committee was tasked with giving legal advice to the Organization and its bodies, as well as with the development of international air law. For the purposes of this latter function, Assembly Resolution A1-48, also adopted at the First Session of the Assembly, set out the procedure for the development and approval of draft conventions in the field of air law.[133] Resolution A1-46 was later revised in 1953 by Resolution A7-5 and Resolution A1-48 was replaced by Resolution A7-6[134] and later superseded by Resolution A31-15.[135] Essentially, the procedure for the approval of draft conventions involves the following steps:

(1) Study of the problems involved by the Secretariat, guided if necessary by a Secretariat study group.
(2) Submission of the Secretariat's report, including if possible a draft text, to the Legal Committee or a rapporteur, or both.
(3) Discussion of the report of the Secretariat by the Legal Committee, which may appoint a subcommittee, or and if it considers the draft text mature enough, approval and submission of its report to the Council.
(4) Discussion of the report of the Legal Committee by the Council, which may take such action as it deems fit, including circulating the draft text to Contracting States and international organizations for comment within a period of not less than four months.

130. See on this matter generally S. Rosenne, 'Conferences and Congresses, International', in *Encyclopedia of Public International Law*, ed. Bernhardt Vol. I (1992), 739 et seq.
131. See *Legal Committee – Constitution – Procedure for Approval of Draft Conventions – Rules of Procedure, Doc. 7669.*
132. This constitution was later revised by Resolution A7-5, *ICAO Doc.* 9848, Part I. See below.
133. Assembly Resolution A1-46; see also Assembly Resolution A7-5, operating clause 2.
134. Resolution A7-6 was consolidated at the 31st Session of the Assembly into Resolution A31-15: *Consolidated statement of continuing ICAO policies in the legal field, ICAO Doc.* 9848, Part V and became Appendix B of Resolution A31-15.
135. See Resolution A31-15, Appendix 3.

(5) Convening if appropriate, of a diplomatic conference by the Council, the opening of which shall not be less than six months from the date of transmission of the draft text to Contracting States.

It should be noted that for the adoption of a text by the diplomatic conference, at least a two-thirds majority is required, in line with the Rules of Procedure for Diplomatic Conferences.[136]

On the basis of the procedure for the development and approval of draft conventions (Resolution A1-48, A7-6 and A 31-15), the Organization has developed a large number of international air law instruments, which were subsequently adopted by a diplomatic conference.

For nearly all of these international air law instruments, which are legally binding for those states having ratified them, the Organization serves as depositary.

Depositary functions should be distinguished from registration. Under Article 83 of the Convention, the Organization, and more specifically the Council, is entrusted with the task to register all aeronautical agreements and arrangements submitted to it by Contracting States, and to render them public. Contracting States shall submit all aeronautical agreements or arrangements they conclude, whether bilateral or multilateral, to the Organization for registration (Articles 81and 83). It is a requirement that any such agreements or arrangements be 'not inconsistent' with the Convention.[137]

Furthermore, under Article 83*bis* of the Convention, agreements or arrangements for the transfer of certain functions and duties in connection with the lease, charter or interchange of aircraft shall not become effective until they are registered and rendered public by the Organization.[138]

On this basis, the Organization has registered close to 5,000 agreements and arrangements.[139] It publishes lists of newly registered agreements from time to time, and is in the course of publishing them electronically on its Website.[140]

---

136. See e.g. Rule 20 (1) of the Rules of Procedure for the International Conference on Air Law, Montreal, 10 May 1999–28 May 1999, in: *Proceedings of the Conference, Doc. 9775*, Vol. II-Documents DCW Doc. No. 2, dated 9 Nov. 1998. These 'Provisional Rules of Procedure' were adopted without change as the definitive Rules of Procedure of the Conference at its first meeting. They follow a model which is used for all diplomatic conferences convened under the auspices of ICAO.
137. See the wording of Art. 83, first Sentence, of the Convention: 'Subject to the provisions of the preceding Article, any Contracting State may make arrangements not inconsistent with the provisions of this Convention'.
138. See Art. 83*bis*, para. b) of the Convention. On this matter, see *Guidance on the Implementation of Article 83bis of the Convention on International Civil Aviation,* ICAO Circular 295 (2003).
139. As of 02/02/2011, in a series of consecutive filings, 4938 registrations had been effected with ICAO.
140. See <www.ICAO.int>, Key activities, Bureau activities, Legal, Aeronautical Agreements ('DAGMAR').

D. STANDARD-SETTING FUNCTIONS

Under Article 54, Subparagraph (l), the Council is vested with competence to adopt, in accordance with the provision of Chapter VI of the Convention, international standards and recommended practices to designate them, for convenience, as Annexes to the Convention; and to notify in each such case all Contracting States of the action taken.[141] Under Article 54, Subparagraph (m), the Council is empowered to consider recommendations of the Air Navigation Commission for amendment of the Annexes and to take action in accordance with Chapter XX of the Convention.[142]

In accordance with Article 54, Subparagraph (l) and Chapter VI of the Convention, the Council has over the years since 1947 adopted eighteen Annexes to the Convention

In accordance with Article 54, Subparagraph (m), the Council has kept the eighteen Annexes up-to-date by adopting from time to time amendments to the Annexes, in accordance with the procedure[143] set out in Chapter XX of the Convention. Chapter XX consists of Article 90, paragraphs (a) and (b), which provide that the adoption by the Council of the Annexes described in Article 54, Subparagraph (l) shall require the vote of two-thirds of the Council at a meeting called for that purpose and shall then be submitted by the Council to each Contracting State. Any such Annex or any amendment of an Annex shall become effective within three months after its submission to the Contracting States or at the end of such longer period of time as the Council may prescribe, unless in the meantime a majority of the Contracting States register their disapproval with the Council. Furthermore, the Council shall immediately notify all Contracting States of the coming into force of any Annex or amendment thereto.[144]

The status of the Annexes to the Convention is governed by Articles 37 and 38 of the Convention. These provisions clarify that the Annexes do not have the same legally binding force as the articles of the main body of the Convention.[145] One reason is that they are not subject to ratification, and that they are a form of 'technical international legislation'.[146] Article 37 provides that each Contracting

141. Article 54 (l) should be read in conjunction with Arts 37 and 38 of the Convention; it has been supplemented by Assembly Resolution A35-14, Appendix A and D, *ICAO Doc.* 9848; and more recently A37-15, Appendix A
142. Chapter XX (Annexes) of the Convention contains only one provision, namely Art. 90 – *Adoption and Amendment of Annexes.*
143. Article 90 of the Convention and Appendices A and D of Resolution A35-14, *ICAO Doc.* 9848; Appendix A of Resolution A37-15.
144. Article 90 para. b) of the Convention.
145. This is clear from the wording 'undertakes to collaborate in securing the highest practicable degree of uniformity' in Art. 37, as well as the term 'impracticable' in Article 38.
146. See on this matter Buergenthal, *ibid.* (n. 1), 57 et seq. See also Cheng, *ibid.* (n. 67), 63 et seq.; Le Geoff, 'Les Annexes techniques à la Convention de Chicago', *Revue Générale de l'Air*, 19 (1956): 146 et seq.; R. Mankiewicz, 'L'adoption des annexes à la Convention de Chicago par le Conseil de l'Organisation internationale de l'aviation civile', in *Beiträge zum Internationalen Luftrecht*, ed. L. Brandt (Festschrift zu Ehren von Alex Meyer: 1954), 82 et seq.

State undertakes to collaborate in securing the highest practicable degree of uniformity in regulations, standards, procedures, and organization in relation to aircraft, personnel airways, and auxiliary services in all matters in which such uniformity will facilitate and improve air navigation. For this purpose, ICAO shall adopt and amend from time to time, as may be necessary, international standards and recommended practices and procedures dealing with matters concerned with the safety, regularity, and efficiency of air navigation as may from time to time appear appropriate.[147]

Article 38 deals with departures from international standards and procedures, and provides that any State which finds it impracticable to comply in all respects with any such international standard or procedure shall give immediate notification to ICAO.[148] The same applies if any State finds it impracticable to bring its own regulations or practices into full accord with any international standard or procedure after amendment of the latter, or when it deems necessary to adopt regulations or practices differing in any particular respect from those established by an international standard. Any notification to ICAO under Article 38 shall set out the differences between the State's own practice and that established by the international standard.[149]

In the case of amendments to international standards, any State which does not make the appropriate amendments to its own regulations or practices shall give notice to the Council within sixty days of the adoption of the amendment to the international standard, or indicate the action it proposes to take.[150] In any such case, the Council shall make immediate notification to all other States of the difference that exists between one or more features of an international standard and the corresponding national practice of that State.[151]

Under Article 38, obligations to notify only relate to departures from international standards or procedures, but not to departures from recommended practices: such recommended practices are only 'recommended' and therefore their non-observance will have no legal effect.[152] International standards and procedures, on the other hand, shall be followed, unless a given State has notified a departure, or 'filed a difference', as the term is now usually referred to.[153]

---

147. Article 37, second Sentence, of the Convention.
148. This rule is to be regarded as a legally binding obligation on Contracting States ('shall give immediate notification'). This interpretation has played an important role during the DGCA Conference in 1997, which recommended the establishment of a universal and mandatory safety oversight audit programme. See *Report of the DGCA Conference on a Global Strategy for Safety Oversight*; *ICAO Doc.* 9707.
149. Article 38, first Sentence, of the Convention. See also Assembly Resolution A36-13 Appendix D, operating clause 2 and Associated Practices, superseded by Assembly Resolution A37-15.
150. Article 38, second Sentence, of the Convention.
151. Article 38, last Sentence, of the Convention.
152. See the definition of 'recommended practice', above (n. 140); Art. 38 mentions only international standards and procedures, but not recommended practices in relation to the obligation to immediately file a difference.
153. See A36-13, Appendix D, Associated Practice 3, superseded by A37-15.

Therefore, Articles 37 and 38 leave only two alternatives to States, either to follow an international standard or procedure, or to immediately file a difference.

In the practice of ICAO, therefore, international standards have been clearly distinguished from recommended practices.[154] While the main body of each of the eighteen Annexes will typically consist of international standards, any paragraphs of text that have the status of a recommended practice will be clearly and visibly set out as such through appropriate print image.[155] Furthermore, international procedures have been laid down specifically for air navigation services (Procedures for Air Navigation Services [PANS]).[156] These are also set apart from Standards and Recommended Practices (SARPs), but are in practice treated on the same footing in most respects:

An *'international standard'* in the sense of Articles 37, 38 and 54 is defined as

> any specification for physical characteristics, configuration, material, performance, personnel or procedure, the uniform application of which is recognized as necessary for the safety or regularity of international air navigation and to which contracting States will conform in accordance with the Convention;[157] in the event of impossibility of compliance, notification to the Council is compulsory under Article 38 of the Convention.

A 'recommended practice' in the sense of Articles 37 and 54 is defined as:

> any specification for physical characteristics, configuration, material, performance, personnel or procedure, the uniform application of which is recognized as desirable in the interest of safety, regularity or efficiency of international air navigation and to which contracting States will endeavour to conform in accordance with the Convention.[158]

SARPs and PANS have become essential tools for the planning processes of ICAO, both on the global and regional basis, as well as for the planning processes of Contracting States. They are amended as necessary to reflect changing requirements and techniques and thus, *inter alia*, to provide a sound basis for regional planning and the provision of facilities and services.[159] A high degree of stability shall be maintained to enable the Contracting States to maintain stability in their national regulations. According to the respective provisions of ICAO Resolution

154. See the Foreword to the Annexes, where this difference is highlighted, e.g. *Doc. AN 1*, Foreword.
155. While standards are shown as consecutive paragraphs in normal print, recommended practices are usually designated as such and are printed in italics. See *Doc. AN 1*.
156. See in particular the PANS-OPS, *Doc. 8168*; PANS/ATM, *Doc. 4444*; PANS/ABC, *Doc. 8400*; and the SUPPS, *Doc. 7030*.
157. ICAO Assembly Resolution A36-13: *Consolidated statement of continuing ICAO polices and associated practices relating specifically to air navigation*, Appendix A; Assembly Resolution A37-15 Appendix A no longer contains this definition.
158. *Ibid.*, (n. 157).
159. Assembly Resolution A37-15, Appendix A, in: Resolutions adopted at the 37th session of the Assembly (provisional edition), November 2010.

A 37-15, Appendix A, 'no Annex or PANS document shall be amended more frequently than once per calendar year'.[160]

E. Judicial and Quasi-judicial Functions

Under Chapter XVIII of the Convention, the Council is entrusted with certain judicial functions regarding disputes between Contracting States; such judicial functions of the Council are also foreseen in certain multilateral and bilateral agreements, in particular the International Air Services Transit Agreement, whereby the Council is entrusted with the judicial settlement of disputes between Contracting States.[161]

Article 84 of the Convention provides the following:

> If any disagreement between two or more contracting States relating to the interpretation or application of this Convention and its Annexes cannot be settled by negotiation, it shall, on the application of any State concerned in the disagreement, be decided by the Council.

The procedure to be applied by the Council in hearing the dispute is laid down in the Rules of Procedure for the Settlement of Differences (ICAO Doc. 7782/2).[162] Under these Rules of Procedure, the Council functions as a judicial body; it may decide on the basis of written submissions of the parties (memorials and counter-memorials),[163] and on the basis of oral hearings.[164] It shall, before proceeding to give a decision, attempt to bring about a settlement between the parties, through inducing direct negotiations or through conciliation.[165] For this purpose, the Council may appoint a Conciliator. Only if these attempts fail, the Council shall proceed to give judgment.

In accordance with Article 84 of the Convention, any such decision of the Council may be appealed, either to an ad-hoc arbitral tribunal[166] or to the International Court of Justice (ICJ).[167] In case of lack of agreement by an ad-hoc tribunal and non-acceptance of the jurisdiction of the ICJ, a special arbitral

160. *Ibid.,* (n. 159), Appendix A, operating clause 8.
161. See Art. II, s. 1, of the *International Air Services Transit Agreement*, *Doc. 7500*. A similar dispute settlement clause is also contained in the *International Air Transport Agreement*, *UNTS* Vol. 171, 387, Art. 4 s. 2.
162. These Rules of Procedure were adopted in 1957, and revised in 1975, *Doc. 7782/2*.
163. Articles 2 (c)-(g) and 4 of the Rules of Procedure for the Settlement of Differences, *ibid.*, (n. 157).
164. See Art. 11 of the Rules of Procedure, *ibid.*
165. Articles 6 and 14 of the Rules of Procedure, *ibid.*
166. This option has so far not been applied in practice.
167. In the case *Pakistan v. India* (1971), India appealed to the ICJ against the decision of the Council to reject the preliminary objections of India, in which India had challenged the jurisdiction of the Council. See *Appeal relating to the Jurisdiction of the ICAO Council*, Judgment, ICJ Reports (1972), 46-179; ICJ Pleadings, *Appeal Relating to the Jurisdiction of the ICAO Council;* see also below.

tribunal set up under Article 85 will hear the appeal. The decision of an ad-hoc arbitral tribunal, of the ICJ, or of a special arbitral tribunal under Article 85 shall be final and binding.[168]

In application of these provisions, the Council has dealt with the following disputes under Chapter XVIII:

(1) *India v. Pakistan (1952)*[169] regarding the legality of a prohibited zone established by Pakistan, under Articles 5, 6 and 9 of the Convention. The dispute was settled through direct negotiations between the parties induced by the Council.

(2) *UK v. Spain (1967)*[170] regarding the legality of a prohibited zone established by Spain in the vicinity of Gibraltar Airport under Article 9 (a) of the Convention. The dispute was deferred *sine die* and subsequently settled by direct negotiation.

(3) *Pakistan v. India (1971)*,[171] regarding the suspension of flights of Pakistani aircraft over Indian Territory, based on Article 5 of the Convention. India submitted preliminary objections against the jurisdiction of the Council, which were rejected by the Council. India appealed to the International Court of Justice, which confirmed the Council's decision. The parties thereafter jointly suspended the proceedings before the Council and settled the dispute through direct negotiations.

(4) *Cuba v. United States (1996)*,[172] regarding the denial by the United States of rights of overflight for Cuban aircraft over US territory for scheduled flights between Cuba and Canada. The Council, after hearing the parties' submissions, appointed its President as Conciliator.[173] As a result of the conciliation, the parties reached a settlement which was formally registered with the Council, and which provided for overflight rights for Cuban aircraft over US territory, subject to certain restrictions.

(5) *United States v. 15 Member States of the European Union (2000)*,[174] regarding the legality of the so-called hush kit Regulation of the EU[175]

168. See Art. 86, third Sentence, of the Convention. See also Art. 19 of the *Rules of Procedure for the Settlement of Differences, Doc.* 7782.

169. *Report of the Council* 1952, *ICAO Doc.* 7367, A7-P/1, 74-76 (1953); ICAO Doc. C-WP/1169 (1952); ICAO Council, 16th Session, *Doc. 7291*, C/845, 11 (1952); *Doc. 7328* (C/853), 129; C-WP/1341 (1952). For the settlement between the parties, see Council, 18th Session, *Doc. 7361* (C/858), 15 et seq.

170. See *Annual Report of the Council – 1967*, *ICAO Doc.* 8724 (1968), 116 et seq.; A16-P/3.

171. See on this matter ICJ Reports (1972), *ibid.*, (n. 162); K. Hailbronner, 'Jurisdiction of the ICAO Council Case', in *Encyclopedia of Public International Law*, ed. Bernhardt Vol. III (1997), 62 et seq. with further references.

172. See Decision of the Council, C-DEC 154/16; C-WP 10864 (Restricted); C/DEC 149/7; C-DEC 150/17; C-DEC 152/14 and C-DEC 153/14.

173. C-DEC 149/7 and Art. 14, paras 2 and 3 of the *Rules for the Settlement of Differences, Doc. 7782/2*; see also C-DEC 150/17, C-DEC 152/14 and C-DEC 153/14.

174. See C-DEC 170/16; C-WP/12075, C-DEC 169/11, C-DEC 166/12 and C-DEC 161/6.

175. Regulation (EC) No. 925/1999.

> under the Convention and related provisions. The fifteen EU Member States submitted preliminary objections to the jurisdiction of the Council, which were rejected by the Council. After hearing the parties on the substance, the Council appointed its President as Conciliator.[176] As a result of the conciliation process, the 'hush kit' Regulation was repealed by the EU and replaced by an EC Council Directive acceptable to all the parties,[177] including the United States. The case was thereupon settled between the parties and the settlement was formally registered with the Council.[178]

These judicial functions should be distinguished from quasi-judicial functions under Articles 54 (n), 54 (j), and 54 (k) of the Convention.[179]

Under Article 54 (n), the Council 'shall consider any matter relating to the Convention which any Contracting State refers to it'. From time to time, Contracting States make written submissions to the Council, in which they complain about one or more other Contracting States, and request the Council to settle the dispute or difference. Unless such complaints are made expressly under Article 84 and follow the formalities of the *'Rules for the Settlement of Differences'*,[180] such complaints are usually handled as referrals under Article 54 (n). This means, *inter alia*, that the Rules of Procedure for the Council[181] apply instead of the Rules for the Settlement of Differences. Consequently, the Council will hear such cases in a quasi-judicial capacity, but without the procedures and legal formalities foreseen in the Rules for the Settlement of Differences. The Council will invite the parties to the complaint to be present in the Council and to make written and/or oral statements, and will then discuss the matter in the presence of the parties to the complaint.[182] The Council may, as a result of the discussion, express views, make statements, issue recommendations, or make decisions in the form of a Council Resolution as may be appropriate, under the Rules of Procedure for the Council.[183]

In this quasi-judicial capacity, the Council has dealt with numerous complaints, for example, the *Republic of the Congo v. Rwanda and Uganda*[184]

176. See C-DEC 161/6; PRES AK/823, dated 11 Jun. 2002; see the progress reports on the conciliation C-DEC 163/17; 164/11; 168/5 and 169/11.
177. EC Council Directive DIR (EC) 2002/30/EC,
178. See C-MIN 170/16; C-WP/12075; C-DEC 170/16. For the revised EC Council Directive, see DIR (EC) 2002/30/EC,
179. See Buergenthal, *ibid.*, 11 (n. 4) and 123 et seq.
180. *ICAO Doc.* 7782.
181. *ICAO Doc.* 7559/5. It is submitted that the procedure under the *Rules of Procedure for the Council*, which allows for greater flexibility from a procedural viewpoint, is better tailored to the political role which the Council plays in relation to the Contracting States of ICAO.
182. Article 53 of the Convention, Art. 32 of the Rules of Procedure for the Council, *ibid.*, (n. 175).
183. *Doc. 7559/2.*
184. Council – 155th Session, C-DEC 155/1, para. 13; 156th Session, C-DEC 156/10; C-MIN 156/10; Memorandum AK/639; Council Declaration adopted on 10 Mar. 1999.

(state hijacking of civil aircraft and other matters); *PLO v. Israel*[185] (destruction of Gaza Airport); *Cuba v. US*[186] (violation of Cuban airspace); *Samoa and Tonga v. Fiji* (amendment to the common Nadi/Auckland oceanic FIR boundary[187]); and other cases.

Theoretically, complaints may also be brought under Article 54 (j) or (k), when a Contracting State is alleged to have committed an infraction of the Convention, or to have failed to carry out a recommendation or determination of the Council, or to have remedied an infraction after notification of the Council. However, in practice, these provisions have been rarely used. A related study of the secretariat has concluded that infractions, in the sense of the Convention, are limited to particularly grave breaches of the Convention.[188]

F. Audit Functions

1. Universal Safety Oversight Audit Programme

The implementation of SARPs is governed by Articles 33, 37 and 38 of the Convention. Article 33 of the Convention requires Contracting States to recognize as valid certificates of airworthiness and personnel licenses issued by another Contracting State, provided that the requirements under which such documents were issued are equal to or above the minimum standards established under the Convention.[189] Article 37 requires each Contracting State to collaborate in securing the highest practicable degree of uniformity in regulations and practices in all matters in which such uniformity will facilitate and improve air navigation. Article 38 requires Contracting States which find it impracticable to comply in all respects with such standards or procedures to give immediate notification to ICAO of the differences.

It became more and more obvious throughout the 1980s and 1990s that these provisions were not followed by many Contracting States. In the absence of any systematic notification of differences by States, neither the Organization nor Contracting States had any clear and objective information on the degree of actual implementation of the technical Annexes. This situation was increasingly seen as presenting a major safety issue.[190]

185. Council – 165th Session, C-MIN 165/9; C-WP/11790 and 11791 revised; see also AVSEC-Conf/02-IP/29.
186. Council – 159th Session, C-MIN 159/1; C-DEC 159/1; see also the Council Resolution adopted on 27 Jun. 1996, C-DEC 148/20; C-MIN 159/1, paras 28 et seq.
187. See C-WP/11723, C-WP/11427, C-DEC 161/11, C-DEC 163/2, C-DEC 163/6 and C-DEC 164/5.
188. See Infractions of the Convention on International Civil Aviation, C-WP/11186, submitted by the Secretary General at the request of the Council (C-DEC 156/7, 158/1).
189. See the wording of Art. 33 of the Convention. M.B. Jennison, 'The Chicago Convention and Safety after 50 years', *Ann ASL* XX (1995): Part I, 283 et seq.
190. See the DGCA Conference Report (1997), Doc. 9707; Assembly Resolution A29-13; *Improvement of Safety Oversight, ICAO Doc.* 9790.

Consequently, upon recommendation of a special Conference of Directors General of Civil Aviation, the Assembly at its 32nd Session in 1998 established the Universal Safety Oversight Audit Programme (USOAP)[191] effective on 1 January 1999.

The USOAP comprises the following elements:[192]

- regular, mandatory, systematic and harmonized safety audits, which shall be carried out by ICAO;
- such programme shall apply to all Contracting States;
- greater transparency and increased disclosure shall be implemented in the release of audit results;
- the programme shall comprise a systematic reporting and monitoring mechanism on the implementation of safety-related standards and recommended practices.

In its first phase, the scope of the programme included audits relating to Annex 1: Personnel Licensing, Annex 6: Operation of Aircraft, and Annex 8: Airworthiness of Aircraft.[193] The audits were performed by audit teams of ICAO, composed of experts from the secretariat and from Contracting States, other than the audited state. The audits were performed in accordance with an administrative framework, including a standard Memorandum of Understanding and the ICAO Safety Oversight Manual.[194]

In the first phase of audits, 1999–2001, nearly 180 out of the then 188 Member States were visited and audited.[195] In the second phase, 2001–2004, a number of follow-up audits were performed, and the focus shifted to resolving deficiencies identified by the USOAP programme and encouraging quality assurance for related technical cooperation projects.[196]

In the third phase, 2004–2007, the Assembly widened the scope of follow-up audits to comprise all safety-related Annexes[197] and took steps to increase

---

191. Assembly Resolution A32-11: *Establishment of an ICAO Universal Safety Oversight Audit Programme*; on this subject, see M. Milde, Aviation Safety Oversight Audits and the Law', *AnnASL* XXVI (2001): 165 et seq.
192. DGCA Conference Report (1997), *Doc. 9707*; *ICAO Safety Oversight Audit Manual, ICAO Doc. 9735*, AN/960.
193. The main purpose of limiting audits to these three Annexes was to provide a focused starting point. See DGCA Conference Report (1997) *Doc. 9707*; 2279th Report to Council by the President of the Air Navigation Commission, C-WP/10898 (16/06/98), 2.
194. *ICAO Doc.* 9734; on the Standard MOU, see Sample Memorandum of Understanding between (State) and ICAO Regarding Safety Oversight Audit, in: *ICAO Safety Oversight Audit Manual, ICAO Doc. 9735*, AN/960
195. See Annual Report of the Council for 2001, *Doc 9786*; *Annual Report of the Council for 2002, Doc. 9814*; *Annual Report of the Council for 2003*, *Doc. 9826*, and Supplement.
196. Resolution A33-9, Clauses 1-9; the Assembly adopted at its 35th Session Resolution A35-7: *Unified strategy to resolve safety-related deficiencies*, supplementing A33-9.
197. Assembly Resolution A35-6, *Doc.* 9848 – Assembly Resolutions in Force (as of 8 Oct. 2004), superseding A33-8.

transparency by making all final audit reports available to all Contracting States.[198] Furthermore, access was provided for all Contracting States to the Audit Findings and Differences Database (AFDD) developed and maintained by ICAO.[199] The Assembly also decided on a 'unified strategy' to resolve safety-related deficiencies and on a combination of measures to assist States in resolving safety-related deficiencies, amended in 2010 to emphasize regional cooperation and assistance.[200]

For the phase beyond 2010, the Assembly decided to apply the 'continuous monitoring approach'(CMA) involving a continuous information exchange between States and ICAO focussing on key safety provisions in Annexes 1, 6, 8, 11, 13, and 14 and providing for the sharing of significant safety concerns (SSC) with interested stakeholders.

2. Universal Aviation Security Audit Programme

Following the events of 11 September 2001, a high-level Ministerial Conference on Aviation Security held in February 2002 recommended adopting an ICAO Aviation Security Plan of Action,[201] including, *inter alia*, the establishment of an Aviation Security Audit Programme. It called for the establishment of a comprehensive programme of regular, mandatory, systematic, and harmonized aviation security audits to be carried out by ICAO in all Contracting States.[202]

The ICAO Aviation Security Plan of Action was adopted accordingly by the Council in June 2002, including the ICAO USAP.[203] The USAP was launched in November 2002.

The audit programme comprises the following elements:[204]

- regular, mandatory, systematic, and harmonized aviation security audits of all ICAO Contracting States;
- audits conducted at both national and airports levels;
- evaluation of States' aviation security oversight capabilities;
- evaluation of the actual security measures in place at selected key airports;

198. See Clause 7 of A35-6.
199. *Ibid.,* (n. 197).
200. Assembly Resolutions A35-7, *ibid.,* (n. 197), A36-4: *Application of a continuous monitoring approach for the ICAO USOAP beyond 2010*, and A37-5: *The Universal Safety Oversight Audit Programme (USOAP) continuous monitoring approach, ibid* (n.159).
201. High-level, Ministerial Conference on Aviation Security, 19 Feb. 2002–20 Feb. 2002, Report. For the Declaration issued, *Ann ASL* XXVI (2001): 441.
202. Assembly Resolution A35-9, Appendix E: *The ICAO Universal Security Audit Programme*, Operative Clause 1.
203. Council 166th Session (June 2002). See A. Kotaite, *Aviation Safety and Security – Two Sides of the Same Coin.* Keynote Address to the Aviation Study Group at Linacre College, Oxford University, 27 Jun. 2003, 2-3
204. Assembly Resolution A35-9 Appendix E, Operative Clauses 1-4.

- audits to be carried out in the basis of a bilateral memorandum of understanding (MOU) signed between each Contracting State and ICAO; and
- coordination with security-related audit programmes at regional and sub-regional levels.

The methodology for the USAP is similar to that used for the USOAP programme, including the audit visit, the drafting of a preliminary report, and the drafting of a final report, comprising an action plan formulated in cooperation with the audited State.[205]

The USAP is, for the time being, financed from the voluntary contributions received from states for that purpose[206] following the High-level, Ministerial Conference. It is envisaged that the USAP be progressively integrated into the Regular Programme Budget of ICAO.

The ICAO Security Audit Reference Manual[207] was issued in April 2004, setting forth the elements, methodology, and procedures for the conduct of the programme.

By the end of 2007, 181 of the 190 ICAO Contracting States had been audited and 172 follow-up visits took place. As from January 2008, a second audit cycle was started with a modified methodology and from 2008 to 2011, 100 further audits were conducted under the second cycle. Significant security concerns (SSeC's) are addressed through a mechanism approved by the Council in 2010.[208]

On the basis of the audits, ICAO has developed a database on findings, which will assist in addressing deficiencies.

G. The Annexes to the Convention

1. Airspace: Annexes 2, 4 and 11

Annex 2: Rules of the Air contains a set of agreed upon rules of the air to ensure the safety of aircraft in flight. They consist of general rules, visual flight rules (VFR), and instrument flight rules (IFR).[209] Flight under VFR is permitted if a flight crew is able to stay clear of clouds by at least 5,000 ft (1,500 m) horizontally and 1,000 ft

205. A. Kotaite *ibid.,* (n. 203,) 2 et seq. However, it was not sufficient to audit only the security oversight arrangements in Member States, but it was necessary to include installations and equipment in situ, namely at the major airports in each Member State. See L. Weber, *ibid.,* (Ch. 2, n. 18), 307.
206. See Assembly Resolution A35-10, sixth whereas clause, *ICAO Doc.* 9848. A36-18: *Financial contributions to the Aviation Security Plan of Action.*
207. *ICAO Doc.* 9807.
208. On the second audit cycle, see AVSECP/22-IP/5. On the mechanism dealing with SSeC's, see C-DEC 189/3
209. *Doc. AN* 2, 9th edn (1990), incl. Amendments 1-37. See s. 3.2; *Pilot Skills to make 'Look-out' more effective in Visual Collision Avoidance*, ICAO Circular 213.

(300 m) vertically and maintain forward visibility of at least 8 km.[210] Save for certain exceptions, flights must be performed under IFR in the absence of these conditions and by night. Most commercial aircraft fly by IFR at all times.

A flight plan must be filed with air traffic services units for all flights that will cross international borders and for most other flights that are engaged in commercial services. However, regardless of the flight plans, the pilot is responsible for avoiding collisions while the aircraft is in the air, in accordance with the 'see-and-avoid' principle,[211] aided by collision avoidance systems, collision hazard information, and the advisories from air traffic control units. Flights operating under IFR are to be separated by air traffic control.[212]

Annex 2 also contains rules and recommendations relating to interception of civil aircraft.[213] The recommendations, contained in Attachment A to the Annex, apply with regard to the procedures that military aircraft of Contracting States should apply when intercepting civil aircraft.[214]

Annex 4:Aeronautical Charts provides SARPs for three series of aeronautical charts available for planning and visual navigation, each with a different scale. ICAO small-scale charts provide a general purpose chart series for long-range flight planning. ICAO 1:1,000,000 charts provide complete world coverage with uniform presentation of data at a constant scale, and are used, *inter alia*, for the production of other charts. The ICAO 1:500,000 chart series gives more detail and is used by low-speed, short- or medium-range aircraft operating at low or intermediate altitudes, as well as for pilot and navigation training.[215]

Aeronautical charts may also be distinguished by the purpose for which they are used. The ICAO series consists of seventeen different chart types, each intended to serve a special purpose.[216] For example, the en-route charts contain the air traffic service system, radio or other navigation aids and other aeronautical information essential to en-route navigation. The ICAO plotting charts are useful in complementing the more complex en-route charts over extensive oceanic and sparsely settled areas. Area charts are useful in the transition from en-route phase to final approach, and from take-off to the en-route phase. Instrument approach charts facilitate the graphic presentation of instrument approach procedures; visual approach charts fulfil a similar purpose for VFR approach procedures. Aerodrome

210. When flying below 10,000 ft, the flight visibility minimum is 5 km. See Annex 2, s. 4.1 and Table 3.1.
211. *Ibid.,* (n. 209), Chs 4 and 5.
212. *Doc. AN 2*, ss 5.2 and 3.6.
213. *Doc. AN 2*, ss 5.2 and 3.6.
214. *Doc. AN 2*, s. 3.8 and Attachment A. On the co-ordination of civil and military aircraft operations, see Assembly Resolution A35-14, Appendix P.
215. *Aeronautical Chart Manual, ibid.,* (n. 79); *Aeronautical Chart Catalogue, Doc. 7101*; *Aeronautical Information Services Manual, Doc. 8126.*
216. *Aeronautical Chart Manual, Doc. 8697*; AN 4. See also *Aeronautical Information Services Manual, Doc. 8126*; *Aeronautical Information Services Provided by States, Doc. 7383*; *Location Indicators, Doc. 7910.*

charts and aerodrome obstacle charts provide illustrations of the layout and facilities of aerodromes and of the obstacles in their vicinity.[217]

In recent years, electronic charting and mapping has progressed rapidly, and electronic versions of ICAO charts have been produced. The ICAO SARPs and resultant maps are constantly updated so as to reflect changes of all aviation-relevant data.

Annex 11: Air Traffic Services sets out the types of air traffic control services to be provided to VFR flights and IFR flights, respectively. It specifies the air traffic control services, consisting of clearances and ATC information, to achieve vertical, longitudinal, and lateral separation between aircraft. It also specifies the contents of clearances, the coordination of clearances between ATC units, and the coordination of transfer of control responsibility from one ATC unit to another.[218]

For cases of dense traffic exceeding the capacity of a particular airport or adjacent airspace or air routes, the Annex provides for ATC units to impose restrictions on the traffic flow, as required, and the parameters therefore.[219] Increasing airspace congestion in some parts of the world and affecting certain air routes, and the resulting need to rationalize traffic flows in these areas, have given rise to the development of Air Traffic Management (ATM). ATM seeks to optimize air traffic flows in defined geographical areas by continuous flow management supported by advanced surveillance technology, reduced separation minima, and flow management techniques developed in the 1990s.[220]

Annex 11 also contains procedures for alerting services, setting in motion all appropriate rescue and emergency organizations and services, as well as ATS requirements for AFS and AMS communications, including recording requirements, identification of air traffic services routes, and requirements for designation for significant waypoints, whether marked by radio aids or unmarked.[221] The SARPs set out in Annex 11 are supplemented by Procedures for Air Navigation Services (PANS).[222]

---

217. *Aeronautical Chart Manual, Doc. 8697*; *Aircraft Characteristics Data Bank (ACDB)*, Vols 1 to 6.
218. *Doc. AN-11*; *Doc. 9426, Air Traffic Services Planning Manual.*
219. This concept involves strategic airspace management (airspace infrastructure planning, and ATM requirements for communications, navigation and surveillance) as well as tactical airspace management (dynamic use of airspace, civil/military co-ordination). See *Doc. AN 11* and Doc. *9426*.
220. The latter involve air traffic flow management systems, air traffic flow management procedures, and air traffic management flow integration, See *AN-11*; *Procedures for Air Navigations Services – Air Traffic Management (PANS – ATM), Doc. 4444.*
221. On Search and Rescue aspects, see AN 11, Ch. 5, *Doc. 9731* and Circular 185; on ATS requirements, see *AN 11*, Ch. 6 and *Doc. 9426.*
222. PANS-ATM, Doc. 4444. See also the related *Air Traffic Services Planning Manual, Doc. 9426* and the *Manual of Air Traffic Services Data Link Applications, Doc. 9694.*

2. Aircraft: Annexes 6, 7 and 8

Annex 6: Operation of Aircraft consists of Part I: International Commercial Air Transport – Aeroplanes; Part II: International General Aviation – Aeroplanes; and Part III: International Operations – Helicopters. It covers not only operations properly speaking, but also aircraft performance criteria, communications and navigation equipment, maintenance, flight documents, responsibilities of flight personnel, responsibilities of states for supervising aircraft operations, responsibilities of operators in relation to the aircraft and flight crew, and other matters.

An important aspect of aircraft performance criteria is the safe operation of twin engine aircraft over extended land and ocean ranges (ETOPS).[223] The performance criteria for such operations have been gradually extended to larger ranges, and continue to be under active review.[224]

The advent of very large aircraft, such as the A380, is giving rise to further revision of related performance criteria and operations rules.[225]

Annex 7: Aircraft Nationality and Registration,[226] which is based on Articles 17 to 20 of the Convention, sets out standards and procedures for the use of letters, numbers, and other graphic symbols to be used for the purposes of nationality and registration marks of aircraft. It also specifies where these will be located on different types of aircraft.[227]

All aircraft engaged in international air navigation, whether commercial, non-commercial or general aviation, must bear nationality and registration marks so as to permit identification.[228] The Annex sets out procedures for selection by ICAO Contracting States of nationality marks from the nationality symbols used in the radio call signs allocated by the International Telecommunications Union (ITU).[229]

Article 7 of the Convention permits joint operating organizations. The Annex therefore defines the terms *common mark, common mark registering authority,* and *international operating agency,* so as to allow aircraft operated by joint operating organizations or agencies to be registered on other than a national basis.[230] Each international operating agency may be assigned a distinctive common mark, selected from symbols allocated by the ITU. In practice, these facilities have only been used in a few rare cases. The Annex also sets forth *a model registration certificate* for use by Contracting States.[231] Each aircraft must carry its registration certificate on board at all times.

223. *Annex 6,* Part I, Ch. 4, s. 4.7: Additional Requirements for extended range operations by aeroplanes with two turbine power units (ETOPS).
224. Attachment E to Annex 6, Part I; *Airworthiness Manual, Doc. 9760.*
225. See *Operations of New Larger Aeroplanes at Existing Aerodromes*, ICAO Circular, 2004.
226. *Doc. AN 7*, 5th edn, incorporating Amendments 1-5, Corrigendum 1 (14/08/2007).
227. *Doc. AN 7*, s. 3: Location of Nationality, Common and Registration Marks.
228. Article 20 of the Convention; under Art. 19, the registration or transfer of registration of aircraft in any Contracting State shall be made in accordance with its laws and regulations.
229. See ss. 2, 4 and 5 of Annex 7; for the ITU.
230. *Annex 7*, see Definitions and ss 2.1, 2.2, 2.4 and note after 2.4.
231. *Annex 7*, s. 7, Figure 1.

Annex 8: Airworthiness of Aircraft[232] contains broad standards which define, for application by national airworthiness authorities, the minimum basis for the mutual recognition of Certificates of Airworthiness for the purpose of flight of aircraft of other States into and over their territories.[233]

The issuance of Certificates of Airworthiness itself is subject to national regulations and national codes of airworthiness, for which Annex 8 provides only a broad framework. Thus, for example, aircraft produced in the United States are issued certificates in accordance with Federal Aviation Regulations (FARs).[234]

Certificates of Airworthiness are based on the Type Certificate, which attests the conformity of the aircraft type with all applicable requirements of the respective national safety regulations regarding aircraft design.[235] While the Type Certificate is not mentioned in the Convention, and was for many years regulated only nationally, a recent major revision of Annex 8 has included the Type Certificate for the first time[236] as an internationally recognized and regulated document.

The technical standards dealing with certification of aeroplanes *include minimum requirements* related to performance, flying qualities, structural design and construction, engine design and installation, instrument and equipment design and installation, and operating limitations. They require the availability of an aircraft manual setting out the design and performance characteristics, maintenance requirements, and operating limitations of the aircraft.

3. Aviation Personnel: Annex 1

Annex 1: Personnel Licensing contains standards and recommended practices for the licensing of flight crew members (pilots, flight engineers), air traffic controllers, and maintenance engineers/technicians/air traffic controllers, and maintenance engineers/technicians. The SARPs describe the skills necessary to ensure proficiency, the medical standards required and periodic medical examinations, and other exigencies for the different types of personnel licenses set out in the Annex. Licensing is the act of authorizing defined activities, which are otherwise prohibited in the absence of such license, because of the inherent risk of such activities being improperly performed without proper training, proficiency, and fitness. Licensing is performed at the level of Contracting States under national legislation that is in line with the SARPs of Annex 1.[237]

---

232. See *Doc. AN 8 – Airworthiness of Aircraft*, 9th edn (2001), incorporating Amendments 1-98; Amendment 99, applicable as of 20/5/06, *Doc. AN 8/E/06.*
233. See Art. 33 of the Convention – *Recognition of Certificates and Licenses.*
234. US Federal Aviation Regulations (*CFR 14*), Parts 21, 23, 25; for engines, see Parts 33-35; for noise standards, see Part 36.
235. See *Annex 8* (n. 232), Ch. 1, Standard 1.4
236. Amendment 99 to Annex 8, adopted by the ICAO Council on 2 Mar. 2001; see on this matter L. Weber/H. Holderbach, 'Type Certification of Commercial Aircraft Calls for Enhanced International Rules' *ICAO Journal* 56, no. 2 (2001): 4 et seq.
237. See Annex 1, 10th edn (2006), including Amendments 1-169-B (18/11/2010); see also ICAO *Doc. E P1/8000*, 2.

Related training manuals provide guidance to states for the scope and depth of training curricula.[238] They also provide guidance for the training of other aviation personnel such as aerodrome emergency crews, flight operations officers, radio operators, and other related functions.

4. Airports: Annex 14

Annex 14: Aerodromes sets out standards, recommended practices, and procedures for the planning, design, operation and facilities/equipment of airports of all types and sizes. The specifications for essential components of an airport, that is, the runways, taxiways, aprons, terminal, gate facilities, emergency and rescue facilities, and other essential facilities are provided.[239] Similarly, specifications for the marking and lighting of essential ground facilities are spelled out. Specifications are also provided for the airspace requirements in the vicinity of the airport, in particular for take-off, landing, and hold operations of aircraft.[240]

Up-to-date information on the condition of facilities at airports is vital today for the safety of civil aviation. Therefore, the Annex specifies the type of information to be available (e.g., strength of pavements, condition of runway surfaces, construction sites at the airport, etc.), how it is to be reported, and to whom. In Volume II, specifications for heliports are provided. Annex 14 is supplemented by the ICAO Airport Services Manual.[241]

5. Operations: Annex 6

Annex 6: Operation of Aircraft has been discussed under 2. above, with further references.

6. Security: Annex 17

Annex 17: Security sets out standards and recommended practices for measures to safeguard civil aviation and its facilities against acts of unlawful interference. It also provides the basis for the ICAO Civil Aviation Security Programme.

The Annex requires each Contracting State to establish its own national civil aviation security programme. It provides a framework and a number of parameters for such a programme, including inspection, screening and control measures to be

---

238. See the ICAO *Training Manual, Doc. 7192*; *Manual of Procedures for Establishment and Management of a State's Personnel Licensing System, Doc. 9379*; *Human Factors Training Manual, Doc. 9683*.

239. *ICAO Doc.* AN 14, Vol. I (Aerodrome Design and Operations); *Aerodrome Design Manual, Doc. 9157*, Part 1 (Runways), Part 2 (Taxiways, Aprons and Holding Bays), Part 3 (Pavements), Part 5 (Electrical Systems); *Airports Planning Manual, Doc. 9184*; *Airport Services Manual, Doc. 9137*, Part 1 (Rescue and Fire Fighting); Part 7 (Airport Emergency Planning).

240. *ICAO Doc.* AN 14, Vol. I; *Airport Services Manual, Doc. 9137*, Parts 6 and 8.

241. *Ibid.*, (n. 240); see also *Aerodrome Design Manual, Doc. 9157*; *Airport Planning Manual, Doc. 9184; Heliport Manual Doc. 9261*; and *SMGCS Manual, Doc. 9476*.

taken at airports, passenger/baggage screening, access control to restricted areas,[242] et cetera. It also provides procedures for the coordination of those involved in security programmes, including airline operators, who shall develop and apply their own complementary security programme under the supervision of government authorities.[243]

As referred to above in F.2, the work of the Organization in this field has focused on amendments to counter the new and emerging threats to civil aviation in the wake of 11 September 2001, and on developing and implementing the ICAO USAP.[244] This programme, which was developed pursuant to the high-level Ministerial Conference of February 2002 in Montreal,[245] provides for the mandatory audit of all 190 ICAO Contracting States and their national aviation security programmes and facilities.[246] The Annex is supplemented by the ICAO Aviation Security Manual.[247]

In the 1960s and early 1970s, the Organization developed three international instruments, namely:

- the Convention on Offences and Certain other Acts Committed on Board Aircraft (Tokyo Convention, 1963);[248]
- the Convention for the Suppression of Unlawful Seizure of Aircraft (The Hague Convention, 1970);[249] and
- the Convention for the Suppression of Unlawful Acts against the Safety of Civil Aviation (Montreal Convention, 1971).[250]

The main purpose of these conventions was to render hijacking, taking of hostages, and similar criminal acts to become international criminal offences, punishable by severe penalties, to establish the principle of 'prosecute or extradite',[251] and to affirm the authority of the aircraft commander and flight crew to take appropriate measures on board.

The principles of the Montreal Convention of 1971 were later extended to apply to unlawful acts of violence at international airports, by the Montreal Supplementary Protocol of 1988.[252] The main principles of the Montreal Convention were also later incorporated in a number of UN conventions on terrorism.

---

242. *Doc. AN 17*, Ch. 3, ss 3.1 et seq.
243. *Doc. AN 17*, Ch. 3, s. 3.3.
244. On the USAP, see above s. F.2 for more details.
245. *High-level, Ministerial Conference on Aviation Security*, 19 Feb. 2002–20 Feb. 2002, *Report*.
246. Assembly Resolutions A37-17, Appendix E; A36-20, Appendix E; A35-9, Appendix E.
247. *Doc. 8973* – Restricted.
248. *UNTS* Vol. 704 (1969), 219 et seq.; *ICAO Doc.* 8364.
249. *UNTS* Vol. 860 (1973), 105 et seq.; *ICAO Doc.* 8920.
250. *UNTS* Vol. 974 (1975), 177 et seq.; *ICAO Doc.* 8966.
251. Article 7 of the Hague Convention of 1970; Art. 7 of the Montreal Convention of 1971.
252. *Protocol for the Suppression of Unlawful Acts of Violence at Airports Serving International Civil Aviation Supplementary to the Convention for the Suppression of Unlawful Acts against the Safety of Civil Aviation*, done at Montreal on 23 Sep. 1971, signed on 29 Feb. 1988, *ICAO Doc.* 9518.

In 1991, the Organization developed the Convention on the Marking of Plastic Explosives for the Purpose of Detection (MEX Convention, 1991),[253] which provides for the mandatory marking of all plastic explosives by chemical markers, which are detectable by appropriate equipment.

Finally, in September 2010 the Beijing Convention and Protocol were developed in order to close a number of gaps in the existing international instruments with regard to new and emerging threats.[254] The make the acts of organizing, instigating and abetting an act of unlawful interference an international crime, and also criminalize the use of bacteriological, chemical or nuclear substances (BCN) for committing such act of unlawful interference, or the act of transporting them for that purpose. The Beijing instruments are not yet in force.

These aviation security conventions have contributed to a significant gradual reduction in the number of unlawful acts. Their effect was augmented by a similar improvement in effectiveness of aviation security measures taken at national and international airports. For these measures, Annex 17 – *Security* provides applicable standards and recommended practices, which have been constantly updated.

7. Other Annexes

Other Annexes which provide for Standards and Recommended Practices in their specific areas are Annex 3: Meteorological Service for International Air Navigation; Annex 5: Units of Measurement to be Used in Air and Ground Operations; Annex 10:Aeronautical Telecommunications; Annex 12: Search and Rescue; Annex 13: Aircraft Accident Investigation; Annex 15: Aeronautical Information Services; Annex 16: Environmental Protection; and Annex 18: The Safe Transport of Dangerous Goods by Air.

II. INTERNATIONAL AIR TRANSPORT ASSOCIATION (IATA)

A. Historical Background

Parallel to the setting up of ICAO, and in accordance with the compromise agreed at the Chicago Conference, the International Air Transport Association (IATA) was set up on 19 April 1945 during the International Air Transport Conference of international airlines held at Havana, Cuba.[255]

253. *ICAO Doc.* 9571.

254. Convention on the Suppression of Unlawful Acts Relating to International Civil Aviation, signed on 10 September 2010 at Beijing (Beijing Convention 2010); and Protocol Supplementary to the Convention for the Suppression of Unlawful Seizure of Aircraft, signed on 10 September 2010 at Beijing (Beijing Protocol 2010)

255. R.Y Chuang, *The International Air Transport Association* (Leiden: Sijthoff, 1972), 26 et seq.; K. Hailbronner, 'International Air Transport Association', in *Encyclopedia,* ed. R. Bernhardt *ibid.,* (n. 9), II (1995), 1047 et seq.; see also A. D. Groenewege, *Compendium of International*

The main objective was to re-establish an industry body that would provide the machinery for setting fares and rates on international routes, subject to governmental approval. Another objective was to re-establish a global trade association body of the international airlines.[256] Therefore, the new IATA was set up with a two-tier structure, comprising the IATA conference machinery for the setting of fares, rates, and conditions, subject to government approval, and the IATA trade association machinery.[257] Both tiers became part of the 'new IATA', which was incorporated in late 1945 as a non-profit association under Canadian law by Special Act of Parliament of Canada,[258] with headquarters in Montreal.

In further application of the compromise reached at the Chicago Conference, the United Kingdom and the United States met at Bermuda in spring 1946 to negotiate the first post-war bilateral Air Services Agreement.[259] The purpose of this agreement, which came to be known as the 'Bermuda Agreement', was to settle the terms of traffic rights for transatlantic scheduled air services between the two countries, including routes, frequency, capacity, and the setting of fares and rates, thus regulating the economic terms of these services on an essentially bilateral basis.[260] The only multilateral element was contained in the tariff clause which provided that the setting of fares and rates would be entrusted, when possible, to the conference machinery of IATA. The Bermuda Agreement became a model for a large number of bilateral air services agreements which were subsequently concluded by many countries during the post-war period.[261] Thus, the setting up of

---

Civil Aviation, 3rd edn (Montreal: IADC, 2003), 224 *et seq.*; L. Weber, 'Internationaler Luftverkehrsverband' (International Air Transport Association/IATA), in *Handwörterbuch Internationale Organisationen,* U.Andersen/W.Woyke (eds), 2nd edn (Opladen: Leske und Budrich, 1995), 219 et seq.

256. The 'International Air Traffic Association' (also called 'old IATA') had operated from 1919 to 1945, with headquarters at The Hague, the Netherlands. It had pioneered trade association work for the emerging international airlines which were members, namely 29 airlines from 24 countries in 1939, in particular in such matters as interlining, standardization of tickets and forms, traffic matters and accountancy. See in particular Groenewege, *ibid.*, (n. 255), 220 et seq.

257. On the IATA structure, see IATA Act of Incorporation, IATA Articles of Association, in:, *IATA Handbook, Rules and Regulations* (Montreal, February 2001).

258. *An Act to Incorporate International Air Transport Association*, Statutes of Canada, 1945, Ch. 51 (Assented to 18 Dec., 1945), as amended by Statutes of Canada, 1974-75-76, Ch. III (Assented to 27 Feb. 1975).

259. UK-US Agreement dated 11 Dec. 1946, *UKTS* No. 3 (1946); See J.C. Cooper, 'Air Transport and World Organization', in *Explorations in Aerospace Law*, ed. I.A. Vlasic (Montreal: McGill University Press, 1968), 357 et seq.; G. Cribbett, 'The Influence of Bilateral Agreements, Tariffs and Subsidies in International Air Transport', *Journal of Aeronautical Science of India* 3 (1951): 1 et seq.; M. Gillilland, 'Bilateral Agreements', in *The Freedom of the Air,* E. McWhinney & M.A. Bradley (eds) (Leiden/Dobbs-Ferry, Oceana/ Sijthoff: 1968), 159 et seq.

260. B. Cheng, *The Law of International Air Transport, ibid.*, (n. 16), 422 et seq.; B. Cheng, 'Beyond Bermuda', in *International Air Transport: Law, Organization and Policies for the Future*, ed. N.M. Matte (Toronto/Paris: Carswell/Pedone, 1976), 81 et seq.; N.M. Matte, *Treatise on Air-Aeronautical Law* (Montreal: McGill/Carswell, Toronto, 1981), 144 et seq.

261. P.P.C. Haanappel, 'Bilateral Air Transport Agreements: 1913-1980', *International Trade Law Journal* 5 (1979): 241 et seq., 245; see also A.F. Lowenfeld, 'A New Takeoff for International Air Transport', *Foreign Affairs* 54 (1975): 36 et seq.

ICAO, the setting up of IATA, and the conclusion of the Bermuda Agreement of 1946 constituted the three main and interrelated elements for the implementation of the compromise that had been negotiated at the Chicago Conference.[262]

B. Structure

As a non-profit corporate entity under Canadian law, IATA is governed by the rules laid down in the Act of Incorporation,[263] on the one hand, and the Articles of Association,[264] on the other hand.

The Act of Incorporation sets out the purposes, aims, and objectives of the Association,[265] namely:

(a) to promote safe, regular and economical air transport for the benefit of the peoples of the world, to foster air commerce and to study the problems connected therewith;
(b) to provide means for collaboration among the air transport enterprises engaged directly or indirectly in international air transport service;
(c) to co-operate with the International Civil Aviation Organization and other international organizations.

The Act also determines the location of the head office,[266] powers to make by laws, rules, and regulations, powers to own property and make financial transactions, rules on officers' tenure of office, powers to exercise its functions abroad, and power to adopt and use a corporate seal.[267]

The Articles of Association, which were first adopted at Havana, Cuba, in April 1945 and have undergone major revisions at the Annual General Meeting (AGM) in Amman, Jordan, in 1997 and at subsequent AGMs,[268] lay down the main organizational rules of the Association.

The two governing bodies of IATA are the Annual General Meeting (AGM),[269] at which all members of the Association are represented, and the

---

262. See s. I.A. above.
263. *An Act to Incorporate International Air Transport Association*, *ibid.*, (n. 258).
264. *IATA Articles of Association,* adopted at the 53rd Annual General Meeting held in Amman (Jordan), 3 Nov. -4 Nov. 1997, as last amended by the 61st AGM held in Tokyo, 29 May–31 May 2005, see <www.iata.org/about/corporate-secretary/>. See also: *IATA Handbook*, Rules and Regulations (Montreal, Ref. No. 1000), Ch. 2.
265. Section 3 of the *Act of Incorporation, ibid.* (n. 258).
266. Under s. 4 of the Act, the head office shall be located in Montreal, Canada, or at such other place as the AGM may determine.
267. Sections 4-10 of the *Act of Incorporation, ibid.* (n. 258).
268. See below (n. 269); the following references to the Articles of Association refer to the 2005 version adopted at the 61st AGM in Tokyo; for earlier versions, see *IATA Handbook*, *ibid.* (n. 264); Groenewege, *ibid.* (n. 255), 133.
269. The Articles of Association refer to the 'General Meeting', Art. VIII, which may be convened either as 'Annual General Meeting', Art IX, or as 'Special General Meeting', Art X.

Board of Governors (also known as the Executive Committee),[270] which is composed of not more than thirty-one persons (according to recent practice, thirty persons) who are Chief Executive Officers of Member Airlines.[271]

The Annual General Meeting is responsible for the election of the members of the Board of Governors, of the Standing Committees, and of other committees or bodies, for the adoption of the financial statements, and for the approval of the annual dues and fees for members.[272] In principle at least, it has ultimate authority to exercise all the powers of IATA.

The Board of Governors is the main executive body.[273] In accordance with Article XII of the Articles of Association, it has wide-ranging powers of management, including the general management and control of the business, affairs, funds, and property of IATA. In particular, it appoints the Director General, who is the Chief Executive Officer of IATA;[274] it also determines IATA policy within the framework of AGM Resolutions, and takes action with respect to the limitation, suspension, or termination of membership in IATA.[275]

In actual practice, the Board of Governors is therefore the main decision-making body of IATA. It usually meets twice a year, or more often as required, and is supported by Board Committees, Industry Committees, the Director General and the Secretariat. Board Committees include the Chair Committee, the Audit Committee, and the Strategy and Policy Committee.[276] The Industry Committees (formerly called Standing Committees) include the Cargo Committee, the Environment Committee, the Financial Committee, the Industry Affairs Committee, the Legal Committee, and the Operations Committee.[277] Industry Committees are set up under the control of the Director General, subject to Board approval, and report through him to the Board.[278] Each of the Industry Committees may set up working groups or ad-hoc task forces for specific subject matters, subject to the approval of the Director General,[279] and numerous such groups have been set up.

The IATA Traffic Conferences, which were established shortly after the Havana meeting in 1945, are semi-autonomous bodies subject only to policy

270. Article XII of the Articles of Association.
271. Article XII para.1.of the Articles of Association, which also mentions the Chairman of the Board, President or Managing Director of a Member Airline as eligible.
272. Article IX para. 3 of the Articles of Association; see also Hailbronner, *ibid.* (n. 255); Weber, *ibid.* (n. 255).
273. Article XII of the Articles of Association; Weber, *ibid.* (n. 255).
274. Article XII paras 3 f. and 4.a. of the Articles of Association.
275. Articles XII para.3 d., V para. 5 b. and c., and XII para.3.o. of the Articles of Association.
276. Article VII (1) of the Rules and Regulations of the Board of Governors.
277. Article VII (4) of the Rules, *ibid.* (n. 285); see also the Rules and Regulations of the Industry Committees, Annex 1 at <www.iata.org/about/corporate-secretary/>, setting out the mandate for each of the Industry Committees.
278. Article XII 4.d. of the Articles of Association; Art. VII (3) of the Rules, *ibid.* (n. 264).
279. Article VII (8) of the *Rules and Regulations of the Board of Governors*; Art. III (7) of the *Rules and Regulations of the Industry Committees.*

guidance by the Board of Governors.[280] They are regulated by the Provisions for the Conduct of the IATA Traffic Conferences[281] and the Traffic Conference Rules and Procedures,[282] and constitute the conference machinery of IATA.

Traffic Conferences were set up for the following subject matters:[283]

- Tariff-Coordinating Conferences: for the coordination of passenger fares and cargo rates, also referred to as tariffs.
- Services Conferences: for matters relating to passenger and cargo services, including handling, documentation, procedures, rules and regulations, reservations, ticketing, schedules, and automation standards.
- Agency Conferences: for matters relating to relationships between airlines and recognized sales agents and other intermediaries, but excluding remuneration levels, both for passenger and cargo.

All Active Members of IATA (international scheduled carriers) are in principle entitled to be members of the above Traffic Conferences with a right to vote.[284] Associate Members of IATA (essentially domestic scheduled carriers) are entitled to Conference membership without a right to vote.[285]

During the period from the 1940s to the late 1970s, all international scheduled air transportation was subject to tariff coordination by the IATA Tariff Conference machinery.[286] All Active Members of IATA were therefore automatically members of the Tariff Coordinating Conferences. This was pursuant to the compromise formula agreed at the Chicago Conference of 1944 and first implemented at Bermuda in 1946.

As from 1979, membership in Tariff Coordinating Conferences became voluntary. As a result of the US Show Cause Order,[287] as well as deregulation in the United States and air transport liberalization in Europe,[288] price competition

280. Article II (4) of the *Rules and Regulations of the Board of Governors*; in addition, the Director General has authority under Art. VI (1) (iv) of the *Rules and Regulations of the Board of Governors* to provide guidance to the Traffic Conferences to ensure that Board policies are taken into account. The latter provision, which is new, refers however to implementation guidance rather than policy guidance, which is reserved to the Board of Governors.

281. See *IATA Handbook*, Rules and Regulations, Ref. No. 1000, 81 et seq.

282. *IATA Handbook*, *ibid.* (n. 281), 104–108.

283. Articles IV 1. to 9. of the *Provisions for the Conduct of the IATA Traffic Conferences*, *ibid* (n.281).

284. Articles II 4. to 10. of the *Provisions, ibid.* (n. 281).

285. Articles II 1. to 3. of the *Provisions*, *ibid.* (n. 290).

286. See R.Y.Chuang, *The International Air Transport Association – A case study of a Quasi-Governmental Organization* (Sijthoff, Leiden: 1976), 62 et seq.

287. US CAB Order 78-6-78 dated 9 Jun. 1978. See K.H. Bòckstiegel, '*CAB v. IATA* – Documentation on Air Law Aspects in the Legislative Hearing on IATA Traffic Conferences', [Washington, October 1979] *ZLW* 29 (1980): 3 et seq.; B.Rein & R. McDonald, 'The Legislative Hearing on IATA Traffic Conferences – Creative Procedures in a High Stakes Setting', in *Essays in Air Law*, ed. A. Kean (Martinus Nijhus Publishers, The Hague 1982), 235 et seq.

288. M.S. Cohen, 'New Air Service and Deregulation: A study in transition', *JALC* 44 (1979): 696 et seq.; P.P.C. Haanappel et al. (eds), *EEC Air Transport Policy and Regulation, and their implications for North America* (Deventer/Boston: Kluwer, 1990).

between scheduled carriers on international routes gained more importance in the 1980s and 1990s and tariff coordination declined, retaining significance mainly as benchmark activity for competitive pricing on international trunk routes.[289] In many secondary markets, it has nevertheless remained a recognized pricing tool for airlines and governments.

C. Membership

Any airline operating international air services is in principle eligible to become an Active Member of IATA.[290] Active Members have the right to vote at any IATA meetings in which they participate. Active Members should be distinguished from Associate Members, who do not have a right to vote, but have otherwise the same rights and privileges as Active Members.[291]

Any airline operating domestic air services is in principle eligible to become an Associate Member of IATA.[292]

To become an Active or Associate Member, an applicant airline must meet one of the following criteria:[293]

- be sponsored by at least two Active Members; or
- have operated an air service for a period of not less than two years, having performed at least 5 million revenue ton kilometres per year; or
- its membership is considered to be in IATA's interest by the Board of Governors.

Membership requires approval of the Board and payment in full of all fees (including application and entrance fees) and dues for the current year.[294] A new member must also undergo the IATA Operational Safety Audit (IOSA).[295] Thereafter, for every year of active or associate membership, the dues as prescribed by the Board shall be paid. The dues to be paid by each member are based on a formula that takes into account the revenue ton kilometres carried by the member during the previous year as well as GNP of its home State. Dues and fees once paid are not refundable.[296]

289. S. Shaw, *Airline Marketing and Management*, 2nd edn (London: Pitman Publishing Ltd, 1985), 113 et seq.
290. Article V para. 1.a.i. *Articles of Association*. In practice, only airlines operating scheduled international air services have joined IATA as Active Members.
291. Article V para. 2 *Articles of Association*.
292. *Ibid.* (n. 291), para. 1.a.ii.In practice, only airlines operating scheduled domestic air services have joined IATA as Associate Members.
293. Article V para. 3.a. *Articles of Association*.
294. Article V para. 3.c. *Articles of Association*.
295. The IOSA programme now applies to all IATA member airlines, which shall undergo the Operational Safety Audit of IATA by the end of 2007. See <www.iata.org/membership/airlines>.
296. Article V para. 4.g. *Articles of Association*.

Membership may be placed 'in limitation' when a member is in arrears in the payment of dues and interest for a period of more than ninety days.[297] During the period that the limitation is in effect, the member loses all rights and privileges of membership, unless the Board has agreed to alternative financial arrangements.

Termination of membership may occur as a result of one of the following events:

- resignation by the member, giving thirty days notice;[298]
- termination by the Board in case of bankruptcy, receivership, voluntary assignment, or cessation of air services, thirty days from the event;[299]
- termination by the Board as a result of the member having become ineligible, ninety days after the event;[300]
- termination by the Board in case of breach of the Articles of Association, or of a regulation thereunder, or in case of an act or omission by the member prejudicial to the aims of IATA, of if the member has been placed in limitation for more than two years;[301]
- termination by a two-thirds vote of the Annual General Meeting at any time.[302]

A member that had its membership terminated may invoke its right to be heard by the Board or may resort to arbitration under the IATA Arbitration Rules.[303] In both cases, the effect of termination shall be suspended pending a decision. The decision of the arbitral tribunal shall be final and binding.

The 1997 revision of the articles of Association has inserted a new Article VI, under which the Board may establish a class of membership known as 'IATA Affiliates' and determine the criteria for membership and rights and duties thereof. However, in practice, this provision seems to have remained unused.

Instead, the Board has established the 'Strategic Partnership' programme, which allows interested non-airline parties, such as suppliers and service providers to the air transport industry, to directly interact with IATA and its member airlines.[304] Strategic Partners formally register with IATA and pay a fee, in return for which they have access to contact information, events, exhibitions, a directory, and use of the Strategic Partner logo.

D. Regulatory Functions

Since the 1940s, most of IATA's members, in particular the international scheduled carriers, were State-owned and State-controlled entities. However, starting in

297. Article V para. 5.b. *Articles of Association.*
298. *Ibid.*, para. 5.a.
299. *Ibid.*, para. 5.c.ii.
300. *Ibid.*, para. 5.c.i.
301. *Ibid.*, para. 5.c.iv.
302. *Ibid.*, para. 5.c.v.
303. *Ibid.*, para. 6.a. and b.
304. See <http://iata.org/membership/strategic>

the 1980s, a wave of privatization occurred in the international airline industry, continuing through the 1990s. As a result, the vast majority of the members of IATA today are privately owned, privately controlled airlines. As an international association of mostly private entities, IATA can therefore be regarded as a non-governmental international organization.[305]

Nevertheless, in accordance with the functions envisaged for it when it was refounded in 1945, IATA has been entrusted by governments with important regulatory functions relating to international air transport.

1. Tariff Coordination Conferences

In line with the compromise formula agreed upon at the Chicago Conference in November/December 1944[306] and starting with the Bermuda Agreement of 1946,[307] governments have entrusted IATA with tariff coordinating functions for international air routes.

The classic tariff clause in a Bermuda-type bilateral agreement, which was prevalent in the 1950s and 1960s, contained the following paragraph:[308]

> The tariffs shall, if possible, be agreed in respect of each route between the designated airlines concerned, in consultation with other airlines operating on the same route or any section thereof. Such agreement shall, where possible, be reached through the rate-fixing machinery of the International Air Transport Association. The tariffs so agreed shall be subject to the approval of the Contracting Parties.

Similarly, the ECAC 'Standard Clauses for Bilateral Agreements' of 1959 provided that:[309]

> agreements shall, where possible, be reached through the rate-fixing machinery of the International Air Transport Association.

The principle underlying this delegation of rate-making functions was that the international airlines, acting through the tariff coordination conference machinery of IATA ('rate-fixing machinery'), would agree on fares and rates for international

305. See on this question R. Chuang, *ibid.* (n. 255), 2 et seq., 154 et seq., who tends to classify IATA as a mixed entity; similarly P.P.C. Haanappel, *Pricing and Capacity Determination in International Air Transport – A Legal Analysis* (Antwerp, Boston, London, Frankfurt: Kluwer, 1984), 72 et seq., who takes the view that it is a private organization as to form, but in fact a 'quasi-public international organization'. Since the 1980s, not only the nature of its members has however gradually changed, but also the importance of IATA's tariff co-ordination activities has declined significantly.
306. See above s. I.A.
307. UK-US Agreement dated 11 Dec. 1946, *UKTS* No. 3 (1946.)
308. B. Cheng, *The Law of International Air Transport* (London: Stevens, 1962), 446.
309. *Standard Clauses for Bilateral Agreements*, Report, *ICAO Doc.* 7977, ECAC/3-1 (1959), 57, Art. 7 para. 2.

routes, subject, however, to government approval of such fares and rates.[310] A similar conference system for the fixing of fares and rates on international routes had existed for many years in the maritime shipping sector[311] and worked reasonably well. The compromise found at the Chicago Conference in 1944 had excluded fare- and rate-fixing functions from the jurisdiction of the newly established ICAO.[312] Direct government-to-government negotiations on fares and rates for international air services were regarded as not practical. The compromise provided therefore that the fare and rate negotiations would be left to the airlines, but that all fares and rates agreed upon would be subject to government approval before they could become effective. This latter condition was seen as keeping governments in ultimate control of the system of fares and rates on international air routes.[313] Whether this was subsequently actually the case, is another matter.

The tariff-coordination machinery of IATA consists essentially of tariff coordination conferences, at which fare or rate packages are negotiated, agreed, and voted upon, and the fare and rate approval process, during which the airline members submit the agreed package to their respective governments for approval with a view to bringing the package into force by an intended effectiveness date.

The tariff coordination conferences comprise passenger conferences, which are responsible for coordinating passenger fares,[314] and cargo conferences with responsibility for cargo rates.[315] Each of these consist of area conferences (a conference each for Area 1: the Americas, Area 2: Europe, Africa, and the Middle East, and Area 3: Asia, Australia, and Oceania), for the routes between these areas, and a worldwide conference.[316] When an international airline joins IATA Tariff Coordination, it becomes an automatic voting member of the area conferences where it has third and fourth freedom rights.[317] Under certain conditions, it can also choose to become a voting member in other area conferences.

At tariff coordination conferences, fares or rates are usually first discussed route by route in smaller groups, with only the carriers serving the respective route participating. The results of these preliminary discussions are then put together into a so-called fare package,[318] or in the case of cargo, a rate package, which is then

310. Chuang, *ibid.* (n. 255), 29-31; Hailbronner, *ibid.* (n. 255), 1049; Haanappel, *ibid.* (n. 305), 27 et seq., 37 with further references.
311. *The Liner Conference System*, UN Doc.TD/B/C.4/62/Rev.1 (*UNCTAD Report* 1970).
312. See above s. I.A.
313. Groenewege, *ibid.* (n. 255), 320; Chuang, *ibid.* (n.255), 29 et seq.
314. *Provisions for the Conduct of the IATA Traffic Conferences, ibid.* (n. 281), s. IV. Para. 5.
315. *Provisions, ibid.*, s. IV. Para. 7.
316. *Provisions, ibid.*, s. I. paras 1–4 and the *First Schedule to the Provisions*, which lists all Tariff Co-ordinating Conferences in detail; however, under s. I. para. 6 of the *Provisions,* the Board of Governors may increase or decrease the number of Traffic Conferences and change the names, alter the boundaries and determine the respective headquarters thereof.
317. *Provisions, ibid.*, s. II. paras 6 (ii) and 7 (ii); see also paras 6 (iii) and (iv) and 7 (iii) and (iv).
318. The term 'package' denotes a bundle of related fare or rate agreements, or proposals for such agreements. It is used in the practical work of the Tariff Co-ordinating Conferences, but does usually not appear in the official texts, which only use the terms 'agreement' and 'Resolution',

submitted and discussed either by subarea groups or directly by the plenary conference. If as a result of the discussions, *consensus* is found, the entire fare or rate package will be put to a vote. In order to pass, an unanimous vote in favour of the package is required.[319]

Each package will usually state the intended effectiveness date,[320] which is the date by which all necessary government approvals are due to be obtained and at which the new fares or rates are to become legally effective and applicable for all air carriers concerned. Typically, a period of three-six months is given for this, that is, from the end of the conference to intended effectiveness.

The government approval process is triggered by the submission of the fare or rate package to each government concerned by the respective carrier or carriers. It is the carriers, not IATA, that apply for approval. Such approval is normally obtained within the specified time period, that is, before the effectiveness date. In case the package or a particular fare or rate is disapproved, or is not approved by the intended effectiveness date, a so-called open rate situation[321] arises. This means that the package or particular fare or rate cannot enter into force; instead, the effectiveness of the previously applicable package or particular fare or rate is then usually extended, until the disapproval issue is resolved.

Because of the antitrust sensitivity of tariff co-ordination under the competition laws of the United States, of the European Union, and of a number of other countries, the activities of the IATA rate-fixing machinery have been subject to close governmental antitrust scrutiny for many years. In the United States, the IATA machinery was approved and immunized by the CAB from the operation of the US antitrust laws as from February 1946, subject, however, to a number of important conditions.[322] Later, the Show Cause Order[323] of the US CAB of 1978 triggered a new governmental review,[324] resulting eventually in important changes in the procedural IATA provisions governing the tariff coordination conferences.

---

in line with the terms used in the *Provisions for the Conduct of the IATA Traffic Conferences, ibid.* (n. 281).

319. See the all-important unanimity rule in the *Provisions, ibid.* (n. 281), s. VIII para. 12 and s. IX para. 4.

320. See s. VIII para. 1, second Sentence, of the *Provisions, ibid.* This has been the subject of an interpretation by the IATA Executive Committee to the effect that any resolution for which approval by the US Government is required shall be declared effective only upon approval by the US Government. See the *Provisions, ibid.* (n. 281) relating to s. VIII para. 1.

321. See Chuang, *ibid.* (n. 255), 72, 73.

322. 6 CAB Reports 639 (1946), Agreement No. 493; this approval and immunization was limited to one year, but was thereafter extended on a yearly basis until 1955, when the Board gave its permanent approval. See on this subject Chuang, *ibid.* (n. 255), 111 et seq.

323. CAB Order 78-6-78 (9 Jun. 1978); see CAB Order 82-3-77 (12 Mar. 1982) and CAB Docket 3285; also K.H. Böckstiegel, '*CAB v. IATA* – Documentation on Air Law Aspects in the Legislative Hearing', [Washington, October 1979 on IATA Traffic Conferences], *ZLW* 29 (1980): 3 et seq.; J.L. Magdelénat, 'The Story of the Life and Death of the CAB Show Cause Order', *Air Law* 5 (1980): 3 et seq.; B. Rein and R. McDonald, 'The 'Legislative Hearing' on IATA Traffic Conferences – Creative Procedure in a High Stakes Setting', in, *Essays in Air Law*, ed. A. Kean (The Hague, Boston, London: Nijhoff, 1982): 235 et seq.

324. See CAB Docket 32851 and CAB Order 82-3-77, *ibid.* (n. 323).

In particular, membership in tariff coordination conferences became voluntary for IATA members,[325] and the US carriers then left the tariff coordination machinery (only to rejoin a few years later). Similarly, as from 1986 the European Union applied the competition rules of the Rome Treaty to air transport,[326] but decided in 1988 in view of the beneficial effects of interlining to grant a block exemption[327] for tariff coordination activities subject to a number of conditions. The European Commission proposed in 2004/2005 to discontinue the EU block exemption[328] for tariff coordination on intra-European routes. If the exemption is withdrawn, this will not render tariff coordination illegal *per se* under EU law, but the carriers participating in tariff coordination and IATA would be exposed to potential competition law enforcement action by the European Commission and potential court action by private parties.[329] As of April 2011, a decision on this matter has not yet been taken.

In view of privatization of many international scheduled carriers, increased competition between them, the importance of airline alliances and code-sharing, and a liberalized regulatory regime on many international routes, the role of tariff co-ordination has evolved since the 1980s.[330] On North Atlantic routes, most intra-European routes, and routes between pairs of states having concluded bilateral agreements with a liberalized tariff clause, air carriers compete on fares and rates.[331] Tariff coordination for those routes has either evolved to a benchmarking function for business class and first class fares only,[332] or has been discontinued.

325. *Provisions, ibid.*, s. II paras 6 (i) and 7 (i), which were inserted in the wake of the *US Show Cause Order*.
326. L. Weber, 'The EEC Internal Air Transport Market and its Impact on the Airline Industry', in *EEC Air Transport Policy and Regulation, and their Implications for North America*, P.P.C. Haanappel/G. Petsikas/R. Rosales/J. Thaker (eds) (Deventer/Boston: Kluwer, 1990): 49 et seq.; the triggering element was the decision of the European Court of Justice in the '*Nouvelles Frontières'* Case (1986) *ECR* 1459 (*Ministère Public v. Lucas Asjes and others*).
327. Council Regulation No. 3976/87 of 14 Dec. 1987, *OJ* No. L 374 (1987), 9; Commission Regulation (EEC) No. 2671/88 of 26 Jul. 1988, *OJ* No. L 239 (1988), 9; later replaced by Commission Regulation (EEC) No. 1617/93 of 25 Jun. 1993, *OJ* No. L 155 (1993), 18, as amended by Commission Regulation (EC) No. 1083/99 of 26 May 1999, *OJ* No. L 131 (1999), 27.
328. European Commission, DG Competition, *Consultation Paper Concerning the Revision and possible Prorogation of Commission Regulation 1617/93*; see also European Commission, *Press Release IP/05/1432* of 16 Nov. 2005.
329. Previous to the exemptions granted in Regulations (EEC) No. 1617/93 and (EC)1083/99, tariff co-ordination relating to routes to/from the EU had proceeded without a protective block exemption. See on this matter Weber, *ibid.* (n. 326), 58 et seq.; on enforcement of the competition rules, see also I. van Bael/J-F.Bellis, *Competition Law of the EEC*, 2nd edn (CCH editions Bicester Oxfordshire 1990), 470 et seq.
330. European Commission, Consultation Paper, *ibid.* (n. 328).
331. For a lucid summary of the competitive environment in these markets, see H. Wassenbergh, 'The International Airline Industry, The Straitjacket of Competition Law', *AnnASL*29 (2004): 185 et seq.
332. While market-pricing and rebates are general practice in the economy fare sector in many markets, this is much less the case in the business fare and first class fare sectors, even in liberalized markets.

On other international routes, however, tariff coordination activities have retained their significance as facilitator of interlining and price regulation under the respective bilateral air transport agreements.

2. Passenger and Cargo Services Conferences

The IATA conference machinery also comprises the Procedures Conferences[333] for passenger and cargo matters, respectively. Passenger Procedures Conferences consist of Passenger Services Conferences and Passenger Agency Conferences.[334] On the cargo side, there are Cargo Services Conferences and Cargo Agency Conferences.

Passenger Services Conferences have the mandate to take action on matters relating to passenger services, including passenger and baggage handling, documentation, procedures, rules and regulations, reservations, ticketing, schedules, and automation standards.[335] More specifically, this includes the making and updating of industry standards for reservations procedures, ticket specification and issuance procedures (including e-tickets), passenger and baggage check-in procedures, baggage tag specifications, standard traffic handling codes and messages, automation standards, interline procedures, fraud prevention procedures, procedures for the handling of incapacitated passengers, and other matters.[336] Particularly important from a legal viewpoint is the making and updating of industry-accepted Notices and Conditions of Contract and General Conditions of Carriage, which provide standard clauses that virtually all IATA member airlines follow. They generally therefore determine the contractual terms and conditions for the carriage of passengers on IATA member carriers.[337]

The Notices and Conditions of Contract[338] which are set out in IATA Resolutions 724, 724a, and 724b, provide for a uniform text of Conditions of Contract for passenger tickets, as well as for a uniform text of Notices and Advice to Passengers on limitation of liability, on baggage liability limitations, and on air transport-related taxes and fees.

---

333. See the term as it is used in the *Provisions*, *ibid.*, ss I.1.(i) and 2.(i), II.4.and 5., IV.3.and 4., and VIII.7. and 8.
334. See s. I.1.(i) of the *Provisions*; for the terms of reference of the Procedures Conferences, see ss IV.3 and 4 of the *Provisions.*
335. Section IV. para. 3.(i) of the Provisions, *ibid.* (n. 282).
336. See IATA Passenger Services Conference Resolutions Manual, *IATA Ref. No. 9096*; the main subjects are: Passenger Services Standards and Procedures; Passenger Reservations Systems; Passenger Fares and Rules Exchange Standards; Passenger and Airport Data Interchange Standards; Incapacitated Passengers Standards and Procedures; Baggage Tracing Services.
337. It is general practice among IATA member carriers to incorporate the IATA Conditions of Contract and IATA General Conditions of Carriage into their own documents, in some cases with additional clauses or wording to satisfy local legal or other requirements.
338. See Resolution 724 Attachments A, B and C; Resolution 724b, in: IATA Passenger Services Conference Resolutions Manual, *ibid.* (n. 336).

The General Conditions of Carriage (Passenger and Baggage),[339] which are found in IATA Recommended Practice 1724, provide for a uniform text of conditions of carriage, regulating the following matters:

- Applicability.
- Tickets (including validity).
- Fares, Taxes, Fees and Charges.
- Reservations.
- Check-in and Boarding.
- Refusal and Limitation of Carriage.
- Baggage.
- Schedules, Delays, Cancellation of Flights.
- Refunds.
- Conduct Aboard Aircraft.
- Arrangements for Additional Services.
- Administrative Formalities.
- Successive Carriers.
- Liability for Damage.
- Time Limitation on Claims and Actions.
- Other Conditions.
- Interpretation.

In the case of most international carriers, the General Conditions of Carriage are incorporated by reference into the passenger contract of carriage by virtue of a notice to the passenger,[340] which appears on the ticket or, in the case of an e-ticket, is part of a notice section of the ticket. In principle, a carrier's General Conditions of Carriage are to be available for inspection upon request by any passenger at carrier's points of sale or check-in.

In setting the terms of contract between scheduled air carriers and passengers on a world-wide basis, the IATA Passenger Services Conference sets relevant industry standards and performs important regulatory functions, which, if left to governments, would be difficult to achieve internationally.

The Passenger Services Conference is assisted by a number of committees reporting to it, namely the Reservations Committee, the Passenger Forms and Procedures Committee and the Airport Services Committee.[341]

---

339. IATA Recommended Practice (RP) 1724, Passenger Services Conference Resolutions Manual, *ibid.* (n. 336).
340. For the model for such notice, see *the Notice and Conditions of Contract*, IATA Resolution 724, Attachment 'A', Clause 2., in: IATA Passenger Services Conference Resolutions Manual, *ibid.*
341. Section X. para. 2.(i) of the Provisions. The Reservations Committee has the mandate to deal with all procedures and policy issues relating to reservations rules and regulations, including transmission of reservations services for use by customers and agents; the Passenger Forms and Procedures Committee is tasked with the simplification and improvement of manual and automated passenger ticketing, documentation, rules and procedures. The Airport Services Committee is responsible for simplifying and improving passenger and baggage handling,

The Cargo Services Conferences are responsible for the development and maintenance of the respective standards for cargo industry procedures,[342] including the Air Waybill Conditions of Contract and General Conditions of Carriage for Cargo (IATA Resolutions 600b and 600b (II) and Recommended Practice 1601, respectively). The Air Waybill Conditions of Contract and the General Conditions of Carriage for Cargo have the same defining role for the contractual terms of carriage of air cargo as the respective documents have for carriage of passengers. The Conference is supported in its work by the Cargo Services Conference Management Group, whose task it is to manage the ongoing work programmes of the Conference.[343]

3. Passenger and Cargo Agency Conferences

The IATA Passenger and Cargo Agency Conferences have the mandate to take action on matters relating to relationships between airlines and recognized passenger sales agents and other passenger or cargo intermediaries, but excluding remuneration levels.[344]

They regulate the legal and commercial relationship between the airlines in their role as principals and their accredited sales agents and other intermediaries, including the terms and conditions of the important sales agency agreements, except for remuneration levels.[345] Agency remuneration was traditionally regulated through IATA tariff coordination conferences fixing uniform remuneration levels,[346] but has progressively become the subject of market regulation in the course of the last fifteen years. This development is mainly the result of technological developments (carriers being able to offer reservations and ticketing directly over the Internet), changes in the role of sales intermediaries (travel agents and corporate travel departments) and government action in favour of a more competitive environment.

Passenger and Cargo Agency Conferences are responsible for defining the conditions and procedures for sales agent accreditation, for the sale of air transportation through sales agents and intermediaries, and for the handling and processing of ticket stock, air waybills, and other accountable traffic documents. They also set the rules the processing and accounting of sales revenues, the organizational structure and mode of functioning of the IATA Billing and Settlement Plan (BSP)[347]

---

procedures, forms, regulations and automated systems and message standards, for providing overall policy direction and general management for airport services standards and procedures, and for publishing recommendations concerning ramp services.

342. Section IV. para. 4.(i) of the Provisions, *ibid.* (n. 281).
343. Section X. para. 3.(i) of the Provisions.
344. Section IV. paras 3.(ii) and 4.(ii) of the *Provisions, ibid.* (n. 281).
345. Section IV. of the Provisions, *ibid.*
346. Section IV. paras 6 and 8 of the *Provisions, ibid.*
347. *IATA Billing and Settlement Plan Manual for Airlines*, Ref. No. 5666-04M; *Billing and Settlement Plan Quick Reference Handbook*, Ref.No.5666-04Q; *IATA Resolution 850*, Attachment B.

and the Cargo Accounts Settlement System (CASS),[348] and other matters relating to the principal-agent relationship between airlines and sales intermediaries. They therefore play a highly important role in ensuring that a global distribution and sales network for the international carriers is in place, operates successfully, and remains fully adapted to the rapid changes in the marketplace.

The Passenger Agency Conference is assisted in its task by several committees reporting to it, namely the Passenger Agency Procedures Committee,[349] the Billing and Settlement Plan Committee,[350] and the Passenger Agency Training Committee.[351] Similarly, the Cargo Agency Conference is assisted by the Cargo Agency Procedures Committee,[352] the Cargo Accounts Settlement System Committee[353] and the Cargo Agency Training Committee,[354] Coordination with the travel agents and cargo agents/intermediaries is ensured through the IATA/ UFTAA and IATA/FIATA Consultative Councils.[355]

E. Other Functions

Among the numerous other functions and services that are provided by IATA, the following should be mentioned:

1. Multilateral Interline Traffic Agreements (MITA)

They consist of MITA Passenger, MITA Cargo, MITA Service Charges-United States, and the IATA Interline Cargo Claims Agreement.[356] They regulate the issuance and mutual acceptance of interline tickets, air waybills, and MCOs, interline checking of baggage, mishandled baggage, claims and indemnities, interline service charges, interline billing and settlement, and other matters regarding interline traffic.[357] The entire interline system is administered by the IATA Secretariat.

---

348. IATA Cargo Accounts Settlement System: *Export Procedures Manual*, Ref. No. 9213; *IATA Cargo Accounts Settlement Systems Quick Reference Handbook*, Ref. No. 9425.
349. Section X.2.(ii).A of the Provisions.
350. Section X.2.(ii).B of the Provisions.
351. Section X.2.(ii).C of the Provisions.
352. Section X.3.(ii).A of the Provisions.
353. Section X.3.(ii).B of the Provisions.
354. Section X.3.(ii).C of the Provisions.
355. Universal Federation of Travel Agents' Associations, and International Federation of Freight Forwarders' Associations, respectively. The IATA/UFTAA Consultative Council was set up by virtue of IATA Resolution 800c, the IATA/FIATA Consultative Council by virtue of IATA Resolution 801c.
356. IATA Resolutions 780 (passenger), 660 (cargo) and 660b (cargo handling), in: *IATA Multilateral Interline Traffic Agreements Manual*, Ref. No. 9092.
357. For the interline rules regarding passengers and baggage, see *IATA Resolution 780*, Arts 2-10 and the MITA Manual, *ibid.*, Ref.No.9092. The text of the MITA agreements is reflected in the respective resolutions. However, the agreements themselves are signed by the participating airlines in hardcopy format. They are also open to non-IATA carriers.

2. Clearing House

The main function of the IATA Clearing House[358] is the mutual settlement and offset of claims and counterclaims between participating carriers arising from interline carriage and interline services under MITA. It settles and offsets claims between carriers once a month. The functioning of the Clearing House is governed by the IATA Clearing House Regulations.[359] It is open for participation by IATA and non-IATA carriers.

3. Billing and Settlement Plan (BSP)

The main function of the Billing and Settlement Plan[360] is the standardized and automated billing, accounting, and settlement of passenger sales revenues between sales agents and intermediaries, on the one hand, and IATA carriers, on the other. It operates by making use of regional or local clearing banks and data processing centres, which provide services to the BSP and its participating carriers and agents, and by providing standardized ticket stock and procedures.[361] It has resulted in an important leap in efficiency for carriers and agents in the billing, accounting and settlement of sales proceeds.

4. Cargo Accounts Settlement System (CASS)

The CASS[362] is the equivalent of the BSP in relation to cargo by providing standardized and automated billing, accounting and settlement facilities for cargo carriers and their sales agents and. intermediaries.

5. IATA Currency Clearance Service (ICCS)

The ICCS[363] is a centralized cash management tool, which provides participating carriers with information, collection, currency conversion, and/or repatriation of their international sales proceeds flowing from BSBs, CASSes, GSAs and Credit Card Settlements. It also provides account reconciliation and administration services.

---

358. *Manual of IATA Clearing House Regulations and Procedures*, Ref. No. 9248.
359. *IATA Handbook, Rules and Regulations*, Ref. No. 1000, Ch. 8, 110 et seq.; for more detail on the functioning of the Clearing House, see Groenewege, *ibid.* (n. 255), 308; the Clearing House Manual, *ibid.* (n. 358); *IATA Clearing House – Rates of Exchange*, Ref. No. 9249 and 5926.
360. IATA Billing and Settlement Plan Manual for Airlines, *ibid.* (n. 347); *Billing and Settlement Plan Manual for Passenger Sales Agents*, Ref. No. 9270.
361. *IATA Resolution 850*, Attachments A and B.
362. *IATA Cargo Accounts Settlement Quick Reference Handbook*, Ref. No. 9425; see also the related *Manuals 9210, 9211, 9212 and 9213*; *IATA Resolution 851*, Attachments A and B.
363. The ICCS is part of the IATA Treasury Services. See on this subject Groenewege, *ibid.* (n. 255), 309; see also *IATA Annual Report* (2001), *World Air Transport Summit and 57th Annual General Meeting* (Madrid 27 May 2001–29 May 2001), 87 et seq.

6. Airline and Airport Designator Service

The Airline and Airport Designator Service of IATA provides two-letter or numerical-alpha designators to airlines and three-letter designators to airports around the world.[364] These designators are universally recognized and used, in particular, in aeronautical telecommunications and messaging systems.

7. Training Services

The IATA Training and Development Institute (ITDI)[365] provides classroom and distance training courses for airline and other aviation staff. In-company courses, self-study courses, and regional training courses are also offered. Its curriculum comprises mainly short-duration (two days to two weeks) professional training courses aimed at enhancing skills and knowledge in the industry, including the developing world. It also offers a certificate programme, which requires the participation in a number of related courses to obtain a certificate. In 2010, the ITDI offered more than 200 scheduled classroom courses in six different regional training centres and e-learning training programmes at locations worldwide.[366]

364. *IATA Coding Directory, Ref. No. 9095*; see also *IATA City Code Directory, Ref. No. 626.*
365. *IATA Training and Development Institute, 2011 Training Schedule* (Montreal 2011); see also Groenewege, *ibid.* (n. 255), 333.
366. *IATA, Training and Development Institute, ibid.*

Chapter 4

From Regulation to Deregulation

Elmar M. Giemulla, Heiko van Schyndel, and Angela Marina Donato

I. AVIATION PRIOR TO LIBERALIZATION

In 1944 in Chicago, three international documents dealing *inter alia* with market access were adopted with implications in the multilateral regulation of international air transport:

- The Convention on International Civil Aviation, signed in Chicago on 7 December 1944,[1] which is the most important document, containing the constitution of the International Civil Aviation Organization (ICAO) and certain Articles that bear on the topic of economic regulation.
- A second instrument is the International Air Services Transit Agreement,[2] in which two freedoms of the air are regulated, recognizing the multilateral exchange of rights of overflight and non-traffic stops for scheduled air services among its contracting States.
- A third instrument is the International Air Transport Agreement,[3] containing the five freedoms of the air for scheduled international air services. This

---

1. 15 *UNTS* 295, *ICAO Doc.* 7300.
2. 84 *UNTS* 389; *ICAO Doc.* 7500.
3. 171 *UNTS* 387; *ICAO Doc.* App. IV-2187.

Elmar M. Giemulla & Ludwig Weber, *International and EU Aviation Law: Selected Issues*, pp. 129–192.

document came initially into force only for nineteen States, eight of which renounced it at a later time.

It is important to note that the main objective of the international conference and the air transport agreement, that is the creation of a multinational framework to regulate air transport services, was not reached; all regulation in this field was defined later on by bilateral agreements.

The first and most important bilateral agreement on air transport services was signed by the United States (US) and the United Kingdom (UK) in Bermuda on 11 February 1946,[4] and was composed of a final act, an agreement and an annex.

It represented a compromise between advocates of detailed regulation and those of non-regulation of basic matters, such as capacity and tariffs. In effect, it established the so-called Bermuda-I-type Agreement as a kind of blueprint for many other bilateral air transport agreements to follow.

It is important to remember that this agreement was the result of a compromise between the two approaches to the regulation of international air transport services that had emerged at the Chicago Conference, but had been left unresolved.

On the one hand, it was held that there should be no regulation of capacity or tariffs, nor specific definitions of routes, while on the other hand, that capacity should be predetermined and tariffs established by the airlines involved through International Air Transport Association (IATA), subject to the approval of both State parties.

The system of commercial air transport, as it was established by the system of the Chicago Convention and Bermuda I bilaterals,[5] has largely been formed by the policy of protection of the national carrier, that is, a scheduled airline in which the State concerned secured influence for itself, usually by means of majority participation, and which – in return for this protection – had to maintain essential air services. Protection has been achieved in two different ways: first, against foreign competitors (other scheduled airlines), and second, against domestic competitors (scheduled airlines as well as charter carriers). This has led, among other things, to a long-standing strict distinction being drawn between scheduled and charter air services.

A. Protection against Foreign Competitors

International air transport, particularly in the form of scheduled and charter services, is based on rights of access, which the different States grant to one another by multilateral or bilateral air service agreements or which is granted by one State to an air transport enterprise upon application.[6] It is self-evident that these rights of access are of major importance to the States concerned both from the point of view

4. Agreement between the United Kingdom and United States, 11 February 1946, 60 Stat. 1499, *TAIS* 1507, 3 *UNTS* 253 (No. 36) and *UKTS* (1946), 3.
5. For details see Ch. 1 s. II. B.2.a.ii.2.
6. *Ibid.*

of transport policy and economy; it is also clear that the airlines involved are dependent upon those States – in positive as well as in negative ways.[7]

Internationally, the rights of access are generally described by reference to the five freedoms of the air, but these categories are not exclusive and can also be combined.[8] These rights are usually granted by the Transport Agreement (containing the first two 'technical' freedoms, see above) and (for the remaining 'commercial' freedoms) in bilateral air services agreements (BASAs) in which the two governments involved try to protect their economies and their (national) carriers.

B. Protection against Domestic Competitors

Domestic protection of scheduled air services has mainly been achieved by shielding them from charter airlines. While the latter operate mostly in the context of the tourist business, the former are principally concerned with the carriage of business traffic. Both these groups have different interests in flying: a tourist usually plans his flight far in advance, and will have a fixed date for his return flight before even starting the journey; another decisive factor will be the fare. With business travellers, the fare will often be relatively insignificant in comparison with other considerations. The ticket will usually be paid for by a company, which will generally be able to deduct the cost as a business expense from taxation. A businessperson will try to coordinate flights with operational necessities. For him, the regularity, punctuality, and reliability of an airline, which enable the flexibility of business travel, are the decisive considerations.

Initially, this strict separation of the two types of air transport was a definite policy of national governments. For a long time, civil aviation law has generally been used to protect national carriers against charter airlines and other scheduled airlines, and scheduled airlines generally against charter airlines.

C. Limited Competition

However, it would be incorrect to create the impression that there was no competition at all before 1978. Even before then, a number of the bilateral air service agreements concluded among the members of the EEC contained provisions for multiple designation and thereby the possibility of competition.[9] In that connection, Niester[10] is right to point out that nine out of the then bilateral air service

7. As to the exchange of rights of access in general see Schwenk/Giemulla, *Handbuch des Luftverkehrsrechts* (Handbook on Aviation Law) (Heymanns Verlag, 3rd edn 2005), 643 et seq.; Diersch, *Der internationale Gelegenheitsluftverkehr* (Peter Lang, 1981), 11 et seq.; 56 et seq.; Basedow, § 8 I 2.
8. For details see Ch. 2, s. III. B. 2. a. i.
9. Single designation was normal at least until the late seventies, because in most States there was only one airline anyway.
10. Gröner, *Regulierung und Wettbewerb im europäischen Luftverkehr* (Regulating Competition in European Air Traffic) (Duncker & Humblot GmbH, 1989), 88.

agreements concluded among the EEC Member States contained provisions for multiple designations and thereby the possibility of competition.[11] Furthermore, the capacity fixing provisions of some of the Bermuda Type I[12] enabled the airlines to fix capacity shares according to the expected demand, with controls only introduced afterwards. Normal provisions on rights of access and the fixing and approval of tariffs also contained some flexibility, so it is not the case that there was no, or only little, scope for competition within the EEC before 1979, the year when the EEC Commission issued its first memorandum on a future air transport policy.[13]

D. First Step towards Liberalization

On 23 July 1977, the original Bermuda Agreement was replaced by a Bermuda II Agreement,[14] more detailed than the first. The liberal period was a direct consequence: different States adopted more-liberal bilateral agreements, with the removal of capacity restraints, reduced government involvement in tariff matters, and increased market access and competition.

As a result of the Bermuda II Agreement, the US and the UK approved routes designated by each of the parties so as to cover all international traffic without involving the interests of third countries, the only exception being the exercise of the fifth freedom of the air. In this case, the development of air transport services must be adjusted to the needs of the air traffic between the country of origination and the country of the final destination, as well as to the needs of the air traffic in the area crossed by the air carriers of the contracting parties, taking into account the local and regional services.

II. DEREGULATION IN THE UNITED STATES

A. The Policy of Deregulation

The first efforts made within the Western World to deregulate aviation took place in the US.[15] Already in 1977, the Chairman of the Civil Aeronautics Board (CAB), who had been appointed by President Carter, took the first steps towards this objective by giving preference to those airlines offering the lowest fares in the allocation of air transport licenses. Next, the CAB enabled the airlines to lower their airfares to 50% below the 'Standard Industry Fare Level' (SIFL).

---

11. Earlier, single designation was normal at least from the end of the Second World War until the late seventies because in most States there was only one airline anyway.
12. I.e., the previous definition of the capacities was renounced. See in addition Schwenk/Giemulla, *Handbuch des Luftverkehrsrechts* (*Handbook on Aviation Law*) (Heymanns Verlag, 3rd edn 2005), 643 et seq.
13. See below Section IV.A.2.(a).
14. Agreement between the Government of the United States of America and the Government of the United Kingdom of Great Britain and Northern Ireland concerning Air Service, 23 July 1997, 1079*UNTS* 21 (No. 16509) and *UKTS* (1977) 76.
15. For further details see Ebke/Wittmann, Wettbewerb im Linienluftverkehr: Erste Erfahrungen mit der Deregulierung in den USA, *RIW 36* (1990), 963.

Following the Airline Deregulation Act of 1978,[16] which amended the Federal Aviation Act of 1958, and the International Air Transportation Competition Act of 1979,[17] control over the US domestic aviation industry was first reduced and then, by additional steps, removed completely.

Initially, on 31 December 1981, the CAB lost its authority to allocate routes. One year later, it also lost its authority in relation to tariffs. On 1 January 1985 the authority of the CAB to approve or disapprove airline mergers passed to the Department of Transportation (DOT), as did also the responsibility for the 'Essential Air Service' programme and international air transport. The US Postal Service was given authority to grant air transport subsidies. On 1 January 1989, merger control passed to the Federal Department of Justice. On 1 January 1984, the CAB presented a report to the US Congress on the subject of whether or not public interest demanded the further existence of the CAB and its functions.[18] On 1 January 1985, the CAB was finally dissolved.[19]

B. Effects of Deregulation

In February 1990, the US DOT presented its report 'Secretary's Task Force on Competition in the US Domestic Airline Industry'. The then US Minister of Transportation (Mr Skinner), who had commissioned it, concluded that 'Air travellers have benefited under deregulation through more service at lower cost'.[20] Also, the German Deregulation Commission[21] in its first report 'Market Opening and Competition' (March 1990),[22] evaluated the results of the deregulation of American air traffic 'positively as a whole' because against the greater variety of lines, the gain on prosperity and the increase of the employee numbers solely the concentration of the air traffic would stand as a disadvantage, which, however, was only partially a result of the deregulation and could have been fought against by a stricter application of the Competition Act. The development of air traffic in the US after 1978 represents a valuable and empirically verified source of information, which could be considered in the formation of the European air traffic market.[23] For this reason, this should be traced in the following.

---

16. 92 Stat. 1705, Pub. L. 95-504; see also Goetz/Dempsey, Airline Deregulation Ten Years After: Something Foul in the Air, *JALC* (1989), 927.
17. 94 Stat. 35 (1980). For further details see Olson/Trapani, Who Has Benefited From Regulation of the Airline Industry?, *Journal of Law & Economics* (Vol. 24, April 1981), 75.
18. 49 USG app. § 1551 (c) and (d).
19. See in detail Kark, *The Liberalization of European Civil Aviation and the Competition Act of European Community* (Frankfurt, 1989), 23 et seq.
20. See Knibb, 'DOT hails deregulation "success"', *Airline Business (*April 1990), 16.
21. An 'independent expert commission for pulling down of market-adverse regulations'. Members of the Commission are, among others, Basedow, Donges, Ewers and Sievert.
22. Volume VIII No. 236.
23. The same opinion has been stated by Ebke/Wittman, *ibid.*, 967.

1. Number of Airlines

In 1978, there were only thirty-six scheduled US airlines. By 1984, their number had increased to 123.[24] As early as 1979, a wave of mergers commenced because the airlines had come to believe that two prerequisites were essential for survival: a certain minimum size and a wide network of domestic routes. Both were possible to achieve by buying up competitors. As a result, the structure of the US market has changed considerably: in 1979, the top nine US airlines held a market share of 'only' 85%. By 1987, the market share of the top eight airlines that dominated the market rose to about 92%.[25] By 1988, the three leading airlines (Texas Air, United Airlines, and American Airlines) operated more than 53% of total airline services.[26]

2. Airports: Hub-and-Spoke Systems

Deregulation also led to changes in the way the market operated: passengers were increasingly carried on connecting rather than direct flights (through the hub-and-spoke system). Though this has brought certain inconveniences[27] for passengers, it has provoked economic advantages for the airlines.[28] However, in many cases this system led to dominance at the hub by one airline: in 1988, in Memphis, Northwest Airlines offered more than 80% of the total passenger and cargo capacity at Memphis, whereas its competitor Delta Airlines had to be content with only 10.7%. At Minneapolis/St. Paul, Northwest jumped from 45% in 1977 to 82% in 1989. At St. Louis, the home base airline TWA held 82.5%

---

24. The number of airlines which came to exist in the meantime was even higher still, as during this period approximately 50% of those airlines operating in 1978 and almost two-thirds of the airlines founded since then had vanished from the market as a result of almost 160 insolvencies and mergers; see Desel, Zehn Jahre Deregulation: Oligopol im US-Luftverkehr, *Lufthansa-Yearbook* (1988), 154.
25. Market shares are calculated on the basis of miles per seat sold.
26. Figures quoted by Desel, *ibid.*, 158 et seq. According to Ebke/Wittmann, *RIW* (1990), 964, the DOT report (see *supra*) shows a similar result: the report stated that the market share held by the five (ten respectively) biggest US airlines was nearly 69 (85%) in 1979, 60 (78%) in 1984 and 74 (94%) in 1988. See also Haanappel, Air Transport Deregulation in Jurisdictions other than the United States, *AASL* (Vol. XIII, 1988), 79/82 et seq.
27. I.e., the necessity to change planes and a longer flight time see Goetz/Dempsey, *JALC* (1989), 951; Ebke/Wittmann, *RIW* (1990), 964. This becomes clear from an example given by the Dempsey report (see *supra*): in 1978 it was possible to fly nonstop from Boston to San Francisco. Nowadays the passenger must take an American Airlines flight via Dallas: instead of flying 2,459 miles nonstop he must accept that the distance has become 24% longer (3,024 miles) and that flight time has increased by 4 hours. Where the fares are calculated by miles flown he must also accept higher fares.
28. Connecting flights will be taken by passengers fed in by a variety of flights, i.e., the market for the connecting flight is independent of the original market for the original flight into the hub. This leads to a higher rate of capacity utilization and consequently a more profitable operation. Furthermore, the hub-and-spoke-system simplifies the planning of aircraft utilization and the performance of routine maintenance work.

(compared to 40% in 1977), followed by the second biggest airline Western Airlines, which offered merely 4.2% of the total passenger capacity.[29] Obviously, there is hardly real competition when the second biggest operator at a hub holds not even 20% of the market share of its competitor. Nevertheless, at some US hubs (e.g., Chicago, Denver, Atlanta, and Dallas/Ft. Worth) there is strong competition, although two airlines, holding almost equal market shares, dominate most of the market.

3. Pricing

Pricing also underwent considerable changes. Between 1978 and 1985 fares went down – compared to a constant dollar rate – by more than 15%. Because of a fierce price war, the share of discount fares rose to such an extent that regular fares became the exception rather than the rule. According to Desel,[30] more than 90% of the revenues in domestic US traffic in 1987 came from discount fares, which on average were 60% cheaper than regular fares. It is obvious that such fares could hardly, if at all, cover the costs. Since then, however, this tendency has not just been brought to a halt, but even reversed: by 1988, the fare per mile had already recovered to the level of 1978, and it has further increased since then. Nowadays the average fare per mile is 2.6% higher than it was before deregulation. Meier[31] stated that the US fares war was fought on the backs of airline employees, whose wages were cut drastically: the wages of all employees, paid by the (then) eight biggest airlines, are said to have decreased by 33% between 1978 and 1984.

4. Airline Safety

One significant result of US deregulation was the impact it had on airline safety, which has been described in the Dempsey report[32] as follows:

- The average age of aircraft went up by 21% from 10.3 years (in 1979) to 12.5 years (in 1988). More than 50% of the aircraft used in the US were 16 or more years old.
- The experience of the responsible pilots had itself diminished: in 1983 a pilot could be first used as a captain after an average of 2,300 flight hours. The threshold was reduced in 1988 on 800 flight hours. While in 1983 only 2% of the captains had less than 2,000 flight hours experience, this percentage was already 14% in 1988.
- Maintenance costs were reduced: in 1977 they accounted for 13% of total expenses, while in 1982 they went down to 8%. In 1988 they reached 11%. It should also be borne in mind that the costs of maintenance rise by about 2% for every year an aircraft ages.

29. Figures quoted by Desel, *ibid.*, 159.
30. *Ibid.*, 161.
31. At: Gröner, *Regulierung und Wettbewerb im europäischen Luftverkehr*, 62.
32. See also the summary at Dempsey, *AASL* (1989), 21/29 et seq.

- The average number of ground mechanics per aircraft was reduced by 2% from 19 (in 1982) to 17 (in 1987). Considering that the aircraft used keep growing older (see above), and for this reason need more maintenance and repair work, this trend is particularly disquieting.
- The number of near misses has increased continuously since 1982: in 1982 there were 311, but five years later there were 1058.

Despite an increasing level of air transport, neither the number of air traffic controllers nor the number of inspectors at the aviation authorities has visibly increased. This makes it difficult to maintain the safety standards that had been achieved in the US before deregulation.

After a press release,[33] the US government also requested the American airlines to convert the 1,368 older airplanes to the newest safety standards by mid 1994.

Thus, even if it were correct that, today, passengers are offered more flights at lower fares, it is arguable that this advantage is counteracted by considerable and serious disadvantages.[34] US legislators, recognizing the problems connected with the high concentration, introduced a number of bills to animate the competition, which was decreasing again with the shrinking number by competing airline companies. So have, by the way, the restrictions in the sale of route rights (approved by the DOT after examining the appropriateness of the price), slots, and gates at airports (at the discretion of the DOT to give advantage to an offer by which to enhance competition) been proposed.[35] For Computerized Reservation Systems (CRS), the contract duration should be limited to a maximum of a year, and it is prohibited for operators to prevent travel agencies to use other systems. Furthermore, it should be permissible for passengers to transfer non-refundable tickets to another person.

5. Substantial Ownership and Effective Control

The traditional concepts of ownership and effective control of air carriers were set up first at the beginning of 1926 when the Air Commerce Act of the United States sets out the requirement that at least 51% of the equity with voting rights remain in the hands of citizens of that country, and that two-third of the executive management be composed of US citizens.

Many reasons were cited as bases for this provision, including, military, economic, and political ones. The Civil Aeronautic Act of 1938 was even more

33. *Handelsblatt* (Trade Journal) of 10 Jun. 1991, 1.
34. Deregulation which has taken place in other States is not considered here. On this see Donato, *RBDA* (South America: 1989), 18; Fitzgerald, *AASL* (Canada: 1989), 47; Petsikas, *Airline deregulation and competition in the Canadian air transport industry today, and prospects for the future* (Thesis McGill, 1989); Haanappel, *AASL* (New Zealand, Australia and Canada, 1988), 79/89.
35. See Bill HR 2074 of the delegated by the Congress 'chief star' ('*New Airline Competition Enhancement Act*').

demanding: 75% in the equity and, as members of the management, the President plus two-thirds of the members of upper management shall be US citizens. Later, the same requirements were maintained in the Federal Aviation Act of 1958.

Despite efforts of the US DOT to lower these requirements through Congress, as well as the terms of the Atlantic Agreement signed with the European Commission, no modifications were made.

III. LIBERALIZATION IN THE EUROPEAN COMMUNITY

A. The Influence of European Law

The immediate legal initiative towards present changes in Europe came from the Treaty for the establishment of the European Economic Community[36] (EEC Treaty; later EC Treaty, now TFEU[37]).

1. The Provisions Relevant to Air Transport

The principal provisions of the Treaty on the Functioning of the European Union (TFEU) that are relevant to air transport are Articles 90 et seq. (Title VI Transport), and Articles 101 et seq. (Title VII Common Rules on Competition, Taxation and Approximation of Laws, Chapter 1 Rules on Competition, Section 1 Rules Applying to Undertakings).

Articles 90 et seq. concern the adoption by the Member States of a common transport policy, while Articles 101 et seq. prohibit undertakings from making anti-competition agreements and participating in concerted practices (Article 101), and from abusing a dominant position (Article 102).

According to Article 100, paragraph 1 the provisions concerning a common transport policy (Articles 90 et seq.) apply only to transport by rail, road, and inland waterways. Since the European air transport industry had traditionally been subject to a number of multilateral and bilateral agreements,[38] it was not possible for the Member States to adopt a common aviation policy without violating those agreements. Therefore, Article 100, paragraph 2 leaves it to the European Parliament and the Council to decide whether, to what extent, and by what procedure appropriate provisions may be laid down for (sea and) air transport. This means, among other things, that the decision whether there should be a common transport policy at all was not taken by the TFEU, but was left to the European Parliament and the Council.

36. EEC Treaty of 25 Mar. 1957 (*BGBl.* 1957 II 766, corrected 1678, and 1958 II, 64), came into force on 1 Jan. 1958, publication on 27 Dec. 1957 (*BGBl.* 1958 II). See in detail about the *Ordinance on transport markets in the European Community* in Basedow, *ibid.* Art. 9.

37. TFEU (*OJ* No. C 83 of 30 March 2008, 47).

38. In particular the Chicago Convention of 7 Dec. 1944, 15 *UNTS*. 295, *BGBl.* 1956 II, 411 besides numerous bilateral air services agreements, in which a strict division of the capacities was arranged without exception.

For some time, various interest groups promoted the opinion that Article 80, paragraph 2 EC Treaty (now, 100, paragraph 2 TFEU) referred to the EC Treaty as a whole. If this were correct, it would have meant in particular that the competition rules of Articles 81 et seq. EC Treaty (now, 101 et seq. TFEU) could not automatically have been applied to air transport but only upon the express, and indeed, unanimous decision of (the European Parliament and) the Council (see Article 80, paragraph 2 EC Treaty; now, 100, paragraph 2 TFEU in connection with Article 71, paragraph 1 EC Treaty; now, 91, paragraph 2 TFEU). Another, even more restrictive, opinion held Articles 74 et seq. EC Treaty (now 94 et seq. TFEU) to be an independent part of the Treaty to which the other provisions should not apply at all. Such commentators pointed to the fact that the Treaty did not speak of a common market with respect to air transport (as it did, for instance in the case of agriculture), but only of a common transport policy.[39]

On the one hand, the consideration that the universality principle is the basis for the EC Treaty/TFEU speaks against this opinion. This principle requires that aviation be integrated with the other industries.[40] Moreover, from a systematic law point of view, it should be considered that Article 100, paragraph 2 TFEU (formerly, 80, paragraph 2 EC Treaty) is the concluding clause of Articles 90 et seq. TFEU (formerly, 70 et seq. EC Treaty) and thus of the Title VI TFEU, whose Title VII begins with Articles 101 et seq. (formerly, 81 et seq. EC Treaty). It goes without saying that in all other respects Article 100, paragraph 2 TFEU (formerly, 80, paragraph 2 EC Treaty) is to be considered in connection with Article 100, paragraph 1 TFEU (formerly, 80, paragraph 1 EC Treaty). There, it is expressed by the wording 'on the strength/grounds' of Articles 90 et seq. TFEU (formerly, 70 et seq. EC Treaty). Thus, the Commission of the EC has always supported the view that the reservation of Article 100, paragraph 2 TFEU (formerly, 80, paragraph 2 EC Treaty) refers exclusively to the provisions of the special Title: Transport in Articles 90 et seq. TFEU (formerly, 70 et seq. EC Treaty), and therefore the general provisions are directly applicable to aviation.[41]

The European Court of Justice (ECJ) put an end to this quarrel in its 'French Seamen Decision'[42] by stating that Article 84, paragraph 2 EEC Treaty (now, 100, paragraph 2 TFEU) by no means excluded the applicability of the Treaty to sea and air transport.

---

39. See, e.g., Wohlfahrt, at: Wohlfahrt/Everling/Glaesner/Sprung, EEC, *Comment on the Treaty* (Frankfurt, 1960), Art. 74 para. 4.
40. See, e.g., Ipsen, *European Community Law* (Tübingen, 1972), 867 et seq.; Stabenow, 'The International Factors in Air Transport under the Treaty Establishing the European Economic Community', *Journal of Air Law and Commerce* 33 (1967), 117 et seq.
41. Memorandum (of the Commission) on the Interpretation and Application of the EEC Treaty to Sea Transport and Aviation from 12 Nov. 1960, in *European Parliament, meeting documents 1961–1962*, doc. 4, appendix II; see also Rehm, The Treatment of Aviation in the European Community – The EC on the way to a single policy of Air Transport, *ZLW* (1985), 201.
42. ECJ of 4 Apr. 1974, *Commission of the European Communities v. The Republic of France*, C-167/73, ECR (1974), 359; aff'd European Court of Justice of 12 Oct. 1978, *Commission of the European Communities v. The Kingdom of Belgium*, C-156/77, ECR (1978), I-1881.

However, the Council did not take the logical step of beginning to build the foundations for a common air transport policy. Various proposals of the Commission either provoked no response or were postponed from one meeting of the Council to the next.[43] For this reason, the European Parliament accused the Council in 1983 of inactivity of this question (after Article 232, paragraph 1 EC Treaty; formerly, 175, paragraph 1 EEC Treaty, now, Article 265 TFEU). This inactivity accusation had an essential result: The ECJ convicted the Council of its inactivity in introducing freedom of the service and the possibility of intra-European cabotage. However, the Court did not prescribe a period of time for the implementation.[44] According to the 'master plan' on transport policy that it had adopted in 1985, the Council aimed to accomplish the realization of the freedom to provide services in the transport field within seven years.[45]

2. The Beginnings of Action by the EEC Institutions

a. The First Memorandum of the Commission (1979) and the First Legislation

Prompted by the judgment of the ECJ, the Commission stated its point of view in a memorandum (on 4 July 1979) on a future air transport policy.[46] The foremost objective of this memorandum was to start a discussion about the terms of a common European air transport policy. It was followed by proposals regarding tariffs, interregional air services, and the application of competition rules to the air transport sector. The proposal regarding regional services was adopted in 1983, but in a rather diluted form.[47] Although this did not result in a bigger change, it was the first breakthrough in which common rules were introduced for market access. Independent from bilateral agreements, airlines of Member States were granted limited rights of access to the markets of other Member States.

According to the First Memorandum, the various activities named in Article 3 of the EEC Treaty were intended to effect the realization of the objectives set out in Article 2. One of these objectives is the promotion of a harmonious development of economic activities, and one of the activities by which that should be achieved is

---

43. See, e.g., Basedow, 'Der europäische Verkehrsmarkt als Rechtsproblem' (The European Transport Market as a legal Problem), *TranspR*, H. 11/12 (1989), 403/403; Krauss, 'Possibilities and Limits of a Common Transport Policy of the European Community', *ZVerkWiss* 47 (1976): 122 et seq.; Ebke/Wenglorz, 'Die zweite Stufe der Liberalisierung des Linienverkehrs in der EG: Open Skies in Europa?' (The Second Stage of the Liberalization of the Scheduled Air Traffic in the EC: Open Skies in Europe?), *RIW* 36 (1990), 468, 470.
44. ECJ, seg. 1985, 1513/1600 et seq.
45. See in detail Ebke/Wenglorz, *ibid.*, 471.
46. Contributions of the European Communities to the development of aviation – Memorandum of the Commission, Document COM (79) 311 final, published in *Bulletin of the European Communities*, Appendix 5/79 (hereinafter: First Memorandum); as to the development see also Haanappel, *AL* (1989),122 et seq.
47. Directive of the Council of 25 Jul. 1983 concerning the approval of interregional scheduled air services for the transport of passengers, mail and cargo between EEC countries (83/416/EEC).

the institution of a system ensuring that competition is not disturbed. Therefore, in the air transport industry, the aim would be to build up a network of intra-EEC air routes free of national limitations on market access, which would be able to offer all its customers useful and efficient services at the most reasonable prices possible. For this purpose, low tariffs should be made widely available, and restrictions upon market access reduced both for existing as well as for newly founded airlines.

The Commission conceded that full freedom of market access could be realized only in the long term, whereas a more flexible tariff system could be created right away. The same applied to the introduction of new scheduled flights. To secure the observance of the competition rules, which were part of the general provisions of the Treaty, the Council would have to adopt a regulation for the application of these rules.[48] Besides the Council Directive mentioned above concerning the authorization of interregional scheduled air services, the following further legislation was adopted in the initial stages:

- The Council Directive of 20 December 1979 on the limitation of noise emissions from subsonic aircraft (80/51/EEC).[49]
- The Council Resolution of 20 December 1979 setting up a consultation procedure for the relations between Member States and other countries in the field of air transport and for action relating to such matters within international organizations (80/50/EEC).[50]
- The Council Directive of 16 December 1980 on future cooperation and mutual assistance between the Member States in the field of air accident investigation (80/1266/EEC).[51]
- The Council Recommendation of 13 July 1981 on the carriage of express low-weight cargo by air.[52]

b. The Commission's Second Memorandum (1984)

The Commission left the bilateral system basically unchanged in its Second Memorandum[53] of 15 March 1984. Furthermore, the governments' control of their own airlines was left unaffected. The memorandum tried to define the main anticompetitive factors of this system.

The following examples were cited: the necessity of double approval of tariffs; the requirement of tariff coordination between two reciprocal carriers; capacity control; and control of market access rights and diplomatic intervention to protect airlines against adverse economic effects. In the Second Memorandum, the

48. First Memorandum, 23.
49. *OJ* No. L 18 of 24 Jan. 1980, 26.
50. *OJ* No. L 18 of 24 Jan. 1980, 24.
51. *OJ* No. L 375 of 31 Dec. 1980, 32.
52. *OJ* No. L 203 of 23 Jul. 1981, 51.
53. *Commission of the European Communities, Civil Aviation Memorandum No. 2*: Progress on the Way towards a common Aviation Policy, *Doc. COM (84) 72 final.*

Commission also made several concrete proposals for a future framework for air transport. With regard to tariffs, it suggested leaving the calculation of tariffs to the airlines themselves – within certain limits, so that the airlines were able to adjust their prices to new competitive situations and demands.

c. *The Asjes Case (Nouvelles Frontières) (1986)*

The *Nouvelles Frontières* decision[54] of the ECJ was a decisive breakthrough for European air law: the court found that the provisions on competition in the EEC Treaty are to be applied, in principle, in their entirety to air transport as well, and, therefore, all previous procedures on the agreement of aviation fares stood in contradiction to the EEC Treaty.

The essential statement of this judgment is the observation of the ECJ that the Council, despite a corresponding proposal on the part of the Commission (especially in the Second Memorandum), disloyally did not enact the necessary implementation rules in the sense of 83 EC Treaty (now, Article 103 TFEU) for the application of the competition rules. The Court of Justice explained then that, on grounds of legal certainty, the competition rules could become predictable and equally applied only if the measures of the authorities of the Member States or the Commission according to 84 EC Treaty (now, Article 104 TFEU) and 85 EC Treaty (now, Article 105) of the Treaty were met.

The *Asjes* decision put instruments in the hands of General Directorate 'Competition' of the Commission (DG IV) to enforce the competition rules of the EEC Treaty also in the field of air traffic. This had been introduced already under Commissioner Peter Sutherland and was continued by Sir Leon Brittan – very much to the displeasure of General Directorate 'Transport' (DG VII), that itself, under the management of Commissioner Stanley Clinton-Davis and also under his successor Karel van Miert, worried, just the same, much about industrial, political, and traffic interests.

d. *The Single European Act (1987)*

The Single European Act, which came into force on 7 July 1987, amending and supplementing the EEC Treaty,[55] provided for the realization of the internal market within the EEC. Air transport is not excluded from this. Furthermore, the Council need no longer make decisions unanimously; a qualified majority is sufficient (Article 16 SEA).

---

54. Judgment of the ECJ of 30 Apr. 1986, *Ministère Public v. Asjes et al.*, joined C-209 to C-213/84, *ECR* (1986), I-1425; see also the review by Adenauer-Frowein, *ZLW* (1986), 193 et seq.; Sedemund/Montag, *NJW* (1986), 2146; Guillaume, *RFDA (*1987), 193 et seq.; Karte, 124 et seq.
55. Common European Act of 28 Feb. 1986, *OJ* No. L 169 of 29 Jun. 1987, 1.

e. *The Ahmed Saeed Case (1989)*

With this judgment,[56] which was delivered on a reference from the First Civil Division of the German Federal Court of Justice (*Bundesgerichtshof* [BGH]) of 30 January 1986,[57] the ECJ made another decision on the application of the competition rules to air transport. Before the judgment, on 14 December 1987, the Council had adopted several pieces of legislation aimed at liberalizing air transport between EEC Member States and promoting competition. Those regulations had some influence upon the judgment.

In detail, the Court of Justice declared:

(1) Pursuant to Article 101, paragraph 2 TFEU (formerly, Article 81, paragraph 2 EC Treaty), bilateral and multilateral agreements on airline tariffs are automatically void:
   - insofar as they concern tariffs for flights between airports in one and the same Member State or between one such airport and an airport in a non-EEC State, either where the authorities of the Member State in which one of the airlines involved has its principal place of business have – in accordance with Article 101 TFEU (formerly, 81 EC Treaty) – declared the agreement incompatible with Article 101 TFEU (formerly, 81 EC Treaty), or where the Commission has declared incompatibility with Article 104 TFEU (formerly, 84 EC Treaty) pursuant to Article 105 TFEU (formerly, 85 EC Treaty);
   - insofar as they concern tariffs for international flights between airports in EEC countries, where no application in accordance with Article 5 of Regulation No. 3975/87 for exemption from the prohibition of Article 101, paragraph 1 TFEU (formerly, Article 81, paragraph 1 EC Treaty) has been submitted to the Commission, or where such application has been made, but has met with a negative response from the Commission within ninety days after publication of the application in the *Official Journal*, or where the period of ninety days has expired without a response from the Commission but the six years' period of validity of the exemption as provided by Article 5 has expired or where the Commission has set aside the exemption within this period.

(2) The application of tariffs to scheduled flights on the basis of bilateral or multilateral agreements may constitute – in certain circumstances:
   - abuse of a dominant position on the market concerned, particularly if an undertaking in a dominant position has succeeded in imposing on other

56. ECJ, of 11 Apr. 1989, *Ahmed Saeed Flight Tours and Silver Line Travel Agency v. Central office for combating unfair competition*, C-66/86, *ECR* (1989), 803; or *ZLW* (1989), 124 (with remarks by Mölls); or *ETL* (1989), 229; see also Balfour, *AL* (1990), 237/243 et seq.
57. *NJW* (1986), 1432.

airlines the application of excessively high, or excessively low, tariffs or the exclusive application of only one tariff on a certain route.

(3) Article 10 EC Treaty and 86 EC Treaty (now, 106 TFEU) are to be interpreted to the effect that:
   - they prohibit the national authorities from encouraging the conclusion of tariff agreements contravening Article 81, paragraph 1 EC Treaty (now, Article 101, paragraph 1 TFEU) or 82 EC Treaty (now, Article 102 TFEU);
   - they preclude the approval of tariffs resulting from such agreements by the national authorities;
   - they do not preclude a limitation of the effects of the competition rules insofar as it is indispensable for the performance of a task of general interest which airlines are required to carry out, provided that the nature of this task as well as its effects on the tariff structure are clearly established.

Mölls[58] has rightly pointed out that aside from these immediate legal consequences, the judgment will probably cause the EEC States to examine their bilateral air service agreements for terms contravening the competition rules established by the EEC Treaty, and which for this reason would be incompatible with their duties under Articles 5 and 90.

It also prohibits them, namely, to maintain measures that could eliminate the practical effectiveness of the competition regulations. For the price competition in air transport, this could be the most important consequence of the judgment.

B. The Three 'Liberalization Packages'

1. The First Package (December 1987)

On 14 December 1987, the Council of the European Communities adopted several legal instruments intended to achieve a liberalization of air transport between the members of the Community over a period of three years and to promote competition. These instruments are listed below:

- Regulation No. 3975/87 laying down the procedure for the application of the rules on competition to undertakings in the air transport sector.[59]
- Regulation No. 3976/87 on the application of Article 85, paragraph 3 of the Treaty to certain categories of agreements and concerted practices in the air transport sector.[60]
- Directive 87/601 on fares for scheduled air services between Member States.[61]

---

58. Mölls, *Europäischer Gerichtshof, Urteil vom 11. April 1989 (Rechtssache 66/86). 'Wettbewerb – Flugtarife', ZLW (1989),* 142 et seq. ((It is German text and in the German language 'is used instead of the English'))
59. *OJ* No. L 374 of 31 Dec. 1987, 1.
60. *OJ* No. L 374 of 31 Dec. 1987, 9.
61. *OJ* No. L 374 of 31 Dec. 1987, 12.

- Decision 87/602 on the sharing of passenger capacity between air carriers and scheduled air services between Member States and on access for air carriers to scheduled air service routes between Member States.[62]

The First Package's provisions on fares (in Fares Directive 87/601) did not remove all restrictions of competition, but introduced a scheme of fare zones, within which the airlines were to be allowed to act freely. Only regular fares still needed approval; the airlines were free to set discount fares provided the fares proposed lay within one of the so-called zones of flexibility (discount zone: 90% to 50% of the regular fare as a reference figure; deep-discount zone: 65% to 45% of the regular fare), and provided they met certain conditions such as advance reservation, no change of reservation without paying an extra fee, and so on. This means that discount fares could not be offered (without approval) for all kinds of flight reservations.

By the first package of measures, further principles were prescribed for orienting the fares[63] and especially the obligation to orient the fares at the average prices on a certain route (reference prices). Furthermore, it removed the legal obligation to coordinate fares with the reciprocal carrier; perhaps, nevertheless, the agreements being made must comply with the rules of Council Regulation No. 3976/87, Article 4, paragraph 1. Furthermore, the First Package restricted the scope of the pools and liberalized the access to routes between a hub and a region as well as between regions, however, with the exception of Israel, North Italy, and Spain.

2. The Second Package (November 1990)

The second package continued the way to liberalization:

a. Fares

The Commission had proposed, with regard to flights within the Community, to introduce the more liberal system of double disapproval for the introduction of all fares.[64] This system, which had already been adopted by some EEC Countries, is simpler and, therefore, enables quicker decisions, since the proposed fares were considered approved if neither of both aviation authorities involved had notified the applicant airline of its disapproval and the reasons for it. After vehement objection by several aviation associations and the European Parliament,[65] the Council refrained from immediately introducing the system of double disapproval

62. *OJ* No. L 374 of 31 Dec. 1987, 19.
63. See Kramer, *EuZW* (1991), 16 for the until then usual fare formation by the airlines and the corresponding regulations of the bilateral air traffic agreements which the multilateral IATA agreements on fares usually take as a base.
64. See Art. 4, para. 3 of the Commission's Proposal of 8 Sept. 1989 (COM (89), 373 final, printed in *OJ* No. C 258 of 11 Oct. 1989, 4.
65. See also the Visser-Report, *ibid.*, 38.

for all fares within the EEC, and instead stated its intention to adopt this system with effect from 1 January 1993.

The system for regulating fares established by Council Regulation No. 2342/90 of 24 July 1990[66] was a hybrid system: the system of double disapproval was applied to certain fares,[67] to others the concept of double approval applied,[68] and within the so-called zones of flexibility that of automatic approval.[69] Fare setting in general was made more flexible[70] than it had been[71] by the introduction of three fare zones based on the economy fare (as the reference fare): zone 1 (normal economy fare: 105% to 95% of the reference fare), zone 2 (discount zone: 94% to 80%), and zone 3 (deep-discount zone: 79% to 30%), for which the conditions were eased considerably. In principle, the fares continue to be subject to approval by the Member States involved (Article 4, paragraph 1), but on the other hand, the authorities, provided certain conditions are satisfied, must allow airlines to set fares as they wish within the flexibility zones (Article 4, paragraph 3a). This has been called 'automatic approval'.

Finally, pursuant to Article 3, paragraph 5, Member States were allowed to permit an airline of another Member State, operating a direct scheduled air service, to match prices already offered by a charter airline, provided that both services were equivalent in terms of quality and conditions. This clause had its origin in demands by the southern EEC Countries – particularly Spain – which wanted to have a greater share of the yearly tourist traffic between north and south. In the medium term, this has speeded up the blurring of the distinction between scheduled and charter services.

b. Access to the Market and Sharing of Capacity

Market access for EEC airlines and the sharing of seating capacities in scheduled air traffic was further liberalized by Council Regulation No. 2343/90 of 24 July 1990,[72] which replaced the preceding Decision 87/602. It also replaced Regulation No. 83/416 concerning interregional scheduled air services for which there is now no separate regime. This resulted from the fact that liberalization of access in accordance with Regulation No. 2343/90 (Articles 4 and 8) was not dependent on any conditions concerning the categories of airports concerned.

---

66. *OJ* No. L 217 of 11 Aug. 1990, 1.
67. In case of more than 105% of the reference fare (see Art. 4, para. 4).
68. To fares outside the zones of flexibility.
69. See Art. 4, para. 3.
70. However, sooner or later this higher flexibility may lead to restrictions on the exchange ability of flight tickets. So-called interline agreements (mutual acceptance of flight documents) may become more difficult to implement and enforce, and as a result passengers' freedom of movement may be impaired.
71. See *supra* para. 4 and Regulation No. 87/601/EEC which was set aside at the same time.
72. *OJ* No. L 217 of 11 Aug. 1990, 8.

In the Preamble, it had been pointed out that the establishment of bilateral capacity sharing was not compatible with the principles of the inner market and, therefore, the limitations in such bilateral agreements should be reduced gradually.

i. Access to the Market

By the so-called Fifth Freedom, the traffic between two transport airports lying in two different European States under certain conditions/requirements could be increased from 30% to 50% of the seasonal capacity of the previous year (Article 8). However, contrary to the proposal of the EC Commission, the Fifth Freedom traffic could take no price leadership (Article 3, paragraph 6).

The Regulation applied neither for the demand air traffic, nor for the freight traffic, for which at a later time a special regulation should be made.

ii. Multiple Designation

The circumstances in which a Member State had to accept the designation of more than one airline of another Member State have been increased, compared with the circumstances established by the First Package: in accordance with Article 6, multiple designation was to be accepted, as from 1 January 1991, if there were more than 140,000 (previously 180,000) passengers, or more than 800 (previously 1,000) return flights on a specific route per year. As from 1 January 1992, the thresholds had been lowered to 100,000 passengers or 600 flights.

iii. Sharing of Capacity

The First Package had provided for obligatory permissible capacity shares of 55%:45% until 30 September 1989, and 60%:40% from 1 October 1989.[73] Since 1 November 1990 it had been possible for each Member State to increase the share of capacity offered by its airlines, as compared to the capacity offered by airlines from another Member State by 7.5% compared to the previous corresponding season, provided that each Member State is entitled to a minimum share of 60% in any case (Article 11, paragraph 1). Thus, since November 1990, it had been possible for a Member State to reach 67.5%, and from November 1991 a proportion of 75%: 25% was possible. In cases in which there had been adequate reason (Article 12, paragraphs 1 and 2), the Commission could, upon application of one of the Member States, limit the permissible increase in capacity for the relevant bilateral partner to a percentage below 7.5% (Article 12, paragraph 2). The EEC Commission expected stronger impulses on competition to come from this rise in capacity limits.

In addition, an innovation promotion clause was introduced. It enabled a Member State to grant an airline two years of protection for passenger flights not exceeding a seating capacity of eighty seats on routes connecting two regional airports, by not obliging the Member State to give its approval to a reciprocal carrier unless this carrier also intended to employ an aircraft with not more than

73. See Art. 3, paras 1 and 2 of 87/602/EEC.

eighty seats, or if the route is only one leg of a connection and not more than eighty seats were offered to the customers.

iv. Exceptions

The Regulation did not apply either to cargo services, for which a special regulation had been adopted, or to charter flights. As to the latter, the Preamble stated that it is necessary to take measures to alleviate the impact of charter traffic on the opportunities of airlines of those Member States that were a destination of charter traffic, but that any measures taken should limit or regulate charter traffic.

Article 1 contained provisions whereby the application of the Regulation were suspended or temporarily excluded with respect to the airports of Gibraltar,[74] Porto, the Greek Islands, and the Atlantic Islands forming the Azores. On the other hand, the exceptions made by Article 6, paragraph 2 of Decision 87/602 in favour of certain airports in Spain, Italy, Denmark, and Ireland have been withdrawn.

c. *No Regulations on Charter Traffic*

The reason why the Second Package did not apply to charter services was that charter traffic services have always been characterized by strong competition and had already been substantially liberalized. Obviously, the Commission saw no need for regulation at that moment.

The policy of (temporary) non-regulation of charter services should only be continued so long as it did not bring about discrimination against charter services in favour of scheduled services. There had been already some danger of this: charter airlines, which were not allowed to transport mail and cargo,[75] either were not allowed to, or only to a limited extent,[76] sell seats to the final customer. These seats, however, although available to all interested passengers, were not displayed on the CRS, because these systems showed scheduled air services only. If the charter carriers were given access to the reservation systems, the demand for passenger services could be satisfied much better than before – to the advantage of the passengers. It, therefore, seemed desirable that the Commission should consider whether the CRS Code of Conduct should be applicable to charter services as well.

3. The Necessity of Supporting Measures

Various forecasts expected a rapid development of air traffic within the last years of the twentieth century: the German Research Institute for Aerospace (*Deutsche Forschungsanstalt für Luft- und Raumfahrt* [DLR]) expected the volume of air

74. See C-298/89 – *Gibraltar v. Council* (*ECR* 1993), I-3605 for Gibraltar's challenge to this suspension.
75. This use of significant dead capacity could help to reduce costs.
76. As a rule, 15% of the seating capacity.

transport to double – compared to 1986 – by the turn of the millennium.[77] A doubling[78] or even a tripling of passenger demand by the turn of the millennium was also expected by the aerospace industry.

As airspace and airports in Europe are already considerably congested, European air transport will be faced with serious problems, if not collapse,[79] in the near future. The causes of the problems will then lie in the inadequacy of the regulation of air traffic control in European airspace and the lack of capacity at large international airports, whose expansion has been rendered almost impossible by lack of space or public opposition. Within recent years, the European Parliament has made several constructive proposals. The Association of European Airlines (AEA) published a report on the extension or revival of European air traffic control. Unfortunately, with the introduction of the necessary proposals with regard to the planned completion of the Internal Market, the Council (of the Ministers of Transport) as well as the governments of the EC Member States have allowed no serious activities to be realized.[80]

A sound development of air transport in a liberalized market requires not only a solution to the problems mentioned above, but also supporting social[81] and technical measures. On the one hand, this enables free exchange of aircraft and spare parts as well as of maintenance work and, on the other hand, a uniform training system enables exchange of personnel and, thus, a greater freedom of movement and flexibility of aircrews. At the same time, this ensures, at least to some extent, that no 'social dumping' takes place and that the established air safety standards are maintained. Thus, the Commission presented proposals and drafts concerning related subjects that were mentioned in its September 1989 communication.[82] Those proposals concerned the following particular subjects:

- denied boarding compensation;
- the licensing of persons employed in air traffic, particularly pilots and air-traffic controllers;
- flight duty time limits;
- minimum safety and social standards;
- standards of airworthiness; and
- a code of conduct for the allocation of slots at airports.

77. See Usster, *Lufthansa-yearbook* 1990, 40; see also the study of the planning Bureau of the Airspace Users *'The Crisis of the European Air Safety'* (1989), 17.
78. See Wilken, *Lufthansa-yearbook* (1990), 154 (on the basis of 1987).
79. According to a report which the American Stanford Research Institute (SRI) made at the request of IATA, European air traffic is threatened with collapse by the end of the 1990s at the latest, unless remedial measures are taken imminently.
80. For the legal possibilities and urgent necessity of an EC initiative for the reform of the European Air Traffic.
81. Contrary to the opinion of the Trade Unions (see *ÖTV-Report Luftfahrt No. 3* (July 1990), 3) this does not necessarily lead to rising wages, and adjustment of working conditions, to the highest level within the entire EEC! (ÖTV – Gewerkschaft Öffentlicher Dienst, Transport und Verkehr – Former (German) Union of Public Services, Transport and Communications Workers).
82. COM (89) 373 final.

4. Further Steps towards the Internal Market

a. Measures of February 1991

On 17 and 18 December 1990, the Council of the European Communities (comprising, in this case, the Ministers of Transport) met to take another important step towards the liberalization of air transport services: the matters discussed were two proposals of the Commission, one concerning the liberalization of air cargo transport,[83] and the other concerning compensation for denied boarding in connection with scheduled air services.[84] However, the Council merely agreed on these proposals in principle, and the Commission was asked to work out further details. On 4 February 1991, the two proposals were finally adopted by the Council.

The liberalization measures of Regulation (EEC) No. 2343/90[85] were applied to combined passenger and cargo services, but cargo-only air services remained unaffected. A specific regulation was essential, because air cargo services had become an important part of the air transport industry from an economic point of view, and played an important role in the development of economy, particularly of the economies of peripheral EEC States. In the opinion of the Council,[86] some EEC States 'depend heavily on air cargo services for their connections with the rest of the Community'.

The Regulation on the Operation of Air Cargo Services,[87] which came into force on 11 February 1991, was an important step towards liberalization of market access and the setting of rates for these kinds of services. Its principal provisions apply only to Community air cargo carriers. The Council planned to adopt rules for the licensing of air cargo carriers and route licensing within the Community by 1 July 1992. Air cargo carriers should be entitled to operate third, fourth, and fifth freedom services between Member States, provided such carriers would be licensed in another Member State and authorized by such other State to exercise those rights. Fifth freedom rights should only have been granted, however, for a service that would form an extension of an air service from, or a preliminary stage of an air service to, the aircraft's state of registration.[88] To ensure operational flexibility, air cargo carriers should be allowed to combine services and use the

83. COM (90) 63 final: *OJ* No. C 88 of 6 Apr. 1990, 7. As regards the statement of the Bundesrat (Senate of the Federal Parliament representing the German states) see *BR-Drucks. 235/90* of 1 Jun. 1990. The amendment proposals made by the European Parliament have been published in *OJ* No. C 9 of 15 Jan. 1991, 4.
84. COM (90) 99 final, *OJ* No. C 129 of 24 May 1990, 13; as regards the statement made by the Bundesrat in its 319th meeting (21 Sep. 1990) see *EuZw* (1990), 234.
85. *OJ* No. L 217 of 11 Sep. 1990.
86. See recital of Reg. No. 294/91.
87. Council Regulation (EEC) No. 294/91, *OJ* No. L 36 of 8 Feb. 1991, 1
88. Thus, the route London-Paris could be served by an aircraft registered in Germany only if it has been part, e.g., of a Frankfurt-London-Paris or London-Paris-Frankfurt service.

same flight number, and at any point on a route carry out intermediate reloading when this involved one change of aircraft only.

The setting of rates was not subject to any regulation.[89] Freight rates should be agreed freely between Community air cargo carriers and their contractual partners. The Commission did not have a right of disapproval,[90] which was still provided in Article 8, paragraph 4 of the proposal.

On 4 February 1991, a further regulation on a denied boarding compensation in scheduled air transport[91] was adopted, which became effective on 8 April 1991. It established the minimum requirements that are to be stipulated in the rules to be established by the airlines (Article 3, paragraph 1).[92]

b. Authorization of the Commission on Preventive Measures against Anticompetitive Practices

By Council Regulation (EEC) No. 1284/91[93] of 14 May 1991, Article 4a has been inserted into Regulation No. 3972/87,[94] which enabled the Commission to prompt action if it was concerned urgently to prevent or stop anticompetitive practices until a decision was taken in accordance with Article 4, paragraph 1 under the condition that the existence of an air traffic service or the existence of an airline was seriously jeopardized by the anticompetitive practices. On the basis of a changed proposal of the European Parliament,[95] it was specified that the provisional decision taken applies only for six months and only once it could be prolonged by up to a further three months.

Article 1 of Regulation No. 3975/87 EEC, however, limited the scope of this provision to 'international' air traffic, so that Article 4a did not extend to domestic traffic of a Member State.

5. The Third Package (June 1992)

a. The Case History

On 17 July 1991, the Commission submitted drafts of three regulations,[96] with which the third and last phase of the liberalization of air traffic in the European Community (EC) was introduced and by which the EC air transport policy regarding the domestic market should be completed. The proposals included the topics of

89. Thus the proposal of the German Bundesrat in its statement of June 1990 (*BR-Drucks. 235/90 – final*).
90. COM (90) 63 final.
91. Council Regulation (EEC) No. 295/91, *OJ* No. L 36 of 8 Feb. 1991, 5.
92. These had to be available for inspection at travel agencies and at the check-in counters of the airlines (Art. 3, para. 2).
93. *OJ* No. L 122 of 17 May 1991, 2.
94. *OJ* No. L 374 of 31 Dec. 1987, 2.
95. *OJ* No. C 398 of 24 Jan. 1991, 321.
96. COM (91) final; Council document 8207/91.

operating licenses for air carriers, market access, and formation of fares. The system of double disapproval, which had been contained already in the basic structure of the Second Package, was accepted with the regulations on fare formation with some few changes.

The Commission had examined the question under discussion, namely, whether the non-scheduled air services, which in terms of passengers-kilometres had been carrying out 65% of all transportation by air within the Community, had to be safeguarded by special regulations. The Commission was of the opinion that a strong case for establishing two sets of rules did not exist. Therefore, the same rules on operating licenses, market access, and fares (with specific provisions on IT-fares) were attached.[97] According to the Commission's intention, the practice of free pricing for non-scheduled air services and air cargo should not be modified:[98] the automatic approval regime for fares charged in conjunction with Inclusive Tour arrangements (IT fares) or group travel should be kept.[99]

On 24 March 1992, the Council of the Transport Ministers met and agreed on the fundamentals of the suggestions; however, it still demanded the inclusion of certain protection regulations as well as of some changes, and postponed the final decision for the next meeting.[100] On 22 June 1992, the transport ministers of the EC Member States adopted the so-called Third Package of Liberalization. With it the establishment of the Single Aviation Market in Europe was guaranteed. The regulations of the Third Package, which after 1993 entered into force either immediately or gradually, had now been made applicable not only for scheduled but also for charter airlines.

b. *The Third Package (1992) in Detail*

The last step to European liberalization in air transport was taken by means of the third package.

i. Fares

From January 1993 onwards, the EC airlines, on the basis of Regulation No. 2409/92 (EEC),[101] were free to set fares on flights (Article 5, paragraph 1). As long as those fares were economically reasonable, that is, they were not purely dumping prices, they were approved automatically by the government. The principle of double disapproval was given up: the government of a Member State concerned could intervene only if, under the cost situation of the enterprise, a proposed fare was considered either too high or too low.

---

97. See *Official Reasons*, 16 et seq. (18).
98. See page 74 of the *Official Reasons*.
99. See Art. 4 of the draft.
100. The proposed amendments of the European Parliament are in the printed material *PE 160, 903* from 8 Apr. 1992, 35 et seq.
101. *OJ* No. L 240 of 24 Aug. 1992, 15.

Whether a price was too high at the disadvantage of the users was measured on whether, with the fixed prices, the airline, under its economic situation, in particular its fully assigned costs[102] on a long-term basis, could operate at least by covering those costs. Price reductions could be forbidden if the market forces lead to a continuous decline of the airfares, which stood out clearly against seasonal fluctuations, and resulted in extensive losses for the affected air services of all airlines concerned.

If a Member State concerned had objections against a proposed fare, then it had to inform the air carrier and the other government involved about its objections and notify them that the fare was not acceptable. If the matter could not be settled by the involved parties themselves, then there was the possibility to appeal to the European Commission.

Basically, the possibility for free price structuring was not harmless, in particular, for the charter flight companies, because now a better possibility was offered for the scheduled flight companies to adapt or undersell their scheduled airfares to those of charter flight traffic and thus step into the competition in the market segment of vacation air journeys still more directly than so far. One who regards the special fares of the scheduled flight companies critically will have to recognize that, indeed, with Regulation (EEC) 2409/92, a price war was loudly declared on the main routes (in particular to tourist destinations in the US and in the Far East), which persists still today.

The system valid so far for the definition of charter flight fares and freight rates had been maintained. Under Article 3, the seat fares,[103] charter fares,[104] and freight rates could freely be agreed upon on the basis of the agreements between the air transport contract parties. The air companies[105] working in the EC had, upon request, to notify the public about all airfares and standard freight rates (Article 4). Since *airfare* in the sense of Article 2 was only the tariff that the passenger paid to the airline is meant, the publication obligation did not refer to the seat or charter prices.

Only the Community air carriers had been entitled to introduce a 'new product'[106] or fares lower than those existing for identical products (the so-called price leaders) (Article 1, paragraph 3).

ii. Market Access

By Council Regulation No. 2408/92,[107] Community air carriers were permitted by the State(s) concerned to exercise traffic rights on routes within the Community

102. Including an appropriate capital return.
103. I.e., the price which the charter operator (tour operator) paid to the airline (Art. 2, para. b).
104. I.e., the price which the passenger paid to the charter operator (tour operator) (Art. 2, para. c).
105. Thus not only the EC carriers.
106. This term is not defined. It could be understood as marketing instruments such as frequent flyer programmes.
107. *OJ* No. L 240 of 24 Aug. 1992, 8.

(Article 3). Therefore, airlines of EC Member States gained in principle access to each other's internal markets.

However, this right to cabotage (eighth freedom) had come into force unrestrictedly only as of 1 April 1997. Until then, airlines were permitted only 'consecutive' cabotage. This meant that those flights had to originate or end in the home country of the carrier (Article 3). For example, Air France was allowed to operate cabotage between Frankfurt and Berlin, only if the flight originates in a French airport or ends there (so-called consecutive cabotage). In addition, during the transition period, the carrier's service on the domestic route in another EC Country will be limited to 50% of its applicable average seasonal capacity on the primary route (e.g., Paris-Frankfurt). Thus, if Air France offered 20,000 seats between Paris and Frankfurt, it would be allowed a maximum of only 10,000 seats between Frankfurt and Berlin as a domestic service under the (limited) cabotage right. The right of the fifth and seventh freedoms[108] had already been allowed since 1993. Thus, from then on, Lufthansa, for example, could operate between Paris and London without any restriction. However, a British charter carrier such as Monarch Airlines or Britannia, could also operate a flight from London or Frankfurt to Samos/Greece. That could be interesting when not all seats from Great Britain have been sold and, therefore, were supposed to be taken up in the Federal Republic of Germany for the improvement of the passenger seat load factor. Within the seventh freedom, such a carrier could even station an aircraft at Frankfurt to operate services from there directly to Samos.

Under Article 7, two or more Community air carriers were permitted to combine operated air services under the same flight number (code-sharing).

iii. Operating License

Starting 1 January 1993, certain criteria apply, which airlines in commercial air transport have to meet to receive or maintain their operating licenses. Any carrier that meets the specified financial criteria on capital provision[109] and safety standards can receive an operating license pursuant to Regulation No. 2407/92 (EEC),[110] which allows the carrier to operate air services anywhere in the EC Member States. A condition for an operating license is the possession of a valid Air Operator's Certificate.

With it a license for operating leased equipment must be obtained in advance to ensure compliance with safety standards and legal responsibility. Leasing contracts regarding aircraft with crews (wet lease) are possible under special conditions, if the demanded safety requirements (Articles 8 and 10) are fulfilled.

108. This freedom allows an airline from one country to operate services between two other countries without any connecting flight to its home country.

109. Exception was made for carriers with aircraft of less than 20 tons maximum take-off weight and/or less than 20 seats.

110. *OJ* No. L 240 of 24 Aug. 1992, 1.

C. Further Measures in 1992

1. The European Economic Area Treaty

The European Economic Area (EEA) Treaty,[111] signed on 2 May 1992, covering seventeen nations, created a single Free Trading Zone. The Treaty incorporated the twelve EC Member States and five States of the European Free Trade Association (EFTA). As a result of the referendum of 6 December 1992, in which the Swiss voted not to join the EEA, Switzerland was unable to ratify the Treaty.[112] This delayed the planned implementation of the Treaty for some time.

Certain existing EC legislation, including the Second Package and rules on competition and State aid, was specifically referred to in the Treaty and became part of the law of each EEA State. These were Council Regulation No. 3975/87[113] implementing the competition rules; Commission Regulation No. 4261/88[114] on complaints, applications, and hearing; Council Regulation No. 2299/89[115] on a code of conduct for CRS; Council Regulation No. 2342/90[116] on fares; Council Regulation No. 2343/90[117] on access and capacity; Council Regulation No. 294/91[118] on cargo services; Council Directive 80/1266[119] on air accident investigation; Council Decision 80/50[120] on a consultation procedure regarding relations between Member States and third countries; and Council Regulation No. 295/91[121] on denied boarding compensation. The Second Package, therefore, had come into force with the EEA Treaty.

Any new EC legislation drawn up after 2 May 1992 had to be discussed in the EEA Joint Committee.[122] No decision should be made by the Council before a consultation and a decision of the Joint Committee. Such a decision was binding on the EEA States. Thus, the Third Package required a decision as described above.

111. *OJ* No. L 1 of 3. Jan. 1994, 3.
112. It is, however, possible that a separate air transport agreement between the EC and Switzerland containing the air transport elements of the EEA Treaty could be drawn up.
113. *OJ* No. L 374 of 31 Dec. 1987, 1.
114. *OJ* No. L 376 of 31 Dec. 1988, 10.
115. *OJ* No. L 220 of 29 Jul. 1989, 1.
116. *OJ* No. L 217 of 11 Aug. 1990, 1.
117. *OJ* No. L 217 of 11 Aug. 1990, 8.
118. *OJ* No. L 36 of 8 Feb. 1991, 1.
119. *OJ* No. L 375 of 31. Dec. 1980, 32.
120. *OJ* No. L 18 of 24 Jan. 1980, 24.
121. *OJ* No. L 36 of 8 Feb. 1991, 5.
122. It consisted of representatives of the seventeen EEA States. The office of the President was to alternate every six months between the Commission and a representative of the EFTA States.

2. The Agreement between EEC and Norway and Sweden

On 12 June 1990,[123] the European Parliament invited the Council to authorize the Commission to negotiate with the EFTA States,[124] first of all with Norway and Sweden, as Denmark, a partner of the Scandinavian aviation consortium SAS, was already an EC Member State.[125] By its decision of 18 June 1990, the Council authorized the Commission to open negotiations with Norway and Sweden using as a basis the negotiating directives drafted for the purpose of the negotiations between the Community and the EFTA States.

At its meeting on 26 March 1992 in Brussels, the Council accepted the integration of Norway and Sweden into the EC aviation regulations. Anticipating the EEA Agreement, the Council adopted on 22 June 1992 the Agreement between the EEC and the Kingdoms of Norway and Sweden by order of the Community.

The Agreement was structured in six chapters, an Annex and three Protocols. Chapter I dealt with the scope of the Agreement and established that the *acquis communautaires* and interpretation of the Court of Justice of the European Communities and of the Commission should be applicable. The next chapter contained a transcription of the competition article of the Treaty. Chapter III created the rights for the Commission to implement the competition articles and the Regulations and Directives that formed part of the *acquis* directly in Norway and Sweden. The following chapter established a Joint Committee and spelled out its tasks. It contained provisions for consultations and a procedure to ensure that future Community legislation concerning air transport would also become part of the Agreement. Chapter V contained provisions for consultations and a procedure to deal with relations with third countries and with international organizations. The last chapter dealt with provisions regarding entry into force and review of the Agreement. Article 19, paragraph 3 stated that the Agreement expired on the day on which an agreement between the EC and the EFTA States on the EEA was put into force. Since the conclusion of the Agreement, the Community had adopted new legislation,[126] including the so-called Third Package. According to Article 12, this was to be integrated in the Agreement. The parties were afraid that the entry into force of the EEA Agreement could give rise to a backwards change in the Community and in Norway and Sweden, since the new legislation would not immediately be part of the EEA Agreement but would become applicable in the EFTA States only when the necessary procedures to supplement the legislation in the EEA had been completed.[127]

123. Doc. A-3-131/90.
124. Then Austria, Iceland, Finland, Norway, Sweden and Switzerland and Liechtenstein.
125. See Doc. A3-131/90, *OJ* No. C 262 of 14 Oct. 1985, 44.
126. The Agreement of 28 Jul. 1993 was adopted by the Council by Decision 93/453/EEC of 22 Jul. 1993.
127. For details see *Recommendation for a Council Decision* (The opening of negotiations between the EEC, the Kingdom of Norway and the Kingdom of Sweden on a modification of their Agreement on civil aviation) COM (93) 265 final, presented by the Commission on 9 Jun. 1993, 1 a-b.

3. The Agreement between the EC and United States on Trade with High-Altitude Civil Aircraft

With the intent to create more favourable conditions for the international trade with high-altitude civil airplanes and to avoid trade distortions that result from the direct or indirect State aid of the development and production of such airplanes, the EEC and the government of the US had signed an Agreement on 17 July 1992 on the basis of which the GATT Agreement for trade with civil airplanes should apply to trade with high-altitude civil airplanes. By the Decision of 13 July 1992 (92/496/EEC)[128] the Council had accepted the Agreement in the name of the Community.

4. Allocation of Slots

To prevent negative effects on the process of liberalization, uniform rules for the allocation slots within the EEC were necessary. The Commission took a first step by Regulation No. 2671/88 of 26 July 1988,[129] and another one by Regulation No. 84/91 of 5 December 1990.[130] In June 1990, it produced a first draft of a more extensive code of conduct and presented it to the Member States. However, it was withdrawn by the Commission because the representatives of the Departments of Transport rejected it.

In August 1990, a second draft had been presented.[131] The proposal provided that the allocation of slots should continue on the basis of 'grandfather rights',[132] as happened under IATA procedures,[133] but suggested a number of changes to enable market access for new competitors at airports where capacity is scarce. At each of the coordination airports, a slot pool should be created, consisting of newly created, unused, and surrendered slots.[134] At least 50% of these slots would be given to new competitors. An airline unable to get any, or any additional, slots on a route that was served by two airlines only, would be considered a 'new entrant' and given slots from the pool. Not only those airlines wanting to approach a certain airport for the first time, but also airlines having served that airport during the preceding season, and wanting more slots now than it had then, were considered 'special new entrants'. A requirement of such an entitlement to allocation should be, however, that the airline is not given more than four slots on that day, and that it has already demanded more slots during the preceding flight schedule period.[135]

At its meeting in October 1992, the Council again rejected a further Commission proposal, being reluctant to interfere with the so-called grandfather

128. *OJ* No. L 301 of 17 Oct. 1992, 31.
129. *OJ* No. C 257 of 4 Oct. 1988, 6.
130. *OJ* No. L 10 of 15 Jan. 1991, 14.
131. Draft No. 523/90 of 30 Sep. 1990.
132. This means that the previous user of a slot should be guaranteed the right of continued use for the next corresponding season as well.
133. Scheduling Procedure Guide (SPG).
134. Such are slots which are used less than 65% within two months.
135. Meaning summer/summer, winter/winter.

rights. But at the Transport Council meeting on 7 December, Transport Ministers reached agreement on a regulation concerning slot allocation, which, after being revised in some details, was published on 18 January as Regulation No. 95/93.[136] Slot allocation at a coordinated airport is now to be carried out by a coordinator assisted by a coordination committee. Grandfather rights are preserved if a carrier uses at least 80% during a season.[137] Slots may be exchanged between carriers or by one carrier between different routes not withstanding whether this is based on a mutual agreement or results from a complete or partial takeover of an airline by another.[138] New entrants are to have priority in the allocation of slots from the pool created from new, surrendered, or unused slots.[139]

D. The Development after the Establishment of the Single Market

The Third Package offered many good opportunities for the airlines to find and create markets. Nevertheless, almost nothing happened for a long time. One has to consider that the airline industry had to recover from the Gulf War trauma, during which much of the international traffic collapsed dramatically. Almost every airline lost a lot of money. Therefore, everyone was so concerned about survival that no one was looking at anything else. Ideas of developing and opening of new markets were less important at first.

1. The Third Package under Test

a. Viva Air

Viva Air, a then independent but wholly owned subsidiary of Iberia, which had been flying to Paris/Orly Airport, had complained that it has been refused permission by the French Civil Aviation Authorities to operate on the Madrid-Paris/ Charles de Gaulle route. On 3 July 1993, the Commission ruled that Viva has the right to fly into Paris/Charles de Gaulle airport. This was considered a milestone decision of the Commission for the establishment of the Single Market. It contains three important points, as described below.

The Commission has clearly confirmed that the Third Package does not automatically authorize Community air carriers to exercise traffic rights and simply commence services on any route after having filed fares with the Member States

136. *OJ* No. 14 of 22 Jan. 1993, 1, lastly amended by Regulation (EC) No. 793/2004 of the European parliament and of the Council of 21 Apr. 2004 amending Council Regulation (EEC) No. 95/93 on common rules for the allocation of slots at Community airports published in *OJ* No. L 138 of 30 Apr. 2004, 50.
137. Exception is made for specific reasons, such as grounding of aircraft type, airspace use restrictions cancellations by tour operations, strike and so on.
138. Except for an initial period in respect of new entrants.
139. For details, see below D.5.

and obtained slots. Member States may impose a formal authorization procedure, but they have to keep the notification requirements to a minimum and to grant the authorization within a very short time.

The Commission further confirmed that an application for traffic rights cannot be refused on the grounds that the airline does not possess the necessary slots and that the possession of a slot does not automatically confer traffic rights.

Even if two carriers are parent company and subsidiary but both separate legal entities, they must be considered as separate Community air carriers. Therefore, both of them can claim their own traffic rights on the same route.

b. TAT

On 27 April 1994, the European Commission requested the air routes Paris-Marseilles, Paris-Toulouse, and Paris-London with takeoff and landing at Orly Airport to be opened for competition by the French Government. These decisions were taken after the French airline TAT, a subsidiary company of British Airways, had tried in vain to attain air route rights from the French Government on the aforementioned routes.

Up to the time of the decision, the traffic distribution rules of the Paris airport system (Orly, Roissy-Charles de Gaulle, and Le Bourget) were established by the Ministry of Transport Decree of December 1993. It provided that (in contrast to the flight connections between France and Spain, and Greece and Portugal, which could be flown from both airports) all remaining intra-Community air services must be operated exclusively from Roissy-Charles de Gaulle Airport. On this Decree, the French Government based its refusal for admission of TAT air route services. According to the opinion of the Commission, this regulation had discriminatory effects because the French domestic flights, which are also connecting flights to a certain extent, take place mainly from Orly Airport. In the opinion of the Commission, this is in conflict with the principles of the EC Single Market and represents an unjustified obstacle to free offer of air services within the EC.

For the air services from Paris to Marseille and Toulouse, the French Government had granted an exclusive right to Air Inter, a subsidiary company of Air France, for takeoff and landing at Orly Airport. The company had arranged with the French Government to take the monopoly over certain domestic routes until the year 2000, on condition that it covered a series of short and unprofitable routes so as to contribute to the French Government's efforts for regional development. The Commission considered the maintenance of the exclusive concession for the Orly airport discrimination and, moreover, referred thereto the commitment of France on the occasion of taking over of UTA airline by Air France in 1990 to open for competition different domestic connections with Paris, to which the two routes that were object of the decision also belonged.

The deregulation policy can only be successful if the EC Commission ensures that there is and will be competition in the aviation industry. Therefore, it has to carefully watch what is going on. Incumbent airlines are leasing airport gates and check-in facilities under long-term, exclusive contracts, which make it hard for new entrants to enter the market. Furthermore, the big established airlines fight new entrants with dumping fares.

There is no question that it is difficult to define what predatory and what still sane competition are. In the *Akzo* Case, the European Court of Justice applied a complex approach under which pricing behaviour must be deemed predatory. If a carrier deliberately schedules a flight that it knows is and will be unprofitable, there is no doubt that it is acting with anticompetitive intent. This is the case if the carrier's revenue from a service does not cover its average variable costs of operations or if revenue does not cover the average total cost of operation.[140]

A proof that an airline made a market intentionally unprofitable is given when the surviving carrier raises its fares again, as soon as the beaten new entrant has withdrawn its service.

2. Liberalization of Ground Handling Services

The provision of ground handling services is an essential element of competition between air carriers. As a result of the EC air transport liberalization, carriers are able to compete through the destinations and connections they serve, fares, and quality of services. However, the ground handling of passengers and cargo is just as important in enabling air carriers to gain and keep the favour of their customers.[141]

Ground handling costs constitute a large portion of the airlines' operating costs.[142] However, this part of costs is beyond the control of the carrier; bringing them down is almost impossible as long as ground-handling services were – as has been the case – the almost exclusive domain of national companies,[143] the former flag carrier, or the airport operator[144] itself. Often, such monopoly was abused by excessive handling charges at various airports for foreign carriers, while the costs were reduced for the national carrier. Sometimes the high fees were accompanied by inferior quality of service. Carriers operating in a liberalized market should not be prevented by monopolies from making savings[145] or improving quality.

On 15 October 1996, the EC Council adopted Directive 96/67/EC on Access to the Ground Handling Services at European Airports.[146] Then the Member States

140. See ECJ, C-62/86 – *Akzo v. Commission, ECR* (1991), I-3359, at Nos 71, 72.
141. Airlines need to brand their own handling product: When something goes wrong only the airline (not the service provider) gets the blame! But without freedom of choice in ground handling service, airlines cannot provide their passengers with an appropriate quality of service.
142. According to Doorten (*Airline Business*, March 1994, 36), it is about 18% of total airline operating costs (excluding fuel costs).
143. E.g., SEA in Milano or AENA/Spain.
144. E.g., in Germany and Greece.
145. Handling rates were on average 30% higher at airports with a handling monopoly than airports with a choice of services. See Doorten, *Airline Business* (March 1994), 36.
146. *OJ* No. L 272 of 25. Oct. 1996, 36.

had to enact the necessary legal and administrative regulations by 25 October 1997 and to convert the Directive into national law (Article 23).

According to the market-opening schedule laid down in the new Directive, airlines and handling service providers would get more and more access to the handling market in the years to follow, and the ramp handling monopolies at European airports would definitely be abolished.

As a general rule, the freedom of self-handling for air carriers was introduced in the beginning of 1998 and third party handling generally was allowed one year later. Regarding particular handling service components (baggage handling, ramp handling, fuel and oil handling, freight, and mail handling), EC Member States may limit the number of service providers, provided that there are no fewer than two for each service category.

In cases of space and capacity constraints, airports can claim exemptions of limited duration from the market-opening requirement. In any case, ramp-handling monopolies have been abolished by the end of 2002. Since the beginning of 2001, at least one of the authorized service suppliers may not be directly or indirectly controlled by the airport operator or any air carrier who has carried more than 25% of the passengers or cargo at the airport in question.

3. Denied Boarding Regulations

The Commission was considering the need to revise Regulation No. 295/91,[147] which established common rules for a denied boarding compensation, as it felt that there would no longer be any justification for distinguishing between passengers travelling on scheduled flights and those using non-scheduled flights on leisure airlines. Its analysis came to the following conclusions:

- all passengers must be sufficiently covered on flights from a Community airport;
- passengers must be adequately informed about their rights to compensation in the event of boarding being denied; and
- fines/penalties should be imposed on carriers who do not comply with these requirements.

The Commission, therefore, planned to do the following:

- abolish the distinction between scheduled and non-scheduled flights;
- increase the requirements for air carriers to provide passengers with information, especially regarding payment of compensation;
- increase the compensation thresholds (it was planned to propose 200 ECU for flights of up to 3,500 km and 400 ECU for flights of more than 3,500 km);

147. *OJ* No. C 120 of 18 Apr. 1998, 18, meanwhile repealed by Regulation (EC) No. 261/2004 of the European Parliament and of the Council of 11 Feb. 2004 establishing common rules on compensation and assistance to passengers in the event of denied boarding and of cancellation or long delay of flights, and repealing Regulation (EEC) No. 295/91, *OJ* No. L 46 of 17 Feb. 2004, 1.

- make it quite clear that, if a passenger fails to comply with any additional conditions laid down by the air carrier, such as reconfirming the reservation within a certain period of time before the flight, the air carrier is not allowed to withdraw the right to compensation in the event of boarding being denied;
- spell out that a passenger has a right to receive compensation even if boarding is denied because the aircraft planned to be sued for the flight has been replaced by an aircraft of smaller capacity; and
- spell out that it is the responsibility of the air carrier operating the flight to pay compensation to the passenger, whether or not he caused the overbooking.

On 11 February 2004, the European Parliament and the Council finally adopted Regulation (EC) No. 261/2004, establishing common rules on compensation and assistance to passengers in the event of denied boarding and of cancellation or long delay of flights, and repealing Regulation (EEC) No. 295/91.[148] This Regulation repeals Council Regulation 295/91/EEC, which established common rules for a denied boarding compensation system in scheduled air transport.

It establishes minimum rights for passengers when they are denied boarding against their will, their flight is cancelled, or their flight is delayed. The Regulation raises the standards of protection set by Regulation 295/91/EEC both by strengthening the rights of passengers and ensuring that air carriers operate under harmonized conditions in a liberalized market.

Since the distinction between scheduled and non-scheduled air services is weakening, such protection should apply to passengers not only on scheduled but also on non-scheduled flights, including those forming part of package tours.

Furthermore, the protection accorded to passengers departing from an airport located in a Member State are extended to those leaving an airport located in a third country for one situated in a Member State, when a Community carrier operates the flight.

a. Denied Boarding

When an operating air carrier reasonably expects to deny boarding on a flight, it shall first call for volunteers to surrender their reservations in exchange for benefits under conditions to be agreed between the passenger concerned and the operating air carrier.

If an insufficient number of volunteers comes forward to allow the remaining passengers with reservations to board the flight, the operating air carrier may then deny boarding to passengers against their will.

If boarding is denied to passengers against their will, the operating air carrier shall immediately compensate them.

148. *OJ* No. L 46 of 17 Feb. 2004, 1.

Passengers will receive compensation from the airline or travel operators amounting to:

- EUR 250 for all flights of 1,500 kilometres or less.
- EUR 400 for all intra-Community flights of more than 1,500 kilometres and for all other flights between 1,500 and 3,500 kilometres.
- EUR 600 for all flights exceeding 3,500 kilometres.

This will create a strong incentive to make volunteering attractive and a powerful deterrent to denying boarding.

In addition to financial compensation, passengers denied boarding will continue to benefit from the choice between reimbursement of their ticket and an alternative flight, and meals, refreshments, and hotel accommodation.

b. Cancellation

When airlines or tour operators cancel flights on their own responsibility, passengers will have the right to compensation at the rate fixed for denied boarding, unless they are informed two weeks before the scheduled time of departure, or they are informed on due time and rerouted at a time very close to that of their original flight.

In addition, in case of cancellations, passengers are entitled to three other rights:

Meals and refreshments; hotel accommodations, when a cancellation obliges a passenger to stay overnight; and reimbursement, when a cancellation delays a passenger for at least five hours.

c. Long Delay

The Regulation introduces a three-tier system:

- in the event of long delays (two hours or more, depending on the distance of the flight), passengers must in every case be offered free meals and refreshments plus two free telephone calls, telex or fax messages, or e-mails;
- if the time of departure is deferred until the next day, passengers must also be offered hotel accommodations and transport between the airport and the place of accommodation;
- when the delay is five hours or longer, passengers may opt for reimbursement of the full cost of the ticket together with, when relevant, a return flight to the first point of departure.

d. Upgrading and Downgrading

If an air carrier places a passenger in a class lower than that for which the ticket was purchased, the passenger must be reimbursed within seven days, as follows:

- 30% of the price of the ticket for all flights of 1,500 kilometres or less;

- 50% of the price of the ticket for all intra-Community flights of more than 1,500 kilometres, except flights between the Member States and the French overseas departments, and for all other flights between 1,500 and 3,500 kilometres;
- 75% of the price of the ticket for all other flights, including flights between the Member States and the French overseas departments.

The Regulation has been criticized because, among others, it was based on Article 80, paragraph 2 of the EC Treaty (transport) rather than on Article 153 (consumer protection); because it deals with private law matters already covered by the transport laws of the EC Member States, and therefore, the most proper legal form would have been a directive rather than a regulation; because it fails to or does not very clearly distinguish the three causes (denied boarding, cancellation, and delay); and because it establishes a kilometre-based compensation scheme instead of a money back policy.[149]

Notwithstanding this criticism, the Regulation remains unchanged since its adoption.

4. Liability Regime

In 1996, the Commission made a proposal to update the Warsaw Convention's liability limits, as they found them to be unacceptable. On 9 October 1997, the Council published Regulation No. 2027/97.[150] The European carriers will be subject to strict liability up to a sum of the equivalent SDR 100,000.[151] Above this limit, air carriers are also liable, but they have the possibility of defending themselves (presumed liability).

As the Commission was aware of the fact that it would be very costly to try to insure against unlimited liability, the Regulation, therefore, specifies that a Community air carrier must be insured up to at least to the equivalent of SDR 100,000 per passenger and thereafter up to a reasonable level.

---

149. See Haanappel, The New EU Denied Boarding Compensation Regulation of 2004, *ZLW* (2005), 22; Führich, Sonderbeilage *MDR* 7/2007: Die Fluggastrechte der VO (EG) Nr. 261/2004 in der Praxis; Schmid, Die Verordnung (EG) Nr. 261/2004 – Europäischer Verbraucherschutz mit Nachbesserungsbedarf, *ZLW* (2005), 373; *id.*, Fluggastrechte – Unehrliches Lamentieren der Airlines, Editorial, *NJW* 5/2006; *id.*, Die Bewährung der neuen Fluggastrechte in der Praxis, *NJW* (2006), 1841; *id.*, Fluggastrechte in der Praxis – Ein Überblick über Entscheidungen zur Verordnung (EG) Nr. 261/2004 mit Anmerkungen, *NJW* (2007), 261; *id.*, Die Verordnung (EG) Nr. 261/2004 – eine 'Sagrada familia' des Fluggastrechts? Oder: Droht der Rückbau der Fluggastrechte durch den Europäischen Gerichtshof?, *RRa* (2008); 202, Müller-Rostin, Rechtliche Unsicherheiten bei der Neuregelung von Fluggastrechten – eine kritische Würdigung der VO (EG) Nr. 261/2004 und zugleich eine Erwiderung zu Schmid, *NJW* (2006), 1841; *NZV* (2007), 242; *id.*, Verordnung (EG) Nr. 261/2004: Ein Zwischenruf, *RRa* (2007), 256; Rennig, Der 'letzte Zielort' i. S. d. Art. 7 Abs. 1 Satz 2 der Verordnung (EG) Nr. 261/2004, *RRa* (2008), 58; Wagner, Verbesserung der Fluggastrechte durch die Verordnung (EG) Nr. 261/2004?, *VuR* (2006), 337.
150. See also: Giemulla/Schmid, *NVZ* (1998), 225.
151. SDR – special drawing rights, a currency account unit of the International Monetary Fund.

An advance payment is obligatory in case of need. However, in the event of death, an advance payment of not less than the equivalent of SDR 15,000 per passenger must be paid. This rule is to be applied within fifteen days in case of accident (Article 5).

The Regulation had consequences not only within the European Union (EU), but also for other European countries with which the EU has association agreements, which directly or indirectly commit these countries to harmonize their legislation with the legislation of the EU.

The Commission's intention is to apply this Regulation to airlines from third countries, too. The Regulation, therefore, obliges third country airlines, which apply lower standards, to inform the passengers. But the Regulation is silent on the question of what will happen if a non-EC-carrier does not follow this rule.

On 28 May 1999 in Montreal, a new international liability agreement was signed as 'Montreal Convention' that replaced the previous Warsaw Convention. Meanwhile, after its ratification by more than thirty signatory States, it has entered into force, but not, however, for the majority of the EC States. In accordance with the Decision of the Council about the conclusion of the Montreal Convention by the EC,[152] the deposit of the ratification documents of the EC should be made together with those of the Member States (to put it more precisely – with the ones that have not been deposited yet). At that time also that the changed Regulation 2027/97 entered into force, it includes the regulations of the Montreal Convention and supplements them.

5. Allocation of Slots

On the basis of the steady growth of the European aviation market in the last years, problems emerged by which the interested air carriers opposed the smooth distribution of slots of an airport.

Since, in the meantime, the airport capacities are becoming more and scarcer, slots represent a precious commodity and are regarded as limiting factors for the growing air traffic.[153]

If one recalls that, according to a study of the UK Civil Aviation Authority, already in 1998, twenty-seven of the forty-four inner-European routes showed an annual increase of more than 400,000 passengers, at which all these flights had as a starting point one of Europe's four busiest airports (Frankfurt, Dusseldorf, London Heathrow, and Gatwick),[154] the problem becomes very clear.

In the first place, the legal nature of slots is defined controversially. The established aviation companies that get allotted the same sequence of slots again in each following flight plan period on the basis of the grandfather

152. *OJ* No. L 194 of 19 Jul. 2001, 38.
153. Beside the overloaded airspace and likewise overloaded air traffic control.
154. CAA (ed.), *The Single European Aviation Market – The first five years* (London: 1998), marginal number 180.

rights[155] regard slots as a property-similar right. Others consider them to have the status of a legal utilization entitlement or a participation-right only.[156]

The definition of the legal nature of slots has effects first of all on their transferability. The trade with the commodity slot is an open industry secret. Many smaller aviation companies financially keep above water by transfer against payment of slots allocated to them; some even discontinue their aviation business completely since the mere commercialization of their slots is economically more appealing.

How transferability of slots is allowable on the basis of the current European legal grounds is answered differently according to placement of interests. Regulation 95/93[157] in Article 8, paragraph 4 admittedly provides for the general possibility for the exchange and the transfer of slots, but makes no statements[158] concerning the exact requirements and the question whether such a transfer can be accompanied by monetary payments.

One can observe that in case there is – according to Article10 of Regulation 95/93 – a decline in the – in terms of the Regulation - 'normal cases' for the fate of unused slots of an air carrier in the slot pool, there – as an exception provided for by the Regulation makers – appears the possibility to consider a transfer between the carriers.

According to Article 8, paragraph 4 of Regulation 95/93, the exchanges and also the transfers of slots require the confirmation of the airport coordinator who must watch for the observance of fair competition between the involved air carriers. Since these transfers must themselves be measured according to these strict competition-safeguarding standards, quite a limited transfer possibility is assumed.[159]

For the first time, this problem was the object of a legal decision of the English High Court in 1999 in the law case *Regina v. Airport Co-Ordination Ltd.*[160] In this model case, it was determined by the High Court that an exchange is admissible also with economically completely unequally worthy slots – as a single crucial criterion, the High Court considered the equal value of the number of the exchanged slots.[161]

---

155. The 'grandfather rights' originate with 80% usage of the allotted series of slots in each current flight plan period at the airport ('use-it-or-lose-it-rule').
156. See on that in detail Giemulla/Schmid, 'Once again: whom does the time belong to?' (Nochmals – Wem gehört die Zeit? Rechtsprobleme der Slot-Zuteilung), *ZLW* (Vol. 3,1995), 258 et seq.
157. *OJ* No. L 14 of 22 Jan. 1993, 1.
158. See on that in detail Kilian, 'Slot allocation und Slot trade', *TranspR,* 2000, 159–168.
159. See Giemulla/Schmid, *ibid.*
160. In 1997 Air UK traded valuable slots held by it in London Heathrow for the same number of economically less worthy slots allotted to British Airways, whereupon Air UK did not return these unused slots in the pool to make the reallocation to another air carrier possible.
161. Whether money payments flowed on this occasion, it could not be proved and therefore was not component of the judgment either, but it was considered as highly probable.

The decision came under vehement criticism,[162] since consequently such fictitious exchange agreements would open the door and thereby new candidates that are to be satisfied to 50% from the slot pool (consisting of unused and newly created slots), would seize the chance of the allotment of an economically reasonable slot.

The grounds for this discussion have been eluded with the entering into force of the amendment of Regulation 95/93.[163] In its proposal for amendment, the Commission made it clear that any form of unilateral transfer should be inadmissible.

Thus, whereas the amended Regulation accepts, for reasons of maintaining the necessary flexibility within a group of air carriers with corporate links, that slots can be transferred from a parent company to its subsidiary and/or also between subsidiaries of one and the same parent company, and/or as part of business takeover, it clearly forbids any other form of transfer of slots.[164] The observance of this prohibition shall be achieved on the grounds of strict control by annual reports of the airport coordinators.

The planned changes in accordance with Article 14 of Regulation 95/93 serve first of all the observance of its original goals, namely, the impartial, transparent, discrimination-free distribution of the slots for the purposes of an efficient utilization of airports with capacity bottlenecks.

In the course of that, even further proposals for a more flexible and more fair allocation of slots were presented by the Commission and were adopted by the Council, although with some changes.

Thus, a fully revised regulation of partially clarified functions will be observed in the future and will counteract the main difficulty of the balance of interests of new and established carriers with a strengthened independent coordinator, who can sanction the air carriers by withdrawal of the already allotted slots if these don't keep to the predetermined rules because of fictitious exchange agreements or regular and deliberate operation during a different time from the released timings.

Therefore, the practice should also be counteracted when economically interesting slots once allotted go to a regular 'hoard' if the relevant company doesn't use the slots economically so as to make sure that these can be used with demand. Especially at severely congested airports, this is against efficient utilization and necessary slots' mobility.

---

162. This was based not least on the completely different concepts across the range of legal interpretations of European 'common law countries', on the one hand, and 'civil law countries' on the other hand; see Kilian, *ibid.*

163. About the stage reached in the proceedings: Proposal of the Commission of 20 Jun. 2001, COM(2001) 335 final. (*OJ* No. C 270 E of 25 Sep. 2001, 131); Opinion of the Economic and Social Committee (*OJ* No. C 125 of 27 May 2002, 8); Amended Proposal of the Commission COM(2002) 623 final <http://europa.eu.int/eurlex/de/com/pdf/2002/com2002_0623de01.pdf>; European Parliament legislative resolution (*OJ* No. C 261 E of 30 Oct. 2003, 116).

164. COM(2001) 335 final., 19. recital.

Furthermore, Article 2a[165] of the new version of Regulation 95/93 determines decisively that a slot is no ownership right but only an entitlement to use a public property – the slot. The right on utilization of the airport infrastructure can be renewed if the air carriers prove to have used the slots effectively.[166]

Simultaneously, the flow of information between coordinators, airports, air traffic control, and airport users shall improve, and the independence and impartiality of the airport coordinator, strengthened through his competence, will be guaranteed.

The new definition of the concept of 'new entrant' in Article 2b of the new version of Regulation 95/93 provides for a better balance between the interests of established and new air carriers. On the one hand, it becomes so reduced that actual new entrants come into the use of the allotment of 50% of the slot pool only in times of code-sharing, franchising, or a joint operation. On the other hand, the concept now also includes carriers that to a great extent are present at the relevant airport.

Furthermore, to follow international terminology, the terms *schedules facilitated airport* and *coordinated airport* have been introduced instead of *coordinated* and *fully coordinated* respectively.

Further changes of Regulation 95/93 are described below.

a. 11 September 2001

The terrorist attacks of 11 September 2001 led to a significant lower demand in air tickets first of all on the air transport connections between Europe and the US, and between the Near and Middle East, but also within Europe. The American airspace was closed for air traffic for four days – until 14 September 2001. Admittedly, the European companies were not affected by these measures to the same extent as the American ones. However, by the end of 2002, they also had to be ready for a traffic reduction of 8% within Europe and 22% on the North Atlantic routes.[167]

The inhibition in bringing back the confidence in carriers' airplanes was clearly perceptible. Therefore, the air carriers could not use the slots remaining from the summer 2001 scheduling season and consequently had to return those in accordance with Article 10 of Regulation 95/93. The same applied for the slots already allotted at the IATA Scheduling Conference in July 2001 for the winter 2001/2002 scheduling season.

165. 'The entitlement established under this Regulation, of an air carrier to use the full range of airport infrastructure necessary to operate an air service at a coordinated airport on a specific date and time for the purpose of landing and take-off as allocated by a coordinator in accordance with this Regulation'.

166. I.e., to understand the renewed confirmation of the 'use-it-or-lose-it-rule'.

167. In the first week of October 2001, the flights in the US dropped by 32%; the advance bookings for October and November 2001 reduced for the intra-European flights by 16%, 5%, and even by 42% for flights to the Near and the Middle East. See COM (2002) 7 final.

The unavoidable consequence was, of course, that the air carriers actually, therefore, could not observe the demanded 80% usage and, therefore, had lost their slots according to Article 10, paragraph 3 of Regulation 95/93.

According to Article 4, paragraphs 5 and 6 of Regulation 95/93, the coordinator exclusively shall be responsible for the allocation of slots and he must carry out his duties in an independent manner and in a neutral, non-discriminatory, and transparent way (Article 4, paragraphs 2 and 3 of Regulation 95/93).

Admittedly, Article 10, paragraph 5a of Regulation 95/93 sees a possible deviation from this rule if the non-utilization is based on unpredictable and unavoidable circumstances, but because of the guaranteed independence of the coordinators, neither the Commission nor the Member States can obligatorily determine which of those are considered as exceptional circumstances regarding the allocation of slots.

Therefore, it was necessary to treat the problem uniformly and to impose the obligation on the coordinators to recognize the traditional rights for the summer 2001 and winter 2001/2002 scheduling seasons by a mere publication of broad guidelines.[168]

Therefore the Commission's proposal to introduce a new Article 10a[169] in Regulation 95/93, which to attend to this problem, was followed by this the issuance of Regulation (EC) 894/2002.[170]

Consequently, without the 80% usage, the air traffic companies were entitled also to the same series of slots during the next scheduling season.

However, for the winter, the arrangement was in contrast to the one for the summer in a way that the air carriers, to keep the grandfather rights, had to declare the return of the slots and probably to apply for those again for winter 2003/2004.

b. The War in Iraq and SARS

The new Article 10b[171] was inserted in Regulation 1554/2003 of 22 July[172] for the same reasons. The background was, first, the war that broke out in Iraq in March 2003 and the fear of terrorist attacks in aviation arising again on the basis of lasting hostilities. The thereby evoked decline of demand led also to serious effects on the European air carriers.

---

168. This had previously happened in the US and in Japan already.
169. Article 10a (The events of 11 Sep. 2001): 'For the purpose of Art. 10, para. 3, coordinators shall accept that air carriers are entitled to the same series of slots during summer scheduling season 2002 and winter scheduling season 2002/2003 as had been allocated to them on the date of 11 Sep. 2001 for the summer scheduling season 2001 and the winter scheduling season 2001/2002 respectively.'
170. *OJ* No. L 142 of 3 May 2002, 3.
171. Article 10b. 'For the purpose of Art. 10, para. 3, coordinators shall accept that air carriers are entitled to the same series of slots during the summer 2004 scheduling season as were allocated to them during the summer 2003 scheduling season.'
172. *OJ* No. L 221 of 4 Sep. 2003, 1.

The outbreak of the lung disease SARS (Service Acute Respiratory Syndrome) in South Asia at the beginning of the summer 2003 scheduling season following it made its contribution to worsening the economic situation of the air carriers.[173] Consequently, the air carriers were not in the position to use all slots (economically reasonable) once again because of lack of demand on the basis of an unpredictable event. To intercept some of the resulting disadvantages, the coordinators, through inserting the new Article 10b, made the commitment to allocate the air carriers the same series of slots during the summer 2004 scheduling season as were allocated to them during the summer 2003 scheduling season.

c. Regulation (EC) No. 793/2004

The Regulation[174] focuses on the introduction of transparent and equitable procedures. This affects in particular the definition of slot capacity available for allocation, the process of allocation, and the monitoring of the correct use of slots.

Clearly linked to the effectiveness of such system is the status of the coordinator, who must be truly independent from any vested interests and must have the necessary financial resources to accomplish the tasks assigned to him by the Regulation.

This Regulation also introduces a series of technical improvements in the form of clearer definitions and priorities among the slot allocation criteria, in a balanced manner so as to maintain the level of undistorted competition. To that end the Regulation is designed to do the following:

- introduce the possibility for incumbent air carriers to retime slots with grandfather status under certain conditions;
- expressly prohibit slot exchanges in the absence of any transparent and non-discriminatory market-based mechanism for accessing airports;
- require, so as to avoid the worsening of competitive conditions at particularly congested European airports, that slots exchanged between air carriers must be used, thus curbing slot trades dressed-up as slot exchanges.

6. Protection of EC Carriers from Unfair Pricing Practices and Subsidization from Non-EU Countries

On 21 April 2004, the European Parliament and the Council adopted Regulation No. 868/2004/EC, concerning protection against subsidization and unfair pricing practices causing injury to Community air carriers in the supply of air services from countries not members of the EC.[175] The purpose of this legislative act is to

173. For substantiation see COM(2003) 207 final of 24 Apr. 2003.
174. Regulation (EC) No. 793/2004 of the European Parliament and of the Council of 21 April 2004 amending Council Regulation (EEC) No. 95/93 on common rules for the allocation of slots at Community airports, *OJ* No. L 138 of 30 Apr. 2004, 50.
175. *OJ* No. L 162 of 30 Apr. 2004, 1.

protect Community airline services from unfair pricing practices and subsidization from non-EU countries.

This Regulation lays down the procedure to be followed to provide protection against subsidization and unfair pricing practices in the supply of air services from countries not members of the EC insofar as injury is thereby caused to the Community industry. This Regulation shall not preclude the prior application of any special provisions in air services agreements between Member States and countries not members of the EC. In addition, this Regulation shall not preclude the application of any special provisions in agreements between the Community and countries not members of the EC. This Regulation is based on definitions and standards currently in use at a multilateral level and by the Community to overcome distortions caused by certain subsidies in the trade in goods. Furthermore, this Regulation is without prejudice to the consultation and conflict-resolution mechanisms provided for under the bilateral agreements among Member States; recourse should be had to the Community's anti-Subsidy Regulation only in cases in which a satisfactory solution cannot be arrived at through the bilateral agreements.

More specifically, the Regulation:

- defines the regressive measures to be taken against such unfair practices;
- determines when a subsidy shall be deemed to exist and according to that principles it should be countervailable, in particular whether the subsidy has been targeted at certain enterprises or sectors or is contingent upon air service supply to third countries;
- lays down clear and detailed guidance as to the factors that may be relevant for the determination of whether the subsidized or unfairly priced air services provided by non-Community air carriers have caused injury or are threatening to cause injury; to demonstrate that the pricing practices related to the supply of such air services cause injury to the Community industry, attention should be given to the effect of other factors, and consideration should be given to all relevant and known factors and economic indicators which have a bearing on the state of the industry, and in particular prevailing market conditions in the Community;
- specifies who may lodge a complaint and the information that such a complaint should contain; a complaint should be rejected where there is insufficient evidence of injury to proceed;
- lays down the procedure to be followed in the investigation of unfair practices by non-Community carriers; this procedure should be limited in time;
- lays down the manner in which interested parties should be given notice of the information which the authorities require; interested parties should have ample opportunity to present all relevant evidence and to defend their interests;
- sets out the rules and procedures to be followed during the investigation, in particular the rules whereby interested parties are to make themselves known;
- lays down the conditions under which provisional measures may be imposed;

– provides that the level of measures should not exceed the value of subsidies or the non-commercial advantages granted as the case may be or the sum corresponding to the injury caused, where this is lower;
– provides that measures should remain in force only for as long as it is necessary to counteract the subsidies or unfair pricing practices causing injury. Preference should be given to duties when it comes to the imposition of measures; where duties prove not to be appropriate, other measures may be considered;
– specifies procedures for the acceptance of undertakings eliminating or offsetting the countervailable subsidies or unfair pricing practices and the injury caused in lieu of the imposition of provisional or definitive measures;
– provides for review of the measures imposed in cases in which sufficient evidence is submitted of changed circumstances.[176]

7. Recast of the Third Package

On 24 September 2008, the Third Liberalization Package was renewed and modified by Regulation (EC) No. 1008/2008 of the European Parliament and of the Council on common rules for the operation of air services in the Community (RECAST).[177] The Regulation supersedes the previously existing Regulations Nos. 2407/92, 2408/92, and 2408/92. These three regulations of the so-called Third Liberalization Package were consolidated into a single text. The purpose of this Regulation is to ensure a more effective functioning of the internal aviation market, to increase the safety of aviation services, and to improve protection of passengers that include, *inter alia*, the terms of fares and rates. Regulation No. 1008/2008 concerns the issue of operating licenses to air carriers, leasing of aircraft, regulation on access of Community air carriers to air routes in the Community, and regulation on fares and rates for aviation services.

a. Operating Licenses

The rules for granting, cancellation, or suspension of operational licenses, inspection of air carriers and their access to the market aim to ensure greater competition in air transport and thus simultaneously contribute to enhancement of the quality of aviation services for the public.

While retaining Member States' control of the supervision of carriers' operating licenses, the Regulation attempts to unify the Community's rules governing the granting and supervision of such licenses. The regulation pays significant attention to the so-called financial health of air carriers, both from the viewpoint of passenger protection against non-fulfilment of obligations and from the viewpoint of the possible impact of an unfavourable financial situation on the

176. <www.europarl.europa.eu/oeil/resume.jsp?id=220482&eventId=1402&backToCaller=NO&language=en>.
177. *OJ* No. L 293 of 31 Oct. 2008, 3.

safety of the operation. It establishes more stringent initial (i.e., on the application for a license) and continued monitoring of the financial health of operators in the Community.

The Regulation strengthens the licensing authorities' ability to ground operators that hold an Air Operator Certificate (AOC) but do not meet the required air licensing standards. The conditions for licensing authorities to grant licenses are codified, and a licensing authority is denied the ability to grant a license unless certain operating conditions (e.g., relating to place of business and corporate control of the operator) and financial conditions (e.g., an undertaking can show it is able to meet its financial obligations for a period of twenty-four months) are met. The Regulation places importance on the ability of the competent authorities to assess on a continuing basis the financial performance of operators as a condition of maintaining an operating license. If an authority is no longer satisfied that the operator is able to meet its financial obligations for a twelve-month period, the license may be suspended or revoked.

Additional monitoring obligations are placed on the national licensing authorities, requiring them to conduct regular reviews of operators' compliance with the regulatory requirements. Operators are required to provide their audited accounts within six months of the end of the financial year. Continual review of an operator's financial status by the competent licensing authority is also provided for, as is the requirement of operators to provide their competent authorities with material business plans, such as any intended mergers and acquisitions. Should the competent authority conclude that such plans will have a significant bearing on the finances of the operator, the operator is required to submit a revised business plan to assess its continued suitability to hold a license.

b. Leasing of Aircraft

The Regulation allows unrestricted leasing arrangements for aircraft registered in the Community, particularly with regard to wet-leasing (leasing including crew), subject, however, to strict safety standards. Lease arrangements with aircraft registered in third countries are to be allowed only in exceptional circumstances in which, among other conditions, strict safety standards have been shown to be met, and it is not possible or reasonable to lease alternative aircraft registered within the Community.

c. Access of Community Air Carriers to Intra-European Air Routes

The Regulation aims to complete the internal aviation market. It removes remaining restrictions so that, when operating intra-Community air services, operators are granted freedom to combine air services and to enter into code-sharing arrangements (without prejudice to the Community competition rules applicable to operators). Once a Community operator has obtained an AOL from its national licensing authority, it needs no additional permits or authorizations to operate intra-Community air services; likewise, the Regulation removes any restrictions on the ability of operators to run intra-Community air services arising from bilateral agreements between Member States.

The public service obligations (PSOs) imposed on Community operators are now simplified. A Member State, having consulted interested parties, may impose PSOs with respect to air services between an airport in their State and an airport serving a peripheral or development region, or on a less popular route, where such route is considered vital for the economic and social development of the region that the airport serves. In assessing the need for such services, the Member State is to have regard to, among other things, the proportionality between the envisaged obligation and the economic development needs of the region concerned and the availability and suitability of other modes of transport to meet such needs. Should no operator have commenced or demonstrated that it is about to commence air services in accordance with the required PSOs on a route, the Member State may limit access to such a route to only one operator for a period of up to four years, or five years when the route serves an airport in an outermost region. Where such limits are imposed, the services shall be assigned by public tender.

The Regulation allows Member States to control, without discrimination on grounds of nationality or identity of operators, the distribution of air traffic between airports that (1) serve the same city or conurbation; (2) are served by adequate transport infrastructure; and (3) are linked to one another and offer necessary services to operators.

d. Fares and Rates for Aviation Services

A fundamental change is the regulation of the method of introduction and publication of air services fares. Air carriers are obliged to state the full and final fare of air tickets as well as a breakdown thereof by individual items, including airport and other charges. The price must be thus presented from the beginning of the order or demand for a specific service. The target is to prevent (former) misleading practices of many airlines that often publish only a portion of the actual fare. The transparent procedure obligation enables the customer to simply compare fares and rates, and thus market competition is increased. Price discrimination of passengers pursuant to the domicile country and automatic increase of prices for various supplementary services are also prohibited without the explicit consent of the customer.

IV. LIBERALIZED BILATERAL AIR SERVICES AGREEMENTS

A. Consequences of US Deregulation and EC Liberalization

After 1992, the US had concluded separate liberal bilateral agreements with a number of EC members. Most of the then sixteen individual bilateral agreements that the US had concluded with various European countries were already of the 'open skies' type.[178]

In 1994, the EC Commission claimed for external competence (which meant that the new bilateral agreements were illegal). Since most of the governments of the EU Member States did not share that view, the EC Commission requested the ECJ to declare the bilateral agreements as null and void. In 2002, the Court of Justice held that:

- the bilateral agreements are only illegal insofar as they provide fifth freedom rights to US carriers and to other EC members with conditions contrary to EC law;
- Article 80, paragraph 2 of the EC Treaty grants the Commission external competence in air transport only if expressly mandated by the Council. Article 80, paragraph 2 read: 'The Council may, acting by a qualified majority, decide whether, to what extent and by what procedure appropriate provisions may be laid down for sea and air transport';
- All existing bilateral agreements with third countries remain in force as long as they are not overruled by an EC bilateral.

In 2003, the Council gave the Commission the mandate for negotiations with the US.

B. The Open Skies Agreement USA/EC

The new Open Skies Agreement USA/EC was signed in March 2007.[179] It replaced and superseded previous open skies agreements between the US and individual European countries. The agreement was signed in Washington, D.C., on 30 April 2007, and became (provisionally) effective on 30 March 2008. It forms a regulatory framework for a market covering more than 60% of global air traffic.[180]

The main elements of the new agreement are given below.[181]

1. Removal of Restrictions on Route Rights

- Any EC airline will be able to fly from any European city to any American city and from there onwards to third destinations (outside the US). Conversely, any US airline will be allowed to fly into any EC airport and from there to third destinations (also inside the EC).
- This will mainly affect London Heathrow (more than 40% of all flights from Europe to America), and where, up to recently, only four carriers

178. See e.g.,: Mendelsohn, 'The United States and the European Union in International Aviation', *Issues in Aviation Law and Policy* 13 (2008): 271.
179. *OJ* No. L 134 of 25 May 2007, 4.
180. See AEA, <http://files.aea.be/News/News020408.pdf>.
181. For an excellent analysis see Mendelsohn *above*.

(British Airways, Virgin Atlantic, American Airlines, and United) had authorization to fly the transatlantic route.
- The UK achieved a delay in the application of the agreement (from October 2007 until 30 March 2008) so as to give Heathrow time to finish building its new terminal for British Airways.

2. Cabotage

- While US airlines can fly within Europe (except for cabotage), European airlines are not allowed to fly domestic US routes.
- However, European carriers have the right to establish subsidiaries in the United States, which can carry domestic traffic.

3. Foreign Ownership

- European companies can buy up to 100% of non-voting shares in US airlines, but not more than 25% of voting rights.
- As a new rule, vice versa.

4. Suspension Clause

- The EC obtained a 'suspension clause', which commits the US to opening up its domestic market and loosening its rules on foreign investment and ownership by mid-2010.
- Negotiations must begin 'no later than sixty days after 30 March 2008'.
- Negotiations have already started again (at least formally).

C. The European Common Aviation Area (ECAA)

In 1996, the EC Council gave the Commission a mandate to negotiate a multilateral agreement with the then candidate countries, as well as Iceland and Norway. The reason was to open up markets between Europe and its neighbours. Later on (in 2002), negotiations were discontinued in view of the impeding accession wave. At the same time, the mandate had been extended to the Balkan region.

On 9 June 2006, the ECAA Agreement[182] was signed by almost all of the twenty-seven EU Members, the EC itself, Norway, Iceland, Croatia, the Former Yugoslav Republic of Macedonia, Albania, Bosnia and Herzegovina, and Kosovo

182. Multilateral Agreement between the European Community and its Member States, the Republic of Albania, Bosnia and Herzegovina, the Republic of Bulgaria, the Republic of Croatia, the former Yugoslav Republic of Macedonia, the Republic of Iceland, the Republic of Montenegro, the Kingdom of Norway, Romania, the Republic of Serbia and the United Nations Interim Administration Mission in Kosovo on the establishment of a European Common Aviation Area, *OJ* No. L 285 of 16 Oct. 2006, 3.

(UNMIK as Kosovo representative under Security Council Resolution 1244). The last two EU Member States to sign it were Slovakia and Latvia, respectively, on 13 June 2006 and 22 June 2006. Finally, of the initially expected countries, Serbia signed on 29 June 2006 and Montenegro on 5 July 2006. Currently, the ratification process is ongoing in almost all of these countries. Hungary finished the ratification on 31 July 2006.

The ECAA will amount to a full extension of the EC internal air transport market to the Western Balkans. It entails the complete liberalization of cross-border traffic among signatories, an adoption of the aviation-related *acquis* and comprehensive sector restructuring at the national level. It is expected to trigger rapid traffic growth, encourage foreign investment in the sector, and act as an important catalyst for broader regional integration. To reap those benefits, the countries of the Western Balkans will have to implement an ambitious reform agenda in a short time span. This includes the following:

– Legislation that liberalizes market access, traffic rights, and fares;
– regulation on airport ground handling and slot allocation;
– safety and security regulations;
– rules on competition and State aid;
– the *acquis* related to air traffic management and the Single European Sky; and
– environmental standards and consumer rights pertaining to aviation.

The implementation of the agreement will take place in three stages. In the first stage, third and fourth freedom rights will be fully liberalized. This means that all airlines licensed within the ECAA area may fly to and from their countries to any ECAA destination, without frequency or capacity restrictions. The second stage will involve a liberalization of the fifth freedom, allowing airlines to pick up passengers on a stopover in another country before dropping them off in a third. Before a country can move to the second stage of the ECAA, however, it needs to implement a basic package of the aviation *acquis,* which mainly relates to safety and security rules. The third stage comprises a liberalization of remaining freedoms and full transposition of the aviation *acquis*. No explicit target dates for stages one and two have been set, and each country can progress at its own pace, once it meets the required conditions. It should be noted that a 'pre-ECAA' step towards liberalization was already taken in May 2006, when the countries of South East Europe signed a series of horizontal agreements with the EC, modifying the nationality clauses in their bilateral agreements with EU Countries. This permits any EU airline to fly from another EU Country to a destination somewhere in Southeast Europe on the same conditions as for a domestic airline'.[183]

183. European Commission – World Bank, Office for South East Europe, The European Common Aviation Area and the Western Balkans: Domestic Reforms and Regional Integration in Air Transport (February 2007), <www.seerecon.org/gen/Documents/SEE%20Air%20Transport%20_9%20February%2007_.pdf>, 4.

V. TOWARDS A LIBERALIZED MULTILATERAL AIR SERVICE AGREEMENT

Despite criticism of the bilateral system in favour of a multilateral one, the former is still in force. Nevertheless, the ICAO, receptive of the worldwide change in the international air transport field, initiated studies on worldwide air transport liberalization.

The first step was the Worldwide Air Transport Colloquium,[184] which convened in April 1992 to informally discuss the new regulation concepts and policies for international air transport. This meeting concentrated top government, air carrier, airport, and academic delegates in a positive exchange of different views.

The Fourth Air Transport Conference was held in November 1994[185] to explore air transport regulation policies on the basis of the aforementioned colloquium conclusions. It is important to take into account the need of the ICAO to assert its leadership in the economic regulation of air transport in anticipation of the conclusion of the Uruguay Round negotiations and the signing of the General Agreement on Trade in Services (GATS).[186]

GATS was an important attempt to offer the first potentially worldwide, multilateral alternative to the bilateral regimen of air transport service agreements.

Despite these efforts, until now, the Air Transport Annex of GATS covered only three air transport activities: aircraft repair and maintenance, the sale and marketing of air transport and computer reservation systems, with the exclusion of the 'grandfather rights', that is, the commercial freedoms of the air.

The GATS is the result of the Group of Negotiations on Services GNS, which entered into effect on 1 January 1995. The regulatory scope of WTO covers goods, services, intellectual property, with integrated dispute settlement. The principles of GATS are the following:

- Market access or specification of the levels of access to be granted other parties through the four modes of supply.
- National treatment, such as treatment of foreign services and suppliers of services no less favourable than that accorded a parties' own services and service suppliers.
- Most Favoured Nation (MFN) treatment, which means non-discrimination, the provision of treatment to all parties no less favourable than that accorded to any party.

Other general principles in the GATS referred, among others, to the following:

- Transparency in prompt publication of all relevant rules and regulations, administrative guidelines, and all other decisions, rulings, or measures of general application that pertain to or affect the operation of the agreement,

184. See Krämer, World wide Air Transport Colloquium, *ZLW* 1992, 276.
185. Report on the conference: *ICAO Doc 9644*.
186. 1869 *UNTS* 183.

with the exception of certain information that is confidential or otherwise contrary to the public interest;
- Increasing participation of less developed countries, to be achieved by improving their access to technology, distribution channels, and information networks, and by the liberalization of market access in sectors.

The Annex on air transport excludes from the scope of the GATS, traffic rights, however, granted or services related to the exercise of traffic rights with the exception of three activities, such as:

- Aircraft repair and maintenance services mean such activities undertaken on an aircraft or a part thereof while it is withdrawn from service and which do not include maintenance;
- Selling and marketing of air transport services which are the opportunities for the air carrier concerned to sell and market freely its air transport services including all aspects of marketing such as market research, advertising, and distribution. These activities do not include the pricing of air transport services or the applicable conditions;
- Computer reservation systems (CRS) services, that is, services provided by computerized systems that contain information about air carriers' schedules, availability, fares and fare rules, through which reservations can be made or tickets may be issued.

ICAO continue to exert the global leadership role in the air transport system, coordinating the process of liberalization and ensuring the safety and security with the appropriate communication and cooperation with other intergovernmental organizations like WTO participating in the review of the Annex Air Transport of GATS.

The Air Transport Conference reaffirming the principles of the Chicago Convention (1944):

- emphasized the principle of effective participation by all States in the international air transport arena, agreed on the possible coexistence of several regulatory regimes, and supported gradual, orderly, progressive, and safeguarded change towards market access;
- supported broadening air carrier ownership and control criteria to include greater foreign investment possibilities, but not to liberalize the right of establishment;
- agreed on the need for exempting inter-airline cooperation such as code-sharing and tariff coordination, from competition laws and their extra-territorial application, and indicated the need for a mechanism to correct competitive abuses; and
- in addition, recommended special, preferential measures to be taken for developing countries.

The report and the conclusions of this conference offer a set of new regulatory arrangements for the air community, to be used by States at their discretion.

At this point, it is interesting to remember that a number of contracting States, such as Australia, Japan, and African and certain Latin American states, opposed the multilateral approach and all-out liberalization of market access before studying all the benefits, concerns, and risks of the process. They were still in favour of the bilateral system, which offered them the best protection in a competitive market.

They expressed that any liberalization should be evolutionary, progressive, and gradual, and could be successfully accomplished in the bilateral framework. At the same time, multilateral market liberalization could also start at the regional or subregional level among states of equal economic size and power.

An alternative to market access liberalization could be the relaxation of air carrier national ownership and control criteria. There was support for the idea of modifying the national ownership requirement of the investment possibilities for carriers, or of extending it to states that are parties to an agreement, or to groups having 'a community of interests'.

From 24 to 29 March 2003, in Montreal, the Worldwide Air Transport Conference[187] on 'Challenges and Opportunities of Liberalization' was held. It resulted in an important declaration of Global Principles for the Liberalization of International Air Transport, recommendations on model clauses and model air transport agreements, and many other relevant issues.

As did its predecessor, the fourth Worldwide Air Transport Conference in 1994,[188] it reaffirmed that the basic principles of sovereignty, fair and equal opportunity, non-discrimination, interdependence, harmonization, and cooperation set out in the Chicago Convention (1944) had served international air transport well and continue to provide the basis for future development of international civil aviation.

The main focus as well as the general principles recognized that ICAO and its contracting States, together with the air transport industry and other stakeholders in civil aviation, will work to:

- ensure high and improving levels of safety and security;
- promote the effective and sustainable participation in and benefit from international air transport by all States, respecting national sovereignty and equality of opportunity, taking into consideration the differing levels of economic development among States through the maintenance of the principle of 'community of interest' and the fostering of preferential measures for developing countries;
- strive to limit its environmental impact;
- safeguard fair competition adequately and effectively; and
- facilitate the provision of resources, particularly for developing countries.

The preservation of safety and security are vital concerns. Both must remain of paramount importance in the operation and development of international air

187. <www.icao.int/icao/en/atb/atconf5/>.
188. Report on the conference: *ICAO Doc 9644*.

transport, and States must accept their primary responsibility for ensuring regulatory oversight of safety and security, irrespective of any change in the economic regulatory arrangements.

VI. NATIONAL CARRIER: SUBSTANTIAL OWNERSHIP AND EFFECTIVE CONTROL

A. Background of the Concept

As one may know the International Air Services Transit Agreement of 1944[189] states in Article 1, section 6:

> Each Contracting State reserves its right to refuse the certificate or authorization to air carrier of scheduled services that is substantially owned and effectively controlled by nationals of the Contracting State . . . .

The treatment of air carrier ownership and control at regional and international levels is, insofar, an important regulation issue in commercial aviation in general and in the deregulation/liberalization process in particular.

The topic has a strong relationship with political criteria regarding the nationality of air carriers.

The Chicago Convention of 1944 contains previsions in Articles 17 and 18 referring to the nationality of aircraft, but it does not cover the topic of nationality of the air carrier. Traditionally, the nationality of air carriers is based on the criteria of substantial ownership and effective control. This concept originated at a time when national carriers were owned by the designating State or its nationals, and, due to defence, economic, or political reasons, were viewed as playing an important strategic role. When States participate in a bilateral air transport service agreement, they do not only negotiate the necessary market access rights in favour of their partner states, but they also approve the airline or airlines that were designated to exercise those rights. When the State was the only owner of the air carrier, all financial issues were covered, if necessary, by the State budget, and very often, financial subsidies and other types of assistance were made available, based on the public service character of scheduled air transport provided by carriers.

Some of the reasons cited to justify the traditional concept are the following:

- National air carriers are considered a strategic asset.
- Aircraft of nationally owned companies should be available for national defence or emergency needs.
- Foreign-owned airlines should be excluded from the domestic market.
- During the World Wars, there was a need to know if the ownership and the control of air carriers were in the hands of the enemies. Currently, this vision has been transferred to the economic field.

189. 84 *UNTS* 389; *ICAO Doc. 7500.*

- National carriers could be an important tool in the development of tourism and other activities with close relations to air transport, and could benefit the national economy.
- National air carriers bring opportunities into the labour field, taking into account the high degree of specialization in the field.
- A situation of potentially non-reciprocated benefits can be prevented when an air carrier from one State uses another State's rights.

Arguments against the traditional concept of nationality of air carriers are that it:

- represents an obstacle to foreign investment for air carriers who need it;
- creates a negative environment for fair competition;
- is often masked through alliances of air carriers looking to overcome limitations.

Presently (in air transport more than in other economic activities, due to increasing cost pressures – particularly fuel and labour costs), air carriers are in need of capital, particularly foreign investment, to satisfy their financial needs. Due to the trend of liberalization in market access, important changes have taken place regarding the concept of air carrier nationality. In the current state of operational and commercial competition (which occurs in a number of ways, including cooperative arrangements such as airline alliances, code-sharing, joint ventures, and franchise operations, some of which have involved transnational investment), air carriers must face huge challenges to survive. In the era of globalization of national economies, the transfer of the economic and financial responsibilities from the State to the private entities has long started, expressed as the well-known 'privatization process'. This trend reached Latin America ten years after first appearing in the world scenario.

Nowadays, achieving this necessary balance involves great difficulties. In the international arena, the high pressure of competition invites many States to subsidize, a controversial policy condemned by ICAO's Fifth Air Transport Conference, held in Montreal 2003.

B. Meaning of Substantial Ownership and Effective Control

What is the meaning of substantial ownership and effective control of the air carrier? The answer to this question is not merely an academic exercise: it has important economic implications, because under certain circumstances, a State could revoke the prior authorization given to an air carrier if, for any reasons, it lost the conditions required.

Substantial ownership generally means that the amount of ownership of the air carrier held by a party is more than 50%.

The other criterion, '*effective control*' of the air carrier, is more complex. The element of substantial ownership can often be fixed by public or other information of shareholders. The second element, 'effective control', may be exercised in different ways, many of which may not be readily apparent. A prestigious Italian lawyer, Giuseppe Ferri, expressed that, to understand the concept of effective control of a company, it is necessary to be face-to-face with a person who can direct the economic activities of the company.

The question is whether one can gather the majority or the proportion of equity that suffices to secure the adoption of resolutions or decisions of the company.

For example, air carrier management may exercise effective control over certain operations, such as opening a new route, while financial entities or a government might exercise effective control for the purpose of increasing the air carrier's capital, merging it with another air carrier or dissolving the company.

In business, there are many ways to secure control of a company, through the equity of the participants or shareholders. The controls could be exercised from within or outside the company. In the first case, there is a direct relationship with the amount of equity when the participation is less than 2% of the capital, the right to vote is absent, and internal control cannot be achieved. When the equity is more than 10%, the situation changes – even more so if it is possible to exercise significant pressure in the assemblies or ordinary meetings of the companies.

The commercial law doctrine expresses that it is also necessary to gain administrative or management control with influence on the superior level of executives to obtain management control of the company.

In this case, it may be possible to obtain 'voting trust', gaining the right to vote in the company without ownership of the equities.

Outside control of the company can be achieved through a private partnership with the state.

Another tool could be secured or unsecured financial loans, or through mortgages. The holdings could represent control of the companies, with the indirect transferences of investment from a healthy company to another in poor financial condition.

In common law, holdings are possible when one company is a partner of another and has more than half of its equity share and can exercise the integration of its management council.

Due to the complexity of determining effective control of the air carrier, the States examine this on a case-by-case basis, applying their national laws and regulations concerning corporate responsibility in decision-making.

C. Exceptions from the Concept

Following the model of Recommendation VIII adopted in 1944 by the Chicago Convention in line with the provisions of the International Air Services Transit Agreement of 1944,[190] practically all bilateral air transport service agreements offered the same formula on the nationality of the air carrier.

190. 84 *UNTS* 389; *ICAO Doc. 7500.*

Nevertheless, there are exceptions, particularly in the establishment of some transnational carriers, such as the SAS, created by three Scandinavian countries; Air Afrique,[191] created by eleven African states; and Gulf Air, established by four Middle Eastern states.

In those cases, agreements were signed by the States to designate their multinational air carriers to serve a third State, with, obviously, the necessary modifications to the ownership and control provisions to allow that the multinational air carriers be authorized to exercise the commercial rights negotiated with the third State.

In addition, the regional organizations offer another, more flexible option to the traditional concept of nationality of airlines.

Along these lines, the Andean Community[192] allows a Member State to – at the level of national law – specify the conditions of development of a designated air carrier of another Member State. Resolutions 297, 320, 360, and 361 of the Commission refer to an air carrier entitled to operate services within the Pact in line with the national laws of the Pact state designating the airline. This concept was adjusted at the tenth Ordinary Meeting of the Andean Committee of Airlines (February 2002), where the following important conditions for the establishment of the Andean air carriers were specified: the main domicile or real and effective headquarters of the airline (i.e., its management and main base of management) must be located in the territory of one of the Member States; and the crew of the aircraft possess certificates granted by a Member State in addition to the operational control and technical management of the fleet under the air carrier.

The Caribbean Community Air Service Agreement created in 1996, composed of Antigua and Barbuda, Bahamas, Belize, Barbados, Dominica, Guyana, Jamaica, Montserrat, Saint Kitts and Nevis, Santa Lucia, San Vicente and the Grenadines, Suriname, and Trinidad and Tobago, allows the ownership and control of the airlines by one or more Member States or their nationals.

As regards the Fortaleza Agreement, concluded in 1996 (and integrated by Argentina, Bolivia, Brazil, Chile, Paraguay, and Uruguay, and later by Peru), Article 5 states that the designation of the air carrier is subject to the requirements of the law belonging to the Member State.

In Europe, according to Council Regulation No. 2407/92[193] (now: No. 1008/2008[194]), an air carrier is to be considered as belonging to the Community, if it is owned by the majority and effectively controlled by Member States or their nationals, with its principal place of business and registered office located in a Member State.

191. Air Afrique was a Pan-African airline mainly owned by many West African countries. It was established as the official transnational carrier for francophone West and Central Africa, under the premise that many of these countries had not the economical capability of affording the creation and maintenance of a national airline. It was liquidated in 2002.

192. Established in 1991, based on the Andean Pact, concluded by five Latin American states, Bolivia, Colombia, Ecuador, Peru, and Venezuela.

193. *OJ* No. L 240 of 24 Aug. 1992, 1.

194. *OJ* No. L 293 of 31 Oct. 2008, 3.

Another exception to the traditional concept of nationality of air carriers is the Multilateral Kona Agreement signed between Brunei, Chile, the US, New Zealand, Singapore, and later, Peru and Samoa. It permits the designated airline of a party to be one whose effective control is vested in the designating party, is incorporated, and has its principal place of business in the territory of the designating party.

Fifty-two African states in line with the Yamoussoukro Decision of 1999, during the fifth Worldwide Air Transport Conference (March 2003), stressed their opinion in favour of foreign investment in air carriers. Along these lines, it was recommended that all Member States adopt the ICAO formula, which is more flexible than the traditional concept of nationality of air carriers. The Yamoussoukro Declaration on a New African Air Transport Policy, which was signed by the Ministers of Civil Aviation of African States in October 1988 (and later revised in September 1994), established a programme for the integration of African airlines and guidelines for cooperation in the air transport field. One of the main changes introduced by this Declaration was Article 6, concerning the selection criteria of the air carrier in bilateral air service agreements. For these purposes, the air carrier must:

- be established in line with the national law of the designating State.
- have a place, central control, and principal place of business in the territory of the designating State.
- be under the effective control of the designating State or its citizens.
- be authorized to operate by the designating State in conformity with the standards contained in Annex 6 of the Chicago Convention. In addition, there are other technical requirements concerning the legal status of the aircraft and mandatory assurance and compliance, similar to those recommended by the ICAO.

Non-compliance with any of the conditions indicated above gives the State the right to withdraw the permission of the operations. This new African Air Policy involved forty-five Member States.

Another exception to the concept of nationality is the Pacific Island Air Services Agreement, known as the Vava'u Agreement (Australia, Cook Islands, Micronesia, Fiji, Kiribati, Nauru, New Zealand, Niue, Palau, Papua, New Guinea, Republic of Marshall Islands, Samoa, Salomon Islands, Tonga, Tuvalu, and Vanuatu), which adopts two steps of transition to a new community system of ownership and control of the air carriers: the first beginning six months after the agreement enters into force, and the second, twenty-four months later. The first step is to permit designation of the air carrier that has substantial ownership and effective control of one or more contracting States or their citizens. In this period, a State without a national carrier can designate an air carrier belonging to another State, provided that the place of residence and principal place of business is in the territory of the designating State – a valuable option to prepare for a more flexible status. In addition, cross-ownership among Member States is permitted, foregoing the substantial ownership and effective control requirements in any country of the region. This kind of flexibility allows better market access.

D. New Concept of Nationality of the Air Carrier

A new formula emerged from the fifth Worldwide Air Transport Conference, held in Montreal in 2003, containing a wise balance of all the elements. Among different views expressed in the fifth Conference, it is important to remember that the European Civil Aviation Conference (ECAC) and their Member States considered that, in view of the economic situation of many airlines, the need to make international financial resources more accessible for aviation, and the wish of the air transport industry to have the same commercial freedom enjoyed by other sectors of the economy could be met by three key principles:

- States should accommodate any other State that wishes to liberalize its ownership and control restrictions unilaterally or as part of a group of like-minded states.
- With appropriate assurances on safety, consideration should be given to designation of airlines based in a third country.
- ICAO Member States should develop a common approach to liberalizing ownership and control requirements while ensuring high standards in aviation safety.

The IATA advocated four steps to liberalize airline ownership and control:

- Distinguish between commercial control conferred by ownership and regulatory control exercised by the licensing authority.
- Remove restrictions on ownership.
- Make regulatory control the responsibility of the designating State.
- Provide control of safety and security through adoption and implementation of the relevant ICAO Model Clauses.

It was interesting to hear the position of the International Transport Workers Federation (IFT), which doubted the beneficial effects claimed by proponents of liberalizing the national ownership and effective control criteria and believed that such action would lead to the FOCs – a situation that prevails in the maritime industry. The IFT recommended that the national ownership and control criteria are retained in the interest of stability, reliability, and economic security of air transport, that states retain effective regulatory tools to meet the public interest dimension of air transport, and that the ICAO identify measures to prevent safety and security 'dumping'.

In the US, it became clear that, under new regimes that change the traditional rules involving airline ownership and control, the responsibility and lines of authority for safety and security oversight must remain clear. There must be a clear point of contact for safety and security, which in almost all cases will be the state of the operator, regardless of the extent to which it has delegated execution of its responsibilities to others.

The International Federation of Air Line Pilots Association (IFALPA), considered that the proposed changes to the ownership and control criteria did not address the labour and social implications and that the general rule that a designated airline must be substantially owned and effectively controlled by a national of the designating country should be preserved as an essential safeguard against the use of FOCs, which would undermine labour and social standards.

At the same time, a few States were in favour of retaining the use of the traditional national ownership and control criteria, particularly in bilateral air services agreements, to take into account the disparities in economies, scope of the markets, and competitiveness of airlines of the partners in the agreement, as well as to ensure reciprocity.

In the ICAO, the issue ran a long course since the year 1983, when a group of small countries proposed the new concept of 'community of interest' as fostering access to additional capital not available within the region (Resolution A24-12[195]).

Later, during the fourth Worldwide Air Transport Conference in 1994,[196] the criteria of the principal place of business plus a solid link with the designating State were admitted, as a result of studies developed by a Panel of Experts (ATRP/9-4) with emphasis as a *sine-qua-non*-requirement to preserve safety and security.

Finally, in the fifth Conference, a model clause was proposed for discretionary use and as one among a number of available options:

> Article X: Designation and Authorization
> (a) Each Party shall have the right to designate in writing to the other Party (an airline) (one or more airlines) (as many airlines as it wishes) to operate the agreed services (in accordance with the Agreement) and to withdraw or alter such designation.
> (b) On receipt of such a designation, and of application from the designated airline, in the form and manner prescribed for operating authorization with minimum procedural delay, provided that:
> (1) the designated airline has its principal place of business * (and permanent residence in the territory of the designating Party,
> (2) the Party designating the airline has and maintains effective regulatory control** of the airline,
> (3) the Party designating the airline is in compliance with the provisions set forth in Article X (Safety) and Article Y (Aviation Security), and
> (4) the designated airline is qualified to meet other conditions prescribed under the laws and regulations normally applied to the operation of international air transport services by the Party receiving the designation.
> (c) On receipt of the operating authorization of paragraph 2 a designated airline may at any time begin to operate the agreed services for which it is designated, provided that the airline complies with the applicable provisions of this Agreement.
> Integral Notes:
> * Evidence of principal place of business is predicated upon the airline being established and incorporated in the territory of the designating party in

195. <www.icao.int/icao/en/assembl/a24/docs/a24_res01.djvu>.
196. Report on the conference: *ICAO Doc 9644*.

accordance with relevant national laws and regulations, has a substantial amount of its operations and capital investment in physical facilities in the territory of the designating party, pays income tax, registers and bases its aircraft there, and employs a significant number of nationals in managerial technical and operational positions.
** Evidence of effective regulatory control is predicated upon but is not limited to the airline holding a valid operating license or permit issued by the licensing authority such as an AOC meets the criteria of the designating party for the operation of international air services, such as proof of financial health, ability to meet public interest requirements, obligations for assurance of service; and the designating party has and maintains safety and security oversight programmes in compliance with ICAO standards.

The conditions set forth in paragraph 2 of this Article should also be used in the article on revocation of authorization.

In conclusion, although there has been a gradual relaxation of rules, many countries maintain limitations on foreign investment in and control of air carriers. These restrictions can impede the long-term restructuring of the industry.

E. Practical Solutions to Overcome Restrictions in Foreign Investment

Alliances, code-sharing, and other forms of cooperation between airlines can circumvent some of the problems, but there are no transparent alternatives to obtain the level of flexibility air carriers need.

Air carrier alliances – voluntary unions of airlines held together by various commercial cooperative arrangements – are a relatively recent and rapidly evolving global phenomenon in the air transport field.

Alliances may be internal, domestic, regional, intercontinental, or global and can be of any size, for any particular objective, or for any length of time.

Modern alliances differ from traditional airline cooperation. One well-known example is pooling, which usually involves an inter-airline agreement on tariffs and sharing capacity, cost, and revenue, whereas alliances are normally built around possible synergies and complementary route structures and services.

An alliance agreement may contain different elements such as code-sharing, blocked space, cooperation in marketing, pricing, frequent flyer programmes, and coordination in scheduling, joint ventures, and franchising.

Among the most important alliance groupings are Star Alliance – founded in 1997 by Air Canada, Lufthansa, SAS, Thai Airways International and United Airlines –, Sky Team – founded in 2000 by AeroMexico, Air France, Delta Air Lines and Korean Air –, Oneworld – founded in 1998 by American Airlines, British Airways, Cathay Pacific and Quantas.

It is important to take into account that the partnership of each alliance group can be unstable.

Code-sharing is becoming a more common practice between carriers. After all, it is an excellent tool of competition in the current framework of international air transport characterized by liberalization and globalization.

The practical applications of code-sharing vary widely, and it is considered one of many air carrier strategies used to improve participation. Other strategies include cooperation between and among air carriers in joint services and marketing, blocked space arrangements, management expertise and training, and investment, as indicated before.

Code-sharing involves the use by an airline of its designator code on an aircraft operated by another airline, which itself uses its designator code on that aircraft. This can result in a single, common, or combined air carrier designator code for two or more air carriers for a certain flight connection, although the connections (or individual segments of the connection) are only operated with aircraft of one of these carriers.

It is promoted as a marketing tool by the airlines and used to integrate their schedules and operations with those of other airlines.

It could represent an important advantage for developing countries, as it offers the possibility of serving very thin routes at minimal cost and using unused rights.

However, code-sharing has negative impacts, such as consumer deception, due to the bias in the display of code-shared flights. We also need to bear in mind the possible anti-competitive effects when a thin code-shared market may be monopolized by code-sharing partners and drive out competition.

To give adequate guidelines to its Member States (190), the ICAO prepared a Study on the Implications of Airline Code-Sharing, which touches upon, among other aspects, the different types and forms of code-sharing; the effects of the new formula on traffic development; market access; competition; and economic, legal, consumer, security and facilitation aspects.

This study was prepared on the instructions of the Council as one of the follow-up actions of the November 1994 Worldwide Air Transport Conference. It was circulated to all Member States. Also, consumer issues are being addressed by the ICAO Code of Conduct for the Regulation and Operation of CRSs. As is well-known, the obligations in the Code for states, systems vendors, air carriers, and subscribers are based on fair competition, transparency and non-discrimination, and it contains a provision on the display of code-shared flights. For instance, displaying code-shared flights more than three times can result in the undesirable practice of 'screen padding'.

This is why the ECAC prepared a recommendation on 'Consumer information/protection needs in connection with code-shared air services'. This document recognizes the necessity, in the interests of safety and passenger protection, of greater transparency with regard to the delimitation of operational and technical responsibilities for code-shared services. It is important to take into account that the ECAC recommendation is based on the knowledge of potentially deceptive and misleading practices against the consumer, and also on the fact that the contracting carrier retains the ultimate responsibility for ensuring that passenger needs are satisfied.

In other words, the practice of code-sharing has benefits and disadvantages. It can be abused and be counterproductive and offers enormous scope for interpretation, and in most cases, the passenger must be covered in the most transparent way with clear rules, particularly in terms of the liability of the carriers during travel.

Code-sharing was initially designed in the US domestic market to circumvent some of the constraints of the 1978 Airline Deregulation Act period, particularly when Allegheny, now USAir, wanted to keep service on a number of routes for which its fleet was ill-suited and on which it was losing money. After its beginnings as a domestic phenomenon, code-sharing has emerged in the international markets in 1988 with more than 400 different alliances.

According to the ICAO Manual on the Regulation of International Air Transport, code-sharing is the 'use of the flight designator code of one air carrier on a service performed by a second air carrier, which service is usually also identified (and may be required to be identified) as a service of, and being performed by, the second carrier'. According to the IATA Resolution 762, amended later in 1993, code-sharing entails the use by an airline of its designator code on an aircraft operated by another airline, which itself also uses its designator code on that aircraft. This can result in a single, or combined, air carrier designator code by two or more air carriers for a certain flight connection, although the connection or individual segments of the connection are only operated with aircraft of one of those carriers.

Two-letter designator codes are provided by the ICAO to identify the airlines on passenger tickets, computer reservation systems, airline guides, and airport information boards. Under a code-sharing agreement, the connecting flights being operated by two separate airlines may be listed as being a single carrier service.

There are a number of cases that serve to illustrate the mechanism of code-sharing in practical terms. For instance, American Airlines and LAN have signed an agreement to provide new code-share services between the US and Chile. Under this formula, LAN will lease and operate an AA 767 on the New York-Santiago route three times a week. AA will code-share on these flights and will lease and operate a LAN 767 for one daily round trip between New York and LAX, and then, LAN will operate the aircraft on a continuing service between JFK and Santiago.

In summary, code-sharing is an agreement between air carriers whereby one party operates a particular service, while allowing another party to hold out at the same time the same service under that other party's designator code, in addition to or in place of the code of the operating carrier.

At the international level, code-sharing can allow carriers to access behind gateway feed traffic despite restricted cabotage rights, nationality clauses in bilateral agreements, and constraints on foreign ownership. For these reasons, governments need to weigh the pros and cons carefully on a case-by-case basis.

Another matter of concern is passenger liability. Code-sharing flights are regarded as successive carriage flights under the Warsaw System and Montreal Convention of 1999, and thus passenger liability rests with the carrier with which the passenger enters into a contract, although the actual carrier may have liability under the Guadalajara Convention of 1961. Potential problems arise when the operating carrier has different contractual terms on liability from the code-sharing partner, under the umbrella of the Warsaw System.[197]

Code-sharing can have implications for some other aspects, such as safety and security standards, regulated in the Chicago Convention of 1944 and its Annexes. For these reasons, it is important that clear lines of accountability and responsibility be established for the parties involved in a code-sharing arrangement, as technical and operational regulations may vary from one airline to another.

Another commercial practice is airline franchising, which involves a franchiser carrier granting a right to use various of its corporate identity elements, for instance its flight designator code or marketing logos, to a franchise carrier to market or deliver the latter's air service products, subject to standards and controls so as to maintain the level of quality of the franchiser.

This commercial tool was initiated in the US in the early 1980s. It usually involves a major carrier with smaller regional airlines, with the latter acting as feeders.

In the same line with the aforementioned commercial practices, franchising has implications in market access rights, competition, and consumer protection.

With reference to market access rights, concerns may arise when the franchisee airline operates services on routes where it has its own underlying route or traffic rights, but it flies its aircraft and holds out its service using the franchiser's brand.

Concerning consumer protection, since franchising, like code-sharing, involves an operator using the brand and code of another airline, it may have similar deceptive effects on passengers. This is why many regulatory rules of code-sharing need to apply to franchising, as well as all safety and security requirements.

VII. THE CONGESTION OF AIRPORTS AND POSSIBLE SOLUTIONS

Airport congestion represents one of the greatest challenges in a large number of countries, particularly, in the US and in European states.

A congested airport is one whose capacity for handling traffic is inadequate to accommodate demand. Several problems arise in connection with congested airports. A number of methodologies have been developed in recent years to overcome these challenges – the use of 'time slots' is the most popular measure.

Every State applies different policies regarding the administration of slots. For instance, it is common to auction slots. This involves the allocation of infrastructure, which increases capacity, bringing it more in line with a competitive framework.

197. For more details see Chapter 7.

There are many methods for slot auctioning that reduce some of the problems related to accumulation, and permit the matching of slots at origins and destinations. One of the difficulties is the non-divisibility of time slots: any auction process also entails a relatively complex set of operational criteria. In the US, the purchase, sale, and lease of domestic slots is permitted at certain airports, subject to the Federal Aviation Administration's High Density Rule.

Another method is the creation of committees that operate at most airports that allow air carriers the opportunity to coordinate their landing and takeoff needs across a network of airports.

Nevertheless, this poses problems, causing the exclusion or, at the very least, limiting the scope of new entrants. It is not a market-based approach, and the negotiated procedure involved does not adequately take into account the cost of slots.

Authorities may administrate slot allocation seeking to meet wider social or economic objectives than airlines. Operating such a system requires a large bureaucracy, given the detailed requirements of flights.

The application of codes of conduct for airport scheduling committees represents a good solution for a self-regulation approach within an administrative structure. The IATA criteria may be the best way to combat the complexity of slot allocation. Participation in the Airline Schedule Coordination Conferences, which are held twice yearly approximately four months prior to each scheduling season, is open to any air carrier, member or non-member of the IATA.

The criteria of 'grandfather rights', 'historical precedent', and the 'use-it-or-lose-it' rules give priority to scheduled services, but also to discrete slot assignment in the case of slots used in a previous equivalent season.

Changes in flight schedules are accommodated between air carriers on a voluntary basis.

There is no doubt that issues at capacity-constrained airports will involve problems related to competition, for instance, the avoidance of excessive concentration and the abuse of a dominant position. For this reason, states provide some flexibility to use alternate airports and cities that can accommodate new entrants.

The ICAO prepared a study, 'Regulatory Implications of the Allocation of Flight Departure and Arrival Slots at International Airport', as Circular 283,[198] which provides a broad policy framework and practical guide, which States may use at their discretion. This guide analyses the existing situation, trends for airports where demand by air carriers to use the airport exceeds its capacity, the regulatory framework involved, and the means by which governments, airports, and air carriers have sought to alleviate or minimize this situation. It also assesses existing and potential mechanisms for dealing with a chronic shortage of airport capacity and suggests possible improvements or alternatives to the existing systems.

---

198. For Foreword, Table of Contents and Executive Summary of Circular 283 see <www.icao.int/icao/en/atb/epm/Ecp/C283_en.pdf>.

Also, the Worldwide Air Transport Conference held in Montreal in 2003,[199] discussed the problem of market access at capacity-constrained airports and associated issues of slot allocation. The conclusion was that:

> Consideration should be given to request for preferential treatment from those States whose airports are not slot-constrained but whose air carriers are unsuccessful in obtaining slots at slot-constrained airports, consistent with relevant national legislation and international obligations.

Most importantly, slot allocation should be fair, non-discriminatory and transparent, and should take into account the interests of all stakeholders. It should also be globally compatible, aimed at maximizing effective use of airport capacity, simple, practicable, and economically sustainable.

199. <www.icao.int/icao/en/atb/atconf5/>.

Chapter 5
Rights in Aircraft

Ludwig Weber

I. GENEVA CONVENTION OF 1948

A. Introduction

The Geneva Convention of 1948 on the International Recognition of Rights in Aircraft,[1] which had eighty-nine States parties as of early 2011, is based on the principles of national registration and mutual recognition with respect to nationally registered property rights in aircraft, in particular, those collateralizing the aircraft for credit provided for the purpose of financing its acquisition or for securing its lease.

The principle of mutual recognition as set out in the Geneva Convention is in line with the thinking behind Article 33 of the Chicago Convention.[2] However, the principle of national registration under the Geneva Convention entailed important limitations in relation to searches and in relation to procedure for obtaining judgment for recognition and enforcement of registered rights in the aircraft.[3]

1. Convention signed at Geneva on 19 Jun. 1948, *ICAO Doc. 7620; T.I.A.S. No. 2847 (1948).*
2. Article 33 of the Convention on International Civil Aviation, *ICAO Doc.* 7500, provides for the mutual recognition of certificates and licenses between Contracting States, provided that the requirements under which such certificates or licenses were issued are equal to or above the minimum standards established under the ICAO Annexes.
3. On the Geneva Convention, see N. M. Matte, *Treatise of Air-Aeronautical Law* (Montreal-Toronto: 1981), 543–579 with further references; Beaumont and Shawcross, *Air Law*, 2 Vols, Issue 101 (Butterworths Law, September 2005), 182 et seq. with references.

Elmar M. Giemulla & Ludwig Weber, *International and EU Aviation Law: Selected Issues*, pp. 193–221.

B. Historical Background

The first draft for a convention on rights in aircraft was developed as early as 1931 by the *Comité International Technique d'Experts Juridiques Aériens* (International Technical Committee of Legal Air Experts) (CITEJA).[4] At the Chicago Conference in November/December 1944, a recommendation was passed at the initiative of the United States to work towards the conclusion of an international convention on the transfer of title to aircraft and related matters.[5]

The 1931 draft of the CITEJA was therefore transmitted to the first Provisional Assembly of Provisional International Civil Aviation Organization (PICAO) in 1946. After modifications made by CITEJA at its last session in November 1946 and by the International Civil Aviation Organization (ICAO) Legal Committee in 1947, it was submitted to the second Session of the ICAO Assembly in May/June 1948, which formally adopted it.[6] It was initially signed by twenty States.

C. Principles and Main Provisions

The fundamental principle of the Convention is the principle of mutual recognition of certain rights in aircraft among Contracting States, provided they have been properly constituted and publicly recorded as defined in Article I of the Convention.[7]

These rights comprise (1) property rights in aircraft; (2) rights to acquire aircraft by purchase coupled with possession of the aircraft; (3) right to possession of aircraft under a lease of at least six months; and (4) mortgages, hypotheques, and similar rights in aircraft, contractually created as security for payment of indebtedness. The principle of mutual recognition applies on conditions that (1) these rights have been constituted in accordance with the law of the Contracting State in which the aircraft is registered; and (2) that they are recorded in a public record of that State.[8]

The obligation to recognize such rights, constituted and recorded under foreign national law, is not dependent on equivalence, that is, the existence of a corresponding right or rights under the national legal system, provided the rights constituted and recorded under foreign law fall into one of the four categories set out in Article I(1) of the Convention. The mutuality of the obligation to recognize such rights applies automatically among all Contracting States,[9] and does therefore not

4. Comité international technique d'experts juridiques aériens (International technical committee of air law experts).
5. First whereas clause of the preamble of the Geneva Convention, *ICAO Doc*. 7620; on the historical aspects, see N. M. Matte, *ibid*. (n. 3), 543–546.
6. N. M. Matte, *ibid*., 544.
7. On the principle of mutual recognition, see below; this principle serves mainly as a basis for enforcement in a foreign jurisdiction, where the creditor would otherwise be unable to provide evidence of the existence of a valid right.
8. Article I (1), in particular sub-paras (i) and (ii), of the Convention.
9. Provided the conditions of Art. I (1), sub-paras (i) and (ii), are fulfilled, this provision sets out a multilateral obligation flowing from a multilateral treaty.

depend on any reciprocity within the framework of the Convention. On the other hand, any Contracting State may prohibit the recording of any right in its own public record if such rights cannot validly be constituted according to its national law.[10]

As regards the public record referred to in Articles I(1)(ii), II, and III of the Convention, it is a national record or registry. It is for each Contracting State to decide on its form of organization and name.[11] However, the public record must be maintained and operated by an authority of that State, must make provision for the regular recording of rights in aircraft, and must provide for the issuance of recording certificates in conformity with Article III of the Convention.[12] Reasonable charges may be levied for the maintenance of the public record.[13]

The effects of the recording of any right in the public record are set out in Articles I(2) and II(2) of the Convention. Under Article I(2), rights in aircraft entered on the public record shall not be subject to priority of other, unrecorded rights. Under Article II(2), other effects of the recording of rights in aircraft, except as otherwise provided in the Convention, shall be determined by the national law of the State of registration. Although the clarity of these provisions leaves much to be desired, it was the objective of the Convention to apply the priority of recordings rule, that is, recorded rights take priority over unrecorded rights, but for the rest to leave other priority aspects, for example, to what extent earlier recordings take priority over later recordings, to be determined by the rules of national law.[14]

Some special rules on priority are set out in Articles IV, V, and X of the Convention. Article IV provides for the priority of certain salvage and special preservation claims over other recorded rights under the circumstances set out therein. Article V provides for the extension of the priority of a right under Article I(1)(d) of the Convention to accrued interest for up to three years. Similarly, Article X provides for the extension of the priority of a right under Article I to certain spare parts[15] as set out in the Article.

The rules on enforcement are set out in Articles VI to X of the Convention, which mention attachment or sale of the aircraft.[16] In the case of sale of the aircraft, the enforcement proceedings shall generally be governed by the national law of the state where the sale takes place, Article VII(1). However, in line with Article VII(2), a six-week delay for the sale, a four-week public notice of the sale at the place of registration of the aircraft, and a concurrent notification of

10. Article II (3) of the Convention.
11. Articles I (1) (ii), II and III make it clear that it is up to each Contracting State to decide on the way its national recording system or registry is organized. In principle, it may either be operated separately from the national aircraft registry, or as a part or subdivision thereof.
12. See Articles III (1), (2) and (4) of the Convention.
13. Article III (4) of the Convention.
14. Articles I (2) and II (2) of the Convention.
15. For the definition of 'spare parts', see Art. X (4) of the Convention; on this subject, see Matte, *ibid.* (n. 3), 575–576.
16. Attachment is mentioned only passingly in Art. V. It is somewhat surprising that other remedies in enforcement, such as administration of the asset, are not mentioned. The same applies for injunctive relief. On enforcement issues, see W. Schwenk/E. Giemulla, *Handbuch des Luftverkehrsrechts*, 3rd edn (Heymanns, Köln: 2005), 348 et seq.

the recorded owner and of all holders of recorded rights are mandatory. Article VII(5) provides some special rules in favour of persons having suffered injury or property damage on the ground.[17]

Articles VIII and IX govern transfer of property and transfer of registration of the aircraft as a result of a sale in execution. Such sale, if effected in conformity with Article VII, shall transfer property in such aircraft free from all rights not assumed by the purchaser.[18] As regards the transfer of registration, it shall require either a sale in conformity with Article VII, or otherwise the satisfaction of or consent by the holders of recorded rights.[19]

The Convention does not regulate searches for title or for other recorded rights, which is a matter of considerable practical importance. Searches are therefore purely subject to national procedural law governing the respective national record or registry. Similarly, the Convention does not regulate requirements of required documentation or evidence in relation to recordings,[20] nor does it regulate the procedure for dealing with such evidence, including remedies and injunctive relief.[21] All these matters are left to procedure under national law.

D. Issues of Practical Application of the Convention

Searches in relation to aircraft before a transaction takes place, so as to ascertain whether and to what extent it is subject to existing recorded rights, are not regulated or even mentioned in the Convention. Such searches may be complex, time-consuming, and costly. Several national registries may have to be searched, sometimes in different languages and involving corresponding legal counsel at the place of each foreign national registry.

The procedure for obtaining judgment for the enforcement of nationally registered rights in aircraft, when the validity of such rights or of their registration is contested,[22] can be equally complex, particularly if such procedure is only the

17. See on this specific subject N. M. Matte, *ibid.* (n. 3), 572–575.
18. Article VIII of the Convention.
19. Article IX of the Convention. However, this provision does not give any specific remedy to the party wishing to transfer the registration. This can be of practical importance in cases where the national aircraft registry refuses to deregister the aircraft, e.g., where it does not wish to become involved in a private law dispute as to whether or not the holders of recorded rights were fully satisfied or whether the sale was in conformity with Article VII of the Convention.
20. Although some rules on recordings are contained in Articles II (1) and III (1) of the Convention, all other matters regarding evidence for the purpose of enforcement are governed by national law, namely *lex fori*. This means that the requirements of evidence may differ, depending on where enforcement is sought.
21. In practice, injunctive relief and other speedy remedies are in many cases important in order to take control of the aircraft and take further steps to preserve its value. This perspective had not been fully realized in the 1930s and 1940s when the Convention was drafted.
22. The conditions set out in Art. I (1) sub-paras (i) and (ii) of the Convention are essential for the recognition and potential subsequent enforcement of a right in an aircraft. Therefore, recalcitrant debtors will contest that these conditions are fulfilled, since if successful such objections will strike at the basis of the subsequent enforcement remedies of the creditor.

starting point for the enforcement of such rights.[23] The procedure may require that the proceedings be brought in the jurisdiction of the national public record or registry.[24] Any judicial decision which results may then require foreign judicial recognition for purposes of enforcing it, by for example arresting or impounding the aircraft in another jurisdiction. The Geneva Convention itself provides the roots for such complexity in its Articles II and VII.

Other difficulties arise as a result of the numerous exceptions which Contracting States may prescribe for the implementation of the Geneva Convention.[25]

Finally, *enforcement proceedings* have sometimes encountered difficulties when the aircraft in question is moved away from the jurisdiction or jurisdictions where such proceedings have been initiated.

As a result, the Geneva Convention has only been of limited value in facilitating credit transactions involving aircraft in international operations.[26] Such aircraft could only serve under certain conditions and with restrictions as collateral for loans and other credit transactions. Instead, other forms of guarantees, additional collateral, and/or alternative risk management have had to be used to satisfy lenders.

II. CAPE TOWN CONVENTION AND PROTOCOL OF 2001

A. Introduction

With the adoption of the Cape Town Convention[27] and Protocol[28] on 16 November 2001, the international aviation community took the necessary steps to go beyond the inherent limitations of the Geneva Convention in facilitating the financing of aircraft, engines, and helicopters involved in international operations.

The Cape Town Convention and Protocol of 2001 aim principally at doing away with the need to resort to alternative or additional collateral and/or guarantees, in favour of pure asset-based financing and leasing.[29]

23. See S. McGairl, 'The Proposed Unidroit Convention: International law for asset finance (aircraft)', *Uniform Law Review* NS – IV no. 2 (1999): 439 et seq., 448–449; see Arts I, II and VII of the Geneva Convention, ICAO Doc. 7620.
24. See the reference to the law of the Contracting State where the right in question was recorded, in Art. II (2); and Art. I (1) (i), establishing a link between the State of Registry of the aircraft and the law under which the recorded rights have been constituted.
25. See Articles II (2) and (3), IV (4) (b), VII (3), (5), X (3), XII of the Geneva Convention, *ICAO Doc*. 7620.
26. L. Weber, 'The New Registry for International Interests in Aircraft Equipment under the Cape Town Convention and Protocol of 2001', *ZLW 55* (2006): 1 et seq.; S. McGairl, *ibid.* (n. 23), 448–449.
27. Convention on International Interests in Mobile Equipment, signed at Cape Town on 16 Nov. 2001, *ICAO Doc*. 9793.
28. Protocol to the Convention on International Interests in Mobile Equipment on Matters Specific to Aircraft Equipment, signed at Cape Town on 16 Nov. 2001, *ICAO Doc*. 9794.
29. See A. Saunders/J. Walter, Proposed Unidroit Convention on International Interests in Mobile Equipment as applicable to Aircraft Equipment through the Aircraft Equipment Protocol: Economic Impact Assessment, September 1998, reproduced in: *Air and Space Law XXIII* (1998),

The main idea behind the Cape Town Convention is the creation of conditions conducive to acceptance by lenders and lessors of the asset as sufficient collateral for a credit transaction[30] regarding that asset. This involves the creation of international interests under a multilateral convention, and the creation of an international registry where such international interests can be registered. Hence, this system no longer relies on national registrations and on the mutual recognition of national registrations, as the Geneva Convention of 1948. Registrations and searches can be centrally effected. Rights and interests registered in the International Registry can be enforced in Contracting States in a similar manner as if they were nationally registered.

B. Historical Background

The Convention and Protocol were adopted as a result of a joint project of the International Civil Aviation Organization (ICAO) and the International Institute for the Unification of Private Law (UNIDROIT), at a Diplomatic Conference held in Cape Town in October/November 2001 under the joint auspices of both organizations.[31] The Diplomatic Conference also adopted a resolution, under which a Preparatory Commission for the International Registry was set up,[32]

339 et seq. See also M. Arundell/F.S. Wilson, 'The Need for International Secured Transactions and Leasing Rules for Aircraft Engines through the Proposed Unidroit Convention', *Air and Space Law XXIII* no. 6 (1998): 283 et seq.; D. Clancy and G. Voss, 'Facilitating Asset-based Financing and Leasing of Aircraft Equipment through the Proposed Unidroit Convention: Manufacturer's Perspective', *Air and Space Law XXIII* no. 6 (1998): 287 et seq.; N. de la Pena, 'Reforming the legal framework for security interests in mobile property', *Uniform Law Review* NS – IV no. 2 (1999): 347 et seq.; on the Economic Impact, see also T. J. Gallagher, 'Assessment of the Anticipated Economic Benefits of the Unidroit Convention', *Air and Space Law* XXIII no. 6 (1998): 294 et seq.

30. See J. Wool, 'The case for a commercial orientation to the proposed Unidroit Convention As Applied To Aircraft Equipment', *Uniform Law Review* NS – IV no. 2 (1999): 289 at 292; Wool, 'The Next Generation of International Aviation Finance Law: An Overview of the Proposed Unidroit Convention on International Interests in Mobile Equipment as Applied to Aircraft Equipment', *Air and Space Law*, XXIII no. 6 (1998): 243–276. See, however, for a critical view, B. J. H. Crans, 'The Unidroit Convention on International Interests in Mobile Equipment and the Aircraft Equipment Protocol: Some Critical Observations', *Air and Space Law* XXIII no. 6 (1998): 277 et seq.
31. The author had the privilege of serving as Co-Secretary General of the Diplomatic Conference which adopted the Convention and the Protocol and as Secretary of the various ICAO bodies which were involved in the government consultation process. On the Diplomatic Conference, see H. G. Bollweg/C. Henrichs, 'Das Übereinkommen von Kapstadt: Diplomatische Konferenz beschließt Übereinkünfte über Sicherungsrechte an Luftfahrtausrüstung', *ZLW* 51 no. 2 (2002): 186 et seq.
32. Resolution No. 2 of the Diplomatic Conference, relating to the Establishment of the Supervisory Authority and the International Registry for Aircraft Objects, in: *Final Act of the Diplomatic Conference to Adopt a Mobile Equipment Convention and an Aircraft Protocol held under the joint auspices of the International Civil Aviation Organization and of Unidroit at CapeTown from 29 Oct. 2001 to 16 Nov. 2001, ICAO Doc.* (2002).

with the task of establishing the International Registry foreseen under Articles 16 et seq. of the Convention and Article XVIII of the Protocol, and ensuring that it becomes operational by the time the Convention and Protocol enter into force.[33]

C. MAIN PROVISIONS OF THE CONVENTION

1. Creation of an International Interest

The Convention provides in its Article 2 for the constitution and effects of an international interest in certain categories of mobile equipment and associated rights. An international interest is defined in Article 2(2) as an 'interest, constituted under Article 7, in a uniquely identifiable object of a category of such objects listed in paragraph 3 and designated in the Protocol: (a) granted by the chargor under a security agreement; (b) vested in a person who is the conditional seller under a title reservation agreement; or (c) vested in a person who is the lessor under a leasing agreement.'

Under Article 7, the constitution of the interest requires that the agreement creating or providing for the interest (a) is in writing; (b) relates to an object of which the chargor, conditional seller, or lessor has power to dispose; (c) enables the object to be identified in conformity with the Protocol; and (d) in the case of a security agreement, enables the secured obligations to be determined.

The categories of objects mentioned in Article 2(2) of the Convention are listed in Article 2(3) as follows: '(a) airframes, aircraft engines, and helicopters; (b) railway rolling stock; and (c) space assets'.[34]

In relation to objects falling within these categories, no further requirements, such as requirements of mobility or internationality, are stipulated. They are considered to follow from the nature of the object.[35]

However, for the Convention to apply to them, it is necessary that two other conditions are fulfilled:

(1) a Protocol applicable to that category of objects must be in force;[36] and
(2) the debtor must be situated in a Contracting State[37] at the time of the conclusion of the agreement creating or providing for the international interest.

33. Final Act, *ibid.* (n. 32), Resolution No. 2, Operational Clause 4, para. (1).
34. For each of the categories of objects listed in Art. 2 (3) of the Convention, a separate Protocol to the Convention is foreseen, see Art. 49 (1) of the Convention. So far, two Protocols have been adopted, the Aircraft Protocol and the Luxembourg Protocol on Railway Rolling Stock, of which only the Aircraft Protocol has entered into force so far.
35. Sir R. Goode, Official Commentary on the Convention on International Interests in Mobile Equipment and Protocol Thereto on Matters Specific to Aircraft Equipment, *Unidroit* (Rome: 2002), 59.
36. Article 49 (1) of the Convention.
37. Article 3 (1) of the Convention. The fact that the creditor is situated in a non-Contracting State does not affect the applicability of the Convention, Art. 3 (2) of the Convention.

In relation to the first condition, the 'Aircraft Protocol' which covers airframes, aircraft engines, and helicopters entered into force on 1 March 2006.[38] As of early 2011, no other protocols relating to the Convention had entered into force. In relation to the second condition, it is necessary to ascertain for each interest whether or not the debtor is situated in a Contracting State. For this purpose, a Contracting State Search[39] can be carried out electronically in the International Registry. In case the debtor is a multinational entity or in other cases of doubt, Article 4 of the Convention provides an interpretation of the term *situated in a Contracting State.*

2. Priority Rules

The effects of an international interest referred to in Article 2(1) and duly registered include default remedies, priority requirements, and effectiveness in the debtor's insolvency.[40] Default remedies and effectiveness in insolvency are discussed below.

The most important effect of a registration is priority: a registered interest has priority over any other interest subsequently registered and any unregistered interest.[41] This rule is fundamental to the registration system under the Cape Town instruments. The economic value of an interest in an aircraft object will in many cases depend on its registration and priority ranking.

The priority rule applies to subsequently registered interests, but also to nationally registered interests that are not registered on the International Registry: The term *unregistered interest* refers to all interests that are not registered in the International Registry, regardless of whether they may be registered elsewhere.[42] Therefore, a nationally registered interest[43] will not enjoy the protection under the Cape Town Convention, unless:

(1) it is also registered in the International Registry;[44]

---

38. For the date of entry into force of the Protocol and the current parties to it, see the website of the depositary at <www.unidroit.org/english/implement/i-2001-aircraftprotocol.pdf>. As of 1 Apr. 2011, the Protocol had 36 States parties. For the definition of the terms airframe, aircraft engine and helicopter, see Art. I of the Protocol.
39. For the definition and rules governing Contracting State search and Contracting State Search Certificates, see s. 7.5 of the Regulations for the International Registry, and ss 13.4 to 13.6 of the Procedures for the International Registry, *ICAO Doc.* 9864.
40. See Goode, *ibid.* (n. 35), Comments on Art. 2 of the Convention, 59.
41. See Art. 29 (1) of the Convention
42. See on this matter R. Goode, ibid. (n. 35), 107–108.
43. Nationally registered interests may fall into two categories: Firstly, interests arising from 'internal transactions' in the sense of Art. 50 of the Convention which are transactions limited in scope and effects to the Contracting State where they are transacted; and secondly, other interests which, without being 'internal transactions', satisfy the criteria of Art. 7 of the Convention. The latter category of interests may therefore be registered in the International Registry, even though they may already be registered on a national registry.
44. National registration will not bar registration in the International Registry; however, see Art. 50 of the Convention, under which a Contracting State may exclude internal transactions from the scope of the Convention. See in this context also Art. 50 (2) of the Convention.

(2) it is covered by a declaration under Article 60(3) of the Convention made by the respective Contracting State;[45] or
(3) it is the subject of a notice of national interest under Articles 16(1)(d), 50(3) of the Convention.[46]

Registrations must be valid and complete to have the affects of the priority rule under Article 29(1) of the Convention.[47]

To be valid, they must satisfy the consent requirements of Article 20 of the Convention, that is, all required consents must have been given in writing. For the registration of an international interest, a prospective international interest, or for the assignment or prospective assignment of an international interest, the consent of the other party to the transaction is required.[48] The same applies for amendments or extensions of registrations. For subordinations, the consent of the holder of the subordinated interest is necessary.[49] In the case of a discharge of a registration, the consent of the holder of the interest to be discharged is required.[50] The consent shall be given within a period of thirty-six hours from notification. In the absence of consent, the registration shall be automatically aborted.[51]

A registration shall be complete upon entry of the required information into the International Registry data base so as to be searchable.[52] The registration shall be searchable when the International Registry has assigned to it a sequentially ordered file number and a time stamp, and when the registration information, including the file number, is stored in durable form and may be accessed at the International Registry.[53]

3. Default and insolvency-related Remedies

The basic default remedies of the chargee (who will usually be the creditor under the related credit agreement) and of the conditional seller or lessor are set out in Chapter III (Articles 8-15) of the Convention. In relation to aircraft objects, important additional default remedies (deregistration, export authorization,

45. A declaration under Art. 60 (3) of the Convention has the effect of bringing pre-existing rights or interests, which may include nationally registered interests and 'internal transactions', into the scope of the Convention and Protocol, after a minimum period of three years. So far, no Contracting State has yet made such a declaration.
46. Giving notice of a national interest is foreseen in Arts 16 (1) (d) and 50 (3) of the Convention, and the latter provision clarifies that the priority rule of Art. 29 of the Convention applies to such a notice; however, as regards transactions involving the national interest once registered, Art. 50 (3) clarifies that the priority rule under Art. 29 (1) applies only to assignments or subrogations under the applicable law.
47. See Art. 19 (1) and (2) of the Convention.
48. See Art. 20 (1) of the Convention; ss 5.3 (f), 5.4 (b), 5.5 (b), 5.9 (b) of the Regulations for the International Registry.
49. See Art. 20 (2) of the Convention; s. 5.7 (b) Regulations.
50. See Art. 20 (3) of the Convention; s. 5.6 (b) Regulations.
51. See Art. 12 (b) of the Procedures for the International Registry.
52. See Art. 19 (2) of the Convention.
53. See Art. 19 (3) of the Convention.

speedy relief, insolvency) are provided in Chapter II (Articles IX-XVI) of the Aircraft Protocol.

The default remedies are triggered by an event of default.[54] The notion of default is defined in Article 11 of the Convention as the events agreed in writing between the debtor and the creditor as constituting a default or, if not so agreed, a default that substantially deprives the creditor of what it is entitled to expect under the agreement.[55]

In the case of default of the chargor,[56] the chargee may, under Article 8, exercise any of the following remedies:[57]

(a) take possession or control of the object;
(b) sell or grant a lease;
(c) collect or receive income or profits from *the management or use of the object.*

These remedies may be exercised as self-help remedies, that is, without prior court order mandating or authorizing them,[58] if the chargor has at any time so agreed and subject to a declaration under Article 54(2) by a Contracting State. The agreement of the chargor to self-help remedies will, if given, normally be stipulated in the security agreement, lease agreement, or conditional sales contract. However, it may also be stipulated at any time after the signing of such agreement.[59] Certain already existing practices of parts of the aircraft financing industry to require inclusion of self-help remedy clauses in aircraft security and/or lease agreements were taken into account when these provisions were drafted.

The declaration under Article 54(2) of the Convention is a mandatory declaration;[60] consequently, even if the chargor has agreed to self-help remedies in the security agreement, it is necessary to ascertain from the declaration of the Contracting State concerned that self-help remedies are permitted.[61]

In case a declaration under Article 54 (2) excludes or prohibits self-help remedies, and/or the chargor has not agreed to them, the remedies set out in

54. Events of default may be defined as between debtor and creditor, e.g., in the credit agreement, conditional sales agreement or lease agreement. If they are not so defined and the agreement merely refers to the term default, the definition set out in Art. 11 (2) applies.
55. See Goode, *ibid.* (n. 35), Comment on Art. 11, 76–77.
56. The term *chargor* is not defined in Art. 1 of the Convention. It refers to a person who charges a piece of his property with a security interest under a security agreement in favour of the *chargee*, usually to secure an obligation under a credit agreement. See the definition of *debtor* in Art. 1 (j) of the Convention.
57. On the remedies in Art. 8, see Goode, *ibid.* (n. 35), Comment on Art. 8, 70–72.
58. Article 11 (1) and (2) of the Convention.
59. Goode, *ibid.* (n. 35), 70–71.
60. Goode, *ibid.*, Comment on Arts 54, 29 and 159.
61. See the wording of Art. 54 (2) of the Convention. So far, all Contracting States have deposited a declaration under Art. 54 (2), (although Nigeria has since withdrawn its declaration on 27 Mar. 2007, effective 1 Oct. 2007). All declarations so far deposited expressly permit self-help remedies, except that of Columbia which expressly prohibits them. See the depositary's website, *ibid.* (n. 38).

Article 8(1) of the Convention may only be exercised as judicial remedies, that is, by application to the competent court for an order authorizing or directing any of the remedies.[62]

A further remedy is provided in Article 9 of the Convention, which provides for the vesting of the object in or towards satisfaction of the secured obligations. Under Article 9(1), the chargee and all the interested persons (chargor and any other persons giving guarantee or having rights in or over the object[63]) may agree that ownership, or any other interest of the chargor in the object, shall vest in the chargee. In case such agreement is not obtained, the chargee may apply to the competent court to obtain an order that ownership, or any other interest of the chargor in the object, shall vest in the chargee.[64] The court shall only so order if the amount of the secured obligations is commensurate with the value of the object, taking into account any payments to be made by the chargee to any of the interested persons.[65]

In the event of a default under a title reservation agreement or under a lease agreement, the conditional seller or lessor has special remedies under Article 10 of the Convention. He may either:

(a) terminate the agreement and take possession or control of the object, unless a declaration under Article 54(2) excluding or prohibiting self-help remedies has been made; or
(b) apply for a court order authorizing or directing the taking of possession or control of the object.[66]

The default remedies provided for in Chapter III of the Convention, whether regular or speedy relief remedies must be exercised in a commercially reasonable manner. The principle of commercial reasonableness[67] is important for the

62. Article 8 (2) in conjunction with Arts 8 (1) and 54 (2).
63. For the definition of the term *interested person*, see Art. 1 (m) of the Convention; it includes (i) the debtor, (ii) any person who, for the purpose of assuring performance of any of the obligations in favour of the creditor, gives or issues a suretyship or demand guarantee or a standby letter of credit or any other form of credit insurance, and (iii) any other person having rights in or over the object.
64. Article 9 (2) of the Convention.
65. Article 9 (3) of the Convention; for the effects of such vesting as against third parties, see Art. 9 (5) of the Convention.
66. Article 10 (a) and (b) of the Convention; in relation to aircraft objects, see also Art. XVI of the Protocol. As owner of the object, the lessor or conditional seller needs only the remedies of termination and taking of possession. Further remedies, such as sale or lease, do not require consent. Art. 10 will not be applied to conditional sales with reservation of title in those jurisdictions which treat such agreements as security agreements; instead, Arts 8 and 9 will be applied. See on this matter Goode, *ibid.* (n. 35), 75 et seq.
67. Article 8 (3) of the Convention, Art. IX (3) of the Protocol; it should be noted that the principle, which does not apply to the remedies set out in Art. 10, applies nevertheless to all remedies given in the Convention with respect to aircraft objects, by virtue of Art. IX (3) of the Protocol. See on the principle of commercial reasonableness and on the commercial orientation of the Cape Town instruments, J. Wool, 'The case for a commercial orientation to the proposed UNIDROIT Convention as applied to aircraft equipment', *Uniform Law Review* NS – IV no. 2 (1999): 289 et seq. and 301et seq.

protection of the debtor[68] against excessive action of the creditor, given the fact that the latter will normally be in a strong position as a result of the use of his standard terms and conditions in his credit and security agreements[69] and the availability of self-help remedies. Under Article 8 (3) of the Convention, a remedy shall be deemed to be exercised in a commercially reasonable manner, if exercised in conformity with a provision of the security agreement, except where such a provision is manifestly unreasonable.

Furthermore, the exercise of any of the aforementioned remedies under the Convention shall, in accordance with Article 14, observe the procedure prescribed by the applicable national law.

4. Interim Relief

The creditor may also under Article 13 of the Convention obtain from a competent court interim relief pending final determination of its claim, in case time is of the essence so as to preserve the value of the object or preserve realization of proceeds.

Such speedy relief[70] shall be available subject to the following conditions being fulfilled, as stipulated by Article 13(1):

(a) the debtor has at any time agreed that speedy relief remedies shall be available in case of default, for example in the credit agreement; and
(b) the Contracting State of the court where application is made has not made a declaration under Article 55 excluding speedy relief or the remedy applied for.[71]

The speedy relief remedies may include one or more of the following orders:[72]

(a) Preservation of the object and its value;
(b) Possession, control, or custody of the object;
(c) Immobilization of the object; and
(d) Lease or management of the object and the income therefrom, except where the latter is covered by (a) to (c).[73]

Before making any such order, the court may require notice of the application to be given to any of the interested persons, according to Article 13(2) of the Convention. While the provisions of Article 13 build on the form of interim relief commonly

68. Goode, *ibid.* (n. 35), 71; for debtor protection, see also Art. XVI of the Protocol.
69. The same applies with respect to standard lease agreements and conditional sales with reservation of title. See on this matter Goode, *ibid.* (n. 35), 71.
70. Article 13 (1) of the Convention, Art. X (2) and (3) of the Protocol.
71. Declarations under Art. 55 of the Convention are non-mandatory opt-out declarations, see Goode, *ibid.* (n. 35), 29. So far, none of the Contracting States has made any declaration under Article 55, see the depositary's website, *ibid.* (n. 38).
72. Article 13 (1) of the Convention; see also Article X (2)-(5) of the Protocol.
73. These remedies do not include sale of the object and application of the proceeds of the sale. However, with respect to aircraft objects, these remedies are available under Article X (3) of the Protocol, to the extent that the debtor and the creditor have specifically so agreed, e.g., in the credit agreement or the security agreement. See Goode, *ibid.* (n. 35), 79.

available in national legal systems, they are to be interpreted in accordance with the Convention, not by reference to national law.[74] This is a result of the fact that Article 13, and the remedies provided thereunder, are an integral part of the Cape Town Convention System.

In accordance with Article 8(3) of the Convention, the principle of commercial reasonableness shall also apply to the exercise of the speedy relief remedies of Article 13. Furthermore, in line with Article 14, the exercise of speedy relief remedies shall observe the procedure prescribed by the applicable national law.

5. Insolvency Rules

Under the basic rule of Article 30 of the Convention, a duly registered international interest is effective in insolvency proceedings against the debtor, provided the registration occurred prior to the commencement of the proceedings.[75] In accordance with this rule, the international interest is 'insolvency-proof'. Nevertheless, any applicable rules of national law on fraudulent preference[76] und on enforcement of property rights relating to property under the control or supervision of an insolvency administrator[77] remain in principle unaffected, according to Article 30(3) of the Convention.

In relation to aircraft objects, Article XI of the Aircraft Protocol modifies Article 30(3) of the Convention and introduces more detailed rules. However, Article XI of the Protocol applies only when the Contracting State of the primary insolvency jurisdiction has made a declaration pursuant to Article XXX(3) of the Protocol.[78] Such declaration must indicate whether Alternative A or B of Article XI is applicable.

Under the insolvency rules of Alternative A, which are inspired by modern United States law insolvency procedures, including debtor-in-possession rules,[79] a waiting period shall apply during which the debtor may remain in possession of the aircraft object.[80] During this period, the creditor is only entitled to interim relief

74. Goode, *ibid.* (n. 35), Comment on Art. 13, 78.
75. Article 30 (1) of the Convention. The international interest must have been registered in conformity with the Convention prior to the commencement of the insolvency proceedings in order to be effective in such proceedings.
76. Article 30 (3) (a) of the Convention; *fraudulent preference* involves transfer of property by an insolvent party to one of his creditors with a view to giving such creditor a preference over other persons, see P.S. James, *Introduction to English Law*, 7th edn (London: 1969), 500.
77. For the definition of *insolvency administrator*, see Art. 1 (k) of the Convention; for the definition of *insolvency proceedings*, see Art. 1 (l) of the Convention.
78. Declarations pursuant to Art. XXX (3) of the Protocol have been made by all States Parties to the Protocol, except Ireland and the United States, see the website of the depositary, *ibid.* (n. 38). In the absence of such a declaration, Art. XI of the Protocol does not apply and only Art. 30 (3) of the Convention in conjunction with national law relating to bankruptcy proceedings applies.
79. In particular s. 1110 of the US Bankruptcy Code, 15 U.S.C. s. 1110; J. Wool, *ibid.* (n. 67), 298 with further references.
80. Article XI, Alternative A, (2), (5) and (7) of the Protocol; the waiting period shall be a period specified in a declaration of the Contracting State which is the primary insolvency jurisdiction, Art. XI, Alternative A, (3) of the Protocol.

remedies, subject however to the debtor's obligation to preserve the aircraft object and maintain its value.[81] An agreement may be made to that effect with the debtor-in-possession. During the waiting period, the debtor-in-possession may cure all defaults and agree to perform all future obligations under the agreement. In this case, he may retain possession of the aircraft object, provided no further default in the fulfilment of these obligations occurs. If the debtor does not cure all defaults and agree to perform all future obligations, possession of the aircraft object shall pass to the creditor at the end of the waiting period.[82]

The insolvency rules of Alternative B, designed to accommodate modern civil law insolvency procedures,[83] operate with a notice period during which either the insolvency administrator or the debtor will be in possession of the aircraft object. Within that period, at the creditor's request, the insolvency administrator or the debtor must give notice to the creditor whether he will cure all defaults and perform all future obligations, or whether he will transfer to the creditor possession of the aircraft object.[84] The court may require any additional step, or the provision of any additional guarantee, in accordance with the applicable national law. Pending a decision of the court regarding the claim and the international interest, the aircraft object may not be sold.[85]

These provisions seek to reflect the realities of modern structured finance, in particular, to facilitate capital market financing and asset-based credit by ensuring that within a specified and binding time-limit, a choice is made.[86] The creditor must be put into the position to secure within a binding time-limit either (a) recovery of the object; or (b) the curing of all defaults and performance of all debtor's future obligations.[87] This applies regardless of whether the debtor remains in possession or whether the insolvency administrator takes over. The removal of uncertainty and delay arising from the insolvency procedure and preservation of the aircraft and its value are the principal objectives of the insolvency rules under the Convention and the Protocol.

6. Transactions Covered

Under Article 2(2) of the Convention, the principal transactions that may give rise to an international interest are security agreements, conditional sale agreements with reservation of title, and lease agreements.

81. Article XI, Alternative A, (5) (a) and (b) of the Protocol.
82. Article XI, Alternative A, (2) and (7) of the Protocol; under para. (7), a second waiting period shall not apply in respect of a default in the performance of such future obligations.
83. On the differences between Alternatives A and B, see Goode, *ibid.* (n. 35), 199 et seq.
84. Article XI, Alternative B, (2) of the Protocol. The notice period, the length of which is specified in a declaration of the Contracting State concerned pursuant to Art. XXX (3) of the Protocol, begins to run only from the time the creditor's request is received by the debtor or the insolvency administrator, Goode, *ibid.* (n. 35), 202.
85. Article XI, Alternative B, (6) of the Protocol.
86. Goode, *ibid.* (n. 35), Comment on Art. XI Protocol, 200.
87. See Goode, *ibid.* (n. 35), 200 et seq.

Article III of the Protocol extends the application of the Convention to outright (unconditional) sales as well as to prospective sales of aircraft objects.[88] As a result, the buyer as well as the prospective buyer of an aircraft object may register the sale or prospective sale in the International Registry like an international interest. The buyer's and prospective buyer's legal position is thereby considerably strengthened in view of the priority rules and insolvency provisions.

It should be noted that under Chapter IX of the Convention, the assignment of an international interest, the prospective assignment of an international interest, and an international interest acquired through subrogation are also covered by its provisions and may therefore be registered in the International Registry.[89]

Furthermore, under Article 40 of the Convention, certain non-consensual rights or interests, as formally declared by a Contracting State,[90] are registrable and, once registered, are governed by the provisions of the Convention. These should be distinguished from non-consensual rights or interests under national law formally declared by a Contracting State under Article 39 of the Convention,[91] which are not registrable and to which the Convention (other than Article 39) does not apply.

D. The International Registry under the Cape Town Convention and Protocol

1. Establishment of the International Registry

The Preparatory Commission was given full authority as Provisional Supervisory Authority for the establishment of the International Registry, under the guidance and supervision of the ICAO Council. ICAO was also invited by the Diplomatic Conference to accept the functions of definitive Supervisory Authority upon the entry into force of the Convention and the Protocol, and entrusted with the task of administering the start-up funds contributed by Contracting States for the establishment of the International Registry.[92]

In accordance with its mandate under Resolution No. 2, the Preparatory Commission set up by the Diplomatic Conference held three meetings between

88. See the wording of Art. III as well as the comments of Goode, *ibid.* (n. 35), 183–186.
89. For further details, see Arts 31–38 of the Convention and Goode, *ibid.* (n. 35), 117 et seq.
90. As of 1 Apr. 2011, 20 out of 36 States Parties to the Convention had made a declaration under Art. 40; for details, see the list of the depositary, *ibid.* (n. 38).
91. So far, all 16 States Parties to the Convention have made a declaration under Art. 39 (1) (a), which relates to national non-consensual rights or interests. Most States Parties have also made a declaration under Art. 39 (1) (b), which relates to the right to arrest or detain aircraft for non-payment of charges, such as air navigation charges. See the list of the depositary, *ibid.* (n. 38).
92. Final Act. *Ibid.* (n. 32), Resolution No. 2, Operational Clauses 1 and 5, *in fine*. The ICAO Council had first accepted *in principle* the functions of Supervisory Authority of the International Registry at its 161st session in November 2000 (C-DEC 161/9), and later accepted these functions definitively at its 175th session in June 2005 (C-Dec 175/15 and C-DEC 175/16).

May 2002 and January 2005. At its first meeting,[93] it agreed on the terms and conditions for the global public tender (including the technical specifications for the International Registry); the global public tender was thereupon issued in early 2004.[94]

As a result, a number of tenders were received, of which four tenders were considered compliant with the technical specifications. The tenders were evaluated in line with the procedures of the ICAO Procurement Code and were then submitted to the second meeting of the Preparatory Commission in May 2004.[95] Of the four tenders evaluated, the Preparatory Commission selected the tender of Aviareto Ltd, a joint venture of *Société Internationale de Télécommunication Aéronautique* (SITA) and the Irish government.[96] Aviareto was subsequently awarded a contract by ICAO/the Preparatory Commission to establish the International Registry and to operate it for a period of five years. The contract was signed on 23 November 2004.[97]

At its third meeting,[98] the Preparatory Commission adopted regulations for the International Registry,[99] foreseen in Article 17(2)(d) of the Convention. It also set the minimum insurance coverage for the International Registry, at USD 10 million, in line with Article 28(4) Convention and Article XX(5) of the Protocol, and approved a fee schedule,[100] in accordance with Article 17(2)(h) of the Convention.

Subsequently, the Commission also adopted administrative procedures for the International Registry, foreseen in Article 17(2)(e) of the Convention.[101]

In accordance with the contract between ICAO/the Preparatory Commission and Aviareto Ltd, the International Registry System was established progressively between June 2004 and November 2005. Provisional acceptance tests for the system were carried out in August 2005, and final acceptance tests in October 2005, resulting in the issuance of the Final Acceptance Certificate on 17 November 2005.

Meanwhile, the process of ratification of the Cape Town Convention and Protocol went ahead. The instruments require eight ratifications to enter into force.[102] The first State to ratify was Panama, on 28 July 2003; Ethiopia, Nigeria, Pakistan, the United States, Oman, and Ireland followed; the eighth ratification

93. The first meeting was held from 8 May 2002 to 10 May 2002 in Montreal; for action taken by the Preparatory Commission, see PCIR/1 – Report.
94. See State Letter LE 3/41.1 – 04/0 dated 16 Jan. 2004.
95. The second meeting was held from 27 May 2004 to 28 May 2004 in Montreal; for action taken by the Preparatory Commission, see PCIR/2 – Report.
96. See PCIR/2 – Report, agenda Item 3: Selection of the Registrar of the International Registry, paras 3.1 to 3.2.4; Aviareto International Registry Proposal, dated 14 Apr. 2004, Vols. 1 and 2.
97. Contract No. 40160 for the Establishment and Operation of the International Registry for International Interests in Mobile Equipment (Aircraft Equipment), signed 23 Nov. 2004; Amendment No. 1 to Contract No. 40160 signed on 4 Nov. 2005.
98. The third meeting was held from 17 Jan. 2005 to 18 Jan. 2005, see PCIR/3 – Report.
99. See PCIR/3 – Report, Agenda Item 7: Regulations for the International Registry, paras 7:1 to 7:11 and Attachment D to the Report.
100. PCIR/3 – Report, Agenda Item 5: User Fees, paras 5.1 to 5.3.
101. The Procedures were adopted by correspondence. They were issued on 26 Oct. 2005.
102. See Art. XXVIII (1) Protocol and Art. 49 (1) (a) – (c) Convention.

was deposited on 2 November 2005 by Malaysia,[103] bringing both instruments into force as of 1 March 2006, in accordance with the terms of Article XXVIII(1) of the Protocol and Article 49(1) of the Convention.

As of 1 March 2006, the International Registry became operational and the Regulations and Procedures for the International Registry entered into force.[104] The ICAO Council took over the functions of Supervisory Authority, and the mandate of the Preparatory Commission lapsed. The Council is advised by a Commission of Experts, which consists of not more than fifteen members nominated by signatory and Contracting States to the Cape Town Convention and Protocol.[105]

2. The International Registry System

In accordance with Chapter IV of the Cape Town Convention, the international registry system consists of the International Registry and the Supervisory Authority.

The International Registry is established for the registration of international interests as defined in Article 2 Convention[106] as well as of prospective international interests, assignments and prospective assignments of such interests, acquisitions of such interests by subrogation, registrable non-consensual rights and interests, notices of national interests, and subordinations of interests.[107] In line with the scope of the Protocol,[108] the scope of the mandate of the International Registry is limited to interests in aircraft objects, that is, airframes, aircraft engines, and helicopters.[109] In accordance with Article III of the Protocol, the Registry may also register contracts of sale and prospective sales of aircraft objects.[110]

---

103. See Convention on International Interests in Mobile Equipment, List of parties, Website of Unidroit (Depositary of the instruments) at <www.unidroit.org/>; see also the list of Parties for the Protocol, *ibid.*
104. Section 18 of the Regulations and s. 21 of the Procedures.
105. Resolution No. 2 of the Diplomatic Conference, *ibid.* (n. 32), operational clause 2.
106. They are defined as interests 'constituted under Article 7, in a uniquely identifiable object of a category of such objects listed in para. 3 and designated in the Protocol: (a) granted by the chargor under a security agreement; (b) vested in a person who is the conditional seller under a security agreement; (b) vested in a person who is the conditional seller under a title reservation agreement; or (c) vested in a person who is the lessor under a leasing agreement.' For a critical view, see Crans, *ibid.* (n. 30), 264 et seq.
107. See Art. 16 (1) (a) to (e) of the Convention. On the various types of registrable international interests, see R. Goode, Convention on International Interests in Mobile Equipment and Protocol thereto on Matters Specific to Aircraft Equipment, Official Commentary (Rome: September 2002), Art. 16 – the International Registry, 82 et seq.
108. See Art. II para. 1 of the Protocol.
109. See Art. I para. (2) (c), in conjunction with sub-paras (a), (b) and (e), of the Protocol; Art. 2 para. 3 (a) of the Convention.
110. Under the provisions of the Convention, Contracts of sale and prospective sales are not registrable. However, due to their practical importance in the field of aircraft object transactions, the Protocol extends the scope of registrable interests to these transactions. See on this matter R. Goode, *ibid.* (n. 35), 183.

The International Registry is an electronic notice-based registry: Registration, modifications of registrations, and discharges may only be effected through electronic means by use of the Internet, and not in hardcopy;[111] furthermore, it is sufficient for the user to give notice to the Registry in the form of electronically transmitted information in accordance with the applicable Regulations and Procedures for the International Registry.[112] The user is not required to submit evidence in the form of signed hardcopy documents, and the Registry is not obligated to check the veracity of the information submitted by users; neither is the Registry responsible or liable for incorrect, misspelled, or otherwise erroneous information transmitted by users.[113]

The authority of each user can, however, be ascertained and checked through the mandatory user registration system, which involves *inter alia* the allocation of a unique digital certificate to each user for the purposes of authentification.[114] Access to the Registry for purposes of registration is restricted to registered users only.[115]

The Supervisory Authority has the mandate to establish the International Registry to appoint and dismiss the Registrar, to supervise the operation of the Registry, and 'to do all things necessary to ensure that an efficient notice-based electronic registration system exists to implement the objectives of this Convention and the Protocol'.[116] The Supervisory Authority shall report periodically to Contracting States concerning the discharge of its obligations under the Convention and Protocol.[117]

On 26 October 2005, the Supervisory Authority[118] issued Regulations and Procedures for the International Registry in conformity with Article 17, paragraphs 2(d) and 9(e) of the Convention.[119] The Regulations provide rules, *inter alia*, on the information required to effect the different types of registrations, amendments and discharges, rules on searches, on operational complaints and on relations with designated entry points. The procedures are administrative in nature and address administrative items required by the Regulations as conditions of use of the

111. See R. Goode, *ibid.* (n. 35), 16: 'The registration provisions are predicated on the assumption that the system will be electronic and available on-line, so that the checking of registration applications, registration itself and responses to searches will be effected automatically by computer and will not involve human intervention.'
112. Regulations and Procedures for the International Registry, issued on 26 Oct. 2005, *ICAO Doc.* 9864 (1st edn 2006).
113. See Art. 28 para. 2 Convention, s. 14 of the Regulations, s. 15 of the Procedures for the International Registry.
114. See ss 5 (e), 6 (c) and 7 (e) of the Procedures for the International Registry.
115. See s. 7 (e) of the Procedures for the International Registry.
116. Article 17 para. 2 (i) of the Convention.
117. Article 17 para. 2 (j) of the Convention.
118. In accordance with Resolution No. 2 of the Cape Town Diplomatic Conference, (see above n. 32), the Preparatory Commission for the International Registry was the Supervisory Authority until entry into force of the Cape Town instruments. As from 1 Mar. 2006, the date of entry into force of the Cape Town instruments, the ICAO Council assumed the functions of Supervisory authority.
119. See s. 1, last Sentence, of the Procedures for the International Registry.

International Registry, or otherwise relating to the technical operation and administrative processes of the International Registry.[120] The Regulations and Procedures, being issued by the Supervisory Authority, regulate the Registry and the relationship to its users from a public-law viewpoint.

Certain private-law aspects between the Registry and its users are governed by terms and conditions which are displayed on the Registry's website.

3. Access to the International Registry

In order to effect registrations or amendments thereto and discharges therefrom, users must first register and pay a fee in accordance with the Fee Schedule.[121] A member of the general public, without being a registered user, may only perform searches in the International Registry, but may not make registrations. To perform a search, he/she must first pay a search fee and must have the required aircraft object information available for such searches.[122]

In order to become a registered user, a person or entity must first submit all required information through the registry's user registration website. In addition, a registry user entity (transacting user entity[123] or professional entity[124]) shall appoint an administrator and shall transmit all required information regarding that administrator to the Registry. The administrator shall be 'the person with authority to act on behalf of a registry user entity on administrative matters in dealings with the International Registry'.[125]

When the International Registry concludes:

(a) that such entity and administrator are who they assert they are; and
(b) on the basis of the information submitted, and without undertaking specific legal analysis, that the latter is entitled to act as administrator of the former, in each case following the standards and procedures set out in the International Registry Procedures, approval of the entity and of the administrator shall be given.[126]

---

120. See s. 1, last Sentence, of the Procedures for the International Registry.
121. Fee Schedule, approved by the Supervisory Authority, Appendix to the Procedures for the International Registry, issued on 26 Oct. 2005. See ICAO Doc. 9864, P-23.
122. Sections 7.1 to 7.3 of the Regulations; s. 13 para. 9a) and 9b) of the Procedures. The information required for searches against an aircraft object are a manufacturer's name, a manufacturer's generic model designation, and a manufacturer's serial number of the aircraft object; and in the case of an airframe or helicopter, the State of Registry of an aircraft of which is part, or the aircraft nationality or registration mark.
123. Transacting user entity is defined as legal entity or natural person intending to be named party in one or more registrations. See s. 2.1.11 of the Regulations.
124. Professional user entity is defined as a firm or other grouping of persons providing professional services to transacting user entities in connection with the transmission of information to the International Registry relating to registrations; professional user is defined as an individual employee, member or partner of a professional user entity.
125. See s. 2.1.1 of the Regulations.
126. See s. 4.1 of the Regulations.

Under the Procedures, the Registrar may make such reasonable identity checks of a proposed administrator as the Registrar considers necessary in relation to that person's undertaking such function.[127]

Once the entity and its administrator[128] are approved by the Registry, the administrator has the authority to approve persons who are employees, officers, members or partners of his entity, as registry users. Each administrator and each registry user, as a result of the approval process, is provided with a unique digital certificate, which for security purposes shall allow the Registry to authenticate that person's submissions to the Registry. The digital certificate shall be kept secure, and shall not be transferred to any other computer, except to a replacement computer under the certificate holder's control, in which case he/she shall first apply to the Registrar for such transfer.[129]

While an administrator is deemed to be authorized to act on behalf of the registry user entity which he/she represents when making registrations, a registry user must first receive authorization from his/her administrator to work on a specific aircraft object before making registrations.[130] The registry user must expressly represent to the Registrar that he/she is so authorized when providing user identity and registration information.

The International Registry can be accessed via the public internet under the URL's <www.internationalregistry.aero> and <www.internationalregistry.org>.[131] It is available in English; other languages are envisaged to be added[132] when the financial means therefore are available.

The International Registry is accessible 24 hours a day, seven days a week, except for maintenance requirements or in case of technical problems. Advance notice of any interruption in access and expected service resumption is to be provided to the maximum extent practicable via the website.[133]

In certain Contracting States, registrations may have to be effected through so-called designated entry points,[134] which are entry points designated by the Contracting State at the time of ratification of the Cape Town instruments.[135] In the case of 'authorizing entry points', the transmission of information required for registration shall first be authorized by the designated entry point, before such

127. See s. 5 (n) of the Procedures for the International Registry.
128. Those shall only be one administrator for any registry user entity. However, in case of absence or illness, an acting Administrator may be appointed, subject to approval by the Registry, who shall act in the administrator's stead. See ss 5 (c) and (f) of the Procedures for the International Registry.
129. See ss 5 (e) and 6 (c) of the Procedures for the International Registry.
130. See s. 6 (b) of the Procedures for the International Registry.
131. See s. 7 (a) of the Procedures for the International Registry. Both Uniform Resource Locators (URL'S) are equivalent.
132. See the discussions of the Preparatory Commission for the International Registry (PCIR) at its first meeting, PCIR/1 – Report, Agenda Item 8, para. 8.1; s. 7 (b) of the Procedures.
133. See s. 7, (d) Procedures for the International Registry.
134. See Article 19 (5) of the Convention and Article XIX of the Protocol.
135. Section 12 of the Regulations for the International Registry. The Regulations, in s. 12.1, distinguish between 'authorizing entry points' and direct entry points'.

transmission can be effected by the registering person to the international Registry.[136] In the case of 'direct entry points', information required for registration shall or may be directly transmitted to the International Registry through the entry point.[137] In practice, existing national registries will in some cases be designated as entry points.[138] Such designations require subsequent arrangements between the International Registry and the designated entry point to govern the electronic transmission of registration information from or authorized by such entry point to the International Registry.[139]

4. Registration Requirements

In accordance with Article 18 of the Convention, the Protocol and the Regulations for the International Registry specify the criteria for the identification of an aircraft object for effecting a registration, for making searches, and for ensuring the confidentiality of information and documents of the International Registry.[140] For effecting a registration, the regulations specify in section 5 in considerable detail the information required for each type of registration;[141] in relation to the identity of the registering person and of the named parties, the name, address and electronic address is required.[142] In relation to the aircraft object, the type of aircraft object, the manufacturer's generic model designation and the manufacturer's serial number assigned to the aircraft object are required. In addition, the information listed in sections 5.3 to 5.11 of the Regulations is required.[143]

For making searches, Article XX(1) of the Protocol specifies that the manufacturer's name, model designation and serial number are required, supplemented as necessary to ensure uniqueness.[144] Section 7.1 of the Regulations provides for

136. See s. 12.1, subs. (a) of the Regulations for the International Registry.
137. See s. 12.1, subs. (b) of the Regulations for the International Registry; R. Goode, *ibid.* (n. 35), 212et seq.
138. See e.g., the Declaration of the United States under Article XIX of the Cape Town Protocol made on 28 Oct. 2004 at the time of deposit of its instrument of ratification of the Protocol, List of Parties to the Protocol, Unidroit website, *ibid.* (n. 38).
139. See s. 12.4 of the Regulations for the International Registry.
140. Article XX Protocol and ss 5 and 7 of the Regulations for the International Registry.
141. Section 5, subss 5.3 to 5.11 set out the information required for the registration of the different categories of interests, namely: an international interest (including also a prospective international interest, an international interest acquired through subrogation, a notice of a national interest, and a registrable non-consensual right or interest); a contract of sale or a prospective sale; an assignment of an international interests, a prospective assignment of an international interest, an assignment of an international interest, a prospective assignment of an international interest, an assignment of a registrable non-consensual interest; a discharge of a registration (other than a registration relating to a contract of sale); a registration of a subordination of an international interest, a prospective international interest, a national interest or a registrable non-consensual interest; a registration of a pre-existing right or interest required by virtue of a declaration under Article 60 (3) of the Convention; an amendment to a registration.
142. See ss 5.2 and 21.4 of the Regulations for the International Registry.
143. Sections 5.3 (c), 5.4 (a), 5.5 (a), 5.6 (a), 5.7 (a) and 5.9 (a) of the Regulations for the International Registry.
144. See on this matter R. Goode, *ibid.* (n. 35), 212et seq.

such supplemental requirements in the case of airframes and helicopters, for which the State of Registry, or the aircraft nationality or registration mark, is also required.[145]

For ensuring the confidentiality of information and documents, section 9 of the Regulations provides that all information in the International Registry shall be confidential, except where it is provided in response to a search, made electronically available to enable users to effect, amend or discharge registrations, provided to the Supervisory Authority at the latter's request, or used for statistical purposes.[146]

The Registrar will, in accordance with Article 18(4) of the Convention, arrange for registrations to be entered into the International Registry data base and made searchable in chronological order of receipt, and the file shall record the date and time of receipt.[147] The Registrar will also provide prompt electronic confirmation of a registration to the named parties, the registering person and all other persons entitled to receive notice. The confirmation shall contain all registered information, and the date and the time of registration.[148] A notice will be sent to the named parties, the registering person and other entitled persons in any previous registration relating to that aircraft object.[149]

5. Effects of Registration

The *effects of an international interest* referred to in Article 2(1) and duly registered concern in particular default remedies, priority rules and effectiveness in the debtor's insolvency.[150]

6. Amendments and Discharges of Registrations

Amendments and discharges of registrations follow in principle the same rules as registrations. However, as regards corrections of incorrectly made registrations and as regards discharges, Article 25 of the Convention provides for some special rules.

In case of registrations which 'ought not to have been made' or in case of incorrectly made, misspelled, or otherwise erroneous registrations, the holder of the registration shall, without undue delay, procure its discharge or amendment after written demand by the debtor.[151] Under the Procedures for the International

145. See ss 7.1 (d) and (e) of the Regulations for the International Registry.
146. See s. 9 of the Regulations and s. 10 of the Procedures for the International Registry. As regards statistics, the Registrar shall publish an annual statistical report.
147. See on this matter R. Goode, *ibid.* (n. 35), 89 et seq.
148. See s. 6.3 of the Regulations for the International Registry; ss 12 (b) and (c) Procedures for the International Registry.
149. See s. 6.3 of the Regulations.
150. Default remedies have been discussed under Ch. 5 II. 3. *supra*. Priority rules have been discussed under Ch. 5 II. C.2. supra. Effectiveness in insolvency is discussed under Ch. 5 II. C.5. *supra*.
151. See Art. 25 (4) Convention; such written demand shall be delivered to debtor's address stated in the registration.

Registry, any amendment to a registration even if only correcting a misspelling or other similar error, shall be treated procedurally like a registration.[152]

Furthermore, Article 25, paragraphs 1 to 3 sets out rules on mandatory discharge of a registration. In particular a registration shall be discharged without undue delay when the obligations secured by a registered security interest, or a national interest specified in a registered notice of a national interest, have been discharged, or the conditions of transfer of title under a registered title reservation agreement have been fulfilled.[153] The same applies when the obligations giving rise to a registered non-consensual right or interest have been discharged. Article XX(2) of the Protocol specifies that, in case if a registered prospective international interest, registered prospective assignment of an international interest or registered prospective sale, the discharge shall be effected within five working days after receipt of the written demand.

7. Searches

In accordance with Article 22 of the Convention, searches in the International Registry may be performed by any person concerning registered interests[154] or registered prospective interests. Such searches may be made by means of a 'priority search' or of an 'informational search', in accordance with section 7.1 of the Regulations.

A priority search is a search for registration information using the three criteria in Article XX(1), that is, manufacturer's name, model designation, and serial number assigned to the aircraft object. The registration information shall be searchable for the purposes of Articles 19(2) and (6) of the Convention and Article XX(1) of the Protocol;[155] thus, only information that is the result of a valid and complete registration shall be searchable. Upon request, the Registrar shall issue a 'priority search certificate' in response to a priority search.[156] In case there is registered information on the aircraft object in question, the search certificate shall list the registered information in chronological order, and in a manner that indicates the transactional history of each registered interest. In case there is no registered information in the International Registry on the aircraft object, the search certificate shall state that fact.[157]

An informational search is a search, other than a priority search, resulting in an 'informational search listing'.[158] This is a list of all matching aircraft objects

152. See ss 12 (a) and (b) of the Procedures.

153. See Art. 25 (1) Convention. This would usually apply where the loan secured by the registered interest has been repaid, or where the last instalment under a credit sale with reservation of title has been paid.

154. See s. 7.1 of the Regulations: 'A search may be performed by any person that complies with the International Registry procedures, whether or not that searching person has a specific interest.' See also s. 13 of the Procedures.

155. See s. 7.2 of the Regulations for the International Registry.

156. See s. 7.4 of the Regulations and ss 13 (d) and (e) of the Procedures.

157. See Art. 22 (2) (2) (a) and (b) of the Convention, and s. 7.4 of the Regulations.

158. See s. 7.3 of the Regulations and s. 13 (b) and (c) of the Procedures. An informational search listing will not generate a search certificate. The Registrar shall not be liable in respect of the content of an informational search listing.

described by the manufacturer's name, model designation, and serial number(s), and if available in the International Registry, the State of Registry of an aircraft of which it is a part, or the aircraft nationality or registration mark.[159] The facility to perform such an informational search does not make that information 'searchable' for the purposes of Article 19(2) and (6) of the Convention and Article XX(1) of the Protocol.[160] The object of an informational search is to provide the searching person with sufficient information to perform a priority search.

A Contracting State search may also be performed, with the aim of ascertaining for any specific Contracting State whether it has ratified the Convention and the Protocol, and any declarations, designations, or withdrawals thereof made by the Contracting State under the Convention and Protocol.[161] The result of a Contracting State search shall be a 'Contracting State Search Certificate', which shall list the effective date of ratifications,[162] declarations, designations[163] and withdrawals, and attach in electronic form a copy of all such instruments deposited by the Contracting State with the depositary.[164]

8. Effects of Registration as against third Parties

The most important effect of a registration as against third parties, namely, the operation of the priority rule under Article 29 of the Convention, has already been mentioned above.[165]

The priority rule applies in favour of a registered interest, in relation to any subsequently registered or unregistered interest. It applies even if the registered interest was acquired or registered with actual knowledge of the existence of another interest, which was then subsequently registered or remained unregistered.[166] The same applies, even as regards value given by the holder of a registered interest with knowledge of the existence of another interest, which was then subsequently registered or remained unregistered.[167] The mere existence of an unregistered interest, even if registered nationally, does not protect its holder against other registrations in the international Registry which may take precedence. The only adequate protection is to register that interest without delay, after it has come into existence.

Similarly, in the case of a sale of an aircraft object, the buyer acquires it, subject to any interest registered at the time of sale, but free from any unregistered

159. See s. 7.3, second Sentence, of the Regulations and s. 13 (b) of the Procedures.
160. Section 7.3, third Sentence of the Regulations.
161. Section 7.5 of the Regulations and s. 13 (d) of the Procedures.
162. Under the applicable rules of public international law, acceptance, approval or accession produce equivalent effects to ratification, namely for the state to be bound by a treaty; therefore, acceptance, approval or accession shall also be listed in the Contracting State Search Certificate.
163. 'Designations' are designations of entry points under Art. XIX of the Protocol; they may sometimes also be called 'declaration'. See the designation made by the United States under Art. XIX of the Protocol, Unidroit website, *ibid.* (n. 38).
164. See s. 7.5 (c) of the Regulations.
165. See *supra*, Ch. 5 II C.2.
166. See Art. 29 (2) (a) Convention.
167. See Art. 29 (2) (b) Convention.

interest, even if he has actual knowledge of the existence of such competing, unregistered interest.[168] The same principle applies also to a conditional buyer and to a lessee.[169] Article XIV(1) of the Protocol clarifies that the rule also applies when an interest was registered 'subsequent' to the acquisition of the aircraft object under a registered sale.[170]

Under Article 29(5) of the Convention, the holders of competing interests or rights may make an agreement on modifying the priority of the competing interest, for example, by agreement on subordination. This will usually imply some form of counter value or compensation for the holder of the subordinated interest. However, an assignee of such subordinated interest will not be bound by such agreement, unless the subordination was registered at the time of the assignment.[171]

There are also important third party effects of registration in insolvency or bankruptcy proceedings. The priority rule of Article 29(1) of the Convention will protect the holder of the registered interest, if the interest was registered prior to the commencement of the insolvency proceedings.[172] However, the interest must be effective under the applicable law.[173] The rules on fraudulent preference, or bankruptcy fraud under the national applicable law, remain unaffected. The same applies to rules of procedures on enforcement under insolvency administration.[174]

Under Article XI, Alternative A, paragraph 12, non-consensual rights or interests, or rights of arrest or detention covered by a declaration under Article 39(1) of the Convention, may exceptionally take priority over registered interests if the declaration so provides.[175] In this case, priority will apply even if the non-consensual right or interest or right of arrest or detention is not registered.

---

168. See Arts 29 (3) (a) and (b) Convention.
169. See Art. 29 (4) Convention. See on this matter Bollweg/Henrichs, *ibid.* (n. 31), 192 et seq.
170. See Art. XIV (1) of the Protocol. Art. XIV is entitled 'Modification of priority provisions'. However, in substance paras (1) and (2) of this Article do not modify but clarify the application of Art. 29 (3) and (4) to aircraft objects.
171. This applies even if the assignee has actual knowledge of the subordination agreement; in this regard the principles underlying Art. 29 (2) (a), (3) (b) and (4) (b) apply. The registration (or non-registration) of the subordination agreement is solely relevant.
172. See Art. 30 (1) of the Convention.
173. Article 30 (2) of the Convention provides that 'nothing in this Article impairs the effectiveness of an international interest in the insolvency proceedings where that interest is effective under applicable law'.
174. See Art. 30 (3) of the Convention.
175. Article 39 (1) (a) of the Convention provides the option for a Contracting State to give certain non-consensual right or interests priority over registered international interests; examples are those rights or interests which enjoy priority in bankruptcy proceedings under national law, such as claims for unpaid taxes, claims for unpaid wages due to an insolvent employer or similar claims. Art. 39 (1) (b) gives the same option with regard to the right of arresting or detaining aircraft for non-payment of public service charges, in particular for providers of air navigation services. This so-called 'Eurocontrol clause' was inserted into the Convention in order to permit the continuation of the existing enforcement mechanisms under national law, where existing, in relation to unpaid air navigation charges, including those of Eurocontrol. In case of declarations under Art. 39 (1) (a) or 39 (1) (b) of the Convention, it is the declaration itself, which is available on the Registry's website (Art. 23 of the Convention) which gives public notice, instead of an individual registration in the Registry.

9. Liability of the Registrar

Under Article 28 of the Convention, the Registrar 'shall be liable for compensatory damages for loss suffered by a person directly resulting from an error or omission of the Registrar and its officers and employees or from a malfunction of the international registration systems ...'. This provision takes account of the fact that the International Registry is an electronic system with a minimum of human intervention. In principle, the liability of the Registrar is not based on fault, but is a strict liability for errors and omissions of the Registrar and its staff, or for system malfunctions.[176]

However, in case of system malfunction, the Registrar is not liable in case of *force majeure*, namely, when the malfunction is caused by an event of an inevitable and irresistible nature, which could not be prevented by using the best practices in current use in the field of electronic registry design and operation, including those related to backup and systems security and networking.[177] The notion of 'best practices' is key to this exception; it encompasses a number of current requirements relating to electronic registry design and operation, including state-of-the-art protection against viruses and system corruption, rapid identification and rectification of a system irregularity or malfunctions, backup of data by use of a secondary site, use of a digital certificate system to permit authentification of users, and other related measures.[178] The International Registry applies all of these measures. During the establishment phase of the Registry (June 2004-November 2005),[179] the Registry, under the guidance of the Supervisory Authority, followed a 'best practice' approach that has sought to benefit from the best available expertise internationally in the field of electronic registry design, including software design and system security.[180] Such best practice also was applied during the operational phase as from 1 March 2006.

Furthermore, the Registrar shall also not be liable 'for factual inaccuracy of registration information received by the Registrar or transmitted by the Registrar in the form in which it received that information, nor for acts or circumstances for which the Registrar and its officers and employees are not responsible and arising prior to receipt of registration information at the International Registry'.[181] This rule is the result of the fact that the International Registry is an electronic, notice-based registry, which does not check on the contents of the information registered, and in which the registering users are responsible for the accuracy of the

176. See on this matter R. Goode, *ibid.* (n. 35), 4 et seq.; Bollweg/Henrichs, *ibid.* (n. 31), 194.
177. See Art. 28 (1) of the Convention.
178. See R. Goode, *ibid.* (n. 356), 105, providing a list of elements to illustrate the term 'best practices'.
179. The establishment phase for the International Registry under Contract 40160 between ICAO/ Preparatory Commission and the Registrar commenced in June 2004 and terminated on November 2005 with the Final Acceptance and issuance of the Final Acceptance Certificate.
180. This included a best practice audit performed by a third party expert entity, as well as a system security audit performed by a third party expert entity.
181. See Art. 28 (2) of the Convention.

information. This is clearly spelled out in sections 4(c) and 15(a) of the Procedures for the International Registry.[182]

In accordance with Article 28(4) of the Convention and Article XX(5) and (6) of the Protocol, the Registrar shall be covered by appropriate insurance arrangements. The Supervisory Authority has determined the minimum coverage to be USD 10 million.[183] Accordingly, all operations of the International Registry will be covered under the Registry's insurance policy in accordance with the terms of the policy.

10. Other Matters

In line with Article 17(2)(e) of the Convention, a procedure for complaints against the Registrar is set out in section 8 of the Regulations and section 14 of the Procedures for the International Registry. Similarly, section 15 of the Procedures regulates the procedure for claims against the Registrar.

The claims procedure concerns 'operational complaints', that is, complaints relating to the operation of the International Registry which are matters relating to general procedures and policies of the International Registry and do not involve specific adjudication by the Registrar or the Supervisory Authority.[184]

Any such complaints shall be submitted to the Registrar either through the 'operational complaints' section of the website or by e-mail. They shall include full, written facts statements. The Registrar shall acknowledge receipt promptly and shall normally respond within fifteen calendar days. If the matter is not satisfactorily addressed by the Registrar within thirty days, the complainant may submit complains to the Supervisory Authority.[185]

As regards claims for monetary losses, section 15 of the Procedures provides that such claims shall first be notified to the Registrar by post or fax and e-mail, including a full fact statement. There shall be a consultation period of three months, during which the parties shall attempt to resolve the claim. If this is unsuccessful, the parties are encouraged to engage in mediation, conciliation, arbitration, or other dispute resolution, but the claimant may nevertheless bring proceedings in the Irish courts against the Registrar.[186] The Irish courts have exclusive jurisdiction in accordance with Article 44 of the Convention.

---

182. See also s. 3.2 Regulations for the International Registry.
183. See Preparatory Commission for the International Registry, Report on the Third Meeting, PCIR/3 – Report, Agenda *item* 4.
184. See s. 8.2 Regulations. The question may arise whether matters relating to an individual registration, search or certificate when they do not involve specific adjudication by the Registrar or the Supervisory Authority, can be the subject of an 'operational complaint', given the language of s. 8.2. Such cases will undoubtedly arise. The language in s. 8.2 may suggest that neither the Registrar nor the Supervisory Authority should deal with such 'individual' operational complaints. In practice, this issue will need to be addressed through interpretation of s. 8.2 of the Regulations in light of the Convention and Protocol.
185. See ss 14 (a)-(e) of the Procedures for the International Registry.
186. See ss 15 (a)-(d) of the Regulations for the International Registry; Art. 44 Convention.

E. Conclusions

The entry into operation of the new International Registry for the International Internship in aircraft objects has been of interest to international airlines, leasing companies, banks and other financial institutions involved in aircraft financing, export credit institutions, law firms involved in aircraft transactions, national registries, and governments.[187] These parties benefit directly or indirectly from the advantages which flow from the use of the Registry's facilities. Apart from the advantages of a 'one-stop shop' facility, the risk reduction aspects of asset-based financing under the Cape Town instruments are attracting many of these parties to use the Registry.[188] Risk reduction is, in particular, the result of the uniform system of remedies in case of debtor default, which is laid down in Chapter III of the Convention and Chapter II of the Protocol. This uniform system, which creditors may use in lieu of national remedies and which they may enforce as provided for under the Convention and Protocol,[189] provides creditors and debtors alike with a foreseeable, transparent, and effective set of tools for managing and reducing the risks flowing from default. Appropriate debtor protection rules have been built in, so as to protect against undue exercise of creditor's rights.

According to an economic study carried out in 2005,[190] which updated an earlier economic impact assessment of 1998,[191] the Convention, Protocol, and Registry are providing enhanced opportunities for airlines, especially in developing countries, to benefit from lower secured financing rates. The study estimated that the difference in the secured and unsecured interest rate would be approximately 2.5% (or 250 basis points).[192] This difference would lead to interest savings between 13% and 20% per dollar of principal borrowed for aircraft financings that are not already covered by protections comparable to those provided by the Protocol. The range of resulting savings estimated by the study for a twenty-year period is USD 5.5 to 6 billion for high-income countries and USD 1.0 to 1.5 billion for low-income countries. As regards governments, the study estimated that the Cape Town instruments would likely result in a reduction in sovereign guarantee requirements for airline financing, with a consequent improvement in overall

187. See M.J. Stanford, 'A broader or a narrower band of beneficiaries for the proposed new international regimen? Some reflections on the merits of the Convention/Protocol structure in facilitating the former', *Uniform Law Review* IV (NS), no. 2 (1999): 242 et seq.
188. On these aspects, see H. W. Fleisig, 'The proposed Unidroit Convention on Mobile Equipment: Economic consequences and issues', *Uniform Law Review*, IV (NS), no. 2 (1999): 253.
189. See Arts 8–15 of the Convention and Arts IX-XVI of the Protocol.
190. See Economic Benefits to the Aviation Industry under International Secured Transactions Law Reform: the Cape Town Convention and the International Registry on Mobile Assets, Study prepared for SITA by A. Saunders, A. Stinivasan and I. Walter, N.Y. University Stern School of Business, 22 Feb. 2005.
191. See Proposed Unidroit Convention on International Interests in Mobile Equipment as Applicable to Aircraft Equipment through the Aircraft Equipment Protocol: Economic Impact Assessment, Study by A. Saunders and J. Walter, (INSEAD and New York University Salomon Centre, September 1998).
192. Economic Benefits Study, *ibid.* (n. 190), 3.

sovereign debt ratings.[193] As regards airlines and their shareholders, the study concluded that the Cape Town instruments would likely result in credit rating improvement, leading to further reductions in interest cost generally for these air carriers, and likely increase in stock market valuation which the authors believed to be in the order of at least 10%.[194] In the five years since the entry into force of the Cape Town instruments, the actual interest savings for aircraft financing, although sizeable, seem not to have reached the above estimated figures so far. However, it remains to be seen whether additional benefits will accrue in the future.

The International Registry is the first and so far only global registry for aircraft, engines, and helicopters. The economic benefits therefore also extend to transactions related to engines and helicopters. The parties involved in transactions regarding engines and helicopters can equally benefit from a range of more flexible financing arrangements.[195]

193. Economic Benefits Study, *ibid.* (n. 190), 4.
194. Economic Benefits Study, *ibid.* (n. 190), 4 et seq.
195. Economic Benefits Study, *ibid.* (n. 190), 5 et seq. with particular regard to aircraft engines.

Chapter 6
Liability in International Law (Private Air Law)

Elmar M. Giemulla and Heiko van Schyndel

I. PRIVATE AVIATION LAW: HISTORICAL OVERVIEW

A. Beginnings

In private aviation law, the first question to focus on was whether and to what extent the owner has to allow overflight over his property. In addition, legal disputes about the air carrier's liability in international carriage by air led to very different results in the early years of private aviation law because different legal provisions could be applied to carriages of the same flight according to the points of contact of International Private Law (IPL).

The 1920s can be considered as the beginning of the international aviation development, that is, of the systematic use of the aircraft as an important means of transport for both fast and safe carriage of people, mail and goods over longer distances and across international borders. An international transport network had already developed by the beginning of the Second World War. Aviation law developed just as quickly and vigorously as aviation itself.

The 1929 Warsaw Convention (WC)[1] met the need for legal unification, which was initially adapted to the further development through additional agreements.

1. Authentic French Text: *II Conférence Internationale de Droit Privé Aerién*, 4–12 Octobre 1929, Varsovie 1930, 220 et seq.; for British translation, see Schedule to the United Kingdom

Elmar M. Giemulla & Ludwig Weber, *International and EU Aviation Law: Selected Issues*, pp. 223–284.

B. Development until the Second World War

In 1925, the first diplomatic conference on private aviation law was held in Paris, initiated by the French government. Delegates from forty-eight nations attended the conference. The result of this first international conference on private aviation law, which was held from 27 October to 6 November 1925, was the presentation of a draft for an agreement on documents of carriage and the liability of the air carrier in international aviation.

Furthermore, the International Technical Committee of Legal Air Experts (CITEJA) was established at the recommendation of the conference – a permanent commission of aviation law experts who were to further develop the presented draft. The CITEJA partially significantly redesigned the draft and presented a pre-draft for an agreement 'on documents of carriage and liability of the carrier relating to international carriage by air' to the second international conference on private aviation law, which was held in Warsaw from 4 to 12 October 1929.

The second diplomatic conference on private aviation law was held in Warsaw in 1929. Forty-four nations had been invited to this conference; however, only thirty-two countries were represented (including the German Reich). The United States (US) had only sent an observer. At the end of the conference, the Convention for the Unification of Certain Rules relating to International Carriage by Air (WC[2]) was signed by twenty-three nations (including the German Reich). The Convention regulates questions concerning the organization of documents of carriage and the liability of the carrier for people as well as for damage to goods and damage occasioned by delay in international carriage by air.[3] In accordance with Article 37, paragraph 2 of the Convention, it came into force ninety days after the fifth nation had deposited the ratification documents – on 13 February 1933. By the end of 1933, twelve countries already were members of the WC. Germany became a member on 29 December 1933 by law from 30 November 1933.[4] The US used the option provided by Article 39 WC and joined the Convention by a notification addressed to the Government of the Republic of Poland on 31 July 1934. President Roosevelt proclaimed the Convention ninety days later – when it came into force.[5] As a US Convention, it is part of the Constitution.[6]

Carriage by Air Act, 1932; 22 & 23 Geo.5, ch. 36; for American translation, see [49 Stat. 3000; T.S 876].

2. Authentic French Text: *II Conférence Internationale de Droit Privé Aerién*, 4–12 Octobre 1929, Varsovie 1930, 220 et seq.; for British translation, see Schedule to the United Kingdom Carriage by Air Act, 1932; 22 & 23 Geo.5, ch. 36; for American translation, see [49 Stat. 3000; T.S 876].
3. *RGBl.* 1933 II, 1039; Meyer, *Freiheit der Luft als Rechtsproblem* (*Freedom of Air Space as a Legal Problem*), 31; Schwenk/Giemulla, *Handbuch des Luftverkehrsrechts* (*Handbook on Aviation Law*) (Heymanns Verlag, 2004), 12, 362.
4. See notification in *RGBl.* 1933 II, 1039.
5. 49 Stat. 3000, T. S., Note 876; also see 1934 *USA v. R* 245, reprint in 49 U.S.C. § 1502 Note 1982.
6. U. S. Constitution Article VI, Cl. 2; *Air France v. Saks*, 470 U.S. 392, 105 S. Ct. 1338, 84 L. Ed. 2 d 289,1985 = 18 Avi 18, 538; *TWA v. Franklin Mint*, 466 U.S. 243, 104 S. Ct. 1776, 8 c L. Ed. 2d 273, 1984; *Kapar v. Kuwait Airways*, US District Court, DC, 20 Avi 18, 421.

The third diplomatic conference on private aviation law was held in Rome in 1933 and resulted in the 'Convention for the Unification of Certain Rules relating to the Precautionary Arrest of Aircraft'[7] and the so-called Rome Convention. The Convention on Precautionary Arrest of Aircraft[8] was signed in Rome on 29 May 1933 and was to ensure that aviation was not disturbed by acts by creditors of the owners or operators of aircraft. The Convention exempted aircraft appropriated to a State service and aircraft in service on a regular line of public transport, and aircraft registered in another contractual State of any precautionary arrest in pursuit of a private interest, and did not apply to precautionary arrest for public reasons nor to insolvency law.[9] The Rome Convention, the Convention for the Unification of Certain Laws relating to Damage Caused by Foreign Aircraft to Third Parties on the Surface[10], was also signed in Rome on 29 May 1933 and was supplemented by an additional protocol that was signed at the fourth diplomatic conference on private aviation law in Brussels on 29 September 1938[11].

The fourth diplomatic conference on private aviation law was held in Brussels in 1938 and adopted the Convention for the Unification of Certain Laws relating to Assistance and Salvage of Aircraft or by Aircraft in Distress at Sea[12] on 29 September 1938.

The same aviation law in the area of private aviation law was in place globally before the Second World War broke out, since the conferences organized by CITEJA were open to all states.[13]

It was only shortly after its adoption that the WC started being criticized, initially by the affected aircraft carriers that found the provisions on the air consignment note to be too restrictive (see Articles 8 et seq. WC). However, works on revising the WC, which were manifested in a draft developed by the CITEJA in Rio de Janeiro in 1935, were interrupted by the breakout of Second World War.

C. Development after the Second World War

In the post-war period, reform efforts were continued by the Legal Committee of the International Civil Aviation Organization (ICAO), which had been newly appointed (the CITEJA was dissolved in 1947). Various international conferences were held, but at first without any concrete results: Cairo (1946), Madrid (1951), Paris (1952), and again Rio de Janeiro (1953). Criticism of the WC had by then increased and shifted significantly. Above all, it came from the US, where the

7. 192 *LNTS* 289; *RGBl.* 1935 II, 301; Meyer, *supra*, 31.
8. Sometimes it is called 'Convention on Precautionary *Attachment* of Aircraft'.
9. Meyer, *ibid.*, 32.
10. VI *Hudson* 334; (1937) JAL 312.
11. (1939) JALC 281.
12. (1939) JALC 277; Meyer, *ibid.*, 35.
13. *Ibid.*, 61; Riese, *Luftrecht: das internationale Recht der zivilen Luftfahrt unter besonderer Berücksichtigung des schweizerischen Rechts* (Koehler, Stuttgart, 1949), 87.

maximum limits of liability, especially for damage to people, of Gold Francs 125,000 (≈ USD 8,300) had proven to be unacceptably low.

1. Hague Protocol

Finally, a diplomatic conference was held at The Hague from 6 to 28 September 1955.[14] However, the result was not – as had been hoped – a general revision of the WC, but simply the signing of an additional protocol by twenty-five of the forty-four States represented at the conference, meaning that the WC in its original version was not replaced by the Hague Protocol (HP)[15], but remained valid. It was simply modified by the HP for the States that had joined the HP as well. The WC and the HP are considered a unified document by the contractual parties of the HP, which is referred to as The HP (1955) Amending the Warsaw Convention (WC/HP). The HP came into force on 1 August 1963, ninety days after the thirtieth ratification document had been deposited with the Government of the Republic of Poland (see Article 22 HP). The HP also came into force in the Federal Republic of Germany on 1 August 1963.[16]

Since these maximum limits of liability were insufficient for the US, they did not join the HP. When the US became more and more dissatisfied with the WC in the following years, the US administration finally felt obligated to act. Denunciation was made by a notification addressed to the Government of the Republic of Poland on 15 November 1965 and would have become effective on 15 May 1966 pursuant to Article 39, paragraph 2 WC, had the US not revoked it one day before.

2. Supplementary Guadalajara Convention

A Supplementary Convention to the WC was concluded in Guadalajara in 1961.[17] The Supplementary Guadalajara Convention (SGC)[18] was the result of a conference that was held from 29 August to 18 September 1961. Eighteen of the forty attending States signed the Convention during the conference. After having been ratified by five States, it came into force on 1 May 1964. While the HP not only included some amendments but also several variations to the provisions of the WC, the SGC only included amendments, namely, the extension of liability to other aircraft carriers or third parties.

As early as 1955, the ICAO had already recognized the problem of charter traffic, which had not yet been of any significance when the WC came into force in its original version. The SGC had been preceded by two drafts: The 1957 Madrid or

14. For details see: *ICAO-Legal-Committee*, Report on the revision of the Warsaw Convention, ICAO International Conference on Private Air Law (The Hague, Sept. 1955), Vol. 2, at 93; *ICAO Doc.* 7686 – LC/140 [1956], Vol. I: Minutes, and Vol. II: Documents.
15. 478 *UNTS* 371; 10 *ILM* 613.
16. See notification of 14 Aug. 1964, *BGBl.* II, 1295; with publication from 8 Jun. 1965, *BGBl.* II, 907.
17. *ICAO Doc.* 8301-LC/149-1 and 8302-LC/149-2.
18. 500 *UNTS* 32.

Tokyo draft and the 1960 Paris or Montreal draft, which formed the basis for discussions held in Guadalajara.

The general subject matter of the SGC was the legal relationships that arise from hiring, chartering and exchanging aircraft. The liability regime of the WC is extended from the contractual to the so-called actual air carrier (for details on these terms, see Article 1 SGC).

3. Montreal Interim Agreement

With the date of the American denunciation coming closer, and because of the great significance of US air traffic, many international airlines felt the need to sign an agreement that had been concluded between several air carriers of the International Air Transport Association (IATA) and the American Civil Aeronautics Board (CAB) on 4 May 1966 (the so-called Montreal Interim Agreement[19]; official designation, Agreement CAB 18, 900). The content of the Montreal Interim Agreement allowed the US to revoke its denunciation of the WC through notification to the Polish Government. However, the legal nature of the Montreal Interim Agreement is not that of an international legal institution, which would simply apply between airlines and their passengers.

Because of its restricted application to carriage of flight passengers from and to the US or stopping over in the US, the Montreal Interim Agreement has led to a split in the international liability system.

4. Guatemala City Protocol

Afterwards, efforts to re-establish a unified liability system did not cease on an international level. In 1967, British airlines also started feeling the pressure of the public opinion as a result of the low liability limits.[20] The ICAO recognized that the Montreal Interim Agreement was limited in time and appointed an expert commission that was to work on revising the WC. In 1971, delegates from fifty-five nations met in Guatemala City to establish the changes to the actual liability in the WC itself based on a draft presented by the ICAO Expert Commission and especially to react to the conditions set forth by the US when revoking its denunciation notification on 14 May 1966, which had so far not been met, namely, the increase of the maximum limit of liability to USD 100,000 in the long term.[21]

On 8 March 1971, the Guatemala City Protocol was signed by twenty-one States.[22] In accordance with the original request by the US, the liability amounts were increased to Gold Francs 1.5 million (USD 100,000).

---

19. (1966) USAvR 450.
20. For details see Cohen, *AL* (1983), 146 et seq./157.
21. For details see: ICAO-International Conference on Air Law, Guatemala City, *ICAO Doc.* 9040-LC/167-1, 167-2 (1971); on the conference, also see Schmidt-Räntsch, *ZLW* (1972), 3 et seq.; Mankiewicz, *JALC* (1972), 519 et seq.
22. 478 *UNTS* 371; 10 *ILM* 613; *ICAO Doc.* No. 8932 (1971).

5. Additional Montreal Protocols

The International Conference on Aviation Law in Montreal from 3 to 25 September 1975 resulted in the first three of four Additional Montreal Protocols of 25 September 1975. These Protocols – at least indirectly – also dealt with liability matters, namely, with the relevant currency.[23] The Additional Montreal Protocols Nos 1,[24] 2,[25] and 3[26] helped change the currency unit relevant for calculating the liability amount internationally to Special Drawing Rights (SDR).[27] Protocol No. 4[28] reacted to the fact that the Guatemala City Protocol left the freight regulations of the WC unchanged.

It took a long time for the Additional Montreal Protocols to come into force. President Ford presented them to the US Senate for adoption as early as 14 January 1977, but on 8 March 1983, neither the Additional Protocols nor the Guatemala City Protocol achieved the required two-thirds majority. The Reagan Administration also tried to obtain approval of Protocols Nos 3 and 4 by the Senate in 1988, but this attempt was also unsuccessful. Finally, Montreal Protocols Nos 1, 2, and 4 came into force after more than twenty years; the two first aforementioned Protocols on 15 February 1996, and the latter Protocol on 14 June 1998. Protocol No. 4 came into force for the US on 4 March 1999.

6. Malta Agreement

With the general tendency of Western industrial nations to increase the liability amounts, a number of Western European governments held a series of consultations after 1974 so as to encourage their national carriers to include higher liability amounts in their contracts. Finally, as a result of the Malta Agreement (MA) of 1 July 1976,[29] airline carriers of several European countries changed their conditions of carriage for international flights and increased the maximum liability amount for damages to people to approximately DM 150,000. This does, however, not apply to flights subject to the Montreal Interim Agreement. Liability for luggage and goods remains regulated by the WC or the HP. Various air carriers providing commercial non-scheduled services have followed this example and have raised their liability limits accordingly.

As early as 1955, the ICAO had already recognized the problem of charter traffic, which had not been of any significance when the WC went into force in its

23. See *ICAO Doc.* No. 9154 – LC/174-1,174-2 (1975).
24. 2097 *UNTS* 28.
25. 2097 *UNTS* 69.
26. Not in force.
27. For the calculation system of SDR, see *RFDA* (1975), 138; du Pontavice, *AD-MA* (1982), 33.
28. 2145 *UNTS* 36.
29. For more details see: McGilchrist, 'Special Contracts and the Malta Agreement', *LMCLQ* 1977, 366 et seq.; Müller-Rostin, 'Neue Haftungsgrenzen für Personenschäden bei internationalen Luftbeförderungen', *ZLW* 25 (1976), 336 et seq.

original version. The SGC had been preceded by two drafts: The 1957 Madrid or Tokyo draft and the 1960 Paris or Montreal draft, which formed the basis for discussions held in Guadalajara.

It must be noted that the WC and its additional Conventions did not expire, despite its successor, the Montreal Convention (MC), meanwhile going into force.[30] It still applied to round trips from a country that had not yet joined the MA and for one-way flights between two countries that had both not yet joined the MA (see Article 1 WC/HP and Article 1 MA).

D. Development towards the Montreal Convention

The 1990s saw many efforts to reform the Warsaw System or to find other ways to conserve it as a legal base for international carriage by air. Furthermore, over the last years, various international organizations have worked towards increasing the maximum liability amounts or changing the Warsaw System structurally.

1. Initial Proposal for a Council (EC) Regulation on Air Carrier Liability in Case of Accidents

Early 1993 saw the first movement through a European Commission initiative. The Directorate General for Transport (DG VII) called a meeting of the Member States, which was held on 18 January 1993, with Norway and Sweden attending as well. The aim of the initiative was to include EC Member States and States that had concluded 'carriage-by-air-agreements' with the EC, the reason for which being not only the notion that the existing liability amounts were too low, but also the need for a unified regulation for all EC Member States. Finally, it was deemed necessary to ensure quick settlement of indemnity processes by paying out a minimum amount (as had been regulated in Germany and in France for quite some time).

A working group was established on 23 March 1993, which was to draft an EC Directive on air carrier liability with increased maximum liability limits, which was to be binding for EC carriers and for non-EC carriers that provided services touching down in the EC. Furthermore, the European Commission assessed the possibility of totally abandoning maximum liability limits or increasing these limits to 250,000/300,000 ECU. Finally, the EC agreed to increase the maximum liability limits to SDR 500,000.

On 15 February 1996, the Commission finally presented a Proposal for a Council (EC) Regulation on air carrier liability in case of accidents.[31]

30. For details on the relationship between the MA and the Agreements on the Warsaw Liability System, see Art. 55 MA.
31. COM (95) 724, final, *OJ* No. C 104 of 10 Apr. 1996, 18; the amended draft COM (96) 663, final – *OJ* No. C 29 of 30 Jan. 1997, 10.

2. The ECAC Initiative

The ECAC Working Group on Intra-European Air Transport Policy (EURPOL), established at the initiative of the European Civil Aviation Conference (ECAC), agreed during its meeting in November 1993 that a new maximum liability limit of SDR 250,000 would restore the indemnity amount that was to be guaranteed by the Montreal Protocols. Accordingly, a recommendation by the ECAC to its thirty-two Member States adopted on 24 June 1994[32] included a request to the governments to encourage air carriers to increase liability limits for damages to people in their conditions of carriage to SDR 250,000. The system of liability for suspected default fixed in the WC was to be maintained.

3. The IATA Intercarrier Agreement

The IATA agreed to completely abandon maximum liability limits during conferences of its members in Washington, D.C. and Kuala Lumpur in 1995 through a private law agreement between the signatory air carriers in which they pledged to change their conditions of carriage accordingly. Almost all commercial air carriers have signed the IATA Intercarrier-Agreements (IIA). The following is a list of the most important elements of these IIA:[33]

- The IIA has been designed as an umbrella accord. The signatory air carriers must specify their detailed rights and obligations in their conditions of carriage and tariffs. They pledge to not refer to the maximum liability limits of Article 22 in the event of death or bodily injury of passengers, that is, liability limits are basically non-existent in these cases. The actual damage is the only compensatory damage. It is calculated based on the applicable law of the passenger's domicile.
- In the Agreement on Measures to Implement the IATA Intercarrier Agreement (MIA),[34] the air carriers pledge to waive the defence of lack of negligence for indemnity claims of up to SDR 100,000 (Article 20). Every company will have the option to only waive this defence for certain routes. Up to this amount, the air carriers, therefore, undergo strict liability. Furthermore, they explicitly have the chance to file a request that the court should apply the law of the passenger's domicile, as long as applying the law of the passenger's domicile does not conflict with the law of the assigned court. Furthermore, the air carriers have the right not to let the waiver of applying liability limits take effect towards social insurance agencies.

---

32. Recommendation ECAC/16-1, Air Carrier's Liability with Respect to Passengers, *BAnz.* of 3 Dec. 1994, 12446.
33. The text is printed in *ZLW* (1996), 23 and in *TAQ* (1996/97), 13/119; on the IIA; also see Böckstiegel, *ZLW* (1996), 18; Clark, *ZLW* (1996), 353; *id.*, *LAL* (1996), Nos 16, 1, 3; Müller-Rostin, *ZLW* (1999), 324; *id.*, Festschrift for Herber, 245 et seq.; Hellebrandt, 253 et seq.
34. Printed in *TAQ* 1996/97, 16/121.

– The Agreement on Provisions Implementing the IATA Intercarrier Agreement to be Included in Conditions of Carriage and Tariffs (IPA)[35] is initially only binding for US American airline carriers. In addition to the waiver of application of liability limits and subjection to strict liability for damages up to SDR 100,000, the signatory carriers of the IPA pledge to apply the law of the passenger's domicile and to allow the passenger a 'fifth place of jurisdiction' at his domicile.

4. Council (EC) Regulation on Air Carrier Liability in Case of Accidents

The same liability regulations were finally included in EC Regulation 2027/97, on Air Carrier Liability in Case of Accidents of 9 October 1997.[36] This EC Regulation came into force on 18 October 1998 and is a directly enforceable law in each of the EC Member States. It initially takes up liability for damages to passengers as per the WC, now as per the MC, but – as opposed to these two documents – does not include liability regulations for the 'air carrier', but only for the 'Community air carriers', which are defined as air transport undertakings that require an EC operating license as per Council Regulation (EC) No. 2407/92.[37] In addition to the aforementioned liability regulations of the IIA, and based on these agreements, it concretizes the insurance (Article 3(1b)) and advance payment obligations of initially no less than SDR 15,000, now SDR 16,000 (Article 5) ,which have already been established by Regulation No. 2407/92. Finally, the air carriers must include liability regulations in their conditions of carriage (Article 6).

5. The Montreal Convention

The Legal Committee of the ICAO approved the text of a Convention draft for the modernization of the Warsaw System in May 1997 (Document C-WP/10613 of 2 June 1997). The object of the suggested changes to the Warsaw System, which was to be re-established as one single document, was for indemnity proceedings to be simplified and significantly reduced in length for the majority of victims of aircraft accidents or their families.

On 28 May 1999, the new Convention[38] was signed by 52 of the 122 States attending the conference, including 18 European states (including Germany) and 18 African states, as well as the USA. However, thirty States had to ratify the Convention for it to come into force. The EC also signed the Convention (on

---

35. Printed in *TAQ* 1996/97, 122.
36. *OJ* No. L 258 of 17 Oct. 1997, 1; on the EC-regulation No. 2027/97; see in detail: Ruhwedel, *TranspR* (1998), 13; Gansfort, *ZLW* (1998), 263; Giemulla/Schmid, *NZV* (1998), 225; Tonner, *RRa* (1998), 211; Müller-Rostin, *TranspR* (1998), 229/232; Schmid, *RRa* (1999), 3; Saenger, *NJW* (2000), 169/172.
37. *OJ* No. L 240 of 24 Aug. 1992, 1.
38. 2242 *UNTS* 350.

9 December 1999). On 5 April 2001, the Council of the European Union (EU) approved the MC.[39]

The MC came into force on 4 November 2003, after the US had been the thirtieth country to ratify it sixty days before. Germany and the other EC Member States at the time (except for two Member States that had already deposited their ratification documents), as well as the EC itself, deposited their ratification documents on 29 April 2004 (before the EC was enlarged by ten additional countries on 1 May 2004).

6. Regulation (EC) No. 889/2002

A complete harmonization between the MC and regulations in the EC was achieved with Regulation (EC) No. 889/2002 of the Parliament and the Council of the EU of 13 May 2002 on changing the Council Regulation (EC) No. 2027 on Air Carrier Liability in Case of Accidents.[40] The maximum liability amounts and legal remedies were adjusted to the liability standards of the MC for all carriages effectuated by European air carriers, irrespective of the route (domestic flight, inner-community flight, or international flight) on which the accident occurred.

II. LIABILITY ARISING FROM AN AIR CARRIAGE AGREEMENT IN ACCORDANCE WITH INTERNATIONAL LAW

A. Introduction

International air carriage, which developed rapidly in the 1920s, demanded proper treatment by the law. To accommodate this requirement, in the years 1925 in Paris, 1929 in Warsaw, two international conferences were held. It was the aim of these conferences to create a certain degree of unification in international air carriage, which affected many countries, with different languages, customs, regimes, and legal systems. Furthermore, by way of a limitation of the liability of the air carriers, the aspiring aviation industry was supposed to be prevented from immediately having its flame of life extinguished by possibly ruinous claims for damages or no longer affordable insurance premiums. As a result of the conferences, the Convention for the Unification of Certain Rules Relating to International Carriage by Air (WC[41]) was put forward for signature and immediately signed

39. *OJ* No. L 194 of 18 Jul. 2001, 38.
40. *OJ* No. L 140 of 30 May 2002, 2.
41. Authentic French Text: *II Conférence Internationale de Droit Privé Aerién*, 4–12 Octobre 1929, Varsovie 1930, p.220 et seq.; for British translation, see Schedule to the United Kingdom Carriage by Air Act, 1932; 22 & 23 Geo.5, ch. 36); for American translation, see [49 Stat. 3000; T.S 876].

by twenty-three participating countries. It came into force on 13 February 1933, ninety days after the deposition of the fifth ratification document, in accordance with its Article 37, paragraph 2. At the end of 1933, twelve countries were already members of the WC.

The WC constituted an attempt at unification concerning certain legal questions; however, the maximum liability limits laid down therein, or also those laid down in the Hague Protocol, to that extent amending the WC, were increasingly felt to be too low. In addition, over the decades, consumer-friendly tendencies, which relieved the passenger or freight consignor of having to prove fault on the part of the air carrier if the liability limits should be exceeded, gained acceptance.

Furthermore, the seventy-year history of the WC is the history of its alterations and additions – with the consequence that the Warsaw Liability System became increasingly opaque and partially bestowed upon the claimant conclusions that were felt to be virtually random.

Following years of efforts to create a renewed unification and revision of the system, finally, within the scope of a diplomatic conference of around 120 countries, which took place in Montreal from 10 to 28 May 1999, the successor to the WC was concluded, the Convention for the Unification of Certain Rules for International Carriage by Air (the so-called MC[42]). This came into force on the sixtieth day after the deposition of the thirtieth ratification document (by the US) on 4 November 2003 and amends some aspects of the previous liability regulations of the WC considerably.

As, however, not all countries in the international community had signed the WC, along with all its supplementary agreements, and not all countries (by a long shot) have implemented the MC, international contractual liability law is still a patchwork.

Furthermore, the conventions specified do not regulate the air carriers' liability comprehensively, but only cover certain essential matters. In addition, the respective applicable national law applies (e.g., in regard to the question of what is to be recognized as damage and how the latter is to be calculated). The respective applicable (national) law is to be determined in accordance with the rules of IPL. Starting points for the choice of law can emerge from the agreements of the parties to the contract, the destination or place of departure of the aircraft, the nationality of the air carrier or the passenger, the branch of the air transportation company and the nationality of the aircraft. The decision on the specific point of contact is (partially) the responsibility of the court called upon, which, however, first has to decide on its jurisdiction. The WC and MC name four respectively five possible jurisdictions. In the event of actions by aggrieved passengers against an air carrier resulting from one and the same accident, various legal systems can be applied, as different places of departure and destinations, nationalities, or transportation agreements can hold good for these. The same is true of freight conveyance.

42. 2242 *UNTS* 350.

It is common to the specified conventions that the liability is dependent upon the following conditions:

- the existence of a carriage agreement;
- the existence of international carriage; and
- if applicable, that the carriage is remunerated.

1. The Existence of a Carriage Agreement

Neither the Warsaw System nor the MC contains a definition of air transport contracts. However, the carriage without contract is not included in the legal international scope or framework. Should passengers or freight be contractually conveyed, this occurs on the basis of a so-called air carriage agreement. As by far the majority of transportations are of a contractual nature, the air carriage agreement has very great practical significance. The relevant liability regulations of the WC and MC do not contain any express provisions on the carriage agreement. Rather, the conclusion of such an agreement is a prerequisite.

In principle, the parties concerned can make such contractual arrangements as they please (WC, Article 22; paragraphs 1 and 27 MC 1999). Article 22, paragraph 2 of the WC gives the parties the right to agree to a higher limit of liability, although, for registered baggage, that limit cannot exceed the passenger's or consignor's actual interest in delivery at destination. On the other hand, Article 33 of the WC specifically authorizes the carrier to refuse to enter into a contract of carriage and to establish general or special conditions of carriage. The parties cannot agree on limits of liability lower than those established by the Convention (Articles 23 and 26 MC 1999). For instance, clauses that exclude the liability of the carrier in case of contributory negligence are considered null and void.

In all air transport contracts, the carrier is the party that has entered into a contract for carriage in its own name and has undertaken to execute its duties. The principal duty of the air carrier is to ensure that the carriage is performed at the agreed date and hour. The subject of the air carriage agreement consists in conveying persons or items by air from one place to another, or also, as in the case of sightseeing flights, back to the starting point. Thus, success in conveyance is specifically required of the air carrier.

The carrier is under no obligation to perform the carriage itself. He can arrange to have it performed by another person or an actual or substitute carrier. This substitute carrier is considered the actual carrier according to the definition in the Guadalajara Convention (1961), in the case of an independent contractor.

The air carriage agreement in accordance with the WC or MC is essentially informal. It materializes through corresponding declarations of intent by the air carrier and the passenger, as the two parties to the agreement. This can occur in different ways and involve the additional participation of further persons. The simplest form of conclusion prevalent in non-commercial air carriage consists in the air carrier and passenger directly agreeing upon conveyance. Tickets are not usual in this case. In commercial air transport, on the other hand, transportation documents are the rule. Missing transportation tickets may, however, result in legal disadvantages for the air carrier (see Article 3, paragraph 2, Sentence 3 WC). The parties to the contract in the case of the air carriage agreement are the air carrier and the passenger or the consignor of freight/merchandise.

According to continental European understanding, an air carrier is any party that contractually undertakes, in its own name, to convey persons or goods/merchandise by air. This definition relies exclusively upon the declarations of intent of the parties to the contract. Accordingly, therefore, any party can be an air carrier, even if it cannot in any way fulfil the obligation of conveyance itself, but, for example, uses an air transportation company, which supplies the actual prerequisites for the fulfilment of the transportation service, as an assistant for this purpose. In the Anglo-Saxon legal circle, this is, however, different. There, the actual conveyance is of relevance. According to the latter, an air carrier is only the party actually carrying out the air carriage.

The essential features of liability arising from the carriage agreement are as follows: the increase in the so-called general risk to life consciously and voluntarily accepted by the passenger through boarding an aircraft, that is, the voluntary acceptance of typical risks of air carriage by the passenger, prohibits the opposing party (in this case, the air carrier) from taking the opportunity of evading liability entirely (Article 20, paragraph 1 WC) or for losses exceeding SDR 100,000 until 29 December 2009, respectively SDR 113,100 since 30 December 2009 per passenger (Article 20 in conjunction with Article 21, paragraph 1 MC), at least by proving that it has done everything conceivable to avoid damage. For this reason, Articles 20 WC and MC provide for the production of such exonerating evidence by the air carrier. On the other hand, if the air carrier cannot produce the exonerating evidence, it has an increased risk of liability in this case, since – conversely – fault on its part does not have to be proven by the passenger. The fault is substituted here by taking on the 'care' of the passenger (or his luggage). The period of time relevant for this purpose is defined in Article 17 WC and Article 17 MC as being that the passenger was on board the aircraft when the damaging event took place or that the latter took place during boarding or disembarkation.

Mere courtesy relationships or carriage without the air carrier's awareness (a 'fare dodger' or stowaway) do not fall within the scope of validity of the Convention, as likewise contracts the purpose of which are not carriage of persons or items, such as rental agreements, charter agreements, or service agreements. The WC or the MC do not, therefore, apply, for example, to the crews on duty flying with the aircraft. In the event of mere courtesy conveyance, a willingness to enter into a commitment between the parties concerned is lacking. In contrast to a gratuitous courtesy agreement, only an actual courtesy relationship, without any contractual commitment, exists. The passenger cannot claim any benefit. In the event of aviation accidents, the carrier is only liable to him in tort, without the carrier, however, being able to appeal to mitigation of liability. Liability in tort can be excluded in advance, except for intent. Declarations of release from liability along those lines are usual when carrying passengers on the basis of courtesy conveyance, and create clear relationships. They can also occur tacitly. However, the gratuitous nature of the carriage does not alone suffice for the assumption of an exclusion of liability. In practice, the delimitation of courtesy conveyance of air carriage agreements involves difficulties from two perspectives. In many cases, ambiguity exists concerning the willingness to enter into a commitment of the parties involved if a written agreement is lacking and they lose their lives in the event of plane crashes. On the other hand, the term *remuneration* is indeterminate. Paid carriage is, in fact, always based on carriage agreements; however, it can be very difficult, in individual cases, to determine when remuneration is involved.

2. The Internationality of the Carriage

The carriage must be international. Pursuant to Article 1 WC or Article 1 MC, only carriage in the case of which, in accordance with the agreements of the parties to the contract, the country of departure and the destination lie within the territories of two contracting States, or, following an intermediary landing abroad, in the territory of the country of departure, are 'international'. Thus, two countries must always be involved, of which, in the event of an intermediary landing, the other country does not have to be a party to the WC or MC. Flying over without an intermediary landing, on the other hand, does not suffice. The intermediary landing is, however, not to be understood technically as a mere break on a single flight, but must function as an agreed partial destination of the carriage. Should a round trip be agreed upon within the scope of a holiday journey, the conveyance service owed forms a unity. The destination is then not the intermediary landing point, but the point of departure. The intermediary landing point is, however, the destination of the (outward) journey.

The conventions are also applied to carriage between a member of the WC or MC and a non-contracting State if the passenger is, in accordance with the agreement, set down there and, after a specific length of stay, is supposed to be conveyed back again into the territory of the Member State. This is, in particular, the case in the event of a sightseeing flight starting off from a Member State, which, after a stopover in a non-member country, brings the passenger back into the country of origin. That also applies to so-called successive carriage, in the case of which several successive air carriers are involved, and, in accordance with the wishes of the parties involved, the carriage is supposed to be uniform. In that respect, it is irrelevant whether the carriage agreement has been concluded in the form of a single agreement or a series of agreements (Article 1, paragraph 3 WC and Article 1, paragraph 3 MC).

Carriage also does not lose its international character through actually taking a different course than anticipated, for example, by a flight with a destination abroad already having to be interrupted within the country of origin or the accident triggering the claim for damages occurring on the domestic section of the route. Domestic feeders are also part of international carriage, if the carriage is, in accordance with the agreement, supposed to be continued to a destination abroad.

The carriage between two points inside the territory of one contracting party, without stop convened in the territory of another State, is not considered international air transport according to the definition in the Convention (Article 1 WC).

3. Remunerability of the Carriage

Carriage must, as a rule, be carried out in exchange for remuneration (Article 1, paragraph 1, Sentence 1 WC/MC). It can, however, be gratuitous if it is carried out by an air transportation company (Article 1, paragraph 1, Sentence 2 WC/MC). The term 'remuneration' is not explained in the conventions and gives rise to interpretation difficulties. The term 'remuneration' is to be construed narrowly, as it can be assumed from it that the conventions are, in the first place, geared towards commercial carriage. It is to be assumed that the significance of the term 'carriage in exchange for remuneration' in no way lies only in the delimitation in regard to courtesy relationships. Rather, the feature of remunerability serves only to include in the scope of application of the WA or MC those private flights for which, according to the interest in the situation, treatment in accordance with a convention appears appropriate in accordance with the conditions of commercial air carriage. Therefore, the interest of the passenger in a free flight is not what is to be focused upon, but rather the economic interest of the air carrier in the carriage. The proprietary interest pursued by the air carrier with the carriage does not need to be geared solely towards money, but can also exist in services and work performed. Arguably, this interest of the air carrier in undertaking the carriage must be sufficiently important that, to that extent, there is no proper and radical difference from a commercial air transportation company. General rules on when carriage is to be viewed as remunerated or gratuitous cannot be established. The specific circumstances of the individual case at hand are decisive, in particular, the parties' declared intentions when the carriage is undertaken. Whether reimbursement of the net costs is also sufficient as remuneration for a flight appears doubtful, in view of the tenor of the convention.

Carriage agreements concerning employees being transported by air transportation companies gratuitously are covered by the scope of validity of the Convention if free flights are granted to them outside their service obligations.

B. Liability in Accordance with the Conventions of the Warsaw System

The Warsaw System (i.e., the WC and the associated supplementary agreements concluded) still continues to apply today for the countries that have not yet dissolved it through the MC. It is still, therefore, of significance today – even if its significance is dwindling. Therefore, it will first be elucidated below in accordance with the historical sequence.

1. Introduction

Viewed chronologically, the WC is the first Convention on the Unification of Certain Rules relating to International Carriage by Air. However, it restricts the unification to rules on the transportation documents (ticket, luggage receipt, and air waybill) and the associated legal relationships, as well as the air carrier's liability for bodily injury and damage to property resulting from the carriage. Insofar, it must be kept in mind that the title of the WC indicates that it is concerned with only 'certain aspects' of private law governing international transport by air, it does not deal with the legal capacity of the parties in the contract, nor the form, validity, cancellation, violation and non-execution of the contract, the legal status of the air carriers, its agents and servants and the basis of their liability, and so on. All these issues must be dealt with in accordance with national law, which means the law of the court seized of the case (Articles 21 and 22, paragraphs 1, 25, 28; paragraphs 2 and 29; paragraph 2, and under the MC 1999, Articles 33 and 46).

The Convention does not apply to the carriage of mail and postal packages (Article 2, paragraph 2) – this is subject to the rules of International Postal Union. The Hague Protocol, amended by the WC and confirmed by Montreal Protocol Number 4, redrafts the article as follows: 'In the carriage of postal items, the carrier shall be liable only to the relevant postal administration in accordance with the rules applicable to the relationship between the carriers and the postal administrations.'

2. Transportation Documents

The Warsaw System provides for three documents of carriage by air: the passenger ticket, the baggage check, and the air waybill.

Article 3, paragraph 1 WC stipulates that, when conveying persons by air, a ticket with a specific minimum content is to be issued. The ticket itself is of no significance for the legal validity of the carriage agreement, because, according to the WC, the carriage agreement does not require any form. The WC does not contain any formal regulations on how the ticket should look. For these reasons, it is also not possible to pose requirements that are too high in that respect. Also, no *pro forma* form is required to be used. A normal sheet of paper or a letter addressed to the passenger may likewise be considered to be a ticket. The original version of the WC prescribes the following minimum details for the ticket:

(a) place and date of issue;
(b) point of departure and destination;
(c) the anticipated intermediary landings; the air carrier may, however, contractually stipulate that, if compelling grounds exist, it may alter the latter without the carriage thereby losing its capacity as international carriage as a result;
(d) name(s) and address(es) of the air carrier(s);
(e) the fact that the carriage is subject to the liability system of this convention.

These details must, in addition, be provided in a particular type size (at least 10 points).[43]

Article 3, paragraph 2 WC underlines the function of the ticket as mere documentary evidence; however, it specifies a sanction in the event that a ticket is not issued at all or that the prescribed reference to the limitation of liability of the WC is missing from it. The air carrier may in these cases not appeal to the regulations of the Convention restricting or excluding liability.

Article 4 WC determines that, when conveying the luggage, a luggage receipt is to be issued. This must likewise contain certain minimum details (in addition to the details specified in Article 3 WC, also the number of the ticket and, if applicable, the amount of the declared value), unless it is physically connected to a ticket corresponding to the regulations of Article 3 WC or its text is incorporated in the ticket. Such combined transportation documents are predominantly used these days in the practice of air carriage. Article 4 WC concerns only the luggage checked in. The latter is understood to mean all items that the passenger surrenders to the air carrier, either in advance or when boarding the flight, with the intention to take it back again at the destination. Hand luggage is not covered by the regulation of Article 4 WC. Article 4, paragraph 2, Sentence 3 WC establishes the consequences of not adhering to particular regulations of paragraph 1: the air carrier worsens its liability situation if it accepts the luggage into its care without issuing a luggage receipt or if the luggage receipt does not contain the reference required in paragraph 1(c).

Article 5, paragraph 1 WC establishes that, when conveying goods, the air carrier can require the consignor to issue and hand over an air waybill, and the consignor can demand that the air carrier accepts this official document. The airfreight agreement itself does not require any form. Materialization is independent of handing over the freight to the air carrier. It is also irrelevant whether an air waybill is issued or not (Article 5, paragraph 2 WC). Freight forwarders are contractual air carriers if it is not clearly recognizable that they do not wish to be active as air carriers themselves. In this case, the conclusion of an air carriage agreement, and not a freight forwarding transaction, is concerned. The airfreight forwarder is generally viewed as an air carrier.

Three copies of the air waybill are issued, with a copy each for the consignor (the so-called third copy of the air waybill), the recipient, and the air carrier. The copy for the air carrier is signed by the consignor. The copy intended for the recipient is signed by both the consignor and the air carrier. It accompanies the goods during carriage. The third copy of the air waybill is signed by the air carrier and handed over to the consignor following acceptance of the goods. It is, therefore, simultaneously a receipt. It is incumbent upon the consignor to issue the air waybill; however, it can instruct third parties in that respect, especially the air carrier. In this case, pursuant to Article 6, paragraph 5 WC, it is presumed until evidence is provided to the contrary that the air carrier has acted as the consignor's agent. Article 8 WC establishes the details that the air waybill is supposed to

43. *Chan v. Korean Air Lines*, 109 S. Ct. 1676 (1989).

contain, but does not have to contain. The issuing of the air waybill and the details contained in it are of significance for the air carrier's liability. Should the air carrier have accepted the goods without an air waybill having been issued, it cannot appeal to the restricted liability. The same applies if a series of details required is not contained in the air waybill.

The air waybill is, according to its legal nature, first, documentary evidence and, pursuant to Article 11 of the WC, substantiates a refutable presumption concerning the correctness of the details on weight, measurements and packaging of the goods and the number of freight items. Furthermore, it provides evidence on the conclusion of the carriage agreement, the receipt of the goods by the air carrier, and the validity of the conditions of carriage.

In addition, the air waybill has an identity-establishing function, as can be seen from the legal relationships between the consignor, freight carrier and recipient. They are regulated in Articles 10, 12, and 13 WC. According to Article 10 WC, the consignor is liable to the air carrier for the correctness of the details and declarations on the goods that it lists in the air waybill, and is obliged to compensate the latter for any damages arising resulting from incorrect, inexact, or incomplete declaration, and in fact also if third parties suffer losses. A similar obligation is incumbent upon the consignor pursuant to Article 16 WC concerning the provision of goods documentation, which is required for customs and other reasons of public law.

3. Liability of the Air Carrier for Bodily Injury

The regulations on the liability of the air carrier are contained in Chapter 3, Articles 17–30 WC. The liability system can be summarized as follows:

(a) liability without fault, restricted in its total amount, when exonerating evidence by the air carrier is lacking (Articles 17–20 WC);
(b) unrestricted liability in the event of gross negligence (Article 25 WC);
(c) no liability if exonerating evidence is produced (Article 20 WC);
(d) no or restricted liability in the event of contributory fault on the part of the claimant (Article 21 WC).

The liability of the air carrier pursuant to Article 17 WC for death, bodily injury, or damage to health assumes an accident on board the aircraft or when boarding or disembarking. An accident is an event, a physical circumstance, that unexpectedly takes place not according to the usual course of things. If the event on board an aeroplane is an ordinary, expected, and usual occurrence, then it cannot be termed an accident.[44] It is doubtful whether liability is inapplicable if the accident does not have a direct causal connection with the operation of the aircraft.

In the event of (restricted) liability, the maximum amount of liability, pursuant to Article 22 WC, is limited to Gold Francs 125,000. Should it be possible, according to the national law of the court appealed to, to fix the compensation in the form

44. *DeMarines v. KLM* – US District Court [EDP], 14 Avi 18, 212.

of a regular payment, its capital value may not exceed this maximum amount. Instead of the amount in Gold Francs, the corresponding amounts in national/European currency apply. The maximum amounts of liability in accordance with the WC have been deemed too low by many countries. That is the essential reason for the revision of the WC in this respect by the HP of 1955[45], which, *inter alia*, led to the maximum amounts of liability being doubled.

Pursuant to Article 25 of the WC, the air carrier is, however, liable without restriction if it has caused the damage deliberately or through negligence, which, according to the law of the court appealed to, is equated with intent.

The restriction on the amount of total liability of the air carrier can – except in the event of gross negligence on the part of the air carrier – only be dispensed with if a ticket has not been issued, or issued incorrectly (Article 3, paragraph 2 WC). An appeal to the provisions of the Convention excluding or restricting liability is excluded in this case.

The air carrier is, however, pursuant to Article 20 WC, not at all liable if it proves that it and its assistants have implemented all necessary measures to protect against damage or that they were not able to implement these measures. This evidence is just as difficult to provide as evidence of gross negligence on the part of the air carrier by the passenger. Should an accident or 'act of God' be determined, the air carrier is discharged; however, in the event of an unresolved cause of damage, the exonerating evidence has not been provided and the fault of the air carrier is presumed.

Pursuant to Article 21 WC, fault on the part of the claimant, in the event of damage arising, can lead to the exclusion or reduction of liability on the part of the air carrier, insofar as this is provided for in accordance with national law. The burden of proof for contributory fault is incumbent upon the air carrier. Should the liability of the air carrier pursuant to Article 20 WC for presumed fault be assumed, it is obvious that Article 21 WC should be interpreted accordingly, that is, to assume contributory fault if the claimant has not implemented all necessary measures which he could have to protect against or reduce the damage.

The air carrier is also liable for the damage incurred by its assistants when carrying out their duties. The original failure to equate the assistants with the air carrier in regard to the limitation of liability was deficient in that the assistants may be more liable than the air carrier. Through the HP version of Article 25A WC, this regulation, which was felt to be unjust, has been remedied.

Article 23 WC contains a general prohibition on the exclusion of the liability of the air carrier. In other words, the amounts of liability cannot be reduced; however, they may, by agreement, be increased. Should, however, the liability of the air carrier lie outside the scope of validity of the Convention, such as, for example, concerning damage that it has not caused through an accident, Article 23 WC does not contradict an exclusion of liability. Any agreements setting a deadline concerning the notification of damage in the event of loss of airfreight also fall under the prohibition of Article 23 WC.

---

45. 478 *UNTS* 371; 10 *ILM* 613.

In the case of successive transportation, the passenger or the other parties entitled to claim can only make a claim against the air carrier that carried out the conveyance in the course of which the damage occurred (Article 30 WC). The first air carrier may, however, by agreement, accept liability for the entire carriage.

4. Liability of the Air Carrier for Damage to Property

a. Items Carried by Passengers Themselves

The WC does not contain any regulation on the liability of the air carrier for damage to items that the passenger carries on or with his person. Therefore, in this respect, in principle, there is no liability in accordance with the WC. As far as the amount is concerned, it is limited by Article 22, paragraph 3 WC to Gold Francs 5,000. Whether it, in principle, exists is geared towards the respective applicable national law.

b. Luggage Checked In

Pursuant to Article 18 of the WC, the air carrier is required to compensate the damage arising through destruction, loss, or damage of checked in luggage or goods if the event through which the damage was caused occurred during air carriage. Other than in the event of bodily injury, the cause does not need to be an accident. The term ‘event’ also covers causes that do not need to occur suddenly, as with an accident.

The amount of the liability is restricted with the possibility of providing exonerating evidence. Pursuant to Article 20, paragraph 2 WC, the possibility of exoneration is made easier through the fact that the air carrier is already freed from liability by proving that the damage occurred through defective steering, guiding, or navigation of the aircraft and that it and its assistants have otherwise implemented all necessary measures to provide protection against damage. This so-called nautical fault of the crew has been adopted by the WC on the basis of maritime regulations. It is justifiably no longer contained in the HP version.

The limited liability of the air carrier not only ceases to apply in the event of intent and gross negligence (Article 25 WC), but also, if, after accepting the luggage, it entirely refrains from issuing a luggage receipt, or omits certain details (Article 4 WC).

The maximum amounts of liability for loss of and damage to luggage amount to Gold Francs 250 per kilogramme of luggage (around EUR 27.35). When the value is declared and a surcharge to be agreed paid, the liability is increased up to the limit of the amount declared.

In the event of successive transportation by several successive air carriers, the passenger may make a claim against either the first or the last air carrier involved in the carriage or the air carrier has carried out the part of the carriage during which the damage occurred. These air carriers are liable to the passenger jointly and severally (Article 30, paragraph 2 WC). It is therefore not, as in the case of bodily injury, only the air carrier directly involved in the cause of the damage that is liable.

5. Air Freight (Cargo)

a. Definition of Air Freight (Cargo)

The Warsaw System does not contain definitions of airfreight (cargo), nor does it prohibit the carriage of certain kinds of cargo, or regulate such matters as the carriage of dangerous goods as airfreight.

Nevertheless, the Chicago Convention (1944)[46], in Articles 35 and 36, sets out the following principles:

> Article 35
>
> (a) No munitions of war or implements of war may be carried in or above the territory of a State in aircraft engaged in international navigation, except by permission of such State. Each State shall determine by regulations what constitutes munitions of war or implements of war for the purposes of this Article, giving due consideration, for the purposes of uniformity, to such recommendations as the International Civil Aviation Organization may from time to time make.
>
> (b) Each contacting State reserves the right, for reasons of public order and safety, to regulate or prohibit the carriage in or above its territory of articles other than those enumerated in paragraph (a) provided that no distinction is made in this respect between its national aircraft engaged in international navigation and the aircraft of the other States so engaged, and provided further that no restriction shall be imposed which may interfere with the carriage and use on aircraft of apparatus necessary for the operation or navigation of the aircraft or the safety of the personnel or passengers.

Article 36 of the Chicago Convention (1944) states that

> Each contracting State may prohibit or regulate the use of photographic apparatus in aircraft over its territory.

In addition, Annex 18 of the Chicago Convention refers to the safe carriage by air of dangerous goods.

b. Air Waybill

In Articles 5–16, the WC, in the first instance, contains regulations on the air waybill, as well as on certain rights and obligations arising from the airfreight agreement. The air waybill is to be made out by the consignor (WC, Article 6,

---

46. 15 *UNTS* 295, *ICAO Doc.* 7300.

paragraph 1). If the air carrier makes it out, he is deemed, subject to proof to the contrary, to have done so on behalf of the consignor (Article 6, paragraph 5 WC). The issuing of the air waybill and the details contained in it are of significance for the air carrier's liability. Should the air carrier have accepted the goods without an air waybill having been issued, he cannot appeal to restricted liability. The same applies if a series of details required is not contained in the air waybill. The air waybill has a function of establishing identity.

In the case where there is one or more air waybill, each must be made out in three original parts. The first is for the carrier, the second, which accompanies the shipment, is for the consignee, and the third, after signature by the carrier, is handed to the consignor when the shipment has been accepted (Article 6, paragraphs 2 and 13; paragraph 1).

The portion of the air waybill belonging to the carrier must be signed by the consignor and the portion for the consignor by the carrier. The portion for the consignee must be signed by both carrier and consignor, Article 6, paragraph 2. The signature of the carrier may be stamped; the signature of the consignor may be printed or stamped (Article 6, paragraph 4).

Certain elements required by Article 8 of the WC are mandatory, such as the indication of the points of departure and destination.

If the points of departure and destination are located in the territory of one contracting party when one or more stopping points are considered, at least one of these stops must be indicated. Finally, an indication of weight must be included.

If the consignor has made a declaration of the value of the cargo at delivery, it must also be recorded in the air waybill, and an additional payment may be required (Article 22, paragraph 2(a), WC).

The consignor is responsible for the correctness of the elements and statements concerning the cargo appearing in the air waybill, whether the consignor has entered them himself or has had them entered by the carrier, customs broker, or freight forwarder (Article 10, paragraph 1 and Article 6, paragraph 5).

The consignor must furnish any information and attach to the air waybill any documents necessary to meet the formalities of customs or police before the cargo can be delivered to the consignee (Article 16, paragraph 1, WC).

As indicated previously, the air waybill must contain a number of particulars, but the weight must be indicated to fulfil requirements that are the responsibility of the carrier.

c. *Rights and Obligations of Consignors of Cargo*

Articles 10 and 12, in addition to Article 16 of the Warsaw System, recognize the right of the parties to a contract for the carriage of goods. The legal relationships between the consignor, freight carrier and recipient are regulated in Articles 10, 12, and 13 WC.

According to Article 10 WC, the consignor is liable to the air carrier for the correctness of the details and declarations on the goods that it lists in the air waybill, and is obliged to compensate the latter for any damages arising resulting from incorrect, inexact, or incomplete declaration, and in fact also if third parties suffer losses. A similar obligation is incumbent upon the consignor pursuant to Article 16 WC concerning the provision of goods documentation, which is required for customs and other reasons of public law.

Pursuant to Article 12, the consignor is required to accord the air carrier a right of disposal over the goods in exchange for cost reimbursement. It can request return at the point of departure or destination, or that the goods are held during a landing, brought back to the point of departure, or delivered to a recipient other than the one specified on the air waybill. The identity-establishing function of the third copy of the air waybill handed over to the consignor following acceptance of the goods becomes clear in Article 12, paragraph 3 WC. According to the latter, the air carrier is liable to the legitimate owner of the air waybill for the damage that the latter has suffered through the air carrier not permitting the air waybill concerning the goods to be exhibited, when it has been provided by the consignor; for it is possible that the consignor procures credit with the third copy of the air waybill, for example, collects the purchase price for the goods delivered by it, and is then in possession of the goods as a non-entitled party. In case of doubt, a consignor that cannot exhibit the third copy of the air waybill is non-entitled. The liability of the air carrier pursuant to Article 12, paragraph 3 WC can also be extended to the case that the air carrier untruthfully issues a third copy of the air waybill, without having accepted the freight. Since Article 12 WC is subject to party autonomy, it is largely amended by the conditions of carriage in favour of the air transportation company. Furthermore, the air carrier does not need to comply with an order by the consignor concerning the goods if it is not possible for it to do this, that is, in practice also if damage would be incurred to it as a result (Article 12, paragraph 2 WC).

The claims to damages pursuant to Articles 10 and 12 WC are independent provisions in regard to Articles 17–19 WC. The consignor or air carrier is, therefore, liable regardless of fault, any exonerating evidence and the maximum amounts of liability. Whether the consignor is obliged, beyond the grounds specified in Articles 10 and 16 WC, to compensate the air carrier for damage arising from the agreement or tort depends upon the respective applicable national law. According to German Law, such liability is possible.

Should the consignor not, pursuant to Article 12 WC, possess the goods, the recipient is entitled to request the air carrier to hand over the air waybill and deliver the goods in return for payment of the amount owed (Article 13 WC). In line with Article 13, the consignor must pay the agreed freight as well as the expenditures incurred by the carrier in the execution of orders given by the consignor in the exercise of his right of disposition of the cargo; for instance, customs duties and the cost of delivery of the cargo at the place of the consignee or to its final recipient, provided that the consignor has not already paid, or agreed on the air waybill to pay these charges. The air carrier is required to notify the recipient of the arrival.

In the event of loss of the goods, the intended recipient has a claim to damages pursuant to Article 18 WC. The loss is presumed if it has still not arrived at the destination seven days after the anticipated date of arrival. Should the goods not be lost, the recipient can demand damages for delay. The consignor and recipient may also assert rights of disposal or receipt in their own names if they are acting on behalf of a third party (Article 14 WC).

The liability system when conveying freight is, in addition, the same as for luggage checked in (Article 18 WC). Likewise, successive carriage is handled in the same way, that is, the consignor can make a claim against the first air carrier, the recipient against the last air carrier, and both the consignor and the recipient against the air carrier on whose transportation section the damage occurred.

Should individual items be lost from shipments consisting of several items – in general, termed a partial loss – it is of significance in regard to various notification deadlines whether damage requiring notification or a loss not requiring notification exists. Should the items in a consignment form one unit, damage is concerned if one or more items thereof are not delivered; however, in the event of independently itemized items, loss is concerned, for which a notification deadline is not prescribed.

Airfreight replacement carriage in the form of 'trucking' raises the question of whether, and to what extent, the WC applies to it. Concerning mixed carriage by various carriers, Article 31 WC expressly makes clear that its regulations only apply to the air carriage route. Pure feeder services belong to the air carriage.

When the cargo has been returned to the consignor because the consignee has not accepted it or could not be found, the consignor must file a complaint within the time limit set forth in Article 26, paragraphs 2 and 3 to achieve compensation for damages to or partial loss of the cargo.

d. Rights and Obligations of Consignees of Cargo

The consignee, being the beneficiary of the contract of carriage, has the right on arrival of the goods at the place of destination to the delivery of the second part of the air waybill that has been made out for him and has travelled with the cargo and the cargo itself (Article 13 WC). The carrier is obligated to give notice as soon as the goods arrive (Article 13, paragraph 2 WC).

The right of the consignee normally begins with the arrival of the cargo (Article 13, paragraph 1). It is important to take into account that the right of the consignor on disposition of the cargo ceases at that very moment.

Some argue that the right of the consignee begins upon receipt of the notice of arrival, made by the carrier. However, in the case that the goods have not arrived, the right of the consignee begins either at the expiration of seven days after the date on which they ought to have arrived or when the carrier admits their loss (Article 13, paragraph 3 WC).

In addition, the consignee has the right to refuse the air waybill or the cargo (Article 12, paragraph 4 WC). This right does not affect the relation with the consignor nor the mutual relations of third parties whose rights are derived from the consignor or from the consignee (Article 15, paragraph 1 WC).

Furthermore, the consignee can exercise the rights given to the consignor in line with Article 12 WC. This privilege belongs only to the consignee indicated on the air waybill and not to any other person, even though the person may have an interest in the cargo.

6. Losses Caused by Delay

Pursuant to Article 19 WC, the air carrier is required to compensate damage arising through delay in the air carriage of passengers, luggage, or goods. Contrary to Article 18, paragraph 1 WC, which expressly makes reference to the luggage checked in, it must be assumed that Article 19 WC also refers to hand luggage. Damage caused by delay is conceivable in the event that the passenger surrenders hand luggage or items of clothing to the cabin crew for safekeeping.

Because of a lack of further specification, the regulation concerning delay pursuant to Article 19 WC raises various problems. In particular, it is questionable when a consignment is delayed and what damage must be compensated. Article 19 WC only alludes to air carriage, without, as in Article 18, paragraph 2 WC, defining it. The latter is understood to mean the 'entire transport', that is, the delay has occurred during carriage if the persons or goods do not arrive at the destination at the agreed time, in regard to which minor deviations are irrelevant. The storage after landing until delivery still belongs to the air carriage. In case law, on the other hand, a differentiation is predominantly made between the carriage of persons and the carriage of goods, and the delay determined in accordance with the periods mentioned in Articles 17 and 18, paragraph 2 WC. Should the delay, as in the case of easily perishable goods, lead to their destruction, the claim pursuant to Article 19 WC, as well as Article 18 WC, can be asserted.

In principle, an exclusion of liability for losses caused by delay is, pursuant to Article 23 of the WC, null and void. The liability system and amounts of liability are the same as in the case of bodily injury (see B.3.) and damage to property (see B.4.).

7. Alterations and Additions by the Hague Protocol

The authors of the WC were obviously aware of the necessity of later revision, as Article 41 WC expressly provides for each party to the agreement already being able to organize the assembly of a new international conference, to bring about some improvements to the Convention, two years after the Convention came into force. This conference assembled from 6 to 28 September 1955 at The Hague, with forty-four countries participating, and, after the groundwork for such a Convention had been carried out within the scope of the ICAO, published at the HP, named after the venue, for signature. The HP was signed at the conference by twenty-five countries. It only came into force, however, on 1 August 1963, after it had received the necessary number of thirty ratifications.

The HP is in the form of a protocol to the WC, which partially amends the provisions of the WC and partially supplements them. What is in many cases not recognized is that it is important for the WC to remain in force alongside the HP. This coexistence was and is certainly unsatisfactory; however, it cannot be avoided, as only a portion of the countries wished to adopt the provisions of the HP. In relation to the Member States of the HP, the WC/HP applies, and, in relation to the Member States of the WC, the WC applies in its original form. However, it also continued to be possible for a country that had, until that time, not belonged to either the WC or the HP to only be a member of the WC. Naturally, it was hoped that the HP would be accepted by the Member States of the WC, and that the countries that were members of neither would accede to the HP version. This proved, however, to be a false estimation. The US, for example, was for a long time not a member of the HP (only in the course of the ratification of the MC was the HP also ratified) and, despite the existence of the HP, some countries have continued to only accept the WC.

The starting point for the revision of the WC was, however, initially formed by the airlines' wish for a simpler regulation regarding the transportation documents, expressed even prior to the Second World War. Furthermore, in the ICAO, attempts at total revision of the WC were apparent, in regard to which the focal points, besides the transportation documents, lay in the liability amounts and the unrestricted liability of the air carriers.

a. Transport Documents

The regulations on the transportation documents have been simplified in relation to the WC. First, fewer details are required (omitted in regard to the ticket, for example, are the details on the place and date of issue, as well as on the name and address of the air carrier). Furthermore, the lack of specific details in the transportation documents no longer has the consequence of the unlimited liability of the air carrier. Should, however, no transportation document at all be issued, or should the reference to the liability restrictions in accordance with the Convention have been omitted from them, the air carrier has unlimited liability. The liability of the consignor concerning details in the air waybill (Article 10, paragraph 2 WC) is limited to the liability that incurred with reference to a third party, i.e., if the air carrier is responsible towards the latter. In Article 15, paragraph 3 WC, it is made clear that the regulations of the WC do not stand in opposition to the negotiability of the air waybill.

b. Liability System

Article 20, paragraph 2 WC, according to which the air carrier can be freed from liability if it proves that the damage occurred through nautical fault and all necessary remedial actions have been taken, has been deleted. The regulation had not, in practice, acquired any meaning.

The most important amendment consisted in the doubling of the maximum amounts of liability from Gold Francs 125,000 to Gold Francs 250,000 for bodily injury, while the liability amounts for damage to property have remained unchanged. In particular the US, the courts of which generally deem higher amounts of compensation than those of the WC appropriate, advocated the increase specified.

Article 23 WC is supplemented to the extent that an exclusion of liability by the air carrier is admissible for losses that result from the nature of the goods conveyed or defects associated with them.

In regard to Article 25 WC, according to which the unlimited liability of the air carrier comes into force in the event of intent or equivalent negligence, according to the HP version, liability is unlimited if it is proven that the damage has been caused by an act or omission on the part of the air carrier or its assistants, either committed with the intention of causing damage or carelessly and in the awareness that damage would probably occur. As a result, this boils down to the unlimited liability of the air carrier being tempered. In fact, it does have unlimited liability in the event of intent, including conditional intent and deliberate gross negligence, not, however, as with the version of the WC, in the case of inadvertent gross negligence. Furthermore, it is important in regard to the version of the WC that uniform grounds for liability exist, and that reliance is not placed upon negligence equivalent to intent in accordance with the law of the court appealed to, which could lead to very different results. The constituent fact of 'carelessness' requires that the air carrier or its assistants have, in a particularly blatant manner, flouted the safety interests of the persons and goods entrusted to their care; only such an obvious infringement of the unquestionable obligatory code of conduct for protecting these interests clearly shown in the situation in question fulfils the form of misconduct termed *témérairement* (reckless, foolhardy, or daring) in the relevant French version. Concerning the constituent element of 'in the awareness that damage would probably occur', it is disputed whether it is to be assessed objectively or subjectively. Viewed objectively, the conduct of an average, a judicious person in a comparable situation is to be taken as a starting point, while it is supposed to be decisive, in accordance with the subjective opinion, whether, in the specific case at hand, the awareness of the occurrence of damage existed, and not whether the conduct of an average person ought to have been present.

Article 25A HP determines that the same limitations of liability apply to the air carrier's assistants as to the air carrier if a direct claim is filed against them by the claimant, and that a total claim may be made against the air carrier and its assistants for up to the sum of the maximum amounts of liability.

c. Other Provisions

Furthermore, the HP also contains some purely editorial amendments, for example, concerning the terms 'international carriage' (Article 1, paragraph 2 HP) and 'successive carriage' (Article 1, paragraph 3 HP). Instead of the term 'traveller', 'passenger' is used, which is supposed to express that contractual carriage is concerned. The deadlines for notifying the damage pursuant to Article 26, paragraph 2 WC amount to seven days for luggage, fourteen days for freight, and twenty-one days for damage caused by delay, in comparison to three, seven, and fourteen days previously.

Article 34 determines, in accordance with its new version that the provisions of Articles 3–9 on the transportation tickets are not to be applied to carriage that is carried out under extraordinary circumstances and not within the scope of regular air carriage.

8. Amendments and Additions through the Montreal Agreement (1966) and the Malta Agreement

Since especially the US deemed the liability amounts in accordance with the WC, and also those in accordance with the HP, too low, it pressed for an increase and terminated the WC. A special conference under the auspices of the ICAO (1-15 February 1966) brought no results. The US, however, withdrew the termination of the WC again after the airlines operating to and from the US or Canada had undertaken, through the Montreal Agreement of 1966[47], to increase the amounts of liability to USD 75,000, including the costs of legal pursuit, or USD 58,000, excluding these costs, and to dispense with the exonerating evidence pursuant to Article 20, paragraph 1 WC in the event of bodily injury. As a result, a strict liability existed for bodily injury. The Montreal Agreement, only intended as a provisional regulation until a further supplementary agreement to the WC should come into force, had yet further repercussions, insofar as numerous airlines also introduced similar liability regulations (of their own). Accordingly, these were in many cases incorporated into the respective conditions of carriage. Concerning the European region, in this connection, the so-called Malta Agreement[48] should be mentioned, which, following an initiative by some European air transportation companies, led to a joint consultation among air transportation companies concerning higher liability amounts.

9. Alterations and Additions by the Guatemala Protocol

Within the ICAO, the attempts to revise the WC, with the aim of improved liability regulations for the benefit of passengers, continued even after the Montreal Agreement. At the conclusion of a State conference under the auspices of the ICAO in Guatemala, on 8 March 1971 the Guatemala Protocol[49] was signed by twenty-one of the fifty-five countries represented there. However, it has never come into force. Of the thirty ratifications required for it, only twelve had been deposited by 1 May 2007. The Guatemala Protocol reflected the tendency already becoming apparent in the Montreal Agreement to increase the amounts of liability and to avert liability resulting from negligence.

---

47. (1966) USAvR 450.
48. For more details see: McGilchrist, ‘Special Contracts and the Malta Agreement’, *LMCLQ* 1977, 366 et seq.; Müller-Rostin, ‘Neue Haftungsgrenzen für Personenschäden bei internationalen Luftbeförderungen’, *ZLW* 25 (1976), 336 et seq.
49. 10 *ILM* 613 (1971).

The amounts of liability were supposed to be increased to *Poincaré* Francs 1.5 million, which, at the conclusion of the Protocol, corresponded to a value of USD 100,000. A special revision clause was supposed to enable the simplified increasing of this amount to Gold Francs 187,500 in the future, in that five years after the Protocol entering into force, a State conference was supposed to be convened. The increase was supposed to be able to be prevented only if this conference opposed it with a two-thirds majority. Furthermore, in accordance with the Protocol, the exonerating evidence pursuant to Article 20 WC was supposed to be dropped. The air carrier would as a result be liable, without regard to fault, for all claims relating to air carriage, that is, also in the event of 'acts of God'. Only when death or bodily injury is based on the passenger's state of health, liability on the part of the air carrier is not supposed to occur. Furthermore, the air carrier is supposed to retain the possibility of exoneration pursuant to Article 21 WC in the event of contributory fault on the part of the passenger. The air carrier is also only supposed to be liable in the event of intent or equivalent forms of fault within the scope of the maximum amounts of liability. This provision, foreign to the German legal system, was less convincingly substantiated, by stating that the air carrier was now subject to strict liability. The limitation of liability, also in the event of fault, is supposed to even that out. According to the new regulation provided for by the Protocol, it would have occurred irrespective of whether the air carrier issued the ticket in proper form or not. Contrary to the losses incurred through an accident, in regard to the losses caused by delay, the provision up to now is supposed to be retained, that is, the air carrier is supposed to be able to provide exonerating evidence in this case.

The Guatemala Protocol only refers to damage to persons and luggage, and leaves the freight regulation unchanged. It no longer differentiates between luggage checked in and hand luggage, and introduces a uniform maximum amount of liability of Gold Francs 15,000 per passenger for his entire luggage and clothing. That signifies an increase of around 50% in relation to the standards of WC/HP. The liability for luggage is, in principle, subject to the same regulation as liability for bodily injury. Without regard to the possibility of exoneration, the objective liability intended with the latter is, apart from contributory negligence on the part of the claimant, only supposed to be disregarded if the damage results from the nature of the luggage itself. Concerning losses caused by delay, the existing principle of liability resulting from negligence is retained with a reversed burden of proof (Article 20 WC).

The maximum amounts of liability amount to Gold Francs 62,500 for conveyance of passengers. Concerning delayed luggage, the same amounts as for losses through destruction, loss, or damage are supposed to apply.

The Article 25A WC/HP is supposed to permit the possibility of additional regulations concerning compensation for damages in comparison to the previous rigid liability system. As a result, it should make things easier for countries that, because of their high standard of living, appear to still find the liability amounts in accordance with the Guatemala Protocol too low to accept. This additional provision concerning damage, which is left to the individual countries to introduce if they wish, should not disadvantage the air carriers. One of the possible financing models is supposed to consist of additional compensation payments being provided out of funds that could be supplied by compulsory payments upon purchasing air tickets.

In addition to the places of jurisdiction listed in Article 29 WC, the claimant should also be able to file an action before the court in the district of which the air carrier has a branch, if it is domiciled in the associated contracting State.

The Guatemala Protocol has the same status as the HP and would thus have led to a third version of the WC, which would have existed alongside the Warsaw and Hague versions already existing side by side. Such a state of affairs has rightly often been bewailed, because, in view of the latter, there can be no question of the legal unity aimed for with the WC.

10. Alterations and Additions by the Montreal Protocols

The Guatemala Protocol has, as mentioned, left the freight provisions of the WC unchanged. The State Conference of Montreal (3-25 September 1975) served the purpose of its revision, as in particular the regulations on the air waybill, no longer appeared up-to-date. The result of the amendments to the freight law resolved at the conference is contained in Protocol No. 4,[50] while Protocols Nos 1,[51] 2,[52] and 3[53] only regulate matters concerning currency.

Through Protocol No. 4, Articles 6–16 WC are partially revised. The focal point is formed by the possibility created through Article 5, paragraph 2 of using electronic data processing (EDP) facilities instead of the conventional air waybill. According to the latter, with the consignor's consent, 'other means' than the air waybill may be utilized to provide evidence of carriage.

Instead of the air waybill, the consignor receives an acknowledgement of receipt, with which the freight can be identified and which enables it to obtain access to the data on the freight conveyance stored in the EDP system. The acknowledgement of receipt only contains details on the point of departure and destination, and the weight of the freight. Since a weight specification is not provided for according to the currently valid law, it will in future be prescribed. The receipt is also equated with the air waybill in regard to Article 10 WC (liability of the consignor for details on the air waybill) and Article 11, paragraph 2 WC (details on the freight).

The liability system is being adapted to the regulation concerning bodily injury provided for at that time through the Guatemala Protocol. Objective liability is also supposed to apply to damage to air freight, and exonerating evidence for the air carrier is, in principle, supposed to be dispensed with. Besides the contributory

50. 2145 *UNTS* 36.
51. 2097 *UNTS* 28.
52. 2097 *UNTS* 69.
53. Not in force.

fault on the part of the claimant, exemption from liability through exonerating evidence is only possible in the case of:

(1) liability for losses caused by delay; and
(2) the cases expressly and conclusively listed in Article 18, paragraph 3, namely:
   (a) defects in the quality of the freight;
   (b) defective packaging not undertaken by the air carrier or its assistants;
   (c) war or armed conflict; and
   (d) State measures in connection with the import, export, or transit of freight.

As in the Guatemala Protocol, with the introduction of objective liability for damage to freight, the possibility of disregarding the maximum amounts of liability if fault on the part of the air carrier is proven ceases to apply. That also applies in the case of intent. The amounts of liability (Gold Francs 250 per kilogramme) remain unchanged. However, it has been converted to the Special Drawing Right (SDR) as a basis for assessment. The penalties imposed pursuant to Article 9 of the WC in the event of filling in the air waybill incompletely have not been applicable anymore.

In the WC, up to now the amounts of liability have been given in Gold Francs. Pursuant to Article 22, paragraph 4 WC, a Gold Franc refers to a unit of currency of 65.5 mg gold with a fineness of 900/1,000. Since the official price of gold has been abandoned by the International Monetary Fund, the Gold Franc has become inappropriate as a basis for assessment, as it is subject to great currency fluctuations. As a more stable basis for assessment, SDR have, therefore, been preferred by many countries. This opinion prevailed at the conference in Montreal against the resistance of the countries not affiliated with the International Monetary Fund. The latter may, however, accept the Protocol with a reservation, so that, for them, the Gold Franc continues as the basis for assessment. The liability limit for freight was fixed at SDR 17 and incorporated into Protocol No. 4, on the freight regulation. Conversion into the national currency is effected, according to its assessment, at the time at which the damages are to be paid.

The change in the basis for assessing the amounts of liability could not remain restricted to damage to freight. It was, therefore, logical that the conference also took SDR, instead of the Gold Franc, as a basis for settling claims for both bodily injury and damage to luggage. This occurred through three protocols, in regard to which each protocol amends the corresponding regulations of the three existing Conventions in the Warsaw liability system, namely:

(a) the WC in its original form (Protocol No. 1);
(b) the HP version of the WC (Protocol No. 2);
(c) the Guatemala Protocol version of the WC (Protocol No. 3).

The Montreal protocols have to date not all come into force. The protocols that have come into force are Protocols Nos 1 and 2 (15 February 1996) and No. 4 (14 June 1998). What has not yet come into force, as a result of a lack of the thirty ratifications required, is Protocol No. 3, which has to date only been ratified by twenty-one countries. Protocol No. 3 coming into force would not effect any alteration in the status of the ratifications for the Guatemala Protocol and could, therefore, not accelerate the latter's coming into force. Acceptance of Protocol No. 3 has accession, but not the ratification of the Guatemala Protocol, as a consequence. The latter will only come into force once the necessary number of ratifications has been reached.

11. Alterations and Additions by the Supplementary Guadalajara Agreement

Concerning the involvement of persons other than the air carrier in the carriage, its assistants, agents, successive air carriers within the meaning of the WC, and third parties actually executing the carriage within its sphere of interest come into consideration. The assistants are employees or authorized agents of the air carrier, which cooperate with it in the carriage. The agents conclude carriage agreements for it as representatives. The successive air carriers are persons who, in the event of successive carriage, are involved on a section of the route as independent air carriers. The WC regulates this case from two perspectives, in that, through Article 1, paragraph 3, the entire carriage is uniformly qualified as international carriage and subjects each of the air carriers involved to its liability system, with the consequence that a claim can be made against it by the claimant for the section of the route for which it is responsible. The successive air carrier may not be confused with the third parties who are in fact involved in the carriage and actually carry it out, but, however, do not have a contractual relationship with the passenger, like that of the air carrier involved in the successive carriage. The legal status of these third parties within the scope of the carriage is the subject of the Supplementary Guadalajara Agreement[54].

The starting points for the Supplementary Guadalajara Agreement lay in the legal circumstances, which can be substantiated by rent, charter, and exchange of aircraft. As a rule, this is the circumstance that one air transportation company charters an aircraft to another, in that it actually carries out the carriage for the latter, and the latter, as the air carrier, concludes the carriage agreements with the passengers. In accordance with the WC, the Supplementary Guadalajara Agreement extends the air carrier's liability to the charterer, although the latter is not involved in the carriage agreement. It terms him the executing air carrier, and the other the contractual air carrier. Thus, at the same time, it is made clear that the contractual air carrier does not need to implement the carriage itself.

The preparatory work for the agreement goes back to the year 1954, with a recommendation by the ECAC, which regulates legal problems concerning rental, charter, and exchange of aircraft through an international agreement. A regulation was not possible in connection with the Civil Law Conference on Aviation at The Hague, however; in the final act, the ICAO was requested to continue to

54. 500 *UNTS* 32.

examine this problem. The draft of the agreement prepared by the Legal Committee of the ICAO was the subject of the State Conference of Guadalajara from 29 August to 18 September 1961, in which forty countries took part, of which eighteen signed the agreement at the Conference. It entered into force on 1 May 1964, following ratification by five countries.

The Guadalajara Agreement does not amend the WC, but supplements it. To that extent it can be distinguished from the HP, which, besides additions, also contains amendments. In addition, it is an independent agreement, which is not in the form of a supplementary protocol. Theoretically conceivable, if also improbable, is membership of a country in the Guadalajara Agreement without simultaneously being a member of the WC.

Article 1 defines the contractual air carrier as a person who has, as a party to an agreement with a passenger or a consignor, or a person acting for the passenger or consignor, concluded a carriage agreement that is subject to the WC, and the executing air carrier as a person other than the contractual air carrier, which, due to an authorization granted by the contractual air carrier, executes the intended carriage, in whole or in part. It is expressly made clear that the successive air carrier is not covered by this definition when carrying out successive carriage. The authorization of the executing air carrier presumes, until evidence is provided to the contrary, that agents and representatives are not air carriers. They do in fact conclude the carriage agreement, however, for another party, and do not take on any contractual obligations towards the passenger in regard to the carriage. The executing air carrier has operational control over the use of the aircraft. It is the aircraft-operating agency. The landlord, who loses its capacity as an operating agency, is, therefore, not the executing air carrier.

Through Article 2 of the Agreement, besides the contractual air carrier, the executing air carrier is also subject to the liability regulations in accordance with the WC. Should the executing air carrier only be involved on a section of the route, its liability is only for this section. The contractual air carrier, on the other hand, is liable for the entire carriage. Whether the executing air carrier is liable in accordance with the original version of the WC or in accordance with the HP depends upon the version applicable to the contractual air carrier. Pursuant to Article 3, the two air carriers are liable jointly and severally, that is, the conduct of the executing air carrier and its assistants is attributed to the contractual air carrier; however, conversely, the conduct of the contractual air carrier is also attributed to the executing air carrier and its assistants, but with the restriction that the latter does not have the unlimited liability of the contractual air carrier and that, without its consent, agreements between the contractual air carrier and the passengers are not applicable to it if they justify obligations extending beyond the WC or a waiver of rights in accordance with the WC or contain a declaration of value pursuant to Article 22 WC. The internal legal relationships between the contractual and executing air carriers are not affected by the Agreement (Article 10). It is up to them how they execute the settlement of liability if a claim is made against one of them. The maximum amounts applicable for the limited liability form the threshold value of the joint and several liabilities (Article 6). Both air carriers can have an action filed against them for the carriage undertaken by the executing air carrier, either individually or jointly, at the plaintiff's option. The air carrier sued can request the other one to take part in the proceedings. The consequences of this third-party notice depend upon the law of the court appealed to (Article 7). A place of jurisdiction for the action exists anywhere where the contractual air carrier can be sued, pursuant to Article 28 WC, or at the court having jurisdiction for the domicile or principal place of business of the executing air carrier (Article 8). Orders or objections in accordance with the WC are, in principle, effective without regard to whether they are issued to the contractual or the executing air carrier (Article 6). Orders by the consignor within the scope of its right of disposal pursuant to Article 12 WA are, however, only to be directed towards the contractual air carrier. The assistants of the two air carriers, against whom a claim is made outside the scope of the carriage agreement, for example, based on tort, are only liable to a restricted extent, in accordance with the HP version of Article 25A WC, insofar as a degree of fault on their part that would carry with it unlimited liability on the part of the air carrier cannot be proven (Article 5).

12. Combined Forms of the WC and Agreements Amending It

The repeated amendments of, and additions to, the WC have inevitably increased the complexity and fragmentation of the liability regulations concerning international air carriage. This is the consequence of the original version of the WC continuing to apply alongside the new regulations. The problems associated with the coexistence of the WC and HP correspondingly apply in relation to the Guatemala Protocol and the Montreal Protocols. This state of affairs can only be changed by as many countries as possible acceding to the MC (the latest respective version of the WC).

In summary, it can be determined that a large number of combined forms of the WC and further agreements exist (in that respect, it is to be taken into account that these regulations are, in fact, partially not yet in force; however, on the other hand, their content has partially already been anticipated through the interim Montreal Agreement under Private Law):

(1) WC of 1929.
(2) WC of 1929, supplemented by the Additional Montreal Protocol No. 1 of 1975.
(3) WC of 1929, supplemented by the HP of 1955 (WC/HP).
(4) WC/HP, supplemented by the Additional Montreal Protocol No. 2 of 1975.
(5) WC/HP, supplemented by the Guatemala Protocol of 1971 (not yet in force).
(6) WC/HP/Guatemala Protocol, supplemented by the Additional Montreal Protocol No. 3 of 1975 (not yet in force).
(7) WC/HP, supplemented by the Additional Montreal Protocol No. 4 of 1975.

All of these combined forms are, finally, supplemented by the Additional Guadalajara Agreement of 1961.

Leaving aside the Guadalajara Agreement, the Guatemala City Protocol, and the Montreal Protocols, concerning direct links between two contracting States of the various conventions, the following constellations are conceivable:

		*Contracting State 1 (Point of Departure)**					
	Convention	MC	MC + WC	WC	WC/HP	WC + WC/HP	MC + WC/HP
Contracting State 2 (Destination)	MC	MC	MC				MC
	MC + WC	MC	MC	WC		WC	MC
	WC		WC	WC		WC	
	WC/HP				WC/HP	WC/HP	WC/HP
	WC + WC/HP			WC	WC/HP	WC/HP	WC/HP
	MC + WC/HP	MC	MC		WC/HP		MC

* Concerning all cases not classified, the respective applicable national law applies.

13. Special Problem: Liability on Code-Sharing Flights

For the participating airlines, code-sharing flights are regarded as successive carriage flights under the WC, and passenger liability therefore rests with the airline operating the flight. However, it must be observed that three conditions must converge for carriage to be considered successive transport under Article 1(3) of the WC: (1) the willingness of the carriers to consider the transportation a single journey, (2) the existence of one contract or a series of contracts with a linkage between each contract, and (3) the carriage must be international in terms of the Warsaw System. This Article of the WC puts the emphasis on the intention of the partners in a global operation that covers different carriers. The internal relationship between the carriers is not covered by the Convention. In sum, a carriage to be performed by successive carriers is deemed to be one undivided carriage if it has been regarded by the parties as a single operation, even though it involves a series of contracts. The intention of the parties with respect to the single operation may be expressed at the time the contract is made or later during its execution.

Generally, each successive carrier is liable only if the accident or delay of the passenger or the loss, destruction, delay of, or damage to registered baggage or cargo has occurred during that part of the carriage that has been performed under its supervision, per Article 30, paragraphs 2 and 3. It must be recalled that in spite of the Guadalajara Convention, which applies the limits recognized by the WC, the passenger or his representative can take action only against the carrier that performed the carriage during which the accident or the delay occurred, except in the case where, by express agreement, the first carrier has assumed liability for the whole journey. However, the first carrier is liable for delay during the second stage of the voyage when the passenger was delayed because no reservation had been made by the first carrier.

In itself, the criterion of the Convention seems clear and without doubt. However, it is necessary to consider in a specific way the different permutations of code-sharing. Problems may occur where the operating carrier's contractual terms of liability differ from those of the code-sharing partner, due to the erosion of the uniformity intended by the framers of the WC. The core of the problem is that under a code-sharing agreement, the connecting flights are operated by two separate airlines, but may be listed as being a single carrier service.

The contractual relationship between the carrier and the actual carrier setting out the latter's liability depends mainly on the contractual document binding on the two parties. If this is the case, the liability of the actual carrier will be governed by the terms of the ticket. The liability of the actual carrier exists in the contract if the contractual document specifies the actual carrier as a party to the transaction.

The question that arises is whether these provisions are applicable to code-sharing or whether it is the text of the Guadalajara Convention that should be applied, depending on the operations if they involve a connection (successive transport) or a point-to-point service. At this point, we need to consider the linkage with the features of the Guadalajara Convention, particularly if the countries in which the airlines are registered are not signatories to this Convention.

Among the Warsaw instruments, Guadalajara has a great importance for our purposes. Indeed, the Convention signed at Guadalajara on 18 September 1961 is supplementary to the WC, and extended its provisions to the actual carrier in cases where the latter was not identical with the contracting carrier. This Convention has been in force since 1964 and its depository is the Government of Mexico. It has been ratified by a total of eighty-five Member States.

Article II of the Guadalajara Convention specifies that the contracting carrier and the actual carrier are both subject to the WC, that is, to the same regime of liability, and second, that the acts and omissions of the one are deemed to be the acts and omissions of the other. This latter feature is known as the regime of reciprocal representation. Under the principle of joint and several liability, each of the two carriers could be sued and condemned without taking into account that the omission might be imputed to one or the other. In other words, the principle required that the obligation is a single one and that the debtor would be liable only once.

Subsequently, in relation to the carriage performed by the actual carrier, an action for damages may be brought, at the option of the plaintiff, against that carrier or the contracting carrier, or against both together or separately. Article VII specifies that:

> If the action is brought against only one of those carriers, that carrier shall have the right to require the other carrier to be joined in the proceedings, the procedure and effects being governed by the law of the court seized of the case.

Both the Warsaw and the Guadalajara Conventions, however, can apply only *mutatis mutandis* with regard to the respective rights and duties of the contracting and the actual carrier and to their reciprocal relationship. Their adaptations are the subject matter of Articles II-X of the Guadalajara Convention.

C. The Route from the Warsaw System to the Montreal Convention

1. Introduction

After – in spite of numerous alterations to the details – the conventional and balanced Warsaw Liability System remained untouched in its essential content for decades, in the last few years of the 1990s it was subjected to considerable pressure. Other than in the case of the former attempts at reform, it was no longer merely an (understandable) dissatisfaction with the maximum liability limits, which were felt to be too low, that was concerned, but also a thorough, if also less systematic, revision of the entire contractual liability system.

The relevant practical amendments were, however, not initially executed at the level of international law, but were implemented on the basis of agreements by air transportation companies under private law. As a result, these agreements have made the necessity of working out a new convention under international law clear to the countries involved in world air traffic and accelerated its conclusion.

2. The IATA Intercarrier Agreement

Through the (private law) IATA Intercarrier Agreement on Passenger Liability (hereinafter, ICA) or the implementing instruments of 1995, a large number of air transportation companies have mutually undertaken in favour of the passengers to no longer wish to exploit certain benefits for the air carriers provided for in the WC. To be specific, they have undertaken among themselves to incorporate the following regulations into the carriage agreements, that is, their General Conditions of Carriage, for the benefit of the passengers:

- Through the ICA itself the air transportation companies have, first, undertaken that, in future, they no longer intend to invoke the maximum liability limits of Article 22 WC in the event of death or bodily injuries to passengers. The bastion of the maximum liability limits has, therefore, been voluntarily and entirely given up by the air transportation companies.
- Through the MIA,[55] the air transportation companies have undertaken that they, in principle, no longer intend to provide the exonerating evidence possible pursuant to Article 20 WC for claims for damages up to SDR 100,000 (this waiver can be limited to particular routes).

55. *TAQ* 1996/97, 16, and 121.

– Through the IPA,[56] the North American air transportation companies have additionally undertaken to grant the passenger a 'fifth place of jurisdiction' at his place of residence and to agree the applicability of the law of the place of domicile.

With these measures (exclusively under private law), the WC, as a legal instrument under international law, has, in fact, formally remained unaffected; however, in its practical application, it has run into difficulties. This is even true if the voluntary nature of the agreements, and thus the legal principle of *volenti non fit injuria*, is pointed out. The voluntary and unconditional acceptance of risk up to SDR 100,000 at least constitutes a financial threat to those air transportation companies that, due to their competitive position, have no other option but to be affiliated to the ICA. In particular, for smaller companies or those from non-industrialized nations, this carries with it considerable financial risk. That appears to be virtually a pillage if an air transportation company could actually provide the exonerating evidence, that is, if it could prove that it had done everything possible to avoid damage, even if this risk is insurable. In addition, the 'avoidance effect' inherent in every threat of liability (i.e., the attempt to do everything to avoid a case of liability, by taking precautions) is neutralized.

This effect has been increased even further through the second (apparent) concession to the position of the passengers, namely, the voluntary waiver of the maximum liability limits. On closer inspection, this alleged concession to the passengers transpires after all to be a (jointly organized) favour for the benefit of the air transportation companies, for, from this time on, there were certainly no more tiresome discussions – if applicable, within the scope of judicial proceedings – on the cause of an accident and the extent to which the air transportation company contributed to it. In fact, until now, an air transportation company could also get out of the latter through the objection of the maximum liability limit simply not being raised in the negotiations with the victims or their surviving dependents concerning compensation for damage. However, this was constantly tainted with the aftertaste that the air transportation company wished to avoid disagreeable insights into its internal structure and organization through voluntary payments, thus in themselves unnecessary. As all the air transportation companies acceding to the ICA had waived the maximum liability limit from the outset, and for all cases, this aftertaste had evaporated. An expedient clarification of the matter in the individual case, necessary for preventing damage, was thereby 'voluntarily' blocked from the outset.

D. Liability in Accordance with the Montreal Convention

The aforementioned agreements under private law were virtually dissolved by a new international agreement on international carriage taking up its basic

56. *TAQ* 1996/97, 122.

principles. Through the Convention for the Unification of Certain Rules for International Carriage of 28 May 1999 (MC),[57] the Warsaw Liability System for damage to passengers and goods in international civil aviation has been modernized, and international law – up to now regulated by various conventions – with differing regional scopes of validity has – once again – been summarized in uniform regulations. The MC can, therefore, rightly be termed the first successful consolidation of all additional conventions, which have partially not entered into force.

Following ratification by the thirtieth country to sign, the Agreement came into force on 4 November 2003. It entirely replaces the previous liability system of the WC (in air traffic between its contracting States). Article 55 establishes the priority of application of the MC to the extent that several conventions have been signed by a country.

In particular, the differences to the regulations of the EC emerging will be explained below.

1. The New Liability Regime

The MC provides for the following individual regulations:

> The air carrier is liable pursuant to Article 17, paragraph 1 of the MC for death and bodily injury to passengers if the cause of the latter were an accident which occurred on board the aircraft or when boarding or disembarking. This formulation closely follows Article 17 WC. The MC has in addition, largely already previously adopted the agreements of the IIA concluded between the airlines as a binding agreement under International Law on a voluntary basis. In the same way as the latter – other than the Warsaw Liability System – the MC no longer recognizes maximum liability limits for bodily injury. The air carrier is entitled to assert the objection of contributory fault on the part of the passenger.
>
> As far as the amount of liability is concerned, the following applies: In the event of proven damage the air carrier was/is automatically liable up to an amount of SDR 100,000 until 29 December 2009, respectively SDR 113,100 since 30 December 2009. Above this amount he may provide exonerating evidence. For this purpose Article 21, paragraph 2 MC requires proof that these losses are not attributable to a wrongful act or omission on the part of the air carrier or its assistants or also a third party, even if it was only committed negligently. The air carrier is consequently supposed to be able to be exonerated in the event of any (negligent) act or omission.
>
> In addition, the wrongful act formulation constitutes a welcome advance in regard to the 'necessary measures' standard of Article 20 WC, which was bewildering and its application difficult. However, also the future possibility of exoneration in the event of misconduct by a third party appears

57. 2242 *UNTS* 350.

complicated, as the latter is only conceivable if the air carrier proves that the damage is 'exclusively' attributable to the latter. It does not have this possibility if it has only contributed to a minor part of the damage, or if the latter has, in the first instance, been caused by a third party.

In the events of death and bodily injury to passengers, the air carrier is required to make immediate advance payments to the surviving dependents to satisfy their direct economic needs (Article 28 MC).

Attempts to also provide for obligatory compensation for damage for purely emotional loss (i.e., loss which is not associated with bodily injury) remained unsuccessful. However, an interpreting statement was accepted by the members of the delegation, according to which case law can be developed in accordance with which compensation for damage could be awarded, in accordance with National Law, for mental injuries. It is debatable whether this statement is legally effective. As the MC also does not itself produce any findings on the scope of the obligation to pay compensation in the event of passengers being killed or suffering bodily injury, claimants or parties entitled to claim are referred to National Laws.

The following regulations apply to liability for damage to luggage. Pursuant to Article 17, paragraph 2 MC, the air carrier is liable for the destruction, loss of or damage to luggage checked in if the event causing it occurred on board the aircraft or during a period of time in which the luggage checked in was in the care of the air carrier, and in fact up to an upper limit of SDR 1,000 until 29 December 2009, respectively SDR 1,131 since 30 December 2009. The air carrier is, however, not liable if, and to the extent that, the damage is attributable to the nature of the luggage or an inherent defect. In the event of luggage not checked in, including personal items, the air carrier is liable if the damage is to be attributed to its fault or the fault of its assistants.

Pursuant to Article 18 MC, the air carrier is liable for loss, destruction, and damage to goods if the event through which the damage was caused occurred during air carriage, and in fact up to an upper limit of SDR 17 until 29 December 2009, respectively SDR 19 since 30 December 2009 per kilogramme. It may, however, be exonerated if the damage occurred through an inherent defect or through inappropriate packaging.

Pursuant to Article 19 WC, the air carrier is required to compensate damages that arise through delay in the air carriage of passengers (upper limit: SDR 4,150 until 29 December 2009, respectively SDR 4,694 since 30 December 2009 per passenger), luggage (upper limit: SDR 1,000 until 29 December 2009, respectively SDR 1,131 since 30 December 2009), or goods (upper limit: SDR 17 until 29 December 2009, respectively SDR 19 since 30 December 2009 per kilogramme). However, it can be exonerated by proving that it and its assistants have taken all reasonable measures to avoid the damage or that it was not possible to implement such measures. Conversely, should the passenger succeed, in the event of a delay to his/her person or luggage, in proving fault on the part of the air carrier (within the meaning of

Article 22, paragraph 5 MC), the limits specified do not apply. This possibility does not exist for a consignor of freight.

In the MC, the so-called prohibited air alternative transport is subject to the regulations of Aviation Law. Prohibited air alternative transport exists if the air carrier, contrary to the agreement, transports goods by road, rail or sea instead of, as agreed, by air. Such prohibited alternative transportation is in future subject to the limited liability of the MC.

2. Contractual/Executing Air Carriers

The MC contains detailed provisions on the contractual and executing air carriers, which are also applicable to code-sharing and wet lease agreements. Articles 39 and 48 MC have in this case assumed the basic principles of the Supplementary Guadalajara Agreement (SGC of 1961).[58] Article 41 of the MC, which has incorporated Article 3, paragraphs 1 and 2 of the SGC, provides for acts and omissions of the executing air carrier and its assistants, insofar as the latter are acting in the execution of their duties, also applying in regard to the carriage executed by the executing air carrier, as those of the contractual air carrier, and vice versa (concerning the details, see the text of the MC). In this way, the MC has introduced a system of joint liability of the contractual and executing air carriers. This benefits the passengers or their surviving dependents.

3. Code-Sharing Flights/Successive Air Carriers

The practical application of code-sharing varies widely, reflecting the increasing complexity of the arrangements, with the spread of franchising and subcontracting. The practice differs from traditional code-sharing in that the passenger is deliberately made to believe that he is travelling on the main carrier rather than an affiliate. This is why the passengers are reminded whenever possible that they will be flying on a partner carrier.

An excellent way to protect the passenger is the formula contained in Article 36 of the MC of 1999, because the principles of solidarity of the code-sharing partners protect the victims and their families against the potential bankruptcy of the current carrier, the real reason for the solidarity.

The MC of 1999 puts the focus on the intention of the parties to consider the successive transport as a single operation, whether it had been agreed upon under the form of a single contract or of a series of contracts. However, obviously, the intention to code-share must be disclosed to the passenger as one of the conditions of the air transport contract.

Also, the MC of 1999 clarifies carrier liability in the case of carriage to be performed by various successive carriers. Each carrier that accepts passengers, and the passenger or any person claiming compensation from it, can take action only against the carrier that performed the carriage during which the accident or the

58. 500 *UNTS* 32.

delay occurred. Such carrier will have a right of action against the first carrier or the last carrier, and both will be jointly and severally liable to the passenger or to the consignor or consignee.

4. The Transportation Documents

The MC poses less-restrictive requirements on the tickets than the WC. Whereas the WC contained an abundance of requirements in regard to passenger information,[59] Article 3 MC only requires minimal passenger information, the lack of which, in addition, has no detrimental consequences for the air carrier. Electronic tickets are now also taken into account.

Furthermore, Article 3 MC provides for the handing over of a transportation document as an individual or collective transportation ticket. This must contain certain obligatory details, such as the point of departure and destination, or possibly intermediary landing point, although non-observance of these rules does not impair the validity of the agreement and the provisions of the MC. Concerning accompanying luggage, the passenger is to be given a luggage receipt, and, in the case of goods being conveyed, the air carrier may choose between handing out an air waybill and any other form of recordal with details on the carriage.

Articles 4 and 16 MC incorporate the requirements of the air waybill, as they were originally laid down in Montreal Protocol No. 4. The most significant change introduced in MC 1999 is the possibility of substituting the traditional form with an electronic one (Article 4), i.e., electronic air waybills are now also permitted. Finally, the air carrier no longer loses the limitation of liability if a reference to this is omitted on the air waybill.

E. Procedure when Settling Claims

The addressee of claims for compensation, pursuant to the WC, WC/HP, or MC, is the air carrier or its legal successors, which is expressly made clear in Article 27 WC, WC/HP, or Article 32 MC. The claims can thus not lapse through the death of the person obliged to be compensated or, in the case of legal persons, by their dissolution, as is partially possible with claims arising from tort in foreign legal systems.

In the case of bodily injury, pursuant to the WC, WC/HP, and MC, no preclusion period exists, within which the claimant has to notify the damage to the party obliged to pay compensation. Such a preclusion period may also not be agreed upon.

Concerning damage to property, on the other hand, Article 26, paragraph 2 WC establishes that the recipient is required to press charges against the air carrier in writing without delay following discovery of the damage, in the case of luggage within three days and in the case of freight within seven days following acceptance,

59. *Chan v. Korean Air Lines*, 109 S. Ct. 1676 (1989).

by noting the details on the transportation ticket or in any other way. The HP has extended these deadlines to seven or fourteen days respectively (Article 26, paragraph 2 WC/HP). The HP has left these deadlines unchanged in relation to the WC/HP (Article 31, paragraph 2 MC). Instead of the recipient, third parties are also entitled to press charges. This is of considerable significance in practice, because freight is, first, frequently accepted by persons other than the recipient following the end of the carriage. Failing to meet the obligation of pressing charges excludes a claim against the air carrier unless the latter prevents the claimant from pressing charges in good time. Whether also the air carrier's mere awareness of the damage makes the failure to observe the deadline insignificant is, on the other hand, questionable. The obligation to adhere to the notification deadline only refers to damage. In the case of destruction or loss, it is assumed that the air carrier is informed on the matter, so that an obligation to press charges can be dispensed with. Partial loss and partial destruction can be viewed as damage, so that they ought to be notified within the deadline. Should the goods be accepted without reservation, pursuant to Article 26, paragraph 1 WC, WC/HP, or Article 31, paragraph 1 MC, a refutable presumption exists that they were found to be in an orderly condition. The recipient must then prove the reverse. The claims to compensation are not lost through accepting the goods without reservation.

In regard to the person of the air carrier authorized to accept the charges, various cases are to be differentiated. Should the air carrier, as a partner to the carriage agreement, execute the carriage itself, the complaint is to be directed towards it or towards persons who are appointed by it to accept the freight. Should an executing air carrier be involved, besides the contractual air carrier, it is sufficient to notify the complaint to one of them. On the other hand, that does not apply in the event that the air carrier serves as a mere assistant, which does not have the status of an executing air carrier within the meaning of the Guadalajara Agreement. The claim is then to be directed towards the contractual air carrier, unless its assistant expressly has a power of attorney to accept the goods.

In the case of successive carriage, it will suffice if the claim is notified, in the event of damage, to the air carrier that has actually executed the carriage and against which the claimant also wishes to make a claim. Should the relevant section of the route not be known, the claim must be notified to the air carrier against which, pursuant to Article 30, paragraph 3 WC or Article 36, paragraph 3 MC, a claim may be made by the consignor or recipient. In the event of the tortfeasor being unknown, that is the first air carrier, for the consignor, and the last air carrier, for the recipient.

Concerning asserting the claim for compensation by way of an action, preclusion periods exist for damage to both persons and property. Pursuant to Article 29 WC or Article 35 MC, the action for compensation for damages may only be filed within a preclusion period of two years. The deadline begins with the day on which the aircraft arrived at the destination or should have arrived there, or on which the carriage was interrupted. For the calculation of the deadline, the law of the court appealed to is decisive. As a preclusion period, it cannot be interrupted or arrested. In the case law of some countries, however, this is partially assessed differently. The claimant may assert the objection of illegal exercising of rights if the air carrier invokes the expiry of the deadline after it has initially prevented the claimant from filing an action in good time.

For the plaintiff, the place of jurisdiction is of considerable significance. In general, it will endeavour to file the action before a local court, as this facilitates the prosecution. On the other hand, difficulties may arise in carrying out execution abroad. Article 28 WC, WC/HP, and Article 31, paragraph 1 MC give the plaintiff a choice among various courts, insofar as these lie within the territory of a party to the agreement, namely, the courts having jurisdiction for:

- the domicile of the air carrier;
- the head office (WC, WC/HP) or main branch (MC) of the air carrier;
- the office of the air carrier through which the transportation agreement has been concluded (the office in the sense of this regulation is also the agency that sold the air ticket, even if it does not belong to the air carrier's company. This interpretation is necessary in the interests of the passenger); and
- the destination (the destination is the airport to which the passenger is, in accordance with the agreement, supposed to be flown. Should a town have several airports, for which different courts have jurisdiction, the court in the district of which the airport is situated is relevant. Should the flights there and back have been booked together, the destination is the airport of departure.).

In addition, Article 33, paragraph 2 grants the passenger a further place of jurisdiction in the event of death and bodily injury, namely, in the contracting State in which the passenger had his permanent place of residence at the time of the accident and in which, or from which, the air carrier transports passengers commercially, and in fact either with its own aircraft or, based on a commercial agreement, with aircraft of another air carrier. This 'fifth place of jurisdiction' appears *inter alia* to be aimed at guaranteeing the passenger or his surviving dependents a place of jurisdiction at his permanent place of residence via both air carriers of a code-sharing agreement, even if only one of them operates air carriage at this location. This would, however, mean that such a code-sharing agreement is viewed as a 'joint carriage service' within the meaning of Article 33, paragraph 3(a).

With the specification of a place of jurisdiction, the right of option for the plaintiff lapses. It may not file an action before several courts simultaneously or divide up the claim between or among various courts. Article 28 WC, WC/HP, or Article 33 MC, as a special regulation, takes precedence over the national provisions or the local jurisdiction. Concerning actions pursuant to WC, WC/HP, or MC, only the places of jurisdiction provided for in this exist, any other places of jurisdiction are not admissible. Article 29 WC, WC/HP, or Article 35 MC only covers those actions against the air carrier the basis for the claims of which directly emerges from Articles 17 et seq. WC, WC/HP, or MC. It does not apply to actions against its assistants or actions for compensation for damages due to non-fulfilment.

Pursuant to Article 32, Sentence 1 WC, WC/HP, or Article 49 MC, all provisions of the carriage and all special agreements concluded by the parties prior to the occurrence of the damage, in which they make provisions on the applicable law or the place of jurisdiction that deviate from the Convention, are null and void. The choice of law and the choice of place of jurisdiction are thus not subject to the disposition of the parties. When transporting freight, however, pursuant to Article 32, Sentence 2 WC, WC/HP, or Article 34 MC, arbitration clauses are admissible to the extent that the compulsory regulations of the Convention are adhered to and the arbitration proceedings take place in a district in which a place of jurisdiction is substantiated pursuant to Article 28, paragraph 1 WC, WC/HP, or Article 33 MC. Following the occurrence of the damage, however, the choice of law, place of jurisdiction, and arbitration agreements are permitted.

F. Comparison of Liability Pursuant to WC, WC/HP and MC

WC	*WC/HP*	*MC*
	Liability for Bodily Injury	
In principle, liability for presumed culpability with the possibility of exonerating evidence.		In principle, liability for presumed culpability.
Liability pursuant to Article 22 WC limited to *Poincaré* Francs 125,000 (Francs 100 = EUR 10.94).	Liability pursuant to Article 22 WC limited to *Poincaré* Francs 250,000 (Francs 100 = EUR 10.94).	For losses in the case of death or bodily injury not exceeding the SDR 100,000/113,100 per passenger, the liability of the air carrier cannot be excluded or limited (Article 21, paragraph 1).
Limitation of liability does not apply, pursuant to Article 25, paragraph 1 WC, if it is proven that the air carrier or its assistants have caused the damage deliberately or through negligence which, according to the law of the court appealed to, is equated with intent.	Limitation of liability does not apply, pursuant to Article 25 WC if it is proven that the air carrier or its assistants have acted with the intention of causing damage, or acted frivolously in the awareness that damage would probably occur.	For losses extending beyond that, it will not be liable if it proves that this damage is not attributable to an illegitimate action or omission by a third party, even if it has only been committed negligently (Article 21, paragraph 2.

WC	*WC/HP*	*MC*
Liability for Items Carried in the Passenger's Care		
Liability up to Francs 5,000 (ca. EUR 547) – Article 22, paragraph 3 WC.		In principle, liability for presumed culpability. When conveying luggage, the air carrier is liable for destruction, loss, damage, or delay only up to an amount of SDR 1,000/1,131 per passenger (Article 22, paragraph 2).
Liability for Luggage (Checked in)		
Liability up to Francs 250 (ca. EUR 27.35) per kilogramme luggage checked in – Article 22, paragraph 2 WC.		In principle, liability for presumed culpability. When conveying luggage, the air carrier is liable for destruction, loss, damage, or delay only up to an amount of SDR 1,000/1,131 per passenger (Article 22, paragraph 2).
The obligation to pay compensation does not occur if the air carrier proves that the damage occurred through defective steering, guiding, or navigation of the aircraft and that it and its assistants have otherwise implemented all necessary measures to provide protection against damage (Article 20, paragraph 2 WC).		

WC	*WC/HP*	*MC*
	Liability for Freight/Goods	
Liability up to Francs 250 (ca. EUR 27.35) per kilogramme of luggage checked in – Article 22, paragraph 2 WC.		When conveying goods, the air carrier is liable for destruction, loss, damage, or delay only up to an amount of SDR 17/19 per kilogramme (Article 22, paragraph 3).
The obligation to pay compensation does not occur if the air carrier proves that the damage occurred through defective steering, guiding or navigation of the aircraft and that it and its assistants have otherwise implemented all necessary measures to provide protection against damage.		
	An exclusion of liability by the air carrier is admissible for losses which result from the nature of the goods transported or the defects associated with them (Article 23 WC/HP).	The air carrier is not liable if, and to the extent that, it proves that the destruction, loss or damage to the goods has been caused by the nature of the goods or an inherent defect in them, defective packaging of the goods by a person other than the air carrier or its assistants, an act of war or armed conflict and/or sovereign activity in

WC	*WC/HP*	*MC*
		connection with the import, export, or transit of goods.
	Liability for Delays	
As above, according to the respective aggrieved legal interests.		In principle, liability for presumed culpability. For losses through delay, the air carrier is liable, when conveying persons, only up to an amount of SDR 4,150/4,694 per passenger (Article 22, paragraph 1).
	Notification Deadlines	
– for luggage – 3 days – for freight – 7 days – for losses caused by delay – 14 days	– for luggage – 7 days – for freight – 14 days – for losses caused by delay – 21 days	– for luggage checked in – 7 days – in the case of goods – 14 days – in the event of delay – 21 days
	Deadlines for Filing an Action	
Two years. The deadline begins with the day on which the aircraft arrived at the destination or on which it should have arrived, or on which the carriage was interrupted.		
	Insurance Requirements	
No regulation.		The contracting States oblige their air carriers to reasonably insure themselves to cover their liability in accordance with this convention.

III. THIRD-PARTY LIABILITY IN INTERNATIONAL AVIATION AND REVISION OF THE ROME CONVENTION

A. Rome Convention

1. History

The principle of IPL according to which the place of the accident decides on the type and amount of compensation claims of the injured parties on the ground against the aircraft operator leads to different results due to the various liability regulations in the individual States. This legal situation has been considered unsatisfactory for several decades, especially because the injured party, as a result of making its claims against a foreign aircraft operator, has no special protection and is dependent on the general rules of international prosecution.

In the 1930s, as a result of the first efforts to harmonize laws within the CITEJA, the Convention for the Unification of Certain Rules Relating to Damage Caused by Foreign Aircraft to Third Parties on the Surface of 29 May 1933[60] was signed during the third Conference on Private Aviation Law in Rome. The Convention grants the injured parties compensation within certain maximum amounts on the basis of strict liability. However, it only gained little significance, as it did not include sufficient regulations on how the claims of the injured parties were to be ensured. The supplementing Protocol signed in Brussels on 29 September 1938[61] was to remedy this shortcoming, but it also remained insignificant.

2. Establishment

As early as 1947, the Legal Committee was working on a revision of the 1933 Convention within the ICAO, which finally led to a new Convention draft that was signed in Rome on 7 October 1952 (Rome Convention)[62]. The Convention entered into force on 4 February 1958, but was only signed and ratified by a fraction of the States. By 1 June 2009, forty-nine States had joined the Convention. The US, Great Britain, France, and the Federal Republic of Germany have not joined the Convention – like almost all other 'big' aviation nations. Canada and Australia initially ratified the Convention, but terminated it again later.

3. Main Content

a. Absolute Liability

The Rome Convention is based on the principle of absolute liability. Absolute liability is a type of liability in which the liability cause is not negligent conduct,

60. VI *Hudson* 334; (1937) JAL 312.
61. (1939) *JALC* 281.
62. 310 *UNTS* 181.

but rather operation of a dangerous item. Liability therefore is a result of realization of the operational risk. The structure of absolute liability is the result of the attempt to achieve a balance of interests between the causer and the injured party in terms of risks resulting from the legislature allowing operation of a dangerous item in the interest of the general public.

i. Principles

The special principles of absolute liability derive from the 'general provisions'[63] that are based on the consideration that liability for damages requires negligent conduct and is not subject to any limit.

Absolute liability is a limited liability for realization of the operational risk of a dangerous item, that is, without requiring negligent conduct of the operator or his staff. The following balance of interest takes place here:

- The disadvantage of the operator of being liable even in the case that there is no negligent conduct on his part is balanced by the advantage of a liability limit.
- Or, the other way round, from the point of view of the injured party: The advantage of not having to prove the operator's negligent conduct is 'bought' by the disadvantage of possibly not being able to claim full compensation.

ii. Exceptions

The possible exceptions derive from this basic interdependency of negligence and liability limit, which are, therefore, part of the nature of absolute liability:

- If the injured party can prove the fault of the operator, referring him to the limits of his claims is not justifiable. Liability according to the 'general provisions' (unlimited liability) then has to be possible.
- The other way around, there is no definite reason to hold an operator (fully or at all) liable when he can prove his non-fault. The operator of a dangerous item, therefore, has the legal option of discharge. Obviously, this aspect allows for variations:

For example, it can be argued that the aspect of risk due to the risk potential of the relevant item is so overwhelming that non-fault of the operator should not have an impact (such as the German aviation law's absolute liability, which does not provide for the possibility of release of liability). In such a case, it might be appropriate to talk about 'strict liability' rather than 'absolute liability'.

Furthermore, it might be appropriate to reduce the possibility of discharge to certain exceptional events (e.g., the German road transport law's absolute liability, which only provides the possibility of release of liability in case of *force majeure*).

63. See for example the reference in § 42 of the German Air Traffic Act (LuftVG).

Finally, it can be argued on a structural basis to not completely neglect the aspect of 'operation of a dangerous item' even in the case of proven non-fault, but rather to allocate part of the risk to the operator for this reason.

b. Limited Liability

In accordance with the Rome Convention, the liability amount is limited and is classified by the weight of the aircraft. Article 11 of the Convention provides:

> [T]he liability for damage giving a right to compensation . . ., for each aircraft and incident, in respect of all persons liable under this Convention, shall not exceed:
>
> (a) Francs 500,000[64] for aircraft weighing 1,000 kilogrammes or less;
> (b) Francs 500,000 plus Francs 400 per kilogramme over 1,000 kilogrammes for air-craft weighing more than 1,000 but not exceeding 6,000 kilogrammes;
> (c) Francs 2,500,000 plus Francs 250 per kilogramme over 6,000 kilogrammes for aircraft weighing more than 6,000 but not exceeding 20,000 kilogrammes;
> (d) Francs 6,000,000 plus Francs 150 per kilogramme over 20,000 kilogrammes for aircraft weighing more than 20,000 but not exceeding 50,000 kilogrammes;
> (e) Francs 10,500,000 plus Francs 100 per kilogramme over 50,000 kilogrammes for aircraft weighing more than 50,000 kilogrammes.
>
> The liability in respect of loss of life or personal injury shall not exceed Francs 500,000 per person killed or injured.

c. Miscellaneous

The aircraft operator is the liability subject. He has unlimited liability when he or his staff have been proven to have caused damage with intent. Contributory negligence by the injured party is taken into account. The Convention only covers damages that have been caused by civil aircraft in flight of another contracting State on the ground surface. However, an accident is not a precondition. Damages that are caused by the simple overflight of an aircraft in accordance with applicable traffic laws[65] are not covered by the Convention. Liability of the operator shall be covered by sufficient liability insurance.

---

64. The sums mentioned in Francs in this article refer to a currency unit consisting of 65 milligrammes of gold of millesimal fineness 900 (Art. 11, para. 4 Rome Convention).
65. Noise damages, see Rinck, *ZLW* (1962), 90.

4. Limited Effect

The low number of ratifications of the Rome Convention mainly has to do with the fact that great aviation nations such as the US and Great Britain do not have any maximum liability amounts for third-party damages. Therefore, the revision efforts of the ICAO, which were concluded with the Montreal Amendment Protocol of 22 September 1978, mainly aimed at liability amounts that would be acceptable to these states. The economic differences between aviation states led to great problems – as had also been the case for liability amounts in the WC. The Montreal Amendment Protocol[66] sets the maximum liability limit for a person entitled to compensation at SDR 125,000, which is approximately EUR 140,000. It has only been ratified by twelve States (last update: 1 June 2009) and entered into force on 25 July 2002.

Apart from the maximum liability amounts, another controversial subject was the efforts of some states to define clear regulations in the Rome Convention for it to be applied to damages from aircraft noise and sonic boom.[67] However, these efforts did not reach a majority, meaning that the question of liability for aircraft noise, which was already disputed when the Convention was established in 1952, remains unsolved.

The low number of ratifications of the Amendment Protocol shows that the Rome Convention is not successful on a global level. From a German perspective, there are concerns with regards to its liability regulations insofar as it only excludes limited liability of the aircraft operator in case of his intent. This is generally a concept foreign to German legislation. At least in the case of conscious intent, further claims against the aircraft operator should be possible.[68]

B. Efforts for a New Regulation of Third-Party Liability in International Aviation

Revision of the Rome Convention on third-party liability in international aviation has again been discussed in various committees and working groups for several years under the aegis of the ICAO. At the end of June 2007, the sixth and last meeting of the Special Group on the Modernization of the Rome Convention established for this purpose was held in Montreal. Delegates from twenty countries and a number of associations who took part as observers were present. While the main issue initially was improving victim protection, the events of 11 September 2001 resulted in the problem of a lack of insurance cover for extreme damages caused by terrorists quickly becoming the main issue. Therefore, the problem of third-party damages was dealt within two Convention drafts, which are hereinafter referred to as Convention I (realization of the general operational risk) and

66. 2195 *UNTS* 372.
67. See Achtnich, *ZLR* (1954), 252.
68. See Rinck, *ZLW* (1962), 101.

Convention II (realization of the terror risk).[69] In accordance with the usual process, the negotiations of the Special Group (which have now been concluded) are to be followed by discussions in the ICAO Legal Committee and then a concluding diplomatic conference.

1. Application Area

From the wording of Article 2(1) of the two Convention drafts, the question arises whether it has to be checked (and confirmed) whether the cause of the accident was purely an operational or a terrorist one. In other words, which Convention applies when a terrorist background has not (yet) been proven?

The answer to this question depends on the relationship of the two Conventions to each other. At least until terrorist attacks have not become a defining concomitant phenomenon of aviation, application of Convention I will from a legal perspective have to be considered the norm and application of Convention II as an exception from this norm. This means that application of Convention I generally has to be assumed, or that the party which wants to draw advantages from application of Convention II has to prove the terrorist background of the event causing the damage. However, this will hardly be possible for such party. If a terrorist background is not obvious (Lockerbie, 9/11) or if it has not (objectively) been confirmed yet, it will not be possible to simply assume it. As long as this uncertainty persists, one will have to assume realization of the general operational risk (Convention I). Press releases or claims of responsibility will not be sufficient for this purpose as they can be guided by interest and, therefore, cannot replace evidence.

Application of Convention I is initially of advantage for the operator. It is only in accordance with this Convention (more precisely: with its Article 3(2)) that he has the option to provide exculpatory evidence for claims beyond the limit of SDR 250,000–500,000. If he is successful, the unlimited liability in accordance with this Convention is no longer a threat to him. This means that it is sufficient for the operator – until confirmation of a terrorist background – to simply argue in the sense of his discharge so as to use this obvious advantage of Convention I. Therefore, he will only want to negotiate damages up to the limit of Article 3(2) in this phase. Only when the terrorist background has been confirmed objectively (or can be proven by the injured party), the 'shift' from Convention I to Convention II has to be made. The previous discharge attempts of the operator are then irrelevant with immediate effect (when not considering Article 17 of Convention II). Its use (or that of the insurances) is only absorbed at a maximum of SDR 700 million. This split of third-party liability may lead to a long legal insecurity, since cases are possible where not one or the other background of the damage can definitely be confirmed.

69. For details see: Bollweg/Schnellenbach, *ZEuP* (*Journal for European Private Law*) (2007), 798 et seq.

2. Liability of the Operator

The liability of the operator is designed generally as an absolute liability in both Conventions; however, both Conventions deviate from this principle in different – and even legally questionable – ways. The question whether the legal institute of absolute liability should even be opened to terrorist risks is absolutely justifiable, since liability for terrorist risks is not about the realization of an operational risk of the dangerous item 'aircraft', but rather about liability for a danger intentionally taken to the aircraft from the outside. The claims of the injured parties obviously are to be directed at the operator through his liability (as the first victim of the attack), because one cannot determine the actual causer of the damage.

The response to this risk to create an absolute liability basis for claim is only justifiable if terrorism is either considered an inseparable part of the phenomenon 'aviation' or if absolute liability is opened to the risk from the outside, for example, arguing that aviation is predestined to be the target of terrorist attacks. However, this would lead to the otherwise strictly separated areas of 'security' (aviation security) and 'safety' (flight safety) being blurred. One also has to take into consideration that the most effective countermeasures to prevent terrorist attacks have to take place on the ground, before passengers and their baggage come on board the aircraft. Today these measures are mainly carried out by public authorities. It is inconsistent with the institute of absolute liability to include measures of other parties, which in addition take place before operation of the aircraft, in the operational risk.

The two Convention drafts meet/contradict the principles of absolute liability (see above A. 3.) as follows.

a. Absolute Liability

Both Conventions in their Articles 3(1) formulate the basic position of any absolute liability, namely, that the liability of the operator of a dangerous item does not depend on his negligent conduct, but on the fact that he has used this item in flight. The question arises whether the time of responsibility is designated correctly with the term *in flight.* Since it is about the liability of the operator for operating a dangerous item, this term should be replaced by *in operation.*[70] This would also cover damaging events before take-off or after landing at the appropriate airport. The explosion of a wide-bodied aircraft on a highly frequented major airport could very well lead to damages similar to those of 9/11. These should be also covered by the Convention.

b. Exculpatory Evidence

Furthermore, the aspect of exculpatory evidence (by the operator) has been considered in both Conventions. Pursuant to Article 3(2) of Convention I, the operator

70. See for example § 33 of the German Air Traffic Act (LuftVG).

can discharge if he proves his non-fault, either directly (a) or only indirectly by proving that the damage was exclusively caused by somebody else's negligent conduct (b). However, the contributory cause by this 'somebody' must not be an act of terrorism since this does not lead to a discharge of the operator, but to application of Convention II.[71]

In the event that the operator successfully provides exculpatory evidence, he is, however, not completely excluded from liability pursuant to Article 3(2) of Convention I, but only for damages exceeding the amount of SDR 250,000–300,000 per injured person. The 'strict liability', which therefore practically applies up to this limit, is legally justifiable when arguing that the operational risk still exists and has to be considered appropriately even in the case of non-fault of the operator. Furthermore, this regulation has to be welcomed from a practical point of view since it allows processing part of the claims without lengthy disputes. Convention I, therefore, is consistent with the structure of absolute liability.

However, the following considerations against the possibility of discharge should be mentioned. If the operator is successful in providing exculpatory evidence pointing at fault of another person (Article 3(2) b), the injured person is basically 'forced' to make further claims against such person. However, since such claims would be subject to the appropriate applicable national law, the effect of Convention I as an international unification convention would be questionable. This is probably the reason why Article 9*bis* (which still is in brackets) excludes liability of a number of third persons, who thereby at least benefit from the absolute liability of the operator in the way that he can naturally only take recourse against them to the amount of his own payment obligation (Article 9). Since this possibility requires discharge of the operator, its effect from the perspective of the 'other person' is like that of a liability limit. It should, therefore, be discussed whether this effect is appropriate and intended.

Convention II on the other hand does not include the possibility of discharge of the operator. It cannot be detected in Article 21 either; since the possibility of release of the operator provided in this article does not constitute a structural possibility of discharge, but simply takes into consideration the contributory fault of the injured person.[72] In accordance with the structural principles of absolute liability detailed above, it is, therefore, justifiable to refer to liability according to Convention II as 'strict liability'. Convention II is, therefore, consistent with the detailed structural principles of absolute liability.

With regards to Convention II, it also seems necessary to grant the operator a possibility of discharge and to not impose liability for misconduct of third parties on him either (as in the current version of Article 5(2)). It could be considered to involve these third persons in the Supplementary Compensation Mechanism (SCM) solution.[73]

71. See Art. 2(1) of the two Conventions.
72. Also see § 34 of the German Air Traffic Act (LuftVG) and Art. 8 of Convention I.
73. Supplementary Compensation Mechanism (SCM).

c. *Liability Limit/Possibility to Break Liability Limit*

Serious concerns must be raised as to whether the design of the aspect of liability limit in both Conventions is compatible with the structural principles of absolute liability – for different reasons.

i. Necessity of a Liability Limit?

The first thing that needs to be mentioned in this regard is that Convention I does not even provide a liability limit. This has an impact on the balance between the advantages and disadvantages of absolute liability. As detailed above, the limited liability of the operator is the balance for the fact that liability does not depend on his fault. Since the last mentioned aspect constitutes the basic thesis of the Convention (Article 3(1)), a liability limit should, for appropriate distribution of advantages and disadvantages, be included.

The counterargument that damages as a result of the general operational risk are naturally limited, at least in comparison to damages caused by the realization of terror risk, which are caused intentionally, is not relevant here either, even though damages caused by terrorism might include aiming at the highest possible damage. However, this cannot be excluded from the very beginning, when only chance plays a part. Therefore, Convention I should also include a liability limit. However, it is doubtful whether SDR 700 million with regards to a wide-bodied aircraft such as the A380 with more than 80 tons of fuel on board would be an appropriate limit. Whether this limit should be possible to break remains to be analysed. Furthermore, the insurance obligation of the operator (Article 7 of Convention I and of Convention II) should be formulated more precisely. The maximum liability amounts according to Article 4 of Convention II are not an indication for this (due to the possibility of recourse of the SCM), especially because Convention I does not provide any liability limit. What is designated appropriate should not be directed by what the insurance market offers, but by the risk to be insured. This is much more significant than SDR 700 million.

In contrast to Convention I, Convention II includes a liability limit (classified depending on the weight of the aircraft) at a maximum of SDR 700 million. Irrespective of whether the amount of the liability limit is economically appropriate, the existence of a liability limit as such corresponds to the structural principles of absolute liability when looking at it in connection with a basis for claim regardless of negligence or fault of Article 3(1).

Both Conventions should set the liability limit where the guarantee obligation of the SCM ends (unless an open SCM was to be created). The current maximum limit of Convention II would then no longer be a maximum liability limit, but would mark the entrance into the guarantee obligation of the SCM.

ii. Possibility to Break the Maximum Liability Limit

However, it is exactly this connection of fault and liability limit that cannot be broken without upsetting the balance of interests. In other words, if the operator has obviously acted with fault or if the injured person successfully provides appropriate evidence, there is no justification to protect the operator by a liability limit. Quite the opposite: It cannot be completely excluded that the operator, considering a definitely calculable liability risk, reduces his efforts to prevent an event of liability for financial or organizational reasons. The purpose of liability law is mainly and particularly compensation of an already occurred damage (compensation effect). In addition, it shall also cause the responsible person to do whatever possible and reasonable in order to prevent another damage (the so-called prevention effect). This requires the operator to have to expect to lose the protection of the liability limit in case of causing damage by negligent conduct, in other words, have unlimited liability.

Irrespective of what degree of fault is taken as a basis, the liability limit of at least Convention II should, therefore, be designed in a way that it can be broken. This conclusion also applies to Convention I if the recommendation made above to provide a liability limit in this Convention will also be followed. There are, in terms of legal construction, two possibilities for breaking such limit.

– Indirect Breaking of the Maximum Liability Limit:

On the one hand, the 'possibility to break' the maximum liability limit can be achieved indirectly by referring to the 'general provisions' in the case of fault (which has to be defined in terms of severity).[74]

However, for bases for liability due to international agreements, this option has a negative effect on the international harmonization efforts, since this means that national law is brought into the picture again.

– Direct Breaking of the Maximum Liability Limit:

Therefore, it should be considered to not achieve the effect of the possibility to break the limit indirectly – by referring to other provisions – but rather to refer directly to the basis for claim in question, that is, include it in the Convention itself. This possibility was, for example, chosen in the WC (Article 25: proof of 'wilful misconduct'). The obvious advantage would be that the liability beyond the maximum limit would also be subject to the international unification convention. Furthermore, compensation payments of the SCM due to Articles 15 et seq. of Convention II would then not refer to bases for liability according to national laws, but rather to those of the Convention itself.

74. In Germany, this would be the provisions on prohibited action (§§ 823 et seq. German Civil Code [BGB]), which do not provide any liability limits, but require fault. This option has for example been chosen in the absolute liability provisions of the German Air Traffic Act (LuftVG) (see § 42).

3. Additional Compensation by SCM

The possibility to legally classify the compensation obligations of the SCM pursuant to Articles 19 et seq. of Convention II depends on whether the strict liability limit of the operator pursuant to Article 4 of Convention II is maintained or whether the possibility to break it shall be provided (in the Convention itself).

a. SCM-Compensation When Maintaining Current Liability Limits

Should the liability limit pursuant to Article 4 be maintained in Convention II, this would mean that the compensation payments of the SCM (second layer) starting beyond the maximum liability limits would not be made 'for foreign fault'; such payments would then rather be made fulfilling one's own obligations. Initially, the fact that the SCM, pursuant to Article 25(2) has a 'right of recourse' especially against the operator in the event that he has acted with severe fault (defined there in detail), initially seems to be a contradiction. This leads to the conclusion that the amount of the compensation obligation of the fund is simply a guarantee obligation, which then again would mean that the liability of the operator would then not be limited to a maximum of 700 million (pursuant to Article 4), but in reality only where the guarantee obligation of the SCM ends (currently an additional SDR 3 billion per event).

This is, however, contradicted by the clear wording of Article 4 of Convention II, pursuant to which 'the liability of the operator shall . . . not exceed . . . ' the provided maximum liability limits. It would be recommendable to not only provide dogmatic clarification, but also to adapt the wording of Article 4 accordingly. Therefore, it is recommended that the liability of the operator is only limited where the guarantee obligation of the SCM ends.

b. SCM-Compensation for Possibility to Break the Liability Limit

If the liability limit pursuant to Article 4 of the Convention (currently a maximum of SDR 700 million) is designed in a way that it is possible to break it, the first question that arises is what reason an injured person should have to prove (gross) fault of the operator if the fund initially pays claims beyond the maximum limit. However, this thought cannot serve as an argument for maintaining the liability limit according to Article 4. It has to be considered that there can be cases of damage that require higher payments than those of the operator pursuant to Article 4 (a maximum of SDR 700 million) plus those of the SCM (up to an additional SDR 3 billion). The possibility to break the liability limit with the help of a proof of fault would then also cover the claims beyond the mentioned SCM payments. Considering that there is probably no insurance available on the market for such claims and that it would probably also greatly exceed the capacity of an air carrier, it would be a political question whether governments would contribute here (if it is not considered to make the guarantee obligation of the SCM open).

The effect of this would be that – beyond the liability limit pursuant to Article 4 – both the SCM as an indirectly injured person (due to its guarantee obligation pursuant to Article 19 of Convention II) and the directly injured persons would be in the same situation of interests: their damage or this part of their damage (directly injured persons) would only be compensated when they prove the fault of the operator (as is already provided for the SCM by Article 25(2)).

Practically, this would mean that the SCM – as provided in the current version of the Convention – would have to prove the fault of the operator to be able to take recourse. For the injured persons, this would, according to the recommendation above, only be necessary beyond the guarantee obligation of the SCM. However, this leads to the following consequence. It would not really be plausible if the operator was liable in the first layer, the SCM's own liability would apply in the second layer, and the operator would again be liable in the third layer. Therefore, the second layer also has to involve liability of the operator, which is then supplemented by the (joint and severable) liability of the SCM.

On the basis of these considerations, it is recommended to set the liability limit of the operator where the guarantee obligation of the SCM ends (upper limit of the second layer). The injured person would then, up to this limit, not have to provide evidence of the (gross) fault of the operator to receive compensation for his damage. For implementing claims beyond this limit (in the third layer), such proof of fault would theoretically be required (if the liability limit is to be designed in a way that it can be broken); however, practically, this would be unnecessary, since the SCM would also want to provide this evidence to take recourse against the operator (for the second layer).

Considering this, providing such evidence of gross fault would most likely not be an insurmountable task for the injured person to successfully claim compensation. The question of (un)reasonableness can only be asked in connection with the possibility to realize his claims in the third layer, namely, insofar as these claims probably exceed the financial capacities of an operator. If one does not want to count on a political solution, the only option that remains is to install the SCM in an open way as a jointly and severally liable debtor (with the connected risk of recourse).

4. Channelling of Liability over the Operator

Further concerns have to be raised about the indemnity of possible other causers by the operator or the SCM provided in the current version of Article 5(2) of Convention II. While this article is formulated as an (objective) exemption from liability of the persons mentioned therein ('no other persons . . . may be obliged to pay compensation . . . '), if read in connection with the current Article 19(1), this would in reality result in indemnity of such persons by the operator or the SCM with the possibility of recourse in the case of gross fault. There would then only be an appropriate reason for recourse when a payment obligation generally exists, but is 'redirected' to somebody else for whatever reasons. The other way around, recourse would not objectively be justifiable if the person taking recourse had not first paid an existing foreign obligation.

a. No Reason for Allocation of Foreign Misconduct to the Operator

With this in mind, the question arises of what the objective reason for the allocation of foreign misconduct to the operator could be. None of the usual reasons (employer, proxy, etc.) is apparent here. The motivation to exclude the direct use of mentioned third persons due to the unwanted effect of application of appropriate national law, might be understandable in the sense of the efforts to make Convention II the only one applicable for damages to be covered by this Convention; however, this is not enough to impose on the operator or the SCM the misconduct of others and the risks of realization of their claims of recourse resulting therefrom.

b. Inclusion of Other Parties Causing the Damage in Absolute Liability

The concerns about this construction are also due to the fact that the privileges of absolute liability are practically transferred to a number of other possible causers of the damage, although they are not the operator of a dangerous item, and there is, thus, no objective reason for the application of the principles of absolute liability. Without the Conventions, they would have to compensate the injured person (which would also include the operator) in accordance with the general basis for liability of the appropriate national law. Fault is a precondition in all of them, and they provide for unlimited liability.

In accordance with Convention II, (limited) liability of the third person (in the form of recourse by the operator or the SCM) only exists when gross fault has been proven as defined in Article 25(1). For absolute liability, this corresponds to the usual possibility to break the maximum liability limit. However, one has to take into account that the third persons are not liable at all in the case of no gross fault, which is not the case for the operator, who, in this case, is at least liable under the liability limits pursuant to Article 4 of Convention II.

They are thereby put on a par with the person subject to absolute liability (i.e., the operator) insofar as they are only liable in the case of gross fault. This already constitutes – as detailed above – an objectively not justifiable privilege. Furthermore, they are also privileged compared to him as they – other than the operator – are not liable in the case of non-fault since they are simply not responsible for the dangerous item 'aircraft'. In addition, they are not liable either in the case of 'normal' fault, although this is provided by the usually applicable bases for a claim (i.e., without the Convention). There is no apparent objective justification for this either.

c. Assumption of Charges Instead of Discharge

Finally, it must be mentioned that the assumption of charges provided by Article 5(2) of the current version turns an essential principle of absolute liability upside down, namely, that the operator can usually use the misconduct of third parties as a reason for discharge. An example for this is provided by Article 3(2) of Convention I, according to which the operator is not liable if he can prove that 'such damage was solely due to the negligence or other wrongful act or omission of another person.'

According to Article 5(2) in connection with Article 19(1) of Convention II (current version), he would not have been able to discharge liability in such a case. Quite the opposite: Liability of other persons is imposed on him, who, on top of that, have damaged him through their misconduct. This has especially severe consequences for him because he can only take recourse in such a case when proving gross fault, which is otherwise refused to him. From a legal perspective, this is extremely questionable. Therefore, the fact that Article 5(2) is no longer included in the current draft version of Convention II must be considered a positive development.

5. Advance Payment Obligation

Reference to the appropriate applicable national law included in Article 6 of Convention I and in Article 6 of Convention II is not enough to cover the important interest behind it. An advance payment obligation only exists in a few countries, but where it is in place,[75] it has proven very meaningful, although the amount is often and rightly considered to be too low.

Therefore, an appropriate advance payment obligation should be introduced on an international level. It is recommended to replace the reference to national law included in both Conventions by an independent obligation for advance payment. The measure of what is appropriate should be guided by the annual income of the deceased.

6. Reduced Compensation

The proportionate reduction of compensation if the amount of all claims exceeds the maximum limits pursuant to Articles 4 and 19 (provided in Article 23 of Convention II) has to be considered extremely questionable, since the first compensations are usually paid out in full in practice. Reductions usually only take place for the remaining claims when it becomes clear that the means to cover the entire event causing the damage will not be sufficient.

75. For example, in the EU Member States in accordance with Regulation (EC) 889/2004.

7. Basis for Definition of SCM Contributions

Article 14(1)(b) and (1)(c) grant air carriers the possibility to evade their contribution obligations with 'soft' arguments. It cannot be excluded that this will threaten financing of the SCM, since many airlines might claim these 'excuses' for themselves.

Chapter 7
Aviation Security

Ludwig Weber

I. HISTORICAL ASPECTS AND OVERVIEW

A. INTRODUCTION

Under Article 44 and the Preamble of the Convention on International Civil Aviation, safety, regularity, and efficiency of international civil aviation are the fundamental objectives of the Convention.[1] While the concept of safety as an absolute prerequisite for all aviation activities[2] is given overriding importance, the notion of security is not mentioned at all in the Convention.

In 1944, when the Convention was drafted, the phenomena of air piracy, sabotage, and other acts of unlawful interference against civil aviation were not yet a matter of specific concern. Nevertheless, the concept of safety of international civil aviation set out in the Convention must be regarded as encompassing security, in the sense of ensuring that the safety of flight will not be affected by human-made, intentional, criminal acts of interference aimed at aircraft, its passengers,

1. See *ICAO Doc.* 7300/9, preamble and Art. 44.
2. On the concept of aviation safety, see the ICAO Global Aviation Safety Plan (*GASP*, 2004 edn).

Elmar M. Giemulla & Ludwig Weber, *International and EU Aviation Law: Selected Issues*, pp. 285–306.

crew, airports, or air navigation installations.[3] Safety and security have appropriately been referred to as 'two sides of the same coin'.[4]

B. Air Piracy

Internationally, issues of aviation security first arose in the 1950s from a number of shoot-downs of civil aircraft by military aircraft, in most cases, for reasons of alleged intrusion into foreign airspace. These cases arose mostly as a result of failed aircraft interceptions. They should be clearly distinguished from hijackings. Today, aircraft interception by military action is no longer treated as an issue of aviation security, but as a separate problem.

Aircraft hijackings became an issue in the aftermath of the revolution in Cuba, when in the 1960s a number of civilian airliners were hijacked and commandeered to land in Cuba.[5] These acts were initially referred to as 'air piracy'. The hijackers were in many cases given red carpet treatment in Cuba, as the hijackers were mostly supporters of the revolutionary regime in Cuba or were portrayed as such. The wave of hijackings increased at the end of the 1960s and early 1970s. The Tokyo Convention of 1963,[6] which aimed at conferring agreed enforcement powers on the aircraft commander to permit him to deal with hijackings on board and to facilitate prosecution,[7] did not have the desired effect of curbing the number of aircraft hijackings.

C. Hijacking and Hostage-Taking

During the 1960s and 1970s, the number of hijackings of civilian airliners increased substantially,[8] in particular in connection with the Middle East conflict, the

3. L. Weber, *International Civil Aviation Organization – An Introduction, Aviation Law and Policy Series*, Vol. 2 (Alphen/Rijn: Kluwer Law International, 2007), 7; similarly P. Dempsey, *Aviation Security: The Challenge of International Law, Address before the ARAVSEC International Conference* (Jeddah, Saudi Arabia, 26–28 Mar. 2007), 2 et seq.
4. A. Kotaite, *Aviation Safety and Security – Two Sides of the Same Coin, Keynote Address to the Aviation Study Group at Linacre College* (Oxford University, 27 Jun. 2003), 2 et seq.
5. G. Guillaume, *Le terrorisme aérien* (Pedone, Paris 1977; Cours IHEI), 7 et seq.; C. Emmanuelli, *Les moyens de prevention et de sanction en cas d'action illicite contre l'aviation civile internationale* (Paris: Pedone, 1974), 159 et seq.; N. D. Joyner, *Aerial hijacking as an international crime* (Dobbs Ferry/Leiden: Oceana/Sijthoff, 1974).
6. *Convention on Offences and Certain Other Acts Committed on Board Aircraft,* signed 14 Sep. 1963 at Tokyo, *ICAO Doc.* 8364. The Convention had its origins in the discussions in ICAO on the legal status of aircraft as from 1950 onwards, and was only partly a response to the rising number of unlawful acts in the 1950s. See G. D. Kyriakopoulos, *La sécurité de l'aviation civile en droit international public* (Athènes-Bruxelles 1999), 62 et seq.
7. R. P. Boyle & R. Pulsifer, 'The Tokyo Convention on Offences and certain other Acts Committed on Board Aircraft', JALC 30 (1964): 305–354; G. F. Fitzgerald, 'Offences and Certain other Acts Committed on Board Aircraft: The Tokyo Convention of 1963', *CanYBIL/ACDI.* VII (1969): 269–297.
8. E. McWhinney, *Aerial Piracy and International Terrorism – The Illegal Diversion of Aircraft and International Law* (Dordrecht/Boston/Lancaster: 1987); Kyriakopoulos, *supra* (n. 6), 52 et seq.

East-West conflict, and smaller regional conflicts. Certain hijackings were also committed by mentally unstable or insane persons. In many cases, hijackings involved the taking of passengers as hostages, so as to obtain the liberation of prisoners, the fulfilment of political demands, ransom, free conduit, or all of these. The term *terrorist act* was increasingly used in the media. In numerous cases, governments ceded and hijackers were let go in exchange for the freeing of hostages.[9]

The international community responded by adopting The Hague Convention of 1970[10] and the Montreal Convention of 1971,[11] so as to outlaw aircraft hijacking and related acts as internationally recognized, serious crimes and to render prosecution, and alternatively extradition, mandatory.[12] In parallel, Annex 17: Security[13] was adopted by the Council of the International Civil Aviation Organization (ICAO) in 1974 as an Annex to the Chicago Convention, laying down preventive measures to protect against hijackings and other acts of unlawful interference, including screening of passengers and baggage.[14] Its standards and recommended practices were gradually implemented by ICAO Member States, involving *inter alia* the installation of screening equipment such as metal detectors and x-ray machines at airports. The increasing number of States ratifying The Hague and Montreal Conventions[15] and applying the screening procedures under Annex 17 finally had a combined effect of effectively deterring and preventing hijacking of aircraft, and the annual number of such unlawful acts fell beginning in the 1980s.[16]

D. VIOLENCE AT AIRPORTS

The bomb explosions at Frankfurt and Tokyo airports in June 1985 and the armed attacks on passengers and airline staff in the terminals of Rome and Vienna airports[17] in December 1985 resulted in a realization that the premises of

9. G. Guillaume, *Le terrorisme aérien* (Pedone 1977), 7; E. Mapelli Y Lopez, Capture illicite d'aéronefs, RFDA (1972): 241 et seq.
10. *Convention for the Suppression of Unlawful Seizure of Aircraft*, signed at The Hague on 16 Dec. 1970, *ICAO Doc.* 8920.
11. *Convention for the Suppression of Unlawful Acts against the Safety of Civil Aviation*, signed at Montreal on 23 Sep. 1971, *ICAO Doc.* 8966.
12. Article 7 Hague Convention 1970 and Art. 7 Montreal Convention 1971. See on this issue Kyriakopoulos, *supra* (n. 6), 122 et seq. with further references.
13. *ICAO Doc.* AN 17, 8th edn (Amendment 11).
14. On the background of Annex 17, see the Foreword to the Annex, *Doc.* AN 17, (v).
15. As of April 2011, the Hague Convention had 185 States Parties and the Montreal Convention 1971 had 188 States Parties.
16. See: US Federal Aviation Administration, Criminal Acts against Civil Aviation (2000; 2001); worldwide figures rose again in the mid-1990s, due to a number of factors, see ICAO, 'Annual Civil Aviation Report', *ICAO Journal* 57 (2002): 12 et seq., 33.
17. See M. Pourcelet, 'Le Protocole du 24 février 1988 pour la répression des actes illicites de violence dans les aéroports servant à l'aviation civile internationale', *RFDA* 175, no. 3 (1990): 290 et seq.; E. Faller, 'Current Legal Activities in ICAO: Development of a Legal Instrument for the Suppression of Unlawful Acts of Violence at Airports Serving International Civil Aviation', *ZLW* 26, no. 3 (1987): 219 et seq.

international airports were not included in the scope of application of the Hague and Montreal Conventions. Consequently, the international community adopted the Montreal Protocol of 1988, on violence at international airports.[18] It extended the application of the Montreal Convention of 1971 to unlawful acts committed at international airports and at air navigation installations.[19]

E. Sabotage of Aircraft

The mid-air destruction of an Air India 747 over the Atlantic in June 1985 and of a PanAm Boeing 747 over Lockerbie in December 1988[20] by a bomb placed on board involving plastic explosives demonstrated the remaining vulnerability of aircraft to such acts of sabotage. As a result, the Montreal Convention of 1991 on the Marking of Plastic Explosives[21] was adopted, which establishes a system of control over the manufacture, sale, and possession of plastic and sheet explosives, and provides for the installation of detection equipment at international airports.[22]

F. The Attacks of 11 September 2001

The attacks of 11 September 2001 raised the resolve of governments, the airline industry, and other parties involved to counter the threat of terrorism and unlawful acts. In June 2002, the Aviation Security Plan of Action[23] was agreed upon in the framework of ICAO, which provided for a Universal Security Audit Programme (USAP)[24] applicable to all ICAO Member States, new stringent standards under Annex 17 - *Security*, and other important measures. The USAP audits, which include the verification of airport security, aim at ensuring the full application of Annex 17 SARPs by Member States, encompassing the implementation of a National Civil Aviation Security Programme by Civil Aviation administrations,[25] and similar Airport and Aircraft Operator Security Programmes.

---

18. *Protocol for the Suppression of Unlawful Acts of Violence at Airports Serving International Civil Aviation,* Supplementary to the Montreal Convention, signed at Montreal on 24 Feb. 1988, *ICAO Doc.* 9518.
19. Pourcelet, *supra* (n. 17); Faller, *supra* (n. 17).
20. See Kyriakopoulos, *supra* (n. 6), 127–135 with further references.
21. *Convention on the Marking of Plastic Explosives for the Purpose of Detection*, signed at Montreal on 1 Mar. 1991, *ICAO Doc.* 9571.
22. Kyriakopoulos, *supra* (n. 6), 248 et seq.; J. Augustin, 'The Role of ICAO in Relation to the Convention on the Marking of Plastic Explosives for the Purpose of Detection', *AnnASL* XVII, no II (1992): 33–69.
23. ICAO Council, 166th Session (June 2002).
24. Assembly Resolution A37-17, Appendix E: *The ICAO Universal Security Audit Programme*; A36-20, Appendix E A35-9, *ICAO Doc.* 9848, VII-6.
25. Annex 17 – *Security*, *ICAO Doc.* AN 17, Standards 3.1.1 to 3.1.8. For details, see below part II.D.

II. INTERNATIONAL CONVENTIONS

A. Tokyo Convention of 1963

The Tokyo Convention,[26] which had its early origins in discussions on the legal status of aircraft rather than in unlawful interference concerns, is aimed at establishing rules on offences committed on board aircraft. Article 1, paragraph 1 defines the applicability of the Convention to criminal offences and other acts jeopardizing the safety or good order and discipline on board.[27] Chapter II establishes international rules on jurisdiction, providing for the jurisdiction of the state of registry of the aircraft over offences and acts against the good order and discipline committed on board of an aircraft in flight.[28]

Chapter III of the Convention (Articles 3–10) defines the powers of the aircraft commander to maintain good order and discipline on board, including the power to restrain an offender on board, to disembark him at the point of first landing, and to deliver him to the competent authorities of the state of landing (Article 6, paragraph 1). Members of the crew and passengers may be mandated with assisting the aircraft commander under delegated authority (Article 6, paragraph 2), but passengers only if they consent.

These rules may, however, be difficult or impossible to apply if, in a case of unlawful seizure of the aircraft, a factual life-threatening situation on board, for example, against crewmembers or passengers, does not allow an attempt to restrain the offender(s). Rules applicable to unlawful seizure of aircraft were added in Article 11 almost as an afterthought.[29] The Convention provides in this regard that the state of landing shall restore control of the aircraft to the lawful commander and facilitate the continuation of the journey. Also in this situation, the application of the rule in Article 11 will depend on an assessment of the threat and the resulting risk for the lives of passengers and crew. In many cases, a stand-off between the aircraft hijackers and the police forces of the state of landing has occurred in practice, resulting either in the use of force on the ground or a decision to let the aircraft proceed to another destination.

Besides these weaknesses, the Convention does not define any offences or criminal acts, but relies entirely on national law.[30] Further, it does not obligate the state of landing to prosecute the offender who has been disembarked or delivered.[31]

---

26. *See supra* (n. 6). The Convention has 185 States Parties (as of April 2011).
27. On the subject of unruly passengers, see ICAO Circular 288 LE/1: *Guidance Material on the Legal Aspects of Unruly/Disruptive Passengers* (June 2002).
28. Articles 3 and 4 of the Convention. On the controversial views regarding the jurisdiction clauses in relation to Art. 1 para.1 of the Convention, see Kyriakopoulos, *supra* (n. 6), 64 et seq.
29. P. Dempsey, Aviation Security: The Challenge of International Law, Address before the ARAVSEC International Conference, Jeddah, Saudi Arabia, 26–28 Mar. 2007, 8.
30. See Art. 1 para. 1 of the Convention.
31. Articles 12 and 13 of the Convention. Art. 13 para. 2 only places a conditional obligation on States which have taken delivery of the offender to take him into custody or 'ensure his presence', namely, 'upon being satisfied that the circumstances so warrant'. Furthermore, Art. 13 para. 4 only provides for a preliminary inquiry into the facts. These provisions leave large loopholes.

In practice, this decision depends mainly on whether the state of landing considers that it has jurisdiction and whether it should be exercised, and therefore leaves a wide gap open. It should be noted that Articles 3 and 4 of the Convention discourage, rather than encourage, the exercise of jurisdiction by the state of landing.[32] Finally, the Convention provides only a weak basis for extradition.

B. Hague Convention of 1970

The Hague Convention of 1970[33] deals specifically with hijacking offences. Article 1 defines the offence of hijacking as follows:

> Any person who on board an aircraft in flight: (a) unlawfully, by force or threat thereof, or by any other form of intimidation, seizes, or exercises control of, that aircraft, or attempts to perform any such act, or (b) is an accomplice of a person who performs or attempts to perform any such act commits an offense . . . .

Under Article 2, each contracting State undertakes to make the offence of hijacking punishable by severe penalties. The term *severe penalties* is not defined, but in practice most contracting States have provided for penalties of not less than five years imprisonment.[34] Article 4 provides that contracting States shall establish jurisdiction over the offence. This is necessary, since states other than the state of registry of the aircraft will normally not exercise nor establish jurisdiction over offences committed on board aircraft in flight.[35] Article 4 has the effect of creating a form of 'universal jurisdiction' (among all contracting States, presently 183) over the offence. It is fully in line with this provision that Article 6 obliges any contracting State in the territory of which the offender is present to take him into custody or to take other measures to ensure his presence: There shall be no 'safe haven' for offenders.[36]

---

32. In particular Art. 4 only provides a narrow basis for exercising jurisdiction by States other than the State of registry of the aircraft; it virtually operates as a presumption that the State of landing does not have jurisdiction over acts of unlawful interference committed on board, and the State of landing will normally not claim jurisdiction save in the exceptional circumstances listed in Art. 4 (a) to (e).
33. See *supra* (n. 10). The Convention has 185 States Parties (as of April 2011).
34. The interpretation of the term 'severe penalty' is not uniform. However, in their implementing legislation many States have provided for not less than five years imprisonment, or for life imprisonment for the offences under the Hague and Montreal Conventions; in very few cases, the death penalty is stipulated. In the Memorandum of Understanding between the US and Cuba of March 1973 to curb hijacking, the parties agreed to apply 'the most severe penalty', *ILM* 12, at 30, 370–375. The US Antihijacking Act of 1974 imposed imprisonment of at least twenty years, and if the offence results in death, life imprisonment, or the death penalty.
35. However, Art. 4 of the Tokyo Convention 1963 has codified those exceptions in which a state other than the state of registry may claim jurisdiction. On international criminal jurisdiction, see Kyriakopoulos, *supra* (n. 6), 82–94.
36. This objective was also a major factor in concluding the Memorandum of Understanding on Hijacking between the US and Cuba, of March 1973, *supra* (n. 34). The number of hijackings

Article 7 establishes the important principle that the contracting State which holds the offender in custody shall either extradite or prosecute him (*aut dedere aut judicare*). This obligation is without exception whatsoever and regardless of whether or not the offence was committed in its territory. Article 7, second Sentence, also stipulates that the offence shall be treated as 'any ordinary offense of a serious nature', thereby excluding that it be treated as a political offence giving rise to the right of asylum.[37] Furthermore, the offence of hijacking shall be deemed to be included as an extraditable offence in any extradition treaty existing between contracting States (Article 8).

While the Convention introduced important new elements into the legal framework for combating unlawful interference, its main weakness is that it covers only hijacking, but not any other acts of violence committed against civil aviation.

C. Montreal Convention of 1971

The Montreal Convention of 1971[38] essentially extends the legal regime of the Hague Convention 1970 to aircraft sabotage and other acts of violence against civil aviation. It includes in its scope acts of violence against passengers or crew on board, against the safety of aircraft and air navigation facilities, as well as communication of false information endangering the safety of civil aviation. It defines the offences, referred to as 'unlawful acts against the safety of civil aviation' in Article 1 and includes attempts to commit any of the offences.

The provisions of the Hague Convention on severe penalties, establishing jurisdiction over the offences, obligation to take the offender into custody, the principle of 'extradite or prosecute', and the basis for extradition are also found in the Montreal Convention.[39]

Although the scope of the Hague Convention of 1970 is limited to hijacking and the Montreal Convention of 1971 covers other offences, in practice, the application of both conventions will often overlap. In most cases, hijackings involve acts of violence or threat of violence against persons on board, and for this reason both conventions will be applicable. Similarly, when explosives are brought on board and are used to threaten the lives of passengers and crew in the course of a

---

and attempted hijackings of US aircraft drastically decreased from more than twenty-five per year prior to the Memorandum of Understanding to one for 1973 and remained low afterwards.

37. Kyriakopoulos, *supra* (n. 6), 117 et seq., 125 et seq.; G. Guillaume, 'La Convention de la Haye du 16 décembre 1970 pour la repression de la capture illicite d'aéronefs', *AFDI* XVI (1970): 35–61; however, K. Hailbronner, *infra* (*Encyclopedia*, n. 39), at 59 takes the contrary view, namely, that unlawful seizure of aircraft may 'still be regarded as a political offence, thereby possibly qualifying the alleged offender for asylum or leniency in prosecution'.
38. See *supra* (n. 11). The Convention has 188 States Parties (as of April 2011).
39. See Hailbronner, 'Civil Aviation, Unlawful Interference with', in *Encyclopedia of Public International Law*, Installment 11(Law of the Sea, Air and Space), (Max Planck Institute for Comparative Public Law and International Law, Heidelberg; Oxford University Press,1995), ed. R. Bernhardt (Amsterdam, New York, Oxford, Tokyo), 57–61, at 59; see also Hailbronner, *Luftpiraterie in rechtlicher Sicht. Von Tokyo bis Montreal* (1972).

hijacking, both Conventions will apply.[40] However, in cases of sabotage against aircraft or air navigation installations, only the Montreal Convention will be applicable. In terms of different types of unlawful interference against civil aviation, the Montreal Convention has by far the widest coverage among the five international instruments.[41]

D. Protocol on Violence at Airports (VIA) of 1988

In the aftermath of the combined attacks against the Rome and Vienna airports in December 1985, it became obvious that the protection under the Tokyo, Hague, and Montreal Conventions was incomplete and that it should be extended to international airports. This was done by the Protocol on Violence at Airports of 1988,[42] which essentially extended the provisions of the Montreal Convention of 1971 to airports serving international aviation.

The Protocol adds two additional offences to those in the Montreal Convention, namely, (a) performing 'an act of violence against a person at an airport serving international civil aviation which causes or is likely to cause serious injury or death', and (2) destroying or seriously damaging 'the facilities of an airport serving international civil aviation or aircraft not in service located thereon or disrupts the services of the airport'. In both cases, it is necessary that 'such act endangers or is likely to endanger safety at that airport'.[43]

While the acts committed on airport premises will normally be strictly localized, the universal jurisdiction of the Montreal Convention as amended by the Protocol will apply. Therefore, if the offenders escape abroad, foreign authorities will exercise jurisdiction, will take them into custody, and either extradite or prosecute.[44]

E. The Convention on the Marking of Plastic Explosives of 1991 (MEX)

This Convention was adopted after the mid-air destruction of Air India flight 182 in 1985 over the Atlantic and of Pan Am flight 103 over Lockerbie, Scotland, in December 1988 by means of explosive devices placed on board.[45] It aims at ensuring that plastic and sheet explosives,[46] which are easy to conceal and difficult

40. See the overlapping offences in Art. 1 Hague Convention and Art. 1 Montreal Convention.
41. See *Kyriakopoulos, supra* (n. 6), 76 et seq.
42. See supra n. 18 and *ICAO Doc.* 9518.
43. Article II of the Protocol, adding a new Art. 1*bis* to Art. 1 of the Montreal Convention of 1971.
44. See Art. III of the Protocol, inserting para. 2*bis* into Art. 5 of the Montreal Convention of 1971.
45. See Kyriakopoulos, *supra* (n. 6), 127 et seq. with further references.
46. Article I(1) of the Convention defines 'explosives' as 'explosive products, commonly known as "plastic explosives" including explosives in flexible or elastic sheet form, as described in the Technical Annex to this Convention'. The Technical Annex, Part 1, sets out a description of explosives.

to detect, can be detected before being placed on board aircraft by passengers, or in baggage, cargo, or mail.

The Convention provides for the obligations of contracting States to (1) prohibit and prevent the manufacture, import, and export of unmarked explosives,[47] (2) destroy existing stockpiles of unmarked explosives after a defined period,[48] and meanwhile (3) exercise strict control over the possession of unmarked explosives.[49] The obligation in (1), to prohibit and prevent the manufacture of unmarked explosives, applies only to producer States of plastic and sheet explosives, while the other obligations apply also to non-producer States. A Technical Annex to the Convention[50] sets out a description of explosives falling under the Convention, as well as a list of detection agents which may be used as chemical markers for newly produced explosives.

These measures seek to ensure that plastic explosives can be detected by appropriate detection equipment installed or to be installed at airports. However, their significance goes beyond civil aviation, since the scope of the Convention is wide enough to apply to all areas in which it is important to protect against the threat of plastic and sheet explosives.[51]

Differently from the four other international instruments mentioned above, this Convention is entirely aimed at prevention of unlawful acts by technological means. In this regard, it supplements the preventive measures provided for in Annex 17 to the Convention on International Civil Aviation.

F. The Beijing Convention and Protocol of 2010

The Beijing instruments were adopted as a result of the events of September 11, 2001 in order to close gaps in the existing international instruments and to deal with new and emerging threats.

They create a number of new international crimes, in particular the acts of organizing, directing or abetting acts of unlawful interference with civil aviation, or of forming a criminal organization for the purpose of committing such acts. Similarly, the use of an aircraft in service for the purpose of causing death injury or damage, and the release or discharge from such aircraft of any biological, chemical, or nuclear substance (BCN) for such purpose is made an international crime. The transportation of explosives or BCN weapons on board an aircraft without lawful authorization is likewise made an international crime.

47. Articles II and III of the Convention, I*CAO Doc.* 9571; see Augustin, *supra* (n. 22), 33 et seq.
48. Article IV paras 2, 3, 4, and 6 of the Convention. On this matter, see Kyriakopoulos, *supra* (n. 6), 249 et seq.; Augustin, *supra* (n. 22), 39 et seq.
49. Article IV paras 1 and 5 of the Convention.
50. See *ICAO Doc.* 9571. The Technical Annex to the Convention has been amended by the International Explosives Technical Commission (IETC) several times since the adoption of the Convention, see the Report of the Fifth Session of the IETC, *Doc. IETC/5*, Part 2-1 (Amendments to the Technical Annex to the Convention).
51. See the scope of the Convention, Arts I-III; on this matter, M. Milde, 'Draft Convention on the Marking of Plastic Explosives', *AnnASL* XV (1990): 180 et seq.; Kyriakopoulos, *supra* (n. 6), 246 et seq.

While the Beijing Convention is a new freestanding Convention which essentially incorporates the provisions of the Montreal Convention 1971 and adds the above-mentioned new offences, the Beijing Protocol amends the Hague Convention 1970. The Beijing instruments apply the jurisdictional rules of the Hague and Montreal Conventions, and also retain the important principle of 'prosecute or extradite' (see II.B. and C. above; see also Chapter 3 I.G.6. above)

III. ANNEX 17 AND RELATED PROVISIONS

A. Annex 17: Security

Annex 17: Security: Safeguarding International Civil Aviation against Acts of Unlawful Interference[52] was adopted by the ICAO Council in March 1974 so as to introduce uniform preventive measures against the then rising numbers of acts of unlawful interference. In particular, hijackings, hijacking attempts, hostage-taking, sabotage against aircraft, and bomb threats were causing major disruption and developed into a major threat to the safety of aircraft, crew, and passengers during this period.[53]

The measures introduced by Annex 17 relate to organization at the level of the public authorities (Chapter 3), preventive security measures relating to aircraft, passengers and cabin baggage, hold baggage, and cargo and mail (Chapter 4), and management of response to acts of unlawful interference (Chapter 5).

1. Organization

The basic principle regarding organization is found in Standard 3.1.2 of the Annex, according to which 'each contracting State shall designate and specify to ICAO an appropriate authority within its administration to be responsible for the development, implementation, and maintenance of the national civil aviation security programme'. In many states, there are overlapping responsibilities between several authorities regarding aviation security,[54] for example, the civil aviation authority, Ministry of the Interior, federal police, state provincial police, airport police and so on. It is, therefore, important to have one authority appointed which will be notified to ICAO as being in charge[55] and which will have a coordinating role.

52. *ICAO Doc.* AN 17.
53. Hailbronner, *supra* (n. 39), 58; McWhinney, *supra* (n. 8).
54. See the *ICAO Security Manual* (*Doc. 8973* – Restricted), part 1: National Organization and Administration. In most States, at least two authorities are involved, namely, the Civil Aviation Administration and the National Police. Furthermore, the Airport Authority or Airport Administration will also have an involvement.
55. Standard 3.1.2 specifies only that the 'appropriate authority' shall be responsible for the development, implementation and maintenance of the NCASP; however, Standards 3.1.5, 3.1.7, and 3.1.8 amplify the scope of responsibilities of the authority, which shall take a key role in coordination of national aviation security activities.

The appropriate authority shall also define and allocate tasks and coordinate activities between and among the departments, agencies, and other organizations of the State, airport, and aircraft operators and other entities concerned by the implementation of the national civil aviation security programme (Standard 3.1.5).[56] A National Civil Aviation Security Committee shall be established for the purpose of coordinating security activities (Standard 3.1.6).[57]

Each airport operator and each aircraft operator shall be required to establish and implement a written security programme for its own operations, which shall meet the requirements of the national programme and which shall be approved by the appropriate authority[58] (Standards 3.2.1 et seq. and 3.3.1).

A national training programme and a national quality control programme shall be established in the framework of the national civil aviation security programme (Standards 3.1.7 and 3.4.1 et seq.).

2. Preventive Security Measures

Chapter 4 deals with aircraft security checks and procedures, screening of passengers and their cabin baggage, and security controls and procedures for hold baggage. It also sets out standards for security controls of cargo, mail, and other goods, and measures relating to special categories of passengers and to access control.

The standards relating to screening of passengers and cabin baggage and those dealing with hold baggage and cargo are the most significant preventive measures. Standard 4.3.1 sets out the principle that all originating passengers and their cabin baggage shall be screened prior to boarding an aircraft engaged in international operations. Standard 4.3.2 provides for adequate security controls for transfer and transit passengers; in this regard, Standard 4.3.3 mandates rescreening if mixing or contact between screened and non-screened persons after the security screening points would otherwise take place.

3. Response Management

Standards 4.4.1 to 4.4.8 and Recommended Practices 4.4.9 to 4.4.10 provide for security control measures and screening for hold baggage. Subchapter 4.7 deals with measures relating to access control. Standard 4.7.1 mandates the establishment of security restricted areas at each international airport and the implementation of procedures and identification systems for persons and vehicles. In regard to the latter, appropriate security controls, including background checks on persons

56. Standard 3.1.5 is the main basis for the coordinating role of the appropriate authority.
57. On the National Committee, see the *ICAO Security Manual, Doc. 8973* – Restricted, Part 1.
58. Such approval requirement is not expressly spelled out in the Annex 17 provisions, but is implied in the terms 'appropriate to meet the requirements of the national civil aviation security programme' set out in Standards 3.2.1 and 3.3.1. In practice, this approval requirement is laid down in national legal provisions of a number of States enacted after the tenth Amendment of Annex 17 was issued.

other than passengers granted unescorted access to security-restricted areas of the airport, shall be implemented.

Chapter 5 of the Annex deals with responses to acts of unlawful interference after they have occurred, or when there is suspicion that they have occurred.

Standards 5.1.1 to 5.1.3 provide the principle that measures and procedures shall be established by each contracting State for safeguarding aircraft on the ground and for inspecting such aircraft, as well as for investigation, in case of well-founded suspicion of an act of unlawful interference, such as concealed explosives or weapons on board.[59]

Standards and Recommended Practices 5.2.1 to 5.2.7 concern the adoption of adequate measures for the safety of passengers and crew of an aircraft subjected to an act of unlawful interference, including assistance while airborne and permission to land. Standard 5.2.4 deals with the standoff situation between aircraft hijackers and police authorities referred to above.[60] It calls for measures to be taken by each contracting State 'to ensure that an aircraft subjected to an act of unlawful seizure that has landed in its territory is detained on the ground unless its departure is necessitated by the overriding duty to protect human life. However, these measures need to recognize the grave hazard attending further flight'. In this regard, Standard 5.2.4 gives more precision to the general obligation in Article 11, paragraph 1, of the Tokyo Convention of 1963 to 'take all appropriate measures to restore control of the aircraft to its lawful commander', in particular as regards the main criteria to be used for these difficult decisions.[61]

Standard 5.3.1 provides for informing ICAO of any security aspects of any act of unlawful interference after it has occurred, and Recommended Practice 5.3.2 deals with the sharing of this information with other contracting States. On this basis, ICAO has created a database on worldwide occurrences of acts of unlawful interference.

B. Other Annexes

It should be noted that certain provisions in other Annexes to the Convention on International Civil Aviation also address important unlawful interference aspects, in particular Annex 2: Rules of the Air, Annex 6: Operation of Aircraft, Annex 9: Facilitation, Annex 10: Aeronautical Telecommunications, Annex 11: Air Traffic

59. Standard 5.1.1 mandates measures for safeguarding aircraft that may be subject to an act of unlawful interference while on the ground; Standard 5.1.2 mandates procedures for inspecting such aircraft; and Standard 5.1.3 mandates arrangements for investigation and disposal of suspected sabotage devices or other potential hazards if such devices or hazards are found.
60. See *supra*, II. A.
61. Standard 5.2.4 provides that: '[e]ach contracting State shall take measures, as it may find practicable, to ensure that an aircraft subjected to an act of unlawful seizure which has landed in its territory is detained on the ground unless its departure is necessitated by the overriding duty to protect human life. However, these measures need to recognize the grave hazard attending further flight. . . . ' .

Services, Annex 13: Aircraft Accident and Incident Investigation, Annex 14: Aerodromes, and Annex 18: The Safe Transport of Dangerous Goods by Air. They concern a number of practically important subject matters, for example, the lockable flight crew compartment door,[62] air operator training programmes,[63] facilitation measures,[64] ATS services to aircraft in the event of an emergency due to unlawful acts of interference,[65] and security measures on aerodromes such as fencing and security lighting.[66] In particular, the security-relevant provisions of Annex 9 – *Facilitation* (see note 64 below) have recently been emphasized as important for reconciling screening measures at airports with the need to ensure the smooth flow of passengers, baggage, and cargo. The security-relevant provisions of Annex 9 and other related standards and recommended practices (SARPs) are set out in the Attachment to Annex 17.

Detailed guidance on the application of the provisions in Annex 17 and other Annexes is provided in the ICAO Security Manual.[67]

IV. LEGAL MANAGEMENT AFTER 11 SEPTEMBER 2001

A. ICAO Assembly Resolution A33-1

The implications of the terrorist attacks of 11 September 2001 were the subject of extensive discussions at the thirty-third session of the ICAO Assembly held from 25 September to 5 October 2001.[68]

In its Resolution A33-1: *Declaration on misuse of civil aircraft as weapons of destruction and other terrorist acts involving civil aviation*,[69] the Assembly strongly condemned these terrorist acts declaring that such acts using civil aircraft as weapons of destruction are contrary to the Convention on International Civil Aviation, in particular its Preamble, Article 4 and Article 44.[70] It also urged contracting States to hold accountable and punish severely those responsible for

62. Annex 6 – *Operations of Aircraft*, Part I – *International Commercial Air Transport – Aeroplanes*, Ch. 13: Security, Standard 13. 1.
63. Annex 6, Standards 13.3.1–13.3.2.
64. Annex 9 – *Facilitation, ICAO Doc.* AN 9, Standards 2.2, 3.2, 3.33–3.34, 4.2, 4.13–4.17, 4.48–4.53, 6.1, Recommended Practices 6.22–6.23, 6.34, 6.44, 6.46, 8.2.
65. Annex 11 – *Air Traffic Services, ICAO Doc.* AN 11, Standards 2.22.1–2.22.2 and Ch. 5. See also Annex 10 – *Aeronautical Telecommunications*, *ICAO Doc.* AN 10, Standards 2.1.4.2.1, 2.1.4.2.3, and 2.1.4.3.
66. Annex 14 – *Aerodromes*, vol. I – *Aerodrome Design and Operations*, Standards 8.4.2–8.4.3 and Recommended Practices 8.4.4–8.4.5 and 8.5.
67. Security Manual for Safeguarding Civil Aviation against Acts of Unlawful Interference, *ICAO Doc.* 8973 – Restricted, 7th revised edn 2008 (five volumes).
68. For a summary, see L. Weber & A. Jakob, 'Activities of the International Civil Aviation Organization (ICAO)', *AnnASL* XXVII (2002): 326 et seq.
69. Assembly Resolutions in Force, *ICAO Doc.* 9790, VII – 1. The current version is contained in: *Resolutions adopted at the 37th Session of the Assembly (Provisional Edition), November 2010*
70. A33-1, Operating Clause 2. See Weber, *supra.* (n. 3), 7.

planning and organizing such acts or for aiding, supporting, or harbouring the perpetrators, and to take within their territories appropriate additional security measures commensurate with the level of threat so as to prevent and eradicate terrorist acts involving civil aviation.

Resolution A33-1 also initiated establishment of an ICAO Universal Security Oversight Audit Programme (USAP) and other measures, and directed the Council to convene at the earliest date a high-level ministerial Conference on aviation security.[71]

B. War-Risk Insurance

Further, Resolution A33-20: *Coordinated approach in providing assistance in the field of aviation war risk insurance* dealt with the problems created by the sudden worldwide cancellation of war risk-insurance coverage for commercial airlines by the aviation insurance market as a reaction to the 11 September events, and initiated a plan for coordinated governmental assistance in this field[72]. As a result of the cancellation of war risk insurance, airlines worldwide were on the verge of halting operations because of domestic legal requirements and also in some cases because of airline board decisions.[73] In light of this development, the President of the ICAO Council appealed to all contracting States by a letter of 21 September 2001 to take the necessary measures to support airline operators and other parties by providing a commitment to cover remaining risks until such time as the insurance markets stabilize.[74] Many States issued temporary commitment letters to their airlines to prevent them from ceasing to operate.[75]

Consequently, the ICAO Secretariat assisted by a study group developed the 'Globaltime' concept, which was approved by the ICAO Council.[76] It provided for the establishment of a global fund operated by a non-profit special-purpose insurance entity under the auspices of ICAO, which would provide non-cancellable third-party aviation war-risk insurance coverage. The scheme was to be funded by insurance premiums collected from participating operators and other insured parties and would be backed by participating State guarantees.[77]

71. A33-1, Operating Clauses 7 and 8.
72. A33-20, *ICAO Doc.* 9790, V-6. See also Weber & Jakob, *supra* (n. 68), 326 and Attachment II.
73. See Working Paper A33-WP/255 – Information and Proposal on Third Party War Risk Insurance, 1 Oct. 2001, presented by IATA. War risk insurance was subsequently reinstated gradually by insurers, but only up to a fraction of the previously available amounts (up to USD 50 million) and against payment of vastly increased premiums. See also R. Margo, 'War Risk Insurance in the Aftermath of September 11', *Air & Space Lawyer* 18 (2003): 1 et seq.
74. See on this matter Weber & Jakob, 'Activities of the International Civil Aviation Organization (ICAO)', *AnnASL* XXIX (2002): 325–365, at 326; Weber & Jakob, 'Activities of the International Civil Aviation Organization (ICAO) in 2002/2003', *AnnASL* XXX (2003): 397–419.
75. A33-20, Seventh Whereas Clause and Second Operating Clause.
76. Council Decision C-DEC 166/4 (28 May 2002).
77. See State Letter LE 4/64-02/55 dated 6 Jun. 2002 and Attachments.

Commencement of Globaltime was conditional upon signature of the Participation Agreement by a sufficient number of States.[78] While the majority of ICAO contracting States signed up by May 2003, the largest contributors (the United States and Japan) refrained from doing so. Therefore, the required threshold for commencement was not reached. However, the Globaltime concept, which is kept dormant, could be activated at any time when needed as a result of sudden cancellation of war risk insurance for aviation operators.

C. Aviation Security Plan of Action

The high-level Ministerial Conference on Aviation Security from 19 to 20 February 2002 agreed on an Aviation Security Plan of Action which was subsequently approved by the ICAO Council[79] in June 2002. The main element of the Plan of Action was the development and implementation of the ICAO Universal Security Audit Programme USAP, to identify and correct deficiencies in the implementation of ICAO security-related standards, along the lines of the already existing ICAO USOAP Audit Programme on safety.

Other elements of the Aviation Security Plan of Action include the following:

(a) development of an effective global response to new and emerging threats, integrating timely measures in specific fields, including airports, aircraft, and air traffic control systems;
(b) strengthening of the security-related provisions in the Annexes to the Convention on International Civil Aviation, using expedited procedures when warranted and subject to overall safety considerations, notably to provide for protection of the flight deck;
(c) close coordination and coherence with audit programmes at the regional and sub-regional level;
(d) processing of the results of the audits by ICAO in a way which reconciles confidentiality and transparency; and
(e) a follow-up programme to assist States in remedying deficiencies in their aviation security capabilities.

This Action Plan has been implemented by ICAO since 2002, resulting in a first cycle of USAP audits during 2002–2004, a second audit cycle during 2005–2007, and a follow-up cycle since 2008. Other important elements of the Action Plan were amendments to security-related ICAO SARPs, increased transparency of USAP audit results, and the establishment of cooperative programmes under ICAO auspices to assist States in remedying deficiencies.

78. Commencement of Globaltime was made conditional upon the signature by a sufficient number of States the sum of whose contribution rates to ICAO should amount to at least 51%, in accordance with A33-26.
79. Council Decisions C-DEC 166/3 and 166/14 (20/6/2002); C-WP 11799 and Discussion Paper No.1.

D. Universal Security Audit Programme

The ICAO USAP provides for regular, mandatory, systematic, and harmonized audits of all ICAO contracting States to promote global aviation security. It aims at an evaluation of aviation security in place in all ICAO contracting States and at identifying and correcting any deficiencies in the implementation of ICAO standards relating to aviation security.[80]

The USAP audits carried out by ICAO review and evaluate each State's aviation security oversight capability as well as the security measures in place at selected airports. The evaluation makes use of eight critical elements of a State's security oversight system, including aviation security legislation, aviation security programmes and regulations, appropriate State authority for aviation security and its responsibilities, personnel qualifications and training, and provision of technical guidance, tools, and security critical information. Obligations relating to certification, approval, and quality control are also evaluated.

In accordance with the Audit Protocol established for USAP audits, audited areas comprise the regulatory framework and the national civil aviation security system, training of personnel, quality control functions, airport operations, aircraft and in-flight security, passenger and baggage security, cargo, catering and mail security, response to acts of unlawful interference, and security aspects of facilitation. An important element evaluated by each audit is the National Civil Aviation Security Programme, in conjunction with the National Quality Control Programme, the National Training Programme and the organization of the appropriate National Authority responsible for aviation security.

By the end of 2007, 181 States had been audited under the USAP programme, and 172 States were the subject of follow-up visits, which were carried out to ascertain progress in the removal of deficiencies. From 2008 to 2010, 100 further audits took place. In its report to the thirty-sixth ICAO Assembly, the Council indicated that the USAP follow-up missions 'have validated a markedly increased level of implementation of ICAO Security Standards, thereby attesting to states' commitment to achieving the objective of the USAP to strengthen aviation security worldwide'.[81]

E. Domestic Legislation

In the aftermath of the events of 11 September 2001, a number of States considered it important to adopt national legislation on aviation security. In particular, the United

80. See Assembly – 37th Session, Executive Committee, A37-WP/32 EX/12; 36th Session, Executive Committee, A36-WP/55 EX/16.
81. Assembly – 36th Session, Executive Committee, *A36-WP/38 EX/9*, 4. For example, as regards national organization and administration, the follow-up audits found an increase in compliance of 24% of audited States. Similarly, as regards certification of screening personnel, the follow-up audits found an increase of 23%. For oversight and enforcement capabilities, the increase was 19%, for training the figure was also 19%. In each case, the difference in the number of fully compliant States between the first audit and the follow-up audit was measured. See also more recently A37-WP/32 EX/12.

States adopted the Aviation and Transportation Security Act of 2001,[82] followed by the Homeland Security Act of 2002.[83] The United Kingdom passed the Antiterrorism, Crime and Security Act 2001[84] (ATCSA), Germany adopted the Aviation Security Act (*Luftsicherheitsgesetz*)[85] of 2005, and France issued a number of decrees, decisions, and ordinances.[86] Similarly, in 2002, the European Union (EU) adopted Regulation No. 2320/2002 establishing common rules in the field of civil aviation security[87] which was later replaced in 2008 by Regulation (EC) No. 300/2008 on common rules in the field of aviation security and repealing Regulation No. 2320/2002.[88] It was supplemented by Commission Regulation (EU) No. 185/2010 of 4 March 2010. Many other States also took legislative measures.

The domestic legislation served in many cases to establish for the first time legal rules on preventive measures such as passenger and baggage screening and its organizational aspects, airline and airport security measures, and to give the authorities a proper legal basis to act. Some States included rules on response management regarding acts of unlawful interference going beyond the Annex 17 rules and related guidance material, including provisions regarding the use of force against aircraft in flight. These latter provisions have given rise to significant legal issues regarding fundamental rights, and certain rules have meanwhile been struck down by the courts.

F. Cooperative Programmes

As a result of ICAO Assembly Resolution A33-1 and the Conclusions and Recommendations of the high-level Ministerial Conference on Aviation

---

82. *Pub. L. 107-71* (19 Nov. 2001). The Act mandated that the airport security function, previously exercised by the airlines under FAA supervision, be fully returned to federal authorities.
83. *49 U.S.C. 114* (2002). For the transfer of the airport security function from the FAA to the TSA, see *49 U.S.C. 45107* (2002).
84. 2001 Ch. 24; see also the earlier UK *Aviation and Maritime Security Act 1990;* the ATCSA was supplemented by the *Prevention of Terrorism Act 2005* of 11 Mar. 2005 (2005, Ch. 2).
85. Luftsicherheitsgesetz of 11 Jan. 2005, *BGBl.* I, 78, amended 5 Jan. 2007, *BGBl.* I. 2–7.
86. *Décret No. 2002-24 du 3 janvier 2002 relatif à la police de l'exploitation des aérodromes et modifiant le code de l'aviation civile; Décret No. 2002-1026 du 31 juillet 2002 relatif à certaines mesures de sûreté et de sécurité du transport aérien et modifiant le code de l'aviation civile; Arrêté du 1er septembre 2003 relatif aux infrastructures, équipements et formations en matière de sûreté du transport aérien ainsi qu'à certaines modalités d'exercice des agréments en qualité d'agent habilité, de chargeur connu, d'établissement connu et d'organisme technique; Arrêté du 12 novembre 2002 relatif aux mesures de sûreté du transport aérien; Arrêté du 28 juin 2005 relatif aux procédures de certification des équipements de détection utilisés pour la sûreté du transport aérien; Ordonnance No. 2005-863 du 28 juillet 2005 relative à la sûreté des vols et à la sécurité de l'exploitation des aérodromes; Arrêté du 2 novembre 2006 modifiant l'arrêté du 12 novembre 2003 relatif aux mesures de sûreté du transport aérien.*
87. *Regulation (EC) No. 2320/2002 of the European Parliament and of the Council of 16 Dec. 2002 establishing common rules in the field of civil aviation security, OJ* No. L 355/1 (30 Dec. 2002).
88. *Regulation (EC) No. 300/2008 of the European Parliament and of the Council of 11 Mar. 2008 on common rules in the field of aviation security and repealing Regulation (EC) No. 2320/2002, OJ* No. L 97 (9 Apr. 2008).

Security,[89] which called for cooperative action, including technical cooperation, the Cooperative Aviation Security Programme Asia Pacific (CASP-AP) was established under the auspices of ICAO in August 2004.[90] It comprised initially fourteen ICAO Member States/administrations in the Asia-Pacific region, and has since grown to a membership of twenty-four States/administrations. Two similar programmes have also been set up in the African region.

The main objective of these cooperative programmes is to assist its members in ensuring compliance with the international aviation security conventions, ICAO SARPs, and related guidance material on aviation security by enhancing the aviation security capabilities of Member States. In the case of CASP-AP, it also aims to achieve a greater degree of harmonization in aviation security matters by creating an aviation security standing structure for Aviation Security (AVSEC) information exchange, cooperation, and coordination, as well as for the training of aviation security personnel.[91]

The CASP-AP programme is governed by a Steering Committee, composed of representatives of all members, and implemented by a Programme Coordinator Office located in Bangkok, Thailand. The financial and human resources of the programme are administered by ICAO.[92]

It is envisaged that similar cooperative programmes also be implemented in other parts of the world where such a need for Member States arises.

V. UNRULY PASSENGERS

The issue of unruly or disruptive passengers concerns offences committed on board aircraft that do not reach the seriousness of acts of unlawful interference. Typical examples are smoking on board aircraft, drinking alcohol resulting in intoxication, refusal to follow instructions by the crew, physical or verbal assault of other passengers or of cabin crewmembers, tampering with safety devices on board, and so on.

These offences do not constitute acts of unlawful interference and do, therefore, generally not fall within the ambit of aviation security regulation. Nevertheless, their rapid increase in the 1990s posed major problems of a practical, regulatory, and legal nature, particularly for the international airlines.[93] At the request of the International Air Transport Association (IATA), the ICAO Council

89. High-level Ministerial Conference on Aviation Security, Montreal 19–20 Feb. 2002, Report. For the Declaration of the Conference, see *AnnASL* XXVI (2001): 441.
90. ICAO Programme Document for the Cooperative Aviation Security Programme: Asia and Pacific Region, 2004 (Restricted).
91. The main purpose of the Standing Structure (CASS) is to promote implementation of Standards 2.3.2 to 2.3.5 and Recommended Practices 2.3.6 and 2.3.8 of Annex 17, which are sometimes neglected.
92. ICAO is the Executing Agency of the Programme. See the Programme Document *supra* (n. 90).
93. See Guidance Material on the Legal Aspects of Unruly/Disruptive Passengers, *ICAO Circular 288* – LE/1 (June 2002), 1.

decided in 1996 to put this subject on the agenda of the ICAO Legal Committee.[94] After review by a Secretariat Study Group, the ICAO Secretariat assisted by the Study Group developed Model Legislation on Certain Offenses Committed on Board Civil Aircraft as guidance material for all ICAO contracting States.[95] In 2001, the thirty-third ICAO Assembly recommended the Model Legislation to contracting States for adoption under national law in Resolution A33-4: Adoption of national legislation on certain offences committed on board civil aircraft (unruly/disruptive passengers[96]). The Model Legislation is set out in the Appendix to this Resolution.[97] A number of contracting States have since incorporated the legislation wholly or in part into their national legislation.

Additionally, the ICAO Secretariat developed guidance material on unruly passengers in ICAO Circular 288: Guidance Material on Legal Aspects of Unruly/ Disruptive Passengers.[98]

VI. CURRENT DEVELOPMENTS IN AVIATION SECURITY

A. General

Since it was set up in 2002, the ICAO USAP audit programme, which verifies oversight capability and implementation at national level, has resulted in measurable improvements.[99] States have placed high priority on aviation security in the post 11 September environment and have committed increasing resources to security measures. Follow-up audits, which are part of the USAP programme, have shown that the overall level of implementation has significantly increased,[100] and the absolute number of acts of unlawful interference has decreased.[101]

B. Risk Assessment Concept

A recent amendment to Standard 3.1.3 of Annex 17 has introduced risk assessment as a formal, systematic concept into security methodology,[102] although it was

94. See *ICAO Circular 288* – LE/1, 2; Weber & Jakob, *supra* (n. 68), 328.
95. *ICAO Circular 288* – LE/1, Appendix.
96. *ICAO Doc.* 9848, Assembly Resolutions in Force (as of 8 Oct. 2004), V – 4 .
97. A33-4, Appendix, *infra* (n. 98).
98. *ICAO Circular* 288 – LE/1.
99. ICAO, Assembly-36th Session, Report on the ICAO Universal Security Audit Programme: Analysis of Audit Findings, *Doc. A36-WP/38 EX/9* (1 Aug. 2007); Addendum No. 1 (2 Aug. 2007).
100. See Appendix C to *Doc. A36-WP/38 EX/9*, Appendix N.1 (2 Aug. 2007).
101. See ICAO, Assembly-36th Session, Developments in the Aviation Security Programme since the 35th Session of the Assembly, *Doc.* A36-WP/55 EX/16, Appendix B, Chart A: *Acts of Unlawful Interference for 2004–2006 compared to 1990–2006.* See also A37-WP/32 EX/12, Appendices.
102. See Amendment 11 to Annex 17, of 30 Nov. 2005, applicable since 1 Jul. 2006 (*Doc. AN 17*).

previously used in practice. The concept provides that each contracting State shall keep under constant review the level of threat to civil aviation within its territory, and establish and implement policies and procedures to adjust relevant elements of its national civil aviation security programme accordingly, based upon a security risk assessment carried out by the relevant national authorities.[103] The methodology for the risk assessment is laid down in the ICAO Security Manual, Doc. 8973.[104]

As unidentified hold baggage and cargo and mail on all-cargo flights are not regulated by standards, the risk assessment concept is particularly important for these categories. In accordance with Recommended Practices 4.5.6 and 4.6.6, each contracting State should establish procedures to deal with unidentified baggage in accordance with a security risk assessment carried out by the national authorities;[105] it should also ensure that security controls to be applied to cargo and mail for transportation on all-cargo aircraft are determined on the basis of a security risk assessment carried out by the relevant authorities.[106]

C. Sky Marshals

Standards 4.7.5, 4.7.7, and 4.7.8 of Annex 17 as amended now regulate the status of the 'In-Flight Security Officer' (IFSO), also referred to as Sky Marshal. The standards provide that only specially selected and trained government personnel shall be deployed as IFSOs, taking into account the safety and security aspects on board an aircraft,[107] which means that private sector outsourcing shall not be applied for such activities, not even in the form of a mandated third party.

The deployment of IFSOs shall be coordinated with the authorities of the state of destination of every flight, since it is important for these authorities to be informed of the deployment in advance of the arrival of the flight.[108]

Furthermore, each deployment is to be treated as strictly confidential;[109] however, the aircraft commander is to be informed of the deployment and the seating of each IFSO in advance of the flight. Special rules in Annex 17 apply with regard to the handling, storage, and use of firearms by IFSOs and other authorized personnel,[110] which were previously regulated on a bilateral or ad hoc basis and which have given rise to a number of problems.

103. Standard 3.1.3 of Annex 17.
104. Security Manual for Safeguarding Civil Aviation Against Acts of Unlawful Interference, *ICAO Doc.* 8973 – Restricted (7th edn 2008), Vol. V Chapt.5, and Appendices 2 and 3.
105. Recommended Practice 4.5.6 of Annex 17.
106. Recommended Practice 4.6.6 of Annex 17. The provisions regarding air cargo screening will be the subject of modifications in the forthcoming Amendment 12 to Annex 17 (effectiveness date 1 July 2011).
107. Standard 4.7.7 of Annex 17.
108. Standard 4.7.7, second Sentence, in conjunction with standard 4.7.5 of Annex 17.
109. Standard 4.7.7, second Sentence, of Annex 17.
110. Standards 4.7.4 to 4.7.6 and 4.7.8 of Annex 17.

D. Liquids, Aerosols, and Gels

After the foiled terrorist attack of August 2006 in London, the ICAO Council issued recommendations in December 2006 restricting the acceptance of liquids, gels, and aerosols (LAGs) in cabin baggage on board aircraft.[111] National implementing rules as well as EC Regulations generally provided for a ban of more than 100 ml of LAGs on board, but were not uniform. Further recommendations were issued by the ICAO Council in March and July 2007,[112] which provided for exceptions for LAGs transported in Security Tamper-evident Bags (STEBs); duty-free items carried in STEBs were to be allowed on board. However, these recommendations were not uniformly applied in national implementing rules and practices, particularly at points of transit.

Consequently, there is a need for further action to render treatment of LAGs uniform, including with regard to duty-free items and authorities' practices at points of transit.[113]

E. Air Cargo Security and Comprehensive AVSEC Strategy

On 29 October 2010, terrorists attempted to insert improvised explosive devices (IED's) into the air cargo supply chain. This plot was foiled, but illustrated the need to strengthen air cargo security measures.[114]

Amendment 12 to Annex 17, which is to become effective on 1 July 2011, introduces a number of changes to chapter 4.6 of Annex 17 with a view to strengthening air cargo security. Furthermore, the ICAO AVSEC Panel is actively working on further additional measures regarding cargo which would be rigorous, consistent, and practical, without hindering international trade.

At the 37th Session of the ICAO Assembly, an ICAO Comprehensive Aviation Security Strategy (ICASS) was adopted which sets forth a Strategic Plan of Action for 2011–2016.[115]

The strategy focuses on seven areas, namely:

(i) Addressing new and existing threats;
(ii) Promoting innovative, effective, and efficient security approaches;
(iii) Promoting the sharing of security relevant information;
(iv) Promoting global compliance and establishing sustainable aviation security oversight capability of States;

111. ICAO State Letter AS 8/11-06/100 dated 1 Dec. 2006 (Confidential).
112. ICAO State Letters AS 8/11-07/26 dated 30 Mar. 2007 and AS 8/11 -07/53 dated 6 Jul. 2007 (Confidential).
113. See on this matter also: ICAO Assembly – 36th Session, A36-WP/171 EX/60 (Singapore) and A36-WP/118 EX/47 (Airports Council International); more recently AVSECP/22-WP/9 (14/03/11, restr.)
114. Strengthening International Air Cargo Security, AVSECP/22-WP/14 (18/3/11)
115. Assembly – 37th Session, A37-WP/18 (28/06/10).

(v) Improving human factors and security culture;
(vi) Promoting the development of mutual recognition for aviation security processes;
(vii) Emphasizing the importance of security among States and Stakeholder.

These focus areas will therefore guide the action of the Organization and of Member States in the period until 2016.

Part II

EU Aviation Law (Selected Issues)

Chapter 8
The European Organization of Aviation

Elmar M. Giemulla and Heiko van Schyndel

I. EC/EU

A. Establishment and Organization

The European Economic Community (EEC), which has been called the European Community (EC) since the entry into force of the Treaty of Maastricht on European Union (TEU) of 7 February 1992[1] and is called European Union (EU) since the entry into force of the Treaty of Lisbon amending the Treaty on European Union and the Treaty establishing the European Community of 13 December 2007[2] was founded in 1957 with the objective of bringing about the economic and political integration of Europe (Treaty of 25 March 1957).[3] It became the most important of the three European Communities established by the Treaties of Rome (EEC[4], ECSC[5], and EAEC, or Euratom[6]) for the continuous European unification process.

1. *OJ* No. C 191 of 29 Jul. 1992, 1. In Germany: *BGBl.* II, 1251, 1252 et seq., in force since 1 Nov. 1993, *BGBl.* 1993 II, 1947.
2. *OJ* No. C 306 of 17 Dec. 2007, 1. In force since 1 Dec. 2009.
3. In Germany: *BGBl.* II, 766.
4. <http://eur-lex.europa.eu/en/treaties/dat/11957E/tif/TRAITES_1957_CEE_1_EN_0001.tif>.
5. <http://eur-lex.europa.eu/en/treaties/dat/11951K/tif/TRAITES_1951_CECA_1_EN_0001.tif>.
6. <http://eur-lex.europa.eu/en/treaties/dat/11957K/tif/TRAITES_1957_EURATOM_1_EN_0001.tif>.

Elmar M. Giemulla & Ludwig Weber, *International and EU Aviation Law: Selected Issues*, pp. 309–332.

The Treaty of Lisbon was, up to this day, the greatest amendment and supplementation of the Treaties of Rome in the course of the further expansion of Europe. The aim of the Treaty is a unified, fully integrated, permanent, and functional union of the EU Member States. The Treaty of Lisbon merged the European Union and the European Community into a single European Union. The word 'Community' was replaced by the word 'Union'. The European Union replaces and succeeds the European Community. Union law is shaped by the following three Treaties: Treaty on European Union[7] (TEU), Treaty on the Functioning of the European Union[8] (TFEU), and Treaty establishing the European Atomic Energy Community[9] EAEC, or Euratom.

At the moment, the EU/EC has twenty-seven Member States, namely:

> Austria, Belgium, Bulgaria, Cyprus, the Czech Republic, Denmark, Estonia, Finland, France, Germany, Great Britain, Greece, Hungary, Ireland, Italy, Latvia, Lithuania, Luxemburg, Malta, the Netherlands, Poland, Portugal, Romania, Slovakia, Slovenia, Spain, and Sweden.

EFTA[10] States, such as Iceland, Liechtenstein, and Norway are connected to the EU through the European Economic Area (EEA) established according to the Agreement on the European Economic Area[11].

Pursuant to Article 13, paragraph 1 TEU, the common bodies of the EU are the following:

- The *European Parliament* shall, jointly with the Council, exercise legislative and budgetary functions. It shall exercise functions of political control and consultation as laid down in the Treaties. It shall elect the President of the Commission (Article 14, paragraph 1 TEU). It has been elected directly since 1979;
- the *European Council*, which consists of the Heads of State or Government of the Member States, together with its President and the President of the Commission (Article 15, paragraph 2), shall provide the Union with the necessary impetus for its development and shall define the general political directions and priorities thereof. It shall not exercise legislative functions (Article 15, paragraph 1 TEU);
- The *Council* is made up of representatives of the governments of the Member States at ministerial level, who may commit the government of the Member State in question and cast its vote. The Council shall, jointly with the European Parliament, exercise legislative and budgetary functions. It shall carry out policy-making and coordinating functions as laid down in the Treaties (Article 16, paragraph 1 TEU);

7. *OJ* No. C 83 of 30 Mar. 2010, 13.
8. *OJ* No. C 83 of 30 Mar. 2010, 47.
9. <http://eur-lex.europa.eu/en/treaties/dat/11957K/tif/TRAITES_1957_EURATOM_1_EN_0001.tif>.
10. *EFTA* – European Free Trade Association.
11. *OJ* No L 1 of 3 Jan. 1994, 3.

- the *European Commission* is the executive body of the EU. Amongst others, it shall ensure the application of the Treaties, and of measures adopted by the institutions pursuant to them, oversee the application of Union law under the control of the Court of Justice of the EU, execute the budget and manage programmes and exercise coordinating, executive and management functions, as laid down in the Treaties (Article 17, paragraph 1 TEU);
- the *Court of Justice of the European Union* (Court of Justice, the General Court and specialized courts) ensures that in the interpretation and application of the Treaties the law is observed (Article 19, paragraph 1 TEU);
- The task of the *European Central Bank* (Articles 129 and 130 TFEU) is to maintain the stability of the European currency, the euro, and control the amount of currency in circulation (Article 128 TFEU)
- the *Court of Auditors* examines the accounts of all revenue and expenditure (Articles 285 and 286 TFEU).

What is important for aviation is the fact that the Commission established a Joint Committee on Civil Aviation (Commission Decision of 30 July 1990[12]) for support of the Commission in planning and implementation of common civil aviation policies. This Committee was replaced by Commission Decision of 20 May 1998, on the establishment of Sectoral Dialogue Committees promoting the dialogue between the social partners at the European level.[13]

B. Responsibilities and Objectives

Under Article 3 TEU, the Union shall establish an internal market, work for the sustainable development of Europe based on balanced economic growth and price stability, a highly competitive social market economy, aiming at full employment and social progress, and a high level of protection and improvement of the quality of the environment and promote scientific and technological advance.

In this context, the activities of the EU also include a common policy in the sphere of transport (Article 90 TFEU), which the Member States are to follow in the sense of the objectives of the Treaty and supervised by the Commission (Article 105 TFEU). The former dispute on the direct application of the predecessor of the TFEU, the Treaty establishing the European Community (ECT),[14] to sea and air transport has been decided by the ECJ in the sense of a universal application of the ECT for all industries and thereby also for aviation, unless exceptions are permitted (e.g., Article 51, paragraphs 1 and 80 paragraph 2 EC (now: Article 58, paragraphs 1 and 100 paragraph 2 TFEU)).[15] This is especially relevant for application of competition rules of Articles 101 et seq. TFEU. Furthermore, the Council – now by qualified majority (Article 16 of the Single European Act [SEA] of

12. *OJ* No. L 230 of 24 Aug. 1990, 22.
13. *OJ* No. L 225 of 12 Aug. 1998, 27.
14. *OJ* No. C 325 of 24 Dec. 2002, 33.
15. *ECJ-ECR,* 1986, 1425–1473; ECJ judgment of 11 Apr. 1989 – Ad: 66/86, *NJW* (1989), 2192.

28 February 1986[16]) – decides 'whether, to what extent, and by what procedure appropriate provisions may be laid down for sea and air transport' (Article 100, paragraph 2 TFEU). Taking into consideration the particularities of air transport, the Council will lay down the following provisions for common aviation policies:

- common rules applicable to international transport to or from the territory of a Member State or passing across the territory of one or more Member States;
- the conditions under which non-resident carriers may operate transport services within a Member State;
- measures to improve transport safety; and
- any other appropriate provisions (Articles 100, paragraph 2, Sentence 2 and 91 paragraph 1 TFEU).

Provisions on the principles of the regulatory system for transport, whose application may seriously threaten the standard of living and employment situation in certain areas as well as operation of transport systems, require a unanimous Council decision. The Council has to take into consideration the necessity of adapting such provisions to the economic development resulting from the establishment of the Common Market (Articles 100, paragraph 2, Sentence 2 and 91, paragraph 3 TFEU).

The principle of subsidiarity (Article 5 TEU) applies to those Council activities which were included in the TEU as an obligation for all activities of the EU. The German Federal Constitutional Court has particularly emphasized the significance of this principle in its Fundamental Decision on the TEU of 12 October 1993.[17]

The principle of subsidiarity basically defines task sharing between the Union and the Member States following the principles:

- of conferred powers, according to which the Union shall act within the limits of the powers conferred upon it by the TEU and TFEU and of the objectives assigned to it therein (Article 4, paragraph 1 TEU);
- of subsidiarity, according to which the Union shall take action in areas which do not fall within its exclusive competence only if and insofar as the objectives of the proposed action cannot be sufficiently achieved by the Member States and can, therefore, by reason of the scale or effects of the proposed action, be better achieved by the Union (Article 5, paragraph 3 TEU); and
- of proportionality, according to which any action by the Union shall not go beyond what is necessary to achieve the objectives of the Treaty (Article 5, paragraph 4 TEU).

For the area of transport, which is essential for positive development of trade and economy, prima facie evidence supports a regulation competence of the Union. The ECJ has always affirmed this for the area of transport as a whole and also for air traffic in particular, although its main focus is on traffic beyond the geographic

16. *OJ* No. L 169 of 29 Jun. 1987. In Germany: *BGBl.* 1986 II, 1102.
17. German Federal Constitutional Court 89, 155 – Maastricht-decision.

area of the EC. After many previous Commission suggestions, the Council decided to establish a 'free market without quantitative limitations' in the area of European inland transport by 1992 since the fundamental and influential ECJ Decision of 30 April 1984, in which it declared the International Air Transport Association (IATA) tariff setting to be incompatible with the competition regulations of the ECT that also apply to scheduled air transport[18] and since the SEA[19] on the establishment of an EC internal market adopted by the heads of government on 14 November 1985.

Since 1987, the EU Ministers of Transport have adopted a whole package of liberalization decisions in the area of air traffic in three steps, especially on the applicability of the EU competition provisions as well as capacity distribution, market access, and fare policy. They aim at loosening national framework conditions and allow for more competition in inner-Union air transport. Especially, operating conditions and admission standards have been mainly harmonized, and the European aviation market has been opened more and more to Union air carriers. These regulations have made bilateralism maintained in air transport with third States outside the EU more and more difficult, since liberalized market conditions mean that joint ventures can gain access to these services more easily and, therefore, could avoid bilateral limitations.[20]

Already when the Commission had taken the last measures to complete the European internal market it wanted to hold negotiations with third States in the name of the Member States in the future. However, neither the Council nor the Member States gave the appropriate mandate to the Commission. Quite the opposite: some EC Member States (Austria, Belgium, Denmark, Finland, Germany, Great Britain, Luxemburg, and Sweden) concluded Open Skies Agreements with the US. The Commission then filed a claim against these eight Member States at the ECJ in December 1998 so as to finally decide the question of competence for concluding international aviation agreements. With its decisions of 5 November 2001,[21] the ECJ ruled that the Member States had violated their obligations from Articles 10 and 43 EC (now: e.g., Articles 20 TFEU), as well as from Council (EEC) Regulation No. 2409/92 of 23 July 1992 on fares and rates for air services,[22] and No. 2299/89 of 24 July 1989 on a code of conduct for computerized reservation systems[23] in the version of the Council (EEC) Regulation No. 3089/93 of 29 October 1993,[24] and that they entered international obligations with the US through agreements

18. *ECJ-ECR,* 1986, 1425-1473, *NJW* (1986), 218.
19. *OJ* No. L 169 of 29 Jun. 1987. In Germany: *BGBl.* 1986 II, 1102 et seq., 1104 et seq.
20. For more details, see the chapter on 'International Public Law'.
21. Case C-466/98, *Commission v. United Kingdom,* [2002] ECR 1-9427; C-467/98, *Commission v. Denmark,* [2002] ECR I-9519; C-468/98, *Commission v. Sweden,* [2002] ECR I -9575; C-469/98, *Commission v. Finland*; C-471, [2002] ECR I -9626, *Commission v. Belgium,* [2002] ECR I-9681; C-472/98, *Commission v. Luxemburg,* [2002] ECR I -9741; C-475/98, *Commission v. Austria,* [2002] ECR I -9797; C-476/98, *Commission v. Germany,* [2002] ECR I -9855.
22. *OJ* No. L 240 of 24 Aug. 1992, 15.
23. *OJ* No. L 220 of 24 Jul. 1992, 1.
24. *OJ* No. L 278 of 11 Nov. 1993, 1.

- which affect the fares of air carriers designated by the US on routes in the Union;
- which affect the computerized reservation systems offered or used in the Member States; and
- which grant the US the right to revoke, cancel, or limit traffic rights when the air carriers designated by the Member States are not owned by such Member States or citizens of such Member States.

It can be summarized that the ECJ decisions only assumed exclusive competence of the Union for certain areas:

(1) for the area of fares for air traffic within the Union.
(2) for the area of computerized reservation systems.
(3) for the area of provisions affecting the right of establishment in accordance with Articles 326 et seq. TFEU.

Otherwise, competence remains with the Member States due to the principle of subsidiarity of Article 5, paragraph 3 TEU.

Council regulations published in the *Official Journal of the European Union* are generally binding and directly applicable in each Member State (Article 288, paragraph 2 TFEU, Article 80, paragraph 3 Basic Law of the Federal Republic of Germany). Council or Commission Directives are published in every Member State concerned and are binding for such States with regard to the objective to be achieved; however, they leave the form and means of implementation up to the States (Article 288, paragraph 3 EC). However, if such Directive includes regulations for the benefit of EU citizens, any Member State that does not implement such Directive in time or not completely is liable for damages.[25] The addressees are notified of decisions that can be made by the Council and the Commission, and such decisions are binding for them in all parts (Article 288, paragraph 4 EC). Recommendations and opinions are not binding (Article 288, paragraph 5 EC).

II. EUROPEAN CIVIL AVIATION CONFERENCE (ECAC)

A. Establishment, Objectives, and Responsibilities

The first efforts of multilateral coordination of European air traffic date back all the way to 1951. Back then, the Council of Europe Consultative Assembly had been presented with three proposals on how to realize this goal:

- the French plan (*Bonnefous* Plan) for a European Transportation Authority;
- an Italian proposal, the *Sforza* Plan for the establishment of a common European airspace organization, a supranational aviation authority, and a European air carrier for air traffic in Europe; and

25. *ECJ-ECR* (1991), 5414.

- its own report by the Council of Europe, developed by the Economic Committee, which recommended a conference to assess the possibility of founding one single European organization that could take over air services between the Member States under certain circumstances.

On 19 March 1953, the Committee of Ministers of the Council of Europe decided to request such a conference being called. On 15 December 1953, the Council of the International Civil Aviation Organization (ICAO) then decided to call a Conference on Conference on Coordination of Air Transport in Europe (CATE) in Strasburg, the seat of the Council of Europe. The conference was held from 20 April to 8 May 1954. A German delegation also attended the conference, although Germany had not yet regained its air sovereignty at that time. A recommendation for founding the ECAC was adopted to continue the work on coordinating air traffic in Europe that had been started during the conference.

The constituent conference of the ECAC was held at the end of 1955, again in Strasbourg. The following tasks were defined for the ECAC:[26]

- general development of air traffic in Europe with the objective of promoting cooperation, better use of available opportunities, and coordinated development of air traffic; and
- discussion of all special problems arising in this area.

Although the number of Member States had initially only grown slowly, the ECAC now includes forty-four States after the political changes in Central and Eastern Europe. The following countries are ECAC members:

> Albania, Armenia, Austria, Azerbaijan, Belgium, Bosnia and Herzegovina, Bulgaria, Croatia, Cyprus, Czech Republic, Denmark, Estonia, Finland, France, Georgia, Germany, Greece, Hungary, Iceland, Ireland, Italy, Latvia, Lithuania, Luxembourg, Malta, Moldova, Monaco, Montenegro, Netherlands, Norway, Poland, Portugal, Romania, San Marino, Serbia, Slovakia, Slovenia, Spain, Sweden, Switzerland, The former Yugoslav Republic of Macedonia, Turkey, Ukraine, and the United Kingdom.

The seat of the ECAC is in Paris.

B. Structure and Work Method

To understand ECAC, it is important to know that the constitutive conference had neither decided on an autonomous institution completely independent of existing organizations, nor on the creation of a subordinate air transport commission on a regional basis (Article 55(a) Chicago Convention), but instead chose a compromise: ECAC decides its own work programme and independently holds conferences and sessions, but works closely together with the ICAO, and especially uses the Secretariat of the ICAO.

26. <www.ecac-ceac.org>.

The institutions of ECAC are the plenum, the Directors General of Civil Aviation, the Coordinating Committee, and Working Committees that are appointed as required by the Directors General of Civil Aviation. Furthermore, the constitution of ECAC allows the creation of so-called associated bodies that are appointed for important tasks in special areas of aviation. This way, the following leading tasks have been taken over within ECAC: the European Air Traffic Control Harmonization and Integration Project (EATCHIP) Board, and the Airport/Air Traffic System Interface (APATSI) Project Board.

ECAC works in very close cooperation with governmental organizations such as the following:

> Council of Europe,[27] International Civil Aviation Organization (ICAO),[28] European Parliament,[29] European Union,[30] Organization for Economic Cooperation and Development (OECD),[31] European Conference of Ministers of Transport (ECMT),[32] EUROCONTROL,[33] Universal Postal Union,[34] and European Aviation Safety Agency (EASA)[35]

and regional organizations such as the following:

> African Civil Aviation Commission (AFCAC),[36] Latin American Civil Aviation Commission (LACAC),[37] and Arab Civil Aviation Commission (ACAC).[38]

The highest institution of ECAC is the plenum. It consists of the representatives of the Member States. Every member has one vote. The plenum elects the President, Vice-Presidents, and the other members of the Coordinating Committee. It defines the work programme of ECAC, decides on the budget, and adopts resolutions, recommendations, and other decisions that are presented to it by the other institutions. The plenum holds a so-called Triennial Session every three years. Special plenary meetings are held in addition to rotational plenary meetings as required. They can also take place on a ministerial level when especially important civil aviation policies are concerned. Meetings of the Directors General of Civil Aviation are called by the Coordinating Committee to discuss developments in aviation policies, make necessary decisions, and prepare the plenary meetings. Apart from the President and Vice-Presidents, the directors of the 'associated bodies' and especially selected members form the Coordinating Committee. The maximum

---

27. <www.coe.fr>.
28. <www.icao.int>.
29. <www.europarl.eu.int>.
30. <http://europa.eu.int/institutions/index_en.htm>.
31. <www.oecd.org>.
32. <www.cemt.org>.
33. <www.eurocontrol.int>.
34. <www.upu.int>.
35. <www.easa.eu.int>.
36. <www.afcac-cafac.org>.
37. <http://clacsec.lima.icao.int/>.
38. <www.acac.org.ma/>.

number is ten. It meets at least once a year. Its task is to coordinate and supervise the work of ECAC and its committees between the plenary meetings.

ECAC does not adopt any decisions that are directly binding for the Member States. In accordance with its Constitution, its tasks are of advisory nature. Accordingly, decisions are made in the form of resolutions, recommendations, or other decisions that are subject to approval of the Member States. ECAC's limitations to advisory functions as well as the possibility to call plenary or other meetings at any time, provide ECAC with an extraordinary amount of flexibility in comparison to other international organizations.

The Member States bear the direct costs of ECAC according to the key applicable to ICAO charges.

C. Focus of ECAC Activities

ECAC has always adapted the focus of its activities to the development and the current requirements of international air traffic. In former years, harmonization of aviation policies of its Member States, especially in the area of approval of tariffs and rates in scheduled air services as well as unification of the entry and departure conditions of the Member States for casual commercial air traffic (definition of charter categories), was the focus of its work. The Multilateral Agreement on Commercial Rights of Non-Scheduled Air Services in Europe of 30 April 1956,[39] which was prepared by ECAC at the initiative of the Committee of Ministers of the Council of Europe, as well as the International Agreement on the Procedure for the Establishment of Tariffs for Scheduled Air Services of 10 July 1967[40] deserve to be mentioned in particular. Another focus was the common representation of aviation interests of the Member States towards third States, especially in North Atlantic traffic towards the US. On the basis of a Memorandum of Understanding concluded in 1982, air services on the North Atlantic could be structured in a much more flexible manner (creation of tariff zones with automatic approval), and an intensive dialogue on new developments in the aviation market, such as computer reservation systems, could be held.

In the mid-1980s, the increased liberalization of air traffic in Europe, which was greatly advanced by the EC, became another new focus of ECAC. ECAC has always looked for a pragmatic compromise between the Member States pushing for a common aviation market and the other Member States.

In June 1987, two international conventions on tariffs and capacities were concluded within ECAC. The contents of these conventions, plus the questions of market access, were the basis of a decisive aviation package, which was adopted by the Council of Ministers of Transport of the EC in December 1987.[41]

---

39. 310 *UNTS* 229; *ICAO Doc.* 7695.
40. 696 *UNTS* 31; *ICAO Doc.* 8681.
41. Giemulla & van Schyndel, *CD-ROM: Europäisches Luftverkehrsrecht*, Einführung (European Aviation Law, Introduction).

It also applies to other areas of aviation, such as safety, defence of external dangers, air traffic control, aviation technology equipment, and facilities that the EC could not have created the necessary regulations, directives, and decisions for the common aviation market as quickly without the preparatory work of the expert committees of ECAC. Cooperation between ECAC and the EC has proven to be very effective over the course of the years. In addition, ECAC has become politically stronger through corresponding decisions of the relevant Ministers, through the leading participation in the EATCHIP, and the APATSI Project, which was established for improving aviation safety in the area of airports. This strengthened political position has led to ECAC adopting focuses of activity that are especially significant for the safety and structure of aviation and its efficient processing in the future. Further activities that should be mentioned include participation in the Air Transport Action Group (ATAG), which develops solutions for overcoming capacity problems in the air and on the ground;, participation in the Group of Experts on the Abatement of Nuisances by Air Transport, which administrations and the industry belong to; execution of the Safety Assessment of Foreign Aircraft (SAFA) programme, which is to be supplemented by the corresponding ICAO Audits; execution of the aviation security standing structure for Aviation Security (AVSEC) Audit programme (safety auditing of airports), and finally, organization of the European Aviation Conference Facilitation Information System in Illegal Immigration (ECAFALIS).

New focuses of activity of ECAC include advisory services and support of its numerous new members on coming closer to meeting traffic and technological standards of the other Member States.

III. JOINT AVIATION AUTHORITIES (JAA)

The JAA[42] were a working group of ECAC, which was founded by ten European states in Cyprus on 11 September 1990 as a foundation of Dutch law succeeding the Joint Airworthiness Authorities. A Secretariat was established in the Dutch town of Hoofddorp to coordinate cooperation. The main task of the JAA was the harmonization of authorization and operation of aircraft and licensing of air traffic personnel. The so-called Arrangement Document of Cyprus has been signed by forty-three States. The following is a list of the last Member States (thirty-seven full members and six so-called member candidates, indicated in italic type):

> *Albania,* Austria, *Armenia, Azerbaijan,* Belgium, Bosnia and Herzegovina, Bulgaria, Croatia, Cyprus, Denmark, Estonia, Finland, France, *Georgia,* Germany, Greece, Hungary, Ireland, Iceland, Italy, Latvia, Lithuania, Luxembourg, Malta, The former Yugoslav Republic of Macedonia, Moldova, Monaco, *Montenegro,* Netherlands, Norway, Poland, Portugal, Romania, Sweden, Switzerland, Serbia, Slovakia, Slovenia, Spain, the Czech Republic, Turkey, *Ukraine,* and the United Kingdom.

42. <www.jaa.nl/>.

The objectives and areas of activity were defined in the Arrangement Document and can be summarized as follows:

- Adjustment of aviation security standards.
- Improvement of aviation security worldwide through expansion of the area of applicability.
- Ensuring international competitiveness through a cost-effective security system.
- Simplification of flight operations through adjustment of the appropriate regulations.
- Application of unified standards in the JAA states to ensure fair competition.

The institutions of the JAA have been the following:

- the JAA Board (JAAB): It considered and reviewed the general policies and the long-term objectives, the working programme and the budget of JAA. The General Directors of the National Aviation Administrations were represented in the Board. Among others, it decided upon the acceptance of new members of the JAA and on any changes to the Cyprus Arrangements. The JAAB met two to three times a year;
- the JAA Committee (JAAC): It was responsible for the introduction and supervision of measures to implement the goals of the Cyprus Arrangements, the creation of proposals for regulations, and the creation of processes and their standardization, especially for the adoption of Joint Aviation Requirements (JARs). The JAAC met two to three times a year. The decision makers of the national aviation administrations who did the preliminary work for the General Directors were represented in the JAAC;
- Special Committees for the individual areas such as regulations, type certificates, maintenance, operation, licensing, and research.

The JAA were not a supranational organization (other than the EC/EU) and, therefore, did not have any sovereign powers; consequently, they could not lay down legal norms or administrative acts. Hence, the JARs developed by the JAA were not legal norms, but mere proposals for regulations that either had to be transferred into Community law (of the EC) or into national law (by the appropriate national lawmakers). In the past, the following JARs have been declared binding by the EC Harmonization Regulation[43] (as Annex II):

- JAR-1: Definitions and Abbreviations.
- JAR-22: Sailplanes and Powered Sailplanes.
- JAR-25: Large Aeroplanes.
- JAR-AWO: All Weather Operations.
- JAR-E: Engines.

---

43. Council Regulation (EEC) No. 3922/91 of 16 Dec. 1991 on the harmonization of technical requirements and administrative procedures in the field of civil aviation, *OJ* No. L 373 of 31 Dec. 1991, 4.

- JAR-P: Propellers.
- JAR-APU: Auxiliary Power Units.
- JAR-TSO: Joint Technical Standard Orders.
- JAR-145: Approved Maintenance Organizations.

The EC Harmonization Regulation (together with its Annex II) was suspended on 28 September 2003 and replaced by regulations drafted by EASA and issued by the Commission.[44]

In addition to these (EC JARs), the following national JARs were put into force by national lawmakers (e. g., by publication of a JAR adopted by the JAA in the German *Federal Gazette* in German translation and by notification in the appropriate national regulation) in Germany. These are the following:

- Luftverkehrs-Ordnung (LuftVO, German Air Traffic Order), with included JAR-TSO German (§ 1).
- Luftverkehrs-Zulassungs-Ordnung (LuftVZO, German Air Traffic Authorization Order), with included JAR-FCL, German (§ 20).
- Betriebsordnung für Luftfahrtgerät (LuftBO, Aircraft Operations Order), with included JAR-OPS 1 and 3, German (§ 1(2), and Implementation Orders (enacted by the Federal Office for Civil Aviation in Germany [LBA]).
- Verordnung zur Prüfung von Luftfahrtgerät (LuftGerPV, Regulation for Examination of Aircraft), with included JAR-21, German (§ 9), as well as the referenced JAR-145 (Maintenance) (§ 11).
- First Implementation Order to the LuftGerPV (enacted by the LBA), with included JAR-66, German (§ 5), certifying staff. Since the right to certify airworthiness is not regulated there, the LBA decided in the notification 'Transferral of activities according to § 108(3) LuftPersV to certifying staff in accordance with JAR-66' of 26 June 2001[45] that the JAR-66 CAT C license will be expanded on the basis of the provisions of the LuftGerPV.
- Regulations for Aviation Personnel (LuftPersV), with included JAR-FCL, German and with included JAR 66, German (§ 111 a(3)) and JAR-147, German (§ 111 a(3)).

However, it has to be noted that when the aforementioned EU Regulations came into force on 28 September 2003, the corresponding German 'regulations' were suspended:

- JAR-21: Certification for Aircraft and Products and Components (JAR-21, German);
- JAR-66: Certifying staff – maintenance (JAR-66, German);
- JAR-147: Approved education organizations – maintenance (JAR-147, German); and
- JAR-TSO: Technical descriptions and standards of aircraft equipment.[46]

44. See below D. European Aviation Safety Agency.
45. *NfL* (Nachrichten für Luftfahrer – German official aviation gazette) II – 57/01.
46. See below D. European Aviation Safety Agency.

A corresponding change of the EC Harmonization Regulation temporarily also replaced the JAR-OPS 1, German with EC Regulations (OPS 1).

At the moment, only the JAR-OPS 3, German, the JAR-FCL 1–4, German, and the JAR-STD A and H are implemented into national law in the corresponding German legal norm through a reference standard.

'On 28 May 2009 the Joint Aviation Authorities held their Farewell event to conclude 40 years of serving European civil aviation. The official closing date is 30 June 2009. JAA's mission to improve overall civil aviation safety by establishing uniform European rules and regulations, and harmonization with parties outside of Europe, will be continued by the European Aviation Safety Agency (EASA) which is located in Cologne, Germany.... The JAA Training Organisation (JAA-TO) will continue with training activities as a Dutch foundation and associated body of ECAC (European Civil Aviation Conference). JAA-TO Headquarters will remain in Hoofddorp. Scheduled training courses are offered in Hoofddorp, Belgrade, London Gatwick, Vienna, Luxembourg, Singapore and Abu Dhabi.'[47]

IV. EUROPEAN AVIATION SAFETY AGENCY (EASA)

The EASA[48] took up work on 28 September 2003. The seat of EASA is Cologne, possibly with future offices to be established in other EU Member States. In recent times, the tasks of the JAA have been increasingly transferred to EASA. The Member States also hand their powers to the EASA step-by-step. The objectives of EASA can be summarized as follows:[49]

- high and uniform level of civil aviation security in Europe;
- high and uniform level of environmental protection;
- facilitation of free traffic of goods, people, and services;
- increase of cost-effectiveness of regulation and licensing processes and avoidance of double work on a national and European level;
- support of Member States in fulfilling their obligations from the Chicago Convention (ICAO Convention);[50] and
- global spreading of the views of the Community on civil aviation security standards and regulations.

Regulation (EC) 1592/2002 (Basic Regulation) has been revised by Regulation (EC) No. 216/2008 of the European Parliament and of the Council of 20 February 2008, on common rules in the field of civil aviation and establishing a EASA, and repealing Council Directive 91/670/EEC, Regulation (EC) No. 1592/2002 and Directive 2004/36/EC.[51]

47. <www.jaa.nl>.
48. <www.easa.eu.int/ws_prod/index.html>.
49. See Art. 2 of the Regulation (EC) No. 1592/2002 of the European Parliament and of the Council of 15 Jul. 2002 on common rules in the field of civil aviation and establishing a European Aviation Safety Agency, *OJ* No. L 240 of 7 Sep. 2002, 1.
50. 15 *UNTS* 295, *ICAO Doc*. 7300.
51. *OJ* No. L 79 of 30 Jul. 2008, 1.

Under this Basic Regulation, EASA has two legislative functions:

- Contribution to 'hard law': Under Article 17, paragraph 2(b), EASA shall assist the Commission by preparing measures to be taken for the implementation of this Regulation. Where these comprise technical rules and in particular rules relating to construction, design, and operational aspects, the Commission may not change their content without prior coordination with the Agency.
- Issuance of 'soft law': Under Article 18(c), the Agency shall, where appropriate, issue certification specifications, including airworthiness codes and acceptable means of compliance, as well as any guidance material for the application of this Regulation and its implementing rules.

On the basis of the EASA Regulation, the EC Commission handed EASA its first work tools:

- the Commission Regulation (EC) No. 1702/2003 of 24 September 2003 laying down implementing rules for the airworthiness and environmental certification of aircraft and related products, parts, and appliances, as well as for the certification of design and production organizations;[52] and
- the Commission Regulation (EC) No. 2042/2003 of 20 November 2003 on the continuing of airworthiness and aeronautical products, parts, and appliances, and on the approval of organizations and personnel involved in these tasks.[53]

Both Regulations include provisions in the Appendices that were formerly known as JARs and were either applicable to European law through Annex II of the Harmonization Directive[54] or had been implemented into the appropriate national law with similar contents and designations, namely:

- Part 21, that is, requirements and processes for certification of aircraft and related products, parts and appliances, and of design and production organizations (Appendix of Regulation (EC) 1702/2003);
- Part M, that is, continuing airworthiness requirements (Appendix I of Regulation (EC) 2042/2003);
- Part 145, that is, the requirements to be met by an organization qualified for the issue or continuation of an approval for the maintenance of aircraft or components (Annex II of Regulation (EC) 2042/2003);
- Part 66, that is, requirements for the issue of an aircraft maintenance license for certifying staff and conditions of its validity and use, for aeroplanes and helicopters of the categories A, B1, B2, and C (Annex III of the Regulation (EC) 2042/2003); and
- Part 147, that is, the requirements to be met by organizations seeking approval to conduct training and examination as specified in Part 66 (Annex IV of the Regulation (EC) 2042/2003).

52. *OJ* No. L 243 of 27 Sep. 2003, 6.
53. *OJ* No. L 315 of 28 Nov. 2003, 1.
54. See above B European Civil Aviation Conference.

These Annexes share the legal character of the respective EC Regulations and are, therefore, directly applicable law in the Member States. Implementation into national law is, therefore, not required.

On the basis of Commission Regulations (EC) Nos 1702/2003, 2042/2003 (including the different parts), and 859/2008 (EU OPS 1), the complete technical legal basis for aviation has gradually been replaced by EASA-influenced or implemented law. The revised and amended Basic Regulation[55] also forms the legal basis for an extension of EASA competences to pilot licenses (Article 7, Annex III), air operations (Article 8, Annex IV), aerodromes (Article 8a, Annex Va), ATM/ANS (Article 8b, Annex Vb), and air traffic controllers licenses. As of 8 April 2008 (the date of the entering into force of this regulation), EASA has also taken over these responsibilities, which were previously in the hands of JAA.

On the basis of these Regulations, EASA is authorized to lay down or take the following individual measures:[56]

- Type certificates.
- Environmental certificates.
- Security information.
- Certification of production organizations.
- Examinations of authorities and companies.
- 'Qualified entities' which are under the supervision and competence of the agency with approval tasks (e.g., technical inspections in connection with approval of products, parts, and appliances).

The institutions of EASA are the following:

- the Administrative Directorate, mainly responsible for appointing the Executive Director and (at the suggestion of the Executive Director) the EASA Directors;
- the Executive Director as legal representative of the EASA. He is completely independent with regard to completing his tasks and is supported by one or several Directors;
- Independent Boards of Appeal responsible for settling disputes between the EASA and the national authorities and organizations.

V. EUROCONTROL

A. Establishment

Given the geographic situation in Europe, it seems obvious not to limit national aviation security within the States' borders. Agreements between the responsible aviation security authorities of neighbouring States have, therefore, partially

55. Regulation (EC) No. 216/2008.
56. See Arts 20 et seq. of the EASA-Basic Regulation.

extended air traffic control in international air traffic to foreign airspace. Aircraft powered by turbines were starting to be used in the beginning of the 1960s, and this development led to a greater need for international cooperation in aviation security because jet planes travel at greater speeds than propeller planes and operate at greater heights. The first signs of an international regulation on aviation security at greater heights that were mainly to be considered for jet planes, the upper airspace, could be observed at a special conference of European ICAO Member States in 1957. The Benelux States and the Federal Republic of Germany declared their intention to establish an international aviation security organization for air traffic control in the upper airspace at a regional flight navigation conference of the ICAO in Geneva in 1958. Other Western European States joined. Final negotiations at a corresponding agreement were held in 1960, and a convention was signed in Brussels on 13 December 1960[57]. The Constitution of the Air Traffic Services Agency that was established by the Convention on the organization EUROCONTROL[58] is part of the Convention.

Currently, members to EUROCONTROL are thirty-nine States and the EU, namely:

> Albania, Armenia, Austria, Belgium, Bosnia and Herzegovina, Bulgaria, Croatia, Cyprus, Czech Republic, Denmark, Finland, France, Germany, Greece, Hungary, Ireland, Italy, Latvia, Lithuania, Luxembourg, Malta, Moldova, Monaco, Montenegro, Netherlands, Norway, Poland, Portugal, Romania, Serbia, Slovakia, Slovenia, Spain, Sweden, Switzerland, The former Yugoslav Republic of Macedonia, Turkey, Ukraine and United Kingdom of Great Britain and Northern Ireland.

Furthermore, it was agreed by the EU on 8 October 2002 that it would also join the revised EUROCONTROL Convention.[59] However, the accession treaty has not been ratified by all members yet. Its entry into force will also have consequences for the structure of the EUROCONTROL institutions.[60]

B. Original Responsibilities and Objectives

Among other matters, the EUROCONTROL Convention in its original version provided for transferral of sovereign powers with executive tasks on the area of air traffic control, which means that the conceptual design of EUROCONTROL was that of a supranational organization.

---

57. 523 *UNTS* 117.
58. <www.eurocontrol.int/>.
59. Protocol on the accession of the European Community to the Eurocontrol International Convention relating to Cooperation for the Safety of Air Navigation of 13 December 1960, as variously amended and as consolidated by the Protocol of 27 Jun. 1997, *OJ* No. L 304 of 30 Sep. 2004, 210.
60. See below 5 Structure and Institutions.

Article 1, paragraph 1 stated:

> The Contracting Parties agree to strengthen their cooperation in the field of air navigation, and in particular to jointly organize aviation security services in the upper airspace.

These objectives were concretized in more detail in the additional provisions of the Convention and the Statute of the agency:

> The Contracting Parties transfer aviation safety services to the Agency in the upper airspace (Article 14).
>
> The Agency shall, for the purpose of completing its tasks, provide all necessary instructions to the air carriers with regards to the powers conferred to the aviation security services . . . (Article 18)
>
> The task of the Agency is to . . . prevent collisions of aircraft; ensuring the efficient and fast process of air traffic . . . (Article 2 Constitution of the Agency).

Joint financing by the Member States was laid down for the services and facilities.

Air traffic control in the upper airspace through EUROCONTROL in the original version of the Convention does not, in terms of its legal character, differ from national air traffic control: it is not only of an advisory nature, but the execution of national sovereign power that had been conferred to EUROCONTROL for the upper airspace also made it a supranational organization with its own sovereign powers. For example, it could collect air navigation charges from its own legislation (Article 20 of the Convention). However, it only operated in this way in the upper airspace above the Benelux countries and Northern Germany. The other States continued to execute their own sovereign power above their respective sovereign territories, for which they were (re)granted power by EUROCONTROL.

C. Amendment of the Convention

The EUROCONTROL Convention that had initially been set out for a period of twenty years would have been due for renewal in 1983. However, it did not take long for doubts to develop as to whether and in what form it was to be renewed, because most Member States were not really willing to meet their obligations resulting from the Convention. The main objective of joint air traffic services by EUROCONTROL in the upper airspace was only achieved to a small extent. Only the Federal Republic of Germany, Belgium, and Luxemburg were prepared to confer air traffic control tasks to EUROCONTROL, so that, since then, air traffic control in the upper airspace as well has mostly been performed by national authorities again. Because, pursuant to the Convention, they did not have the competence to do so, they became active by order of EUROCONTROL. This situation did not leave any other choice than to continue EUROCONTROL with a changed portfolio of responsibilities, since liquidation of the organization was, politically, hardly an option.

D. Responsibilities and Objectives in the Version of the Amendment Protocol

The EUROCONTROL Convention was changed by the Protocol that entered into force on 1 January 1986[61] to the effect that the tasks of air traffic control in the upper airspace were transferred back to the Member States, leaving them the option to instruct the organization to complete such tasks. Essentially, EUROCONTROL now has the following tasks for both the lower and the upper airspace, pursuant to Article 2 of the amended Convention:

- Coordination of national plans for the purpose of establishment of a joint medium-term plan for air traffic control services and air traffic organizations.
- Further development of the air traffic control system through joint examinations and experiments, for example, through the Experimental Centre in Bretigny.
- Cooperation in training and additional training of air traffic control personnel.
- Central tasks in air traffic flow management, for example, through establishment of a central database.
- Joint collection of air navigation charges.

Upon request by the Member States, the following tasks may be entrusted:

- Support for specific tasks such as planning and establishment of air traffic control organizations and air traffic services.
- Provision and operation of all or part of the air traffic control organizations and air traffic services for a Member State.
- Support for the collection of air navigation charges.

Finally, upon request by third States, the organization can take over the task of air traffic flow management, planning of air traffic control services, and collection of air navigation charges for such States. The activities in accordance with the new tasks will be executed by various organizational units. Air traffic flow management is of particular significance in this regard.

E. Structure and Institutions

EUROCONTROL has its own legal personality. The seat of the organization is Brussels. The bodies of the organization are the Commission (in the transitional period until ratification of the Convention by all Member States); the Eurocontrol

61. 1430 *UNTS* 279.

Permanent Commission as the body responsible for the general policies of the organization; the Council (in the transitional period, the Provisional Council) as the body implementing decisions of the Commission and the supervisory body of the agency; and finally, the Eurocontrol Agency as the executive body for the tasks defined by the Convention and the Constitution or assigned to it by the Commission. The Commission consists of representatives of the Member States, which each have only one vote. Decisions have to be unanimous and are generally binding; however, in contrast to the previous version of the Convention, a Member State can deviate from a decision for important reasons of national interest. The principle of majority applies to Directives and Recommendations. The Commission has policy and supervisory powers over the Agency and, therefore, determines the framework of its activity. The Commission is generally responsible for external relations unless the Agency is authorized to do so in individual cases.

The Agency is led by an Executive Committee and a Director General elected by that Committee by qualified majority for a period of five years. The Director General legally represents the organization and can exercise certain powers in the area of budget, allocation, and human resources independently, pursuant to Article 15 of the Constitution. In the Executive Committee, only one representative of a Member State each is entitled to vote in the Commission; however, when making decisions not requiring unanimity, the votes of the Member States are weighted differently. A weighting table is used for this purpose, in accordance with which each Member State has between one and sixteen votes, depending on the annual membership fee. The number of sixteen votes is achieved with 30% share in the budget as the highest possible annual membership fee of a member (Article 8 of the Convention and Article14 of the Constitution). Depending on the type of decision, certain qualified majorities are required, for example 70% of submitted weighted total votes for the election of the Director General.

F. Financing

The organization is mainly financed by the fees of the Member States. The fees are calculated on the basis of a budget structure developed by the Executive Committee of the Agency and approved by the Commission, which defines a coefficient for the individual Member States that depends on the gross domestic product of the individual Member States as defined in the appropriate statistics of the OECD. The annual budget plans are developed by the Executive Committee and approved by the Commission.

G. Air Navigation Charges

In many States, fees are charged for using the services and institutions of air traffic control. Articles 6 and 20 of the original version of the EUROCONTROL Convention provided that the Agency was entitled to collect charges in accordance with its task as a traffic control authority in the upper airspace. For practical reasons, the EUROCONTROL Member States agreed to collect air navigation charges for using their services in the lower airspace, where such charges were to be paid pursuant to national regulations, in the same way as provided for by EUROCONTROL. The Multilateral Agreement relating to the Collection of Route Charges of 8 September1970[62] provided that charges incurred in the lower airspace were to be combined with those for the upper airspace and to be collected as one single charge. The governments of the Member States instructed EUROCONTROL to collect the payable user charges for the lower airspace for them in almost literally identical agreements. Because EUROCONTROL did not execute any air traffic control itself, the charges collected by the organization were passed on to the respective country in accordance with the share of such country in air traffic control of a flight. Some third States, such as Austria and Switzerland, joined this method through agreements with EUROCONTROL. Thereby, the organization was in fact a collection agency for foreign services, although it had sole authorization to collect charges for the upper airspace.[63]

After the Amending Protocol, EUROCONTROL was no longer responsible for air traffic control, which also meant that it lost its authorization to collect charges for it from its own right. Because the method of collecting charges had proven its worth, its legal bases were adapted to this practice. Article 2 of the amended Convention now provides that EUROCONTROL charges, determines, and collects air navigation charges for both members and third states. The new Multilateral Agreement relating to Route Charges of 12 February 1981[64] defines the details. It only covers the route charges for both the upper and the lower airspace, while other air navigation charges, especially those for approach and departure control, remain limited to separate agreements with EUROCONTROL. Third states can again participate in the charges collection system. Their codetermination in the organization is ensured through the Enlarged Commission and the Enlarged Committee of the Agency.

In relation to collection of air navigation charges, which an air carrier had refused to pay, the ECJ, after an order of referral from the Belgian Cour de Cassation, ruled in its decision of 19 January 1994[65] that EUROCONTROL was not an undertaking in the sense of Articles 86 and 90 ECT valid at the time (from the Amsterdam Treaty, Articles 82 and 86 EC), the consequence being that collection of charges could not be a violation of these provisions, which had been claimed by the plaintive air carrier. The decision reads:

'Taken as a whole, EUROCONTROL's activities are connected with their nature, their aim, and the rules to which they are subject, to the exercise of powers relating to the control and supervision of airspace, which are typically those of a

62. 830 *UNTS* 29; *BGBl.* 1971 II, 1153.
63. For details see Schwenk, *ZLW* (Zeitschrift für Luft- und Weltraumrecht – German Journal of Air and Space Law) (1972): 62.
64. See 1430 *UNTS* 123; *BGBl.* 1984 II, 109.
65. Judgment of the Court of 19 Jan. 1994. – *SAT Fluggesellschaft mbH v. Eurocontrol*. – Reference for a preliminary ruling: Cour de cassation – Belgium. – Articles 86 and 90 of the Treaty – Concept of undertaking – International organization. – Case C-364/92, [1994] ECR I-43.

public authority and are not of an economic nature justifying the application of the EEC Treaty rules of competition. Articles 86 and 90 of the Treaty are to be interpreted as meaning that an international organization such as EUROCONTROL does not constitute an undertaking within the meaning of those articles.'

VI. EUROPEAN AIR TRAFFIC CONTROL/SINGLE EUROPEAN SKY

A. Development over the Last Years

Unfortunately, the development of EUROCONTROL was digressive for a long time. Instead of strengthening and further developing this organization, whose existence was much more necessary at the time the Amended Protocol came into force than at the time of its establishment, it has been restricted in its tasks to a level that cannot objectively be justified and that can only be explained by the national selfishness of certain Member States. The barriers at the EC borders have come down; in the airspace, however, they continued to exist for a long time, although they should have been removed from the upper airspace in 1960.

The growing awareness for the necessity of international cooperation in the area of air traffic control must, however, have some influence on EUROCONTROL as an organization established for this exact purpose, even when the current portfolio of tasks is very restrictive for its activities. It can especially be observed that strong impulses towards such cooperation come from the ECAC and the EC while trying to include EUROCONTROL in this development process as much as possible. On the one hand, EUROCONTROL has advisory and planning tasks to improve the situation of aviation in the European airspace; on the other hand, operational possibilities, especially in the area of air traffic flow management, are taken advantage of through use of a central database. Due to the different members of EUROCONTROL and the EC, there are limits as to how much the two organizations can approach each other. However, these limitations have become less and less through the expansion of the EC.

The last years have seen an encouraging development, which can be attributed to the EATCHIP initiated by the ECAC. The aim of this programme was to create a standard air traffic control system in Europe in four phases, under the supervision of EUROCONTROL. Phase 1 was completed by the end of 1991 and revealed the fragmentation of the existing air traffic control systems in a detailed analysis of the current situation. A working programme was developed in phase 2 with the goal of harmonizing these systems. This programme was implemented in phase 3, which was completed by 1998. Phase 4 now aims to develop an integrated standard air traffic control system, the European Air Traffic Management System (EATMS)[66] which will go even beyond harmonization.

66. For details on development see Schwenk, 'Flugsicherung in Europa' (Air traffic control in Europe), *ZLW* (*Zeitschrift für Luft- und Weltraumrecht – German Journal of Air and Space Law*) (1993), 121.

B. General Aspects and Objectives of Creating the Single European Sky

On 23 and 24 March 2000, during a special Council in Lisbon, the European Council summoned the Commission to develop recommendations for management of airspace, air navigation, and air traffic flow. A group of experts from civil and military backgrounds responsible for air traffic control in the Member States was appointed by the Council and presented its report in November 2000. On 10 October 2001, the Commission presented a package of recommendations on common management of the airspace, the appointment of a regulator with extensive competence, further integration of civil and military airspace management, the creation of institutional synergies between the EU and EUROCONTROL, the provision of adapted and new technology, and improved coordination of personnel policy in the area of air traffic control.

The aims were the following:

- improvement and increase of safety;
- more efficient and better integrated air traffic control services on the basis of the provision of a service dependent on the demand;
- restructuring of the European airspace, not based on national borders but rather depending on the air traffic flow; and
- creation of additional capacities and increase of efficiency of the air traffic management system as a whole.

The ambitious plan to establish the legal bases for a Single European Sky by 31 December 2004 was realized. On 2 February 2004, the Council adopted the package of four regulations by written procedure in keeping with the common draft approved by the Conciliation Committee.

This package includes the following regulations:

(1) Regulation (EC) No. 549/2004 of the European Parliament and of the Council of 10 March 2004 laying down the framework for the creation of the Single European Sky (the Framework Regulation).[67] The Framework Regulation lays down the frame of the Single European Sky through general provisions. For better understanding, three main goals must be emphasized:

- to enhance current safety standards and overall efficiency for general air traffic in Europe;
- to optimize capacity, meeting the requirements of all airspace users; and
- to minimize delays. In pursuit of this objective, the aim of this regulation is to establish a harmonized regulatory framework for the creation of the Single European Sky.

(2) Regulation (EC) No. 550/2004 of the European Parliament and of the Council of 10 March 2004 on the provision of air navigation services in

67. *OJ* No. L 96 of 31 Mar. 2004, 1.

the Single European Sky (the Service Provision Regulation).[68] The purpose of the Service Provision Regulation is the definition of common requirements for a safe and efficient, smooth, and interoperable provision of air navigation services in the Union.

Harmonization of the licensing system for controllers shall counteract fragmentation of air navigation, which will have positive effects on flow and regularity of air traffic. Controllers shall be authorized to provide their services in other Member States, as well through mutual recognition of licenses issued by the Member States in all Member States.

(3) Regulation (EC) No. 551/2004 of the European Parliament and of the Council of 10 March 2004 on the organization and use of the airspace in the Single European Sky (the Airspace Regulation).[69] The provisions of the Airspace Regulation are a reaction to the main problems in European airspace management that were part of the reason for the significant increase in delays. Efficient airspace management is an essential precondition for increasing the capacity of the air traffic service system, for best possible satisfaction of different user requirements, and for ensuring airspace use that is as flexible as possible. Given the need for greater flexibility due to the increased use of the airspace, new functional airspace blocks are no longer based on the national borders.

(4) Regulation (EC) No. 552/2004 of the European Parliament and of the Council of 10 March 2004 on the interoperability of the European Air Traffic Management network (the Interoperability Regulation).[70] The Interoperability Regulation aims at an adaptation of the various systems, components, and related processes of the European Air Traffic Management network by defining the basic requirements thereof in cooperation with EUROCONTROL. This also addresses the problem of the industry to have to adapt products to the appropriate national market provisions.

However, implementation of these Regulations encountered great legal problems. Especially, German Federal President Horst Köhler had refused to sign the law on privatization of air traffic control, explaining that the State had a constitutional responsibility of liability with regard to the safety task of 'air navigation'. Therefore, he would have to be able to influence any acting air navigation organization in Germany at any time, which was effectively only possible with a majority share. The German Federal President thereby not only put a stop to the sale of the majority share in German air navigation, but also created an obstacle for a non-national air navigation organization becoming active in a 'functional airspace' including the German airspace.

The Single European Sky regulations adopted in 2004 (SES I) have not delivered the expected results in some important areas. The process of integration within

68. *OJ* No. L 96 of 31 Mar. 2004, 10.
69. *OJ* No. L 96 of 31 Mar. 2004, 20.
70. *OJ* No. L 96 of 31 Mar. 2004, 26.

functional airspace blocks (FABs), regardless of national borders, has encountered numerous hurdles. In particular, air traffic control has been related to the issue of national sovereignty. Obviously, this is a complex argument, but, instead of prompting innovative solutions for exercising sovereignty, it has been used to block cross-border integration. There has been little progress in the overall efficiency of the design and use of the European air network.

This second package is based on four pillars:

- The existing Single Sky legislation needs to be sharpened to deal with performance and environmental challenges.
- The SESAR (Single European Sky ATM Research) programme should help in the development of future technology.
- The competence of the EASA is to be extended to aerodromes, air traffic management, and air navigation services.
- The 'action plan for airport capacity, efficiency and safety' needs to be implemented.

The legislative components of the SES II have been expected to come into effect in 2009 or 2010 at the latest.[71]

71. For details see *ICAO Working Paper*, Conference on the Economics of Airports and Air Navigation Services, Montreal, 15-20 Sep. 2008, CEANS-WP/56, 5/9/08.

Chapter 9

Supranational Law: EU Law

Elmar M. Giemulla and Heiko van Schyndel

European Union (EU) Law consists of the Foundation Treaties of the European Union (primary Union law) and the law that is produced by the organs of the EU (secondary Union law). Under the TFEU,[1] the European legislators are the European Parliament and the Council (of Ministers), usually in co-decision. Pursuant to Article 288 TFEU, legal acts enacted in this manner are either directly applicable law in the Member States (regulations) or have to be transferred to their respective national law (directives).

The principle of conferred powers (Article 5, paragraph 2 TEU) applies to actions of the Union and its organs. In accordance with this principle, the Union only becomes active within the boundaries of its rights and defined objectives conferred to the Union by the TEU and TFEU, meaning that the European Union and its organs require a legal basis in these Treaties that is explicit or at least verifiable by means of analysis for each legal act. The subsidiarity principle (Article 5, paragraph 3 TEU) states that the Union must only become active in areas where it is not exclusively responsible for when and insofar as the objectives of the considered measures cannot sufficiently be achieved on the Member States level.[2]

1. Treaty establishing the European Community (consolidated text), *OJ* No. C 325 of 24 Dec. 2002, 1.
2. Art. 5, para. 3 reads as follows: 'Under the principle of subsidiarity, in areas which do not fall within its exclusive competence, the Union shall act only if and in so far as the objectives of the

Elmar M. Giemulla & Ludwig Weber, *International and EU Aviation Law: Selected Issues*, pp. 333–338.

I. PRIMARY EU LAW

The Treaties of Rome of 25 March 1957 (in force since 1 January 1958), which are the Treaties establishing the European Economic Community (EEC)[3] and the Treaty establishing the European Atomic Energy Community (EAEC),[4] formed the basis of primary EEC law. The first established the EEC, and the second established the EAEC or Euratom. They were the first international organizations to be based on supranationalism, after the European Coal and Steel Community (ECSC) established already in 1952.[5]

These treaties were signed by six European governments: Belgium, France, Italy, Luxembourg, the Netherlands, and the Federal Republic of Germany.

In 1992, the Treaty of Maastricht[6] changed the name of the EEC Treaty to reflect the change of the EEC in becoming the European Community (EC). Hence, the treaty became the Treaty Establishing the European Community (TEC). Since then, the European Communities thus consisted of the European Community, the EAEC, and the ECSC. At the same time, the EU was founded as a result of the Treaty on European Union (TEU), which consisted of two additional, intergovernmental pillars apart from the EC as the supranational pillar, namely the Common Foreign and Security Policy (CFSP) and the Cooperation in Justice and Home Affairs (CJHA). The Maastricht Treaties also created the legal basis for the introduction of a community currency (the euro).

Through the Amsterdam Treaty[7] (amending the treaty to the TEU and the EC treaties), the so-called co-decision procedure between Council and European Parliament was introduced when adopting secondary law.

The ECSC was dissolved by the Treaty of Nice.[8] Since then, the EU was made up of two intergovernmental pillars and a supranational pillar (the EC), which was made up of the EC and the EAEC.

The Treaty of Lisbon merged the European Union and the European Community into a single European Union. The word 'Community' is replaced throughout by the word 'Union'. The Union replaces and succeeds the European Community. However, Union law is still shaped by the following three Treaties: Treaty on European Union[9] (TEU), Treaty on the Functioning of the European

---

proposed action cannot be sufficiently achieved by the Member States, either at central level or at regional and local level, but can rather, by reason of the scale or effects of the proposed action, be better achieved at Union level.'

3. <http://eur-lex.europa.eu/en/treaties/dat/11957E/tif/TRAITES_1957_CEE_1_EN_0001.tif>.
4. <http://eur-lex.europa.eu/en/treaties/dat/11957K/tif/TRAITES_1957_EURATOM_1_EN_0001.tif>.
5. <http://eur-lex.europa.eu/en/treaties/dat/11951K/tif/TRAITES_1951_CECA_1_EN_0001.tif>.
6. *OJ* No. C 191 of 29 Jul. 1992, 1; *OJ* No. C 224 of 31 Aug. 1992, 1.
7. *OJ* No. C 340 of 10 Nov. 1997, 1.
8. *OJ* No. C 80 of 10 Mar. 2001, 1.
9. *OJ* No. C 83 of 30 Mar. 2010, 13.

Union[10] (TFEU) and Treaty establishing the European Atomic Energy Community[11] EAEC, or Euratom.

Primary Union law also includes the Accession Treaties of 1972 (the UK, Ireland, and Denmark),[12] 1979 (Greece),[13] 1985 (Portugal and Spain),[14] 1994 (Finland, Austria, and Sweden),[15] 2003 (Estonia, Latvia, Lithuania, Malta, Poland, Slovakia, Slovenia, the Czech Republic, Hungary, and Cyprus),[16] and 2007 (Bulgaria and Romania).[17] The number of EEC/EC/EU Member States has increased from six in its founding year of 1957 to twenty-seven, representing now more than 450 million people – with more to follow.

As a result of the primary Union law, the EU has extensive aviation competence. Pursuant to Article 100, paragraph 2 TFEU, the European Parliament and the Council may be 'acting in accordance with the ordinary legislative procedure, may lay down appropriate provisions for sea and air transport', and the general procedural provisions of Article 91 (laying down necessary measures) shall apply.

This regulation intends to clearly show that there is a greater room for interpretation in this area with regard to international obligations of the stated carriers than with regard to other carriers. The extended application of the general conditions of the treaty especially leads to regulations on fundamental freedoms of the treaty, especially freedom to provide services, and antitrust and competition law, also applying to aviation without any restrictions.

II. SECONDARY EU LAW

The term *secondary Union law* means legislation laid down by the organs of the EU as a result of primary law procedural provisions (legislation created by the organs or secondary legislation).

The secondary EU law consists of legislative acts, delegated acts, implementing acts and other legal acts. 'Legislative acts' are legal acts adopted by ordinary or special legislative procedure (Article 289 TFEU). 'Delegated acts' are non-legislative acts of general and binding application to supplement or amend certain non-essential elements of a legislative act. They are adopted by the Commission; a legislative act must be drawn up explicitly delegating power to the Commission for this purpose. The objectives, content, scope and duration of the delegation of power are explicitly defined in the legislative act concerned. This delegation of power can be revoked by the Council or the European Parliament at any time.

---

10. *OJ* No. C 83 of 30 Mar. 2010, 47.
11. <http://eur-lex.europa.eu/en/treaties/dat/11957K/tif/TRAITES_1957_EURATOM_1_EN_0001.tif>.
12. *OJ* No. C 73 of 27 Mar. 1972, 1.
13. *OJ* No. C 291 of 19 Nov. 1979, 1.
14. *OJ* No. C 392 of 15 Nov. 1985, 1.
15. *OJ* No. C 241 of 29 Aug. 1994, 1; *OJ* No. C 1 of 1 Jan. 1995, 1.
16. *OJ* No. C 236 of 23 Sep. 2003, 1; *OJ* No. C 227 E of 23 Sep. 2003, 1.
17. *OJ* No. C 157 of 21 Jun. 2005, 1.

A delegated act may enter into force only if no objection has been raised by the European Parliament or the Council within a period set by the legislative act (Article 290 TFEU). 'Implementing acts' are an exception to the principle whereby all the measures required to implement binding EU legal acts are taken by the Member States in accordance with their own national provisions. Where uniform conditions are needed for implementing legally binding EU acts, this is done by means of appropriate implementing acts, which are generally adopted by the Commission, and, in certain exceptional cases, by the Council. However, the European Parliament and the Council lay down in advance the rules and general principles concerning the mechanisms for control by Member States of the Commission's exercise of implementing powers (Article 291 TFEU). Finally, there is a whole set of 'other legal acts' which the Union institutions can use to issue non-binding measures and statements or which regulate the internal workings of the EU or its institutions, such as agreements or arrangements between the institutions, or internal rules of procedure.

To carry out their responsibilities and in accordance with the provisions of the TEU and the TFEU, the institutions of the Union – the European Parliament acting jointly with the Council and the Commission – lay down regulations and directives, make decisions, make recommendations and deliver opinions (Article 288 TFEU).

A. Regulations and Their Legislative Impact

Regulations are binding upon all Member States and are directly applicable within all such States. The Union passes many regulations, and if each had to be separately incorporated into each national legal system before it could be effective, then the Union machinery would grind to a halt. The phrase *directly applicable* obviates this difficulty, making regulations a part of the Member States' national legal systems automatically without the need for separate national legal measures. A regulation 'lay down the same law throughout the Union, regardless of international borders, and apply in full in all Member States. A Member State has no power to apply a regulation incompletely or to select only those provisions of which it approves as a means of ensuring that an instrument which it opposed at the time of its adoption or which runs counter to its perceived national interest is not given effect. Nor can it invoke provisions or practices of domestic law to preclude the mandatory application of a regulation . . . the legal acts do not have to be transposed into national law but confer rights or impose obligations on the Union citizen in the same way as national law. The Member States and their governing institutions and courts are bound directly by Union law and have to comply with it in the same way as with national law'.[18]

Usually, regulations are issued by the European Parliament and the Council (in a co-decision). However, these regulations can provide for the Commission to

18. Borchardt, *The ABC of European Union law*, Luxembourg 2010, 88 et seq.

issue subordinated regulations (s. a. 'delegated acts') that contain details left open by the Council and EP regulations. Since the Commission is advised by a committee of representatives of the Member States, these subordinated regulations are often called 'comitology regulations'.

B. Directives and Their Legislative Impact

Directives are binding as to the end to be achieved while leaving some choice as to the form and method of implementation open to the Member States. As there are variations in the political, administrative, and social arrangements within the Member States, directives were considered a particularly useful framework device, setting out the ends which Member States are to meet in considerable detail. 'Its purpose is to reconcile the dual objectives of both securing the necessary uniformity of Union law and respecting the diversity of national traditions and structures. What the directive primarily aims for, then, is not the unification of the law, which is the regulation's purpose, but its harmonisation . . . A directive is binding on the Member States as regards the objective to be achieved but leaves it to the national authorities to decide on how the agreed Community objective is to be incorporated into their domestic legal systems.'[19]

As a result of the lack of direct applicability, Member States frequently interpret a directive's provisions according to their convenience and needs. This often results in a distinct lack of harmonization EU-wide, the very thing that directives are adopted to avoid.

The European Court of Justice[20] has held that even if directives are not implemented, individuals may nonetheless rely on them, at least in actions against a State. The Court[21] has also held that a Member State can be liable in damages for non-implementation of a directive.

C. Decisions and Their Legislative Impact

Institutions are free to proceed by way of decision in many areas. The TFEU also stipulates areas in which decisions should be the chosen method of policy making. The Council may delegate power to the Commission to make decisions that are within the competence of the Council itself.

The basic characteristics of a decision can be summed up as follows:

- It is distinguished from the regulation by being of individual applicability: the persons to whom it is addressed must be named in it and are the only

19. Borchardt, *The ABC of European Union law*, Luxembourg 2010, 89.
20. Judgment of the European Court of Justice of 19 Nov. 1991, Cases C-6/90 and C-9/90, *Francovich v. Italy*, *ECR* (1991) I-5357.
21. *Ibid.*

ones bound by it. This requirement is met if, at the time the decision is issued, the category of addressees can be identified and can thereafter not be extended. Reference is made to the actual content of the decision, which must be such as to have a direct, individual impact on the citizen's situation. Even a third party may fall within the definition if, by reason of personal qualities or circumstances that distinguish them from others, they are individually affected and are identifiable as such in the same way as the addressee.
- It is distinguished from the directive in that it is binding in its entirety (whereas the directive simply sets out the objective to be attained).
- It is directly binding on those to whom it is addressed. A decision addressed to a Member State may in fact have the same direct effect in relation to the citizen as a directive.[22]

D. Recommendations and Opinions and Their Legislative Impact

Recommendations and opinions have neither binding force nor direct effect. The Commission is imbued with a general power to formulate recommendations or deliver opinions on matters dealt with in the TEU and the TFEU, either where it is expressly so provided, or where the Commission believes that it is necessary to do so.

'They enable the Union institutions to express a view to Member States, and in some cases to individual citizens, which is not binding and does not place any legal obligation on the addressee.

In recommendations, the party to whom they are addressed is called on, but not placed under any legal obligation, to behave in a particular way. For example, in cases where the adoption or amendment of a legal or administrative provision in a Member State causes a distortion of competition in the European internal market, the Commission may recommend to the State concerned such measures as are appropriate to avoid this distortion (Article 117(1), second sentence, TFEU).

Opinions, on the other hand, are issued by the Union institutions when giving an assessment of a given situation or developments in the Union or individual Member States. In some cases, they also prepare the way for subsequent, legally binding acts, or are a prerequisite for the institution of proceedings before the Court of Justice (Articles 258 and 259 TFEU).'[23]

---

22. Borchardt, *The ABC of European Union law*, Luxembourg 2010, 93 et seq.
23. Borchardt, *The ABC of European Union law*, Luxembourg 2010, 95.

Chapter 10

Liability in European Law

Elmar M. Giemulla and Heiko van Schyndel

I. LIABILITY ARISING FROM THE OPERATION OF AIRCRAFT

As already explained in Chapter 6, 'Liability in International Law', in regard to the liability arising from the operation of aircraft, it is necessary to differentiate between the liability arising from air carriage regulations or an air carriage agreement and third party liability. Both areas of application are likewise dealt with in the European regulations – even if with a differing regulatory depth.

A. LIABILITY ARISING FROM AN AIR CARRIAGE AGREEMENT IN ACCORDANCE WITH EUROPEAN LAW

1. Preface

Due to the constantly increasing significance of European legislation, including the field of aviation, the national regulations in the Member States of the European Union (EU) have, in the past few years, been increasingly displaced,

Elmar M. Giemulla & Ludwig Weber, *International and EU Aviation Law: Selected Issues*, pp. 339–355.

and meanwhile have only very restricted validity. This also applies to the regulations on liability arising from the carriage agreement. Here, within the scope of the third liberalization package, Council Regulation (EC) No. 2027/97 of 9 October 1997 on air-carrier liability in the event of accidents[1] was issued, which was correspondingly adapted in connection with the accession of the EC to the Montreal Convention (MC).[2]

2. The Original Version of the EC Liability Regulations

Council Regulation (EC) No. 2027/97 of 9 October 1997 on air carrier liability in the event of accidents has little ability to alter anything in the Warsaw Convention (WC)[3] as the IATA Intercarrier Agreement (IIA)[4] or its implementing instruments. While this ascertainment is obvious for the IIA, as an agreement under private law, the EC/EU Regulation, as a legal instrument governed by public law, in any case having legal effect in the Member States of the EC/EU (Article 249 ECT /now: Article 288 TFEU/), requires explanation. It may justifiably be doubted whether an EC/EU Regulation may at all be able to invalidate, or at least alter, international agreements with countries outside the EU. This question can, however, be debatable in the case at hand, because the regulation did not make any claim to wish to intervene in the regulations of the WC. Rather – just like the IIA and its implementing instruments – it picked up on where the WC provides for flexibility for the benefit of the passengers, namely, in the case of exonerating evidence (Article 20 WC) and the maximum liability limits (Article 22 WC):

- Just as in accordance with the IIA, pursuant to Article 3, paragraph 1 of the EC Regulation, the liability of air transportation companies in the event of death, bodily injury, and damage to health was not subject to any limitation;
- Just as, in accordance with the Agreement on Measures to Implement the IIA, pursuant to Article 3, paragraph 2 of the EC Regulation, the air transportation companies concerned were now obliged to no longer produce any exonerating evidence in the event of losses up to SDR 100,000; and
- Just as in accordance with these agreements under Private Law, the air transportation companies were obliged by Article 6, paragraph 1 of the EC Regulation to include corresponding clauses in their General Terms and Conditions of Carriage.

1. *OJ* No. L 285 of 17 Oct. 1997, 1.
2. 2242 *UNTS* 350.
3. Authentic French Text: *II Conférence Internationale de Droit Privé Aerién*, 4 - 12 Octobre 1929, Varsovie 1930, 220 et seq.; for British translation, see Schedule to the United Kingdom Carriage by Air Act, 1932; 22 & 23 Geo.5, ch. 36); for American translation, see [49 Stat. 3000; T.S 876].
4. The text is printed in *ZLW* (1996), 23 and in *TAQ* (1996/97), 13/119; on the IIA; also see Böckstiegel, *ZLW* (1996), 18; Clark, *ZLW* (1996), 353; *id.*, *LAL* (1996), Nos 16, 1, 3; Müller-Rostin, *ZLW* (1999), 324; *id.*, Festschrift for Herber, 245 et seq.; Hellebrandt, 253 et seq.

Thus, the EC Regulation had, under public law, demanded of the air transportation companies concerned what the air transportation companies which had acceded to the IIA had already voluntarily undertaken.

3. Liability in Accordance with European Law Following the Accession of the EC to the MC

a. Liability of Air Transportation Companies in the Union When Carrying Persons and Their Luggage

Currently applicable to air transportation companies within the Community is Council Regulation No. 2027/97 on air carrier liability in respect of the carriage of passengers and their baggage by air,[5] namely, the version taking into account the European Parliament and Council Regulation (EC) No. 889/2002 of 13 May 2002 amending Council Regulation (EC) No. 2027/97 on air carrier liability in the event of accidents.[6] Through the latter Amendment Regulation, the MC, the subjects of the regulations of which partly fall within the scope of responsibility of the EC/EU, has been partially supplemented and adopted in European law, and, in fact, for both national and international air carriage by the companies specified.

A significant difference between the EC liability regulation and the MC is the respective circle of persons addressed. While the statutory European provisions take as the standard a liability on the part of the Union air transportation companies (i.e., air transportation companies which possess an authorization pursuant to Council Regulation (EEC) No. 2407/92[7]), the MC substantiates a liability on the part of the air carrier – both contractual and executing (see, in regard to these terms, Article 39 MC). European law can therefore only be applied if the tortfeasor is, first, an air transportation company and not any other air carrier; second, it must be a Community air transportation company, that is, the EC liability regulation does not apply to non-EU carriers, even if they execute carriage to and from a Member State of the EU.

A further difference is that it is decisive for the applicability of the MC whether the flight has taken place between two contracting States. Such a restriction does not emerge from the European regulations; they apply – as long as a Community air transportation company is concerned – independently of the question of between which countries the flight has taken place or whether even a domestic flight is concerned.

5. *OJ* No. L 285 of 17 Oct. 1997, 1.
6. *OJ* No. L 140 of 30 May 2002, 2.
7. *OJ* No. L 240 of 24 Aug. 1992, 1.

The basis for any claims (international or EU, or even national law) can be ascertained with the aid of the following overview.

Type of carriage/ Type of air carrier	*International Carriage*	*National Carriage*
'EU air transportation companies' within the meaning of EC Regulation 2027/97, new version	EC Regulation 2027/97, new version in conjunction with the MC	EC Regulation 2027/97, new version, making reference to the MC
'Non-EU air transportation companies' within the meaning of EC-Regulation 2027/97, new version	MC, respective applicable version of the WC, national law	National law
Air carriers with their head office outside the EU	MC, respective applicable version of the WC, national law	As a rule: none (cabotage prohibition)

Concerning the liability of a Community air transportation company for passengers and their luggage, all relevant provisions of the MC apply (i.e., expressly Article 3, paragraph 1 of the EC Liability Regulations), and in fact independently of whether they carry out domestic, intra-Union, or international flights. Since the intra-Union flights are simultaneously international flights, in these cases, the legal status of the MC would already (directly) apply, even without the EC liability regulation. The EC liability regulation therefore only has independent significance for the domestic flights in the individual Member States of the EU, as an EC Regulation is directly applicable law there. As a result, it is achieved, within the meaning of a uniform EU-internal market, that there is no difference in the liability, wherever, and on what routes, air transportation companies within the Community execute carriage.

Concerning the details of the European liability regime, reference can be made to the explanations regarding the MC.

It is clearly determined in Article 3, paragraph 2 of the EC Liability Regulation that the insurance obligation in accordance with Regulation (EEC) No. 2407/92 is to be understood to mean that all persons entitled to compensation for damage receive the full amount to which they have a material claim.

b. The System of Liability Arising from the Carriage Agreement in Accordance with European Law: Comparative Overview: EU Air Carriers and Non-EU Air Carriers

International Carriage by Air Carriers with their Head Office Outside the EU and by Non-EU Air Transportation Companies	*International and National Carriage by EU Air Transportation Companies*
MC	EC Regulation 2027/97, 2004 version
Liability for Bodily Injury	
Fundamental liability for presumed culpability. For losses in the case of death or bodily injury not exceeding SDR 113,100 per passenger, the liability of the air carrier cannot be excluded or limited (Article 21, paragraph 1 MC). For losses extending beyond that, it is not liable if it proves that this damage is not attributable to an illegitimate act or omission on the part of the air carrier or its assistants, even if only negligently committed, or that this damage is exclusively attributable to an illegitimate act or omission by a third party, even if only negligently committed (Article 21, paragraph 2 MC).	Reference to MC (Article 3, paragraph 1 EC Regulation), no supplementary regulation.
Liability for Luggage	
Fundamental liability for presumed culpability. When carrying luggage, the air carrier is liable for destruction, loss, damage, or delay only up to an amount of SDR 1,131 per passenger (Article 22, paragraph 2 MC).	Reference to MC (Article 3, paragraph 1 EC Regulation), no supplementary regulation.
Liability for delays of passengers	
Fundamental liability for presumed culpability. For losses through delay, the air carrier is liable, when carrying	Reference to MC (Article 3, paragraph 1 EC Regulation), no supplementary regulation.

International Carriage by Air Carriers with their Head Office Outside the EU and by Non-EU Air Transportation Companies	*International and National Carriage by EU Air Transportation Companies*
persons, only up to an amount of SDR 4,694 per passenger (Article 22, paragraph 1 MC).	
Liability for Goods	
When carrying goods, the air carrier is liable for destruction, loss, damage, or delay only up to an amount of SDR 19 per kilogramme (Article 22, paragraph 3 MC).	Reference to MC (Article 3, paragraph 1 EC Regulation), no supplementary regulation.
Insurance Requirements	
The contracting States oblige their air carriers to reasonably insure themselves to cover their liability in accordance with this convention (Article 50 MC).	Reference to MC (Article 3, paragraph 1 EC Regulation) Supplementary regulation – implementation for EU air transportation companies: Article 3, paragraph 2 in conjunction with Article 11 of EC Regulation No. 1008/2008: 'Notwithstanding Regulation (EC) No 785/2004, an air carrier shall be insured to cover liability in case of accidents with respect to mail.'

4. Denied Boarding, Cancellation and Long Delays

a. *EEC Regulation No. 295/91*

Council Regulation (EEC) No. 295/91 of 4 February 1991 on establishing common rules for a denied boarding compensation system in scheduled air transport[8] numbered among the first EC regulations which were devoted to protecting the consumer in air carriage. Instead of compensation for damage due to non-fulfilment (denied boarding) as a consequence of overbooking, since 1991, a passenger has already been able, on the basis of the regulation specified, to demand flat-rate compensation, as was already similarly previously provided for in the Conditions of Carriage of the IATA companies. It applied to flights in air transport with places

8. *OJ* No. L 36 of 8 Feb. 1991, 5.

of departure in the EC region. If individual transportation, as opposed to the usual flat-rate travel arrangements, was sold, in the case of charter flights, the regulation likewise was deemed applicable.

In accordance with the regulation, any passenger not carried in consequence of overbooking could request either reimbursement of the price of the flight or to be booked onto the next available flight, or a later flight of his choice. In addition, he had a claim to certain compensation, which was on a scale, according to the length of the delay and distance to the destination. There was also reimbursement of expenses for telephone calls, meals, and accommodation during the waiting period, and any transfer necessary. An 'overbooked flight' concerned a flight for which more passengers possessed a confirmed booking, and had reported on time and in conformity with the other conditions prior to departure, than there were places available (Article 2 d) of the regulation specified).

The compensation regulation only applied to passengers who were carried at generally accepted tariffs. This did not include, for example, the employees of the air transportation company or a travel agency flying at discounted airfares.

The regulation lacked an express provision in the event that, contrary to the flight schedule, a smaller aircraft was used and therefore passengers remained stranded.

b. EC Regulation No. 261/2004

As a further development of the so-called overbooking regulation, Regulation (EC) No. 261/2004 of the European Parliament and of the Council of 11 February 2004 establishing common rules on compensation and assistance to passengers in the event of denied boarding and of cancellation or long delay of flights, and repealing (EEC) No. 295/91[9] was issued. It came into force on 17 February 2005 (Article 19). The regulation extends beyond its forerunner in its scope of regulation, by not only providing compensation for the affected passengers in the event of denied boarding due to overbooking (Article 4), but also in the event of cancellation (Article 5) or long flight delays (Article 6). Furthermore, the scope of the regulation no longer only extends to scheduled flights, but now also covers all other flights.

The regulation applies to passengers who board a flight at airports in the territory of a Member State, and, in fact, including domestic flights. It also applies to passengers who, insofar as the executing air transportation company is a Community air transportation company, board a flight to an airport in the territory of a Member State from an airport in a country outside the EU, unless they have already received a consideration, or compensation and support payments, in this country outside the EU. It does not, on the other hand, apply to passengers who travel free of charge or at a reduced rate which is not available to the public, either directly or indirectly. It does, however, apply to passengers with tickets which were issued within the scope of a customer loyalty programme or other promotional programmes by an air transportation company or travel organization.

9. *OJ* No. L 46 of 17 Feb. 2004, 1.

In the event of denied boarding and short-term cancellation (less than seven or fourteen days prior to the planned departure), the passenger receives compensation payments in the amount of EUR 250 in the case of all flights of a distance of 1,500 km or less, EUR 400 in the case of all intra-Community flights of a distance of over 1,500 km, as well as all other flights covering a distance between 1,500 km and 3,500 km, and EUR 600 in the case of all cancelled flights extending beyond that.

Distance (kilometres)	*Compensation in the Event of Denied Boarding or Cancellation (EUR)*
Up to 1,5000	250
1,500–3,500	400
3,500 and up	600

In the event of delay, the same amounts apply; however, this is dependent on the fulfilment of the additional condition that the flight is delayed by two hours or more, in the case of all flights of a distance of 1,500 km or less, by three hours or more in the case of all intra-Community flights of a distance of over 1,500 km, as well as all other flights of a distance between 1,500 km and 3,500 km, or 4 hours or more in the case of all other flights in relation to the scheduled time of departure.

Distance (kilometres)	*Delay of up to . . . hours*	*Compensation (EUR) – Article 7, paragraph 1*
Up to 1,500	2	250
1,500–3,500	3	400
3,500 and up	4	600

In addition, the passenger has a claim, on the conditions more precisely defined in the regulations, to being provided with the necessary meals, refreshments, and hotel accommodations (if applicable).

B. Third Party Liability in Accordance with European Law

European law does not contain any regulations on the prerequisites for third party liability. The provision for this liability remains exclusively reserved for national regulations, with the exception of Belgium, Italy, and Luxembourg, which are the only EU Member States which have acceded to the Rome Convention.

However, air transportation companies and aircraft operators that fly within the sovereign territory, into the sovereign territory, out of the sovereign territory, or over the sovereign territory of a Member State to which the TEU and the TFEU apply must, pursuant to Regulation (EC) No. 785/2004 of the European Parliament and of the Council of 21 April 2004 on insurance requirements for air carriers and aircraft operators[10] insure the risks arising from third party liability (at least) in the amount specified in Article 7 of this regulation.

The following is stated there: 'For liability in regard to third parties, the minimum sum insured per claim, for each individual aircraft, is as follows:

Category	*MTOM*[11] *(kilogrammes)*	*Minimum Sum Insured (in Millions of SDRs)*
1	< 500	0.75
2	< 1,000	1.5
3	< 2,700	3
4	< 6,000	7
5	< 12,000	18
6	< 25,000	80
7	< 50,000	150
8	< 200,000	300
9	< 500,000	500
10	=/< 500,000	700'

The Member States of the EU have, to that extent, adapted their national legislation to the EC Regulation.

II. PRODUCT LIABILITY ACCORDING TO EUROPEAN LAW

In addition to contractual liability and third party liability, claims from product liability or producer liability also have to be considered in aviation. Defects of the aircraft as a whole or of parts thereof can lead to the producer being liable – the so-called product liability. In aviation, this type of liability has especially become significant as a result of serious plane crashes, where the airlines, which are primarily liable as aircraft operators or air carriers, were able to successfully claim limited liability. The claimants therefore tried to overcome this limited liability and claim against the producers.

10. *OJ* No. L 138 of 30 Apr. 2004, 1.
11. Maximum Take-Off Mass.

A. EUROPEAN PRODUCT LIABILITY: GENERAL

The Council Directive No. 85/374/EEC of 25 July 1985 on the approximation of the laws, regulations and administrative provisions of the Member States concerning liability for defective products[12] as amended by Directive 1999/34/EC of the European Parliament and of the Council of 10 May 1999 amending Council Directive 85/374/EEC on the approximation of the laws, regulations and administrative provisions of the Member States concerning liability for defective products[13] is the result of fifteen years of discussions in the EC.

The EC Commission had already started preparing a European regulation of product liability in 1968. On 23 July 1976, it presented a draft on the regulation of product liability,[14] which was amended[15] after the opinion of the Economic and Social Committee.[16] The Directive was finally adopted on 25 July 1985.

It introduced the principle of liability regardless of negligence or fault. According to this principle, the producer of a defective movable has to replace any damage to a person's physical integrity or property regardless of whether such producer acted with negligence or not. The European Parliament Directive 1999/34/EC of 10 May 1999[17] extended the application area of this type of product liability to primary agricultural products, which had initially not been included in the Directive.

Directive 85/374/EEC does not include any direct provisions on the regulation of individual cases. Being a Directive, it has to be transposed into national law (Article 288 TFEU, formerly: Article 249 ECT). The aim of the Directive is to harmonize national legal provisions on the producer's civil liability as much as possible.

Product liability is an absolute liability, that is, it does not depend on the fault of the producer who circulates a product. The dangerous action which provides the point of contact for the producer's liability is solely placing the product on the market. This liability is reasoned by the fact that whoever places a product on the market as a businessperson has to be responsible for third parties not being harmed by it. The businessperson therefore has to ensure that his product meets the state of technology.

The European product liability law applies to all products circulated in the EEA (including non-EEA producers). It is of equal significance for both consumers and producers. These legal provisions create a balanced relationship between the two groups and aim to bring together consumer interests and domestic market policies (namely, free trade and elimination of distortion of competition).

---

12. *OJ* No. L 21 of 7 Aug. 1985, 29.
13. *OJ* No. L 141 of 4 Jun. 1999, 21; *OJ* No. L 283 of 6 Nov.1999, 20.
14. *OJ* No. C 241 of 14 Oct. 1976, 9.
15. *OJ* No. C 271 of 26 Oct. 1979, 3.
16. *OJ* No. C 115 of 7 May 1979, 61.
17. *OJ* No. L 141 of 4 Jun. 1999, 20.

B. The Provisions of the Product Liability Directive in Detail

The EC Directive on Product Liability states the following principles:

- Liability is objective, that is, irrespective of fault or negligence.
- Liability is connected to a 'product'.
- Every 'producer' is liable.
- The claimant has to prove the damage, the defect and causality between the two.
- Everybody involved in the production chain is jointly and severally liable to financially ensure compensation for damage.
- Liability is relative: the producer is not liable when he can prove existence of certain conditions specifically mentioned in the Directive.
- Due to standard time limits in the EEA, liability is limited with regard to time.
- Clauses that limit or exclude liability towards the claimant are not lawful, that is, liability cannot be excluded by the parties' declaration of intent.

1. Absolute Liability

Article 1 of the Directive includes the provision for absolute liability. The formulation that '(t)he producer shall be liable for damage caused by a defect in his product' makes it clear that liability is not based on the respondent's 'fault' or 'unreasonable' behaviour, that is, on negligence, but only on the fact that a defect in the product has caused the damage.

2. Product

The term *product* is defined in Article 2. It includes 'all movables . . ., even though incorporated into another movable or into an immovable . . .*Product* includes electricity.' This definition includes parts and raw materials as well as finished products.

Defective services are not covered by the application area of the Directive.

3. Liable Parties

Liability regardless of negligence or fault applies to *producers.*

Article 3, paragraph 1 of the Directive uses a list to define this term in more detail. For the purpose of the Directive, producer means

- the producer of finished products;
- the producer of raw materials;
- the producer of component parts; and
- 'any person who, by putting his name, trademark or other distinguishing feature on the product presents himself as its producer'.

Furthermore, *importers*, that is, 'any person who imports into the Community a product for sale, hire, leasing or any form of distribution in the course of his business shall be deemed to be a producer within the meaning of this Directive' (Article 3, paragraph 2).

Article 3, paragraph 3 extends liability even further. Thereby, any *supplier* of a product shall be treated as its 'producer' when the producer or importer of the product cannot be identified. However, he shall not be treated as the 'producer' when 'he informs the injured person, within a reasonable time, of the identity of the producer or of the person who supplied him with the product'. This aspect of the Directive is different from American product liability law, under which (in certain circumstances) all sellers of a product are jointly and severally liable irrespective of their position in the distribution chain.

4. Damage

Pursuant to Article 9 of the Directive, the term *damage* in the sense of Article 1 includes:

- damage caused by death or by personal injuries, and
- damage to, or destruction of, any item of property other than the defective product itself provided that such item of property
  (1) is of a type ordinarily intended for private use or consumption, and
  (2) was used by the injured person mainly for his own private use or consumption.

The Directive does not cover damage to goods that are usually for commercial use.

To avoid litigation in an excessive number of cases, an excess of EUR 500 applies to damages to any item of property.

The Directive does not cover purely economic damages. Thereby, the possibility of claiming compensation for damages to the product itself, for loss of profit, or for other purely economic damages is regulated by the individual national laws.

Compensation for non-material damage is also based on the legal provisions of each individual Member State of the EC (Article 9, Sentence 2).

5. Defect

Article 6, paragraph 1 defines the term *defect* in the sense of the consumer's expectations. It states that, '(a) product is defective when it does not provide the safety that a person is entitled to expect, taking all circumstances into account.' The Directive defines the following circumstances to be especially taken into account for assessment:

- the presentation of the product;
- the use to which it could reasonably be expected that the product would be put; and
- the time when the product was put into circulation.

American product liability law, rather than basing the definition of a defective product on the consumer's expectations, considers the balance between risk and use. Pursuant to American law, a product is defective when it is unreasonably dangerous, that is, when it has features whose danger outbalances the use of the product.

The main types of defects are the following:

- manufacturing defects

  A manufacturing defect means that an individual product does not meet the specifications of the series stated by the producer.
- design defects

  A design defect means that the product itself poses certain risks for the consumer. A design defect is naturally included in every single product of one series. Such a defect is generally determined by remarks on customary aspects, use, state of technology, competing products, and economic factors, as well as the consumer's expectations.
- warning defects

  This is the failure to point out the dangers of a product to the consumer in an adequate manner. There may be a warning defect even when the product has neither a manufacturing nor a design defect. This type of defect includes situations when labels, packaging, user manuals, or security specific explanations in advertisements do not sufficiently warn the consumer about the danger of the product.

6. Burden of Proof

Generally, the claimant has to prove the damage, the defect, and causality between the defect and the damage. The fact that the claimant has suffered damage is not enough to establish the producer's civil liability in the sense of the Directive. The claimant must prove that the damage is the result of a product defect. Because of the technical complexity, such proof can be very difficult and/or very expensive due to the costs for obtaining the required expert opinions. The Directive itself does not define any standard of proof. The most difficult task for the claimant is to convince the producer (or in the case of litigation, the judge) that the product was defective and that there is causality between this defect and the suffered damage. Generally, there is a certain imbalance of 'weapons' between the producer and the claimant, especially with regard to access to information. It is easier for the producer to recognize the source of the problem because he knows the production process.

Therefore, legislation includes some adjustments to facilitate the process for the claimant. In the case of a defect, prima facie evidence might be a possibility, for example, when several users have suffered the same damages, when the producer has violated accident prevention regulations, or when other concrete circumstances suggest that the cause of the defect lies in the sphere of the producer. With regard to the burden of proof for the damage and the causality, general facilitations of burden of proof for liabilities for negligence apply, especially the prima facie evidence when liability of negligence is clear and there is a typical damage for such negligence.

7. Joint Liability

When several producers are liable, they have a joint liability. In these cases, the claimant can contact one of these producers at his own discretion. Such producers' right of recourse against the other producers remains unaffected. This saves the claimant having to contact each individual liable party to receive full compensation.

8. Liability Disclaimer

The producer is not liable if he proves:

(a) that he did not put the product into circulation;
(b) that, having regard to the circumstances, it is probable that the defect which caused the damage did not exist at the time when the product was put into circulation by him or that this defect came into being afterwards;
(c) that the product was neither manufactured by him for sale or any form of distribution for economic purpose nor manufactured or distributed by him in the course of his business;
(d) that the defect is due to compliance of the product with mandatory regulations issued by the public authorities;
(e) that the state of scientific and technical knowledge at the time when he puts the product into circulation was not such as to enable the existence of the defect to be discovered;
(f) in the case of a manufacturer of a component, that the defect is attributable to the design of the product in which the component has been fitted or to the instructions given by the manufacturer of the product (Article 7).

9. Reduction of Liability

Article 8 provides that 'the liability of the producer may be reduced or disallowed when . . . the damage is caused both by a defect in the product and by the fault of the injured person or any person for whom the injured person is responsible.'

However, the liability of the producer shall not be reduced when the damage is caused both by a defect in product and by the act of a third party.

10. Statute of Limitation

If a person suffers damage due to a defective product, he has to claim compensation within three years 'from the day on which the plaintiff became aware, or should reasonably have become aware, of the damage, the defect and the identity of the producer.'

11. Term of Preclusion

The rights conferred upon the injured person pursuant to the Directive shall be extinguished upon the expiry of a period of ten years from the date on which the producer put into circulation the actual product which caused the damage, unless the injured person has in the meantime instituted proceedings against the producer (Article 11).

12. 'Options'

Considering the various legal traditions in the Member States of the Community, the Directive (Articles 15 and 16) allows the Member States to make changes to the mutual regulations in some points ('options'):

- The producer shall not be excluded from liability even if he proves that the state of scientific and technical knowledge at the time when he puts the product into circulation was not such as to enable the existence of a defect to be discovered.
- A producer's total liability for damage resulting from a death or personal injury and caused by identical items with the same defect can be limited to an amount which may not be less than 70 million ECU.

C. Typical Product Liability Cases in Aviation

Typical product liability cases in aviation first and foremost include development- and construction defects, since all aircraft built after a defective model has the same defects. In contrast to construction defects, fabrication defects – including assembly and quality inspection – generally only affect individual aircraft. Missing or faulty manuals can lead to serious accidents.

It is questionable whether the principles of product liability are also applicable to aeronautical companies completing repair- and maintenance work. The conditions in such a company can be compared to those of a manufacturer, so that the claimant does not have the full burden of proof because he cannot have any insight into the complicated work processes. Therefore, including repair, companies in product liability can be partially affirmed. Legislation in the USA is obviously different.[18] The fact that the repair company has a contractual liability towards the aircraft operator as well as against the aircraft operator and a damaged third party

18. See Speiser, Krause & Gans, *Aviation tort law* (Lawyers Co-operative Pub. Co. Rochester, 1980), 587.

in the case of proven negligence from prohibited action, on the other hand, is undisputed.

D. Product Liability and Aviation Law Liability

Generally, product liability claims collide with other claims that the injured person can make against the producer. The following can be claimants: aircraft operators and aircraft owners, aircraft crew, flight passengers, third claimants on the ground, and passengers of another aircraft. The claims of these injured people colliding with product liability claims can be of a general nature or can result from the special provisions of aviation law. If an aircraft has an accident as a result of a manufacturing defect, the following claims can arise:

- Guarantee and compensation claims of the owner from the purchase agreement, for proven fault or negligence from prohibited action and without full proof of negligence from product liability. When the aircraft operator also is the owner, his claims are the same. Otherwise, the operator can only make claims from prohibited action and product liability.
- Crewmembers can make claims against the aircraft operator from their employment contract and against the producer from prohibited action and product liability.
- Flight passengers can make claims against the air carrier, who usually is the aircraft operator, from the transport agreement. Generally, they will only be successful through maximum liability amounts defined by national and international regulations. Furthermore, they can litigate against the producer from prohibited action and product liability.
- The same applies to third claimants. They can make the same claims against the producer as flight passengers and can additionally assert operator liability against the aircraft operator.

In practice, the focus is mainly on claims of the injured flight passengers because they only very rarely manage to achieve unlimited liability of the aircraft operator. They then turn to the producer. Claims of third injured parties are similar, but they are in fact of less significance because mainly the passengers are affected in the case of an airplane accident.

E. Liability Cover and Reform Efforts

The Directive does not include an obligation for the producer to provide financial cover and especially not to take out liability insurance for a sufficient amount to cover possible damages from defective products. At the moment, the Member States are responsible for defining the conditions of such an insurance obligation.

Damage cover for product liability poses great problems. On the one hand, liability risk is very difficult to calculate, and on the other hand, for small suppliers of the final producer, it is disproportionate to the value of the supplied component. Therefore, it is difficult for producers and especially for suppliers to obtain sufficient insurance coverage at acceptable rates. The usual solution is product liability insurance covering not only the final producer, but also the component suppliers (umbrella cover) with exclusion of right of recourse against each other.[19] Such umbrella insurance covers damages to the aircraft itself, to the passengers, and to those involved in loading, as well as uninvolved third parties. However, limitations arise from the fact that certain damages are not subject to the insurance protection.[20]

It is therefore understandable that producers aim for a positive law regulation of product liability with limited liability or for state involvement in liability for non-insured risks. In addition, producers are more and more frequently sued for compensation from product liability when the claimants have not achieved any or only partial compensation from liability regulations in aviation law. A regulation on product liability that is as global as possible should therefore be in the interest of the producers. Points of contact for such a regulation could be found in international aviation conventions and agreements on liability of the air carrier and the aircraft operator. An integrated liability system including producer liability seems to be the obvious solution. It is not satisfactory for claimants if they have to litigate against several opposing parties separately. Channelling of liability appears necessary for processing economic reasons alone.[21] Existing international aviation conventions and agreements also indicate that product liability in aviation should be regulated on a trans-regional level and not necessarily in combination with general product liability. When following a globally existing liability regulation such as the MC or the WC, a regulation on product liability in aviation which at least has the tendency of being universal in nature is certainly easier to realize than a convention that would apply to many different types of products.

19. For details see Dietz, *Produkthaftung* (Product Liability) in: Böckstiegel, Die Produkthaftung in der Luft- und Raumfahrt (Carl Heymanns, 1977), 143 et seq.
20. See Dietz, *ibid.*, 150.
21. See Böckstiegel, *Die Produkthaftung in der Luft- und Raumfahrt* (Product Liability in Aviation and Astronautics) (1978), 258 et seq.

Chapter 11

Aviation Security in the European Union

Elmar M. Giemulla

The architecture of European aviation security is essentially based on Regulation (EC) No. 2320/2002,[1] which in turn mainly goes back to European Civil Aviation Conference (ECAC) Document No. 30, Part II. In addition, International Civil Aviation Organization (ICAO) Annex 17 (security) and Annex 9 (facilitation) was also involved.

The Regulation entered into force on 19 January 2003, and has been amended by the following Regulation (EC) (of the Parliament and the Council):

- Regulation (EC) No. 849/2004.[2]
- Corrigendum to Regulation (EC) No. 849/2004.[3]

1. Regulation (EC) No. 2320/2002 of the European Parliament and of the Council of 16 Dec. 2002 establishing common rules in the field of civil aviation security, *OJ* No. L 355 of 30 Dec. 2002, 1.
2. Regulation (EC) No. 849/2004 of the European Parliament and of the Council of 29 Apr. 2004 amending Regulation (EC) No. 2320/2002 establishing common rules in the field of civil aviation security.
3. Corrigendum to Regulation (EC) No. 849/2004 of the European Parliament and of the Council of 29 Apr. 2004 amending Regulation (EC) No. 2320/2002 establishing common rules in the field of civil aviation security, *OJ* No. L 229 of 29 Jun. 2004, 3.

Elmar M. Giemulla & Ludwig Weber, *International and EU Aviation Law: Selected Issues*, pp. 357–376.

Regulation (EC) No. 2320/2002 has been replaced by Regulation (EC) No. 300/2008,[4] which has entered into force on the twentieth day following its publication, but was applicable only 24 months after entry into force.

I. THE REGULATION (EC) ON AVIATION SECURITY 300/2008

A. Structure and Legal Character of the Regulation (EC) on Aviation Security

The Regulation (EC) on Aviation Security 300/2008 (hereinafter also referred to as Regulation (EC) 300/2008) consists of a relatively short regulation text and two more detailed Annexes. Annex I on 'Common basic standards for safeguarding civil aviation against acts of unlawful interference (Article 4)' is divided into twelve sections, each dealing with one aspect of aviation security, such as airport security, aircraft security, passenger and cabin baggage, hold baggage, cargo and mail, in-flight security measures, or staff recruitment and training.

In contrast to the legally non-binding ECAC Document, the Regulation (EC) on Aviation Security is binding in its entirety and directly applicable in all Member States as per Article 288 TFEU and, therefore, does not, at least not formally, require any further implementation by the national lawmakers. However, this is very doubtful with regard to both facts and legal doctrine, so much so that even the question arises whether the contents of the ECAC Document would in fact not have had to be laid down as EU Directives (which have to be implemented). One simply cannot deny that an obligation, to be complete, does not only require a subject matter, but also an addressee. Although it might make sense to leave the question of the addressees of the numerous obligations up to the national lawmakers because of the differences in legal traditions and administrative structures of the individual Member States, choosing a regulation as the legal instrument should not have been due to the related implementation requirement adequate (so-called limping regulation).

B. The Functionality of the Regulation (EC) on Aviation Security

Despite the 'normal' legal character of the regulation, the Regulation (EC) on Aviation Security does not lay down any norms in the sense of 'legal norms', which are general and binding regulations with external effect. To have the nature of 'legal norms', the norms in the Regulation (EC) on Aviation Security would,

4. Regulation (EC) No. 300/2008 of the European Parliament and of the Council of 11 Mar. 2008 on common rules in the field of civil aviation security and repealing Regulation (EC) No. 2320/2002, *OJ* No. L 97 of 9 Apr. 2008, 72.

therefore, at least have to mention addressees (only then would they be 'binding'). However, this is not the case: The Regulation rather only defines 'standards' that do not include addressees for the areas mentioned in the Annexes. This view is confirmed by the fact that the Regulation (EC) on Aviation Security, Article 4, paragraph 1 does not talk about 'norms', but rather about 'standards' laid down in the Annex of the Regulation. In Article 4, paragraph 5, the Member States require ensuring of the application, which then, from this point of view, no longer refers to compliance with already existing norms, but to turning standards (without an addressee) into binding legal norms, which then have to be applied by the addressees. This constitutes a provision for the legally binding application of originally non-binding standards.

This understanding of the term *norm* (in the sense of standards) also corresponds to the term *standard* as it is generally being used in international aviation. Pursuant to Article 37 of the Chicago Convention, the 'standards' formulated by the ICAO as Annexes to the Convention are to be implemented into national legislation by the Member States. Generally, these standards do not have any addressees as such either (just like the Regulation (EC) on Aviation Security), but Member States have to add addressees and thereby make them binding.

Even when taking this understanding as a basis for analysis, it has to be assumed that the Regulation (EC) on Aviation Security does not lay down any norms in the sense of 'legal norms', but simply standards which have to be upgraded to legal norms by the national lawmakers. The obligation of Member States from Article 4, paragraph 5 seems to confirm this view in a way that they have to ensure application of the standards through upgrading of such standards to the level of legal norms (by way of adoption of a national security programme).

The State orientation of the Regulation (EC) on Aviation Security is not only reflected in the requirement of implementation and supplementation, but also in the Regulation, including a number of obligations directly addressed to the Member States. For example, the Member States are especially obligated to present to the EU Commission the establishment of their aviation security regime in a so-called national civil aviation security programme (Article 10 of the Regulation (EC) on Aviation Security) and the introduced measures for maintaining the standard of aviation security in a national quality control programme (Article 11 of the Regulation (EC)).

C. Additional Regulations Adopted by Comitology Procedure

To appropriately deal with the dynamics of the topic of aviation security when laying down the additional required Regulations, the so-called comitology procedure was chosen for the adoption of implementing regulations (Article 19 of the Regulation (EC) on Aviation Security in connection with Article 291 TFEU and the Regulation (EU) No. 182/2011 of the European Parliament and of the Council of 16 February 2011 laying down the rules and general principles concerning mechanisms for control by Member States of the Commission's exercise of implementing powers[5]), the advantage being that such implementing regulations do not have to go through the normal legislative procedure in the European bodies, but can be laid down by the Commission after deliberation in a committee of national experts. The following implementing regulations (some of which have already been mentioned) have already been developed and laid down in this way:

- Commission Regulation (EC) No. 272/2009 of 2 April 2009 supplementing the common basic standards on civil aviation security laid down in the Annex to Regulation (EC) No. 300/2008 of the European Parliament and of the Council.[6]
- Commission Regulation (EU) No. 1254/2009 of 18 December 2009 setting criteria to allow Member States to derogate from the common basic standards on civil aviation security and to adopt alternative security measures.[7]
- Commission Regulation (EU) No. 72/2010 of 26 January 2010 laying down procedures for conducting Commission inspections in the field of aviation security.[8]
- Commission Regulation (EU) No. 185/2010 of 4 March 2010 laying down detailed measures for the implementation of the common basic standards on aviation security.[9]

Regulation No. 185/2010 (the last one mentioned above) needs to be especially emphasized; it supplements the Regulation (EC) on Aviation Security and its Annex I. This Regulation lays down detailed measures for the implementation of common basic standards for safeguarding civil aviation against acts of unlawful interference that jeopardize the security of civil aviation and general measures supplementing the common basic standards (see Article 1).

---

5. *OJ* No. L 55 of 28 Feb. 2011, 13.
6. *OJ* No. L 91 of 3 Apr. 2009, 7, as amended by Commission Regulation (EU) No. 297/2010 of 9 Apr. 2010 amending Regulation (EC) No. 272/2009 supplementing the common basic standards on civil aviation security (*OJ* No. L 90 of 10 Apr. 2010, 1).
7. *OJ* No. L 338 of 19 Dec. 2008, 17.
8. *OJ* No. L 23 of 27 Jan. 2010, 1.
9. *OJ* No. L 55 of 5 Mar. 2010, 1, as amended by Commission Regulation (EU) No. 357/2010 of 23 Apr. 2010 amending Regulation (EU) No. 185/2010 of 4 March 2010 laying down detailed measures for the implementation of the common basic standards on aviation security (*OJ* No. L 105 of 27 Apr. 2010, 10), Commission Regulation (EU) No. 358/2010 of 23 Apr. 2010 amending Regulation (EU) No. 185/2010 of 4 March 2010 laying down detailed measures for the implementation of the common basic standards on aviation security (*OJ* No. L 105 of 27 Apr. 2010, 12), Commission Regulation (EU) No. 573/2010 of 30 Jun. 2010 amending Regulation (EU) No. 185/2010 laying down detailed measures for the implementation of the common basic standards on aviation security (*OJ* No. L 166 of 1 July 2010, 1) and Commission Regulation (EU) No. 983/2010 of 3 November 2010 amending Regulation (EU) No. 185/2010 laying down detailed measures for the implementation of the common basic standards on aviation security (*OJ* No. L 286 of 4 November 2010, 1).

D. Important Introductions as a Result of EC Regulation 300/2008

Regulation (EC) 300/2008[10] repeals and replaces EC regulation 2320/2008. Although it entered into force on 29 April 2008, it applies only as from 29 April 2010 (see Article 24, paragraph 2).

The following is a list of the most important introductions to the legal situation:

- Structural Introductions:

Under national laws, the legal contents are split up into basic questions (parliamentary acts) and technical details (subordinated regulations). In comparison, under EU law, basic questions are covered by regulations (Council and EP), whereas technical or other details can be left to comitology regulations (Commission together with a committee of national experts). Regulation (EC) 300/2008 makes use of this possibility in Article 4, paragraph 2. Consequently, the function of the national aviation security acts is not to cover detailed questions which are not contained in Regulation (EC) 300/2008 but to deal with basic questions left open by this Regulation (e.g., background checks).

- Drawing up of Security Programmes:

Whereas the Regulation (EC) 2320/2002 had imposed on the Member States to oblige airport operators and air carriers to draw up security programmes, Regulation (EC) 300/2008 creates an immediate obligation of airport operators, air carriers, and, as a new invention, so-called entities. This means that national laws do not have to deal with this obligation as long as they do not create more stringent measures under Article 6.

- Addressees:

Similar to the former Regulation (EC) 2320/2002, Regulation (EC) 300/2008 lists all relevant security measures without naming the addressees for the particular measure. On the other hand, Article 2 of Regulation (EC) 300/2008 names airports, operators, and entities as possible addressees. This means that the assignment of these measures to the addressees is still left to national decisions. There are two options open to the national decision makers:

- First Option: National Aviation Security Act

  The national Aviation Security Act could contain separate provisions for each of the above companies, assigning security measures to each of

10. Regulation (EC) No. 300/2008 of the European Parliament and of the Council of 11 Mar. 2008 on common rules in the field of civil aviation security and repealing Regulation (EC) No. 2320/2002, *OJ* No. L 97 of 9 Apr. 2008, 72.

them. The obvious disadvantage is that the Annex of the Regulation would have to be repeated in the national acts. Furthermore, each amendment of the Annex would have consequences to the national legislature.
- Second Option: Security Programmes
  According to Articles 10 to14, the purpose of the security programmes is to make the above companies comply with Regulation (EC) 300/2008 (including the Annexes). If the total of all five security programmes reflect the entire content of the Annexes (except police tasks) then compliance with the security measures can be guaranteed also this way. The obvious advantage of this option is flexibility. However, this option excludes the security programmes of operators and entities from being submitted to the authorities just upon request. Submission and approval should be obligatory.

• Air Cargo:

Annex 6 of Regulation (EC) 2320/2002 had introduced and defined the terms *regulated agent* and *known consigner.* As a consequence, these terms need not be dealt with in national law. In contrast, Regulation (EC) 300/2008 just mentions these terms in its Annex 6, without defining them in detail. Therefore, it can be assumed that the details will be laid down in a comitology regulation.

II. ALLOCATION OF THE 'OPEN OBLIGATIONS' OF REGULATION (EC) ON AVIATION SECURITY

Regulation (EC) 300/2008, respectively its Annex I, mainly includes the following obligations (most of them without addressees):

- Airport security, including access control and screening of staff (Annex I Nos. 1 and 2),
- Aircraft security, including aircraft inspections (Annex I No. 3) as well as protection of aircraft,
- Screening of passengers and cabin baggage (Annex I No. 4),
- Screening and protection of hold baggage (Annex I No. 5),
- Screening of cargo and mail (Annex I No. 6),
- Air Carrier Mail and materials (Annex I No. 7),
- In-flight supplies (Annex I No. 8),
- Airport supplies (Annex I No. 9),
- In-flight security measures (Annex I No. 10),
- Staff recruitment and training (Annex I No. 11),
- Security equipment (Annex I No. 12).

The 'open obligations' have to be allocated to concrete addressees by the lawmakers of the individual EU Member States by way of adoption of appropriate national provisions.

A. Parameters for Allocation

The Regulation (EC) on Aviation Security has intentionally left open allocation of these obligations since there is no generally binding concept for allocation. The following parameters should form the basis for the decision on allocation of these responsibilities, which is thereby left to the national lawmakers:

- Legal tradition and general structure of a State;
- greatest possible level of professionalism;
- financing questions.

B. The Main 'Open Obligations'

The following parameters should be relevant for allocation of the main 'open obligations' drawn up by the Regulation (EC) on Aviation Security by the national lawmakers.

1. Screening of Passengers and Cabin Baggage

This should be the responsibility of a national authority, as it is a traditional police activity and as it invades privacy and, therefore, affects fundamental rights of private persons. This does not mean that the government, with appropriate authorization underlying principles, cannot transfer tasks 'regarding the carrying out of security measures in accordance with paragraphs 1 to 4 to suitable (natural or legal) persons fulfilling State functions *(Beliehener)*' (see for example, Section 5, paragraph 5 Luftsicherheitsgesetz - German Aviation Security Act). It is also possible that the government uses suitable private persons as pure administrative aides. Therefore, these tasks do not constitute private law rights of the airports or air carriers (which could result from their property right) or an obligation within their (public law) private security obligations, but exercise of sovereign powers, that is, an activity to be executed by the government or on behalf the government. Otherwise, the control personnel would have to be allocated to the aforementioned undertakings (airports or air carriers); their activities would then be part of the contractual relationship between the passenger and such undertaking. However, this would require the private personnel to be trained and equipped in a similar way to the police. Also, with regard to the highest possible level of professionalism, the aforementioned responsibilities are, therefore, rightly in the hands of the State authorities.

This is also confirmed by the aspect of appropriate financing of these responsibilities. In the interest of a responsible execution of these tasks, they should not get caught up in the maelstrom of general economic considerations. This danger would, however, exist if screening and control measures would have to be executed and financed by private institutions (as personal obligations). By collecting a public law charge for financing the service of a State authority, which can, in terms of its nature, also be provided by contractors with State authority or administrative aides, one can also better ensure that this service is executed with the required intensity. Accordingly, Article 5 of Regulation (EC) 300/2008 has left open the issue of Security costs stating that, subject to the relevant rules of Community law, each Member State may determine in which circumstances, and the extent to which, the costs of security measures taken under this Regulation to protect civil aviation against acts of unlawful interference should be borne by the State, the airport entities, air carriers, other responsible agencies, or users. If appropriate, and in conformity with Community law, Member States may contribute with users to the costs of more stringent security measures taken under this Regulation. As far as may be practicable, any charges or transfers of security costs shall be directly related to the costs of providing the security services concerned and shall be designed to recover no more than the relevant costs involved.

2. Screening and Protection of Hold Baggage, Cargo, and Mail

These obligations provided in the Regulation (EC) on Aviation Security (Annex I, Nos. 5 to 7) should also be allocated to a State authority. The analysed aspects for screening of passengers and cabin baggage apply here as well. However, the obligation of airport operators in Germany (under their private security obligations) to 'fetch the passenger when searching hold baggage in accordance with Section 5, or, when searching such baggage in the absence of the passenger, to open any locks the items of luggage are fitted with' (Section 8, paragraph 1, No. 3 Luftsicherheitsgesetz - German Aviation Security Act) has to be analysed in this context. While, when applying the aforementioned parameters, the task of fetching a passenger has appropriately been allocated to the airport operator, since it does not constitute execution of sovereign powers and the necessary personnel, and material (loudspeaker system) is also available to the airport operator, allocating the task of opening the locks of items of baggage in the absence of the passenger to the airport operator must be considered wrong. On the one hand, this process also invades the flight passenger's privacy, especially when opening such item of baggage is only possible with causing damage to such item. On the other hand, it is inconclusive which special knowledge and skills the employees of the airport operator have that would enable them to open items of baggage so as to allow aviation security authorities present to search such item of baggage. Hold baggage is entrusted to the responsible air carrier after check-in (seeRegulation (EC) 785/2004 on insurance requirements), but when the air carrier uses the services of third parties, this is only possible for handling, storage, and transport/loading, but not for security controls.

3. Airport Security, including Access Control and Screening of Staff

Under the heading 'Airport Security', Annex I, No. 1 of the Regulation (EC) on Aviation Security lists a number of measures, including airport planning requirements, access control, screening of staff, items carried, and vehicles, as well as physical security and patrols.

These tasks can only be executed sensibly by State authorities. If such measures are not only to be cosmetic in nature, they might also involve having to use physical force. Any person unjustifiably found on airport grounds has already broken the law through his pure presence and for this reason alone has to be suspected to be up to something worse. Realistically, such person can only be met with (State) sovereign powers all the way to subpoena.

Security related airport planning requirements, on the other hand, are obviously the traditional domain of the private security obligation of the airport operator (see e.g., section 8, paragraph 1 of the German Aviation Security Act).

However, it has to be questioned whether search or screening of its own staff and staff from other companies operating in the airport have been allocated correctly to the airport operator in Germany (see section 8, paragraph 1 No. 5 of the German Aviation Security Act), that is, whether the legal institution of private security obligation might not have been overstretched.

Private security obligations constitute taking private companies into service in the public interest.[11] They shall contribute to the authorities completing their tasks (so far) mainly in a way that they create the structural changes and conditions that are an essential precondition for completing the actual tasks. Private security obligations belong to public law, but these are not sovereign powers.

However, this border is crossed by the obligation to take its own active security measures such as screening of staff. Especially when considering that screening measures (of passengers) have been classified as a State task upon their introduction in Germany due to the necessary invasion of privacy connected with such measures, there is a certain paradigm shift in conferring screening measures to the airport operator. The (non-system) stretching of private security obligations conversely leads to a withdrawal of the State from its traditional monopolist position for invading privacy, which is questionable from a legal perspective.

The counter-argument that screening measures are not invasions, but that such measures happen on a voluntary basis, is not valid either. Although this view cannot be dismissed for the usual process of screening and searching measures, it reaches its limits when a person refuses to be searched or cannot prove access permission. Since State authority would have to be used here, it is artificial to subject this common context in real life to two different legal regimes, namely, to the private security obligations of the airport operator and additionally to State authority.

The 'aspect of the highest possible level of professionalism' only increases these concerns. As analysed in detail above, stopping, holding, searching people, possibly taking their identification, and using direct force all the way to using firearms is a classic form of police intervention. The police have the necessary theoretic (legal) knowledge and practical skills. Providing such knowledge and skills to

11. See instead of all Baumann, *Private Luftfahrtverwaltung* (*Private aviation administration*) (Carl Heymanns Cologne 2002), 25 with further references.

airport operator staff executing these tasks would not only require significant (other) legal changes, but also police-like training and equipment of such staff.

4. Aircraft Security, including Aircraft Inspections and Protection of Aircraft

These obligations included in Annex I, No. 3 of the Regulation (EC) on Aviation Security can be appropriately allocated to various addressees upon application of the parameters mentioned above.

First of all, the obligation of protection of aircraft (Annex I, No. 3.2) can be allocated to the respective air carriers. Protection of security-endangered aircraft by armed personnel can just as appropriately be allocated to State authorities.

The obligation of searching and checking of aircraft (Annex I, No. 3.1. of the Regulation (EC) on Aviation Security) can be allocated to the air carriers under their private security obligations under application of the parameters mentioned above, since they have the most intensive knowledge about where in the aircraft items can be hidden or where it can be manipulated. However, this would also involve stretching this term beyond its traditional understanding.

5. Other 'Open Obligations' to be allocated

The Regulation (EC) on Aviation Security includes a number of other 'standards', which have to be allocated to certain addressees by the national lawmakers of the EU Member States and which are complemented in detail by Commission Regulation (EC) No. 272/2009:

- Pursuant to Annex I, 1.2 of the Regulation (EC) on Aviation Security, the means of controlling access to public areas that are close to aircraft movement areas shall be provided, and arrangements shall be made to ensure that such public areas may be closed at short notice in the event of an increase in threat. Security staff shall patrol these areas when open to the public. The national Aviation Security Acts of the Member States have to expand this 'standard' and allocate it to individual addressees. The aviation security authority and/or the airport operator are both an option.
- Pursuant to Annex I, 1.2.3 and 1.4 of the Regulation (EC) on Aviation Security, vehicles required moving between landside and airside areas shall be issued with a pass specific to the vehicle. The provisions regulating the details of such access authorization shall be *sedes materiae*.
- Annex I, 1.5 of the Regulation (EC) on Aviation Security describes details for physical security of airports. Patrol of the airport grounds provided in this section is originally a State responsibility. The physical security obligation to adequately illuminated aprons and other parking areas and to protect technical and maintenance areas, as well as the individually listed airport facilities by fences or similar measures, however, does not fall under State responsibility.
- Pursuant to Annex I, 3. of the Regulation (EC) on Aviation Security, aircraft not in service shall be subjected to an 'aircraft security search' and aircraft

in service shall be subjected to an 'aircraft security check'. The details are described in this section. Based on the parameters mentioned above, these standards should sensibly be designed as obligations of the air carriers.

- Annex I, 4. of the Regulation (EC) on Aviation Security provides that screened departing passengers shall not mix with arriving passengers who may not have been screened to the standard detailed in the Annex. This requires constructional and structural changes to the airport buildings and appropriate organizational adaptation of processes. These standards can only be met by the airport operators.
- Pursuant to Annex I, 5. of the Regulation (EC) on Aviation Security, hold baggage shall not be placed on board an aircraft unless the measures listed in that section have been taken. This can sensibly not be allocated to one single addressee, but always to the one who has access to the hold baggage during the respective phase in the process. Hold baggage shall be properly marked externally to permit identification with relevant passengers (this obligation could be allocated to the air carrier or to the handling agent); furthermore, prior to loading, hold baggage shall, for example, be held in an area of the airport to which only authorized persons have access (this would consequently have to be designed as an obligation of the airport operator).
- Pursuant to Annex I, 5.2 of the Regulation (EC) on Aviation Security, hold baggage to be carried on an aircraft shall be protected from unauthorized interference from the point at which it is accepted into the care of the carrier until departure of the aircraft on which it is to be carried. This obligation could well be allocated to the airport operator. Allocating this obligation to the air carriers, on the other hand, should be excluded, as they do not have access to the baggage between check-in and loading.
- Annex I, 6.1 of the Regulation (EC) on Aviation Security provides that all cargo, courier, and express parcels intended to be carried on passenger or all-cargo aircraft shall be subjected to the security controls detailed in the Annex before being placed on board the aircraft. Commission Regulation (EC) No. 272/2009, Part F, No. 2.1 then defines the qualifications for a so-called regulated agent; Part F, No. 2.2 defines the criteria for a so-called known consignor – both of them to be approved by the appropriate authority –, and Part F, No. 2.3 describes the criteria for the so-called account consignor to be designated by a regulated agent. Who concretely is obligated to act is only partially conclusive to the reader. National laws have to establish the required legal clarity by formulating the concrete obligations and allocating them to the relevant addressees.

III. AIR CARGO SECURITY

The air carrier can use an authorized so-called regulated agent to carry out security controls for cargo and can also carry out such controls outside airport grounds.

Air carriers or regulated agents can use 'known consignors' of cargo approved by the appropriate authority. 'Account consignors' are to be designated by a regulated agent. This way, the time and effort involved in control of cargo will be reduced significantly.

'Delegation' of security controls to a regulated agent releases the air carrier from control obligations for cargo which would otherwise be his responsibility. Although approval of a regulated agent or a known consignor also means that supervision is transferred to the responsible authority, the air carrier remains obligated to notify the control agency of any obvious breaches of obligation of the regulated agent.

A. Background

Regulation (EC) 300/2008 and Commission Regulation (EC) No. 272/2009, which also extensively deal with cargo security, take up the concept of the air carrier as one of the three 'pillars' of aviation security (beside the airports and the authorities) with regard to cargo by significantly facilitating its obligations of control of cargo when cooperating with a 'regulated agent.'

In contrast to the former Regulation (EC) 2320/2003, the 'known consignor' as the additional part of the chain, is no longer designated by just a private person (the regulated agent), but officially authorized (under public law: Commission Regulation (EC) No. 272/2009, Part F, No. 2). However, account consignors shall be designated by a regulated agent (Part F, No. 3). Due to their 'public responsibilities', it is justified to designate this system as the 'fourth pillar' of aviation security architecture in Europe.

Connecting the cargo chain to the proven construction may be understood as a further development of a proven system; however, this further development has weaknesses that cannot be overlooked and that become obvious when considering that cargo and mail are not only transported by aircraft, but also (in addition or exclusively) by other means of transport. European and consequently also national aviation security law of the Member States might be plausible and conclusive in themselves when assuming that transported goods are usually taken from the producer (consignor) to a forwarding agent and so on, all the way to an aircraft which transports them to their destination. If such goods are also or exclusively transported by road or rail or on waterways, this obviously means that aviation security law cannot be applied to the process and therefore another legal regime has to ensure security of the goods. This leads to an unnecessary complication not only of the question of applicable law, but even more so of a multiplication of the time and effort required for the recognition process for the (known) consignors, who have to subject themselves to the recognition process several times from the perspective of the relevant applicable law.

An appropriate solution, therefore, has to start from the process as a whole; it has to be process-oriented and define common processes for all types of transport from the producer to the consumer. In addition, it has to be designed in an international way and, therefore, has to be at least guided by the US-system (C-TPAT) [12] or be adapted to it.

B. Legal Persons: Regulated Agent, Known Consignor and Account Consignor

1. The Regulated Agent

According to Article 3, No. 26 of Regulation (EC) 300/2008, a 'regulated agent' means an air carrier, agent, freight forwarder, or any other entity who ensures security controls in respect of cargo or mail. The legal person 'regulated agent' thereby has both a private law and a public law aspect. First of all, the regulated agent has to 'conduct business' (private law) with an air carrier, due to which the execution of security measures which are normally the responsibility of the air carrier itself are transferred to the regulated agent. In addition, an (public law) act of State is required which leads to relevant public law obligations. This 'regulation' of the agent is carried out in accordance with Commission Regulation (EC) No. 272/2009, Part F, No. 2.

a. Conducting Business with an Air Carrier

According to No. 1.20 of the Annex to the former Regulation (EC) 2320/2002, the definition of a 'regulated agent' included his conducting business with an air carrier. However, this could not necessarily mean that his commission stemmed from such business relationship. In most cases, he has rather been commissioned by the consignor (producer) of the cargo. 'Conducting business' as was referred to in Regulation (EC) 2320/2002 was, therefore, understood to be of a more factual nature, that is, the regulated agent has to conduct business with an air carrier or enter such business relationships so as to process the order by the consignor. Regulation (EC) 300/2008 does no longer require a formal business relationship with an air carrier.

b. Approval by the Aviation Security Authority

Part F, No. 6.1 of Commission Regulation (EC) No. 272/2009 requires a regulated agent to be 'approved by the appropriate authority' to obtain the legal position of regulated agent. By mentioning several types of decisions, the EC law takes the national laws of the individual Member States into account. In accordance with German law, for example, the legal position of a regulated agent is best justified with the approval, since it shall not only be ensured that he meets certain

---

12. For more details see: <www.cbp.gov/xp/cgov/trade/cargo_security/ctpat/what_ctpat/ctpat_overview.xml>.

requirements, but also that he plays an independent role in the economic and legal environment due to these requirements, especially recognition and supervision of the known consignor.

However, this is not an entrustment with public power (*Beleihung*), as this would require the tasks carried out by the regulated agent originally being tasks within the responsibility of the authority. However, the tasks of the regulated agent in relation to the known consignor are designed as original tasks of the regulated agent or the regulated postal authority or administration by the law-makers. Since completing these tasks is not only in the (private) economic interest of the regulated agent or the regulated postal authority/administration (reduction of time and effort when carrying out security measures), but mainly in the public interest, the regulated agents or the regulated postal authorities/administration thereby receive a virtually authority-like character. This is also confirmed by the tasks conferred to them (recognition and supervision of the known consignor).

The commissioner receives an approval certificate as a 'regulated agent' or 'regulated postal authority/administration' from the appropriate authority which officially notes his status as regulated agent.

c. *Criteria for Approval*

In contrast to the former Regulation (EC) 2320/2002, Commission Regulations (EC) No. 272/2009 and, in particular, No. 185/2010 (Annex, No. 6.3) include criteria for approval of the regulated agent. In order to be approved as a regulated agent, the applicant shall submit documentation on aviation security standards and shall then be subject to an on-site verification to ensure that it fulfils the required standards.

The Regulation leaves it up to the appropriate national authorities to determine the details. It is questionable whether this solution is particularly appropriate, as one has to take into account that significant burdens both with regard to organization and process would be imposed on an 'air carrier, agent, freight forwarder or any other entity' that could be considered as a regulated agent. Furthermore, these burdens would have significant financial consequences as well. The heavier such burdens are, the stricter are the criteria for approval as a 'regulated agent'. This could, when comparing the individual EU Member States, lead to unequal treatment, which could result in significant distortion of competition.

d. *Obligations of the Regulated Agent*

The obligations of the regulated agent and the regulated postal authority/administration are derived from those of the air carrier, that is, they either have to apply the aforementioned security measures to the cargo handed to them by the consignor or have to deal with a consignor who is approved as a 'known consignor' beforehand.

Commission Regulation (EC) No. 185/2010 (Annex, No. 6.3.2) sets forth the following obligations of a regulated agent:

6.3.2 **Security controls to be applied by a regulated agent**

6.3.2.1 When accepting any consignments, a regulated agent shall establish whether the entity from which it receives the consignments is a regulated agent, a known consignor, an account consignor or none of these.

6.3.2.2 The person delivering the consignments to the regulated agent or air carrier shall present an identity card, passport, driving licence or other document, which includes his or her photograph and which has been issued or is recognised by the national authority. The card or document shall be used to establish the identity of the person delivering the consignments.

6.3.2.3 When accepting consignments to which not all required security controls have previously been applied, the regulated agent shall ensure that they are screened in accordance with point 6.2.

6.3.2.4 After the security controls referred to in points 6.3.2.1 to 6.3.2.3 of this Regulation and point 6.3 of a separate Commission Decision have been applied, the regulated agent shall ensure that:

(a) access to these consignments is controlled; and

(b) these consignments are protected from unauthorised interference until they are handed over to another regulated agent or air carrier.

6.3.2.5 After the security controls referred to in points 6.3.2.1 to 6.3.2.4 of this Regulation have been applied, the regulated agent shall ensure that any consignment tendered to an air carrier or another regulated agent is accompanied by appropriate documentation, either in the form of an air waybill or in a separate declaration and either in an electronic format or in writing.

6.3.2.6 The documentation shall be available for inspection by the appropriate authority at any point before the consignment is loaded on to an aircraft and shall provide the following information:

(a) the site specific name and address of the regulated agent that issued the security status and/or its unique alphanumeric identifier as received from the appropriate authority;

(b) a unique identifier of the consignment, such as the number of the (house or master) air waybill;

(c) the content of the consignment;

(d) the security status of the consignment, stating

- 'SPX', meaning secure for passenger, all-cargo and all-mail aircraft, or
- 'SCO', meaning secure for all-cargo and all-mail aircraft only;

(e) the reason that the security status was issued, stating:

- 'KC', meaning received from known consignor, or
- 'AC', meaning received from account consignor, or
- the means or method of screening used, or
- the grounds for exempting the consignment from screening;

(f) the name of the person who issued the security status, or an equivalent identification, and the date and time of issue;

(g) the site specific name and address, or unique identifier received from the appropriate authority, of any regulated agent who has accepted the security status given to a consignment by another regulated agent.

6.3.2.7 In the case of consolidations, the requirements under points 6.3.2.6(c), (e), (f) and (g) will be considered as met, if the regulated agent is able to establish the nature of the contents, the reason that the security status was issued and/or the name of the person who issued the security status and the date and time of issue, respectively, by a verifiable audit trail at any time before the consignment is loaded on an aircraft and afterwards for the duration of the flight or for 24 hours, whichever is the longer.

6.3.2.8 When accepting consignments to which not all required security controls have previously been applied, the regulated agent may also elect not to apply the security controls as referred to in point 6.3.2, but to hand the consignments over to another regulated agent to ensure the application of these security controls. Security controls to be applied by a regulated agent shall also be subject to the additional provisions laid down in a separate Commission Decision.

2. The Known Consignor/the Account Consignor

Pursuant to Article 3 of Regulation (EC) No. 300/2008, a 'known consignor' and an 'account consignor' are:

- No. 27: 'known consignor' means a consignor who originates cargo or mail for its own account and whose procedures meet common security rules and standards sufficient to allow carriage of cargo or mail on any aircraft;
- No. 28: 'account consignor' means a consignor who originates cargo or mail for its own account and whose procedures meet common security rules and standards sufficient to allow carriage of that cargo on all-cargo aircraft or mail on all-mail aircraft.

Whereas a known consignor must be approved by the appropriate authority, an account consignor is to be designated by a regulated agent.

a. The Known Consignor

Commission Regulation (EC) No. 185/2010 (Annex, No. 6.4) contains the following provisions:

6.4.1 **Approval of known consignors**

6.4.1.1 Known consignors shall be approved by the appropriate authority.
The approval as a known consignor shall be site specific.

6.4.1.2 The appropriate authority of each Member State shall define in its national civil aviation security programme as referred to in Article 10 of Regulation (EC) No. 300/2008 the responsibilities for the implementation of the following procedure on the approval of known consignors:

(a) the applicant shall seek approval from the appropriate authority of the Member State in which its site is located.

The applicant shall be provided with the 'Guidance for known consignors' as contained in Attachment 6-B;

(b) the appropriate authority, or independent validator acting on its behalf, shall make an on-site verification of the sites specified in order to assess whether the applicant complies with the requirements of Regulation (EC) No. 300/2008 and its implementing acts.

In order to assess whether the applicant complies with these requirements, the appropriate authority, or independent validator acting on its behalf, shall make use of the 'Validation checklist for known consignors' as contained in Attachment 6-C. This checklist includes a declaration of commitments which shall be signed by the applicant's legal representative or by the person responsible for security at the site.

The appropriate authority, or independent validator acting on its behalf, should take into account whether or not the applicant is a holder of an AEO certificate referred to in point (b) or (c) of Article 14a(1) of Commission Regulation (EC) No. 1875/2006 amending Regulation (EEC) No. 2454/93.

Once the validation checklist is completed, the information contained in the checklist shall be handled as classified information.

The signed declaration shall be retained by the appropriate authority concerned or retained by the independent validator and made available on request to the appropriate authority concerned;

(c) if the appropriate authority is satisfied with the information provided under points (a) and (b), it shall ensure that the necessary details of the consignor are entered into the 'EC database of regulated agents and known consignors' not later than the next working day. When making the database entry the appropriate authority shall give each approved site a unique alphanumeric identifier in the standard format.

If the appropriate authority is not satisfied with the information provided under points (a) and (b) then the reasons shall promptly be notified to the entity seeking approval as a known consignor;

(d) where a known consignor has been approved before 29 April 2010 to ensure that the requirements covered by point 6.4.2 were met, it may be considered as a known consignor for the purposes of Regulation (EC) No. 300/2008 and its implementing acts for up to 3 years after the entry into force of this Regulation;

(e) a known consignor shall not be considered as approved until its details are listed in the 'EC database of regulated agents and known consignors'.

6.4.1.3 A known consignor shall designate at least one person at each site who shall be responsible for the application and supervision of the implementation of security controls at that site. This person shall have successfully completed a background check.

6.4.1.4 A known consignor shall be re-validated at regular intervals not exceeding 5 years. This shall include an on-site verification in order to assess whether the known consignor still complies with the requirements of Regulation (EC) No. 300/2008 and its implementing acts.

An inspection at the premises of the known consignor by the appropriate authority in accordance with its national quality control programme may be considered as an on-site verification, provided that it covers all areas specified in the checklist of Attachment 6-C.

6.4.1.5 If the appropriate authority is no longer satisfied that the known consignor complies with the requirements of Regulation (EC) No. 300/2008 and its implementing acts, it shall withdraw the status of known consignor for the specified site(s).

Immediately after withdrawal, and in all cases within 24 hours, the appropriate authority shall ensure that the consignor's change of status is indicated in the 'EC database of regulated agents and known consignors'.

6.4.1.6 Without prejudice to the right of each Member State to apply more stringent measures in accordance with Article 6 of Regulation (EC) No. 300/2008, a known consignor approved in accordance with point 6.4 shall be recognised in all Member States.

Known consignors approved in accordance with point 6.4.1.2(d) shall also be subject to the additional provision laid down in point 6.4 of a separate Commission Decision.

6.4.2 **Security controls to be applied by a known consignor**

6.4.2.1 A known consignor shall ensure that:

(a) there is a level of security on the site or at the premises sufficient to protect identifiable air cargo and identifiable air mail from unauthorised interference; and

(b) all staff with access to identifiable air cargo or identifiable air mail to which the required security controls have been applied have been recruited and trained in accordance with the requirements of chapter 11; and

(c) during production, packing, storage, despatch and/or transportation, as appropriate, identifiable air cargo and identifiable air mail is protected from unauthorised interference or tampering.

When, for whatever reason, these security controls have not been applied to a consignment, or where the consignment has not been originated by the known consignor for its own account, the known consignor shall clearly identify this to the regulated agent so that point 6.3.2.3 can be applied.

6.4.2.2 The known consignor shall accept that consignments to which the appropriate security controls have not been applied are screened in accordance with point 6.2.1.

b. The Account Consignor

Commission Regulation (EC) No. 185/2010 (Annex, No. 6.5) contains the following provisions:

6.5.1 Account consignors shall be designated by a regulated agent.

6.5.2 In order to be designated as an account consignor, the following procedure shall apply:

(a) the regulated agent shall provide the entity with the 'Aviation security instructions for account consignors' and 'Declaration of commitments – account consignor' as contained in Attachment 6-D. These instructions and declaration shall be provided to the regulated agent by the appropriate authority of the Member State in which its site is located;

(b) the entity shall submit a signed 'Declaration of commitments – account consignor' as contained in Attachment 6-D to the regulated agent, unless the entity is a holder of an AEO certificate referred to in point (b) or (c) of Article 14a(1) of Commission Regulation (EC) No. 1875/2006 amending Regulation (EEC) No. 2454/93.

The entity shall also designate at least one person responsible for security at its premises and shall inform the regulated agent of this person's name and contact details.

Where applicable, the signed declaration shall be retained by the regulated agent and made available on request to the appropriate authority concerned.

Where the requirement to complete a Declaration of Commitments has been waived on the basis of an AEO certificate, an account consignor shall immediately inform the regulated agent if it is no longer a holder of such a certificate;

(c) the regulated agent shall make a validation by establishing the following details of the prospective account consignor:

- the company details, including the bona fide business address, and
- the nature of the business, and
- contact details, including those of the person(s) responsible for security, and
- VAT reference number or company registration number, and
- where the exemption under 6.5.2(b) is applied, the AEO certificate number;

(d) if the regulated agent is satisfied with the information provided under points (b) and (c), then the regulated agent may designate the entity as an account consignor.

6.5.3 The regulated agent shall maintain a database with the information referred to in point 6.5.2(c). The database shall be available for inspection by the appropriate authority.

6.5.4 If there is no activity relating to movements of cargo or mail by air on the account of the account consignor within a period of 2 years, the status of account consignor shall expire.

6.5.5 If the appropriate authority or the regulated agent is no longer satisfied that the account consignor complies with the instructions as contained in Attachment 6-D, the regulated agent shall immediately withdraw the status of account consignor.

6.5.6 When, for whatever reason, the security controls specified in the 'Aviation security instructions for account consignors' have not been applied to a consignment, or where the consignment has not been originated by the account consignor for its own account, the account consignor shall clearly identify this to the regulated agent so that point 6.3.2.3 can be applied.

Chapter 12

Aviation and the European Emissions Trading Scheme

Elmar M. Giemulla and Heiko van Schyndel

An emissions-trading system is a system whereby the total amount of emissions is capped, and allowances in the form of permits to emit CO_2 can be bought and sold to meet emission-reduction objectives. Such a system could serve as a cost-effective measure to limit or reduce CO_2) emitted by civil aviation in the long term, provided that it is open to all economic sectors.[1]

I. BACKGROUND OF THE EU ETS DIRECTIVE

Aircraft engines produce emissions that are similar to other emissions resulting from fossil fuel combustion. However, aircraft emissions are unusual in that a significant proportion is emitted at high altitudes. These emissions give rise to important environmental concerns regarding their global impact and their effect on local air quality at ground level.[2]

1. <www.icao.int/icao/en/env/EmissionsTrading.htm>.
2. <www.icao.int/icao/en/env/aee.htm>.

Elmar M. Giemulla & Ludwig Weber, *International and EU Aviation Law: Selected Issues*, pp. 377–393.

In this regard, the Kyoto Protocol of 1997[3] to the United Nations Framework Convention on Climate Change (UNFCCC)[4] is of particular importance. The protocol, which entered into force on 16 February 2005, requires countries listed in Annex I to the Convention (industrialized countries) to reduce their emissions by 8% during the period from 2008–2012 compared with 1990 levels.

Although, the international aviation contributes to climate change through different aircraft emissions (carbon dioxide and water vapour emissions, contrails or 'aviation smog', indirectly nitrogen oxides) the Kyoto Protocol[5] excluded emissions from international aviation services from national emissions targets, and stipulated that an approach to addressing emissions from international aviation should be developed separately through the International Civil Aviation Organization (ICAO). 'At the sixth meeting of the ICAO Committee on Aviation Environmental Protection in 2004, it was agreed that an aviation-specific emissions trading system based on a new legal instrument under ICAO auspices seemed sufficiently unattractive that it should not then be pursued further. Consequently, Resolution A35-5 of the ICAO's 35th Assembly held in September 2004 did not propose a new legal instrument but instead endorsed open emissions trading and the possibility for States to incorporate emissions from international aviation into their emissions trading schemes. Appendix L to Resolution A36-22 of the ICAO's 36th Assembly held in September 2007 urges Contracting States not to implement an emissions trading system on other Contracting States' aircraft operators except on the basis of mutual agreement between those States.

But since it is imperative that each mode of transport makes its contribution to tackling climate change, ways of limiting greenhouse gas emissions from aviation have to be sought.[6] Recalling that the Chicago Convention recognizes expressly the right of each Contracting Party to apply on a non-discriminatory basis its own air laws and regulations to the aircraft of all States, the Member States of the European Community and fifteen other European States placed a reservation on this resolution and reserved the right under the Chicago Convention to enact and apply market-based measures on a non-discriminatory basis to all aircraft operators of all States providing services to, from or within their territory.'[7]

In accordance with this approach, the European Commission proposed in February 2005 that international aviation should be included in any post-2012 climate change regime. 'Several policy options were examined, including aviation taxes, such as a fuel tax – as kerosene is currently exempted from taxation – but this would have required a unanimous decision in the Council of Ministers and was strongly opposed by the aviation industry.

---

3. Kyoto Protocol to the United Nations Framework Convention on Climate Change, 10 Dec. 1997, *UN Doc.* FCCC/CP/1997/7/Add.1, 37 *ILM* (1998) 22.
4. Framework Convention on Climate Change, 9 May 1992, 31 *ILM* 849.
5. Kyoto Protocol to the United Nations Framework Convention on Climate Change, 10 Dec. 1997, *UN Doc.* FCCC/CP/1997/7/Add.1, 37 *ILM* (1998) 22.
6. <www.bmvbs.de/en/Transport/Aviation-,2969/Environmental-protection.htm>.
7. Preamble of Directive 2008/101/EC, Recital (9).

In a September 2005 Communication, the Commission finally concluded that bringing aviation into the EU's greenhouse gas (GHG) emissions trading system (EU-ETS) would be the most cost-effective way of reducing the climate change impact of aviation.'[8] On 20 December 2006, the Commission adopted a proposal for legislation to include aviation in the European Emissions Trading Scheme (EU ETS).[9] Consequently, the Directive 2008/101/EC that modifies Directive 2003/87/EC requires all aircraft operators flying into or out of any EU airport to participate in the EU ETS from 2012.

On 19 November 2008, the European Parliament and the Council adopted Directive 2008/101/EC amending Directive 2003/87/EC so as to include aviation activities in the scheme for greenhouse gas emission allowance trading within the Community. It was published in the Official Journal on 13 January 2009[10] and according to its Article 3 entered into force on the 20th day following its publication in the Official Journal of the European Union, i.e. on 2 February 2009. EC Member States had one year to transpose the Directive into national law.

The intention of the EC legislator is for the EU ETS to serve as a model for other countries considering similar national or regional schemes, and to link these to the EU ETS over time. Therefore, the EU ETS in the view of the European Parliament and of the Council can form the basis for wider, global action.

The main milestones on the way to include aviation into the EU ETS were/are:

- 20 December 2006: Commission presented draft legislation aimed at including aviation in the Emissions Trading Scheme.
- 26 June 2008: MEPs and the EU's Slovenian Presidency reached a deal on the details of plans to include aviation in the EU's Emissions Trading Scheme as of 2012.
- 8 July 2008: European Parliament backed compromise deal, paving the way for entry into force of the legislation.
- 24 October 2008: EU justice ministers approved a compromise deal on including aviation activities in the EU ETS.
- 7 March 2011: Commission decision on historical aviation emissions establishing a scheme for GHG emission allowance trading within the EU.
- 1 January 2012: Target date for aviation sector to start trading CO_2.
- 1 January 2013: Revised EU ETS due to come into force, covering not only power-intensive industries, but also aviation.[11]

8. See: <www.euractiv.com/en/climate-change/aviation-emissions-trading/article-139728>.
9. Proposal for a Directive of the European Parliament and of the Council amending Directive 2003/87/EC so as to include aviation activities in the scheme for greenhouse gas emission allowance trading within the Community (presented by the Commission), *COM/2006/0818 final* - COD 2006/0304.
10. *OJ* No. L 8 of 13 Jan. 2009, 3.
11. See: <www.euractiv.com/en/climate-change/aviation-emissions-trading/article-139728>.

II. EUROPEAN GREENHOUSE GAS EMISSIONS TRADING SCHEME IN GENERAL

The European Greenhouse Gas Emissions Trading Scheme has been operational since January 2005 for some 10,000 fixed energy intensive installations in the energy, metals, minerals and paper industries. It is the largest multi-country, multi-sector GHG emission trading scheme in the world and covers around 2 billion tones of CO_2 emissions or about 50% of the EU's total emissions. The scheme is based on Directive 2003/87/EC of the European Parliament and of the Council of 13 October 2003 establishing a scheme for GHG emission allowance trading within the Community and amending Council Directive 96/61/EC,[12] which entered into force on 25 October 2003. Emission trading is an economic policy instrument used to control emissions by providing economic incentives for achieving emission reductions. An emission trading system sets a cap on the amount of a pollutant that can be emitted.

Companies under the trading system are given allowances which represent the right to emit a specific amount. Companies that emit in excess of their allowances must buy allowances from an operator that has more allowances than it needs. In the first period, 15% of allowances are to be auctioned.

III. CATEGORIES OF AVIATION ACTIVITIES INCLUDED IN THE EU ETS

From 1 January 2012, all flights which arrive at or depart from an airport situated in the territory of a Member State to which the Treaty applies shall be included in the EU ETS, i.e. all flights arriving at or departing from EU airports are covered, regardless of the nationality of the aircraft operator. The term 'flight' means one flight sector, which is a flight or a series of flights which commences at a parking place of the aircraft and terminates at a parking place of the aircraft.[13]

According to Article 1, paragraph 1 of and Annex 1 to the Directive 2003/87/EC not included are:

(a) flights performed exclusively for the transport, on official mission, of a reigning Monarch and his immediate family, Heads of State, Heads of Government and Government Ministers, of a country other than a Member State, where this is substantiated by an appropriate status indicator in the flight plan;

12. *OJ* No. L 275 of 25 Oct. 2003, 32.
13. Draft Commission Decision on the detailed interpretation of the aviation activities listed in Annex I to Directive 2003/87/EC, Annex 'Guidelines on the detailed interpretation of the aviation activities listed in Annex I to Directive 2003/87/EC', <http://ec.europa.eu/transparency/regcomitology/searchform/OpenAttachment.cfm?zoBvnm93LFk4ZYqoxQyzQ3GIHXuly76zwFnTy1cTiDJvAGu0Y1ej7CE13uqKtKFx6kdqKFcBdrq3r2C35q/P/cNBhVGbvZjFJD0yeqx2XrVxKjB+RHHwdbIM9vZi883u>

(b) military flights performed by military aircraft and customs and police flights;
(c) flights related to search and rescue, firefighting flights, humanitarian flights and emergency medical service flights authorised by the appropriate competent authority;
(d) any flights performed exclusively under visual flight rules as defined in Annex 2 to the Chicago Convention;
(e) flights terminating at the aerodrome from which the aircraft has taken off and during which no intermediate landing has been made;
(f) training flights performed exclusively for the purpose of obtaining a licence, or a rating in the case of cockpit flight crew where this is substantiated by an appropriate remark in the flight plan provided that the flight does not serve for the transport of passengers and/or cargo or for the positioning or ferrying of the aircraft;
(g) flights performed exclusively for the purpose of scientific research or for the purpose of checking, testing or certifying aircraft or equipment whether airborne or ground-based;
(h) flights performed by aircraft with a certified maximum take-off mass of less than 5 700 kg;
(i) flights performed in the framework of public service obligations imposed in accordance with Regulation (EEC) No 2408/92 on routes within outermost regions, as specified in Article 299(2) of the Treaty, or on routes where the capacity offered does not exceed 30 000 seats per year; and
(j) flights which, but for this point, would fall within this activity, performed by a commercial air transport operator operating either:
   - fewer than 243 flights per period for three consecutive four-month periods; or
   - flights with total annual emissions lower than 10 000 tonnes per year.

   Flights performed exclusively for the transport, on official mission, of a reigning Monarch and his immediate family, Heads of State, Heads of Government and Government Ministers, of a Member State may not be excluded under this point.

IV. ALLOCATION OF ALLOWANCES

For the period from 1 January 2012 to 31 December 2012, the total quantity of allowances to be allocated to aircraft operators will be equivalent to 97% of the of historical aviation emissions, i. e. the mean average of the annual emissions in the calendar years 2004, 2005 and 2006. Historical emissions will be calculated from data held on the Eurocontrol billing system. Fifteen per cent of allowances will be auctioned and 3% set aside in a special reserve for new operators and operators whose activity has significantly increased. The remaining allowances will be allocated to operators free of charge in accordance with a benchmark drawn up by the Commission based upon operators' verified tonne-kilometre data.

For the five-year period beginning on 1 January 2013, the total quantity will be equivalent to 95% of historic aviation emissions. Furthermore, on 30 April 2013 and annually thereafter, aircraft operators will have to surrender a number of allowances equivalent to their CO_2 emissions, calculated from the previous year.

V. GENERAL RULES OF THE EMISSION TRADING SCHEME IN AVIATION

In order to reduce the administrative burden on aircraft operators, one Member State will be responsible for each aircraft operator. Member States will be required to ensure that aircraft operators which were issued with an operating license in that Member State, or aircraft operators without an operating license or from third countries whose emissions in a base year are mostly attributable to that Member State, comply with the requirements of the EU ETS.

The administering Member State in respect of an aircraft operator shall be:

(a) in the case of an aircraft operator with a valid operating license granted by a Member State, the Member State which granted the operating license; and
(b) in all other cases, the Member State with the greatest estimated attributed aviation emissions from flights performed by that aircraft operator in the base year.

The European Commission has published[14] and amended[15] a list of aircraft operators that have undertaken a relevant aviation activity on or after 1 January 2006, specifying the administering Member State for each aircraft operator.

The administering Member State should ensure that each aircraft operator submits to the competent authority in that Member State a monitoring plan setting out measures to monitor and report emissions and tonne kilometre data for the purpose of an application for an allocation of allowances that are to be allocated free of charge, and that such plans are approved by the competent authority in accordance with the guidelines adopted pursuant to Article 14 of Directive 2003/87/EC. The total amount of free emission allowances will be divided over all participating aircraft operators based on their transportation performance in 2010 in terms of tonne-kilometres. Based on the number of tonne-kilometres of all aircraft operators in the EU ETS and the total quantity of free emission allowances, the European Commission will set a benchmark on 30 September 2011 for calculating the individual allocation to each participating operator.

The annual issuance of allowances to operators must take place before March of each year. So an aircraft operator will receive the allowances for the year 2012 before March of that same year.

Each aircraft operator under the EU ETS has to have a monitoring plan. This plan lays down the rules that have to be followed when reporting the CO_2 emissions

14. *OJ* L 219 of 22 Aug. 2009, 1.
15. *OJ* L 25 of 29 Jan. 2010, 12.

data under the EU ETS. Each year, before April (or earlier in some countries), the EU ETS installation or aircraft operator has to report the amount of CO_2 emissions that have been emitted in the previous year. This report has to comply with the rules of the monitoring plan and has to be verified by an accredited verifier appointed by the aircraft operator.

Aircraft operators are obliged to match the (verified) emissions with an equal amount of allowances. This is called 'surrendering' of allowances. Each aircraft operator has to surrender the allowances (of the previous year) before 30 April of the ongoing year. If an operator is short of allowances it will have to buy allowances from an installation or aircraft operator that has more allowances than needed to cover the verified emissions. A company that does not surrender enough allowances will be fined and will still be obliged to surrender the missing allowances.

Member States can allow a limited use of credits by the Clean Development Mechanism (CDM) and Joint implementation (JI) for compliance use in the EU ETS. This means that airline operators can use CERs (Certified Emission Reductions) and ERUs (Emission Reduction Units) next to EUAs (EU Allowances) to cover their emissions.

Each aircraft operator may apply for an allocation of allowances that are to be allocated free of charge by submitting to the Competent Authority verified tonne-kilometre data for the calendar year ending 24 months before the start of the period to which it relates, or, in relation to the period from 1 January 2012 to 31 December 2012, - for the year 2010.

VI. PENALTIES

If an aircraft operator does not manage to surrender enough allowances by 30 April of each year to cover its emissions during the preceding year, it must expect not only to be obliged to surrender the additional allowances but also to pay a fine (EUR 100 for each tonne of CO_2 emitted for which the operator or aircraft operator has not surrendered allowances) and from this point on it is no longer in a position to sell allowances. Under the Council decision, the country responsible for administering this airline within the EU emission allowance trading scheme can as an *ultima ratio* revoke or suspend the airline's operating permit.

Article 16, paragraph 5 states:

> In the event that an aircraft operator fails to comply with the requirements of this Directive and where other enforcement measures have failed to ensure compliance, its administering Member State may request the Commission to decide on the imposition of an operating ban on the aircraft operator concerned.

The application of the administering Member State must in line with Article 16, paragraph 6 include the following elements:

(a) evidence that the aircraft operator has not complied with its obligations under this Directive;

(b) details of the enforcement action which has been taken by that Member State;
(c) a justification for the imposition of an operating ban at Community level; and
(d) a recommendation for the scope of an operating ban at Community level and any conditions that should be applied.

After informing all Member States (paragraph 7), holding consultations with the authorities responsible for regulatory oversight of the aircraft operator concerned (paragraph 8) and informing the airline, which should be given the opportunity to comment on its conduct (paragraph 9), the Commission decides on the basis of the request, in accordance with the procedure set out in Article 23, paragraph 2, to impose an operating ban on the aircraft in question (paragraph 10). The Member States must then enforce within their territory the measures decided at Community level and fully inform the Commission of these measures (paragraph 11). The Commission may, if appropriate, make more detailed stipulations regarding the procedure (paragraph 12).

VII. GENERAL TIMEFRAME OF ACTIVITIES REQUIRED UNDER THE DIRECTIVE

31 August 2009	Aircraft Operators to submit benchmarking plans and emissions plans to their respective competent authorities for approval
1 January 2010 and every year thereafter	Aircraft operators to monitor their total CO_2 emissions every year, starting with calendar year 2010. However, 2012 is the first monitoring year for which operators must surrender the correct number of allowances to cover their CO_2 emissions
1 January 2011 – 31 March 2011	Aircraft operators to have their emissions reports verified by a verifier who is approved by the relevant regulator (it is not necessary to have the emissions plan verified)
31 March 2011	Aircraft operators to submit pre-compliance verified benchmark tonne-km reports and annual emissions reports for the monitoring period 1 January 2010 to 31 December 2010
30 September 2011	Commission produces benchmark number for calculating emissions
31 December 2011	Regulator publishes final allocations to each operator

28 February 2012	Regulators issue allowances to operators
31 March 2012	Aircraft operators to submit pre-compliance annual emissions reports for the monitoring period 1 January 2011 to 31 December 2011
31 December 2012	End of first emissions reporting year for which allowances must be surrendered by operators. Submission of first verified emissions report.
April 2013 and every year thereafter	Aircraft operators surrender the correct number of allowances from their registry accounts to cover their CO_2 emissions

VIII. DEBATE ON THE (LEGALITY OF THE) EU ETS

A. The US cons

1. The Legal Objections[16]

The EU's proposal was initially met by a strong reaction from the US Government, which not only denounced the move as illegal, but threatened legal action.[17] This was echoed by a number of other nations - 130, according to the Director General of the International Air Transport Association (IATA).[18] Whether the Obama Administration will continue to press this legal issue is yet to be determined; the government is still grappling hard with the details of how it will meet its own promises to address the climate change issue, particularly in light of the Waxman-Markey bill (HR 2454), which is moving rapidly through Congress as of this writing, and which, *inter alia*, would establish a carbon-trading scheme. The Administration must solidify its position prior to the Conference of the Parties to the UNFCCC in Copenhagen in December 2009, where a successor to the Kyoto regime will be debated. Until that happens, no one can say how the US government will deal with the ETS.

The legal arguments directed against the EU's move have been, in any event, rather vague. There is a serious question whether there are solid legal grounds for an objection, and if so, what can be done about it. The legal arguments advanced normally invoke (1) the proper role of ICAO, (2) the Chicago Convention and

16. Subchapters 1 and 2 taken from: Mark Atwood, *Europe Contra Mundi - The Challenge of the EU's Emissions Trading Scheme*, in: *TQ Online* Vol. 2, No. 3, Summer 2009, 5, 14 et seq. <www.americanbar.org/content/dam/aba/migrated/2011_build/administrative_law/tq2009summer.pdf-2011-03-29>.
17. David Armstrong, *Clearing the Air: Emissions from Commercial Planes Prompt Concerns about Regulating Greenhouse Gases*, S.F. Chron., 14 Feb. 2007, at C-1.
18. IATA Director General and CEO Giovanni Bisignani claims that over 130 countries oppose the EU's inclusion of air carriers in the proposed emissions trading scheme. See Press Release, IATA, Europe Must Abandon 'Tunnel-Vision' On Emissions Trading (25 Jun. 2008), <www.iata.org/pressroom/pr/2008-06-25-02.htm>.

relevant bilateral air service agreements, (3) questions of extraterritorial application of laws, and (4) various practical problems resulting from a piecemeal approach to a global problem.[19]

It is significant that the Kyoto Protocol neither requires nor authorizes the ETS' reach into aviation. Rather, Article 2.2 says, 'The Parties included in Annex I shall pursue limitation or reduction of emissions of greenhouse gases . . . from aviation and marine bunker fuels, working through the International Civil Aviation Organization and the International Maritime Organization, respectively.'[20]

Despite Kyoto's specific deference to ICAO on this matter, the EU contends that ICAO has not acted with sufficient urgency and has expressed disappointment with the lack of progress. This helped justify its decision to take unilateral action on aviation emissions.

The fact is, however, that ICAO has been taking a number of actions to develop a coherent worldwide emissions trading system for aviation. In its October 2004 General Assembly, the organization adopted a resolution (A35-5) that established the goal of limiting or reducing the impact of international aviation GHG emissions on the global climate, and endorsed 'the further development of an open emissions trading system for international aviation.' It also instructed the Council to prepare guidance for States that wish to include airlines in their emissions trading schemes.[21]

At the following General Assembly in 2007, ICAO adopted Resolution A36-22[22] which asked States not to implement emissions trading systems except on the basis of 'mutual consent'. In an unusual move, however, the 42 nations of Europe (including the 27 Member States of the EU) filed a 'formal reserve' to Appendix L of the resolution, expressing 'great disappointment' in ICAO and reserving their rights under the Chicago Convention. Thus, Resolution A36-22 is an unlikely basis for legal action against the EU.

Some parties, notably the Air Transport Association, have advanced arguments based on provisions of the Chicago Convention, particularly Articles 1, 11, 12, 15 and 24. By way of very brief summary:

- Article 1 provides that States shall have *exclusive* sovereignty over the airspace above *their* territory.
- Article 11 provides that laws relating to admission or departure of aircraft from a State's territory must be complied with 'by such aircraft upon entering or departing from or while within the territory of that State'.

19. *See generally*, Janelle Veno, *Flying the Unfriendly Skies: The European Union's New Proposal to Include Aviation in Their Emissions Trading Scheme*, 72 J. Air L. & Com. 429, 659 (Summer 2007); Stephen R. Stegich & Laura A. McGinn, *The EU Emissions Trading Scheme and Aviation*, 16th Annual Aero-Engine Cost Management Conference, February 6–7, 2008.
20. *See also Emissions Trading for International Aviation*, ICAO, 9th Meeting of Directors of Civil Aviation of the Central Caribbean, C/CAR DCA/9 WP/10, 20 Jun. 2007, at 2.1.
21. Published in 2008 as *Guidance on the Use of Emissions Trading for Aviation*, ICAO Doc. 9885.
22. *Consolidated Statement of Continuing ICAO Policies and Practices Relating to Environmental Protection*, ICAO, Sep. 2007.

- Article 12 requires States to ensure that (1) aircraft carrying their mark, wherever they are operating comply with the regulations in force in that location; (2) they keep their own regulations uniform 'to the greatest possible extent' *with those of ICAO*; and (3) *ICAO rules shall govern over the high seas.*
- Article 15 prohibits fees or charges solely for entry into, exit from, or transit over, the territory of any Contracting State.
- Article 24 forbids imposition of duties and other charges on aviation fuel.

The ETS arguably offends Article 1 in that the EU is purporting to exercise regulatory jurisdiction over flights outside its territory. The extraterritorial reach of the rule also may be challenged under customary international law, unless the legislating country can meet the 'effects doctrine' test,[23] thereby justifying its reach. Although this is questionable given the very attenuated actual impact of flights on climate change in Europe.

An Article 11 violation can be alleged because the ETS effectively regulates the ability of an aircraft to enter into the territory of an EU nation, yet compliance is required not simply upon entering or while within European territory, but throughout the entire flight. Further, Article 11 makes entry and exit requirements '[s]ubject to the provisions of this Convention'. The ETS is arguably inconsistent with the Convention in many respects.

The ETS may violate Article 12 in that it is clearly not consistent with the resolutions laid down under the Convention, and it purports to regulate flights over the high seas where only ICAO rules may govern. Article 15 may be violated because the requirement that airlines buy at auction or from other entities at least some of the credits needed to fly may be a de facto charge solely for entry, exit, or transit over European territory.[24] Moreover, the charge would not be related to the cost of providing airports or air navigation facilities, as is required by the Article.[25] Finally, Article 24's prohibition on fuel taxes may be violated in that the allocation of credits – some of which must be purchased – is based on fuel uplift as a proxy for emissions. The ICAO Council has interpreted this article very broadly to include 'import, export, excise, sales, consumption and internal duties and taxes of all kinds'.[26] Some of these same arguments, particularly on taxation, could be made under the air service agreements between the EU (or its individual Member States) and other nations. For example, the 2008 US-EU open-skies agreement contains standard bilateral agreement language very similar to

23. *See* Restatement (Third) of Foreign Relations Law of the United States, §§ 402-403 (1987); *see also* Ruwantissa Abeyratne, *The Authority of the European Union to Unilaterally Impose an Emissions Trading Scheme*, *The Air & Space Lawyer*, 2008, at 5-9.
24. The ICAO Legal Bureau has concluded that 'it would not be legitimate for States to individually establish a charge including environmental costs related to territories they have no sovereignty over.' Secretariat, *Legal Framework and Policy Issues Related to the Use of Emissions-Related Levies*, CAEP/6-WP24, at para. 3.6.5.
25. *See ICAO's Policies on Charges for Airports and Air Navigation Services*, Doc. 9082/7, paras 2–3 (2004).
26. Policy on Taxation in the Field of International Aviation, Doc. 8632 (3d edition, 2000) at 1(a) & (b).

Article 24, exempting fuel from 'taxes, levies, duties, fees and charges'.[27] Moreover, violators of the ETS may be barred from service to the EU, which may violate the Grant of Rights provisions of that and other air transport agreements.

2. Legal Recourse

The implication of these arguments is that the EU may be haled before the Council of ICAO under Article 84 of the Convention, which provides for settlement of disputes between Contracting States. There is a recent and very close precedent for such an action: the dispute between the United States and the EU in 1999–2001 concerning the EU's regulation barring aircraft using 'hush kits' to reduce engine noise to levels below ICAO Annex 16 Chapter 2 levels.[28] That regulation primarily impacted US-manufactured aircraft and hush kits,[29] since the European-made Airbus aircraft achieved the quieter 'Chapter 3' limits without the use of hush kits. The abundant evidence that this rule was adopted with the specific intent of keeping out hush-kitted aircraft of US manufacture made it easy to make out a case under Articles 11 and 15 on deprivation of 'national treatment.' Violations of Articles 33, 37 and 38, regarding mutual recognition of certificates of airworthiness and collaboration in securing uniformity of standards and regulations, were also alleged.

After more than a year of fruitless lobbying of the European Commission, including personal entreaties by President Clinton, the United States filed a petition with the ICAO Council on March 14, 2000. This initiated the legal process laid out in ICAO's 'Rules for the Settlement of Differences',[30] which included months of mediation by Council President Assad Kotaite. The case was fully briefed and argued to the Council, and only after it became clear that the EU would not prevail was a compromise reached that involved adoption of an ICAO resolution[31] promoting a 'balanced approach' to environmental regulation. The EU regulation was rescinded and the United States withdrew its complaint under Article 84.[32] This precedent may light the way for one or more nations to take the EU before the Council. It may not be the United States this time, however, since the US may end up settling privately with Europe (see below). If some nation takes the EU before the Council, the matter would be handled much like the hush-kit dispute. Council members that are party to the dispute may not vote in the Council's decision. The unsuccessful party may appeal the decision either to the International Court of Justice[33] or to an ad hoc arbitral tribunal. The penalties are severe: Article 88

27. Air Transport Agreement between the United States and Member States of the European Union, art. 11, para. 1 & 2(c), *available at* <www.state.gov/e/eeb/rls/othr/ata/e/eu/114768.htm>.
28. Council Regulation 925/99, 1999 O.J. (L 120) 47.
29. The author participated in this dispute as counsel for a coalition of hush kit manufacturers.
30. ICAO, *Rules for the Settlement of Differences* (2d Ed. 1975).
31. Resolution A33/7 (7 October 2001).
32. The case against Belgium, however, was not dropped at that time based on concerns about its imposition of curfews and other operating restrictions.
33. This would be as successor to the Permanent Court of International Justice, which is identified in the Convention.

provides that the Assembly *shall* suspend the voting rights in the Council and Assembly of any Contracting State that is found in violation; Article 87 requires each Contracting State to *refuse entry* into its airspace by aircraft of a Contracting State that the Council finds does not comply with its decision. Thus, it seems unlikely that, if challenged under Article 84, the EU would let the matter go all the way to a Council vote, particularly because it would have no voice in that decision.

3. Legal action

On 16 December 2009, the Air Transport Association of America (ATA) and three US airlines (American, Continental and United) commenced their long-threatened legal action against the inclusion of aviation in the ETS. The claimants brought their case in the Administrative Court in London. The English court permitted various entities to intervene in the case, including IATA, which represents about 230 airlines comprising 93% of scheduled international air traffic; the National Airlines Council of Canada (NACC); and five environmental, non-governmental organizations (the Aviation Environment Federation, WWF-UK, the European Fund for Transport and Environment, the Environmental Defense Fund and Earthjustice). The UK government opposes the claims, but has no objection to referral to the CJEU. As expected the case was referred to the Court of Justice of the EU (CJEU) and a preliminary ruling has been sought from the CJEU on a number of questions concerning the validity of Directive 2003/87, as amended by Directive 2008/101. Under EU law, only the CJEU has authority to declare EU legislation invalid and may render a ruling on these issues that will be binding on all Member States. The CJEU has been asked to prioritize this case in view of its global importance and the requirement under the ETS that carriers surrender allowances effective 1 January 2012.[34]

B. The Position of African States

African States view with the great concern the unilateral imposition of the Emission Trading scheme by the European Union on non-EU carriers. The EC Directive raises serious questions regarding the issues of Chicago Convention and Bilateral Air Services Agreements. It is disputable if this is in conflict with the Chicago Convention, in particular, to

- Article 1: Is ETS a violation of the sovereignty of other Member States?
- Article 15, which permits charges solely for the entry or exit.

Furthermore, the Directive subjects African States and their airlines to the required emission targets an action which is contrary to the provisions of the Kyoto

34. Mark Bisset/Georgina Crowhurst, *Is the EU's Application of its Emissions Trading Scheme to Aviation Illegal?*, <www.clydeco.com/news/articles/is-the-eus-application-of-its-emissions-trading-scheme-to-aviation-illegal.cfm>.

Protocol. There is need to comply with the United Nations Framework Convention on Climate Change (UNFCCC) principle of common but differentiated responsibilities and capabilities.

African States are therefore stating that they:

a) do not support unilateral inclusion of third party airlines in the Emission Trading Scheme (ETS) of European Union (EU) without their mutual consent, as well as the EU proposed geographical scope of the scheme. They believe that while Emission Trading could be a more effective solution than imposition of charges, inclusion of aviation emissions in ETS should follow ICAO guidelines based on mutual agreement of States and airlines involved;
b) believe that since Kyoto Protocol does not set emission targets for developing countries, inclusion of airlines from developing countries in the ETS of EU would amount to setting for them emission targets through the back door;
c) believe that ICAO and Contracting States should adhere to the UNFCCC fundamental principle of common but differentiated responsibilities and capabilities for developing and developed countries;
d) support the ICAO's efforts in minimizing the impact of aviation emission on the environment. African States do not believe that unilateral imposition of aviation emission charges by a region is an effective solution to the problem of emission due to difficulties associated with direct application of those charges to emission reduction and the potential discrimination against aviation in comparison to other more polluting sectors. African States therefore do not support the imposition of aviation emission charges;
e) agree and support that ICAO should be the forum through which to resolve all technical issues relating to the environment;
f) expect that emphasis should be on those measures that reduce emissions and at the same time do not negatively impact the growth of air transport, particularly in the developing countries where the industry is at infancy. Such emphasis should be on the development of better fuel efficient engines, research into alternative fuels, reduction in air traffic delays, fuel burn by aircraft etc.; and
g) expect ICAO and its Contracting States to look closely at the management of interrelationship between noise and emissions. In this regard advocate for removal of night curfews imposed on operation into airports particularly in Europe, since aircraft noise levels have over the years reduced considerably. Retention of the night curfews further increase delays and congestion at those airports with great fuel burn and other operational penalties to airlines, as well as higher emissions into the environment.'[35]

---

35. ICAO Assembly – 36th session, Agenda Item 17: Environmental protection, Working Paper: Environment and Emission Trading Charges (Presented by Nigeria on behalf of African States), A36-WP/251.

The future will show how the non-European aviation community will react on the ETS Directive. Maybe, the ICAO has to decide on the matter. Third countries affected by the Directive that are Contracting States to the Chicago Convention may make recourse to the ICAO Council as an arbitration body to appeal the inclusion of GHG emissions from international aviation in the EU emission allowance trading scheme.

C. THE EU PROS

1. Political Statements

The Commission's Head of Unit for clean air and transport Marianne Klingbeil stressed that 'including aviation in the ETS is not the worst thing that could happen to the industry' but added that the EU would continue to push for a global agreement that would minimize the competitive disadvantage for European airlines. She denies that airlines were being treated any more unfavourably than other sectors, pointing to legislation currently under preparation to limit emissions from cars and ships.

The aviation sector has some of the fastest growth rates today, 'and this attracts attention', she said, adding: 'You ask: does aviation deserve the attention? But does the steel sector deserve it? Does Europe deserve more and more CO_2 emissions? The more coming from one sector, the more other sectors already under the ETS have to pay for it. Is this a fair deal?'

Environment Commissioner Stavros Dimas defended the inclusion of all intra and extra EU flights in the scheme, insisting that his plan is in line with international rules.[36]

2. Legal Arguments

a. Scientific Opinion

Prof. Pache, who holds a chair on Constitutional Law, International Law, International Business Law and Economic Administrative Law at Würzburg University has analysed the question whether the inclusion of emissions from international aviation into the European emissions trading scheme is compatible with international legal provisions. This legal opinion[37] was commissioned by the Federal Environment Ministry. The question of compatibility with international law arises especially with regard to flights between the EU and third countries performed by third country airlines.

36. <www.euractiv.com/en/climate-change/aviation-emissions-trading/article-139728>.

37. E. Pache, *On the compatibility with international legal provisions of including greenhouse gas emissions from international aviation in the EU emission allowance trading scheme as a result of the proposed changes to the EU emission allowance trading directive* (Würzburg 2008); <www.bmu.de/files/pdfs/allgemein/application/pdf/aviation_emission_trading.pdf>.

The opinion comes to the conclusion that including international aviation in the European emissions trading scheme does not conflict with any international legal provisions. The analysis addresses the Kyoto-Protocol, the Framework Convention on Climate Change, the Chicago Convention, bilateral agreements, ICAO secondary legislation, international trade law and principles of general international law.'[38]

b. The UK Case Argumentation[39]

In the case brought into the UK the Treasury Solicitor, defending the claim on behalf of the UK government,[40] argued that the EU is not bound by the Chicago Convention because it is not a signatory to the Convention. The Treasury Solicitor also argued that the requirement that operators forfeit allowances for emissions caused by flights passing over the territory of third countries (or the high seas) does not amount to regulation over the territory of a third country state. The ETS's requirements have no impact whatsoever on the sovereignty of other States, which remain free to impose emissions schemes and other rules on aviation over or into or from their territory. Although the claimants point out that there is a clear risk of multiple regulation, Article 25a of the Directive may operate to exempt flights from a particular country from the ETS where that country has adopted emission-reducing measures.

Furthermore, taking into account claimants' argument that the ETS is contrary to Article 11 insofar as its application is not limited to flights within the airspace of the EU Member State, one can see that Article 11 is an anti-discrimination provision with a specific purpose. It requires that rules applied by a Contracting State within its airspace be applied to aircraft of all nationalities without discrimination, and that the aircraft within that state's airspace comply with those rules. In this respect, the ETS is non-discriminatory because it treats similarly all flights to/from EU Member States. Further, Article 11 concerns laws and regulations relating to the admission and departure of aircraft and their operation and navigation within a Contracting State's territory, and does not apply to environmental legislation regarding emissions trading. Nor does Article 11 state that the only regulations that can apply in relation to a Contracting State's airspace are those made by the State in question.

The arguments of the claimants relating to a probable violation of Article 12 Chicago Convention fail, too. Article 12 has a specific purpose. It requires Contracting States to adopt measures to ensure compliance with rules on flight and manoeuvre in their airspace and uniformity of such rules with those established by

---

38. Legal opinion: Compatibility with international legal provisions of including greenhouse gas emissions from international aviation in the EU emissions trading scheme, <www.bmu.de/english/emissions_trading/doc/42364.php>.
39. Subchapter based on: Mark Bisset/Georgina Crowhurst, *Is the EU's Application of its Emissions Trading Scheme to Aviation Illegal?*, <www.clydeco.com/news/articles/is-the-eus-application-of-its-emissions-trading-scheme-to-aviation-illegal.cfm>.
40. Claimants detailed Statement of Grounds in claim no. CO/15376/2009, *supra* n. 7.

ICAO. It also states that the rules in force over the high seas on flight and manoeuvre shall be those established under the Chicago Convention. Because Article 12 relates to regulations concerning the flight and manoeuvre of aircraft, it seems unlikely that it also would apply to environmental legislation regarding emissions trading. The ETS does not affect the flight and manoeuvre of aircraft, but only the terms for admission to and/or departure from EU territory.

The Treasury Solicitor counters the argument of the claimants that the imposition of a requirement on foreign aircraft to surrender emission allowances would contravene Article 15 of the Convention, which is entitled 'Airport and similar charges' by stating that the ETS is not a 'fee, due or other charge', but rather an administrative scheme that obliges air operators to monitor and report their emissions and gives them the option of whether to operate within their allocated allowances or exceed those allowances by buying additional allowances. Even if an air operator decides to exercise the latter option, the amount that it pays cannot (it is argued) be characterized as a fee, due or charge, particularly given the overall context in which the provision appears. ICAO's Council Resolution on Taxation of International Air Transport states: 'Charges are levies to defray the costs of providing facilities and services for civil aviation', whereas the ETS is not 'designed and applied specifically to recover the costs of providing facilities and services for civil aviation.'

A further counter-argument is that, even if the ETS could be described as a charge, it is not imposed in respect 'solely' of the right of transit over or entry into or exit from territory. The Treasury Solicitor cited the 2007 case of R (Federation of Tour Operators) v HM Treasury,[41] in which the judge found that UK Air Passenger Duty was not a due imposed solely in respect of transit, entry or exit because it was equally payable if the flight did not leave the UK, and was 'essentially an anti-discrimination provision' precluding a State from favouring its national airlines when imposing charges.

41. ICAO Consolidated Resolution in Taxation of International Air Transport (AT-WP/1851, 21/12/98), <www.icao.int/icaonet/dcs/8632.html>.

Appendices

INTERNATIONAL AND EU AVIATION LAW
Selected Issues

APPENDICES

PROF. DR. ELMAR GIEMULLA
PROF. DR. LUDWIG WEBER
DR: HEIKO VAN SCHYNDEL

KLUWER INTERNATIONAL

Table of Contents

Appendices

Appendix 1

Convention[1] on International Civil Aviation

Signed at Chicago, on 7 December 1944

PREAMBLE

WHEREAS the future development of international civil aviation can greatly help to create and preserve friendship and understanding among the nations and peoples of the world, yet its abuse can become a threat to the general security; and

WHEREAS it is desirable to avoid friction and to promote that cooperation between nations and peoples upon which the peace of the world depends;

THEREFORE, the undersigned governments having agreed on certain principles and arrangements in order that international civil aviation may be developed in a safe and orderly manner and that international air transport services may be established on the basis of equality of opportunity and operated soundly and economically;

Have accordingly concluded this Convention to that end.

---

1. Came into force on 4 April 1947, the thirtieth day after deposit with the Government of the United States of America of the twenty-sixth instrument of ratification thereof or notification of adherence thereto, in accordance with Article 91 *b)*.

AIR NAVIGATION

CHAPTER I
GENERAL PRINCIPLES AND APPLICATION OF THE CONVENTION

Article 1

Sovereignty

The contracting States recognize that every State has complete and exclusive sovereignty over the airspace above its territory.

Article 2

Territory

For the purposes of this Convention the territory of a State shall be deemed to be the land areas and territorial waters adjacent thereto under the sovereignty, suzerainty, protection or mandate of such State.

Article 3

Civil and state aircraft

a) This Convention shall be applicable only to civil aircraft, and shall not be applicable to state aircraft.

b) Aircraft used in military, customs and police services shall be deemed to be state aircraft.

c) No state aircraft of a contracting State shall fly over the territory of another State or land thereon without authorization by special agreement or otherwise, and in accordance with the terms thereof.

d) The contracting States undertake, when issuing regulations for their state aircraft, that they will have due regard for the safety of navigation of civil aircraft.

Article 3 *bis*[*]

a) The contracting States recognize that every State must refrain from resorting to the use of weapons against civil aircraft in flight and that, in case of interception, the lives of persons on board and the safety of aircraft must not be endangered. This provision shall not be interpreted as modifying in any way the rights and obligations of States set forth in the Charter of the United Nations.

b) The contracting States recognize that every State, in the exercise of its sovereignty, is entitled to require the landing at some designated airport of a civil aircraft

---

* The 25th (Extraordinary) Session of the Assembly on 10 May 1984 amended the Convention by adopting the Protocol introducing Article 3 *bis*. This amendment came into force on 1 October 1998.

flying above its territory without authority or if there are reasonable grounds to conclude that it is being used for any purpose inconsistent with the aims of this Convention; it may also give such aircraft any other instructions to put an end to such violations. For this purpose, the contracting States may resort to any appropriate means consistent with relevant rules of international law, including the relevant provisions of this Convention, specifically paragraph *a)* of this Article. Each contracting State agrees to publish its regulations in force regarding the interception of civil aircraft.

c) Every civil aircraft shall comply with an order given in conformity with paragraph *b)* of this Article. To this end each contracting State shall establish all necessary provisions in its national laws or regulations to make such compliance mandatory for any civil aircraft registered in that State or operated by an operator who has his principal place of business or permanent residence in that State. Each contracting State shall make any violation of such applicable laws or regulations punishable by severe penalties and shall submit the case to its competent authorities in accordance with its laws or regulations.

d) Each contracting State shall take appropriate measures to prohibit the deliberate use of any civil aircraft registered in that State or operated by an operator who has his principal place of business or permanent residence in that State for any purpose inconsistent with the aims of this Convention. This provision shall not affect paragraph *a)* or derogate from paragraphs *b)* and *c)* of this Article.

Article 4

Misuse of civil aviation

Each contracting State agrees not to use civil aviation for any purpose inconsistent with the aims of this Convention.

Chapter II
Flight over Territory of contracting States

Article 5

Right of non-scheduled flight

Each contracting State agrees that all aircraft of the other contracting States, being aircraft not engaged in scheduled international air services shall have the right, subject to the observance of the terms of this Convention, to make flights into or in transit non-stop across its territory and to make stops for non-traffic purposes without the necessity of obtaining prior permission, and subject to the right of the State flown over to require landing. Each contracting State nevertheless reserves the right, for reasons of safety of flight, to require aircraft desiring to proceed over regions which are inaccessible or without adequate air navigation facilities to follow prescribed routes, or to obtain special permission for such flights.

Such aircraft, if engaged in the carriage of passengers, cargo, or mail for remuneration or hire on other than scheduled international air services, shall also, subject to the provisions of Article 7, have the privilege of taking on or discharging passengers, cargo, or mail, subject to the right of any State where such embarkation or discharge takes place to impose such regulations, conditions or limitations as it may consider desirable.

Article 6

Scheduled air services

No scheduled international air service may be operated over or into the territory of a contracting State, except with the special permission or other authorization of that State, and in accordance with the terms of such permission or authorization.

Article 7

Cabotage

Each contracting State shall have the right to refuse permission to the aircraft of other contracting States to take on in its territory passengers, mail and cargo carried for remuneration or hire and destined for another point within its territory. Each contracting State undertakes not to enter into any arrangements which specifically grant any such privilege on an exclusive basis to any other State or an airline of any other State, and not to obtain any such exclusive privilege from any other State.

Article 8

Pilotless aircraft

No aircraft capable of being flown without a pilot shall be flown without a pilot over the territory of a contracting State without special authorization by that State and in accordance with the terms of such authorization. Each contracting State undertakes to insure that the flight of such aircraft without a pilot in regions open to civil aircraft shall be so controlled as to obviate danger to civil aircraft.

Article 9

Prohibited areas

a) Each contracting State may, for reasons of military necessity or public safety, restrict or prohibit uniformly the aircraft of other States from flying over certain areas of its territory, provided that no distinction in this respect is made between the aircraft of the State whose territory is involved, engaged in international scheduled airline services, and the aircraft of the other contracting States likewise engaged. Such prohibited areas shall be of reasonable extent and location so as not to interfere unnecessarily with air navigation. Descriptions of such prohibited areas in the territory of a contracting State, as well as any subsequent alterations therein, shall be communicated as soon as possible to the other contracting States and to the International Civil Aviation Organization.

b) Each contracting State reserves also the right, in exceptional circumstances or during a period of emergency, or in the interest of public safety, and with immediate effect, temporarily to restrict or prohibit flying over the whole or any part of its territory, on condition that such restriction or prohibition shall be applicable without distinction of nationality to aircraft of all other States.

c) Each contracting State, under such regulations as it may prescribe, may require any aircraft entering the areas contemplated in subparagraphs *a)* or *b)* above to effect a landing as soon as practicable thereafter at some designated airport within its territory.

Article 10

Landing at customs airport

Except in a case where, under the terms of this Convention or a special authorization, aircraft are permitted to cross the territory of a contracting State without landing, every aircraft which enters the territory of a contracting State shall, if the regulations of that State so require, land at an airport designated by that State for the purpose of customs and other examination. On departure from the territory of a contracting State, such aircraft shall depart from a similarly designated customs airport. Particulars of all designated customs airports shall be published by the State and transmitted to the International Civil Aviation Organization established under Part II of this Convention for communication to all other contracting States.

Article 11

Applicability of air regulations

Subject to the provisions of this Convention, the laws and regulations of a contracting State relating to the admission to or departure from its territory of aircraft engaged in international air navigation, or to the operation and navigation of such aircraft while within its territory, shall be applied to the aircraft of all contracting States without distinction as to nationality, and shall be complied with by such aircraft upon entering or departing from or while within the territory of that State.

Article 12

Rules of the air

Each contracting State undertakes to adopt measures to insure that every aircraft flying over or maneuvering within its territory and that every aircraft carrying its nationality mark, wherever such aircraft may be, shall comply with the rules and regulations relating to the flight and maneuver of aircraft there in force. Each contracting State undertakes to keep its own regulations in these respects uniform, to the greatest possible extent, with those established from time to time under this Convention. Over the high seas, the rules in force shall be those established under this Convention. Each contracting State undertakes to insure the prosecution of all persons violating the regulations applicable.

Article 13

Entry and clearance regulations

The laws and regulations of a contracting State as to the admission to or departure from its territory of passengers, crew or cargo of aircraft, such as regulations relating to entry, clearance, immigration, passports, customs, and quarantine shall be complied with by or on behalf of such passengers, crew or cargo upon entrance into or departure from, or while within the territory of that State.

Article 14

Prevention of spread of disease

Each contracting State agrees to take effective measures to prevent the spread by means of air navigation of cholera, typhus (epidemic), smallpox, yellow fever, plague, and such other communicable diseases as the contracting States shall from time to time decide to designate, and to that end contracting States will keep in close consultation with the agencies concerned with international regulations relating to sanitary measures applicable to aircraft. Such consultation shall be without prejudice to the application of any existing international convention on this subject to which the contracting States may be parties.

Article 15

Airport and similar charges

Every airport in a contracting State which is open to public use by its national aircraft shall likewise, subject to the provisions of Article 68, be open under uniform conditions to the aircraft of all the other contracting States. The like uniform conditions shall apply to the use, by aircraft of every contracting State, of all air navigation facilities, including radio and meteorological services, which may be provided for public use for the safety and expedition of air navigation.

Any charges that may be imposed or permitted to be imposed by a contracting State for the use of such airports and air navigation facilities by the aircraft of any other contracting State shall not be higher,

a) As to aircraft not engaged in scheduled international air services, than those that would be paid by its national aircraft of the same class engaged in similar operations, and

b) As to aircraft engaged in scheduled international air services, than those that would be paid by its national aircraft engaged in similar international air services.

All such charges shall be published and communicated to the International Civil Aviation Organization, provided that, upon representation by an interested contracting State, the charges imposed for the use of airports and other facilities shall be subject to review by the Council, which shall report and make recommendations thereon for the consideration of the State or States concerned. No fees, dues or other charges shall be imposed by any contracting State in respect solely of the right of transit over or entry into or exit from its territory of any aircraft of a contracting State or persons or property thereon.

Article 16

Search of aircraft

The appropriate authorities of each of the contracting States shall have the right, without unreasonable delay, to search aircraft of the other contracting States on landing or departure, and to inspect the certificates and other documents prescribed by this Convention.

Chapter III
Nationality of Aircraft

Article 17

Nationality of aircraft

Aircraft have the nationality of the State in which they are registered.

Article 18

Dual registration

An aircraft cannot be validly registered in more than one State, but its registration may be changed from one State to another.

Article 19

National laws governing registration

The registration or transfer of registration of aircraft in any contracting State shall be made in accordance with its laws and regulations.

Article 20

Display of marks

Every aircraft engaged in international air navigation shall bear its appropriate nationality and registration marks.

Article 21

Report of registrations

Each contracting State undertakes to supply to any other contracting State or to the International Civil Aviation Organization, on demand, information concerning the registration and ownership of any particular aircraft registered in that State. In addition, each contracting State shall furnish reports to the International Civil Aviation Organization, under such regulations as the latter may prescribe, giving such pertinent data as can be made available concerning the ownership and control of aircraft registered in that State and habitually engaged in international air navigation. The data thus obtained by the International Civil Aviation Organization shall be made available by it on request to the other contracting States.

Chapter IV
Measures to Facilitate Air Navigation

Article 22

Facilitation of formalities

Each contracting State agrees to adopt all practicable measures, through the issuance of special regulations or otherwise, to facilitate and expedite navigation by aircraft between the territories of contracting States, and to prevent unnecessary delays to aircraft, crews, passengers and cargo, especially in the administration of the laws relating to immigration, quarantine, customs and clearance.

Article 23

Customs and immigration procedures

Each contracting State undertakes, so far as it may find practicable, to establish customs and immigration procedures affecting international air navigation in accordance with the practices which may be established or recommended from time to time, pursuant to this Convention. Nothing in this Convention shall be construed as preventing the establishment of customs-free airports.

Article 24

Customs duty

a) Aircraft on a flight to, from, or across the territory of another contracting State shall be admitted temporarily free of duty, subject to the customs regulations of the State. Fuel, lubricating oils, spare parts, regular equipment and aircraft stores on board an aircraft of a contracting State, on arrival in the territory of another contracting State and retained on board on leaving the territory of that State shall be exempt from customs duty, inspection fees or similar national or local duties and charges. This exemption shall not apply to any quantities or articles unloaded, except in accordance with the customs regulations of the State, which may require that they shall be kept under customs supervision.

b) Spare parts and equipment imported into the territory of a contracting State for incorporation in or use on an aircraft of another contracting State engaged in international air navigation shall be admitted free of customs duty, subject to compliance with the regulations of the State concerned, which may provide that the articles shall be kept under customs supervision and control.

Article 25

Aircraft in distress

Each contracting State undertakes to provide such measures of assistance to aircraft in distress in its territory as it may find practicable, and to permit, subject to control by its own authorities, the owners of the aircraft or authorities of the State in which the aircraft is registered to provide such measures of assistance as may be necessitated by the circumstances. Each contracting State, when undertaking search for missing aircraft, will collaborate in coordinated measures which may be recommended from time to time pursuant to this Convention.

Article 26

Investigation of accidents

In the event of an accident to an aircraft of a contracting State occurring in the territory of another contracting State, and involving death or serious injury, or indicating serious technical defect in the aircraft or air navigation facilities, the State in which the accident occurs will institute an inquiry into the circumstances of the accident, in accordance, so far as its laws permit, with the procedure which may be recommended by the International Civil Aviation Organization. The State in which the aircraft is registered shall be given the opportunity to appoint observers to be present at the inquiry and the State holding the inquiry shall communicate the report and findings in the matter to that State.

Article 27

Exemption from seizure on patent claims

a) While engaged in international air navigation, any authorized entry of aircraft of a contracting State into the territory of another contracting State or authorized transit across the territory of such State with or without landings shall not entail any seizure or detention of the aircraft or any claim against the owner or operator thereof or any other interference therewith by or on behalf of such State or any person therein, on the ground that the construction, mechanism, parts, accessories or operation of the aircraft is an infringement of any patent, design, or model duly granted or registered in the State whose territory is entered by the aircraft, it being agreed that no deposit of security in connection with the foregoing exemption from seizure or detention of the aircraft shall in any case be required in the State entered by such aircraft.

b) The provisions of paragraph *a)* of this Article shall also be applicable to the storage of spare parts and spare equipment for the aircraft and the right to use and install the same in the repair of an aircraft of a contracting State in the territory of any other contracting State, provided that any patented part or equipment so stored shall not be sold or distributed internally in or exported commercially from the contracting State entered by the aircraft.

c) The benefits of this Article shall apply only to such States, parties to this Convention, as either 1) are parties to the International Convention for the Protection of Industrial Property and to any amendments thereof; or 2) have enacted patent laws which recognize and give adequate protection to inventions made by the nationals of the other States parties to this Convention.

Article 28

Air navigation facilities and standard systems

Each contracting State undertakes, so far as it may find practicable, to:

(a) Provide, in its territory, airports, radio services, meteorological services and other air navigation facilities to facilitate international air navigation, in accordance with the standards and practices recommended or established from time to time, pursuant to this Convention;
(b) Adopt and put into operation the appropriate standard systems of communications procedure, codes, markings, signals, lighting and other operational practices and rules which may be recommended or established from time to time, pursuant to this Convention;
(c) Collaborate in international measures to secure the publication of aeronautical maps and charts in accordance with standards which may be recommended or established from time to time, pursuant to this Convention

Chapter V

Conditions to be Fulfilled with respect to Aircraft

Article 29

Documents carried in aircraft

Every aircraft of a contracting State, engaged in international navigation, shall carry the following documents in conformity with the conditions prescribed in this Convention:

a) Its certificate of registration;
b) Its certificate of airworthiness;
c) The appropriate licenses for each member of the crew;
d) Its journey log book;
e) If it is equipped with radio apparatus, the aircraft radio station license;
f) If it carries passengers, a list of their names and places of embarkation and destination;
g) If it carries cargo, a manifest and detailed declarations of the cargo.

Article 30

Aircraft radio equipment

a) Aircraft of each contracting State may, in or over the territory of other contracting States, carry radio transmitting apparatus only if a license to install and operate such apparatus has been issued by the appropriate authorities of the State in which the aircraft is registered. The use of radio transmitting apparatus in the territory of the contracting State whose territory is flown over shall be in accordance with the regulations prescribed by that State.

b) Radio transmitting apparatus may be used only by members of the flight crew who are provided with a special license for the purpose, issued by the appropriate authorities of the State in which the aircraft is registered.

Article 31

Certificates of airworthiness

Every aircraft engaged in international navigation shall be provided with a certificate of airworthiness issued or rendered valid by the State in which it is registered.

Article 32

Licenses of personnel

a) The pilot of every aircraft and the other members of the operating crew of every aircraft engaged in international navigation shall be provided with certificates of competency and licenses issued or rendered valid by the State in which the aircraft is registered.

b) Each contracting State reserves the right to refuse to recognize, for the purpose of flight above its own territory, certificates of competency and licenses granted to any of its nationals by another contracting State.

Article 33

Recognition of certificates and licenses

Certificates of airworthiness and certificates of competency and licenses issued or rendered valid by the contracting State in which the aircraft is registered, shall be recognized as valid by the other contracting States, provided that the requirements under which such certificates or licences were issued or rendered valid are equal to or above the minimum standards which may be established from time to time pursuant to this Convention.

Article 34

Journey log books

There shall be maintained in respect of every aircraft engaged in international navigation a journey log book in which shall be entered particulars of the aircraft, its crew and of each journey, in such form as may be prescribed from time to time pursuant to this Convention.

Article 35

Cargo restrictions

a) No munitions of war or implements of war may be carried in or above the territory of a State in aircraft engaged in international navigation, except by permission of such State. Each State shall determine by regulations what constitutes munitions of war or implements of war for the purposes of this Article, giving due consideration, for the purposes of uniformity, to such recommendations as the International Civil Aviation Organization may from time to time make.

b) Each contracting State reserves the right, for reasons of public order and safety, to regulate or prohibit the carriage in or above its territory of articles other than those enumerated in paragraph *a)*: provided that no distinction is made in this respect between its national aircraft engaged in international navigation and the aircraft of the other States so engaged; and provided further that no restriction shall be imposed which may interfere with the carriage and use on aircraft of apparatus necessary for the operation or navigation of the aircraft or the safety of the personnel or passengers.

Article 36

Photographic apparatus

Each contracting State may prohibit or regulate the use of photographic apparatus in aircraft over its territory.

Chapter VI
International Standards and Recommended Practices

Article 37

Adoption of international standards and procedures

Each contracting State undertakes to collaborate in securing the highest practicable degree of uniformity in regulations, standards, procedures, and organization in relation to aircraft, personnel, airways and auxiliary services in all matters in which such uniformity will facilitate and improve air navigation.

To this end the International Civil Aviation Organization shall adopt and amend from time to time, as may be necessary, international standards and recommended practices and procedures dealing with:

a) Communications systems and air navigation aids, including ground marking;
b) Characteristics of airports and landing areas;
c) Rules of the air and air traffic control practices;
d) Licensing of operating and mechanical personnel;
e) Airworthiness of aircraft;
f) Registration and identification of aircraft;
g) Collection and exchange of meteorological information;
h) Log books;
i) Aeronautical maps and charts;
j) Customs and immigration procedures;
k) Aircraft in distress and investigation of accidents;

and such other matters concerned with the safety, regularity, and efficiency of air navigation as may from time to time appear appropriate.

Article 38

Departures from international standards and procedures

Any State which finds it impracticable to comply in all respects with any such international standard or procedure, or to bring its own regulations or practices into full accord with any international standard or procedure after amendment of the latter, or which deems it necessary to adopt regulations or practices differing in any particular respect from those established by an international standard, shall give immediate notification to the International Civil Aviation Organization of the differences between its own practice and that established by the international standard. In the case of amendments to international standards, any State which does not make the appropriate amendments to its own regulations or practices shall give notice to the Council within sixty days of the adoption of the amendment to the international standard, or indicate the action which it proposes to take. In any such case, the Council shall make immediate notification to all other states of the difference which exists between one or more features of an international standard and the corresponding national practice of that State.

Article 39

Endorsement of certificates and licenses

a) Any aircraft or part thereof with respect to which there exists an international standard of airworthiness or performance, and which failed in any respect to satisfy that standard at the time of its certification, shall have endorsed on or attached to its airworthiness certificate a complete enumeration of the details in respect of which it so failed.

b) Any person holding a license who does not satisfy in full the conditions laid down in the international standard relating to the class of license or certificate which he holds shall have endorsed on or attached to his license a complete enumeration of the particulars in which he does not satisfy such conditions.

Article 40

Validity of endorsed certificates and licenses

No aircraft or personnel having certificates or licenses so endorsed shall participate in international navigation, except with the permission of the State or States whose territory is entered. The registration or use of any such aircraft, or of any certificated aircraft part, in any State other than that in which it was originally certificated shall be at the discretion of the State into which the aircraft or part is imported.

Article 41

Recognition of existing standards of airworthiness

The provisions of this Chapter shall not apply to aircraft and aircraft equipment of types of which the prototype is submitted to the appropriate national authorities for certification prior to a date three years after the date of adoption of an international standard of airworthiness for such equipment.

Article 42

Recognition of existing standards of competency of personnel

The provisions of this Chapter shall not apply to personnel whose licenses are originally issued prior to a date one year after initial adoption of an international standard of qualification for such personnel; but they shall in any case apply to all personnel whose licenses remain valid five years after the date of adoption of such standard.

PART II
THE INTERNATIONAL CIVIL AVIATION ORGANIZATION

CHAPTER VII
THE ORGANIZATION

Article 43

Name and composition

An organization to be named the International Civil Aviation Organization is formed by the Convention. It is made up of an Assembly, a Council, and such other bodies as may be necessary.

Article 44

Objectives

The aims and objectives of the Organization are to develop the principles and techniques of international air navigation and to foster the planning and development of international air transport so as to:

a) Insure the safe and orderly growth of international civil aviation throughout the world;
b) Encourage the arts of aircraft design and operation for peaceful purposes;
c) Encourage the development of airways, airports, and air navigation facilities for international civil aviation;
d) Meet the needs of the peoples of the world for safe, regular, efficient and economical air transport;
e) Prevent economic waste caused by unreasonable competition;
f) Insure that the rights of contracting States are fully respected and that every contracting State has a fair opportunity to operate international airlines;
g) Avoid discrimination between contracting States;
h) Promote safety of flight in international air navigation;
i) Promote generally the development of all aspects of international civil aeronautics.

Article 45*

Permanent seat

The permanent seat of the Organization shall be at such place as shall be determined at the final meeting of the Interim Assembly of the Provisional International Civil Aviation Organization set up by the Interim Agreement on International Civil Aviation signed at Chicago on December 7, 1944. The seat may be temporarily transferred elsewhere by decision of the Council, and otherwise than temporarily by decision of the Assembly, such decision to be taken by the number of votes specified by the Assembly. The number of votes so specified will not be less than three-fifths of the total number of contracting States.

Article 46

First meeting of Assembly

The first meeting of the Assembly shall be summoned by the Interim Council of the above-mentioned Provisional Organization as soon as the Convention has come into force, to meet at a time and place to be decided by the Interim Council.

Article 47

Legal capacity

The Organization shall enjoy in the territory of each contracting State such legal capacity as may be necessary for the performance of its functions. Full juridical personality shall be granted wherever compatible with the constitution and laws of the State concerned.

Chapter VIII
The Assembly

Article 48

Meetings of Assembly and voting

a) The Assembly shall meet not less than once in three years and shall be convened by the Council at a suitable time and place. An extraordinary meeting of the Assembly may be held at any time upon the call of the Council or at the request of not less than one-fifth of the total number of contracting States addressed to the Secretary General.*

---

* This is the text of the Article as amended by the 8th Session of the Assembly on 14 June 1954; it entered into force on 16 May 1958. The original text read as follows:

"The permanent seat of the Organization shall be at such place as shall be determined at the final meeting of the Interim Assembly of the Provisional International Civil Aviation Organization set up by the Interim Agreement on International Civil Aviation signed at Chicago on December 7, 1944. The seat may be temporarily transferred elsewhere by decision of the Council."

* This is the text of the Article as amended by the 14th Session of the Assembly on 15 September 1962; it entered into force on 11 September 1975. The previous text of this Article as amended by

b) All contracting States shall have an equal right to be represented at the meetings of the Assembly and each contracting State shall be entitled to one vote. Delegates representing contracting States may be assisted by technical advisers who may participate in the meetings but shall have no vote.

c) A majority of the contracting States is required to constitute a quorum for the meetings of the Assembly. Unless otherwise provided in this Convention, decisions of the Assembly shall be taken by a majority of the votes cast.

Article 49

Powers and duties of Assembly

The powers and duties of the Assembly shall be to:

a) Elect at each meeting its President and other officers;
b) Elect the contracting States to be represented on the Council, in accordance with the provisions of Chapter IX;
c) Examine and take appropriate action on the reports of the Council and decide on any matter referred to it by the Council;
d) Determine its own rules of procedure and establish such subsidiary commissions as it may consider to be necessary or desirable;
e) Vote annual budgets and determine the financial arrangements of the Organization, in accordance with the provisions of Chapter XII;*
f) Review expenditures and approve the accounts of the Organization;
g) Refer, at its discretion, to the Council, to subsidiary commissions, or to any other body any matter within its sphere of action;
h) Delegate to the Council the powers and authority necessary or desirable for the discharge of the duties of the Organization and revoke or modify the delegations of authority at any time;
i) Carry out the appropriate provisions of Chapter XIII;

---

the 8th Session of the Assembly on 14 June 1954 and which entered into force on 12 December 1956 read as follows:

> "*a*) The Assembly shall meet not less than once in three years and shall be convened by the Council at a suitable time and place. Extraordinary meetings of the Assembly may be held at any time upon the call of the Council or at the request of any ten contracting States addressed to the Secretary General."

The original unamended text of the Convention read as follows:

> "*a*) The Assembly shall meet annually and shall be convened by the Council at a suitable time and place. Extraordinary meetings of the Assembly may be held at any time upon the call of the Council or at the request of any ten contracting States addressed to the Secretary General."

* This is the text of the Article as amended by the 8th Session of the Assembly on 14 June 1954; it entered into force on 12 December 1956. The original text read as follows:

> "*e*) Vote an annual budget and determine the financial arrangements of the Organization, in accordance with the provisions of Chapter XII;".

j) Consider proposals for the modification or amendment of the provisions of this Convention and, if it approves of the proposals, recommend them to the contracting States in accordance with the provisions of Chapter XXI;

k) Deal with any matter within the sphere of action of the Organization not specifically assigned to the Council.

Chapter IX
The Council

Article 50

Composition and election of Council

a) The Council shall be a permanent body responsible to the Assembly. It shall be composed of thirty-six contracting States elected by the Assembly. An election shall be held at the first meeting of the Assembly and thereafter every three years, and the members of the Council so elected shall hold office until the next following election.*

b) In electing the members of the Council, the Assembly shall give adequate representation to 1) the States of chief importance in air transport; 2) the States not otherwise included which make the largest contribution to the provision of facilities for international civil air navigation; and 3) the States not otherwise included whose designation will insure that all the major geographic areas of the world are represented on the Council. Any vacancy on the Council shall be filled by the Assembly as soon as possible; any contracting State so elected to the Council shall hold office for the unexpired portion of its predecessor's term of office.

c) No representative of a contracting State on the Council shall be actively associated with the operation of an international air service or financially interested in such a service.

Article 51

President of Council

The Council shall elect its President for a term of three years. He may be reelected. He shall have no vote. The Council shall elect from among its members one or

---

* This is the text of the Article as amended by the 28th (Extraordinary) Session of the Assembly on 26 October 1990; it entered into force on 28 November 2002. The original text of the Convention provided for twenty-one members of the Council. That text was subsequently amended by the 13th (Extraordinary) Session of the Assembly on 21 June 1961; this amendment entered into force on 17 July 1962 and provided for twenty-seven members of the Council. A second amendment was adopted by the 17th (A) (Extraordinary) Session of the Assembly on 12 March 1971; this amendment entered into force on 16 January 1973 and provided for thirty members of the Council. A third amendment was adopted by the 21st Session of the Assembly on 16 October 1974; this amendment entered into force on 15 February 1980 and provided for thirty-three members of the Council.

more Vice Presidents who shall retain their right to vote when serving as acting President. The President need not be selected from among the representatives of the members of the Council but, if a representative is elected, his seat shall be deemed vacant and it shall be filled by the State which he represented. The duties of the President shall be to:

a) Convene meetings of the Council, the Air Transport Committee, and the Air Navigation Commission;
b) Serve as representative of the Council; and
c) Carry out on behalf of the Council the functions which the Council assigns to him.

Article 52

Voting in Council

Decisions by the Council shall require approval by a majority of its members. The Council may delegate authority with respect to any particular matter to a committee of its members. Decisions of any committee of the Council may be appealed to the Council by any interested contracting State.

Article 53

Participation without a vote

Any contracting State may participate, without a vote, in the consideration by the Council and by its committees and commissions of any question which especially affects its interests. No member of the Council shall vote in the consideration by the Council of a dispute to which it is a party.

Article 54

Mandatory functions of Council

The Council shall:

a) Submit annual reports to the Assembly;
b) Carry out the directions of the Assembly and discharge the duties and obligations which are laid on it by this Convention;
c) Determine its organization and rules of procedure;
d) Appoint and define the duties of an Air Transport Committee, which shall be chosen from among the representatives of the members of the Council, and which shall be responsible to it;
e) Establish an Air Navigation Commission, in accordance with the provisions of Chapter X;
f) Administer the finances of the Organization in accordance with the provisions of Chapters XII and XV;
g) Determine the emoluments of the President of the Council;
h) Appoint a chief executive officer who shall be called the Secretary General, and make provision for the appointment of such other

personnel as may be necessary, in accordance with the provisions of Chapter XI;

i) Request, collect, examine and publish information relating to the advancement of air navigation and the operation of international air services, including information about the costs of operation and particulars of subsidies paid to airlines from public funds;
j) Report to contracting States any infraction of this Convention, as well as any failure to carry out recommendations or determinations of the Council;
k) Report to the Assembly any infraction of this Convention where a contracting State has failed to take appropriate action within a reasonable time after notice of the infraction;
l) Adopt, in accordance with the provisions of Chapter VI of this Convention, international standards and recommended practices; for convenience, designate them as Annexes to this Convention; and notify all contracting States of the action taken;
m) Consider recommendations of the Air Navigation Commission for amendment of the Annexes and take action in accordance with the provisions of Chapter XX;
n) Consider any matter relating to the Convention which any contracting State refers to it.

Article 55

Permissive functions of Council

The Council may:

a) Where appropriate and as experience may show to be desirable, create subordinate air transport commissions on a regional or other basis and define groups of states or airlines with or through which it may deal to facilitate the carrying out of the aims of this Convention;
b) Delegate to the Air Navigation Commission duties additional to those set forth in the Convention and revoke or modify such delegations of authority at any time;
c) Conduct research into all aspects of air transport and air navigation which are of international importance, communicate the results of its research to the contracting States, and facilitate the exchange of information between contracting States on air transport and air navigation matters;
d) Study any matters affecting the organization and operation of international air transport, including the international ownership and operation of international air services on trunk routes, and submit to the Assembly plans in relation thereto;
e) Investigate, at the request of any contracting State, any situation which may appear to present avoidable obstacles to the development of international air navigation; and, after such investigation, issue such reports as may appear to it desirable.

CHAPTER X
THE AIR NAVIGATION COMMISSION

Article 56

Nomination and appointment of Commission

The Air Navigation Commission shall be composed of nineteen members appointed by the Council from among persons nominated by contracting States. These persons shall have suitable qualifications and experience in the science and practice of aeronautics. The Council shall request all contracting States to submit nominations. The President of the Air Navigation Commission shall be appointed by the Council.*

Article 57

Duties of Commission

The Air Navigation Commission shall:

a) Consider, and recommend to the Council for adoption, modifications of the Annexes to this Convention;
b) Establish technical subcommissions on which any contracting State may be represented, if it so desires;
c) Advise the Council concerning the collection and communication to the contracting States of all information which it considers necessary and useful for the advancement of air navigation.

CHAPTER XI
PERSONNEL

Article 58

Appointment of personnel

Subject to any rules laid down by the Assembly and to the provisions of this Convention, the Council shall determine the method of appointment and of termination of appointment, the training, and the salaries, allowances, and conditions of service of the Secretary General and other personnel of the Organization, and may employ or make use of the services of nationals of any contracting State.

Article 59

International character of personnel

The President of the Council, the Secretary General, and other personnel shall not seek or receive instructions in regard to the discharge of their responsibilities from

---

* This is the text of the Article as amended by the 27th Session of the Assembly on 6 October 1989; it entered into force on 18 April 2005. The original text of the Convention provided for twelve members of the Air Navigation Commission. That text was subsequently amended by the 18th Session of the Assembly on 7 July 1971; this amendment entered into force on 19 December 1974 and provided for fifteen members of the Air Navigation Commission.

any authority external to the Organization. Each contracting State undertakes fully to respect the international character of the responsibilities of the personnel and not to seek to influence any of its nationals in the discharge of their responsibilities.

Article 60

Immunities and privileges of personnel

Each contracting State undertakes, so far as possible under its constitutional procedure, to accord to the President of the Council, the Secretary General, and the other personnel of the Organization, the immunities and privileges which are accorded to corresponding personnel of other public international organizations. If a general international agreement on the immunities and privileges of international civil servants is arrived at, the immunities and privileges accorded to the President, the Secretary General, and the other personnel of the Organization shall be the immunities and privileges accorded under that general international agreement.

CHAPTER XII
FINANCE

Article 61*

Budget and apportionment of expenses

The Council shall submit to the Assembly annual budgets, annual statements of accounts and estimates of all receipts and expenditures. The Assembly shall vote the budgets with whatever modification it sees fit to prescribe, and, with the exception of assessments under Chapter XV to States consenting thereto, shall apportion the expenses of the Organization among the contracting States on the basis which it shall from time to time determine.

Article 62

Suspension of voting power

The Assembly may suspend the voting power in the Assembly and in the Council of any contracting State that fails to discharge within a reasonable period its financial obligations to the Organization.

Article 63

Expenses of delegations and other representatives

Each contracting State shall bear the expenses of its own delegation to the Assembly and the remuneration, travel, and other expenses of any person whom it

---

* This is the text of the Article as amended by the 8th Session of the Assembly on 14 June 1954; it entered into force on 12 December 1956. The original text read as follows:

> "The Council shall submit to the Assembly an annual budget, annual statements of accounts and estimates of all receipts and expenditures. The Assembly shall vote the budget with whatever modification it sees fit to prescribe, and, with the exception of assessments under Chapter XV to States consenting thereto, shall apportion the expenses of the Organization among the contracting States on the basis which it shall from time to time determine."

appoints to serve on the Council, and of its nominees or representatives on any subsidiary committees or commissions of the Organization.

Chapter XIII
OTHER INTERNATIONAL ARRANGEMENTS

Article 64

Security arrangements

The Organization may, with respect to air matters within its competence directly affecting world security, by vote of the Assembly enter into appropriate arrangements with any general organization set up by the nations of the world to preserve peace.

Article 65

Arrangements with other international bodies

The Council, on behalf of the Organization, may enter into agreements with other international bodies for the maintenance of common services and for common arrangements concerning personnel and, with the approval of the Assembly, may enter into such other arrangements as may facilitate the work of the Organization.

Article 66

Functions relating to other agreements

a) The Organization shall also carry out the functions placed upon it by the International Air Services Transit Agreement and by the International Air Transport Agreement drawn up at Chicago on December 7, 1944, in accordance with the terms and conditions therein set forth.

b) Members of the Assembly and the Council who have not accepted the International Air Services Transit Agreement of the International Air Transport Agreement drawn up at Chicago on December 7, 1944 shall not have the right to vote on any questions referred to the Assembly or Council under the provisions of the relevant Agreement.

PART III
INTERNATIONAL AIR TRANSPORT

Chapter XIV
INFORMATION AND REPORTS

Article 67

File reports with Council

Each contracting State undertakes that its international airlines shall, in accordance with requirements laid down by the Council, file with the Council traffic reports, cost statistics and financial statements showing among other things all receipts and the sources thereof.

Chapter XV

Airports and Other Air Navigation Facilities

Article 68

Designation of routes and airports

Each contracting State may, subject to the provisions of this Convention, designate the route to be followed within its territory by any international air service and the airports which any such service may use.

Article 69

Improvement of air navigation facilities

If the Council is of the opinion that the airports or other air navigation facilities, including radio and meteorological services, of a contracting State are not reasonably adequate for the safe, regular, efficient, and economical operation of international air services, present or contemplated, the Council shall consult with the State directly concerned, and other States affected, with a view to finding means by which the situation may be remedied, and may make recommendations for that purpose. No contracting State shall be guilty of an infraction of this Convention if it fails to carry out these recommendations.

Article 70

Financing of air navigation facilities

A contracting State, in the circumstances arising under the provisions of Article 69, may conclude an arrangement with the Council for giving effect to such recommendations. The State may elect to bear all of the costs involved in any such arrangement. If the State does not so elect, the Council may agree, at the request of the State, to provide for all or a portion of the costs.

Article 71

Provision and maintenance of facilities by Council

If a contracting State so requests, the Council may agree to provide, man, maintain, and administer any or all of the airports and other air navigation facilities including radio and meteorological services, required in its territory for the safe, regular, efficient and economical operation of the international air services of the other contracting States, and may specify just and reasonable charges for the use of the facilities provided.

Article 72

Acquisition or use of land

Where land is needed for facilities financed in whole or in part by the Council at the request of a contracting State, that State shall either provide the land itself, retaining title if it wishes, or facilitate the use of the land by the Council on just and reasonable terms and in accordance with the laws of the State concerned.

Article 73

Expenditure and assessment of funds

Within the limit of the funds which may be made available to it by the Assembly under Chapter XII, the Council may make current expenditures for the purposes of this Chapter from the general funds of the Organization. The Council shall assess the capital funds required for the purposes of this Chapter in previously agreed proportions over a reasonable period of time to the contracting States consenting thereto whose airlines use the facilities. The Council may also assess to States that consent any working funds that are required.

Article 74

Technical assistance and utilization of revenues

When the Council, at the request of a contracting State, advances funds or provides airports or other facilities in whole or in part, the arrangement may provide, with the consent of that State, for technical assistance in the supervision and operation of the airports and other facilities, and for the payment, from the revenues derived from the operation of the airports and other facilities, of the operating expenses of the airports and the other facilities, and of interest and amortization charges.

Article 75

Taking over of facilities from Council

A contracting State may at any time discharge any obligation into which it has entered under Article 70, and take over airports and other facilities which the Council has provided in its territory pursuant to the provisions of Articles 71 and 72, by paying to the Council an amount which in the opinion of the Council is reasonable in the circumstances. If the State considers that the amount fixed by the Council is unreasonable it may appeal to the Assembly against the decision of the Council and the Assembly may confirm or amend the decision of the Council.

Article 76

Return of funds

Funds obtained by the Council through reimbursement under Article 75 and from receipts of interest and amortization payments under Article 74 shall, in the case of advances originally financed by States under Article 73, be returned to the States which were originally assessed in the proportion of their assessments, as determined by the Council.

Chapter XVI
Joint Operating Organizations and Pooled Services

Article 77

Joint operating organizations permitted

Nothing in this Convention shall prevent two or more contracting States from constituting joint air transport operating organizations or international operating agencies and from pooling their air services on any routes or in any regions, but such organizations or agencies and such pooled services shall be subject to all the provisions of this Convention, including those relating to the registration of agreements with the Council. The Council shall determine in what manner the provisions of this Convention relating to nationality of aircraft shall apply to aircraft operated by international operating agencies.

Article 78

Function of Council

The Council may suggest to contracting States concerned that they form joint organizations to operate air services on any routes or in any regions.

Article 79

Participation in operating organizations

A State may participate in joint operating organizations or in pooling arrangements, either through its government or through an airline company or companies designated by its government. The companies may, at the sole discretion of the State concerned, be state-owned or partly state-owned or privately owned.

PART IV
FINAL PROVISIONS

Chapter XVII
Other Aeronautical Agreements and Arrangements

Article 80

Paris and Habana Conventions

Each contracting State undertakes, immediately upon the coming into force of this Convention, to give notice of denunciation of the Convention relating to the Regulation of Aerial Navigation signed at Paris on October 13, 1919 or the Convention on Commercial Aviation signed at Habana on February 20, 1928, if it is a party to either. As between contracting States, this Convention supersedes the Conventions of Paris and Habana previously referred to.

Article 81

Registration of existing agreements

All aeronautical agreements which are in existence on the coming into force of this Convention, and which are between a contracting State and any other State or between an airline of a contracting State and any other State or the airline of any other State, shall be forthwith registered with the Council.

Article 82

Abrogation of inconsistent arrangements

The contracting States accept this Convention as abrogating all obligations and understandings between them which are inconsistent with its terms, and undertake not to enter into any such obligations and understandings. A contracting State which, before becoming a member of the Organization has undertaken any obligations toward a non-contracting State or a national of a contracting State or of a non-contracting State inconsistent with the terms of this Convention, shall take immediate steps to procure its release from the obligations. If an airline of any contracting State has entered into any such inconsistent obligations, the State of which it is a national shall use its best efforts to secure their termination forthwith and shall in any event cause them to be terminated as soon as such action can lawfully be taken after the coming into force of this Convention.

Article 83

Registration of new arrangements

Subject to the provisions of the preceding Article, any contracting State may make arrangements not inconsistent with the provisions of this Convention. Any such arrangement shall be forthwith registered with the Council, which shall make it public as soon as possible.

Article 83 *bis*[*]

Transfer of certain functions and duties

a) Notwithstanding the provisions of Articles 12, 30, 31 and 32 *a)*, when an aircraft registered in a contracting State is operated pursuant to an agreement for the lease, charter or interchange of the aircraft or any similar arrangement by an operator who has his principal place of business or, if he has no such place of business, his permanent residence in another contracting State, the State of registry may, by agreement with such other State, transfer to it all or part of its functions and duties as State of registry in respect of that aircraft under Articles 12, 30, 31 and 32 *a)*. The State of registry shall be relieved of responsibility in respect of the functions and duties transferred.

---

* The 23rd Session of the Assembly on 6 October 1980 amended the Chicago Convention by introducing Article 83 *bis*. This amendment came into force on 20 June 1997.

b) The transfer shall not have effect in respect of other contracting States before either the agreement between States in which it is embodied has been registered with the Council and made public pursuant to Article 83 or the existence and scope of the agreement have been directly communicated to the authorities of the other contracting State or States concerned by a State party to the agreement.

c) The provisions of paragraphs *a)* and *b)* above shall also be applicable to cases covered by Article 77.

Chapter XVIII
Disputes and Default

Article 84

Settlement of disputes

If any disagreement between two or more contracting States relating to the interpretation or application of this Convention and its Annexes cannot be settled by negotiation, it shall, on the application of any State concerned in the disagreement, be decided by the Council. No member of the Council shall vote in the consideration by the Council of any dispute to which it is a party. Any contracting State may, subject to Article 85, appeal from the decision of the Council to an ad hoc arbitral tribunal agreed upon with the other parties to the dispute or to the Permanent Court of International Justice. Any such appeal shall be notified to the Council within sixty days of receipt of notification of the decision of the Council.

Article 85

Arbitration procedure

If any contracting State party to a dispute in which the decision of the Council is under appeal has not accepted the Statute of the Permanent Court of International Justice and the contracting States parties to the dispute cannot agree on the choice of the arbitral tribunal, each of the contracting States parties to the dispute shall name a single arbitrator who shall name an umpire. If either contracting State party to the dispute fails to name an arbitrator within a period of three months from the date of the appeal, an arbitrator shall be named on behalf of that State by the President of the Council from a list of qualified and available persons maintained by the Council. If, within thirty days, the arbitrators cannot agree on an umpire, the President of the Council shall designate an umpire from the list previously referred to. The arbitrators and the umpire shall then jointly constitute an arbitral tribunal. Any arbitral tribunal established under this or the preceding Article shall settle its own procedure and give its decisions by majority vote, provided that the Council may determine procedural questions in the event of any delay which in the opinion of the Council is excessive.

Article 86

Appeals

Unless the Council decides otherwise any decision by the Council on whether an international airline is operating in conformity with the provisions of this Convention shall remain in effect unless reversed on appeal. On any other matter, decisions of the Council shall, if appealed from, be suspended until the appeal is decided. The decisions of the Permanent Court of International Justice and of an arbitral tribunal shall be final and binding.

Article 87

Penalty for non-conformity of airline

Each contracting State undertakes not to allow the operation of an airline of a contracting State through the airspace above its territory if the Council has decided that the airline concerned is not conforming to a final decision rendered in accordance with the previous Article.

Article 88

Penalty for non-conformity by State

The Assembly shall suspend the voting power in the Assembly and in the Council of any contracting State that is found in default under the provisions of this Chapter.

CHAPTER XIX
WAR

Article 89

War and emergency conditions

In case of war, the provisions of this Convention shall not affect the freedom of action of any of the contracting States affected, whether as belligerents or as neutrals. The same principle shall apply in the case of any contracting State which declares a state of national emergency and notifies the fact to the Council.

CHAPTER XX
ANNEXES

Article 90

Adoption and amendment of Annexes

a) The adoption by the Council of the Annexes described in Article 54, subparagraph *l*), shall require the vote of two-thirds of the Council at a meeting called for that purpose and shall then be submitted by the Council to each contracting State. Any such Annex or any amendment of an Annex shall become effective within three months after its submission to the contracting States or at the end of such longer period of time as the Council may prescribe, unless in the meantime a majority of the contracting States register their disapproval with the Council.

b) The Council shall immediately notify all contracting States of the coming into force of any Annex or amendment thereto.

Chapter XXI
Ratifications, Adherences, Amendments, and Denunciations

Article 91

Ratification of Convention

a) This Convention shall be subject to ratification by the signatory States. The instruments of ratification shall be deposited in the archives of the Government of the United States of America, which shall give notice of the date of the deposit to each of the signatory and adhering States.

b) As soon as this Convention has been ratified or adhered to by twenty-six States it shall come into force between them on the thirtieth day after deposit of the twenty-sixth instrument. It shall come into force for each State ratifying thereafter on the thirtieth day after the deposit of its instrument of ratification.

c) It shall be the duty of the Government of the United States of America to notify the government of each of the signatory and adhering States of the date on which this Convention comes into force.

Article 92

Adherence to Convention

a) This Convention shall be open for adherence by members of the United Nations and States associated with them, and States which remained neutral during the present world conflict.

b) Adherence shall be effected by a notification addressed to the Government of the United States of America and shall take effect as from the thirtieth day from the receipt of the notification by the Government of the United States of America, which shall notify all the contracting States.

Article 93

Admission of other States

States other than those provided for in Articles 91 and 92 *a)* may, subject to approval by any general international organization set up by the nations of the world to preserve peace, be admitted to participation in this Convention by means of a four-fifths vote of the Assembly and on such conditions as the Assembly may prescribe: provided that in each case the assent of any State invaded or attacked during the present war by the State seeking admission shall be necessary.

Article 93 *bis**

a) Notwithstanding the provisions of Articles 91, 92 and 93 above:

1) A State whose government the General Assembly of the United Nations has recommended be debarred from membership in international agencies established by or brought into relationship with the United Nations shall automatically cease to be a member of the International Civil Aviation Organization;
2) A State which has been expelled from membership in the United Nations shall automatically cease to be a member of the International Civil Aviation Organization unless the General Assembly of the United Nations attaches to its act of expulsion a recommendation to the contrary.

b) A State which ceases to be a member of the International Civil Aviation Organization as a result of the provisions of paragraph *a)* above may, after approval by the General Assembly of the United Nations, be readmitted to the International Civil Aviation Organization upon application and upon approval by a majority of the Council.

c) Members of the Organization which are suspended from the exercise of the rights and privileges of membership in the United Nations shall, upon the request of the latter, be suspended from the rights and privileges of membership in this Organization.

Article 94

Amendment of Convention

a) Any proposed amendment to this Convention must be approved by a two-thirds vote of the Assembly and shall then come into force in respect of States which have ratified such amendment when ratified by the number of contracting States specified by the Assembly. The number so specified shall not be less than two-thirds of the total number of contracting States.

b) If in its opinion the amendment is of such a nature as to justify this course, the Assembly in its resolution recommending adoption may provide that any State which has not ratified within a specified period after the amendment has come into force shall thereupon cease to be a member of the Organization and a party to the Convention.

* The 1st Session of the Assembly on 27 May 1947 amended the Chicago Convention by introducing Article 93 bis. This amendment came into force on 20 March 1961.

Article 95

Denunciation of Convention

a) Any contracting State may give notice of denunciation of this Convention three years after its coming into effect by notification addressed to the Government of the United States of America, which shall at once inform each of the contracting States.

b) Denunciation shall take effect one year from the date of the receipt of the notification and shall operate only as regards the State effecting the denunciation.

Chapter XXII
DEFINITIONS

Article 96

For the purpose of this Convention the expression:

a) "Air service" means any scheduled air service performed by aircraft for the public transport of passengers, mail or cargo.
b) "International air service" means an air service which passes through the air space over the territory of more than one State.
c) "Airline" means any air transport enterprise offering or operating an international air service.
d) "Stop for non-traffic purposes" means a landing for any purpose other than taking on or discharging passengers, cargo or mail.

SIGNATURE OF CONVENTION

IN WITNESS WHEREOF, the undersigned plenipotentiaries, having been duly authorized, sign this Convention on behalf of their respective governments on the dates appearing opposite their signatures.

DONE at Chicago the seventh day of December 1944 in the English language. The texts of this Convention drawn up in the English, French, Russian and Spanish languages are of equal authenticity. These texts shall be deposited in the archives of the Government of the United States of America, and certified copies shall be transmitted by that Government to the Governments of all the States which may sign or adhere to this Convention. This Convention shall be open for signature at Washington, D.C.*

* This is the text of the final paragraph as amended by the 22nd Session of the Assembly on 30 September 1977; it entered into force on 17 August 1999. The original text read as follows:

> "DONE at Chicago the seventh day of December 1944 in the English language. A text drawn up in the English, French and Spanish languages, each of which shall be of equal authenticity, shall be open for signature at Washington, D.C. Both texts shall be deposited in the archives of the Government of the United States of America, and certified copies shall be transmitted by that Government to the governments of all the States which may sign or adhere to this Convention."

PROTOCOL[1]

ON THE AUTHENTIC TRILINGUAL TEXT OF THE CONVENTION ON INTERNATIONAL CIVIL A VIATION (CHICAGO, 1944)

Signed at Buenos Aires on 24 September 1968

THE UNDERSIGNED GOVERNMENTS

CONSIDERING that the last paragraph of the Convention on International Civil Aviation, hereinafter called "the Convention", provides that a text of the Convention, drawn up in the English, French and Spanish languages, each of which shall be of equal authenticity, shall be open for signature;

CONSIDERING that the Convention was opened for signature, at Chicago, on the seventh day of December, 1944, in a text in the English language;

CONSIDERING, accordingly, that it is appropriate to make the necessary provision for the text to exist in three languages as contemplated in the Convention;

CONSIDERING that in making such provision, it should be taken into account that there exist amendments to the Convention in the English, French and Spanish languages, and that the text of the Convention in the French and Spanish languages should not incorporate those amendments because, in accordance with Article 94 *a)* of the Convention, each such amendment can come into force only in respect of any State which has ratified it;

HAVE AGREED as follows:

Article I[2]

The text of the Convention in the French and Spanish languages annexed to this Protocol, together with the text of the Convention in the English language, constitutes the text equally authentic in the three languages as specifically referred to in the last paragraph of the Convention.

Article II

If a State party to this Protocol has ratified or in the future ratifies any amendment made to the Convention in accordance with Article 94 *a)* thereof, then the text of such amendment in the English, French and Spanish languages shall be deemed to refer to the text, equally authentic in the three languages, which results from this Protocol.

1. Came into force on 24 October 1968.
2. The text of the Convention in the French and Spanish languages mentioned in this Article will be found in the second and third columns at pages 1 to 44 of this document, subject to what is stated in the second paragraph of the Foreword at page (ii).

Article III

1) The States members of the International Civil Aviation Organization may become parties to this Protocol either by:

a) signature without reservation as to acceptance, or
b) signature with reservation as to acceptance followed by acceptance, or
c) acceptance.

2) This Protocol shall remain open for signature at Buenos Aires until the twenty-seventh day of September 1968 and thereafter at Washington, D.C.

3) Acceptance shall be effected by the deposit of an instrument of acceptance with the Government of the United States of America.

4) Adherence to or ratification or approval of this Protocol shall be deemed to be acceptance thereof.

Article IV

1) This Protocol shall come into force on the thirtieth day after twelve States shall, in accordance with the provisions of Article III, have signed it without reservation as to acceptance or accepted it.

2) As regards any State which shall subsequently become a party to this Protocol, in accordance with Article III, the Protocol shall come into force on the date of its signature without reservation as to acceptance or of its acceptance.

Article V

Any future adherence of a State to the Convention shall be deemed to be acceptance of this Protocol.

Article VI

As soon as this Protocol comes into force, it shall be registered with the United Nations and with the International Civil Aviation Organization by the Government of the United States of America.

Article VII

1) This Protocol shall remain in force so long as the Convention is in force.

2) This Protocol shall cease to be in force for a State only when that State ceases to be a party to the Convention.

Article VIII

The Government of the United States of America shall give notice to all States members of the International Civil Aviation Organization and to the Organization itself:

a) of any signature of this Protocol and the date thereof, with an indication whether the signature is with or without reservation as to acceptance;

b) of the deposit of any instrument of acceptance and the date thereof;
c) of the date on which this Protocol comes into force in accordance with the provisions of Article IV, paragraph 1).

Article IX

This Protocol, drawn up in the English, French and Spanish languages, each text being equally authentic, shall be deposited in the archives of the Government of the United States of America, which shall transmit duly certified copies thereof to the Government of the States members of the International Civil Aviation Organization.

IN WITNESS WHEREOF, the undersigned Plenipotentiaries, duly authorized, have signed this Protocol.

DONE at Buenos Aires this twenty-fourth day of September, one thousand nine hundred and sixty-eight.

PROTOCOL[1]

ON THE AUTHENTIC QUADRILINGUAL TEXT OF THE CONVENTION ON INTERNATIONAL CIVIL A VIATION (CHICAGO, 1944)

Signed at Montreal on 30 September 1977

THE UNDERSIGNED GOVERNMENTS

CONSIDERING that the 21st Session of the Assembly of the International Civil Aviation Organization requested the Council of this Organization "to undertake the necessary measures for the preparation of the authentic text of the Convention on International Civil Aviation in the Russian language, with the aim of having it approved not later than the year 1977";

CONSIDERING that the English text of the Convention on International Civil Aviation was opened for signature at Chicago on 7 December 1944;

CONSIDERING that, pursuant to the Protocol signed at Buenos Aires on 24 September 1968 on the authentic trilingual text of the Convention on International Civil Aviation done at Chicago, 7 December 1944, the text of the Convention on International Civil Aviation (hereinafter called the Convention) was adopted in the French and Spanish languages and, together with the text of the Convention in the English language, constitutes the text equally authentic in the three languages as provided for in the final clause of the Convention;

CONSIDERING accordingly, that it is appropriate to make the necessary provision for the text of the Convention to exist in the Russian language;

CONSIDERING that in making such provision account must be taken of the existing amendments to the Convention in the English, French and Spanish languages, the texts of which are equally authentic and that, according to Article 94 *a)* of the Convention, any amendment can come into force only in respect of any State which has ratified it;

HAVE AGREED as follows:

Article I[2]

The text of the Convention and of the amendments thereto in the Russian language annexed to this Protocol, together with the text of the Convention and of the amendments thereto in the English, French and Spanish languages, constitutes the text equally authentic in the four languages.

1. Came into force on 16 September 1999.
2. The text of the Convention in the Russian language mentioned in this Article will be found in the fourth column at pages 1 to 44 of this document, subject to what is stated in the second paragraph of the Foreword at page (ii).

Article II

If a State party to this Protocol has ratified or in the future ratifies any amendment made to the Convention in accordance with Article 94 *a)* thereof, then the text of such amendment in the Russian, English, French and Spanish languages shall be deemed to refer to the text equally authentic in the four languages, which results from this Protocol.

Article III

1) The States members of the International Civil Aviation Organization may become parties to this Protocol either by:

a) signature without reservation as to acceptance, or
b) signature with reservation as to acceptance followed by acceptance, or
c) acceptance.

2) This Protocol shall remain open for signature at Montreal until the 5th of October 1977 and thereafter at Washington, D.C.

3) Acceptance shall be effected by the deposit of an instrument of acceptance with the Government of the United States of America.

4) Adherence to or ratification or approval of this Protocol shall be deemed to be acceptance thereof.

Article IV

1) This Protocol shall come into force on the thirtieth day after twelve States shall, in accordance with the provisions of Article III, have signed it without reservation as to acceptance or accepted it and after entry into force of the amendment to the final clause of the Convention, which provides that the text of the Convention in the Russian language is of equal authenticity.

2) As regards any State which shall subsequently become a party to this Protocol in accordance with Article III, the Protocol shall come into force on the date of its signature without reservation as to acceptance or of its acceptance.

Article V

Any adherence of a State to the Convention after this Protocol has entered into force shall be deemed to be acceptance of this Protocol.

Article VI

Acceptance by a State of this Protocol shall not be regarded as ratification by it of any amendment to the Convention.

Article VII

As soon as this Protocol comes into force, it shall be registered with the United Nations and with the International Civil Aviation Organization by the Government of the United States of America.

Article VIII

1) This Protocol shall remain in force so long as the Convention is in force.

2) This Protocol shall cease to be in force for a State only when that State ceases to be a party to the Convention.

Article IX

The Government of the United States of America shall give notice to all States members of the International Civil Aviation Organization and to the Organization itself:

a) of any signature of this Protocol and the date thereof, with an indication whether the signature is with or without reservation as to acceptance;
b) of the deposit of any instrument of acceptance and the date thereof;
c) of the date on which this Protocol comes into force in accordance with the provisions of Article IV, paragraph 1.

Article X

This Protocol, drawn up in the English, French, Russian and Spanish languages, each text being equally authentic, shall be deposited in the archives of the Government of the United States of America, which shall transmit duly certified copies thereof to the Governments of the States members of the International Civil Aviation Organization.

IN WITNESS WHEREOF, the undersigned Plenipotentiaries, duly authorized, have signed this Protocol.

DONE at Montreal this thirtieth day of September, one thousand nine hundred and seventy-seven.

Appendix 2
IATA Act of Incorporation

AN ACT TO INCOPORATE INTERNATIONAL AIR TRANSPORT ASSOCIATION*

Whereas Herbert James Symington, Companion of the Most Distinguished Order of St. Michael and St. George, and one of His Majesty's Counsel, of the city of Montreal, in the province of Quebec, president of the unincorporated Association known as "International Air Transport Association", hereinafter called the "unincorporated Association", John Cobb Cooper, executive, and John Elliot Slater, executive, both of the city of New York, in the State of New York, one of the United States of America, members of the Executive Committee of the unincorporated Association, and Hugh Emmett O'Donnell, of the city of Montreal, one of His Majesty's Counsel and Attorney-at-law of the unincorporated Association, have, by their petition on behalf of the unincorporated Association, prayed that it be enacted as hereinafter set forth, and it is expedient to grant the prayer of the petition; Therefore His Majesty, by and with the advice and consent of the Senate and the House of Commons of Canada, enacts as follows:—

Act of Incorporation

1. In this Act, unless the context otherwise requires:—
   (a) "air service" means any air service performed by aircraft for the public transport of passengers, mail or cargo;
   (b) "air transport enterprise" includes those persons, corporate bodies and unincorporated bodies, companies, firms, partnerships, societies and associations, now or hereafter operating an air service for public hire, under

---

* Statutes of Canada, 1945, Chap. 51 (Assented to 18th December, 1945) as amended by Statutes of Canada, 1974-75-76, Chap. 111 (Assented to 27th February, 1975).

proper authority, in the transport of passengers, mail or cargo under the flag of a State eligible for membership in the International Civil Aviation Organization;

(c) "International Civil Aviation Organization" means the organizations provisional and permanent provided for by the Interim Agreement on International Civil Aviation and by the Convention on International Civil Aviation concluded on the 7th day of December, 1944, at the city of Chicago, in the State of Illinois, one of the United States of America, at the International Civil Aviation Conference.

2. The said Herbert James Symington, John Cobb Cooper, John Elliot Slater and Hugh Emmett O'Donnell, and all the present members of the unincorporated Association, together with such other persons, corporate bodies or unincorporated bodies, companies, firms, partnerships, societies and associations, as may hereafter from time to time become associated with them for the purposes of this Act, and become members of the Association hereby incorporated, are incorporated under the name of "International Air Transport Association" hereinafter called "the Association".

3. The purposes, objects and aims of the Association shall be:—

(a) to promote safe, regular and economical air transport for the benefit of the peoples of the world, to foster air commerce and to study the problems connected therewith;

(b) to provide means for collaboration among the air transport enterprises engaged directly or indirectly in international air transport service;

(c) to co-operate with the International Civil Aviation Organization and other international organizations.

4. The head office of the Association shall be at the city of Montreal, in the province of Quebec, or at such other place as the Association may determine by by-law from time to time.

5. The Association may, by by-laws, rules and regulations:—

(a) define and regulate the qualifications, admission, termination, suspension and expulsion of members, determine the different classes of members and their rights, duties and privileges, and fix the fees, subscriptions and dues to be paid by them;

(b) establish an Executive Committee of the Association with executive powers, determine the method of election or appointment thereto or selection thereof, define the constitution, powers, duties, quorum and terms of office of such Executive Committee and fix the number, powers, duties, quorum, terms and conditions of office of the officers and committees of the Association;

(c) fix the time and place for holding the annual meeting and other meetings of the Association and the notice to be given thereof;

(d) provide for the administration and management of the business and affairs of the Association and the furthering of its objects, purposes and aims, and such delegation as it may deem proper of any of its powers to the Executive Committee of the Association, and to any other committee as it may from time to time appoint.

6. (1) In addition to the general powers accorded to it by law and to those set forth elsewhere in this Act, the Association shall have power:—

(a) to acquire the whole or any part of the rights and properties owned or held by, for or on behalf of the unincorporated Association;
(b) to purchase, take on lease or in exchange, hire and acquire by gift, grant, devise, legacy or otherwise and to own and hold any estate, property or rights, real or personal, moveable or immoveable, or any title or interest therein, and to alienate, sell, exchange, manage, develop, lease, hypothecate, mortgage, change, pledge or otherwise deal therewith in such manner as the Association may determine;
(c) to borrow money for the purposes of the Association;
(d) to draw, make, accept, endorse, discount, execute and issue promissory notes, bills of exchange and other negotiable or transferable instruments;
(e) to invest and deal with the monies of the Association not immediately required in such manner as may from time to time be determined;
(f) to carry out all or any of the objects of the Association and do all or any of the above things as principal, agent, contractor or otherwise, and either alone or in conjunction with others;
(g) to do all such other things as are incidental or conducive to the attainment of the objects and the exercise of the powers of the Association.

(2) Nothing in this section shall be deemed to authorize the Association to issue any note payable to the bearer thereof, or any promissory note intended to be circulated as money, or as the note of a bank, or to engage in the business of banking or insurance.

7. The present officers and members of the Executive Committee and of the committees of the unincorporated Association shall subject to the by-laws, rules or regulations of the unincorporated Association continue to hold their offices until their successors shall have been appointed or elected in accordance with the provisions of this Act and of the by-laws, rules or regulations made thereunder.

8. The existing constitution, by-laws and rules of the unincorporated Association, insofar as they are not contrary to law or to the provisions of this Act, shall be the constitution, by-laws and rules of the Association until altered or repealed at an annual or special general meeting of the Association.

9. The Association may exercise its functions throughout Canada or elsewhere and meetings of the Association and of the Executive Committee and any other committees of the Association may be held at any place other than the head office of the Association and either within or without Canada.

10. The Association may adopt and use a corporate seal in such form as may be deemed expedient.

Appendix 3
Articles of Association

ARTICLE I
Title

Articles of Association to regulate the activities and affairs of an association known as the International Air Transport Association ("IATA").

ARTICLE II
Definitions

In these Articles of Association, unless the context otherwise requires:

1. "Act of Incorporation" shall mean An Act to Incorporate the International Air Transport Association, Statutes of Canada, 1945, Chap. 51 (Assented to December 18, 1945) as amended from time to time;

2. "air service" shall mean the public transport of passengers, mail or cargo by aircraft;

3. "airline" shall mean an entity operating an air service;

4. "Articles" shall mean these by-laws, articles of association, rules and regulations adopted pursuant to Section 5 of the Act of Incorporation (hereinafter "Articles");

5. "Board" shall mean the Board of Governors established pursuant to Article VIII(2)(a) of these Articles;

6. "dues" shall mean any prescribed amounts required to be paid by a Member to maintain membership in IATA, and any other duly authorised assessment;

7. "fees" shall mean any prescribed amounts required to be paid by an airline to apply for and to acquire membership in IATA;

8. "IATA Conferences" shall mean the conferences established by a General Meeting pursuant to Article IX(3)(c) of these Articles;

9. "Industry Committees" shall mean the committees established by the Director General with the approval of the Board;

10. "international air service" shall mean any air service operated between the territories of two or more States;

11. "Member" shall mean the member airlines of IATA, admitted pursuant to the terms of Article V of these Articles.

12. "Membership Office" shall mean the person(s) designated by the Director General from time to time, responsible for the membership matters set out herein.

ARTICLE III
Head Office

The Head Office of IATA shall be at Montreal, Canada, or at such other place as a General Meeting may determine by amendment to these Articles.

ARTICLE IV
Mission and Aims of IATA

The mission of IATA is to represent and serve the airline industry. In carrying out this mission IATA shall:

1. Promote safe, reliable and secure air services for the benefit of the peoples of the world;
2. Provide means of collaboration among airlines engaged directly or indirectly in international air transport;
3. Cooperate with the International Civil Aviation Organization and other relevant international organisations.

ARTICLE V
Membership

1. Category of Membership

a. Membership in IATA is available to airlines as:

  i. Active Member: any airline operating an international air service;
  ii. Associate Member: any airline operating an air service other than an international air service.

b. A Member who changes the nature of its business operations such that it is eligible for a different category of membership, shall immediately give written notice of such changes to the Membership Office, and may submit its application for membership in the appropriate category.

2. Rights and Privileges of Members

Except for the right to vote at relevant IATA meetings, which shall be available solely to Active Members, all Members shall enjoy the same rights and privileges attaching to membership in IATA.

3. Qualifications for Membership

a. Unless sponsored by at least two (2) Active Members, an applicant for Active or Associate membership shall have operated an air service for a period of not less than two (2) years, and performed for each such year at least five million (5,000,000) revenue tonne-kilometres. Notwithstanding the foregoing, an airline that does not meet these criteria may be admitted to membership if the Board considers such airline's membership to be in the interest of IATA.

b. All applications for membership in IATA shall be made in the form provided and submitted together with the application fee to the Membership Office. All applications are subject to the approval of the Board.

c. Membership shall become effective once payment in full of all fees and payment of dues for the current year are received and upon approval by the Board.

d. Any airline whose application for membership is not approved by the Board may appeal the decision to the next Annual General Meeting, the decision of which shall be final.

4. Fees and Dues

a. Upon the written request of the Director General, acting on behalf of the Board, a Member shall provide, by the date specified in the request, all data necessary to establish the annual dues payable by the Member. If such data is not provided by the specified date, the Board may prescribe the amount of dues to be paid.

b. Unless otherwise determined by the Board, annual dues shall be payable when invoiced and in the currency or currencies set out in the invoice.

c. Interest on arrears of dues shall accrue and be payable at the rate set by the Board, taking into account prevailing market rates for the relevant currency or currencies, unless due to exceptional circumstances, the Board waives this requirement.

d. A Member giving notice of resignation is liable to pay all dues payable up to and including the year of resignation.

e. Any Member under limitation is liable to pay all dues assessed during the period of limitation.

f. When membership in IATA has been terminated all dues outstanding on the effective date of termination are payable.

g. Payments of fees and dues are not refundable under any circumstances.

5. Membership Resignation, Limitation and Termination

a. Resignation

A Member may resign at any time by giving not less than thirty (30) days written notice to the Membership Office.

b. Limitation

i. Any Member in arrears in the payment of dues and interest for a period of more than ninety (90) days shall be placed in limitation by the Membership Office and lose all rights and privileges of membership during the period that the limitation is in effect, unless the Board has agreed to alternative financial arrangements.
ii. The Membership Office shall indicate in the notice of limitation to the Member the effective date of the limitation, and the conditions to be met for the limitation to be removed.
iii. A limitation on membership rights will be enforced against Members that have payments of USD 3000 or more overdue to IATA for more than 120 days.

c. Termination

i. A Member no longer meeting the criteria for membership may have its membership terminated by the Board ninety (90) days after the occurrence of the event giving rise to its ineligibility.
ii. A Member declared bankrupt or placed in receivership, or making a voluntary assignment for the benefit of its creditors, or ceasing to hold the authority to operate, or otherwise ceasing to carry on the business that qualifies it for membership, may have its membership terminated by the Board effective thirty (30) days from the date of occurrence of such event.
iii. Notwithstanding sections 5.c.i and 5.c.ii, the Board may, upon the written request of the Member concerned, postpone the effective date of termination for a fixed period, as appropriate.
iv. The Board may also terminate membership if:

  1) a Member is in breach of these Articles or any rule or regulation adopted thereunder;
  2) a Member has committed any act or omission which is prejudicial to the aims of IATA;
  3) a Member has been placed in limitation for a period of at least one (1) year.

v. A membership may be terminated at any time by a vote of two-thirds of the Members present and voting at a General Meeting.

6. Right to be Heard and Arbitration

a. A Member that has had its membership terminated by the Board and received a notice of termination may, by written notification to the Corporate Secretary within thirty (30) days of receipt of the notice, invoke its right to be heard by the Board. Invocation of this right shall suspend the effective date of the termination, pending the results of the hearing by the Board.

b. A Member whose membership has been terminated by the Board or by a General Meeting may seek arbitration under the IATA Arbitration Rules.

Invocation of this procedure shall suspend the effective date of the termination, pending the results of the arbitration.

c. The decision of the arbitration tribunal shall be final and binding. If the decision is in favour of IATA, the termination shall be effective on the date of the decision, and the costs of the arbitration shall be borne by the Member. If the decision is in favour of the Member, the termination shall be revoked as of the date of the original termination, and the costs shall be borne or reimbursed by IATA.

7. Voluntary Suspension of Membership

At the written request of a Member, the Board may agree to suspend its membership for a fixed period if the Board considers it in the interest of IATA. During the period of suspension, the Member shall not be required to pay any dues but shall not exercise any rights and privileges of membership.

8. Notice of Resignation, Limitation, Suspension or Termination

The Membership Office shall notify all Members in writing of the resignation, limitation, suspension, and lifting of suspension of a Member or its termination of membership.

9. Re-Application

An airline that ceases to be a Member whether through resignation or termination may re-apply for membership and in such event the Board may specify the terms and conditions to be fulfilled, including payment of any fees and dues, before membership can be effective.

ARTICLE VI
IATA Affiliates

The Board may establish a class of membership known as "IATA Affiliates", and determine the criteria for membership, and the rights and duties thereof.

ARTICLE VII
Annual Budget and Financial Statement

1. The Board shall approve the annual budget and prepare and approve and submit the audited annual financial statement to the next Annual General Meeting. A General Meeting may approve any special assessments and conditions and procedures relating thereto.

2. The approved audited annual financial statement shall be accompanied by a certification by each of the Director General and the Chief Financial Officer to the effect that:

   a. the audited financial statements present fairly the financial conditions, results of operations and cash flows of IATA, and do not contain an untrue statement of material fact or omit to state any material fact; and

b. appropriate disclosure controls and procedures have been established to provide reasonable assurance that all material information is made known to the Director General and the Chief Financial Officer.

ARTICLE VIII
Authority/General Powers

1. A General Meeting is vested with the ultimate authority to exercise all of the powers of IATA.

2. a. There shall be an executive committee to be known as the "Board of Governors" with authority to exercise all such powers of IATA as are not by law, the Act of Incorporation or these Articles required to be exercised by a General Meeting.

b. The Board is accountable to a General Meeting for the overall performance of IATA.

ARTICLE IX
Annual General Meetings

1. The Annual General Meeting shall be convened at a place and time agreed to by a previous Annual General Meeting. In the absence of such decision or should the Board deem it impractical to hold the Meeting at the place and/or time so decided, the Board shall determine the place and/or time of the Meeting.

2. Not less than forty-five (45) days in advance of the Annual General Meeting, Active Members may submit to the Board, through the Corporate Secretary, matters for inclusion on the Agenda. The Corporate Secretary shall provide Members with not less than thirty (30) days written notice of, and the Agenda for, the Annual General Meeting. Upon a majority vote of Active Members present and voting at the Meeting, any other matter may be added to the Agenda.

3. The Annual General Meeting shall:

a. Elect its President;
b. Receive nominations to and elect members of the Board;
c. Establish IATA Conferences and such groups and subordinate bodies as it considers appropriate;
d. Confirm the appointment, term of office and duties of the Director General;
e. Receive and consider reports of the Board, Industry Committees, IATA Conferences, and of the Director General;
f. Approve the audited financial statements for the previous year;
g. On the recommendation of the Board, approve the applicable dues and fees;
h. On the recommendation of the Board, approve the currency or currencies in which, and the time by which, such dues and fees shall be payable;
i. Appoint the external auditor for the current year;
j. Transact any other business as may properly come before the Meeting.

4. The President of the Annual General Meeting shall, before conclusion of the Meeting, appoint a Nominating Committee to make recommendations to the next Annual General Meeting for election to the Board. The composition of and rules applicable to the Nominating Committee shall be as established by a General Meeting.

ARTICLE X
Special General Meetings

A Special General Meeting shall be convened at the written request of not less than one third of the Active Members made to the Corporate Secretary, or may be convened by the Board at any time. The Corporate Secretary shall provide thirty (30) days notice of, and a proposed Agenda for, such meeting. In the case of urgency, the Board may reduce the notice period as it deems appropriate.

ARTICLE XI
Quorum and Voting at General Meetings

A majority of Active Members registered at a General Meeting shall constitute a quorum for the duration of the Meeting. Each Active Member shall have one vote which may be cast solely by its official representative present and voting at the Meeting. No proxy may be appointed by any Member.

ARTICLE XII
Management

1. The Board shall be composed of not more than thirty-one (31) persons elected by the Annual General Meeting from among the Active Members. Allowing for the differences of nomenclature in the Member airlines, members of the Board shall hold any one of the following, or similar, positions: Chairman of the Board; President of the company; Chief Executive; or Managing Director. The terms of office shall be as set by the Annual General Meeting on the recommendation of the Board. Ten (10) members of the Board shall constitute a quorum but decisions shall require approval of a majority of Board members, which approval may be given in writing or by electronically transmitted and recorded means.

2. Should a vacancy arise on the Board, the Board shall elect a replacement from among the representatives of Active Members, who shall hold office until the next Annual General Meeting.

3. The Board:

a. Shall elect its Chairman;
b. Shall meet immediately in advance of the Annual General Meeting, and otherwise as appropriate;
c. Shall be vested with executive powers and duties, including the general management and control of the business, affairs, funds and property of IATA;

d. Shall determine, review and approve IATA policy within the framework of the Act of Incorporation, these Articles and the resolutions of General Meetings;
e. Shall take action in response to specific requests from Members as it deems appropriate;
f. Shall appoint the Director General, subject to the approval of the Annual General Meeting, and determine the term of office, duties and remuneration;
g. Shall appoint the Corporate Secretary, the Chief Financial Officer and such other officers of IATA as deemed appropriate, who shall be subject to the supervision and authority of the Director General;
h. Shall establish subsidiary corporations, industry settlement plan offices, branches, regional and other offices of IATA anywhere in the world as it considers appropriate;
i. Shall approve the Agenda for a General Meeting;
j. Shall approve the Rules and Regulations of the Industry Committees and the Provisions for the Conduct of the IATA Traffic Conferences;
k. Shall establish and determine the membership, duties and functions of any Committee of the Board;
l. Shall either establish and determine the rules and regulations of any Committee of the Board, or authorise any such Committee to adopt its own rules and regulations;
m. Shall recommend to the Annual General Meeting the fees and dues and the time by which they shall be payable, as well as the currency or currencies in which they are to be paid;
n. Shall consider for approval applications for membership in IATA;
o. Shall take such action as may be appropriate with respect to the limitation, suspension or termination of membership;
p. May delegate, as appropriate, authority to Committees of the Board or to the Director General;
q. May adopt and amend its Rules and Regulations as deemed appropriate for the exercise of its executive powers and the performance of its duties.

4. The Director General:

a. Shall be the Chief Executive Officer of IATA and shall exercise, under the authority of the Board, the supervision, direction and control over the business and affairs of IATA, as well as such other functions and duties that a General Meeting or the Board may delegate or assign to the Director General;
b. Shall supervise the mechanisms for the settlement of transactions between airlines, branches, regional and other offices of IATA, and such other entities that the Board may consider appropriate in the interest of IATA;
c. Shall carry out the duties assigned or delegated to the Director General by a General Meeting or the Board, and report on the activities of IATA to the Annual General Meeting;

d. May, with the approval of the Board, establish such Committee(s) to advise on subjects of significant interest to the air transport industry, appoint its members, and dissolve any such Industry Committee(s) at any time.
e. May establish such working groups and ad hoc task forces as necessary to address specific issues concerning the air transport industry, appoint their members and dissolve any such working groups or ad hoc task forces at any time.

ARTICLE XIII
Majority Vote

At any General Meeting or meeting of the Board, or of any committee of IATA, a vote shall be determined by a simple majority of those present and voting, unless a greater majority is otherwise specifically provided by these Articles or the relevant rules and regulations of the particular body. Each Active Member represented by its official representative at a meeting shall have the right to exercise one vote.

ARTICLE XIV
Voting Procedure (General)

i. Voting at any meeting of Members shall take place by a show of hands and any Active Member may request a repeat show of hands. However, a roll call vote or secret ballot may be requested at any time by a majority of the Active Members present and voting at a meeting.

ii. A roll call vote or vote by secret ballot shall be taken in such manner as the chair of the meeting directs.

ARTICLE XV
Telecommunication Meetings

With the consent of at least two-thirds of all Members entitled to participate in the meeting, a meeting of the Board or of any committee or subordinate body of IATA may be conducted by such means of telephone or other telecommunications facilities as permit all participants in the meeting to hear each other.

ARTICLE XVI
Signed Decision

A resolution in writing, signed by all the Members entitled to vote at a meeting of the Board, or of any committee, as the case may be, shall be a decision as valid as if it had been made at such meeting. The decision shall be effective from the date of the last signature. A copy of every signed decision shall be kept by the Corporate Secretary.

ARTICLE XVII
Committee Procedure

Unless otherwise determined by the Board or these Articles, each committee or subordinate body of IATA shall have the power to elect its chair, to regulate its procedure and to fix its quorum; provided that the approval of at least a simple majority of members of the committee or subordinate body, present and voting, shall be required for any decisions.

ARTICLE XVIII
Remuneration

No Member or representative of a Member shall receive any remuneration for their services on the Board, any Industry Committee or any other body of IATA. Nevertheless, nothing herein shall be construed to preclude any Member or representative of a Member from being remunerated under a specific mandate which has been conferred by decision of the Board, the Director General, an Industry Committee or other competent body of IATA.

ARTICLE XIX
The Corporate Secretary

The Corporate Secretary shall perform such duties as are specifically assigned to the Corporate Secretary in these Articles and as may be determined by the Board or the Director General, and in addition, shall act as the Secretary of General Meetings and of the Board.

ARTICLE XX
The Chief Financial Officer

The Chief Financial Officer, shall perform such duties as may be determined by the Board or the Director General.

ARTICLE XXI
Notices

All notices required to be given by IATA or by a Member in accordance with these Articles shall be deemed to have been effectively given upon delivery in person or on the day after electronic transmission or, if sent by registered or certified mail or by courier, on the date shown on the return receipt.

ARTICLE XXII
Languages

The languages of IATA shall be English, French, Spanish, Arabic (translation into Arabic is limited to those documents for a General Meeting as requested by Arabic speaking Active Members) and any other language that may from time to time be requested and as the Board may from time to time agree, provided that the cost of any such additional language shall be borne by the requesting Member(s).

ARTICLE XXIII
Amendment

These Articles may be amended by a two thirds majority vote of Active Members registered and voting at a General Meeting, provided the proposed amendment has properly come before the Meeting in accordance with these Articles.

ARTICLE XXIV
Dissolution

IATA may be dissolved solely by resolution of a General Meeting, approved in writing by two- thirds of all the Active Members, which resolution shall set the effective date for dissolution. In such event any net remaining assets of IATA shall be disbursed to the United Nations. Members shall be responsible for outstanding and contingent liabilities in the same proportion as their last dues relate to the total amount of annual dues assessed.

ARTICLE XXV
Indemnification

Subject to any limitations imposed by applicable law, IATA shall fully indemnify, defend and hold harmless current and former members of the Board, officers, heads of division, or legal counsel of IATA, and their heirs, from and against any and all claims, actions, demands, damages, losses, reasonable costs and expenses arising out of or in connection with the performance of the Indemnified Individual's duties and obligations pursuant to the terms of his or her appointment, engagement or employment, provided that he or she:

1. Acted honestly and in good faith; and
2. In the case of a criminal or administrative action or proceeding that is enforced by a monetary penalty, had reasonable grounds for believing that his or her conduct was lawful.

IATA shall maintain in force insurance for the purposes of giving effect to the indemnity referred to in this Article in such amounts as the Board may from time to time reasonably determine, and as permitted by applicable law.

ARTICLE XXVI
Powers of Attorney

The Director General or the Corporate Secretary may grant powers of attorney for the conduct of the activities of IATA and appoint any person or persons as the attorney or attorneys of IATA to execute and deliver any instrument or to execute and deliver a class or series of instruments.

Appendix 4

Convention on Recognition of Rights in Aircraft (Geneva convention), 1948

CONVENTION ON THE INTERNATIONAL RECOGNITION OF RIGHTS IN AIRCRAFT, SIGNED AT GENEVA, ON 19 JUNE 1948 (GENEVA CONVENTION)

WHEREAS the International Civil Aviation Conference, held at Chicago in November-December 1944, recommended the early adoption of a Convention dealing with the transfer of title to aircraft,

WHEREAS it is highly desirable in the interest of the future expansion of international civil aviation that rights in aircraft be recognised internationally,

THE UNDERSIGNED, duly authorized, HAVE AGREED, on behalf of their respective Governments, AS FOLLOWS:

Article I

1. The Contracting States undertake to recognise:

(a) rights of property in aircraft;

(b) rights to acquire aircraft by purchase coupled with possession of the aircraft;

(c) rights to possession of aircraft under leases of six months or more;

(d) mortgages, hypotheques and similar rights in aircraft which are contractually created as security for payment of an indebtedness;

provided that such rights

(i) have been constituted in accordance with the law of the Contracting State in which the aircraft was registered as to nationality at the time of their constitution, and

(ii) are regularly recorded in a public record of the Contracting State in which the aircraft is registered as to nationality.

The regularity of successive recordings in different Contracting States shall be determined in accordance with the law of the State where the aircraft was registered as to nationality at the time of each recording.

2. Nothing in this Convention shall prevent the recognition of any rights in aircraft under the law of any Contracting State; but Contracting States shall not admit or recognise any right as taking priority over the rights mentioned in paragraph 1 of this Article.

Article II

1. All recordings relating to a given aircraft must appear in the same record.

2. Except as otherwise provided in this Convention, the effects of the recording of any right mentioned in Article I, paragraph 1, with regard to third parties shall be determined according to the law of the Contracting State where it is recorded.

3. A Contracting State may prohibit the recording of any right which cannot validly be constituted according to its national law.

Article III

1. The address of the authority responsible for maintaining the record must be shown on every aircraft's certificate of registration as to nationality.

2. Any person shall be entitled to receive from the authority duly certified copies or extracts of the particulars recorded. Such copies or extracts shall constitute prima facie evidence of the contents of the record.

3. If the law of a Contracting State provides that the filing of a document for recording shall have the same effect as the recording, it shall have the same effect for the purposes of this Convention. In that case, adequate provision shall be made to ensure that such document is open to the public.

4. Reasonable charges may be made for services performed by the authority maintaining the record.

Article IV

1. In the event that any claims in respect of:

(a) compensation due for salvage of the aircraft, or
(b) extraordinary expenses indispensable for the preservation of the aircraft

give rise, under the law of the Contracting State where the operations of salvage or preservation were terminated, to a right conferring a charge against the aircraft, such right shall be recognised by Contracting States and shall take priority over all other rights in the aircraft.

2. The rights enumerated in paragraph 1 shall be satisfied in the inverse order of the dates of the incidents in connexion with which they have arisen.

3. Any of the said rights may, within three months from the date of the termination of the salvage or preservation operations, be noted on the record.

4. The said rights shall not be recognised in other Contracting States after expiration of the three months mentioned in paragraph 3 unless, within this period,

(a) the right has been noted on the record in conformity with paragraph 3, and

(b) the amount has been agreed upon or judicial action on the right has been commenced. As far as judicial action is concerned, the law of the forum shall determine the contingencies upon which the three months period may be interrupted or suspended.

5. This Article shall apply notwithstanding the provisions of Article I, paragraph 2.

Article V

The priority of a right mentioned in Article I, paragraph 1 (d), extends to all sums thereby secured. However, the amount of interest included shall not exceed that accrued during the three years prior to the execution proceedings together with that accrued during the execution proceedings.

Article VI

In case of attachment or sale of an aircraft in execution, or of any right therein, the Contracting States shall not be obliged to recognise, as against the attaching or executing creditor or against the purchaser, any right mentioned in Article I, paragraph 1, or the transfer of any such right, if constituted or effected with knowledge of the sale or execution proceedings by the person against whom the proceedings are directed.

Article VII

1. The proceedings of a sale of an aircraft in execution shall be determined by the law of the Contracting State where the sale takes place.

2. The following provisions shall however be observed:

(a) The date and place of the sale shall be fixed at least six weeks in advance.

(b) The executing creditor shall supply to the Court or other competent authority a certified extract of the recordings concerning the aircraft. He shall give public notice of the sale at the place where the aircraft is registered as to nationality, in accordance with the law there applicable, at least one month before the day fixed, and shall concurrently notify by registered letter, if possible by air mail, the recorded owner and the holders of recorded rights in the aircraft and of rights noted on the record under Article IV, paragraph 3, according to their addresses as shown on the record.

3. The consequences of failure to observe the requirements of paragraph 2 shall be as provided by the law of the Contracting State where the sale takes place. However, any sale taking place in contravention of the requirements of that paragraph may be annulled upon demand made within six months from the date of the sale by any person suffering damage as the result of such contravention.

4. No sale in execution can be effected unless all rights having priority over the claim of the executing creditor in accordance with this Convention which are established before the competent authority, are covered by the proceeds of sale or assumed by the purchaser.

5. When injury or damage is caused to persons or property on the surface of the Contracting State where the execution sale takes place, by any aircraft subject to any right referred to in Article I held as security for an indebtedness, unless adequate and effective insurance by a State or an insurance undertaking in any State has been provided by or on behalf of the operator to cover such injury or damage, the national law of such Contracting State may provide in case of the seizure of such aircraft or any other aircraft owned by the same person and encumbered with any similar right held by the same creditor:

(a) that the provisions of paragraph 4 above shall have no effect with regard to the person suffering such injury or damage or his representative if he is an executing creditor;

(b) that any right referred to in Article I held as security for an indebtedness encumbering the aircraft may not be set up against any person suffering such injury or damage or his representative in excess of an amount equal to 80% of the sale price.

In the absence of other limit established by the law of the Contracting State where the execution sale takes place, the insurance shall be considered adequate within the meaning of the present paragraph if the amount of the insurance corresponds to the value when new of the aircraft seized in execution.

6. Costs legally chargeable under the law of the Contracting State where the sale takes place, which are incurred in the common interest of creditors in the course of execution proceedings leading to sale, shall be paid out of the proceeds of sale before any claims, including those given preference by Article IV.

Article VIII

Sale of an aircraft in execution in conformity with the provisions of Article VII shall effect the transfer of the property in such aircraft free from all rights which are not assumed by the purchaser.

Article IX

Except in the case of a sale in execution in conformity with the provisions of Article VII, no transfer of an aircraft from the nationality register or the record of a Contracting State to that of another Contracting State shall be made, unless all holders of recorded rights have been satisfied or consent to the transfer.

Article X

1. If a recorded right in an aircraft of the nature specified in Article 1, and held as security for the payment of an indebtedness, extends, in conformity with the law of the Contracting State where the aircraft is registered, to spare parts stored in a specified place or places, such right shall be recognised by all Contracting States, as long as the spare parts remain in the place or places specified, provided that an appropriate public notice, specifying the description of the right, the name and address of the holder of this right and the record in which such right is recorded, is exhibited at the place where the spare parts are located, so as to give due notification to third parties that such spare parts are encumbered.

2. A statement indicating the character and the approximate number of such spare parts shall be annexed to or included in the recorded document. Such parts may be replaced by similar parts without affecting the right of the creditor.

3. The provisions of Article VII, paragraphs 1 and 4, and of Article VIII shall apply to a sale of spare parts in execution. However, where the executing creditor is an unsecured creditor, paragraph 4 of Article VII in its application to such a sale shall be construed so as to permit the sale to take place if a bid is received in an amount not less than two-thirds of the value of the spare parts as determined by experts appointed by the authority responsible for the sale. Further, in the distribution of the proceeds of sale, the competent authority may, in order to provide for the claim of the executing creditor, limit the amount payable to holders of prior rights to two-thirds of such proceeds of sale after payment of the costs referred to in Article VII, paragraph 6.

4. For the purpose of this Article the term "spare parts" means parts of aircraft, engines, propellers, radio apparatus, instruments, appliances, furnishings, parts of any of the foregoing, and generally any other articles of whatever description maintained for installation in aircraft in substitution for parts or articles removed.

Article XI

1. The provisions of this Convention shall in each Contracting State apply to all aircraft registered as to nationality in another Contracting State.

2. Each Contracting State shall also apply to aircraft there registered as to nationality:

(a) The provisions of Articles II, III, IX, and

(b) The provisions of Article IV, unless the salvage or preservation operations have been terminated within its own territory.

Article XII

Nothing in this Convention shall prejudice the right of any Contracting State to enforce against an aircraft its national laws relating to immigration, customs or air navigation.

Article XIII

This Convention shall not apply to aircraft used in military, customs or police services.

Article XIV

For the purpose of this Convention, the competent judicial and administrative authorities of the Contracting States may, subject to any contrary provision in their national law, correspond directly with each other.

Article XV

The Contracting States shall take such measures as are necessary for the fulfilment of the provisions of this Convention and shall forthwith inform the Secretary General of the International Civil Aviation Organization of these measures.

Article XVI

For the purposes of this Convention the term "aircraft" shall include the airframe, engines, propellers, radio apparatus, and all other articles intended for use in the aircraft whether installed therein or temporarily separated therefrom.

Article XVII

If a separate register of aircraft for purposes of nationality is maintained in any territory for whose foreign relations a Contracting State is responsible, references in this Convention to the law of the Contracting State shall be construed as references to the law of that territory.

Article XVIII

This Convention shall remain open for signature until it comes into force in accordance with the provisions of Article XX.

Article XIX

1. This Convention shall be subject to ratification by the signatory States.

2. The instruments of ratification shall be deposited in the archives of the International Civil Aviation Organization, which shall give notice of the date of deposit to each of the signatory and adhering States.

Article XX

1. As soon as two of the signatory States have deposited their instruments of ratification of this Convention, it shall come into force between them on the ninetieth day after the date of the deposit of the second instrument of ratification. It shall come into force, for each State which deposits its instrument of ratification after that date, on the ninetieth day after the deposit of its instrument of ratification.

2. The International Civil Aviation Organization shall give notice to each signatory State of the date on which this Convention comes into force.

3. As soon as this Convention comes into force, it shall be registered with the United Nations by the Secretary General of the International Civil Aviation Organization.

Article XXI

1. This Convention shall, after it has come into force, be open for adherence by non-signatory States.

2. Adherence shall be effected by the deposit of an instrument of adherence in the archives of the International Civil Aviation Organization, which shall give notice of the date of the deposit to each signatory and adhering State.

3. Adherence shall take effect as from the ninetieth day after the date of the deposit of the instrument of adherence in the archives of the International Civil Aviation Organization.

Article XXII

1. Any Contracting State may denounce this Convention by notification of denunciation to the International Civil Aviation Organization, which shall give notice of the date of receipt of such notification to each signatory and adhering State.

2. Denunciation shall take effect six months after the date of receipt by the International Civil Aviation Organization of the notification of denunciation.

Article XXIII

1. Any State may at the time of deposit of its instrument of ratification or adherence, declare that its acceptance of this Convention does not apply to any one or more of the territories for the foreign relations of which such State is responsible.

2. The International Civil Aviation Organization shall give notice of any such declaration to each signatory and adhering State.

3. With the exception of territories in respect of which a declaration has been made in accordance with paragraph 1 of this Article, this Convention shall apply to all territories for the foreign relations of which a Contracting State is responsible.

4. Any State may adhere to this Convention separately on behalf of all or any of the territories regarding which it has made a declaration in accordance with paragraph 1 of this Article and the provisions of paragraphs 2 and 3 of Article XXI shall apply to such adherence.

5. Any Contracting State may denounce this Convention, in accordance with the provisions of Article XXII, separately for all or any of the territories for the foreign relations of which such State is responsible.

IN WITNESS WHEREOF the undersigned Plenipotentiaries, having been duly authorized, have signed this Convention.

DONE at Geneva, on the nineteenth day of the month of June of the year one thousand nine hundred and forty-eight in the English, French and Spanish languages, each text being of equal authenticity.

This Convention shall be deposited in the archives of the International Civil Aviation Organization where, in accordance with Article XVIII, it shall remain open for signature.

Appendix 5

Convention on International Interests in Mobile Equipment (Cape Town Convention) 2011

THE STATES PARTIES TO THIS CONVENTION,

AWARE of the need to acquire and use mobile equipment of high value or particular economic significance and to facilitate the financing of the acquisition and use of such equipment in an efficient manner,

RECOGNISING the advantages of asset-based financing and leasing for this purpose and desiring to facilitate these types of transaction by establishing clear rules to govern them,

MINDFUL of the need to ensure that interests in such equipment are recognised and protected universally,

DESIRING to provide broad and mutual economic benefits for all interested parties,

BELIEVING that such rules must reflect the principles underlying asset-based financing and leasing and promote the autonomy of the parties necessary in these transactions,

CONSCIOUS of the need to establish a legal framework for international interests in such equipment and for that purpose to create an international registration system for their protection,

TAKING INTO CONSIDERATION the objectives and principles enunciated in existing Conventions relating to such equipment,

HAVE AGREED upon the following provisions:

Chapter I
Sphere of application and general provisions

Article 1—Definitions

In this Convention, except where the context otherwise requires, the following terms are employed with the meanings set out below:

(a) "agreement" means a security agreement, a title reservation agreement or a leasing agreement;
(b) "assignment" means a contract which, whether by way of security or otherwise, confers on the assignee associated rights with or without a transfer of the related international interest;
(c) "associated rights" means all rights to payment or other performance by a debtor under an agreement which are secured by or associated with the object;
(d) "commencement of the insolvency proceedings" means the time at which the insolvency proceedings are deemed to commence under the applicable insolvency law;
(e) "conditional buyer" means a buyer under a title reservation agreement;
(f) "conditional seller" means a seller under a title reservation agreement;
(g) "contract of sale" means a contract for the sale of an object by a seller to a buyer which is not an agreement as defined in (a) above;
(h) "court" means a court of law or an administrative or arbitral tribunal established by a Contracting State;
(i) "creditor" means a chargee under a security agreement, a conditional seller under a title reservation agreement or a lessor under a leasing agreement;
(j) "debtor" means a chargor under a security agreement, a conditional buyer under a title reservation agreement, a lessee under a leasing agreement or a person whose interest in an object is burdened by a registrable non-consensual right or interest;
(k) "insolvency administrator" means a person authorised to administer the reorganisation or liquidation, including one authorised on an interim basis, and includes a debtor in possession if permitted by the applicable insolvency law;
(l) "insolvency proceedings" means bankruptcy, liquidation or other collective judicial or administrative proceedings, including interim proceedings, in which the assets and affairs of the debtor are subject to control or supervision by a court for the purposes of reorganisation or liquidation;
(m) "interested persons" means:
    (i) the debtor;
    (ii) any person who, for the purpose of assuring performance of any of the obligations in favour of the creditor, gives or issues a suretyship or demand guarantee or a standby letter of credit or any other form of credit insurance;

(iii) any other person having rights in or over the object;

(n) "internal transaction" means a transaction of a type listed in Article 2(2)(a) to (c) where the centre of the main interests of all parties to such transaction is situated, and the relevant object located (as specified in the Protocol), in the same Contracting State at the time of the conclusion of the contract and where the interest created by the transaction has been registered in a national registry in that Contracting State which has made a declaration under Article 50(1);

(o) "international interest" means an interest held by a creditor to which Article 2 applies;

(p) "International Registry" means the international registration facilities established for the purposes of this Convention or the Protocol;

(q) "leasing agreement" means an agreement by which one person (the lessor) grants a right to possession or control of an object (with or without an option to purchase) to another person (the lessee) in return for a rental or other payment;

(r) "national interest" means an interest held by a creditor in an object and created by an internal transaction covered by a declaration under Article 50(1);

(s) "non-consensual right or interest" means a right or interest conferred under the law of a Contracting State which has made a declaration under Article 39 to secure the performance of an obligation, including an obligation to a State, State entity or an intergovernmental or private organisation;

(t) "notice of a national interest" means notice registered or to be registered in the International Registry that a national interest has been created;

(u) "object" means an object of a category to which Article 2 applies;

(v) "pre-existing right or interest" means a right or interest of any kind in or over an object created or arising before the effective date of this Convention as defined by Article 60(2)(a);

(w) "proceeds" means money or non-money proceeds of an object arising from the total or partial loss or physical destruction of the object or its total or partial confiscation, condemnation or requisition;

(x) "prospective assignment" means an assignment that is intended to be made in the future, upon the occurrence of a stated event, whether or not the occurrence of the event is certain;

(y) "prospective international interest" means an interest that is intended to be created or provided for in an object as an international interest in the future, upon the occurrence of a stated event (which may include the debtor's acquisition of an interest in the object), whether or not the occurrence of the event is certain;

(z) "prospective sale" means a sale which is intended to be made in the future, upon the occurrence of a stated event, whether or not the occurrence of the event is certain;

(aa) "Protocol" means, in respect of any category of object and associated rights to which this Convention applies, the Protocol in respect of that category of object and associated rights;
(bb) "registered" means registered in the International Registry pursuant to Chapter V;
(cc) "registered interest" means an international interest, a registrable non-consensual right or interest or a national interest specified in a notice of a national interest registered pursuant to Chapter V;
(dd) "registrable non-consensual right or interest" means a non-consensual right or interest registrable pursuant to a declaration deposited under Article 40;
(ee) "Registrar" means, in respect of the Protocol, the person or body designated by that Protocol or appointed under Article 17(2)(b);
(ff) "regulations" means regulations made or approved by the Supervisory Authority pursuant to the Protocol;
(gg) "sale" means a transfer of ownership of an object pursuant to a contract of sale;
(hh) "secured obligation" means an obligation secured by a security interest;
(ii) "security agreement" means an agreement by which a chargor grants or agrees to grant to a chargee an interest (including an ownership interest) in or over an object to secure the performance of any existing or future obligation of the chargor or a third person;
(jj) "security interest" means an interest created by a security agreement;
(kk) "Supervisory Authority" means, in respect of the Protocol, the Supervisory Authority referred to in Article 17(1);
(ll) "title reservation agreement" means an agreement for the sale of an object on terms that ownership does not pass until fulfilment of the condition or conditions stated in the agreement;
(mm) "unregistered interest" means a consensual interest or non-consensual right or interest (other than an interest to which Article 39 applies) which has not been registered, whether or not it is registrable under this Convention; and
(nn) "writing" means a record of information (including information communicated by teletransmission) which is in tangible or other form and is capable of being reproduced in tangible form on a subsequent occasion and which indicates by reasonable means a person's approval of the record.

Article 2—The international interest

1. This Convention provides for the constitution and effects of an international interest in certain categories of mobile equipment and associated rights.

2. For the purposes of this Convention, an international interest in mobile equipment is an interest, constituted under Article 7, in a uniquely identifiable object of a category of such objects listed in paragraph 3 and designated in the Protocol:

(a) granted by the chargor under a security agreement;
(b) vested in a person who is the conditional seller under a title reservation agreement; or
(c) vested in a person who is the lessor under a leasing agreement.

An interest falling within sub-paragraph (a) does not also fall within sub-paragraph (b) or (c).

3. The categories referred to in the preceding paragraphs are:

(a) airframes, aircraft engines and helicopters;
(b) railway rolling stock; and
(c) space assets.

4. The applicable law determines whether an interest to which paragraph 2 applies falls within sub-paragraph (a), (b) or (c) of that paragraph.

5. An international interest in an object extends to proceeds of that object.

Article 3—Sphere of application

1. This Convention applies when, at the time of the conclusion of the agreement creating or providing for the international interest, the debtor is situated in a Contracting State.

2. The fact that the creditor is situated in a non-Contracting State does not affect the applicability of this Convention.

Article 4—Where debtor is situated

1. For the purposes of Article 3(1), the debtor is situated in any Contracting State:

(a) under the law of which it is incorporated or formed;
(b) where it has its registered office or statutory seat;
(c) where it has its centre of administration; or
(d) where it has its place of business.

2. A reference in sub-paragraph (d) of the preceding paragraph to the debtor's place of business shall, if it has more than one place of business, mean its principal place of business or, if it has no place of business, its habitual residence.

Article 5—Interpretation and applicable law

1. In the interpretation of this Convention, regard is to be had to its purposes as set forth in the preamble, to its international character and to the need to promote uniformity and predictability in its application.

2. Questions concerning matters governed by this Convention which are not expressly settled in it are to be settled in conformity with the general principles on which it is based or, in the absence of such principles, in conformity with the applicable law.

3. References to the applicable law are to the domestic rules of the law applicable by virtue of the rules of private international law of the forum State.

4. Where a State comprises several territorial units, each of which has its own rules of law in respect of the matter to be decided, and where there is no indication of the relevant territorial unit, the law of that State decides which is the territorial unit whose rules shall govern. In the absence of any such rule, the law of the territorial unit with which the case is most closely connected shall apply.

Article 6—Relationship between the Convention and the Protocol

1. This Convention and the Protocol shall be read and interpreted together as a single instrument.

2. To the extent of any inconsistency between this Convention and the Protocol, the Protocol shall prevail.

Chapter II
Constitution of an international interest

Article 7—Formal requirements

An interest is constituted as an international interest under this Convention where the agreement creating or providing for the interest:

(a) is in writing;
(b) relates to an object of which the chargor, conditional seller or lessor has power to dispose;
(c) enables the object to be identified in conformity with the Protocol; and
(d) in the case of a security agreement, enables the secured obligations to be determined, but without the need to state a sum or maximum sum secured.

Chapter III
Default remedies

Article 8—Remedies of chargee

1. In the event of default as provided in Article 11, the chargee may, to the extent that the chargor has at any time so agreed and subject to any declaration that may be made by a Contracting State under Article 54, exercise any one or more of the following remedies:

(a) take possession or control of any object charged to it;
(b) sell or grant a lease of any such object;
(c) collect or receive any income or profits arising from the management or use of any such object.

2. The chargee may alternatively apply for a court order authorising or directing any of the acts referred to in the preceding paragraph.

3. Any remedy set out in sub-paragraph (a), (b) or (c) of paragraph 1 or by Article 13 shall be exercised in a commercially reasonable manner. A remedy shall be

deemed to be exercised in a commercially reasonable manner where it is exercised in conformity with a provision of the security agreement except where such a provision is manifestly unreasonable.

4. A chargee proposing to sell or grant a lease of an object under paragraph 1 shall give reasonable prior notice in writing of the proposed sale or lease to:

(a) interested persons specified in Article 1(m)(i) and (ii); and
(b) interested persons specified in Article 1(m)(iii) who have given notice of their rights to the chargee within a reasonable time prior to the sale or lease.

5. Any sum collected or received by the chargee as a result of exercise of any of the remedies set out in paragraph 1 or 2 shall be applied towards discharge of the amount of the secured obligations.

6. Where the sums collected or received by the chargee as a result of the exercise of any remedy set out in paragraph 1 or 2 exceed the amount secured by the security interest and any reasonable costs incurred in the exercise of any such remedy, then unless otherwise ordered by the court the chargee shall distribute the surplus among holders of subsequently ranking interests which have been registered or of which the chargee has been given notice, in order of priority, and pay any remaining balance to the chargor.

Article 9—Vesting of object in satisfaction; redemption

1. At any time after default as provided in Article 11, the chargee and all the interested persons may agree that ownership of (or any other interest of the chargor in) any object covered by the security interest shall vest in the chargee in or towards satisfaction of the secured obligations.

2. The court may on the application of the chargee order that ownership of (or any other interest of the chargor in) any object covered by the security interest shall vest in the chargee in or towards satisfaction of the secured obligations.

3. The court shall grant an application under the preceding paragraph only if the amount of the secured obligations to be satisfied by such vesting is commensurate with the value of the object after taking account of any payment to be made by the chargee to any of the interested persons.

4. At any time after default as provided in Article 11 and before sale of the charged object or the making of an order under paragraph 2, the chargor or any interested person may discharge the security interest by paying in full the amount secured, subject to any lease granted by the chargee under Article 8(1)(b) or ordered under Article 8(2). Where, after such default, the payment of the amount secured is made in full by an interested person other than the debtor, that person is subrogated to the rights of the chargee.

5. Ownership or any other interest of the chargor passing on a sale under Article 8(1)(b) or passing under paragraph 1 or 2 of this Article is free from any other interest over which the chargee's security interest has priority under the provisions of Article 29.

Article 10—Remedies of conditional seller or lessor

In the event of default under a title reservation agreement or under a leasing agreement as provided in Article 11, the conditional seller or the lessor, as the case may be, may:

(a) subject to any declaration that may be made by a Contracting State under Article 54, terminate the agreement and take possession or control of any object to which the agreement relates; or
(b) apply for a court order authorising or directing either of these acts.

Article 11—Meaning of default

1. The debtor and the creditor may at any time agree in writing as to the events that constitute a default or otherwise give rise to the rights and remedies specified in Articles 8 to 10 and 13.

2. Where the debtor and the creditor have not so agreed, "default" for the purposes of Articles 8 to 10 and 13 means a default which substantially deprives the creditor of what it is entitled to expect under the agreement.

Article 12—Additional remedies

Any additional remedies permitted by the applicable law, including any remedies agreed upon by the parties, may be exercised to the extent that they are not inconsistent with the mandatory provisions of this Chapter as set out in Article 15.

Article 13—Relief pending final determination

1. Subject to any declaration that it may make under Article 55, a Contracting State shall ensure that a creditor who adduces evidence of default by the debtor may, pending final determination of its claim and to the extent that the debtor has at any time so agreed, obtain from a court speedy relief in the form of such one or more of the following orders as the creditor requests:

(a) preservation of the object and its value;
(b) possession, control or custody of the object;
(c) immobilisation of the object; and
(d) lease or, except where covered by sub-paragraphs (a) to (c), management of the object and the income therefrom.

2. In making any order under the preceding paragraph, the court may impose such terms as it considers necessary to protect the interested persons in the event that the creditor:

(a) in implementing any order granting such relief, fails to perform any of its obligations to the debtor under this Convention or the Protocol; or
(b) fails to establish its claim, wholly or in part, on the final determination of that claim.

3. Before making any order under paragraph 1, the court may require notice of the request to be given to any of the interested persons.

4. Nothing in this Article affects the application of Article 8(3) or limits the availability of forms of interim relief other than those set out in paragraph 1.

Article 14—Procedural requirements

Subject to Article 54(2), any remedy provided by this Chapter shall be exercised in conformity with the procedure prescribed by the law of the place where the remedy is to be exercised.

Article 15—Derogation

In their relations with each other, any two or more of the parties referred to in this Chapter may at any time, by agreement in writing, derogate from or vary the effect of any of the preceding provisions of this Chapter except Articles 8(3) to (6), 9(3) and (4), 13(2) and 14.

Chapter IV
The international registration system

Article 16—The International Registry

1. An International Registry shall be established for registrations of:

   (a) international interests, prospective international interests and registrable non-consensual rights and interests;
   (b) assignments and prospective assignments of international interests;
   (c) acquisitions of international interests by legal or contractual subrogations under the applicable law;
   (d) notices of national interests; and
   (e) subordinations of interests referred to in any of the preceding sub-paragraphs.

2. Different international registries may be established for different categories of object and associated rights.

3. For the purposes of this Chapter and Chapter V, the term "registration" includes, where appropriate, an amendment, extension or discharge of a registration.

Article 17—The Supervisory Authority and the Registrar

1. There shall be a Supervisory Authority as provided by the Protocol.

2. The Supervisory Authority shall:

   (a) establish or provide for the establishment of the International Registry;
   (b) except as otherwise provided by the Protocol, appoint and dismiss the Registrar;

(c) ensure that any rights required for the continued effective operation of the International Registry in the event of a change of Registrar will vest in or be assignable to the new Registrar;
(d) after consultation with the Contracting States, make or approve and ensure the publication of regulations pursuant to the Protocol dealing with the operation of the International Registry;
(e) establish administrative procedures through which complaints concerning the operation of the International Registry can be made to the Supervisory Authority;
(f) supervise the Registrar and the operation of the International Registry;
(g) at the request of the Registrar, provide such guidance to the Registrar as the Supervisory Authority thinks fit;
(h) set and periodically review the structure of fees to be charged for the services and facilities of the International Registry;
(i) do all things necessary to ensure that an efficient notice-based electronic registration system exists to implement the objectives of this Convention and the Protocol; and
(j) report periodically to Contracting States concerning the discharge of its obligations under this Convention and the Protocol.

3. The Supervisory Authority may enter into any agreement requisite for the performance of its functions, including any agreement referred to in Article 27(3).

4. The Supervisory Authority shall own all proprietary rights in the data bases and archives of the International Registry.

5. The Registrar shall ensure the efficient operation of the International Registry and perform the functions assigned to it by this Convention, the Protocol and the regulations.

Chapter V
Other matters relating to registration

Article 18—Registration requirements

1. The Protocol and regulations shall specify the requirements, including the criteria for the identification of the object:

(a) for effecting a registration (which shall include provision for prior electronic transmission of any consent from any person whose consent is required under Article 20);
(b) for making searches and issuing search certificates, and, subject thereto;
(c) for ensuring the confidentiality of information and documents of the International Registry other than information and documents relating to a registration.

2. The Registrar shall not be under a duty to enquire whether a consent to registration under Article 20 has in fact been given or is valid.

3. Where an interest registered as a prospective international interest becomes an international interest, no further registration shall be required provided that

the registration information is sufficient for a registration of an international interest.

4. The Registrar shall arrange for registrations to be entered into the International Registry data base and made searchable in chronological order of receipt, and the file shall record the date and time of receipt.

5. The Protocol may provide that a Contracting State may designate an entity or entities in its territory as the entry point or entry points through which the information required for registration shall or may be transmitted to the International Registry. A Contracting State making such a designation may specify the requirements, if any, to be satisfied before such information is transmitted to the International Registry.

Article 19—Validity and time of registration

1. A registration shall be valid only if made in conformity with Article 20.

2. A registration, if valid, shall be complete upon entry of the required information into the International Registry data base so as to be searchable.

3. A registration shall be searchable for the purposes of the preceding paragraph at the time when:

(a) the International Registry has assigned to it a sequentially ordered file number; and
(b) the registration information, including the file number, is stored in durable form and may be accessed at the International Registry.

4. If an interest first registered as a prospective international interest becomes an international interest, that international interest shall be treated as registered from the time of registration of the prospective international interest provided that the registration was still current immediately before the international interest was constituted as provided by Article 7.

5. The preceding paragraph applies with necessary modifications to the registration of a prospective assignment of an international interest.

6. A registration shall be searchable in the International Registry data base according to the criteria prescribed by the Protocol.

Article 20—Consent to registration

1. An international interest, a prospective international interest or an assignment or prospective assignment of an international interest may be registered, and any such registration amended or extended prior to its expiry, by either party with the consent in writing of the other.

2. The subordination of an international interest to another international interest may be registered by or with the consent in writing at any time of the person whose interest has been subordinated.

3. A registration may be discharged by or with the consent in writing of the party in whose favour it was made.

4. The acquisition of an international interest by legal or contractual subrogation may be registered by the subrogee.

5. A registrable non-consensual right or interest may be registered by the holder thereof.

6. A notice of a national interest may be registered by the holder thereof.

Article 21—Duration of registration

Registration of an international interest remains effective until discharged or until expiry of the period specified in the registration.

Article 22—Searches

1. Any person may, in the manner prescribed by the Protocol and regulations, make or request a search of the International Registry by electronic means concerning interests or prospective international interests registered therein.

2. Upon receipt of a request therefor, the Registrar, in the manner prescribed by the Protocol and regulations, shall issue a registry search certificate by electronic means with respect to any object:

(a) stating all registered information relating thereto, together with a statement indicating the date and time of registration of such information; or
(b) stating that there is no information in the International Registry relating thereto.

3. A search certificate issued under the preceding paragraph shall indicate that the creditor named in the registration information has acquired or intends to acquire an international interest in the object but shall not indicate whether what is registered is an international interest or a prospective international interest, even if this is ascertainable from the relevant registration information.

Article 23—List of declarations and declared non-consensual rights or interests

The Registrar shall maintain a list of declarations, withdrawals of declaration and of the categories of non-consensual right or interest communicated to the Registrar by the Depositary as having been declared by Contracting States in conformity with Articles 39 and 40 and the date of each such declaration or withdrawal of declaration. Such list shall be recorded and searchable in the name of the declaring State and shall be made available as provided in the Protocol and regulations to any person requesting it.

Article 24—Evidentiary value of certificates

A document in the form prescribed by the regulations which purports to be a certificate issued by the International Registry is prima facie proof:

(a) that it has been so issued; and
(b) of the facts recited in it, including the date and time of a registration.

Article 25—Discharge of registration

1. Where the obligations secured by a registered security interest or the obligations giving rise to a registered non-consensual right or interest have been discharged, or where the conditions of transfer of title under a registered title reservation agreement have been fulfilled, the holder of such interest shall, without undue delay, procure the discharge of the registration after written demand by the debtor delivered to or received at its address stated in the registration.

2. Where a prospective international interest or a prospective assignment of an international interest has been registered, the intending creditor or intending assignee shall, without undue delay, procure the discharge of the registration after written demand by the intending debtor or assignor which is delivered to or received at its address stated in the registration before the intending creditor or assignee has given value or incurred a commitment to give value.

3. Where the obligations secured by a national interest specified in a registered notice of a national interest have been discharged, the holder of such interest shall, without undue delay, procure the discharge of the registration after written demand by the debtor delivered to or received at its address stated in the registration.

4. Where a registration ought not to have been made or is incorrect, the person in whose favour the registration was made shall, without undue delay, procure its discharge or amendment after written demand by the debtor delivered to or received at its address stated in the registration.

Article 26—Access to the international registration facilities

No person shall be denied access to the registration and search facilities of the International Registry on any ground other than its failure to comply with the procedures prescribed by this Chapter.

Chapter VI
Privileges and immunities of the Supervisory Authority and the Registrar

Article 27—Legal personality; immunity

1. The Supervisory Authority shall have international legal personality where not already possessing such personality.

2. The Supervisory Authority and its officers and employees shall enjoy such immunity from legal or administrative process as is specified in the Protocol.

3. (a) The Supervisory Authority shall enjoy exemption from taxes and such other privileges as may be provided by agreement with the host State.
   (b) For the purposes of this paragraph, "host State" means the State in which the Supervisory Authority is situated.

4. The assets, documents, data bases and archives of the International Registry shall be inviolable and immune from seizure or other legal or administrative process.

5. For the purposes of any claim against the Registrar under Article 28(1) or Article 44, the claimant shall be entitled to access to such information and documents as are necessary to enable the claimant to pursue its claim.

6. The Supervisory Authority may waive the inviolability and immunity conferred by paragraph 4.

Chapter VII
Liability of the Registrar

Article 28—Liability and financial assurances

1. The Registrar shall be liable for compensatory damages for loss suffered by a person directly resulting from an error or omission of the Registrar and its officers and employees or from a malfunction of the international registration system except where the malfunction is caused by an event of an inevitable and irresistible nature, which could not be prevented by using the best practices in current use in the field of electronic registry design and operation, including those related to back-up and systems security and networking.

2. The Registrar shall not be liable under the preceding paragraph for factual inaccuracy of registration information received by the Registrar or transmitted by the Registrar in the form in which it received that information nor for acts or circumstances for which the Registrar and its officers and employees are not responsible and arising prior to receipt of registration information at the International Registry.

3. Compensation under paragraph 1 may be reduced to the extent that the person who suffered the damage caused or contributed to that damage.

4. The Registrar shall procure insurance or a financial guarantee covering the liability referred to in this Article to the extent determined by the Supervisory Authority, in accordance with the Protocol.

Chapter VIII
Effects of an international interest as against third parties

Article 29—Priority of competing interests

1. A registered interest has priority over any other interest subsequently registered and over an unregistered interest.

2. The priority of the first-mentioned interest under the preceding paragraph applies:

(a) even if the first-mentioned interest was acquired or registered with actual knowledge of the other interest; and
(b) even as regards value given by the holder of the first-mentioned interest with such knowledge.

3. The buyer of an object acquires its interest in it:

(a) subject to an interest registered at the time of its acquisition of that interest; and

(b) free from an unregistered interest even if it has actual knowledge of such an interest.

4. The conditional buyer or lessee acquires its interest in or right over that object:

(a) subject to an interest registered prior to the registration of the international interest held by its conditional seller or lessor; and
(b) free from an interest not so registered at that time even if it has actual knowledge of that interest.

5. The priority of competing interests or rights under this Article may be varied by agreement between the holders of those interests, but an assignee of a subordinated interest is not bound by an agreement to subordinate that interest unless at the time of the assignment a subordination had been registered relating to that agreement.

6. Any priority given by this Article to an interest in an object extends to proceeds.

7. This Convention:

(a) does not affect the rights of a person in an item, other than an object, held prior to its installation on an object if under the applicable law those rights continue to exist after the installation; and
(b) does not prevent the creation of rights in an item, other than an object, which has previously been installed on an object where under the applicable law those rights are created.

Article 30—Effects of insolvency

1. In insolvency proceedings against the debtor an international interest is effective if prior to the commencement of the insolvency proceedings that interest was registered in conformity with this Convention.

2. Nothing in this Article impairs the effectiveness of an international interest in the insolvency proceedings where that interest is effective under the applicable law.

3. Nothing in this Article affects:

(a) any rules of law applicable in insolvency proceedings relating to the avoidance of a transaction as a preference or a transfer in fraud of creditors; or
(b) any rules of procedure relating to the enforcement of rights to property which is under the control or supervision of the insolvency administrator.

Chapter IX
Assignments of associated rights and international interests; rights of subrogation

Article 31—Effects of assignment

1. Except as otherwise agreed by the parties, an assignment of associated rights made in conformity with Article 32 also transfers to the assignee:

(a) the related international interest; and
(b) all the interests and priorities of the assignor under this Convention.

2. Nothing in this Convention prevents a partial assignment of the assignor's associated rights. In the case of such a partial assignment the assignor and assignee may agree as to their respective rights concerning the related international interest assigned under the preceding paragraph but not so as adversely to affect the debtor without its consent.

3. Subject to paragraph 4, the applicable law shall determine the defences and rights of set-off available to the debtor against the assignee.

4. The debtor may at any time by agreement in writing waive all or any of the defences and rights of set-off referred to in the preceding paragraph other than defences arising from fraudulent acts on the part of the assignee.

5. In the case of an assignment by way of security, the assigned associated rights revest in the assignor, to the extent that they are still subsisting, when the obligations secured by the assignment have been discharged.

Article 32—Formal requirements of assignment

1. An assignment of associated rights transfers the related international interest only if it:

(a) is in writing;
(b) enables the associated rights to be identified under the contract from which they arise; and
(c) in the case of an assignment by way of security, enables the obligations secured by the assignment to be determined in accordance with the Protocol but without the need to state a sum or maximum sum secured.

2. An assignment of an international interest created or provided for by a security agreement is not valid unless some or all related associated rights also are assigned.

3. This Convention does not apply to an assignment of associated rights which is not effective to transfer the related international interest.

Article 33—Debtor's duty to assignee

1. To the extent that associated rights and the related international interest have been transferred in accordance with Articles 31 and 32, the debtor in relation to those rights and that interest is bound by the assignment and has a duty to make payment or give other performance to the assignee, if but only if:

(a) the debtor has been given notice of the assignment in writing by or with the authority of the assignor; and
(b) the notice identifies the associated rights.

2. Irrespective of any other ground on which payment or performance by the debtor discharges the latter from liability, payment or performance shall be effective for this purpose if made in accordance with the preceding paragraph.

3. Nothing in this Article shall affect the priority of competing assignments.

Article 34—Default remedies in respect of assignment by way of security

In the event of default by the assignor under the assignment of associated rights and the related international interest made by way of security, Articles 8, 9 and 11 to 14 apply in the relations between the assignor and the assignee (and, in relation to associated rights, apply in so far as those provisions are capable of application to intangible property) as if references:

(a) to the secured obligation and the security interest were references to the obligation secured by the assignment of the associated rights and the related international interest and the security interest created by that assignment;
(b) to the chargee or creditor and chargor or debtor were references to the assignee and assignor;
(c) to the holder of the international interest were references to the assignee; and
(d) to the object were references to the assigned associated rights and the related international interest.

Article 35—Priority of competing assignments

1. Where there are competing assignments of associated rights and at least one of the assignments includes the related international interest and is registered, the provisions of Article 29 apply as if the references to a registered interest were references to an assignment of the associated rights and the related registered interest and as if references to a registered or unregistered interest were references to a registered or unregistered assignment.

2. Article 30 applies to an assignment of associated rights as if the references to an international interest were references to an assignment of the associated rights and the related international interest.

Article 36—Assignee's priority with respect to associated rights

1. The assignee of associated rights and the related international interest whose assignment has been registered only has priority under Article 35(1) over another assignee of the associated rights:

(a) if the contract under which the associated rights arise states that they are secured by or associated with the object; and
(b) to the extent that the associated rights are related to an object.

2. For the purposes of sub-paragraph (b) of the preceding paragraph, associated rights are related to an object only to the extent that they consist of rights to payment or performance that relate to:

(a) a sum advanced and utilised for the purchase of the object;
(b) a sum advanced and utilised for the purchase of another object in which the assignor held another international interest if the assignor transferred that interest to the assignee and the assignment has been registered;

(c) the price payable for the object;
(d) the rentals payable in respect of the object; or
(e) other obligations arising from a transaction referred to in any of the preceding sub-paragraphs.

3. In all other cases, the priority of the competing assignments of the associated rights shall be determined by the applicable law.

Article 37—Effects of assignor's insolvency

The provisions of Article 30 apply to insolvency proceedings against the assignor as if references to the debtor were references to the assignor.

Article 38—Subrogation

1. Subject to paragraph 2, nothing in this Convention affects the acquisition of associated rights and the related international interest by legal or contractual subrogation under the applicable law.

2. The priority between any interest within the preceding paragraph and a competing interest may be varied by agreement in writing between the holders of the respective interests but an assignee of a subordinated interest is not bound by an agreement to subordinate that interest unless at the time of the assignment a subordination had been registered relating to that agreement.

Chapter X
Rights or interests subject to declarations by Contracting States

Article 39—Rights having priority without registration

1. A Contracting State may at any time, in a declaration deposited with the Depositary of the Protocol declare, generally or specifically:

(a) those categories of non-consensual right or interest (other than a right or interest to which Article 40 applies) which under that State's law have priority over an interest in an object equivalent to that of the holder of a registered international interest and which shall have priority over a registered international interest, whether in or outside insolvency proceedings; and
(b) that nothing in this Convention shall affect the right of a State or State entity, intergovernmental organisation or other private provider of public services to arrest or detain an object under the laws of that State for payment of amounts owed to such entity, organisation or provider directly relating to those services in respect of that object or another object.

2. A declaration made under the preceding paragraph may be expressed to cover categories that are created after the deposit of that declaration.

3. A non-consensual right or interest has priority over an international interest if and only if the former is of a category covered by a declaration deposited prior to the registration of the international interest.

4. Notwithstanding the preceding paragraph, a Contracting State may, at the time of ratification, acceptance, approval of, or accession to the Protocol, declare that a right or interest of a category covered by a declaration made under sub-paragraph (a) of paragraph 1 shall have priority over an international interest registered prior to the date of such ratification, acceptance, approval or accession.

Article 40—Registrable non-consensual rights or interests

A Contracting State may at any time in a declaration deposited with the Depositary of the Protocol list the categories of non-consensual right or interest which shall be registrable under this Convention as regards any category of object as if the right or interest were an international interest and shall be regulated accordingly. Such a declaration may be modified from time to time.

Chapter XI
Application of the Convention to sales

Article 41—Sale and prospective sale

This Convention shall apply to the sale or prospective sale of an object as provided for in the Protocol with any modifications therein.

Chapter XII
Jurisdiction

Article 42—Choice of forum

1. Subject to Articles 43 and 44, the courts of a Contracting State chosen by the parties to a transaction have jurisdiction in respect of any claim brought under this Convention, whether or not the chosen forum has a connection with the parties or the transaction. Such jurisdiction shall be exclusive unless otherwise agreed between the parties.

2. Any such agreement shall be in writing or otherwise concluded in accordance with the formal requirements of the law of the chosen forum.

Article 43—Jurisdiction under Article 13

1. The courts of a Contracting State chosen by the parties and the courts of the Contracting State on the territory of which the object is situated have jurisdiction to grant relief under Article 13(1)(a), (b), (c) and Article 13(4) in respect of that object.

2. Jurisdiction to grant relief under Article 13(1)(d) or other interim relief by virtue of Article 13(4) may be exercised either:

(a) by the courts chosen by the parties; or
(b) by the courts of a Contracting State on the territory of which the debtor is situated, being relief which, by the terms of the order granting it, is enforceable only in the territory of that Contracting State.

3. A court has jurisdiction under the preceding paragraphs even if the final determination of the claim referred to in Article 13(1) will or may take place in a court of another Contracting State or by arbitration.

Article 44—Jurisdiction to make orders against the Registrar

1. The courts of the place in which the Registrar has its centre of administration shall have exclusive jurisdiction to award damages or make orders against the Registrar.

2. Where a person fails to respond to a demand made under Article 25 and that person has ceased to exist or cannot be found for the purpose of enabling an order to be made against it requiring it to procure discharge of the registration, the courts referred to in the preceding paragraph shall have exclusive jurisdiction, on the application of the debtor or intending debtor, to make an order directed to the Registrar requiring the Registrar to discharge the registration.

3. Where a person fails to comply with an order of a court having jurisdiction under this Convention or, in the case of a national interest, an order of a court of competent jurisdiction requiring that person to procure the amendment or discharge of a registration, the courts referred to in paragraph 1 may direct the Registrar to take such steps as will give effect to that order.

4. Except as otherwise provided by the preceding paragraphs, no court may make orders or give judgments or rulings against or purporting to bind the Registrar.

Article 45—Jurisdiction in respect of insolvency proceedings

The provisions of this Chapter are not applicable to insolvency proceedings.

Chapter XIII
Relationship with other Conventions

Article 45 *bis*—Relationship with the *United Nations Convention on the Assignment of Receivables in International Trade*

This Convention shall prevail over the *United Nations Convention on the Assignment of Receivables in International Trade*, opened for signature in New York on 12 December 2001, as it relates to the assignment of receivables which are associated rights related to international interests in aircraft objects, railway rolling stock and space assets.

Article 46—Relationship with the *Unidroit Convention on International Financial Leasing*

The Protocol may determine the relationship between this Convention and the *Unidroit Convention on International Financial Leasing*, signed at Ottawa on 28 May 1988.

Chapter XIV
Final provisions

Article 47—Signature, ratification, acceptance, approval or accession

1. This Convention shall be open for signature in Cape Town on 16 November 2001 by States participating in the Diplomatic Conference to Adopt a Mobile Equipment Convention and an Aircraft Protocol held at Cape Town from 29 October to 16 November 2001. After 16 November 2001, the Convention

shall be open to all States for signature at the Headquarters of the International Institute for the Unification of Private Law (UNIDROIT) in Rome until it enters into force in accordance with Article 49.

2. This Convention shall be subject to ratification, acceptance or approval by States which have signed it.

3. Any State which does not sign this Convention may accede to it at any time.

4. Ratification, acceptance, approval or accession is effected by the deposit of a formal instrument to that effect with the Depositary.

Article 48—Regional Economic Integration Organisations

1. A Regional Economic Integration Organisation which is constituted by sovereign States and has competence over certain matters governed by this Convention may similarly sign, accept, approve or accede to this Convention. The Regional Economic Integration Organisation shall in that case have the rights and obligations of a Contracting State, to the extent that that Organisation has competence over matters governed by this Convention. Where the number of Contracting States is relevant in this Convention, the Regional Economic Integration Organisation shall not count as a Contracting State in addition to its Member States which are Contracting States.

2. The Regional Economic Integration Organisation shall, at the time of signature, acceptance, approval or accession, make a declaration to the Depositary specifying the matters governed by this Convention in respect of which competence has been transferred to that Organisation by its Member States. The Regional Economic Integration Organisation shall promptly notify the Depositary of any changes to the distribution of competence, including new transfers of competence, specified in the declaration under this paragraph.

3. Any reference to a "Contracting State" or "Contracting States" or "State Party" or "States Parties" in this Convention applies equally to a Regional Economic Integration Organisation where the context so requires.

Article 49—Entry into force

1. This Convention enters into force on the first day of the month following the expiration of three months after the date of the deposit of the third instrument of ratification, acceptance, approval or accession but only as regards a category of objects to which a Protocol applies:

(a) as from the time of entry into force of that Protocol;
(b) subject to the terms of that Protocol; and
(c) as between States Parties to this Convention and that Protocol.

2. For other States this Convention enters into force on the first day of the month following the expiration of three months after the date of the deposit of their instrument of ratification, acceptance, approval or accession but only as regards a category of objects to which a Protocol applies and subject, in relation to such

Protocol, to the requirements of sub-paragraphs (a), (b) and (c) of the preceding paragraph.

Article 50—Internal transactions

1. A Contracting State may, at the time of ratification, acceptance, approval of, or accession to the Protocol, declare that this Convention shall not apply to a transaction which is an internal transaction in relation to that State with regard to all types of objects or some of them.

2. Notwithstanding the preceding paragraph, the provisions of Articles 8(4), 9(1), 16, Chapter V, Article 29, and any provisions of this Convention relating to registered interests shall apply to an internal transaction.

3. Where notice of a national interest has been registered in the International Registry, the priority of the holder of that interest under Article 29 shall not be affected by the fact that such interest has become vested in another person by assignment or subrogation under the applicable law.

Article 51—Future Protocols

1. The Depositary may create working groups, in co-operation with such relevant non-governmental organisations as the Depositary considers appropriate, to assess the feasibility of extending the application of this Convention, through one or more Protocols, to objects of any category of high-value mobile equipment, other than a category referred to in Article 2(3), each member of which is uniquely identifiable, and associated rights relating to such objects.

2. The Depositary shall communicate the text of any preliminary draft Protocol relating to a category of objects prepared by such a working group to all States Parties to this Convention, all member States of the Depositary, member States of the United Nations which are not members of the Depositary and the relevant intergovernmental organisations, and shall invite such States and organisations to participate in intergovernmental negotiations for the completion of a draft Protocol on the basis of such a preliminary draft Protocol.

3. The Depositary shall also communicate the text of any preliminary draft Protocol prepared by such a working group to such relevant non-governmental organisations as the Depositary considers appropriate. Such non-governmental organisations shall be invited promptly to submit comments on the text of the preliminary draft Protocol to the Depositary and to participate as observers in the preparation of a draft Protocol.

4. When the competent bodies of the Depositary adjudge such a draft Protocol ripe for adoption, the Depositary shall convene a diplomatic conference for its adoption.

5. Once such a Protocol has been adopted, subject to paragraph 6, this Convention shall apply to the category of objects covered thereby.

6. Article 45 *bis* of this Convention applies to such a Protocol only if specifically provided for in that Protocol.

Article 52—Territorial units

1. If a Contracting State has territorial units in which different systems of law are applicable in relation to the matters dealt with in this Convention, it may, at the time of ratification, acceptance, approval or accession, declare that this Convention is to extend to all its territorial units or only to one or more of them and may modify its declaration by submitting another declaration at any time.

2. Any such declaration shall state expressly the territorial units to which this Convention applies.

3. If a Contracting State has not made any declaration under paragraph 1, this Convention shall apply to all territorial units of that State.

4. Where a Contracting State extends this Convention to one or more of its territorial units, declarations permitted under this Convention may be made in respect of each such territorial unit, and the declarations made in respect of one territorial unit may be different from those made in respect of another territorial unit.

5. If by virtue of a declaration under paragraph 1, this Convention extends to one or more territorial units of a Contracting State:

(a) the debtor is considered to be situated in a Contracting State only if it is incorporated or formed under a law in force in a territorial unit to which this Convention applies or if it has its registered office or statutory seat, centre of administration, place of business or habitual residence in a territorial unit to which this Convention applies;
(b) any reference to the location of the object in a Contracting State refers to the location of the object in a territorial unit to which this Convention applies; and
(c) any reference to the administrative authorities in that Contracting State shall be construed as referring to the administrative authorities having jurisdiction in a territorial unit to which this Convention applies.

Article 53—Determination of courts

A Contracting State may, at the time of ratification, acceptance, approval of, or accession to the Protocol, declare the relevant "court" or "courts" for the purposes of Article 1 and Chapter XII of this Convention.

Article 54—Declarations regarding remedies

1. A Contracting State may, at the time of ratification, acceptance, approval of, or accession to the Protocol, declare that while the charged object is situated within, or controlled from its territory the chargee shall not grant a lease of the object in that territory.

2. A Contracting State shall, at the time of ratification, acceptance, approval of, or accession to the Protocol, declare whether or not any remedy available to the creditor under any provision of this Convention which is not there expressed to require application to the court may be exercised only with leave of the court.

Article 55—Declarations regarding relief pending final determination

A Contracting State may, at the time of ratification, acceptance, approval of, or accession to the Protocol, declare that it will not apply the provisions of Article 13 or Article 43, or both, wholly or in part. The declaration shall specify under which conditions the relevant Article will be applied, in case it will be applied partly, or otherwise which other forms of interim relief will be applied.

Article 56—Reservations and declarations

1. No reservations may be made to this Convention but declarations authorised by Articles 39, 40, 50, 52, 53, 54, 55, 57, 58 and 60 may be made in accordance with these provisions.

2. Any declaration or subsequent declaration or any withdrawal of a declaration made under this Convention shall be notified in writing to the Depositary.

Article 57—Subsequent declarations

1. A State Party may make a subsequent declaration, other than a declaration authorised under Article 60, at any time after the date on which this Convention has entered into force for it, by notifying the Depositary to that effect.

2. Any such subsequent declaration shall take effect on the first day of the month following the expiration of six months after the date of receipt of the notification by the Depositary. Where a longer period for that declaration to take effect is specified in the notification, it shall take effect upon the expiration of such longer period after receipt of the notification by the Depositary.

3. Notwithstanding the previous paragraphs, this Convention shall continue to apply, as if no such subsequent declarations had been made, in respect of all rights and interests arising prior to the effective date of any such subsequent declaration.

Article 58—Withdrawal of declarations

1. Any State Party having made a declaration under this Convention, other than a declaration authorised under Article 60, may withdraw it at any time by notifying the Depositary. Such withdrawal is to take effect on the first day of the month following the expiration of six months after the date of receipt of the notification by the Depositary.

2. Notwithstanding the previous paragraph, this Convention shall continue to apply, as if no such withdrawal of declaration had been made, in respect of all rights and interests arising prior to the effective date of any such withdrawal.

Article 59—Denunciations

1. Any State Party may denounce this Convention by notification in writing to the Depositary.

2. Any such denunciation shall take effect on the first day of the month following the expiration of twelve months after the date on which notification is received by the Depositary.

3. Notwithstanding the previous paragraphs, this Convention shall continue to apply, as if no such denunciation had been made, in respect of all rights and interests arising prior to the effective date of any such denunciation.

Article 60—Transitional provisions

1. Unless otherwise declared by a Contracting State at any time, the Convention does not apply to a pre-existing right or interest, which retains the priority it enjoyed under the applicable law before the effective date of this Convention.

2. For the purposes of Article 1(v) and of determining priority under this Convention:

(a) "effective date of this Convention" means in relation to a debtor the time when this Convention enters into force or the time when the State in which the debtor is situated becomes a Contracting State, whichever is the later; and
(b) the debtor is situated in a State where it has its centre of administration or, if it has no centre of administration, its place of business or, if it has more than one place of business, its principal place of business or, if it has no place of business, its habitual residence.

3. A Contracting State may in its declaration under paragraph 1 specify a date, not earlier than three years after the date on which the declaration becomes effective, when this Convention and the Protocol will become applicable, for the purpose of determining priority, including the protection of any existing priority, to pre-existing rights or interests arising under an agreement made at a time when the debtor was situated in a State referred to in sub-paragraph (b) of the preceding paragraph but only to the extent and in the manner specified in its declaration.

Article 61—Review Conferences, amendments and related matters

1. The Depositary shall prepare reports yearly or at such other time as the circumstances may require for the States Parties as to the manner in which the international regimen established in this Convention has operated in practice. In preparing such reports, the Depositary shall take into account the reports of the Supervisory Authority concerning the functioning of the international registration system.

2. At the request of not less than twenty-five per cent of the States Parties, Review Conferences of States Parties shall be convened from time to time by the Depositary, in consultation with the Supervisory Authority, to consider:

(a) the practical operation of this Convention and its effectiveness in facilitating the asset-based financing and leasing of the objects covered by its terms;
(b) the judicial interpretation given to, and the application made of the terms of this Convention and the regulations;
(c) the functioning of the international registration system, the performance of the Registrar and its oversight by the Supervisory Authority, taking into account the reports of the Supervisory Authority; and
(d) whether any modifications to this Convention or the arrangements relating to the International Registry are desirable.

3. Subject to paragraph 4, any amendment to this Convention shall be approved by at least a two-thirds majority of States Parties participating in the Conference referred to in the preceding paragraph and shall then enter into force in respect of States which have ratified, accepted or approved such amendment when ratified, accepted, or approved by three States in accordance with the provisions of Article 49 relating to its entry into force.

4. Where the proposed amendment to this Convention is intended to apply to more than one category of equipment, such amendment shall also be approved by at least a two-thirds majority of States Parties to each Protocol that are participating in the Conference referred to in paragraph 2.

Article 62—Depositary and its functions

1. Instruments of ratification, acceptance, approval or accession shall be deposited with the International Institute for the Unification of Private Law (UNIDROIT), which is hereby designated the Depositary.

2. The Depositary shall:

(a) inform all Contracting States of:
  (i) each new signature or deposit of an instrument of ratification, acceptance, approval or accession, together with the date thereof;
  (ii) the date of entry into force of this Convention;
  (iii) each declaration made in accordance with this Convention, together with the date thereof;
  (iv) the withdrawal or amendment of any declaration, together with the date thereof; and
  (v) the notification of any denunciation of this Convention together with the date thereof and the date on which it takes effect;
(b) transmit certified true copies of this Convention to all Contracting States;
(c) provide the Supervisory Authority and the Registrar with a copy of each instrument of ratification, acceptance, approval or accession, together with the date of deposit thereof, of each declaration or withdrawal or amendment of a declaration and of each notification of denunciation, together with the date of notification thereof, so that the information contained therein is easily and fully available; and
(d) perform such other functions customary for depositaries.

IN WITNESS WHEREOF the undersigned Plenipotentiaries, having been duly authorised, have signed this Convention.

DONE at Cape Town, this sixteenth day of November, two thousand and one, in a single original in the English, Arabic, Chinese, French, Russian and Spanish languages, all texts being equally authentic, such authenticity to take effect upon verification by the Joint Secretariat of the Conference under the authority of the President of the Conference within ninety days hereof as to the conformity of the texts with one another.

Appendix 6

Protocol to the Convention on International interests in Mobile Equipment on Matters Specific to Aircraft Equipment

THE STATES PARTIES TO THIS PROTOCOL,

CONSIDERING it necessary to implement the *Convention on International Interests in Mobile Equipment* (hereinafter referred to as "the Convention") as it relates to aircraft equipment, in the light of the purposes set out in the preamble to the Convention,

MINDFUL of the need to adapt the Convention to meet the particular requirements of aircraft finance and to extend the sphere of application of the Convention to include contracts of sale of aircraft equipment,

MINDFUL of the principles and objectives of the *Convention on International Civil Aviation*, signed at Chicago on 7 December 1944,

HAVE AGREED upon the following provisions relating to aircraft equipment:

Chapter I
Sphere of application and general provisions

Article I—Defined terms

1. In this Protocol, except where the context otherwise requires, terms used in it have the meanings set out in the Convention.

2. In this Protocol the following terms are employed with the meanings set out below:

(a) "aircraft" means aircraft as defined for the purposes of the Chicago Convention which are either airframes with aircraft engines installed thereon or helicopters;

(b) "aircraft engines" means aircraft engines (other than those used in military, customs or police services) powered by jet propulsion or turbine or piston technology and:
  (i) in the case of jet propulsion aircraft engines, have at least 1750 lb of thrust or its equivalent; and
  (ii) in the case of turbine-powered or piston-powered aircraft engines, have at least 550 rated take-off shaft horsepower or its equivalent,

  together with all modules and other installed, incorporated or attached accessories, parts and equipment and all data, manuals and records relating thereto;

(c) "aircraft objects" means airframes, aircraft engines and helicopters;

(d) "aircraft register" means a register maintained by a State or a common mark registering authority for the purposes of the Chicago Convention;

(e) "airframes" means airframes (other than those used in military, customs or police services) that, when appropriate aircraft engines are installed thereon, are type certified by the competent aviation authority to transport:
  (i) at least eight (8) persons including crew; or
  (ii) goods in excess of 2750 kilograms,

  together with all installed, incorporated or attached accessories, parts and equipment (other than aircraft engines), and all data, manuals and records relating thereto;

(f) "authorised party" means the party referred to in Article XIII(3);

(g) "Chicago Convention" means the *Convention on International Civil Aviation*, signed at Chicago on 7 December 1944, as amended, and its Annexes;

(h) "common mark registering authority" means the authority maintaining a register in accordance with Article 77 of the Chicago Convention as implemented by the Resolution adopted on 14 December 1967 by the Council of the International Civil Aviation Organization on nationality and registration of aircraft operated by international operating agencies;

(i) "de-registration of the aircraft" means deletion or removal of the registration of the aircraft from its aircraft register in accordance with the Chicago Convention;

(j) "guarantee contract" means a contract entered into by a person as guarantor;

(k) "guarantor" means a person who, for the purpose of assuring performance of any obligations in favour of a creditor secured by a security agreement or under an agreement, gives or issues a suretyship or demand guarantee or a standby letter of credit or any other form of credit insurance;

(l) "helicopters" means heavier-than-air machines (other than those used in military, customs or police services) supported in flight chiefly by the reactions of the air on one or more power-driven rotors on substantially vertical axes and which are type certified by the competent aviation authority to transport:
  (i) at least five (5) persons including crew; or

(ii) goods in excess of 450 kilograms,
together with all installed, incorporated or attached accessories, parts and equipment (including rotors), and all data, manuals and records relating thereto;

(m) "insolvency-related event" means:

(i) the commencement of the insolvency proceedings; or

(ii) the declared intention to suspend or actual suspension of payments by the debtor where the creditor's right to institute insolvency proceedings against the debtor or to exercise remedies under the Convention is prevented or suspended by law or State action;

(n) "primary insolvency jurisdiction" means the Contracting State in which the centre of the debtor's main interests is situated, which for this purpose shall be deemed to be the place of the debtor's statutory seat or, if there is none, the place where the debtor is incorporated or formed, unless proved otherwise;

(o) "registry authority" means the national authority or the common mark registering authority, maintaining an aircraft register in a Contracting State and responsible for the registration and de-registration of an aircraft in accordance with the Chicago Convention; and

(p) "State of registry" means, in respect of an aircraft, the State on the national register of which an aircraft is entered or the State of location of the common mark registering authority maintaining the aircraft register.

Article II—Application of Convention as regards aircraft objects

1. The Convention shall apply in relation to aircraft objects as provided by the terms of this Protocol.

2. The Convention and this Protocol shall be known as the Convention on International Interests in Mobile Equipment as applied to aircraft objects.

Article III—Application of Convention to sales

The following provisions of the Convention apply as if references to an agreement creating or providing for an international interest were references to a contract of sale and as if references to an international interest, a prospective international interest, the debtor and the creditor were references to a sale, a prospective sale, the seller and the buyer respectively:

Articles 3 and 4;
Article 16(1)(a);
Article 19(4);
Article 20(1) (as regards registration of a contract of sale or a prospective sale);
Article 25(2) (as regards a prospective sale); and
Article 30.

In addition, the general provisions of Article 1, Article 5, Chapters IV to VII, Article 29 (other than Article 29(3) which is replaced by Article XIV(1) and

(2)), Chapter X, Chapter XII (other than Article 43), Chapter XIII and Chapter XIV (other than Article 60) shall apply to contracts of sale and prospective sales.

Article IV—Sphere of application

1. Without prejudice to Article 3(1) of the Convention, the Convention shall also apply in relation to a helicopter, or to an airframe pertaining to an aircraft, registered in an aircraft register of a Contracting State which is the State of registry, and where such registration is made pursuant to an agreement for registration of the aircraft it is deemed to have been effected at the time of the agreement.

2. For the purposes of the definition of "internal transaction" in Article 1 of the Convention:

(a) an airframe is located in the State of registry of the aircraft of which it is a part;
(b) an aircraft engine is located in the State of registry of the aircraft on which it is installed or, if it is not installed on an aircraft, where it is physically located; and
(c) a helicopter is located in its State of registry,

at the time of the conclusion of the agreement creating or providing for the interest.

3. The parties may, by agreement in writing, exclude the application of Article XI and, in their relations with each other, derogate from or vary the effect of any of the provisions of this Protocol except Article IX (2)-(4).

Article V—Formalities, effects and registration of contracts of sale

1. For the purposes of this Protocol, a contract of sale is one which:

(a) is in writing;
(b) relates to an aircraft object of which the seller has power to dispose; and
(c) enables the aircraft object to be identified in conformity with this Protocol.

2. A contract of sale transfers the interest of the seller in the aircraft object to the buyer according to its terms.

3. Registration of a contract of sale remains effective indefinitely. Registration of a prospective sale remains effective unless discharged or until expiry of the period, if any, specified in the registration.

Article VI—Representative capacities

A person may enter into an agreement or a sale, and register an international interest in, or a sale of, an aircraft object, in an agency, trust or other representative capacity. In such case, that person is entitled to assert rights and interests under the Convention.

Article VII—Description of aircraft objects

A description of an aircraft object that contains its manufacturer's serial number, the name of the manufacturer and its model designation is necessary and sufficient to identify the object for the purposes of Article 7(c) of the Convention and Article V(1)(c) of this Protocol.

Article VIII—Choice of law

1. This Article applies only where a Contracting State has made a declaration pursuant to Article XXX(1).

2. The parties to an agreement, or a contract of sale, or a related guarantee contract or subordination agreement may agree on the law which is to govern their contractual rights and obligations, wholly or in part.

3. Unless otherwise agreed, the reference in the preceding paragraph to the law chosen by the parties is to the domestic rules of law of the designated State or, where that State comprises several territorial units, to the domestic law of the designated territorial unit.

Chapter II
Default remedies, priorities and assignments

Article IX—Modification of default remedies provisions

1. In addition to the remedies specified in Chapter III of the Convention, the creditor may, to the extent that the debtor has at any time so agreed and in the circumstances specified in that Chapter:

(a) procure the de-registration of the aircraft; and
(b) procure the export and physical transfer of the aircraft object from the territory in which it is situated.

2. The creditor shall not exercise the remedies specified in the preceding paragraph without the prior consent in writing of the holder of any registered interest ranking in priority to that of the creditor.

3. Article 8(3) of the Convention shall not apply to aircraft objects. Any remedy given by the Convention in relation to an aircraft object shall be exercised in a commercially reasonable manner. A remedy shall be deemed to be exercised in a commercially reasonable manner where it is exercised in conformity with a provision of the agreement except where such a provision is manifestly unreasonable.

4. A chargee giving ten or more working days' prior written notice of a proposed sale or lease to interested persons shall be deemed to satisfy the requirement of providing "reasonable prior notice" specified in Article 8(4) of the Convention. The foregoing shall not prevent a chargee and a chargor or a guarantor from agreeing to a longer period of prior notice.

5. The registry authority in a Contracting State shall, subject to any applicable safety laws and regulations, honour a request for de-registration and export if:

(a) the request is properly submitted by the authorised party under a recorded irrevocable de-registration and export request authorisation; and

(b) the authorised party certifies to the registry authority, if required by that authority, that all registered interests ranking in priority to that of the creditor in whose favour the authorisation has been issued have been discharged or that the holders of such interests have consented to the de-registration and export.

6. A chargee proposing to procure the de-registration and export of an aircraft under paragraph 1 otherwise than pursuant to a court order shall give reasonable prior notice in writing of the proposed de-registration and export to:

(a) interested persons specified in Article 1(m)(i) and (ii) of the Convention; and
(b) interested persons specified in Article 1(m)(iii) of the Convention who have given notice of their rights to the chargee within a reasonable time prior to the de-registration and export.

Article X—Modification of provisions regarding relief pending final determination

1. This Article applies only where a Contracting State has made a declaration under Article XXX(2) and to the extent stated in such declaration.

2. For the purposes of Article 13(1) of the Convention, "speedy" in the context of obtaining relief means within such number of working days from the date of filing of the application for relief as is specified in a declaration made by the Contracting State in which the application is made.

3. Article 13(1) of the Convention applies with the following being added immediately after sub-paragraph (d):

"(e) if at any time the debtor and the creditor specifically agree, sale and application of proceeds therefrom",

and Article 43(2) applies with the insertion after the words "Article 13(1)(d)" of the words "and (e)".

4. Ownership or any other interest of the debtor passing on a sale under the preceding paragraph is free from any other interest over which the creditor's international interest has priority under the provisions of Article 29 of the Convention.

5. The creditor and the debtor or any other interested person may agree in writing to exclude the application of Article 13(2) of the Convention.

6. With regard to the remedies in Article IX(1):

(a) they shall be made available by the registry authority and other administrative authorities, as applicable, in a Contracting State no later than five working days after the creditor notifies such authorities that the relief specified in Article IX(1) is granted or, in the case of relief granted by a foreign court, recognised by a court of that Contracting State, and that

the creditor is entitled to procure those remedies in accordance with the Convention; and
(b) the applicable authorities shall expeditiously co-operate with and assist the creditor in the exercise of such remedies in conformity with the applicable aviation safety laws and regulations.

7. Paragraphs 2 and 6 shall not affect any applicable aviation safety laws and regulations.

Article XI—Remedies on insolvency

1. This Article applies only where a Contracting State that is the primary insolvency jurisdiction has made a declaration pursuant to Article XXX(3).

Alternative A

2. Upon the occurrence of an insolvency-related event, the insolvency administrator or the debtor, as applicable, shall, subject to paragraph 7, give possession of the aircraft object to the creditor no later than the earlier of:

(a) the end of the waiting period; and
(b) the date on which the creditor would be entitled to possession of the aircraft object if this Article did not apply.

3. For the purposes of this Article, the "waiting period" shall be the period specified in a declaration of the Contracting State which is the primary insolvency jurisdiction.

4. References in this Article to the "insolvency administrator" shall be to that person in its official, not in its personal, capacity.

5. Unless and until the creditor is given the opportunity to take possession under paragraph 2:

(a) the insolvency administrator or the debtor, as applicable, shall preserve the aircraft object and maintain it and its value in accordance with the agreement; and
(b) the creditor shall be entitled to apply for any other forms of interim relief available under the applicable law.

6. Sub-paragraph (a) of the preceding paragraph shall not preclude the use of the aircraft object under arrangements designed to preserve the aircraft object and maintain it and its value.

7. The insolvency administrator or the debtor, as applicable, may retain possession of the aircraft object where, by the time specified in paragraph 2, it has cured all defaults other than a default constituted by the opening of insolvency proceedings and has agreed to perform all future obligations under the agreement. A second waiting period shall not apply in respect of a default in the performance of such future obligations.

8. With regard to the remedies in Article IX(1):

(a) they shall be made available by the registry authority and the administrative authorities in a Contracting State, as applicable, no later than five working days after the date on which the creditor notifies such authorities that it is entitled to procure those remedies in accordance with the Convention; and
(b) the applicable authorities shall expeditiously co-operate with and assist the creditor in the exercise of such remedies in conformity with the applicable aviation safety laws and regulations.

9. No exercise of remedies permitted by the Convention or this Protocol may be prevented or delayed after the date specified in paragraph 2.

10. No obligations of the debtor under the agreement may be modified without the consent of the creditor.

11. Nothing in the preceding paragraph shall be construed to affect the authority, if any, of the insolvency administrator under the applicable law to terminate the agreement.

12. No rights or interests, except for non-consensual rights or interests of a category covered by a declaration pursuant to Article 39(1), shall have priority in insolvency proceedings over registered interests.

13. The Convention as modified by Article IX of this Protocol shall apply to the exercise of any remedies under this Article.

Alternative B

2. Upon the occurrence of an insolvency-related event, the insolvency administrator or the debtor, as applicable, upon the request of the creditor, shall give notice to the creditor within the time specified in a declaration of a Contracting State pursuant to Article XXX(3) whether it will:

(a) cure all defaults other than a default constituted by the opening of insolvency proceedings and agree to perform all future obligations, under the agreement and related transaction documents; or
(b) give the creditor the opportunity to take possession of the aircraft object, in accordance with the applicable law.

3. The applicable law referred to in sub-paragraph (b) of the preceding paragraph may permit the court to require the taking of any additional step or the provision of any additional guarantee.

4. The creditor shall provide evidence of its claims and proof that its international interest has been registered.

5. If the insolvency administrator or the debtor, as applicable, does not give notice in conformity with paragraph 2, or when the insolvency administrator or the debtor has declared that it will give the creditor the opportunity to take possession of the

aircraft object but fails to do so, the court may permit the creditor to take possession of the aircraft object upon such terms as the court may order and may require the taking of any additional step or the provision of any additional guarantee.

6. The aircraft object shall not be sold pending a decision by a court regarding the claim and the international interest.

Article XII—Insolvency assistance

1. This Article applies only where a Contracting State has made a declaration pursuant to Article XXX(1).

2. The courts of a Contracting State in which an aircraft object is situated shall, in accordance with the law of the Contracting State, co-operate to the maximum extent possible with foreign courts and foreign insolvency administrators in carrying out the provisions of Article XI.

Article XIII—De-registration and export request authorisation

1. This Article applies only where a Contracting State has made a declaration pursuant to Article XXX(1).

2. Where the debtor has issued an irrevocable de-registration and export request authorisation substantially in the form annexed to this Protocol and has submitted such authorisation for recordation to the registry authority, that authorisation shall be so recorded.

3. The person in whose favour the authorisation has been issued (the "authorised party") or its certified designee shall be the sole person entitled to exercise the remedies specified in Article IX(1) and may do so only in accordance with the authorisation and applicable aviation safety laws and regulations. Such authorisation may not be revoked by the debtor without the consent in writing of the authorised party. The registry authority shall remove an authorisation from the registry at the request of the authorised party.

4. The registry authority and other administrative authorities in Contracting States shall expeditiously co-operate with and assist the authorised party in the exercise of the remedies specified in Article IX.

Article XIV—Modification of priority provisions

1. A buyer of an aircraft object under a registered sale acquires its interest in that object free from an interest subsequently registered and from an unregistered interest, even if the buyer has actual knowledge of the unregistered interest.

2. A buyer of an aircraft object acquires its interest in that object subject to an interest registered at the time of its acquisition.

3. Ownership of or another right or interest in an aircraft engine shall not be affected by its installation on or removal from an aircraft.

4. Article 29(7) of the Convention applies to an item, other than an object, installed on an airframe, aircraft engine or helicopter.

Article XV—Modification of assignment provisions

Article 33(1) of the Convention applies as if the following were added immediately after sub-paragraph (b):

"and (c) the debtor has consented in writing, whether or not the consent is given in advance of the assignment or identifies the assignee."

Article XVI—Debtor provisions

1. In the absence of a default within the meaning of Article 11 of the Convention, the debtor shall be entitled to the quiet possession and use of the object in accordance with the agreement as against:

(a) its creditor and the holder of any interest from which the debtor takes free pursuant to Article 29(4) of the Convention or, in the capacity of buyer, Article XIV(1) of this Protocol, unless and to the extent that the debtor has otherwise agreed; and
(b) the holder of any interest to which the debtor's right or interest is subject pursuant to Article 29(4) of the Convention or, in the capacity of buyer, Article XIV(2) of this Protocol, but only to the extent, if any, that such holder has agreed.

2. Nothing in the Convention or this Protocol affects the liability of a creditor for any breach of the agreement under the applicable law in so far as that agreement relates to an aircraft object.

Chapter III
Registry provisions relating to international interests in aircraft objects

Article XVII—The Supervisory Authority and the Registrar

1. The Supervisory Authority shall be the international entity designated by a Resolution adopted by the Diplomatic Conference to Adopt a Mobile Equipment Convention and an Aircraft Protocol.

2. Where the international entity referred to in the preceding paragraph is not able and willing to act as Supervisory Authority, a Conference of Signatory and Contracting States shall be convened to designate another Supervisory Authority.

3. The Supervisory Authority and its officers and employees shall enjoy such immunity from legal and administrative process as is provided under the rules applicable to them as an international entity or otherwise.

4. The Supervisory Authority may establish a commission of experts, from among persons nominated by Signatory and Contracting States and having the necessary qualifications and experience, and entrust it with the task of assisting the Supervisory Authority in the discharge of its functions.

5. The first Registrar shall operate the International Registry for a period of five years from the date of entry into force of this Protocol. Thereafter, the Registrar shall be appointed or reappointed at regular five-yearly intervals by the Supervisory Authority.

Article XVIII—First regulations

The first regulations shall be made by the Supervisory Authority so as to take effect upon the entry into force of this Protocol.

Article XIX—Designated entry points

1. Subject to paragraph 2, a Contracting State may at any time designate an entity or entities in its territory as the entry point or entry points through which there shall or may be transmitted to the International Registry information required for registration other than registration of a notice of a national interest or a right or interest under Article 40 in either case arising under the laws of another State.

2. A designation made under the preceding paragraph may permit, but not compel, use of a designated entry point or entry points for information required for registrations in respect of aircraft engines.

Article XX—Additional modifications to Registry provisions

1. For the purposes of Article 19(6) of the Convention, the search criteria for an aircraft object shall be the name of its manufacturer, its manufacturer's serial number and its model designation, supplemented as necessary to ensure uniqueness. Such supplementary information shall be specified in the regulations.

2. For the purposes of Article 25(2) of the Convention and in the circumstances there described, the holder of a registered prospective international interest or a registered prospective assignment of an international interest or the person in whose favour a prospective sale has been registered shall take such steps as are within its power to procure the discharge of the registration no later than five working days after the receipt of the demand described in such paragraph.

3. The fees referred to in Article 17(2)(h) of the Convention shall be determined so as to recover the reasonable costs of establishing, operating and regulating the International Registry and the reasonable costs of the Supervisory Authority associated with the performance of the functions, exercise of the powers, and discharge of the duties contemplated by Article 17(2) of the Convention.

4. The centralised functions of the International Registry shall be operated and administered by the Registrar on a twenty-four hour basis. The various entry points shall be operated at least during working hours in their respective territories.

5. The amount of the insurance or financial guarantee referred to in Article 28(4) of the Convention shall, in respect of each event, not be less than the maximum value of an aircraft object as determined by the Supervisory Authority.

6. Nothing in the Convention shall preclude the Registrar from procuring insurance or a financial guarantee covering events for which the Registrar is not liable under Article 28 of the Convention.

Chapter IV
Jurisdiction

Article XXI—Modification of jurisdiction provisions

For the purposes of Article 43 of the Convention and subject to Article 42 of the Convention, a court of a Contracting State also has jurisdiction where the object is a helicopter, or an airframe pertaining to an aircraft, for which that State is the State of registry.

Article XXII—Waivers of sovereign immunity

1. Subject to paragraph 2, a waiver of sovereign immunity from jurisdiction of the courts specified in Article 42 or Article 43 of the Convention or relating to enforcement of rights and interests relating to an aircraft object under the Convention shall be binding and, if the other conditions to such jurisdiction or enforcement have been satisfied, shall be effective to confer jurisdiction and permit enforcement, as the case may be.

2. A waiver under the preceding paragraph must be in writing and contain a description of the aircraft object.

Chapter V
Relationship with other conventions

Article XXIII—Relationship with the *Convention on the International Recognition of Rights in Aircraft*

The Convention shall, for a Contracting State that is a party to the *Convention on the International Recognition of Rights in Aircraft*, signed at Geneva on 19 June 1948, supersede that Convention as it relates to aircraft, as defined in this Protocol, and to aircraft objects. However, with respect to rights or interests not covered or affected by the present Convention, the Geneva Convention shall not be superseded.

Article XXIV—Relationship with the *Convention for the Unification of Certain Rules Relating to the Precautionary Attachment of Aircraft*

1. The Convention shall, for a Contracting State that is a Party to the *Convention for the Unification of Certain Rules Relating to the Precautionary Attachment of Aircraft*, signed at Rome on 29 May 1933, supersede that Convention as it relates to aircraft, as defined in this Protocol.

2. A Contracting State Party to the above Convention may declare, at the time of ratification, acceptance, approval of, or accession to this Protocol, that it will not apply this Article.

Article XXV—Relationship with the *Unidroit Convention on International Financial Leasing*

The Convention shall supersede the *Unidroit* Convention on International Financial Leasing, signed at Ottawa on 28 May 1988, as it relates to aircraft objects.

Chapter VI
Final provisions

Article XXVI—Signature, ratification, acceptance, approval or accession

1. This Protocol shall be open for signature in Cape Town on 16 November 2001 by States participating in the Diplomatic Conference to Adopt a Mobile Equipment Convention and an Aircraft Protocol held at Cape Town from 29 October to 16 November 2001. After 16 November 2001, this Protocol shall be open to all States for signature at the Headquarters of the International Institute for the Unification of Private Law (Unidroit) in Rome until it enters into force in accordance with Article XXVIII.

2. This Protocol shall be subject to ratification, acceptance or approval by States which have signed it.

3. Any State which does not sign this Protocol may accede to it at any time.

4. Ratification, acceptance, approval or accession is effected by the deposit of a formal instrument to that effect with the Depositary.

5. A State may not become a Party to this Protocol unless it is or becomes also a Party to the Convention.

Article XXVII—Regional Economic Integration Organisations

1. A Regional Economic Integration Organisation which is constituted by sovereign States and has competence over certain matters governed by this Protocol may similarly sign, accept, approve or accede to this Protocol. The Regional Economic Integration Organisation shall in that case have the rights and obligations of a Contracting State, to the extent that that Organisation has competence over matters governed by this Protocol. Where the number of Contracting States is relevant in this Protocol, the Regional Economic Integration Organisation shall not count as a Contracting State in addition to its Member States which are Contracting States.

2. The Regional Economic Integration Organisation shall, at the time of signature, acceptance, approval or accession, make a declaration to the Depositary specifying the matters governed by this Protocol in respect of which competence has been transferred to that Organisation by its Member States. The Regional Economic Integration Organisation shall promptly notify the Depositary of any changes to the distribution of competence, including new transfers of competence, specified in the declaration under this paragraph.

3. Any reference to a "Contracting State" or "Contracting States" or "State Party" or "States Parties" in this Protocol applies equally to a Regional Economic Integration Organisation where the context so requires.

Article XXVIII—Entry into force

1. This Protocol enters into force on the first day of the month following the expiration of three months after the date of the deposit of the eighth instrument of ratification, acceptance, approval or accession, between the States which have deposited such instruments.

2. For other States this Protocol enters into force on the first day of the month following the expiration of three months after the date of the deposit of its instrument of ratification, acceptance, approval or accession.

Article XXIX—Territorial units

1. If a Contracting State has territorial units in which different systems of law are applicable in relation to the matters dealt with in this Protocol, it may, at the time of ratification, acceptance, approval or accession, declare that this Protocol is to extend to all its territorial units or only to one or more of them and may modify its declaration by submitting another declaration at any time.

2. Any such declaration shall state expressly the territorial units to which this Protocol applies.

3. If a Contracting State has not made any declaration under paragraph 1, this Protocol shall apply to all territorial units of that State.

4. Where a Contracting State extends this Protocol to one or more of its territorial units, declarations permitted under this Protocol may be made in respect of each such territorial unit, and the declarations made in respect of one territorial unit may be different from those made in respect of another territorial unit.

5. If by virtue of a declaration under paragraph 1, this Protocol extends to one or more territorial units of a Contracting State:

(a) the debtor is considered to be situated in a Contracting State only if it is incorporated or formed under a law in force in a territorial unit to which the Convention and this Protocol apply or if it has its registered office or statutory seat, centre of administration, place of business or habitual residence in a territorial unit to which the Convention and this Protocol apply;
(b) any reference to the location of the object in a Contracting State refers to the location of the object in a territorial unit to which the Convention and this Protocol apply; and
(c) any reference to the administrative authorities in that Contracting State shall be construed as referring to the administrative authorities having jurisdiction in a territorial unit to which the Convention and this Protocol apply and any reference to the national register or to the registry authority in that Contracting State shall be construed as referring to the aircraft register in force or to the registry authority having jurisdiction in the territorial unit or units to which the Convention and this Protocol apply.

Article XXX—Declarations relating to certain provisions

1. A Contracting State may, at the time of ratification, acceptance, approval of, or accession to this Protocol, declare that it will apply any one or more of Articles VIII, XII and XIII of this Protocol.

2. A Contracting State may, at the time of ratification, acceptance, approval of, or accession to this Protocol, declare that it will apply Article X of this Protocol, wholly or in part. If it so declares with respect to Article X(2), it shall specify the time-period required thereby.

3. A Contracting State may, at the time of ratification, acceptance, approval of, or accession to this Protocol, declare that it will apply the entirety of Alternative A, or the entirety of Alternative B of Article XI and, if so, shall specify the types of insolvency proceeding, if any, to which it will apply Alternative A and the types of insolvency proceeding, if any, to which it will apply Alternative B. A Contracting State making a declaration pursuant to this paragraph shall specify the time-period required by Article XI.

4. The courts of Contracting States shall apply Article XI in conformity with the declaration made by the Contracting State which is the primary insolvency jurisdiction.

5. A Contracting State may, at the time of ratification, acceptance, approval of, or accession to this Protocol, declare that it will not apply the provisions of Article XXI, wholly or in part. The declaration shall specify under which conditions the relevant Article will be applied, in case it will be applied partly, or otherwise which other forms of interim relief will be applied.

Article XXXI—Declarations under the Convention

Declarations made under the Convention, including those made under Articles 39, 40, 50, 53, 54, 55, 57, 58 and 60 of the Convention, shall be deemed to have also been made under this Protocol unless stated otherwise.

Article XXXII—Reservations and declarations

1. No reservations may be made to this Protocol but declarations authorised by Articles XXIV, XXIX, XXX, XXXI, XXXIII and XXXIV may be made in accordance with these provisions.

2. Any declaration or subsequent declaration or any withdrawal of a declaration made under this Protocol shall be notified in writing to the Depositary.

Article XXXIII—Subsequent declarations

1. A State Party may make a subsequent declaration, other than a declaration made in accordance with Article XXXI under Article 60 of the Convention, at any time after the date on which this Protocol has entered into force for it, by notifying the Depositary to that effect.

2. Any such subsequent declaration shall take effect on the first day of the month following the expiration of six months after the date of receipt of the notification by

the Depositary. Where a longer period for that declaration to take effect is specified in the notification, it shall take effect upon the expiration of such longer period after receipt of the notification by the Depositary.

3. Notwithstanding the previous paragraphs, this Protocol shall continue to apply, as if no such subsequent declarations had been made, in respect of all rights and interests arising prior to the effective date of any such subsequent declaration.

Article XXXIV—Withdrawal of declarations

1. Any State Party having made a declaration under this Protocol, other than a declaration made in accordance with Article XXXI under Article 60 of the Convention, may withdraw it at any time by notifying the Depositary. Such withdrawal is to take effect on the first day of the month following the expiration of six months after the date of receipt of the notification by the Depositary.

2. Notwithstanding the previous paragraph, this Protocol shall continue to apply, as if no such withdrawal of declaration had been made, in respect of all rights and interests arising prior to the effective date of any such withdrawal.

Article XXXV—Denunciations

1. Any State Party may denounce this Protocol by notification in writing to the Depositary.

2. Any such denunciation shall take effect on the first day of the month following the expiration of twelve months after the date of receipt of the notification by the Depositary.

3. Notwithstanding the previous paragraphs, this Protocol shall continue to apply, as if no such denunciation had been made, in respect of all rights and interests arising prior to the effective date of any such denunciation.

Article XXXVI—Review Conferences, amendments and related matters

1. The Depositary, in consultation with the Supervisory Authority, shall prepare reports yearly, or at such other time as the circumstances may require, for the States Parties as to the manner in which the international regime established in the Convention as amended by this Protocol has operated in practice. In preparing such reports, the Depositary shall take into account the reports of the Supervisory Authority concerning the functioning of the international registration system.

2. At the request of not less than twenty-five per cent of the States Parties, Review Conferences of the States Parties shall be convened from time to time by the Depositary, in consultation with the Supervisory Authority, to consider:

(a) the practical operation of the Convention as amended by this Protocol and its effectiveness in facilitating the asset-based financing and leasing of the objects covered by its terms;
(b) the judicial interpretation given to, and the application made of the terms of this Protocol and the regulations;

(c) the functioning of the international registration system, the performance of the Registrar and its oversight by the Supervisory Authority, taking into account the reports of the Supervisory Authority; and
(d) whether any modifications to this Protocol or the arrangements relating to the International Registry are desirable.

3. Any amendment to this Protocol shall be approved by at least a two-thirds majority of States Parties participating in the Conference referred to in the preceding paragraph and shall then enter into force in respect of States which have ratified, accepted or approved such amendment when it has been ratified, accepted or approved by eight States in accordance with the provisions of Article XXVIII relating to its entry into force.

Article XXXVII—Depositary and its functions

1. Instruments of ratification, acceptance, approval or accession shall be deposited with the International Institute for the Unification of Private Law (UNIDROIT), which is hereby designated the Depositary.

2. The Depositary shall:

(a) inform all Contracting States of:
  (i) each new signature or deposit of an instrument of ratification, acceptance, approval or accession, together with the date thereof;
  (ii) the date of entry into force of this Protocol;
  (iii) each declaration made in accordance with this Protocol, together with the date thereof;
  (iv) the withdrawal or amendment of any declaration, together with the date thereof; and
  (v) the notification of any denunciation of this Protocol together with the date thereof and the date on which it takes effect;
(b) transmit certified true copies of this Protocol to all Contracting States;
(c) provide the Supervisory Authority and the Registrar with a copy of each instrument of ratification, acceptance, approval or accession, together with the date of deposit thereof, of each declaration or withdrawal or amendment of a declaration and of each notification of denunciation, together with the date of notification thereof, so that the information contained therein is easily and fully available; and
(d) perform such other functions customary for depositaries.

IN WITNESS WHEREOF the undersigned Plenipotentiaries, having been duly authorised, have signed this Protocol.

DONE at Cape Town, this sixteenth day of November, two thousand and one, in a single original in the English, Arabic, Chinese, French, Russian and Spanish languages, all texts being equally authentic, such authenticity to take effect upon verification by the Joint Secretariat of the Conference under the authority of the President of the Conference within ninety days hereof as to the conformity of the texts with one another.

Annex

FORM OF IRREVOCABLE DE-REGISTRATION AND EXPORT REQUEST AUTHORISATION

Annex referred to in Article XIII

[Insert Date]

To: [Insert Name of Registry Authority]

Re: Irrevocable De-Registration and Export Request Authorisation

The undersigned is the registered [operator] [owner]* of the [insert the airframe/helicopter manufacturer name and model number] bearing manufacturers serial number [insert manufacturer's serial number] and registration [number] [mark] [insert registration number/mark] (together with all installed, incorporated or attached accessories, parts and equipment, the "aircraft").

This instrument is an irrevocable de-registration and export request authorisation issued by the undersigned in favour of [insert name of creditor] ("the authorised party") under the authority of Article XIII of the Protocol to the Convention on International Interests in Mobile Equipment on Matters specific to Aircraft Equipment. In accordance with that Article, the undersigned hereby requests:

(i) recognition that the authorised party or the person it certifies as its designee is the sole person entitled to:
   (a) procure the de-registration of the aircraft from the [insert name of aircraft register] maintained by the [insert name of registry authority] for the purposes of Chapter III of the *Convention on International Civil Aviation*, signed at Chicago, on 7 December 1944, and
   (b) procure the export and physical transfer of the aircraft from [insert name of country]; and

(ii) confirmation that the authorised party or the person it certifies as its designee may take the action specified in clause (i) above on written demand without the consent of the undersigned and that, upon such demand, the authorities in [insert name of country] shall co-operate with the authorised party with a view to the speedy completion of such action.

The rights in favour of the authorised party established by this instrument may not be revoked by the undersigned without the written consent of the authorised party.

* Select the term that reflects the relevant nationality registration criterion.

Please acknowledge your agreement to this request and its terms by appropriate notation in the space provided below and lodging this instrument in [insert name of registry authority].

[insert name of operator/owner]

____

Agreed to and lodged this
[insert date]

By: [insert name of signatory]
Its: [insert title of signatory]

____

[insert relevant notational details]

Appendix 7

Regulations and Procedures for the International Registry

Doc 9864
Addendum No. 1
5/3/09

(Third Edition)

ADDENDUM NO. 1

1. In reference to the final paragraph of Section 5.7 of the Regulations (quoted below), please note that this paragraph will not be in effect until further notice:

> For purposes of the foregoing Section 5.7 (b), both an assignor and an assignee, in the case of an assignment, and a subrogor and a subrogee, in the case of a subrogation, shall be deemed to be parties in whose favour a registration was made unless they electronically elect, in connection with and at the time of the registration of that assignment or subrogation, that (solely for such purposes) one of them shall be deemed to be that party, in which case that entity shall have the sole right to consent to a discharge of such assigned or subrogated international interest. The assignor and assignee or subrogor and subrogee may amend that election in accordance with Section 5.10. The rights established by application of the foregoing shall follow, and apply to, further assignments or subrogations of that assigned or subrogated international interest.

2. A second addendum will be issued when this paragraph comes into effect.

Appendix 7

Doc 9864

Regulations and Procedures for the International Registry

Third Edition—2009

International Civil Aviation Organization

Doc 9864

Regulations and Procedures for the International Registry

Third Edition—2009

International Civil Aviation Organization

Published in separate Arabic, Chinese, English, French,
Russian and Spanish editions by the
INTERNATIONAL CIVIL AVIATION ORGANIZATION
999 University Street, Montréal, Quebec, Canada H3C 5H7

First edition 2006
Second edition 2007
Third edition 2009

ICAO Doc 9864, ***Regulations and Procedures for the International Registry***
Order Number: 9864
Not for sale. This document may be downloaded from:
http://www.icao.int/icao/en/leb/intl_registry/index.html.

TABLE OF CONTENTS

Regulations

Section 1
AUTHORITY

These "Regulations" are issued by the Supervisory Authority pursuant to Article 17 (2) (d) of the *Convention on International Interests in Mobile Equipment*, signed at Cape Town on 16 November 2001 (the "Convention")and Article XVIII of the *Protocol to the Convention on International Interests in Mobile Equipment on Matters specific to Aircraft Equipment*, signed at Cape Town on 16 November 2001 (the "Protocol").

Section 2
DEFINITIONS

2.1 Terms defined in the Convention and the Protocol shall have the same meanings in these Regulations. In addition, the following terms shall have the meanings set out below:

2.1.1 "Administrator" means the person with authority to act on behalf of a registry user entity on administrative matters in dealings with the International Registry, and an "acting administrator" has the meaning set out in Section 4.1.

2.1.2 "Amendment", unless the context suggests otherwise, means any change in registration information, including any change in the duration of a registration, but does not include assignment, subrogation or subordination.

2.1.3 "Authorization" means an electronic authorization given by the administrator of a transacting user entity to one of its transacting users or to a professional user to transmit information to the International Registry to effect or consent to a registration on behalf of that transacting user entity.

2.1.4 "Consent" means an electronic consent to a registration.

2.1.5 "Controlled entity" means a business entity, trust or association of any kind, however established, with capacity to be a named party in registrations, where a transacting user entity electronically asserts that it controls, manages or administers that business entity, trust or association.

2.1.6 "Identity" means the name, address and electronic address of the entity or person in respect of whom the identifying information is sought.

2.1.7 "Named party" means the transacting user entity named in a registration, and a "named representative" means a person named in a registration and acting for others in an agency, trust or other representative capacity.

2.1.8 "Professional user entity" means a firm or other grouping of persons (such as an internal legal department of a transacting user entity) providing professional services to transacting user entities in connection with the transmission, to the International Registry, of information relating to registrations, and a "professional user" means an individual employee, member or partner of a professional user entity.

2.1.9 "Registration" means an interest electronically registered with the International Registry. For the purposes of Sections 4.4 and 6, the term has the extended meaning set out in Section 6.1. A "registering person" means the transacting user, professional user or direct entry point transmitting information to the International Registry to effect a registration.

2.1.10 "Registry user entity" means:

(a) a transacting user entity; or
(b) a professional user entity.

A "registry user" means a transacting user or a professional user.

2.1.11 "Searching person" means a person making a search in accordance with Section 7 of these Regulations.

2.1.12 "Transacting user entity" means a legal entity, natural person or more than one of the foregoing acting jointly intending to be a named party in one or more registrations, and a "transacting user" means an individual employee, member or partner of a transacting user entity or an affiliate of that entity.

2.2 The term or terms:

(a) "entry point", "authorizing entry point" and "direct entry point" have the meanings set out in Section 12.1;
(b) "International Registry Procedures" has the meaning set out in Section 15.1; and
(c) "priority search", "priority search certificate", "informational search listing", "Contracting State search" and "Contracting State search certificate" have the meanings set out in Section 7.

Section 3
GENERAL PROVISIONS

3.1 The International Registry is established as the facility for effecting and searching registrations under the Convention and the Protocol.

3.2 Since the International Registry merely provides notice of registrations, the facts underlying any such registration or registered interest shall determine whether it falls within the scope of the Convention or the Protocol. Without limiting the foregoing, while there will be no technical impediment to the registration of pre-existing rights and interests or assignment thereof, such registrations shall have no legal effect under the Convention and the Protocol, except where, by virtue of a declaration under Article 60 (3) of the Convention, registration thereof is required. The contents of this Section 3.2 shall be prominently displayed by the International Registry as a general cautionary note.

3.3 The Registrar shall perform the functions specified in the Convention, the Protocol, these Regulations and the International Registry Procedures.

3.4 The International Registry shall be accessible 24 hours a day, 7 days a week, except if precluded by maintenance performed outside peak periods, or technical or security problems, as set out in the International Registry Procedures.

3.5 Technical support shall be provided to registering persons, searching persons and administrators by a help desk of the International Registry, which shall be available 24 hours a day, 7 days a week, via telephone and/or electronic mail, as set out in the International Registry Procedures.

3.6 The International Registry may be used for no other purpose than that set forth in Sections 3.1 and 3.2, unless approved in advance by the Supervisory Authority and subject to the terms of that approval.

Section 4
ACCESS TO THE INTERNATIONAL REGISTRY

4.1 No registry user entity or administrator of that entity shall have access to the International Registry unless that entity and administrator are first approved as such by the Registrar and are otherwise in compliance with these Regulations and the International Registry Procedures. For the purposes of the preceding sentence, such approval shall be given when the Registrar reasonably concludes:

(a) that such entity and administrator are who they claim to be; and
(b) on the basis of information submitted, and without undertaking specific legal analysis, that the latter is entitled to act as administrator of the former, in each case, following the standards and procedures set out in the International Registry Procedures.

An administrator may electronically delegate his/her powers to an "acting administrator" from time to time for periods not to exceed three (3) months.

4.2 No registry user shall have access to the International Registry unless that user is first electronically approved as such by the administrator of the subject registry user entity and is otherwise in compliance with these Regulations and the International Registry Procedures. No approved registry user shall be entitled to transmit information to the International Registry to effect a registration unless that user has first received authorization to do so. For the purposes of the preceding sentence, such electronic approval and authorization may be given at the sole discretion of the relevant administrator and may be revoked by such administrator at any time.

4.3 Notwithstanding the preceding paragraphs:

(a) the administrator of a transacting user entity approved by the Registrar may electronically approve a controlled entity as a transacting user entity upon the payment of the fee provided for in Table 1 of the Appendix to the International Registry Procedures; and
(b) in such a case, the rights, powers and obligations of the administrator of the approving transacting user entity and its transacting users, respectively, shall apply equally to the approved transacting user entity.

4.4 Subject to these Regulations and in accordance with the International Registry Procedures, a registration may only be effected, with an authorization, by a registering person, on behalf of the transacting user entity, which is a named party required or permitted to effect that registration under Article 20 of the Convention and Article III of the Protocol.

4.5 No searching person shall have access to the International Registry unless that person is first in compliance with these Regulations and the International Registry Procedures.

Section 5
INFORMATION REQUIRED TO EFFECT REGISTRATION

5.1 In order to effect a registration, use of electronic information provided by the International Registry relating to the aircraft object is mandatory and, where so provided, is the sole means of satisfying the requirements of Section 5.3 (c) (ii) to (iv). For the purposes of the foregoing, "information provided by the International Registry" excludes information submitted in a different format by the registering person. To the extent such information is not so provided at the time the registration data are submitted to the International Registry, it shall be electronically entered by a registering person using the format prescribed in the International Registry Procedures, except as regards named parties (other than those whose consent is not required under Section 5.9) because they must be approved transacting user entities.

5.2 Identity information shall be deemed complete only if each of the three elements contained in the definition of identity is provided.

5.3 The information required to effect the registration of an international interest, a prospective international interest, a notice of a national interest, or a registrable non-consensual right or interest is:

(a) the identity and electronic signature of the registering person and a statement on whose behalf that person is acting;
(b) the identity of the named parties;
(c) the following information identifying the aircraft object:
   (i) type of aircraft object;
   (ii) manufacturer's name;
   (iii) manufacturer's generic model designation; and
   (iv) manufacturer's serial number assigned to the aircraft object;
(d) in the case of an airframe or helicopter, the following information, if known:
   (i) the current and, if different, intended State of Registry for nationality purposes; and
   (ii) the current and, if different, intended aircraft nationality and registration marks assigned pursuant to the Chicago Convention;
(e) the duration of the registration, if the registration is to lapse prior to the filing of a discharge;
(f) in the case of an international interest or a prospective international interest, the consent of the named parties, given under an authorization; and
(g) the names and electronic addresses of persons to which the Registrar is required to send information notices pursuant to Section 6.

5.4 The information required to effect the registration of a contract of sale or a prospective sale is:

(a) the information referred to in Sections 5.3 (a) to (d) and 5.3 (g);
(b) the consent of the named parties, given under an authorization; and
(c) in the case of a prospective sale, the duration of the registration, if that registration is to lapse prior to the time of a discharge.

5.5 The information required to effect the registration of the assignment of an international interest, the prospective assignment of an international interest, the assignment of a registrable non-consensual interest or an international interest acquired through subrogation is:

(a) the information referred to in Sections 5.3 (a) to (d) and 5.3 (g);
(b) the consent of the named parties, given under an authorization;
(c) if the interest being assigned is a registered interest, the file number of the registration relating to that interest; and
(d) if the interest being assigned is not a registered interest, a description of the interest assigned and original debtor thereunder, using the format prescribed by the International Registry Procedures.

5.6 The International Registry may provide a facility permitting the registration of all assignments included in a "block assignment registration request". A "block assignment registration request" shall include:

(a) an electronic certification by the assignor that all of the underlying interests evidenced by registrations on the International Registry in which it is a named party have been assigned to the assignee; and
(b) a consent thereto given by the assignee,

each given under an authorization.

5.7 The information required to discharge a registration, other than a registration relating to a contract of sale is:

(a) the information referred to in Sections 5.3 (a) to (d) and 5.3 (g);
(b) the consent of the named parties benefiting from the registered interest, given under an authorization, but not of the debtor, assignor, subrogor or person subordinating the registered interest, or of the prospective seller in the case of a registration relating to a prospective sale;
(c) the file number of the registration to be discharged; and
(d) the date the discharge is to be effective.

For purposes of the foregoing Section 5.7 (b), both an assignor and an assignee, in the case of an assignment, and a subrogor and a subrogee, in the case of a subrogation, shall be deemed to be parties in whose favour a registration was made unless they electronically elect, in connection with and at the time of the registration of that assignment or subrogation, that (solely for such purposes) one of them shall be deemed to be that party, in which case that entity shall have the sole right to consent to a discharge of such assigned or subrogated international interest. The assignor and assignee or subrogor and subrogee may amend that election in accordance with Section 5.10. The rights established by application of the foregoing shall follow, and apply to, further assignments or subrogations of that assigned or subrogated international interest.

5.8 The information required to effect the registration of the subordination of an international interest, a prospective international interest, a national interest or a registrable non-consensual interest is:

(a) the information referred to in Sections 5.3 (a) to (d) and 5.3 (g), and for the purposes of the foregoing reference to Section 5.3 (b) and for the purposes of Section 5.8 (b), the "named parties" shall be the registry user entities subordinating their interest and benefiting from that subordination;
(b) the consent of the named party whose interest is subordinated, given under an authorization;
(c) if the interest being subordinated or benefiting from the subordination is a registered interest, the file number relating to each such interest; and
(d) if the interest being subordinated or benefiting from the subordination is not a registered interest, a description of such interest and the original debtor thereunder, using the format prescribed by the International Registry Procedures.

5.9 Notwithstanding Sections 5.3 (f), 5.4 (b) and 5.5 (b), the information needed to effect the registration of a pre-existing right or interest required by virtue of a declaration under Article 60 (3) of the Convention need not include the consent of the debtor, assignor, seller or person subordinating the right or interest.

5.10 Subject to Section 5.11, the information required to amend a registration or to amend information contained in an assignment, subrogation or subordination is:

(a) the information referred to in Sections 5.3 (a) to (d) and 5.3 (g);
(b) the consent of the named parties that consented to the registration to be amended, given under an authorization;
(c) the file number of the registration to be amended; and
(d) the amendments to be made.

5.11 The following shall apply in respect of amendments to registrations:

(a) Registration of an amendment of information referred to in Section 5.3 (c) or a change of a category of registration shall be treated as a new registration in respect of the object or category to which the amending registration refers, with priority ranking from the time the amending registration is complete. The named parties to such amendment shall consent to the discharge of the previous registration under an authorization, which shall be effected automatically.
(b) Registration of an amendment in which the information referred to in Section 5.3 (b) has been changed shall require the consent of the named parties that consented to that registration and of the named party to be specified in the amended registration, each given under an authorization.
(c) Registration of an amendment in which the information referred to in Section 5.3 (d) has been changed shall be without prejudice as to whether the original registration complied with Section 12.
(d) Registration of an amendment in which the information referred to in Section 5.3 (e) has been changed shall have no effect on the priority of the original registration for the amended duration of that registration. The foregoing is without prejudice as to whether a new underlying interest has been constituted that requires registration under the Convention.
(e) A change to a user capacity statement or the contact details of a registry user are outside of Section 5.10 and may be made after the Registrar reasonably concludes that such requested change is accurate.

5.12 Without prejudice to Section 12.6, the lack of information referred to in Section 5.3 (d), including where cross-referenced in other sections, does not invalidate a registration.

5.13 The consent requirements of this Section 5 shall be satisfied:

(a) in the case of a registration initiated by a direct entry point in accordance with Section 12.1 (b), when the International Registry receives the consent from all parties whose consent is required under the Convention, the Protocol, and these Regulations; and

(b) in the case of a registration authorized in accordance with Section 12.1 (a), in respect of the submitting party when the International Registry receives such registration together with the authorization.

5.14 Any registration may specify that:

(a) it covers a fractional or partial interest in an aircraft object and, if so, the extent of such interest; and/or
(b) multiple named parties hold or have granted an interest evidenced thereby.

5.15 With respect to an interest referred to in Section 5.14 (a):

(a) an increase or decrease to such interest arising by virtue of a sale or an assignment of an international interest shall be registered as such in accordance with Sections 5.4 or 5.5, respectively;
(b) a decrease in such an interest arising by virtue of payment of a secured obligation shall be partially or wholly discharged in accordance with Section 5.7; and
(c) an amendment changing such interest shall be permitted to correct an error when made in accordance with Section 5.10.

5.16 The International Registry may provide a facility for notice of a change of name to a transacting user entity, where set out in a "name change notification request". For purposes of the foregoing, a "change of name" means either that the transacting user entity has changed its name or that the registered interest has become vested in a new entity created by merger or otherwise by operation of law. In such a case:

(a) the Registrar shall confirm that such changed name has been effected following the standard set out in Section 4.1;
(b) when so confirmed, all registrations on the International Registry in which that transacting user entity is a named party shall, without amending registration information, be annotated to advise of the change of name, such annotation to be included in all priority search certificates;
(c) following the time at which such annotation is made, the new or resulting entity shall be deemed to be a transacting user entity for all purposes of the International Registry; and
(d) the vesting shall have no effect on the priority of the original registration.

Section 6
CONFIRMATION AND NOTICE OF REGISTRATION

6.1 In this section, the term "registration" includes, where appropriate, the amendment, extension or discharge of a registration.

6.2 The Registrar shall provide prompt electronic confirmation of a registration to the named parties, the registering person and all other persons entitled to receive notice of that registration under Section 5. A confirmation shall contain the information set forth in Article 22 (2) (a) of the Convention.

6.3 When a registration is effected relating to an aircraft object, an electronic notice thereof shall be sent to the named parties and registering persons in any other registration relating to that object.

6.4 The confirmation and notice referred to in Sections 6.2 and 6.3, respectively, shall include information specified in Section 5 relating thereto and the file number of the registration.

6.5 Named parties may electronically elect not to receive the notices referred to in Section 6.3. Such elections shall require digital signatures. Registry users may request not to receive electronic notices in respect of one or more registrations.

Section 7
SEARCHES

7.1 Searches of the International Registry may be performed against:

(a) a manufacturer's name;
(b) a manufacturer's generic model designation; and
(c) a manufacturer's serial number of an aircraft object; and in the case of an airframe or helicopter, against:
(d) the State of Registry of the aircraft of which it is part; or
(e) the nationality or registration mark.

Such information may be searched by means of a priority search or informational search, as set out in Sections 7.2 and 7.3, respectively. A Contracting State search may also be made, as set out in Section 7.5. A search may be performed by any person who complies with the International Registry Procedures, whether or not that searching person has a specific interest. All searches shall be performed by electronic means.

7.2 A "priority search" is a search for registration information using the three criteria specified in Article XX (1) of the Protocol, as set out in Section 7.1 (a) to (c). Such information is searchable for purposes of Articles 19 (2) and (6) of the Convention and Article XX (1) of the Protocol.

7.3 An "informational search" is a search other than a priority search, using the criterion set out in Section 7.1 (c) or, when available on the International Registry, Section 7.1 (e), in either case alone or with another criterion set out in that Section. Such informational searches may include the use of symbols specified in the International Registry designed to produce inclusive search results. The results of an informational search, an "informational search listing", shall be a list of all matching aircraft objects, described by the items set out in Section 7.1 (a) to (c) and, if available in the International Registry, the items in Section 7.1 (d) to (e). The facility to perform such an informational search does not make that information "searchable" for the purposes of Articles 19 (2) and (6) of the Convention and Article XX (1) of the Protocol.

7.4 A "priority search certificate" is a certificate issued in response to a priority search. It shall:

(a) set out the information required by Article 22 (2) (a) or (b) of the Convention, as applicable, and comply with Article 22 (3) of the Convention; and
(b) in the case where Article 22 (2) (a) of the Convention applies, list the registered information in both:
  (i) chronological order; and
  (ii) a manner that indicates the transactional history of each registered interest.

7.5 A "Contracting State search" is a search for all declarations and designations, and withdrawals thereof, made under the Convention and the Protocol by the Contracting State specified in the search. A "Contracting State search certificate" is a certificate issued in response to a Contracting State search. A Contracting State search certificate shall:

(a) indicate, in chronological order, all declarations and designations, and withdrawals thereof, by the specified Contracting State;
(b) list the effective date of ratification, acceptance, approval or accession of the Convention and the Protocol, and of each declaration or designation, and withdrawal thereof, by the specified Contracting State; and
(c) attach, in the electronic form set out in the International Registry Procedures, a copy of all instruments deposited by the specified Contracting State relating to items within the scope of Section 7.5 (b).

7.6 Each search certificate and listing shall be issued and made available in electronic form. Upon request, a printed copy of a priority search certificate or Contracting State search certificate shall be provided by the Registrar.

Section 8
OPERATIONAL COMPLAINTS

8.1 Any person may submit a complaint to the Registrar concerning the operation of the International Registry. If not satisfactorily addressed by the Registrar, that complaint may be further submitted by that person to the Supervisory Authority.

8.2 For the purposes of Section 8.1, a matter "concerns the operation of the International Registry" when the matter relates to the general procedures and policies of the International Registry and does not involve specific adjudication by the Registrar or Supervisory Authority.

8.3 A person making a complaint shall substantiate his/her assertions in writing.

8.4 The Supervisory Authority shall consider complaints, and where, on the basis of that consideration, it determines changes to the procedures or policies are appropriate, it shall so instruct the Registrar.

8.5 The International Registry Procedures shall set out details relating to the procedure contemplated by Sections 8.1 to 8.4.

Section 9
CONFIDENTIALITY

All information in the International Registry shall be confidential except where it is:

(a) provided by the Registrar in response to a search under Section 7;
(b) made electronically available to enable registry users to effect, amend or discharge registrations;
(c) provided to the Supervisory Authority at the latter's request; or
(d) used for the purposes of the statistics required by Section 10.

Section 10
STATISTICS

10.1 The Registrar shall maintain updated registration statistics and shall publish them in an annual report. This report shall be electronically accessible to any person.

10.2 The registration statistics under Section 10.1 shall consist of:

(a) transactional volumes and revenues subdivided in each case by registration type and geographic distribution; and
(b) other compilations of non-confidential information requested by the Supervisory Authority.

Section 11
ANNUAL REPORT TO THE SUPERVISORY AUTHORITY

The Registrar shall prepare an annual report, including statistical data referred to in Section 10, and shall submit it to the Supervisory Authority.

Section 12
RELATIONS WITH THE ENTRY POINTS

12.1 A Contracting State may designate an entry point or entry points ("entry point") under Article XIX (1) of the Protocol:

(a) which shall or may authorize the transmission of information required for registration under the Convention and the Protocol to the International Registry ("authorizing entry point"); or
(b) through which information required for registration under the Convention and the Protocol shall or may be directly transmitted to the International Registry ("direct entry point").

12.2 A Contracting State may only designate a mandatory entry point in respect of:

(a) registrations relating to airframes and helicopters for which it is the State of Registry; and/or

(b) registrations of prospective international interests, prospective sales or prospective assignments of international interests in any airframe or helicopter for which it has taken regulatory steps to become the State of Registry.

12.3 A Contracting State designating an entry point shall notify the Depositary and the Supervisory Authority thereof, indicating whether such entry point is an authorizing or direct entry point. The Supervisory Authority shall keep the Registrar informed of such designations, and the Registrar shall maintain a current list thereof that is electronically accessible to users.

12.4 The Registrar shall establish arrangements applicable to the electronic transmission of registration information from, or authorized by, entry points to the International Registry and, after consultations with each designated entry point, shall specify the procedures applicable to that entry point. The foregoing shall not require the establishment of electronically coordinated systems but rather arrangements designed to enhance the efficient use of the International Registry by entry points.

12.5 The International Registry shall provide an electronic warning against a registration that is not effected:

(a) through a direct entry point where use thereof is mandatory; or
(b) in accordance with procedures required by an authorizing entry point;

to the extent agreed between the International Registry and the Contracting State declaring that entry point.

12.6 A registration effected in violation of the terms of a designation under Sections 12.1 and 12.2 is invalid.

Section 13
FEES

13.1 The Registrar shall collect a fee prior to undertaking services relating to the International Registry.

13.2 Fees, including fees arising from operations through an entry point, must be paid to the Registrar prior to the requested operation unless otherwise agreed between the Registrar and such entry point.

13.3 Fees shall be collected according to a schedule issued by the Supervisory Authority, which shall state the amount of fees payable for each service.

13.4 Fees shall be established and adjusted by the Supervisory Authority, as required by the Convention and the Protocol.

Section 14
LIABILITY AND INSURANCE

14.1 For the purposes of Article 28 (1) of the Convention, "loss suffered" means loss or damage resulting from an error or omission of the Registrar and its officers and employees or from a malfunction of the international registration system, except as provided for by Article 28 of the Convention, but does not include loss or damage resulting from lack of access to the International Registry as a result of measures referred to in Section 3.4 of these Regulations.

14.2 Any claim against the Registrar under Article 28 (1) of the Convention:

(a) shall be made in writing within the time period applicable under the laws of the State where the International Registry is located;
(b) shall be subject to consultations between the claimant and the Registrar; and
(c) if not resolved by such consultations, may be pursued by the claimant in accordance with Article 44 of the Convention.

14.3 The International Registry Procedures shall set out details relating to the procedure contemplated by Section 14.2.

14.4 The amount of insurance or financial guarantee required under Article 28 (4) of the Convention and Article XX (5) of the Protocol shall be determined and may be revised by the Supervisory Authority.

Section 15
INTERNATIONAL REGISTRY PROCEDURES

15.1 International Registry Procedures addressing items required by these Regulations or otherwise relating to the technical operation and administrative processes of the International Registry shall be established by the Supervisory Authority.

15.2 Without restricting their content, the International Registry Procedures shall set out the technical and administrative processes for:

(a) effecting, amending and discharging registrations and making and obtaining copies of searches; and
(b) obtaining the approvals and authorizations required to access the International Registry.

Section 16
PUBLICATION

16.1 The authentic version of these Regulations and the International Registry Procedures shall be published in an official publication of the Supervisory Authority.

16.2 The Registrar shall make an electronic version of the authentic texts referred to in Section 16.1, as may be amended as contemplated by Section 17, available to the public at no cost.

Section 17
AMENDMENTS

17.1 Requests for amendments to these Regulations or the International Registry Procedures may be submitted by the Registrar to the Supervisory Authority, which shall consider such amendments.

17.2 The authentic version of any amendments to these Regulations or the International Registry Procedures approved by the Supervisory Authority shall be published in an official publication of the Supervisory Authority.

Section 18
EFFECTIVE DATES

The present Regulations and the initial International Registry Procedures shall take effect on the date the Protocol enters into force. Any amendments to these Regulations or the International Registry Procedures shall take effect one calendar month after the date of their publication unless otherwise determined by the Supervisory Authority.

PROCEDURES

Section 1
AUTHORITY
(Section 15 of the Regulations)

These "Procedures" are issued by the Supervisory Authority of the International Registry under the *Convention on International Interests in Mobile Equipment*, signed at Cape Town on 16 November 2001 (the "Convention"), the *Protocol to the Convention on International Interests in Mobile Equipment on Matters specific to Aircraft Equipment*, signed at Cape Town on 16 November 2001 (the "Protocol"), and the *Regulations for the International Registry* (the "Regulations"). They address administrative items required by the Regulations as conditions to use of the International Registry or otherwise relating to the technical operation and administrative processes of the International Registry.

Section 2
DEFINITIONS

Terms defined in the Convention, the Protocol, and the Regulations shall have the same meaning in these Procedures. In addition, the following terms shall have the meaning set out below:

(a) "Approval" means either:
   (i) an electronic approval, by the Registrar, of an entity as a registry user entity and/or of an individual as that registry user entity's administrator, in accordance with Section 10 below; or
   (ii) an electronic approval, by the administrator, of an individual as a registry user of such registry user entity, in accordance with Section 11 below, and "approve" and "approved" shall be construed accordingly.

(b) "Confirmation" means an electronic confirmation provided in accordance with Section 6 of the Regulations, automatically issued by the Registrar when a registration, amendment or discharge is searchable.

(c) "CPS" means the Registrar's certification practice statement, as displayed on the website.

(d) "Digital certificate" means a digital certificate for use in communications with the International Registry, issued to an administrator or other registry user by the Registrar in accordance with these Procedures and the CPS.

(e) "Final consent" means the electronic consent of the last of the named parties whose consent is required under Article 20 of the Convention in relation to a registration, amendment or discharge.

(f) "Private key" means the private key associated with a digital certificate.

(g) "Website" means the website that provides the public interface of the International Registry and associated content provided by the Registrar under the Uniform Resource Locator (URL): http://www.internationalregistry.aero.

Section 3
FUNCTIONS OF THE REGISTRAR
(Section 3 of the Regulations)

The Registrar shall operate the International Registry and perform the functions assigned to it by the Convention, the Protocol and the Regulations.

Section 4
FUNCTIONS OF THE REGISTRY USER ENTITY
(Section 4 of the Regulations)

For the purpose of using the International Registry, the following functions fall within the scope of responsibility of each registry user entity:

(a) the proper selection and appointment of its administrator;
(b) any actions of its administrator, including any acting administrator, and of its registry users taken in relation to the Registry, which shall be deemed to have been duly authorized by that registry user entity;
(c) the accuracy of the data transmitted to the International Registry on its behalf;
(d) requesting, through its "back-up contact" referred to in Section 5.12 below, that the Registrar revoke the approval of the administrator acting on behalf of a registry user entity if the administrator ceases to be employed by that registry user entity or otherwise ceases to be authorized to act on its behalf;
(e) abiding by the applicable terms and conditions in place from time to time governing use of the International Registry. The applicable terms and conditions can be accessed on the website.

Section 5
FUNCTIONS OF THE ADMINISTRATOR OF A REGISTRY USER ENTITY
(Section 4 of the Regulations)

5.1 An administrator, who may but need not be an employee of a registry user entity, shall be duly appointed by each registry user entity, with authority to act on its behalf for the purposes of the International Registry, and such authority shall be represented during the approval process.

5.2 An administrator should hold appropriate formal professional qualifications commensurate with the requirements of the functions of administrator.

5.3 Each registry user entity may have only one administrator at any given time.

5.4 The administrator of a transacting user entity, who has been approved by the Registrar, is automatically authorized to effect, amend, discharge or consent to registrations in which that entity is a named party.

5.5 An administrator:

(a) shall keep his/her password and digital certificate secure;

(b) shall not transfer his/her digital certificate from the computer on which it was first installed, except to a replacement computer under his/her control, in which case he/she shall first apply to the Registrar for that purpose; and
(c) is permitted to make a secure back-up copy of his/her digital certificate subject to the requirements of the CPS as amended from time to time.

5.6 Where an administrator electronically delegates his/her powers to an acting administrator in accordance with Section 4.1 of the Regulations, that acting administrator shall be deemed to be the administrator for the purposes of these Procedures.

5.7 Where an administrator electronically approves a registry user to act on behalf of a registry user entity in accordance with Section 4.2 of the Regulations, the Registrar shall issue an email to that registry user containing a link to a digital certificate in accordance with these Procedures.

5.8 An administrator shall, through the website:

(a) keep up to date the email address and other details of the administrator and each registry user representing such registry user entity held by the International Registry;
(b) promptly revoke the approval of a registry user representing such registry user entity in the event that such registry user leaves the employment of, or otherwise ceases to be associated with, such registry user entity; and
(c) promptly revoke the authorization of a registry user representing such registry user entity in the event that such registry user is no longer authorized to effect, amend, discharge or consent to one or more registrations in which that entity is a named party.

5.9 In the event that an administrator is to leave the employment of the registry user entity on whose behalf he/she is authorized to act or if there is to be a change of administrator, the administrator shall electronically notify the Registrar thereof in a timely fashion. Should the registry user entity wish to appoint a replacement administrator, such appointment shall be subject to a set-up fee applicable to a new administrator.

5.10 The administrator of a registry user entity shall have the authority, through the website, to block and/or disable the user account of any registry user representing his/her registry user entity. It is the administrator's responsibility to take such action promptly in the event of a security breach relating to any such registry user's user account, of which he/she has actual knowledge, including but not limited to compromise of such registry user's private key.

5.11 The administrator of a registry user entity shall notify the Registrar of any security breach (for example, a breach compromising a private key), of which he/she has actual knowledge, that is expected to result in unauthorized registrations. If the security breach relates to a registry user account, the administrator may block and/or disable the account.

5.12 If the account of an administrator is subject to a security breach that could reasonably be expected to result in unauthorized access to and use of the International Registry, the Registrar and the registry user entity shall cooperate to expeditiously take corrective action appropriate under the circumstances. A registry user entity shall designate a "back-up contact" for these purposes.

5.13 On notification of a security breach, the Registrar may block and/or disable any user account.

5.14 The Registrar may make such reasonable identity checks of a proposed administrator as the Registrar considers necessary in relation to that person undertaking such function. The Registrar may make similar checks of a registry user, where deemed necessary by the Registrar.

5.15 Each administrator may electronically approve further registry users to act on behalf of the registry user entity which that administrator represents (when authorized to do so) and may approve the issue of a digital certificate to each of those registry users.

5.16 The administrator has sole responsibility for the selection of his/her registry user entity's registry users and for ensuring that only individuals who are duly authorized to act on behalf of his/her registry user entity are appointed as registry users from time to time.

Section 6
FUNCTIONS OF THE REGISTRY USER
(Section 4 of the Regulations)

6.1 No individual other than an administrator may effect, amend, discharge or consent to registrations with the International Registry until he/she has been approved as a registry user by the administrator of the registry user entity that such person represents.

6.2 No registry user may transmit information to the International Registry to effect, amend or discharge a registration in respect of an aircraft object unless such registry user has first received authorization to do so in relation to such aircraft object either:

(a) in the case of a transacting user, from the administrator of the transacting user entity that represents it; or
(b) in the case of a professional user, from the administrator of the transacting user entity being such professional user's client.

6.3 Each registry user:

(a) shall keep his/her password and digital certificate secure;
(b) shall not transfer his/her digital certificate from the computer on which it was first installed, except to a replacement computer under his/her control, in which case he/she shall first apply to the Registrar for that purpose; and
(c) is permitted to make a secure back-up copy of his/her digital certificate subject to the requirements of the CPS as amended from time to time.

6.4 Each registry user shall notify his/her respective administrator of any security breach, of which he/she is aware, that is expected to result in unauthorized registrations, including unauthorized use, disclosure or compromise of his/her password or private keys.

6.5 Each registry user acknowledges that his/her respective administrator may make such identity checks as the Registrar considers necessary in connection with such registry user's access to the International Registry.

Section 7
ACCESS TO THE INTERNATIONAL REGISTRY
(Section 4 of the Regulations)

7.1 The International Registry can be accessed via the public Internet under the URL:

http://www.internationalregistry.aero.

7.2 The International Registry will initially be available in English only. It is envisaged that other languages will be added when the necessary financial means are available, taking into account the implications thereof as well as advantages for users.

7.3 To access the International Registry, an administrator, registry user or a searching person requires access to the Internet with a compatible browser(s), as specified on the website. Each such person shall establish his/her own arrangements for:

(a) access to the Internet; and
(b) contracting with, and paying the fees of, any third party Internet service provider.

The International Registry extends only to the access point to the Internet located at the Registrar's hosting location.

7.4 The International Registry shall be accessible 24 hours a day, 7 days a week, except if precluded by maintenance performed outside peak periods, or technical or security problems. Advance notice of any interruption in access, and expected resumption of service, shall, to the maximum extent practicable, be provided via the website.

7.5 Access to the International Registry is conditioned on:

(a) in the case of an administrator and a registry user, having a valid digital certificate and complying with the applicable part of the CPS relating to his/her use and, where required, entering the correct password;
(b) following the steps and procedures provided on the website, including acceptance of the website terms and conditions, and of the CPS, and abiding thereby;
(c) paying, in advance, the fees set by the Supervisory Authority and published on the website; and
(d) complying with these Procedures.

7.6 If an administrator's or a registry user's password is entered incorrectly, that person shall be given the opportunity to re-enter the password or terminate the action. If there are three failed attempts to enter the correct password, the corresponding user account will be blocked until contact has been made with the help desk and the issue giving rise to the failure has been corrected.

Section 8
ENTRY POINTS
(Section 12 of the Regulations)

8.1 The Registrar shall establish arrangements applicable to the electronic transmission of registration information from, or authorized by, entry points to the International Registry designated under Article XIX (1) of the Protocol and Section 12 of the Regulations and, after consultations with each designated entry point, shall specify the arrangements applicable to that entry point. The arrangements applicable, designed to enhance the efficient use of the International Registry by entry points, shall be published on the website.

8.2 All registry users making registrations through a designated entry point or entry points under Article XIX (1) of the Protocol shall comply with the arrangements referred to in the preceding Section 8.1.

Section 9
HELP DESK AND TECHNICAL SUPPORT
(Section 3.5 of the Regulations)

9.1 To access the technical support function of the International Registry, an administrator, registry user or searching person may email or call the help desk, as specified on the website. It is recommended that the "help" pages of the website and email be used, where possible. Any person communicating with the help desk via email is requested to:

(a) specify the nature of the problem or question;
(b) provide his/her full name and company name;
(c) identify which type of user he/she is (e.g. administrator, registry user or searching person); and
(d) provide a main contact telephone number.

The Registrar may, to the extent consistent with applicable privacy law, verify the identity of all callers and log and record all calls to the help desk.

9.2 The terms of Section 3.4 of the Regulations and Section 7.4 of these Procedures shall apply to:

(a) the hours of operation of the help desk, and exceptions thereto; and
(b) notice of interruption and resumption of access to the help desk and its services.

9.3 The initial working languages of the help desk will be English, French and Spanish. It is envisaged that other languages will be added when the necessary financial means are available, taking into account the implications thereof as well as advantages for users.

9.4 Help desk response times will depend on demand and cannot therefore be guaranteed.

9.5 The help desk is for technical support only and cannot provide support on other matters, including legal questions. The help desk cannot respond to queries concerning an administrator's, a registry user's or a searching person's:

(a) computer or network system;
(b) system security policies;
(c) Internet access, including its connectivity and performance; or
(d) browser.

Section 10
SIGN-UP AND APPROVAL—REGISTRY USER ENTITY AND ADMINISTRATOR
(Section 4 of the Regulations)

10.1 In connection with approvals under Section 4.1 of the Regulations, the proposed administrator of a proposed registry user entity shall complete and electronically submit to the Registrar, through the website, the form for approval of:

(a) a registry user entity; and
(b) an administrator of that entity.

Information designated as mandatory on the form shall be provided. Information designated as optional on the form may be provided. Names of organizations and persons must be their correct legal names. In exceptional cases (e.g. where the space on the form is insufficient), prior approval of the Registrar for using a name other than the correct legal name must be sought by email. A proposed registry user entity shall also electronically submit to the Registrar, with proper signature, confirmation that a proposed administrator is entitled to act in that capacity. At the specific request of the Registrar, such confirmation shall be provided in hard-copy on the entity's letterhead with proper signature. All applications for approval shall include acceptance of these Procedures and of the website terms and conditions governing the use of the International Registry.

10.2 All applications for approval must be accompanied by full payment (by credit or debit card) of the appropriate non-refundable fee, together with value added tax (VAT), if required by law. The proposed administrator will be presented with a summary of the amount (in U.S. dollars) to be paid and prompted to enter credit or debit card details. Once the card details have been submitted and validated, payment will be taken from the relevant account and that person will be presented with a confirmation screen and the option to save a digital copy of the invoice.

10.3 All applications for approvals will be acknowledged to the electronic mail address provided on the submitted application form.

10.4 The proposed administrator shall promptly reply to requests for additional information from the Registrar in connection with the approval process. Such requests, made at the sole discretion of the Registrar, shall be consistent with applicable privacy laws.

10.5 If satisfied with the information provided, the Registrar shall issue to the proposed administrator, in electronic form, the Registrar's approval and a notification of the URL at which the administrator can access his/her digital certificate, together with appropriate instructions on its use.

10.6 The Registrar shall issue its approval (if given) as soon as is reasonably practicable and will endeavour to complete the approval process within 48 hours of receipt of the application.

10.7 Once the Registrar has issued its approval, the administrator shall test his/her ability to access the website.

10.8 The Registrar shall not approve a registry user entity or an administrator where the Registrar believes that the requirements of Section 4.1 of the Regulations have not been met. In such a case, the Registrar, if requested in writing shall:

(a) specify in writing, via email, the reasons why such requirements have not been met; and
(b) provide the applicant with a reasonable opportunity to take corrective action.

If not corrected, at the sole discretion of the Registrar, the application shall be declined. Refusal of an application shall not prevent an applicant from making a subsequent application for approval, provided that the requirements of these Procedures are fully complied with in respect thereto, and payment of the appropriate fee together with VAT (if applicable) is made.

10.9 The fee for issuing a replacement digital certificate shall be borne by the registry user entity. A person seeking a replacement digital certificate shall apply to the Registrar and follow the instructions specified on the website.

10.10 The Registrar may revoke the approval of a registry user entity and/or an administrator at any time where, in its view, there exists a material risk of fraudulent registrations or other misuse. In such a case, the Registrar and the registry user entity shall take all reasonable steps to cooperate to expeditiously take corrective action appropriate under the circumstances; the back-up contact designated under Section 5.12 may be used as required. The Registrar may block and/or disable any user account of the registry user entity concerned.

Section 11
SIGN-UP AND APPROVAL—REGISTRY USER
(Section 4 of the Regulations)

11.1 In connection with approval of registry users under Section 4.2 of the Regulations, a proposed registry user seeking to act on behalf of an approved registry user entity shall apply through the website, requesting electronic approval from the administrator of that entity.

11.2 An administrator has the sole right to approve one or more registry users employed by a registry user entity to act on his/her behalf. If the administrator elects to approve such registry users, the administrator shall take that action through the "approved registry user" page on the website, specifying the period of validity of a proposed registry user's access to the International Registry and directing that the associated payment be made.

11.3 Upon receiving the approval of his/her administrator and following successful testing of his/her ability to access the website, a registry user will be issued a digital certificate by the administrator via an email containing a link to the website. The registry user should then download from the website the digital certificate, providing him/her with a private key.

Section 12
EFFECTING, AMENDING AND DISCHARGING REGISTRATIONS
(Sections 5 and 6 of the Regulations)

12.1 To effect, amend or discharge a registration, a registering person shall:

(a) follow the relevant process and instructions specified on the website; and
(b) complete the electronic forms contained on the website, with the relevant information required by Section 5 of the Regulations.

Registration information electronically provided on the website shall be used by a registering person, as required by Section 5 of the Regulations. To the extent such information is not provided, registration information shall be inserted by a registering person following the instructions specified on the website.

12.2 Each named party, other than the registering party, required to consent under Article 20 of the Convention in order for a registration, amendment or discharge to become effective shall be electronically requested to consent thereto, in accordance with Article 18 (1) (a) of the Convention, prior to that registration, amendment or discharge becoming searchable. Once a registering person has entered registration, amendment or discharge information on the website and has digitally signed it, each named party identified in the registration:

(a) will be notified thereof by electronic mail; and
(b) shall be given the opportunity to consent thereto, through the website, for a period of 36 hours.

In the event that any such named party fails to give its consent within the 36-hour period, the registration, amendment or discharge will be automatically aborted.

12.3 Upon receipt of the final consent, the Registrar shall automatically issue a confirmation thereof by email to all parties entitled to receive a confirmation thereof under Section 6 of the Regulations, provided that the email addresses of all such parties have previously been provided.

12.4 An administrator may, at his/her sole discretion, authorize one or more of his/her approved registry users or professional users to effect, amend or discharge a registration. The authorization may cover one or more aircraft objects. Several users may be authorized to work on the same aircraft object or objects, but not simultaneously during the same registration session. An administrator may, at any time, revoke an authorization he/she has given and grant further authorizations to qualifying registry users.

12.5 Upon receipt of a confirmation, any named party wishing to ensure that the respective entry has been correctly made may undertake a priority search.

12.6 Rectification of any error or inaccuracy in a registration, once searchable, may only be effected through an amended registration.

12.7 Initiated, but not completed, registrations, amendments or discharges shall not appear on any search results.

Section 13
MAKING SEARCHES AND OBTAINING SEARCH RESULTS
(Section 7 of the Regulations)

13.1 Any person may, following payment of the required fee, search the International Registry, and that searching person shall:

(a) follow the relevant process and instructions specified on the website; and
(b) complete the electronic forms contained on the website, with the relevant information required by Section 7 of the Regulations.

13.2 The object of an informational search is to provide the searching person with sufficient information to perform a priority search.

13.3 An informational search listing shall be made available in electronic form to the person undertaking the search. For the avoidance of doubt, an informational search will not generate a search certificate. The Registrar shall not be liable in respect of the content of an informational search listing.

13.4 In making a priority search or a Contracting State search, the searching person shall state the name of the person or persons having the benefit of the search. The name of such person or persons shall appear on the priority search certificate or the Contracting State search certificate, as the case may be. Beneficiaries may include:

(a) parties entering into, planning or forbearing from commercial transactions involving a named party of an aircraft object; or
(b) parties providing legal or other professional advice to, or insuring, the parties specified in clause (a) immediately preceding.

13.5 Priority search certificates and Contracting State search certificates will be digitally signed by the Registrar and must be so signed in order to be valid. They shall be stored electronically by the Registrar. An electronic version thereof shall be issued and made available to the searching person. A printed version of either such certificate shall be made available upon payment of the required fee.

13.6 The fees for Contracting State searches undertaken by government authorities in Contracting States for official purposes shall be waived. The fees for other searches performed by such authorities may be waived pursuant to arrangements made with the Registrar.

Section 14
OPERATIONAL COMPLAINTS
(Section 8 of the Regulations)

14.1 In accordance with Section 8 of the Regulations, any person may submit an operational complaint to the Registrar through the "operational complaints" section of the website or by email as specified on the website. The receipt of an operational complaint shall be promptly acknowledged by the Registrar.

14.2 Operational complaints shall include a written statement containing full details of the facts said to give rise to the complaint.

14.3 The Registrar shall respond to the complaint or state why it is not able to do so, within 15 calendar days of receipt of the complaint or, if later, receipt of the full facts statement. The Registrar shall transmit a copy of its reply to the Supervisory Authority.

14.4 If, within 30 calendar days of making the complaint, the person does not consider that the matter has been or is being satisfactorily addressed by the Registrar, that person may submit the complaint to the Supervisory Authority (with a copy to the Registrar) for further consideration. Submission of the complaint to the Supervisory Authority shall be made stating the full facts of the case either by email to LEB@icao.int or by letter or facsimile to:

International Civil Aviation Organization
Supervisory Authority of the International Registry
c/o Legal Affairs and External Relations Bureau
999 University Street
Montréal, Quebec
Canada H3C 5H7

Fax: +1 514-954-8032

14.5 If the Supervisory Authority determines that changes to the procedures or policies of the International Registry are appropriate, it will instruct the Registrar to carry out such changes.

Section 15
CLAIMS AGAINST THE REGISTRAR
(Section 14 of the Regulations)

15.1 Claims may be brought against the Registrar under Article 28 of the Convention for loss suffered as defined in Section 14 of the Regulations. In accordance with Article 28 (2), the Registrar shall not be liable for factual inaccuracy of registration information received by the Registrar or transmitted by the Registrar in the form in which it received that information nor for acts or circumstances for which the Registrar and its officers and employees are not responsible and arising prior to receipt of registration information at the International Registry.

15.2 All such claims shall be notified in writing to the Registrar by post and/or facsimile and by email at:

Aviareto Ltd.
Suite 3
Plaza 255
Blanchardstown Corporate Park 2
Blanchardstown
Dublin 15
Republic of Ireland

fax.: +353 (0)1 829 3508
email: registryofficials@aviareto.aero

and shall include a full statement of the facts giving rise to the claim pursuant to Article 28 of the Convention. Such statement shall be provided to the Registrar within three months of the person becoming aware of the existence of the claim.

15.3 All such claims shall be subject to a consultation period during which the claimant and the Registrar will in good faith attempt to resolve the claim. The consultation period shall be three months from the date the Registrar receives notification of the claim, or the statement of facts (if later). The three-month period may be extended by mutual agreement of the parties.

15.4 If, following the consultation period, the claim has not been resolved, the parties are encouraged to engage in mediation, conciliation, arbitration or other dispute resolution process but the claimant may, subject to the procedural requirements of the applicable law, commence proceedings against the Registrar in accordance with Articles 28 and 44 of the Convention.

15.5 Nothing in these Procedures shall:

(a) operate to extend any limitation period applicable under the applicable law; or
(b) affect a party's right to commence proceedings where otherwise a limitation period would expire.

Section 16
CONFIDENTIALITY
(Section 9 of the Regulations)

The Registrar shall keep all information in the International Registry confidential, except where:

(a) it is provided in response to a priority search, a Contracting State search or informational search, or made electronically available to enable registry users to effect, amend or discharge registrations;

(b) it is requested under Article 27, paragraph 5, of the Convention, or provided to the Supervisory Authority at the latter's request; or
(c) it is used for the purposes of the statistics required by Section 10 of the Regulations for the International Registry.

Section 17
NOTIFICATIONS

The Registrar may notify an administrator or a registry user entity, by email to the current email address provided by or for that person, of any matters affecting the International Registry. Any such notification shall be presumed to have been received 24 hours after it was sent.

Section 18
FEES
(Section 13 of the Regulations)

All applicable fees shall be paid in advance. The current fee schedule is set out in the Appendix to the present Procedures and may be adjusted from time to time by the Supervisory Authority, as provided by the Convention and the Protocol.

Section 19
PUBLICATION
(Section 16 of the Regulations)

19.1 The authentic version of these Procedures shall be published in an official publication of the Supervisory Authority.

19.2 The Registrar shall make an electronic version of these Procedures, as may be amended, available to the public at no cost by publishing it on the website.

Section 20
AMENDMENTS
(Section 17 of the Regulations)

20.1 Requests for amendments to these Procedures may be submitted by the Registrar to the Supervisory Authority, which shall consider such amendments.

20.2 The authentic version of any amendments to these Procedures approved by the Supervisory Authority shall be published in an official publication of the Supervisory Authority.

Section 21
EFFECTIVE DATES
(Section 18 of the Regulations)

These Procedures shall take effect on the date the Protocol enters into force. Any amendments to these Procedures shall take effect one calendar month after the date of their publication unless otherwise determined by the Supervisory Authority.

Appendix
Fee Schedule

1. FEES FOR USING THE INTERNATIONAL REGISTRY

User set-up fee

1.1 No person may register with the International Registry without having paid a "user set-up fee". There shall be three options open to users:

(a) a five-year subscription;
(b) a one-year subscription;
(c) a ten-user, five-year subscription.

1.2 For option (c), the person purchasing the subscription will be nominated as the administrator of the group of users and will be provided with a user credit to set up a further nine individual users in one or more user sessions.

1.3 The user set-up fee payable in respect of a controlled entity shall be levied as follows:

(a) upon approval of the controlled entity by the administrator of an approved transacting user entity, after the coming into force of the Third Edition of the Regulations and Procedures for the International Registry; and
(b) on the next date of the subscription renewal of an approved transacting user entity, where the administrator of said entity approved the controlled entity or the special purpose entity prior to the coming into force of the Third Edition of the Regulations and Procedures for the International Registry.

1.4 User set-up fees are defined in Table 1. These fees include the provision of a public key infrastructure (PKI) certificate that is installed on the user workstation. In the event of this certificate being lost or destroyed, a new certificate will be supplied on payment of a "lost certificate fee" as set out in Table 1.

Registration fee

1.5 A single registration fee shall be charged for all registrations initiated by the same registering party during a "registration session", defined to mean one session with the International Registry permitting "all registrations" relating to:

(a) one airframe and all engines regularly used thereon (or any subset thereof or any individual engine); or
(b) one helicopter.

For this purpose, "all registrations" means all registrations reflecting transactions relating to the object or objects set out in clauses (a) or (b) entered into within a period of 24 hours from the time of the initiation of the first registration, as electronically confirmed by the registering and consenting parties, including those reflecting different or multiple types of registrations permitted under the

Convention and the Protocol without limitation in number (e.g. an international interest (leasing agreement), a second international interest (security agreement), a third international interest (a second security agreement), subordination (of the second international interest to the first), and an assignment of one or more of the international interests). A "registration session" will last for 24 hours for the purposes of the "registration fee".

1.6 That single registration fee shall be defined as the "registration fee", the amount of which is set out in Table 1.

1.7 Spare engines (i.e. further engines beyond the number normally fitted to an airframe) that are to be registered with an airframe during a single registration session will be subject to an additional "spare engine fee", the amount of which is defined in Table 1.

Priority search fee

1.8 A single search fee shall be charged for a priority search session. A "priority search session" is defined to mean "all priority searches" relating to:

(a) one airframe and all engines to be regularly used thereon (or any subset thereof or any individual engine); or
(b) one helicopter;

carried out within a sixty-minute period.

For this purpose, "all priority searches" means all priority searches made within a single sixty-minute period relating to the object or objects set out in clauses (a) or (b), as electronically confirmed by the searching party. That single search fee shall be defined as the "priority search fee," the amount of which is set out in Table 1.

Table 1. Fees

Description	*Fee (in U.S. dollars)*
User set-up fee (5 years)	500
Controlled entity set-up fee (1 year)	180
User set-up fee (1 year)	200
Controlled entity set-up fee (5 years)	400
Ten-user set-up fee (5 years)	2 500
Registration fee	100
Spare engine fee	50
Priority search fee	35
Lost certificate fee	100

2. PROCEDURE FOR ADJUSTMENT OF FEES

2.1 At the end of the initial period (first year of the operational phase), fees shall be reviewed by the Supervisory Authority, in consultation with the contractor. New fees may then be set by the Supervisory Authority, based upon anticipated volume at that point, taking into account:

(a) the contractor's cash reserves for working capital;
(b) the level of insurance required by the Supervisory Authority;
(c) any litigation budget required by the Supervisory Authority or the contractor above that contained in the cost schedule;
(d) the Supervisory Authority costs;
(e) any service enhancements requested by the Supervisory Authority or suggested by the contractor;
(f) the transaction volume achieved by the Registry and the variation from the transaction volume projected by the contractor;
(g) any other relevant factors.

2.2 The same review mechanism set out in paragraph 2.1 may be carried out at the end of the second, third and fourth years of operation.

3. IRISH VAT

Users will be invited to state their country of residence as part of their user profile and, if based in the European Union, will be asked for a company VAT number that will determine the application of Irish VAT (applies to Irish and European Union users). Under current legislation, European VAT is not applicable to services delivered to parties outside of Europe (therefore users outside of the European Union are not subject to VAT).

Appendix 8

Convention on Offences and Certain Other Acts Committed on Board Aircraft

THE STATES Parties to this Convention
HAVE AGREED as follows:

Chapter I—Scope of the Convention

Article 1

1. This Convention shall apply in respect of:

   a) offences against penal law;
   b) acts which, whether or not they are offences, may or do jeopardize the safety of the aircraft or of persons or property therein or which jeopardize good order and discipline on board.

2. Except as provided in Chapter III, this Convention shall apply in respect of offences committed or acts done by a person on board any aircraft registered in a Contracting State, while that aircraft is in flight or on the surface of the high seas or of any other area outside the territory of any State.

3. For the purposes of this Convention, an aircraft is considered to be in flight from the moment when power is applied for the purpose of take-off until the moment when the landing run ends.

4. This Convention shall not apply to aircraft used in military, customs or police services.

Article 2

Without prejudice to the provisions of Article 4 and except when the safety of the aircraft or of persons or property on board so requires, no provision of this

Convention shall be interpreted as authorizing or requiring any action in respect of offences against penal laws of a political nature or those based on racial or religious discrimination.

Chapter II—Jurisdiction

Article 3

1. The State of registration of the aircraft is competent to exercise jurisdiction over offences and acts committed on board.

2. Each Contracting State shall take such measures as may be necessary to establish its jurisdiction as the State of registration over offences committed on board aircraft registered in such State.

3. This Convention does not exclude any criminal jurisdiction exercised in accordance with national law.

Article 4

A Contracting State which is not the State of registration may not interfere with an aircraft in flight in order to exercise its criminal jurisdiction over an offence committed on board except in the following cases:

a) the offence has effect on the territory of such State;
b) the offence has been committed by or against a national or permanent resident of such State;
c) the offence is against the security of such State;
d) the offence consists of a breach of any rules or regulations relating to the flight or manoeuvre of aircraft in force in such State;
e) the exercise of jurisdiction is necessary to ensure the observance of any obligation of such State under a multilateral international agreement.

Chapter III—Powers of the aircraft commander

Article 5

1. The provisions of this Chapter shall not apply to offences and acts committed or about to be committed by a person on board an aircraft in flight in the airspace of the State of registration or over the high seas of any other area outside the territory of any State unless the last point of take-off or the next point of intended landing is situated in a State other than that of registration, or the aircraft subsequently flies in the airspace of a State other than that of registration with such person still on board.

2. Notwithstanding the provisions of Article 1, paragraph 3, an aircraft shall for the purposes of this Chapter, be considered to be in flight at any time from the moment when all its external doors are closed following embarkation until the moment when any such door is opened for disembarkation. In the case of a forced landing, the provisions of this Chapter shall continue to apply with respect to offences and acts committed on board until competent authorities of a State take over the responsibility for the aircraft and for the persons and property on board.

Article 6

1. The aircraft commander may, when he has reasonable grounds to believe that a person has committed, or is about to commit, on board the aircraft, an offence or act contemplated in Article 1, paragraph 1, impose upon such person reasonable measures including restraint which are necessary:

a) to protect the safety of the aircraft, or of persons or property therein; or
b) to maintain good order and discipline on board; or
c) to enable him to deliver such person to competent authorities or to disembark him in accordance with the provisions of this Chapter.

2. The aircraft commander may require or authorize the assistance of other crew members and may request or authorize, but not require, the assistance of passengers to restrain any person whom he is entitled to restrain. Any crew member or passenger may also take reasonable preventive measures without such authorization when he has reasonable grounds to believe that such action is immediately necessary to protect the safety of the aircraft, or of persons or property therein.

Article 7

1. Measures of restraint imposed upon a person in accordance with Article 6 shall not be continued beyond any point at which the aircraft lands unless:

a) such point is in the territory of a non-Contracting State and its authorities refuse to permit disembarkation of that person or those measures have been imposed in accordance with Article 6, paragraph 1 c) in order to enable his delivery to competent authorities;
b) the aircraft makes a forced landing and the aircraft commander is unable to deliver that person to competent authorities; or
c) that person agrees to onward carriage under restraint.

2. The aircraft commander shall as soon as practicable, and if possible before landing in the territory of a State with a person on board who has been placed under restraint in accordance with the provisions of Article 6, notify the authorities of such State of the fact that a person on board is under restraint and of the reasons for such restraint.

Article 8

1. The aircraft commander may, in so far as it is necessary for the purpose of subparagraph a) or b) of paragraph 1 of Article 6, disembark in the territory of any State in which the aircraft lands any person who he has reasonable grounds to believe has committed, or is about to commit, on board the aircraft an act contemplated in Article 1, paragraph 1 b).

2. The aircraft commander shall report to the authorities of the State in which he disembarks any person pursuant to this Article, the fact of, and the reasons for, such disembarkation.

Article 9

1. The aircraft commander may deliver to the competent authorities of any Contracting State in the territory of which the aircraft lands any person who he has reasonable grounds to believe has committed on board the aircraft an act which, in his opinion, is a serious offence according to the penal law of the State of registration of the aircraft.

2. The aircraft commander shall as soon as practicable and if possible before landing in the territory of a Contracting State with a person on board whom the aircraft commander intends to deliver in accordance with the preceding paragraph, notify the authorities of such Sate of his intention to deliver such person and the reasons therefor.

3. The aircraft commander shall furnish the authorities to whom any suspected offender is delivered in accordance with the provisions of this Article with evidence and information which, under the law of the State of registration of the aircraft, are lawfully in his possession.

Article 10

For action taken in accordance with this Convention, neither the aircraft commander, any other member of the crew, any passenger, the owner or operator of the aircraft, nor the person on whose behalf the flight was performed shall be held responsible in any proceeding on account of the treatment undergone by the person against whom the actions were taken.

Chapter IV—Unlawful Seizure of Aircraft

Article 11

1. When a person on board has unlawfully committed by force or threat thereof an act of interference, seizure, or other wrongful exercise of control of an aircraft in flight or when such an act is about to be committed, Contracting States shall take all appropriate measures to restore control of the aircraft to its lawful commander or to preserve his control of the aircraft.

2. In the cases contemplated in the preceding paragraph, the Contracting State in which the aircraft lands shall permit its passengers and crew to continue their journey as soon as practicable, and shall return the aircraft and its cargo to the persons lawfully entitled to possession.

Chapter V—Powers and Duties of States

Article 12

Any Contracting State shall allow the commander of an aircraft registered in another Contracting State to disembark any person pursuant to Article 8, paragraph 1.

Article 13

1. Any Contracting State shall take delivery of any person whom the aircraft commander delivers pursuant to Article 9, paragraph 1.

2. Upon being satisfied that the circumstances so warrant, any Contracting State shall take custody or other measures to ensure the presence of any person suspected of an act contemplated in Article 11, paragraph 1 and of any person of whom it has taken delivery. The custody and other measures shall be as provided in the law of that State but may only be continued for such time as is reasonably necessary to enable any criminal or extradition proceedings to be instituted.

3. Any person in custody pursuant to the previous paragraph shall be assisted in communicating immediately with the nearest appropriate representative of the State of which he is a national.

4. Any Contracting State, to which a person is delivered pursuant to Article 9, paragraph 1, or in whose territory an aircraft lands following the commission of an act contemplated in Article 11, paragraph 1, shall immediately make a preliminary enquiry into the facts.

5. When a State, pursuant to this Article, has taken a person into custody, it shall immediately notify the State of registration of the aircraft and the State of nationality of the detained person and, if it considers it advisable, any other interested State of the fact that such person is in custody and of the circumstances which warrant his detention. The State which makes the preliminary enquiry contemplated in paragraph 4 of this Article shall promptly report its findings to the said States and shall indicate whether it intends to exercise jurisdiction.

Article 14

1. When any person has been disembarked in accordance with Article 8, paragraph 1, or delivered in accordance with Article 9, paragraph 1, or has disembarked after committing an act contemplated in Article 11, paragraph 1, and when such person cannot or does not desire to continue his journey and the State of landing refuses to admit him, that State may, if the person in question is not a national or permanent resident of that State, return him to the territory of the State of which he is a national or permanent resident or to the territory of the State in which he began his journey by air.

2. Neither disembarkation, nor delivery, nor the taking of custody or other measures contemplated in Article 13, paragraph 2, nor return of the person concerned, shall be considered as admission to the territory of the Contracting State concerned for the purpose of its law relating to entry or admission of persons and nothing in this Convention shall affect the law of a Contracting State relating to the expulsion of persons from its territory.

Article 15

1. Without prejudice to Article 14, any person who has been disembarked in accordance with Article 8, paragraph 1, or delivered in accordance with Article 9, paragraph 1, or has disembarked after committing an act contemplated in Article 11, paragraph 1, and who desires to continue his journey shall be at liberty as soon as practicable to proceed to any destination of his choice unless his

presence is required by the law of the State of landing for the purpose of extradition or criminal proceedings.

2. Without prejudice to its law as to entry and admission to, and extradition and expulsion from its territory, a Contracting State in whose territory a person has been disembarked in accordance with Article 8, paragraph 1, or delivered in accordance with Article 9, paragraph 1 or has disembarked and is suspected of having committed an act contemplated in Article 11, paragraph 1, shall accord to such person treatment which is no less favourable for his protection and security than that accorded to nationals of such Contracting State in like circumstances.

Chapter VI—Other Provisions

Article 16

1. Offences committed on aircraft registered in a Contracting State shall be treated, for the purpose of extradition, as if they had been committed not only in the place in which they have occurred but also in the territory of the State of registration of the aircraft.

2. Without prejudice to the provisions of the preceding paragraph, nothing in this Convention shall be deemed to create an obligation to grant extradition.

Article 17

In taking any measures for investigation or arrest or otherwise exercising jurisdiction in connection with any offence committed on board an aircraft the Contracting States shall pay due regard to the safety and other interests of air navigation and shall so act as to avoid unnecessary delay of the aircraft, passengers, crew or cargo.

Article 18

If Contracting States establish joint air transport operating organizations or international operating agencies, which operate aircraft not registered in any one State those States shall, according to the circumstances of the case, designate the State among them which, for the purposes of this Convention, shall be considered as the State of registration and shall give notice thereof to the International Civil Aviation Organization which shall communicate the notice to all States Parties to this Convention.

Chapter VII—Final Clauses

Article 19

Until the date on which this Convention comes into force in accordance with the provisions of Article 21, it shall remain open for signature on behalf of any State which at that date is a Member of the United Nations or of any of the Specialized Agencies.

Article 20

1. This Convention shall be subject to ratification by the signatory States in accordance with their constitutional procedures.

2. The instruments of ratification shall be deposited with the International Civil Aviation Organization.

Article 21

1. As soon as twelve of the signatory States have deposited their instruments of ratification of this Convention, it shall come into force between them on the ninetieth day after the date of the deposit of the twelfth instrument of ratification. It shall come into force for each State ratifying thereafter on the ninetieth day after the deposit of its instrument of ratification.

2. As soon as this Convention comes into force, it shall be registered with the Secretary-General of the United Nations by the International Civil Aviation Organization.

Article 22

1. This Convention shall, after it has come into force, be open for accession by any State Member of the United Nations or of any of the Specialized Agencies.

2. The accession of a State shall be effected by the deposit of an instrument of accession with the International Civil Aviation Organization and shall take effect on the ninetieth day after the date of such deposit.

Article 23

1. Any Contracting State may denounce this Convention by notification addressed to the International Civil Aviation Organization.

2. Denunciation shall take effect six months after the date of receipt by the International Civil Aviation Organization of the notification of denunciation.

Article 24

1. Any dispute between two or more Contracting States concerning the interpretation or application of this Convention which cannot be settled through negotiation, shall, at the request of one of them, be submitted to arbitration. If within six months from the date of the request for arbitration the Parties are unable to agree on the organization of the arbitration, any one of those Parties may refer the dispute to the International Court of Justice by request in conformity with the Statute of the Court.

2. Each State may at the time of signature or ratification of this Convention or accession thereto, declare that it does not consider itself bound by the preceding paragraph. The other Contracting States shall not be bound by the preceding paragraph with respect to any Contracting State having made such a reservation.

3. Any Contracting State having made a reservation in accordance with the preceding paragraph may at any time withdraw this reservation by notification to the International Civil Aviation Organization.

Article 25

Except as provided in Article 24 no reservation may be made to this Convention.

Article 26

The International Civil Aviation Organization shall give notice to all States Members of the United Nations or of any of the Specialized Agencies:

a) of any signature of this Convention and the date thereof;
b) of the deposit of any instrument of ratification or accession and the date thereof;
c) of the date on which this Convention comes into force in accordance with Article 21, paragraph 1;
d) of the receipt of any notification of denunciation and the date thereof; and
e) of the receipt of any declaration or notification made under Article 24 and the date thereof.

IN WITNESS WHEREOF the undersigned Plenipotentiaries, having been duly authorized, have signed this Convention.

DONE at Tokyo on the fourteenth day of September One Thousand Nine Hundred and Sixty-three in three authentic texts drawn up in the English, French and Spanish languages.

This Convention shall be deposited with the International Civil Aviation Organization with which, in accordance with Article 19, it shall remain open for signature and the said Organization shall send certified copies thereof to all States Members of the United Nations or of any Specialized Agency.

Appendix 9

Convention for the Suppression of Unlawful Seizure of Aircraft

PREAMBLE

THE STATES PARTIES TO THIS CONVENTION

CONSIDERING that unlawful acts of seizure or exercise of control of aircraft in flight jeopardize the safety of persons and property, seriously affect the operation of air services, and undermine the confidence of the peoples of the world in the safety of civil aviation;

CONSIDERING that the occurrence of such acts is a matter of grave concern; CONSIDERING that, for the purpose of deterring such acts, there is an urgent need to provide appropriate measures for punishment of offenders;

HAVE AGREED AS FOLLOWS:

Article 1

Any person who on board an aircraft in flight:

(a) unlawfully, by force or threat thereof, or by any other form of intimidation, seizes, or exercises control of, that aircraft, or attempts to perform any such act, or

(b) is an accomplice of a person who performs or attempts to perform any such act

commits an offence (hereinafter referred to as "the offence").

Article 2

Each Contracting State undertakes to make the offence punishable by severe penalties.

Article 3

1. For the purposes of this Convention, an aircraft is considered to be in flight at any time from the moment when all its external doors are closed following embarkation until the moment when any such door is opened for disembarkation. In the case of a forced landing the flight shall be deemed to continue until the competent authorities take over the responsibility for the aircraft and for persons and property on board.

2. This Convention shall not apply to aircraft used in military, customs or police services.

3. This Convention shall apply only if the place of take-off or the place of actual landing of the aircraft on board which the offence is committed is situated outside the territory of the State of registration of that aircraft; it shall be immaterial whether the aircraft is engaged in an international or domestic flight.

4. In the cases mentioned in Article 5, this Convention shall not apply if the place of take-off and the place of actual landing of the aircraft on board which the offence is committed are situated within the territory of the same State where that State is one of those referred to in that Article.

5. Notwithstanding paragraphs 3 and 4 of this Article, Articles 6, 7, 8 and 10 shall apply whatever the place of take-off or the place of actual landing of the aircraft, if the offender or the alleged offender is found in the territory of a State other than the State of registration of that aircraft.

Article 4

1. Each Contracting State shall take such measures as may be necessary to establish its jurisdiction over the offence and any other act of violence against passengers or crew committed by the alleged offender in connection with the offence, in the following cases:

- *(a)* when the offence is committed on board an aircraft registered in that State;
- *(b)* when the aircraft on board which the offence is committed lands in its territory with the alleged offender still on board;
- *(c)* when the offence is committed on board an aircraft leased without crew to a lessee who has his principal place of business or, if the lessee has no such place of business, his permanent residence, in that State.

2. Each Contracting State shall likewise take such measures as may be necessary to establish its jurisdiction over the offence in the case where the alleged offender is present in its territory and it does not extradite him pursuant to Article 8 to any of the States mentioned in paragraph 1 of this Article.

3. This Convention does not exclude any criminal jurisdiction exercised in accordance with national law.

Article 5

The Contracting States which establish joint air transport operating organizations or international operating agencies, which operate aircraft which are subject to joint or international registration shall, by appropriate means, designate for each aircraft the State among them which shall exercise the jurisdiction and have the attributes of the State of registration for the purpose of this Convention and shall give notice thereof to the International Civil Aviation Organization which shall communicate the notice to all States Parties to this Convention.

Article 6

1. Upon being satisfied that the circumstances so warrant, any Contracting State in the territory of which the offender or the alleged offender is present, shall take him into custody or take other measures to ensure his presence. The custody and other measures shall be as provided in the law of that State but may only be continued for such time as is necessary to enable any criminal or extradition proceedings to be instituted.

2. Such State shall immediately make a preliminary enquiry into the facts.

3. Any person in custody pursuant to paragraph 1 of this Article shall be assisted in communicating immediately with the nearest appropriate representative of the State of which he is a national.

4. When a State, pursuant to this Article, has taken a person into custody, it shall immediately notify the State of registration of the aircraft, the State mentioned in Article 4, paragraph 1*(c)*, the State of nationality of the detained person and, if it considers it advisable, any other interested States of the fact that such person is in custody and of the circumstances which warrant his detention. The State which makes the preliminary enquiry contemplated in paragraph 2 of this Article shall promptly report its findings to the said States and shall indicate whether it intends to exercise jurisdiction.

Article 7

The Contracting State in the territory of which the alleged offender is found shall, if it does not extradite him, be obliged, without exception whatsoever and whether or not the offence was committed in its territory, to submit the case to its competent authorities for the purpose of prosecution. Those authorities shall take their decision in the same manner as in the case of any ordinary offence of a serious nature under the law of that State.

Article 8

1. The offence shall be deemed to be included as an extraditable offence in any extradition treaty existing between Contracting States. Contracting States undertake to include the offence as an extraditable offence in every extradition treaty to be concluded between them.

2. If a Contracting State which makes extradition conditional on the existence of a treaty receives a request for extradition from another Contracting State with which it has no extradition treaty, it may at its option consider this Convention as the legal basis for extradition in respect of the offence. Extradition shall be subject to the other conditions provided by the law of the requested State.

3. Contracting States which do not make extradition conditional on the existence of a treaty shall recognize the offence as an extraditable offence between themselves subject to the conditions provided by the law of the requested State.

4. The offence shall be treated, for the purpose of extradition between Contracting States, as if it had been committed not only in the place in which it occurred but also in the territories of the States required to establish their jurisdiction in accordance with Article 4, paragraph 1.

Article 9

1. When any of the acts mentioned in Article 1(*a*) has occurred or is about to occur, Contracting States shall take all appropriate measures to restore control of the aircraft to its lawful commander or to preserve his control of the aircraft.

2. In the cases contemplated by the preceding paragraph, any Contracting State in which the aircraft or its passengers or crew are present shall facilitate the continuation of the journey of the passengers and crew as soon as practicable, and shall without delay return the aircraft and its cargo to the persons lawfully entitled to possession.

Article 10

1. Contracting States shall afford one another the greatest measure of assistance in connection with criminal proceedings brought in respect of the offence and other acts mentioned in Article 4. The law of the State requested shall apply in all cases.

2. The provisions of paragraph 1 of this Article shall not affect obligations under any other treaty, bilateral or multilateral, which governs or will govern, in whole or in part, mutual assistance in criminal matters.

Article 11

Each Contracting State shall in accordance with its national law report to the Council of the International Civil Aviation Organization as promptly as possible any relevant information in its possession concerning:

- (*a*) the circumstances of the offence;
- (*b*) the action taken pursuant to Article 9;
- (*c*) the measures taken in relation to the offender or the alleged offender, and, in particular, the results of any extradition proceedings or other legal proceedings.

Article 12

1. Any dispute between two or more Contracting States concerning the interpretation or application of this Convention which cannot be settled through negotiation, shall, at the request of one of them, be submitted to arbitration. If within six months from the date of the request for arbitration the Parties are unable to agree on the organization of the arbitration, any one of those Parties may refer the dispute to the International Court of Justice by request in conformity with the Statute of the Court.

2. Each State may at the time of signature or ratification of this Convention or accession thereto, declare that it does not consider itself bound by the preceding paragraph. The other Contracting States shall not be bound by the preceding paragraph with respect to any Contracting State having made such a reservation.

3. Any Contracting State having made a reservation in accordance with the preceding paragraph may at any time withdraw this reservation by notification to the Depositary Governments.

Article 13

1. This Convention shall be open for signature at The Hague on 16 December 1970, by States participating in the International Conference on Air Law held at The Hague from 1 to 16 December 1970 (hereinafter referred to as The Hague Conference). After 31 December 1970, the Convention shall be open to all States for signature in Moscow, London and Washington. Any State which does not sign this Convention before its entry into force in accordance with paragraph 3 of this Article may accede to it at any time.

2. This Convention shall be subject to ratification by the signatory States. Instruments of ratification and instruments of accession shall be deposited with the Governments of the Union of Soviet Socialist Republics, the United Kingdom of Great Britain and Northern Ireland, and the United States of America, which are hereby designated the Depositary Governments.

3. This Convention shall enter into force thirty days following the date of the deposit of instruments of ratification by ten States signatory to this Convention which participated in The Hague Conference.

4. For other States, this Convention shall enter into force on the date of entry into force of this Convention in accordance with paragraph 3 of this Article, or thirty days following the date of deposit of their instruments of ratification or accession, whichever is later.

5. The Depositary Governments shall promptly inform all signatory and acceding States of the date of each signature, the date of deposit of each instrument of ratification or accession, the date of entry into force of this Convention, and other notices.

6. As soon as this Convention comes into force, it shall be registered by the Depositary Governments pursuant to Article 102 of the Charter of the United

Nations and pursuant to Article 83 of the Convention on International Civil Aviation (Chicago, 1944).

Article 14

1. Any Contracting State may denounce this Convention by written notification to the Depositary Governments.

2. Denunciation shall take effect six months following the date on which notification is received by the Depositary Governments.

IN WITNESS WHEREOF the undersigned Plenipotentiaries, being duly authorised thereto by their Governments, have signed this Convention.

DONE at The Hague, this sixteenth day of December, one thousand nine hundred and seventy, in three originals, each being drawn up in four authentic texts in the English, French, Russian and Spanish languages.

Appendix 10

Convention for the Suppression of Unlawful Acts against the Safety of Civil Aviation

THE STATES PARTIES TO THIS CONVENTION

CONSIDERING that unlawful acts against the safety of civil aviation jeopardize the safety of persons and property, seriously affect the operation of air services, and undermine the confidence of the peoples of the world in the safety of civil aviation;

CONSIDERING that the occurrence of such acts is a matter of grave concern;

CONSIDERING that, for the purpose of deterring such acts, there is an urgent need to provide appropriate measures for punishment of offenders;

HAVE AGREED AS FOLLOWS:

Article 1

1. Any person commits an offence if he unlawfully and intentionally:

(a) performs an act of violence against a person on board an aircraft in flight if that act is likely to endanger the safety of that aircraft; or

(b) destroys an aircraft in service or causes damage to such an aircraft which renders it incapable of flight or which is likely to endanger its safety in flight; or

(c) places or causes to be placed on an aircraft in service, by any means whatsoever, a device or substance which is likely to destroy that aircraft, or to cause damage to it which renders it incapable of flight, or to cause damage to it which is likely to endanger its safety in flight; or

(d) destroys or damages air navigation facilities or interferes with their operation, if any such act is likely to endanger the safety of aircraft in flight; or

(e) communicates information which he knows to be false, thereby endangering the safety of an aircraft in flight.

2. Any person also commits an offence if he:

(a) attempts to commit any of the offences mentioned in paragraph 1 of this Article; or
(b) is an accomplice of a person who commits or attempts to commit any such offence.

Article 2

For the purposes of this Convention:

(a) an aircraft is considered to be in flight at any time from the moment when all its external doors are closed following embarkation until the moment when any such door is opened for disembarkation; in the case of a forced landing, the flight shall be deemed to continue until the competent authorities take over the responsibility for the aircraft and for persons and property on board;
(b) an aircraft is considered to be in service from the beginning of the preflight preparation of the aircraft by ground personnel or by the crew for a specific flight until twenty-four hours after any landing; the period of service shall, in any event, extend for the entire period during which the aircraft is in flight as defined in paragraph (a) of this Article.

Article 3

Each Contracting State undertakes to make the offences mentioned in Article 1 punishable by severe penalties.

Article 4

1. This Convention shall not apply to aircraft used in military, customs or police services.

2. In the cases contemplated in subparagraphs (a), (b), (c) and (e) of paragraph 1 of Article 1, this Convention shall apply, irrespective of whether the aircraft is engaged in an international or domestic flight, only if:

(a) the place of take-off or landing, actual or intended, of the aircraft is situated outside the territory of the State of registration of that aircraft; or
(b) the offence is committed in the territory of a State other than the State of registration of the aircraft.

3. Notwithstanding paragraph 2 of this Article, in the cases contemplated in subparagraphs (a), (b), (c) and (e) of paragraph 1 of Article 1, this Convention shall also apply if the offender or the alleged offender is found in the territory of a State other than the State of registration of the aircraft.

4. With respect to the States mentioned in Article 9 and in the cases mentioned in subparagraphs (a), (b), (c) and (e) of paragraph 1 of Article 1, this Convention shall not apply if the places referred to in subparagraph (a) of paragraph 2 of this

Article are situated within the territory of the same State where that State is one of those referred to in Article 9, unless the offence is committed or the offender or alleged offender is found in the territory of a State other than that State.

5. In the cases contemplated in subparagraph (d) of paragraph 1 of Article 1, this Convention shall apply only if the air navigation facilities are used in international air navigation.

6. The provisions of paragraphs 2, 3, 4 and 5 of this Article shall also apply in the cases contemplated in paragraph 2 of Article 1.

Article 5

1. Each Contracting State shall take such measures as may be necessary to establish its jurisdiction over the offences in the following cases;

   (a) when the offence is committed in the territory of that State;
   (b) when the offence is committed against or on board an aircraft registered in that State;
   (c) when the aircraft on board which the offence is committed lands in its territory with the alleged offender still on board;
   (d) when the offence is committed against or on board an aircraft leased without crew to a lessee who has his principal place of business or, if the lessee has no such place of business, his permanent residence, in that State.

2. Each Contracting State shall likewise take such measures as may be necessary to establish its jurisdiction over the offences mentioned in Article 1, paragraph 1 (a), (b) and (c), and in Article 1, paragraph 2, in so far as that paragraph relates to those offences, in the case where the alleged offender is present in its territory and it does not extradite him pursuant to Article 8 to any of the States mentioned in paragraph 1 of this Article.

3. This Convention does not exclude any criminal jurisdiction exercised in accordance with national law.

Article 6

1. Upon being satisfied that the circumstances so warrant, any Contracting State in the territory of which the offender or the alleged offender is present, shall take him into custody or take other measures to ensure his presence. The custody and other measures shall be as provided in the law of that State but may only be continued for such time as is necessary to enable any criminal or extradition proceedings to be instituted.

2. Such State shall immediately make a preliminary enquiry into the facts.

3. Any person in custody pursuant to paragraph 1 of this Article shall be assisted in communicating immediately with the nearest appropriate representative of the State of which he is a national.

4. When a State, pursuant to this Article, has taken a person into custody, it shall immediately notify the States mentioned in Article 5, paragraph 1, the State of nationality of the detained person and, if it considers it advisable, any other

interested States of the fact that such person is in custody and of the circumstances which warrant his detention. The State which makes the preliminary enquiry contemplated in paragraph 2 of this Article shall promptly report its findings to the said States and shall indicate whether it intends to exercise jurisdiction.

Article 7

The Contracting State in the territory of which the alleged offender is found shall, if it does not extradite him, be obliged, without exception whatsoever and whether or not the offence was committed in its territory, to submit the case to its competent authorities for the purpose of prosecution. Those authorities shall take their decision in the same manner as in the case of any ordinary offence of a serious nature under the law of that State.

Article 8

1. The offences shall be deemed to be included as extraditable offences in any extradition treaty existing between Contracting States. Contracting States undertake to include the offences as extraditable offences in every extradition treaty to be concluded between them.

2. If a Contracting State which makes extradition conditional on the existence of a treaty receives a request for extradition from another Contracting State with which it has no extradition treaty, it may at its option consider this Convention as the legal basis for extradition in respect of the offences. Extradition shall be subject to the other conditions provided by the law of the requested State.

3. Contracting States which do not make extradition conditional on the existence of a treaty shall recognize the offences as extraditable offences between themselves subject to the conditions provided by the law of the requested State.

4. Each of the offences shall be treated, for the purpose of extradition between Contracting States, as if it had been committed not only in the place in which it occurred but also in the territories of the States required to establish their jurisdiction in accordance with Article 5, paragraph 1 (b), (c) and (d).

Article 9

The Contracting States which establish joint air transport operating organizations or international operating agencies, which operate aircraft which are subject to joint or international registration shall, by appropriate means, designate for each aircraft the State among them which shall exercise the jurisdiction and have the attributes of the State of registration for the purpose of this Convention and shall give notice thereof to the International Civil Aviation Organization which shall communicate the notice to all States Parties to this Convention.

Article 10

1. Contracting States shall, in accordance with international and national law, endeavour to take all practicable measures for the purpose of preventing the offences mentioned in Article 1.

2. When, due to the commission of one of the offences mentioned in Article 1, a flight has been delayed or interrupted, any Contracting State in whose territory the aircraft or passengers or crew are present shall facilitate the continuation of the journey of the passengers and crew as soon as practicable, and shall without delay return the aircraft and its cargo to the persons lawfully entitled to possession.

Article 11

1. Contracting States shall afford one another the greatest measure of assistance in connection with criminal proceedings brought in respect of the offences. The law of the State requested shall apply in all cases.

2. The provisions of paragraph 1 of this Article shall not affect obligations under any other treaty, bilateral or multilateral, which governs or will govern, in whole or in part, mutual assistance in criminal matters.

Article 12

Any Contracting State having reason to believe that one of the offences mentioned in Article 1 will be committed shall, in accordance with its national law, furnish any relevant information in its possession to those States which it believes would be the States mentioned in Article 5, paragraph 1.

Article 13

Each Contracting State shall in accordance with its national law report to the Council of the International Civil Aviation Organization as promptly as possible any relevant information in its possession concerning:

(a) the circumstances of the offence;
(b) the action taken pursuant to Article 10, paragraph 2;
(c) the measures taken in relation to the offender or the alleged offender and, in particular, the results of any extradition proceedings or other legal proceedings.

Article 14

1. Any dispute between two or more Contracting States concerning the interpretation or application of this Convention which cannot be settled through negotiation, shall, at the request of one of them, be submitted to arbitration. If within six months from the date of the request for arbitration the Parties are unable to agree on the organization of the arbitration, any one of those Parties may refer the dispute to the International Court of Justice by request in conformity with the Statute of the Court.

2. Each State may at the time of signature or ratification of this Convention or accession thereto, declare that it does not consider itself bound by the preceding paragraph. The other Contracting States shall not be bound by the preceding paragraph with respect to any Contracting State having made such a reservation.

3. Any Contracting State having made a reservation in accordance with the preceding paragraph may at any time withdraw this reservation by notification to the Depositary Governments.

Article 15

1. This Convention shall be open for signature at Montreal on 23 September 1971, by States participating in the International Conference on Air Law held at Montreal from 8 to 23 September 1971 (hereinafter referred to as the Montreal Conference). After 10 October 1971, the Convention shall be open to all States for signature in Moscow, London and Washington. Any State which does not sign this Convention before its entry into force in accordance with paragraph 3 of this Article may accede to it at any time.

2. This Convention shall be subject to ratification by the signatory States. Instruments of ratification and instruments of accession shall be deposited with the Governments of the Union of Soviet Socialist Republics, the United Kingdom of Great Britain and Northern Ireland, and the United States of America, which are hereby designated the Depositary Governments.

3. This Convention shall enter into force thirty days following the date of the deposit of instruments of ratification by ten States signatory to this Convention which participated in the Montreal Conference.

4. For other States, this Convention shall enter into force on the date of entry into force of this Convention in accordance with paragraph 3 of this Article, or thirty days following the date of deposit of their instruments of ratification or accession, whichever is later.

5. The Depositary Governments shall promptly inform all signatory and acceding States of the date of each signature, the date of deposit of each instrument of ratification or accession, the date of entry into force of this Convention, and other notices.

6. As soon as this Convention comes into force, it shall be registered by the Depositary Governments pursuant to Article 102 of the Charter of the United Nations and pursuant to Article 83 of the Convention on International Civil Aviation (Chicago, 1944).

Article 16

1. Any Contracting State may denounce this Convention by written notification to the Depositary Governments.

2. Denunciation shall take effect six months following the date on which notification is received by the Depositary Governments.

IN WITNESS WHEREOF the undersigned Plenipotentiaries, being duly authorized thereto by their Governments, have signed this Convention.

DONE at Montreal, this twenty-third day of September, one thousand nine hundred and seventy-one, in three originals, each being drawn up in four authentic texts in the English, French, Russian and Spanish languages.

Appendix 11

Protocol for the Suppression of Unlawful Acts of Violence at Airports Serving International Civil Aviation, Supplementary to the connection for the Suppression of Unlawful Acts against the safety of Civil Aviation done at montreal on 23 september 1971

No. 14118. CONVENTION FOR THE SUPPRESSION OF UNLAWFUL ACTS AGAINST THE SAFETY OF CIVIL AVIATION. CONCLUDED AT MONTREAL ON 23 SEPTEMBER 1971[1]

PROTOCOL[2] FOR THE SUPPRESSION OF UNLAWFUL ACTS OF VIOLENCE AT AIRPORTS SERVING INTERNATIONAL CIVIL AVIATION, SUPPLEMENTARY TO THE ABOVE-MENTIONED CONVENTION (WITH FINAL ACT). CONCLUDED AT MONTREAL ON 24 FEBRUARY 1988

1. United Nations, *Treaty Series*, vol. 974, p. 177; for subsequent actions, see references in Cumulative Index No. 17, as well as annex A in volumes 1058, 1107, 1126, 1144, 1195, 1214, 1217 (corrigendum to volume 974), 1259, 1286, 1297, 1308, 1338, 1484, 1491, 1505, 1510, 1511, 1563 and 1579.
2. Came into force on 6 August 1989 in respect of the following States, on behalf of which an instrument of ratification had been deposited with the Governments of the Union of Soviet Socialist Republics, the United Kingdom of Great Britain and Northern Ireland and the United States of America or with the International Civil Aviation Organization, i.e., the thirtieth day after the date of the deposit of the tenth instrument of ratification (7 July 1989), in accordance

with article VI (1), provided that the deposit with the International Civil Aviation Organization of the relevant instruments was the effective deposit for the purpose of article VI (1):

State	Date of deposit of the instrument of ratification	
Byelorussian Soviet Socialist Republic	1 May	1989
German Democratic Republic	31 January	1989
Hungary	7 September	1988
Kuwait	8 March	1989
Marshall Islands	30 May	1989
Peru	7 June	1989
Saudi Arabia	21 February	1989
Turkey	7 July	1989
Union of Soviet Socialist Republics	31 March	1989
United Arab Emirates	9 March	1989

Subsequently, the Protocol came into force for the following States on the thirtieth day after the date of deposit with the International Civil Aviation Organization of their instruments of ratification in accordance with article **VI**(1):

State	Date of deposit of the instrument of ratification	
Chile (With effect from 14 September 1989, provided that the deposit with the International Civil Aviation Organization was the effective deposit for the purpose of article VI (1) of the Protocol.)	15 August	1989
Mauritius (With effect from 16 September 1989, provided that the deposit with the International Civil Aviation Organization was the effective deposit for the purpose of article VI (1) of the Protocol.)	17 August	1989
France* (With effect from 6 October 1989, provided that the deposit with the International Civil Aviation Organization was the effective deposit for the purpose of article VI (1) of the Protocol.)	6 September	1989
Denmark (With a declaration of non-application to the Faeroe Islands. With effect from 23 December 1989, provided that the deposit with the International Civil Aviation Organization was the effective deposit for the purpose of article VI (1) of the Protocol.)	23 November	1989
Austria (With effect from 27 January 1990, provided that the deposit with the International Civil Aviation Organization was the effective deposit for the purpose of article VI (1) of the Protocol.)	28 November	1989

* See p. 505 of this volume for the text of the declaration made upon ratification.

Authentic texts: English, French, Russian and Spanish.
Registered by the International Civil Aviation Organization on 22 December 1990.

THE STATES PARTIES TO THIS PROTOCOL

CONSIDERING that unlawful acts of violence which endanger or are likely to endanger the safety of persons at airports serving international civil aviation or which jeopardize the safe operation of such airports undermine the confidence of the peoples of the world in safety at such airports and disturb the safe and orderly conduct of civil aviation for all States;

CONSIDERING that the occurrence of such acts is a matter of grave concern to the international community and that, for the purpose of deterring such acts, there is an urgent need to provide appropriate measures for punishment of offenders;

CONSIDERING that it is necessary to adopt provisions supplementary to those of the Convention for the Suppression of Unlawful Acts against the Safety of Civil Aviation, done at Montreal on 23 September 1971,[3] to deal with such unlawful acts of violence at airports serving international civil aviation;

HAVE AGREED AS FOLLOWS:

Article I

This Protocol supplements the Convention for the Suppression of Unlawful Acts against the Safety of Civil Aviation, done at Montreal on 23 September 1971 (hereinafter referred to as "the Convention"), and, as between the Parties to this Protocol, the Convention and the Protocol shall be read and interpreted together as one single instrument.

Article II

1. In Article 1 of the Convention, the following shall be added as new paragraph 1 *bis:*

"1 *bis.* Any person commits an offence if he unlawfully and intentionally, using any device, substance or weapon:

(a) performs an act of violence against a person at an airport serving international civil aviation which causes or is likely to cause serious injury or death; or
(b) destroys or seriously damages the facilities of an airport serving international civil aviation or aircraft not in service located thereon or disrupts the services of the airport,

if such an act endangers or is likely to endanger safety at that airport."

2. In paragraph 2 (a) of Article 1 of the Convention, the following words shall be inserted after the words "paragraph 1":

"or paragraph 1 *bis*".

3. United Nations, *Treaty Series,* vol. 974, p. 177.

Article III

In Article 5 of the Convention, the following shall be added as paragraph *2 bis:*

> "*2 bis.* Each Contracting State shall likewise take such measures as may be necessary to establish its jurisdiction over the offences mentioned in Article 1, paragraph 1 *bis*, and in Article I, paragraph 2, in so far as that paragraph relates to those offences, in the case where the alleged offender is present in its territory and it does not extradite him pursuant to Article 8 to the State mentioned in paragraph 1 (a) of this Article."

Article IV

This Protocol shall be open for signature at Montreal on 24 February 1988 by States participating in the International Conference on Air Law held at Montreal from 9 to 24 February 1988. After 1 March 1988, the Protocol shall be open for signature to all States in London, Moscow, Washington and Montreal, until it enters into force in accordance with Article VI.

Article V

1. This Protocol shall be subject to ratification by the signatory States.

2. Any State which is not a Contracting State to the Convention may ratify this Protocol if at the same time it ratifies or accedes to the Convention in accordance with Article 15 thereof.

3. Instruments of ratification shall be deposited with the Governments of the Union of Soviet Socialist Republics, the United Kingdom of Great Britain and Northern Ireland and the United States of America or with the International Civil Aviation Organization, which are hereby designated the Depositaries.

Article VI

1. As soon as ten of the signatory States have deposited their instruments of ratification of this Protocol, it shall enter into force between them on the thirtieth day after the date of the deposit of the tenth instrument of ratification. It shall enter into force for each State which deposits its instrument of ratification after that date on the thirtieth day after deposit of its instrument of ratification.

2. As soon as this Protocol enters into force, it shall be registered by the Depositaries pursuant to Article 102 of the Charter of the United Nations and pursuant to Article 83 of the Convention on International Civil Aviation (Chicago, 1944).[4]

4. United Nations, *Treaty Series,* vol. 15, p. 295. For the texts of the Protocols amending this Convention, see vol. 320, pp. 209 and 217; vol. 418, p. 161; vol. 514, p. 209; vol. 740, p. 21; vol. 893, p. 117; vol. 958, p. 217; vol. 1008, p. 213, and vol. 1175, p. 297.

Article VII

1. This Protocol shall, after it has entered into force, be open for accession by any non-signatory State.

2. Any State which is not a Contracting State to the Convention may accede to this Protocol if at the same time it ratifies or accedes to the Convention in accordance with Article 15 thereof.

3. Instruments of accession shall be deposited with the Depositaries and accession shall take effect on the thirtieth day after the deposit.

Article VIII

1. Any Party to this Protocol may denounce it by written notification addressed to the Depositaries.

2. Denunciation shall take effect six months following the date on which notification is received by the Depositaries.

3. Denunciation of this Protocol shall not of itself have the effect of denunciation of the Convention.

4. Denunciation of the Convention by a Contracting State to the Convention as supplemented by this Protocol shall also have the effect of denunciation of this Protocol.

Article IX

1. The Depositaries shall promptly inform all signatory and acceding States to this Protocol and all signatory and acceding States to the Convention:

(a) of the date of each signature and the date of deposit of each instrument of ratification of, or accession to, this Protocol, and
(b) of the receipt of any notification of denunciation of this Protocol and the date thereof.

2. The Depositaries shall also notify the States referred to in paragraph 1 of the date on which this Protocol enters into force in accordance with Article VI.

IN WITNESS WHEREOF the undersigned Plenipotentiaries, being duly authorized thereto by their Governments, have signed this Protocol.

DONE at Montreal on the twenty-fourth day of February of the year One Thousand Nine Hundred and Eighty-eight, in four originals, each being drawn up in four authentic texts in the English, French, Russian and Spanish languages.

[*For the signatures, see p. 492 of this volume.*]

Appendix 12

Convention on the Marking of Plastic Explosives for the Purpose of detection

THE STATES PARTIES TO THIS CONVENTION,

CONSCIOUS of the implications of acts of terrorism for international security;

EXPRESSING deep concern regarding terrorist acts aimed at destruction of aircraft, other means of transportation and other targets;

CONCERNED that plastic explosives have been used for such terrorist acts;

CONSIDERING that the marking of such explosives for the purpose of detection would contribute significantly to the prevention of such unlawful acts;

RECOGNIZING that for the purpose of deterring such unlawful acts there is an urgent need for an international instrument obliging States to adopt appropriate measures to ensure that plastic explosives are duly marked;

CONSIDERING United Nations Security Council Resolution 635 of 14 June 1989, and United Nations General Assembly Resolution 44/29 of 4 December 1989 urging the International Civil Aviation Organization to intensify its work on devising an international regime for the marking of plastic or sheet explosives for the purpose of detection;

BEARING IN MIND Resolution A27-8 adopted unanimously by the 27th Session of the Assembly of the International Civil Aviation Organization which endorsed with the highest and overriding priority the preparation of a new international instrument regarding the marking of plastic or sheet explosives for detection;

NOTING with satisfaction the role played by the Council of the International Civil Aviation Organization in the preparation of the Convention as well as its willingness to assume functions related to its implementation;

HAVE AGREED AS FOLLOWS:

Article I

For the purposes of this Convention:

1. "Explosives" mean explosive products, commonly known as "plastic explosives", including explosives in flexible or elastic sheet form, as described in the Technical Annex to this Convention.
2. "Detection agent" means a substance as described in the Technical Annex to this Convention which is introduced into an explosive to render it detectable.
3. "Marking" means introducing into an explosive a detection agent in accordance with the Technical Annex to this Convention.
4. "Manufacture" means any process, including reprocessing, that produces explosives.
5. "Duly authorized military devices" include, but are not restricted to, shells, bombs, projectiles, mines, missiles, rockets, shaped charges, grenades and perforators manufactured exclusively for military or police purposes according to the laws and regulations of the State Party concerned.
6. "Producer State" means any State in whose territory explosives are manufactured.

Article II

Each State Party shall take the necessary and effective measures to prohibit and prevent the manufacture in its territory of unmarked explosives.

Article III

1. Each State Party shall take the necessary and effective measures to prohibit and prevent the movement into or out of its territory of unmarked explosives.

2. The preceding paragraph shall not apply in respect of movements for purposes not inconsistent with the objectives of this Convention, by authorities of a State Party performing military or police functions, of unmarked explosives under the control of that State Party in accordance with paragraph 1 of Article IV.

Article IV

1. Each State Party shall take the necessary measures to exercise strict and effective control over the possession and transfer of possession of unmarked explosives which have been manufactured in or brought into its territory prior to the entry into force of this Convention in respect of that State, so as to prevent their diversion or use for purposes inconsistent with the objectives of this Convention.

2. Each State Party shall take the necessary measures to ensure that all stocks of those explosives referred to in paragraph 1 of this Article not held by its authorities

performing military or police functions are destroyed or consumed for purposes not inconsistent with the objectives of this Convention, marked or rendered permanently ineffective, within a period of three years from the entry into force of this Convention in respect of that State.

3. Each State Party shall take the necessary measures to ensure that all stocks of those explosives referred to in paragraph 1 of this Article held by its authorities performing military or police functions and that are not incorporated as an integral part of duly authorized military devices are destroyed or consumed for purposes not inconsistent with the objectives of this Convention, marked or rendered permanently ineffective, within a period of fifteen years from the entry into force of this Convention in respect of that State.

4. Each State Party shall take the necessary measures to ensure the destruction, as soon as possible, in its territory of unmarked explosives which may be discovered therein and which are not referred to in the preceding paragraphs of this Article, other than stocks of unmarked explosives held by its authorities performing military or police functions and incorporated as an integral part of duly authorized military devices at the date of the entry into force of this Convention in respect of that State.

5. Each State Party shall take the necessary measures to exercise strict and effective control over the possession and transfer of possession of the explosives referred to in paragraph II of Part 1 of the Technical Annex to this Convention so as to prevent their diversion or use for purposes inconsistent with the objectives of this Convention.

6. Each State Party shall take the necessary measures to ensure the destruction, as soon as possible, in its territory of unmarked explosives manufactured since the coming into force of this Convention in respect of that State that are not incorporated as specified in paragraph II d) of Part 1 of the Technical Annex to this Convention and of unmarked explosives which no longer fall within the scope of any other sub-paragraphs of the said paragraph II.

Article V

1. There is established by this Convention an International Explosives Technical Commission (hereinafter referred to as "the Commission") consisting of not less than fifteen nor more than nineteen members appointed by the Council of the International Civil Aviation Organization (hereinafter referred to as "the Council") from among persons nominated by States Parties to this Convention.

2. The members of the Commission shall be experts having direct and substantial experience in matters relating to the manufacture or detection of, or research in, explosives.

3. Members of the Commission shall serve for a period of three years and shall be eligible for re-appointment.

4. Sessions of the Commission shall be convened, at least once a year at the Headquarters of the International Civil Aviation Organization, or at such places and times as may be directed or approved by the Council.

5. The Commission shall adopt its rules of procedure, subject to the approval of the Council.

Article VI

1. The Commission shall evaluate technical developments relating to the manufacture, marking and detection of explosives.

2. The Commission, through the Council, shall report its findings to the States Parties and international organizations concerned.

3. Whenever necessary, the Commission shall make recommendations to the Council for amendments to the Technical Annex to this Convention. The Commission shall endeavour to take its decisions on such recommendations by consensus. In the absence of consensus the Commission shall take such decisions by a two-thirds majority vote of its members.

4. The Council may, on the recommendation of the Commission, propose to States Parties amendments to the Technical Annex to this Convention.

Article VII

1. Any State Party may, within ninety days from the date of notification of a proposed amendment to the Technical Annex to this Convention, transmit to the Council its comments. The Council shall communicate these comments to the Commission as soon as possible for its consideration. The Council shall invite any State Party which comments on or objects to the proposed amendment to consult the Commission.

2. The Commission shall consider the views of States Parties made pursuant to the preceding paragraph and report to the Council. The Council, after consideration of the Commission's report, and taking into account the nature of the amendment and the comments of States Parties, including producer States, may propose the amendment to all States Parties for adoption.

3. If a proposed amendment has not been objected to by five or more States Parties by means of written notification to the Council within ninety days from the date of notification of the amendment by the Council, it shall be deemed to have been adopted, and shall enter into force one hundred and eighty days thereafter or after such other period as specified in the proposed amendment for States Parties not having expressly objected thereto.

4. States Parties having expressly objected to the proposed amendment may, subsequently, by means of the deposit of an instrument of acceptance or approval, express their consent to be bound by the provisions of the amendment.

5. If five or more States Parties have objected to the proposed amendment, the Council shall refer it to the Commission for further consideration.

6. If the proposed amendment has not been adopted in accordance with paragraph 3 of this Article, the Council may also convene a conference of all States Parties.

Article VIII

1. States Parties shall, if possible, transmit to the Council information that would assist the Commission in the discharge of its functions under paragraph 1 of Article VI.

2. States Parties shall keep the Council informed of measures they have taken to implement the provisions of this Convention. The Council shall communicate such information to all States Parties and international organizations concerned.

Article IX

The Council shall, in co-operation with States Parties and international organizations concerned, take appropriate measures to facilitate the implementation of this Convention, including the provision of technical assistance and measures for the exchange of information relating to technical developments in the marking and detection of explosives.

Article X

The Technical Annex to this Convention shall form an integral part of this Convention.

Article XI

1. Any dispute between two or more States Parties concerning the interpretation or application of this Convention which cannot be settled through negotiation shall, at the request of one of them, be submitted to arbitration. If within six months from the date of the request for arbitration the Parties are unable to agree on the organization of the arbitration, any one of those Parties may refer the dispute to the International Court of Justice by request in conformity with the Statute of the Court.

2. Each State Party may, at the time of signature, ratification, acceptance or approval of this Convention or accession thereto, declare that it does not consider itself bound by the preceding paragraph. The other States Parties shall not be bound by the preceding paragraph with respect to any State Party having made such a reservation.

3. Any State Party having made a reservation in accordance with the preceding paragraph may at any time withdraw this reservation by notification to the Depositary.

Article XII

Except as provided in Article XI no reservation may be made to this Convention.

Article XIII

1. This Convention shall be open for signature in Montreal on 1 March 1991 by States participating in the International Conference on Air Law held at Montreal from 12 February to 1 March 1991. After 1 March 1991 the Convention shall be open to all States for signature at the Headquarters of the International Civil Aviation Organization in Montreal until it enters into force in accordance with

paragraph 3 of this Article. Any State which does not sign this Convention may accede to it at any time.

2. This Convention shall be subject to ratification, acceptance, approval or accession by States. Instruments of ratification, acceptance, approval or accession shall be deposited with the International Civil Aviation Organization, which is hereby designated the Depositary. When depositing its instrument of ratification, acceptance, approval or accession, each State shall declare whether or not it is a producer State.

3. This Convention shall enter into force on the sixtieth day following the date of deposit of the thirty-fifth instrument of ratification, acceptance, approval or accession with the Depositary, provided that no fewer than five such States have declared pursuant to paragraph 2 of this Article that they are producer States. Should thirty-five such instruments be deposited prior to the deposit of their instruments by five producer States, this Convention shall enter into force on the sixtieth day following the date of deposit of the instrument of ratification, acceptance, approval or accession of the fifth producer State.

4. For other States, this Convention shall enter into force sixty days following the date of deposit of their instruments of ratification, acceptance, approval or accession.

5. As soon as this Convention comes into force, it shall be registered by the Depositary pursuant to Article 102 of the Charter of the United Nations and pursuant to Article 83 of the Convention on International Civil Aviation (Chicago, 1944).

Article XIV

The Depositary shall promptly notify all signatories and States Parties of:

1. each signature of this Convention and date thereof;
2. each deposit of an instrument of ratification, acceptance, approval or accession and date thereof, giving special reference to whether the State has identified itself as a producer State;
3. the date of entry into force of this Convention;
4. the date of entry into force of any amendment to this Convention or its Technical Annex;
5. any denunciation made under Article XV; and
6. any declaration made under paragraph 2 of Article XI.

Article XV

1. Any State Party may denounce this Convention by written notification to the Depositary.

2. Denunciation shall take effect one hundred and eighty days following the date on which notification is received by the Depositary.

IN WITNESS WHEREOF the undersigned Plenipotentiaries, being duly authorized thereto by their Governments, have signed this Convention.

DONE at Montreal, this first day of March, one thousand nine hundred and ninety-one, in one original, drawn up in five authentic texts in the English, French, Russian, Spanish and Arabic languages.

TECHNICAL ANNEX

PART 1: DESCRIPTION OF EXPLOSIVES

I. The explosives referred to in paragraph 1 of Article I of this Convention are those that:

(a) are formulated with one or more high explosives which in their pure form have a vapour pressure less than 10^{-4} Pa at a temperature of 25°C;
(b) are formulated with a binder material; and
(c) are, as a mixture, malleable or flexible at normal room temperature.

II. The following explosives, even though meeting the description of explosives in paragraph I of this Part, shall not be considered to be explosives as long as they continue to be held or used for the purposes specified below or remain incorporated as there specified, namely those explosives that:

(a) are manufactured, or held, in limited quantities solely for use in duly authorized research, development or testing of new or modified explosives;
(b) are manufactured, or held, in limited quantities solely for use in duly authorized training in explosives detection and/or development or testing of explosives detection equipment;
(c) are manufactured, or held, in limited quantities solely for duly authorized forensic science purposes; or
(d) are destined to be and are incorporated as an integral part of duly authorized military devices in the territory of the producer State within three years after the coming into force of this Convention in respect of that State. Such devices produced in this period of three years shall be deemed to be duly authorized military devices within paragraph 4 of Article IV of this Convention.

III. In this Part:

"duly authorized" in paragraph II a), b) and c) means permitted according to the laws and regulations of the State Party concerned; and

"High explosives" include but are not restricted to cyclotetramethylene-tetranitramine (HMX), pentraerythritol tetranitrate (PETN) and cyclotri-methylenetrinitramine (RDX).

PART 2: DETECTION AGENTS

A detection agent is any one of those substances set out in the following Table. Detection agents described in this Table are intended to be used to enhance the detectability of explosives by vapour detection means. In each case, the introduction of a detection agent into an explosive shall be done in such a manner as to achieve homogeneous distribution in the finished product. The minimum concentration of a detection agent in the finished product at the time of manufacture shall be shown in the said Table.

Table

Name of detection agent	*Molecular formula*	*Molecular weight*	*Minimum concentration*
Ethylene glycol dinitrate (EGDN)	$C_2H_4(NO_3)_2$	152	0.2% by mass
2,3-Dimethyl-2,3-dinitrobutane (DMNB)	$C_6H_{12}(NO_2)_2$	176	0.1% by mass
para-Mononitrotoluene (p-MNT)	$C_7H_7NO_2$	137	0.5% by mass
ortho-Mononitrotoluene (o-MNT)	$C_7H_7NO_2$	137	0.5% by mass

Any explosive which, as a result of its normal formulation, contains any of the designated detection agents at or above the required minimum concentration level shall be deemed to be marked.

Appendix 13

ICAO Annex 17 – Security (Safeguarding International Civil Aviation against Acts of Unlawful Interference)

TABLE OF CONTENTS

ATTACHMENT TO ANNEX 17

FOREWORD

Historical background

The material included in this Annex was developed by the Council pursuant to the following two resolutions of the Assembly:

Resolution A1710: Implementation by States of Security Specifications and Practices adopted by this Assembly and further work by ICAO related to such Specifications and Practices

. . . . . .

THE ASSEMBLY:

. . . . . .

(3) REQUESTS the Council, with the assistance of the other constituent bodies of the Organization, to develop and incorporate, as appropriate, the material in the Appendices to this Resolution as Standards, Recommended Practices and Procedures in existing or new Annexes or other regulatory documents or guidance material of the Organization.

Resolution A1810: Additional Technical Measures
for the Protection of the Security of
International Civil Air Transport

. . . . . .

THE ASSEMBLY:

(1) REQUESTS the Council to ensure, with respect to the technical aspects of air transportation security, that:

(a) the subject of air transportation security continues to be given adequate attention by the Secretary General, with a priority commensurate with the current threat to the security of air transportation;

. . . . . .

Following the work of the Air Navigation Commission, the Air Transport Committee and the Committee on Unlawful Interference, and as a result of the comments received from Contracting States and interested International Organizations, to whom draft material had been circulated, Standards and Recommended Practices on Security were adopted by the Council on 22 March 1974, pursuant to the provisions of Article 37 of the Convention on International Civil Aviation, and designated as Annex 17 to the Convention with the title "Standards and Recommended Practices — *Security* — Safeguarding International Civil Aviation against Acts of Unlawful Interference".

Table A shows the origin of subsequent amendments together with a list of the principal subjects involved and the dates on which the Annex and the amendments were adopted by the Council, when they became effective and when they became applicable.

Introduction

In order that a comprehensive document may be available to States for implementation of the security measures prescribed by this Annex, an Attachment hereto reproduces extracts from other Annexes, *Technical Instructions for the Safe Transport of Dangerous Goods by Air* (Doc 9284), PANSATM and PANS-OPS bearing on the subject of action to be taken by States to prevent unlawful interference with civil aviation, or when such interference has been committed.

Guidance material

The *Security Manual for Safeguarding Civil Aviation Against Acts of Unlawful Interference* (Doc 8973 — Restricted) provides detailed procedures and guidance on aspects of aviation security and is intended to assist States in the implementation of their respective national civil aviation security programmes required by the specifications in the Annexes to the Convention on International Civil Aviation.

Action by Contracting States

Applicability. The provisions of the Standards and Recommended Practices in this document are to be applied by Contracting States.

Notification of differences. The attention of Contracting States is drawn to the obligation imposed by Article 38 of the Convention, by which Contracting States are required to notify the Organization of any differences between their national regulations and practices and the International Standards contained in this Annex and any amendments thereto. Contracting States are invited to keep the Organization currently informed of any differences which may subsequently occur, or of the withdrawal of any difference previously notified. A specific request for notification of differences will be sent to Contracting States immediately after the adoption of each amendment to this Annex.

Contracting States are also invited to extend such notification to any differences from the Recommended Practices contained in this Annex, and any amendment thereto, when the notification of such differences is important for the safety of air navigation.

Attention of States is also drawn to the provisions of Annex 15 related to the publication of differences between their national regulations and practices and the related ICAO Standards and Recommended Practices through the Aeronautical Information Service, in addition to the obligation of States under Article 38 of the Convention.

Promulgation of information. Information relating to the establishment and withdrawal of and changes to facilities, services and procedures affecting aircraft operations provided according to the Standards and Recommended Practices specified in this Annex should be notified and take effect in accordance with Annex 15.

Use of the text of the Annex in national regulations. The Council, on 13 April 1948, adopted a resolution inviting the attention of Contracting States to the desirability of using in their own national regulations, as far as practicable, the precise language of those ICAO Standards that are of a regulatory character and also of indicating departures from the Standards, including any additional national regulations that were import-ant for the safety or regularity of air navigation. Wherever possible, the provisions of this Annex have been written in such a way as would facilitate incorporation, without major textual changes, into national legislation.

General information

An Annex is made up of the following component parts, not all of which, however, are necessarily found in every Annex; they have the status indicated:

1. — *Material comprising the Annex proper:*
   a) *Standards* and *Recommended Practices* adopted by the Council under the provisions of the Convention. They are defined as follows:
   Standard: Any specification for physical characteristics, configuration, matériel, performance, personnel or procedure, the uniform application of which is recognized as necessary for the safety or regularity of international air navigation and to which Contracting States will conform in accordance with the Convention; in the event of impossibility of compliance, notification to the Council is compulsory under Article 38 of the Convention.
   Recommended Practice: Any specification for physical characteristics, configuration, matériel, performance, personnel or procedure, the uniform application of which is recognized as desirable in the interests of safety, regularity or efficiency of international air navigation, and to which Contracting States will endeavour to conform in accordance with the Convention.
   b) *Appendices* comprising material grouped separately for convenience but forming part of the Standards and Recommended Practices adopted by the Council.
   c) *Definitions* of terms used in the Standards and Recommended Practices which are not self-explanatory in that they do not have accepted dictionary meanings. A definition does not have an independent status but is an essential part of each Standard and Recommended Practice in which the term is used, since a change in the meaning of the term would affect the specification.
2. — *Material approved by the Council for publication in association with the Standards and Recommended Practices:*
   a) *Forewords* comprising historical and explanatory material based on the action of the Council and including an explanation of the obligations of States with regard to the application of the Standards and Recommended Practices ensuing from the Convention and the Resolution of Adoption.
   b) *Introductions* comprising explanatory material introduced at the beginning of parts, chapters or sections of the Annex to assist in the understanding of the application of the text.
   c) *Notes* included in the text, where appropriate, to give factual information or references bearing on the Standards or Recommended Practices in question, but not constituting part of the Standards or Recommended Practices.
   d) *Attachments* comprising material supplementary to the Standards and Recommended Practices, or included as a guide to their application.

Table A. Amendments to Annex 17

Amendment	*Source(s)*	*Subject(s)*	*Adopted* *Effective* *Applicable*
1st Edition	Council action in pursuance of Assembly Resolutions A17-10 and A18-10	—	22 March 1974 22 August 1974 27 February 1975
1	Council action in pursuance of Assembly Resolution A21-23	Change in status of 3.1.2 and 5.1.2 to a Standard; compilation and dissemination of information related to an aircraft being subjected to an act of unlawful interference.	31 March 1976 31 July 1976 30 December 1976
2	Proposals of some States and Council action in pursuance of Assembly Resolution A22-17	Transfer of specifications appearing in Chapter 9 of Annex 9 — *Facilitation* (Seventh Edition) to Annex 17; new provision in Chapter 5 concerning measures to be taken to control transfer and transit passengers and their cabin baggage; and amplification of the note to 5.2.4 (Annex 17, Chapter 5) on measures and procedures to prevent unauthorized access to specified areas on an aerodrome.	15 December 1977 15 April 1978 10 August 1978
3	Proposals of some States and the Secretariat and Council action in pursuance of Assembly Resolution A22-17	Specifications were added on the review of the level of threat by States, the development of training programmes, the isolation of security	13 December 1978 13 April 1979 29 November 1979

		processed passengers, the inspection of aircraft for concealed weapons or other dangerous devices and the adoption of measures for the safety of passengers and crew of unlawfully diverted aircraft. A number of specifications were amplified and the status of one was changed to a Standard, related to the segregation and special guarding of aircraft liable to attack during stopovers.	
4 (2nd Edition)	Proposals of some States and an international organization and Council action in pursuance of Assembly Resolution A22-17	A specification was added on the transportation of persons in custody, and two specifications revised to provide for aircraft which were leased, chartered or interchanged. The status of a specification dealing with the safety of passengers and crew of an aircraft subjected to an act of unlawful interference was changed to a Standard; the provisions of a specification dealing with the prevention of sabotage were amplified and Chapter 1 — Applicability, deleted.	15 June 1981 15 October 1981 26 November 1981
5	Proposals of the Committee on Unlawful Interference and Council action in pursuance of Assembly Resolution A22-17	The note to Chapter 1 — Definitions was deleted. A specification setting out the action required for the transportation of weapons on board aircraft by law enforcement and other	30 November 1984 14 April 1985 21 November 1985

Table A. (Cont'd)

Amendment	*Source(s)*	*Subject(s)*	*Adopted Effective Applicable*
		duly authorized persons was modified. A specification on the carriage of weapons in all other cases was added and the note to a specification dealing with the safeguarding of unattended aircraft was clarified.	
6 (3rd Edition)	Proposals of the Committee on Unlawful Interference with the assistance of an Ad Hoc Group of Experts — Unlawful Interference and Council action in pursuance of Assembly Resolution A22-17	On the instruction of the Council this amendment was undertaken as a matter of urgency by the Committee on Unlawful Interference with the assistance of an Ad Hoc Group of Experts on aviation security which had been appointed on the instruction of the Council. As a consequence 11 new specifications were introduced into the Annex and 19 specifications were adopted as Standards.	19 December 1985 19 March 1986 19 May 1986
		Special effective and applicable dates for 5.1.4 are shown in the adjacent column. The Council recommended that those States that are able to implement the substance of 5.1.4 do so as soon as it is feasible and practicable before the applicable date.	19 October 1987 19 December 1987

7 (4th Edition)	Proposals of the Committee on Unlawful Interference with the assistance of the Aviation Security Panel and Council action in pursuance of Assembly Resolution A26-7	This amendment includes: a) a reorganization of the chapters of the Annex directed at a rationalization of the sequence of objectives, obligations and necessary actions relating to organization, preventive security measures and management of response; b) the introduction of important new provisions to reflect developments and assist States in confronting new situations which arose from grave acts of unlawful interference against civil aviation, since the last revision of Annex 17 in 1985; and c) the amendment or fine tuning of existing provisions consequential to a) and b), as well as to reflect the experience gained in the implementation of such measures.	22 June 1989 30 October 1989 16 November 1989
8 (5th Edition)	Proposals of the Committee on Unlawful Interference with the assistance of the Aviation Security Panel (AVSECP) and Council action in pursuance of Assembly Resolution A27-7	This amendment includes the introduction of important new provisions in relation to the comprehensive security screening of checked baggage, security control over cargo, courier and express parcels and mail, variations to procedures relating to security programmes, pre-flight checks of international aircraft, and measures relating to the incorporation of security consideration into airport	11 September 1992 16 December 1992 1 April 1993

Table A. (Cont'd)

Amendment	*Source(s)*	*Subject(s)*	*Adopted* *Effective* *Applicable*
		design for the purpose of assisting States in the consistent and uniform implementation of such measures.	
9 (6th Edition)	Proposals of the Committee on Unlawful Interference with the assistance of the Aviation Security Panel (AVSECP) and Council action in pursuance of Assembly Resolution A31-4	This amendment includes the introduction of new provisions in relation to the pre-employment checks and capabilities of persons engaged in implementing security controls, baggage accountability and authorization, measures to be applied to catering supplies and operators' stores and supplies, tests for programme effectiveness, and need for notification to the State of known or presumed destination of aircraft under a seized condition.	12 November 1996 31 March 1997 1 August 1997
10 (7th Edition)	Proposals of the Aviation Security Panel (AVSECP) and Council action in pursuance of Assembly Resolution A33-1	This amendment includes the introduction of various definitions and new provisions in relation to the applicability of this Annex to domestic operations, international cooperation relating to threat information, appropriate authority, National Aviation Security Committee, national quality control, access control,	7 December 2001 15 April 2002 1 July 2002

		passengers and their cabin and hold baggage, in-flight security personnel and protection of the cockpit, code-sharing/collaborative arrangements, Human Factors and management of response to acts of unlawful interference. The status of a number of specifications was changed to Standards.	
11 (8th Edition)	Proposals of the Committee on Unlawful Interference with the assistance of the Aviation Security Panel (AVSECP) and Council action in pursuance of Assembly Resolution A35-9	This amendment includes provisions to further clarify the wording of existing Standards and Recommended Practices (SARPs) to facilitate both their common interpretation by Contracting States and their ease of auditing under the ICAO Universal Security Audit Programme (USAP). The amendment addresses the following: applicability of Annex 17; reinforcement of national civil aviation security control programme provisions; in-flight security officers (IFSOs); general aviation and aerial work; one-stop security concept for passengers and baggage; risk assessment concept; security for all-cargo operations; and definitions.	30 November 2005 10 April 2006 1 July 2006

This Annex has been adopted in six languages — English, Arabic, Chinese, French, Russian and Spanish. Each Contracting State is requested to select one of those texts for the purpose of national implementation and for other effects provided for in the Convention, either through direct use or through translation into its own national language, and to notify the Organization accordingly.

The following practice has been adhered to in order to indicate at a glance the status of each statement: *Standards* have been printed in light face roman; *Recommended Practices* have been printed in light face italics, the status being indicated by the prefix **Recommendation**; *Notes* have been printed in light face italics, the status being indicated by the prefix *Note*.

Any reference to a portion of this document which is identified by a number includes all subdivisions of that portion.

CHAPTER 1. DEFINITIONS

Acts of unlawful interference. These are acts or attempted acts such as to jeopardize the safety of civil aviation and air transport, i.e.:

- unlawful seizure of aircraft in flight,
- unlawful seizure of aircraft on the ground,
- hostage-taking on board aircraft or on aerodromes,
- forcible intrusion on board an aircraft, at an airport or on the premises of an aeronautical facility,
- introduction on board an aircraft or at an airport of a weapon or hazardous device or material intended for criminal purposes,
- communication of false information such as to jeopardize the safety of an aircraft in flight or on the ground, of passengers, crew, ground personnel or the general public, at an airport or on the premises of a civil aviation facility.

Aerial work. An aircraft operation in which an aircraft is used for specialized services such as agriculture, construction, photography, surveying observation and patrol, search and rescue, aerial advertisement, etc.

Aircraft security check. An inspection of the interior of an aircraft to which passengers may have had access and an inspection of the hold for the purposes of discovering suspicious objects, weapons, explosives or other dangerous devices, articles and substances.

Aircraft security search. A thorough inspection of the interior and exterior of the aircraft for the purpose of discovering suspicious objects, weapons, explosives or other dangerous devices, articles or substances.

Airside. The movement area of an airport, adjacent terrain and buildings or portions thereof, access to which is controlled.

Background check. A check of a person's identity and previous experience, including where legally permissible, any criminal history, as part of the assessment of an individual's suitability to implement a security control and/or for unescorted access to a security restricted area.

Cargo. Any property carried on an aircraft other than mail, stores and accompanied or mishandled baggage.

Certification. A formal evaluation and confirmation by or on behalf of the appropriate authority for aviation security that a person possesses the necessary competencies to perform assigned functions to an acceptable level as defined by the appropriate authority.

Commercial air transport operation. An aircraft operation involving the transport of passengers, cargo or mail for remuneration or hire.

Corporate aviation. The non-commercial operation or use of aircraft by a company for the carriage of passengers or goods as an aid to the conduct of company business, flown by a professional pilot employed to fly the aircraft. (Note that corporate aviation is a subset of general aviation.)

Disruptive passenger. A passenger who fails to respect the rules of conduct at an airport or on board an aircraft or to follow the instructions of the airport staff or crew members and thereby disturbs the good order and discipline at an airport or on board the aircraft.

General aviation operation. An aircraft operation other than a commercial air transport operation or an aerial work operation.

Human Factors principles. Principles which apply to design, certification, training, operations and maintenance and which seek safe interface between the human and other system components by proper consideration to human performance.

Human performance. Human capabilities and limitations which have an impact on the safety, security and efficiency of aeronautical operations.

Regulated agent. An agent, freight forwarder or any other entity who conducts business with an operator and provides security controls that are accepted or required by the appropriate authority in respect of cargo or mail.

Screening. The application of technical or other means which are intended to identify and/or detect weapons, explosives or other dangerous devices, articles or substances which may be used to commit an act of unlawful interference.

Note. — Certain dangerous articles or substances are classified as dangerous goods by Annex 18 and the associated Technical Instructions for the Safe Transport of Dangerous Goods by Air *(Doc 9284) and must be transported in accordance with those instructions. In addition, the* Security Manual for Safeguarding Civil Aviation Against Acts of Unlawful Interference *(Doc 8973 — Restricted) provides a list of prohibited items that must never be carried in the cabin of an aircraft.*

Security. Safeguarding civil aviation against acts of unlawful interference. This objective is achieved by a combination of measures and human and material resources.

Security audit. An in-depth compliance examination of all aspects of the implementation of the national civil aviation security programme.

Security control. A means by which the introduction of weapons, explosives or other dangerous devices, articles or substances which may be used to commit an act of unlawful interference can be prevented.

Security inspection. An examination of the implementation of relevant national civil aviation security programme requirements by an airline, airport, or other entity involved in security.

Security restricted area. Those areas of the airside of an airport which are identified as priority risk areas where in addition to access control, other security controls are applied. Such areas will normally include, *inter alia,* all commercial aviation passenger departure areas between the screening checkpoint and the aircraft, the ramp, baggage make-up areas, including those where aircraft are being brought into service and screened baggage and cargo are present, cargo sheds, mail centres, airside catering and aircraft cleaning premises.

Security survey. An evaluation of security needs including the identification of vulnerabilities which could be exploited to carry out an act of unlawful interference, and the recommendation of corrective actions.

Security test. A covert or overt trial of an aviation security measure which simulates an attempt to commit an unlawful act.

Unidentified baggage. Baggage at an airport, with or without a baggage tag, which is not picked up by or identified with a passenger.

CHAPTER 2. GENERAL PRINCIPLES

2.1 Objectives

2.1.1 Each Contracting State shall have as its primary objective the safety of passengers, crew, ground personnel and the general public in all matters related to safeguarding against acts of unlawful interference with civil aviation.

2.1.2 Each Contracting State shall establish an organization and develop and implement regulations, practices and procedures to safeguard civil aviation against acts of unlawful interference taking into account the safety, regularity and efficiency of flights.

2.1.3 Each Contracting State shall ensure that such an organization and such regulations, practices and procedures:

a) protect the safety of passengers, crew, ground personnel and the general public in all matters related to safeguarding against acts of unlawful interference with civil aviation; and
b) are capable of responding rapidly to meet any increased security threat.

2.1.4 **Recommendation. —** *Each Contracting State should ensure appropriate protection of aviation security information.*

Note 1. — Guidance material on achieving civil aviation security objectives through application of the Standards and Recommended Practices in the following chapters is to be found in the Security Manual for Safeguarding Civil Aviation Against Acts of Unlawful Interference *(Doc 8973 — Restricted).*

Note 2. — The comprehensive aviation security training material to assist States in achieving civil aviation security objectives is contained in the ICAO Training Programme for Aviation Security comprising a series of Aviation Security Training Packages (ASTPs).

2.2 Applicability

2.2.1 Each Contracting State shall apply the Standards and shall endeavour to apply the Recommended Practices contained in Annex 17 to international civil aviation operations.

2.2.2 Each Contracting State shall ensure that measures designed to safeguard against acts of unlawful interference are applied to domestic operations to the extent practicable, based upon a security risk assessment carried out by the relevant national authorities.

2.3 Security and facilitation

Recommendation. — *Each Contracting State should whenever possible arrange for the security controls and procedures to cause a minimum of interference with, or delay to the activities of, civil aviation provided the effectiveness of these controls and procedures is not compromised.*

2.4 International cooperation

2.4.1 Each Contracting State shall ensure that requests from other Contracting States for additional security measures in respect of a specific flight(s) by operators of such other States are met, as far as may be practicable. The requesting State shall give consideration to alternative measures of the other State that are equivalent to those requested.

2.4.2 Each Contracting State shall cooperate with other States in the development and exchange of information concerning national civil aviation security programmes, training programmes and quality control programmes, as necessary.

2.4.3 Each Contracting State shall establish and implement procedures to share with other Contracting States threat information that applies to the aviation security interests of those States, to the extent practicable.

2.4.4 Each Contracting State shall establish and implement suitable protection and handling procedures for security information shared by other Contracting States, or security information that affects the security interests of other Contracting States, in order to ensure that inappropriate use or disclosure of such information is avoided.

2.4.5 **Recommendation.** — *Each Contracting State should share, as appropriate, and consistent with its sovereignty, the results of the audit carried out by ICAO and the corrective actions taken by the audited State if requested by another State.*

2.4.6 **Recommendation.** — *Each Contracting State should include in each of its bilateral agreements on air transport a clause related to aviation security, taking into account the model clause developed by ICAO.*

2.4.7 **Recommendation.** — *Each Contracting State should make available to other Contracting States on request a written version of the appropriate parts of its national civil aviation security programme.*

2.4.8 **Recommendation.** — *Each Contracting State should notify ICAO where it has shared information under 2.4.5.*

2.5 Equipment, research and development

2.5.1 **Recommendation.** — *Each Contracting State should promote research and development of new security equipment, processes and procedures which will better achieve civil aviation security objectives and should cooperate with other Contracting States in this matter.*

2.5.2 **Recommendation.** — *Each Contracting State should ensure that the development of new security equipment takes into consideration Human Factors principles.*

Note. — Guidance material regarding Human Factors principles can be found in the manual on Human Factors in Civil Aviation Security Operations *(Doc 9808) and in Part 1, Chapter 4, of the* Human Factors Training Manual *(Doc 9683).*

CHAPTER 3. ORGANIZATION

3.1 National organization and appropriate authority

3.1.1 Each Contracting State shall establish and implement a written national civil aviation security programme to safeguard civil aviation operations against acts of unlawful interference, through regulations, practices and procedures which take into account the safety, regularity and efficiency of flights.

3.1.2 Each Contracting State shall designate and specify to ICAO an appropriate authority within its administration to be responsible for the development, implementation and maintenance of the national civil aviation security programme.

3.1.3 Each Contracting State shall keep under constant review the level of threat to civil aviation within its territory, and establish and implement policies and procedures to adjust relevant elements of its national civil aviation security programme accordingly, based upon a security risk assessment carried out by the relevant national authorities.

Note. — Guidance material regarding threat assessment and risk management methodologies can be found in the Security Manual for Safeguarding Civil Aviation Against Acts of Unlawful Interference *(Doc 8973 — Restricted).*

3.1.4 Each Contracting State shall require the appropriate authority to define and allocate tasks and coordinate activities between the departments, agencies and other organizations of the State, airport and aircraft operators and other entities concerned with or responsible for the implementation of various aspects of the national civil aviation security programme.

3.1.5 Each Contracting State shall establish a national aviation security committee or similar arrangements for the purpose of coordinating security activities between the departments, agencies and other organizations of the State, airport and aircraft operators and other entities concerned with or responsible for the implementation of various aspects of the national civil aviation security programme.

3.1.6 Each Contracting State shall require the appropriate authority to ensure the development and implementation of a national training programme for personnel of all entities involved with or responsible for the implementation of various aspects of the national civil aviation security programme. This training programme shall be designed to ensure the effectiveness of the national civil aviation security programme.

3.1.7 **Recommendation.** — *Each Contracting State should ensure that trainers and training programmes meet standards defined by the appropriate authority.*

3.1.8 Each Contracting State shall ensure that the appropriate authority arranges for the supporting resources and facilities required by the aviation security services to be available at each airport serving civil aviation.

3.1.9 Each Contracting State shall make available to its airport and aircraft operators operating in its territory and other entities concerned, a written version of the appropriate parts of its national civil aviation security programme and/or relevant information or guidelines enabling them to meet the requirements of the national civil aviation security programme.

3.2 Airport operations

3.2.1 Each Contracting State shall require each airport serving civil aviation to establish, implement and maintain a written airport security programme appropriate to meet the requirements of the national civil aviation security programme.

3.2.2 Each Contracting State shall ensure that an authority at each airport serving civil aviation is responsible for coordinating the implementation of security controls.

3.2.3 Each Contracting State shall ensure that an airport security committee at each airport serving civil aviation is established to assist the authority mentioned under 3.2.2 in its role of coordinating the implementation of security controls and procedures as specified in the airport security programme.

3.2.4 Each Contracting State shall ensure that airport design requirements, including architectural and infrastructure-related requirements necessary for the implementation of the security measures in the national civil aviation security programme, are integrated into the design and construction of new facilities and alterations to existing facilities at airports.

3.3 Aircraft operators

3.3.1 Each Contracting State shall ensure that commercial air transport operators providing service from that State have established, implemented and maintained a written operator security programme that meets the requirements of the national civil aviation security programme of that State.

3.3.2 **Recommendation**. — *Each Contracting State should ensure that each entity conducting general aviation operations, including corporate aviation operations, using aircraft with a maximum take-off mass greater than 5 700 kg, has established, implemented and maintained a written operator security programme that meets the requirements of the national civil aviation security programme of that State.*

3.3.3 **Recommendation**. — *Each Contracting State should ensure that each entity conducting aerial work operations has established, implemented and maintained a written operator security programme that meets the requirements of the national civil aviation security programme of that State. The programme shall contain operations features specific to the type of operations conducted.*

3.3.4 **Recommendation.** — *Each Contracting State should take into account the ICAO model as a basis for operators' or entities' security programmes under 3.3.1, 3.3.2 and 3.3.3.*

3.3.5 **Recommendation.** — *Each Contracting State should require operators providing service from that State and participating in code-sharing or other collaborative arrangements with other operators to notify the appropriate authority of the nature of these arrangements, including the identity of the other operators.*

3.4 Quality control

3.4.1 Each Contracting State shall ensure that the persons implementing security controls are subject to background checks and selection procedures.

3.4.2 Each Contracting State shall ensure that the persons implementing security controls possess all competencies required to perform their duties and are appropriately trained according to the requirements of the national civil aviation security programme and that appropriate records are maintained up to date. Relevant standards of performance shall be established and initial and periodic assessments shall be introduced to maintain those standards.

3.4.3 Each Contracting State shall ensure that the persons carrying out screening operations are certified according to the requirements of the national civil aviation security programme to ensure that performance standards are consistently and reliably achieved.

3.4.4 Each Contracting State shall require the appropriate authority to develop, implement and maintain a national civil aviation security quality control programme to determine compliance with and validate the effectiveness of its national civil aviation security programme.

3.4.5 Each Contracting State shall ensure that the implementation of security measures is regularly subjected to verification of compliance with the national civil aviation security programme. The priorities and frequency of monitoring shall be determined on the basis of risk assessment carried out by the relevant authorities.

3.4.6 Each Contracting State shall arrange for security audits, tests, surveys and inspections to be conducted on a regular basis, to verify compliance with the national civil aviation security programme and to provide for the rapid and effective rectification of any deficiencies.

3.4.7 Each Contracting State shall ensure that the management, setting of priorities and organization of the national civil aviation security quality control programme shall be undertaken independently from the entities and persons responsible for the implementation of the measures taken under the national civil aviation security programme. Each Contracting State shall also:

a) ensure that the personnel carrying out security audits, tests, surveys and inspections are trained to appropriate standards for these tasks in accordance with the national civil aviation security programme;
b) ensure that the personnel carrying out security audits, tests, surveys and inspections are afforded the necessary authority to obtain information to carry out these tasks and to enforce corrective actions;
c) supplement the national civil aviation security quality control programme by establishing a confidential reporting system for analysing security information provided by sources such as passengers, crew and ground personnel; and
d) establish a process to record and analyse the results of the national civil aviation security quality control programme, to contribute to the effective development and implementation of the national civil aviation security programme, including identifying the causes and patterns of non-compliance and verifying that corrective actions have been implemented and sustained.

3.4.8 Each Contracting State concerned with an act of unlawful interference shall require its appropriate authority to re-evaluate security controls and procedures and in a timely fashion take action necessary to remedy weaknesses so as to prevent recurrence. These actions shall be shared with ICAO.

CHAPTER 4. PREVENTIVE SECURITY MEASURES

4.1 Objective

Each Contracting State shall establish measures to prevent weapons, explosives or any other dangerous devices, articles or substances, which may be used to commit an act of unlawful interference, the carriage or bearing of which is not authorized, from being introduced, by any means whatsoever, on board an aircraft engaged in civil aviation.

4.2 Measures relating to access control

4.2.1 Each Contracting State shall ensure that the access to airside areas at airports serving civil aviation is controlled in order to prevent unauthorized entry.

4.2.2 Each Contracting State shall ensure that security restricted areas are established at each airport serving civil aviation designated by the State based upon a security risk assessment carried out by the relevant national authorities.

4.2.3 Each Contracting State shall ensure that identification systems are established in respect of persons and vehicles in order to prevent unauthorized access to airside areas and security restricted areas. Identity shall be verified at designated checkpoints before access is allowed to airside areas and security restricted areas.

4.2.4 Each Contracting State shall ensure that background checks are conducted on persons other than passengers granted unescorted access to security restricted areas of the airport prior to granting access to security restricted areas.

4.2.5 Each Contracting State shall ensure that the movement of persons and vehicles to and from the aircraft is supervised in security restricted areas in order to prevent unauthorized access to aircraft.

4.2.6 Each Contracting State shall ensure that, at a minimum, a proportion of persons other than passengers being granted access to security restricted areas, together with items carried, are screened. The proportion shall be determined in accordance with risk assessment carried out by the relevant national authorities.

4.2.7 **Recommendation.** — *Each Contracting State should ensure that identity documents issued to aircraft crew members provide a harmonized and reliable international basis for recognition and validation of documentation to permit authorized access to airside and security restricted areas by conforming to the relevant specifications set forth in Doc 9303,* Machine Readable Travel Documents.

4.2.8 **Recommendation.** — *Each Contracting State should ensure that checks specified in 4.2.4 be reapplied on a regular basis to all persons granted unescorted access to security restricted areas.*

4.3 Measures relating to aircraft

4.3.1 Each Contracting State shall ensure that aircraft security checks of originating aircraft engaged in commercial air transport movements are performed or an aircraft security search is carried out. The determination of whether it is an aircraft security check or a search that is appropriate shall be based upon a security risk assessment carried out by the relevant national authorities.

4.3.2 Each Contracting State shall ensure that measures are taken to ensure that passengers of commercial flights disembarking from the aircraft at any time do not leave items on board the aircraft.

4.3.3 Each Contracting State shall require its commercial air transport operators to take measures as appropriate to ensure that during flight unauthorized persons are prevented from entering the flight crew compartment.

Note. — Provisions for security of the flight crew compartment of aircraft engaged in commercial air transportation are contained in Annex 6, Part I, Chapter 13, Section 13.2.

4.3.4 Each Contracting State shall ensure that an aircraft subject to 4.3.1 is protected from unauthorized interference from the time the aircraft search or check has commenced until the aircraft departs.

4.3.5 **Recommendation. —** *Each Contracting State should ensure that security controls are established to prevent acts of unlawful interference with aircraft when they are not in security restricted areas.*

4.4 Measures relating to passengers and their cabin baggage

4.4.1 Each Contracting State shall establish measures to ensure that originating passengers of commercial air transport operations and their cabin baggage are screened prior to boarding an aircraft departing from a security restricted area.

4.4.2 Each Contracting State shall ensure that transfer passengers of commercial air transport operations and their cabin baggage are screened prior to boarding an aircraft, unless it has established a validation process and continuously implements procedures, in collaboration with the other Contracting State where appropriate, to ensure that such passengers and their cabin baggage have been screened to an appropriate level at the point of origin and subsequently protected from unauthorized interference from the point of screening at the originating airport to the departing aircraft at the transfer airport.

Note. — See guidance material on this issue in the Security Manual for Safeguarding Civil Aviation Against Acts of Unlawful Interference *(Doc 8973 — Restricted).*

4.4.3 Each Contracting State shall ensure that passengers and their cabin baggage which have been screened are protected from unauthorized interference from the point of screening until they board their aircraft. If mixing or contact does take place, the passengers concerned and their cabin baggage shall be rescreened before boarding an aircraft.

4.4.4 Each Contracting State shall establish at an airport measures for transit operations to protect transit passengers' cabin baggage from unauthorized interference and protect the integrity of the security of the airport of transit.

4.5 Measures relating to hold baggage

4.5.1 Each Contracting State shall establish measures to ensure that originating hold baggage is screened prior to being loaded onto an aircraft engaged in commercial air transport operations departing from a security restricted area.

4.5.2 Each Contracting State shall ensure that all hold baggage to be carried on a commercial aircraft is protected from unauthorized interference from the point it is screened or accepted into the care of the carrier, whichever is earlier, until departure of the aircraft on which it is to be carried. If the integrity of hold baggage is jeopardized, the hold baggage shall be re-screened before being placed on board an aircraft.

4.5.3 Each Contracting State shall ensure that commercial air transport operators do not transport the baggage of passengers who are not on board the aircraft unless that baggage is identified as unaccompanied and subjected to additional screening.

4.5.4 Each Contracting State shall ensure that transfer hold baggage is screened prior to being loaded onto an aircraft engaged in commercial air transport operations, unless it has established a validation process and continuously implements procedures, in collaboration with the other Contracting State where appropriate, to ensure that such hold baggage has been screened at the point of origin and subsequently protected from unauthorized interference from the originating airport to the departing aircraft at the transfer airport.

Note. — See guidance material on this issue in the Security Manual for Safeguarding Civil Aviation Against Acts of Unlawful Interference *(Doc 8973 — Restricted).*

4.5.5 Each Contracting State shall ensure that aircraft commercial air transport operators transport only items of hold baggage which have been individually identified as accompanied or unaccompanied, screened to the appropriate standard and accepted for carriage on that flight by the air carrier. All such baggage should be recorded as meeting these criteria and authorized for carriage on that flight.

4.5.6 **Recommendation.** — *Each Contracting State should establish procedures to deal with unidentified baggage in accordance with a security risk assessment carried out by the relevant national authorities.*

4.6 Measures relating to cargo, mail and other goods

4.6.1 Each Contracting State shall ensure that security controls are applied to cargo and mail, prior to their being loaded onto an aircraft engaged in passenger commercial air transport operations.

4.6.2 Each Contracting State shall ensure that cargo and mail to be carried on a passenger commercial aircraft are protected from unauthorized interference from the point security controls are applied until departure of the aircraft.

4.6.3 Each Contracting State shall establish a process for approval of regulated agents, if such agents are involved in implementing security controls.

4.6.4 Each Contracting State shall ensure that operators do not accept cargo or mail for carriage on an aircraft engaged in passenger commercial air transport operations unless the application of security controls is confirmed and accounted for by a regulated agent, or such consignments are subjected to appropriate security controls.

4.6.5 Each Contracting State shall ensure that catering, stores and supplies intended for carriage on passenger commercial flights are subjected to appropriate security controls and thereafter protected until loaded onto the aircraft.

4.6.6 **Recommendation. —** *Each Contracting State should ensure that security controls to be applied to cargo and mail for transportation on all-cargo aircraft are determined on the basis of a security risk assessment carried out by the relevant national authorities.*

4.7 Measures relating to special categories of passengers

4.7.1 Each Contracting State shall develop requirements for air carriers for the carriage of potentially disruptive passengers who are obliged to travel because they have been the subject of judicial or administrative proceedings.

Note. — See guidance material on this issue found in the Security Manual for Safeguarding Civil Aviation Against Acts of Unlawful Interference *(Doc 8973 — Restricted).*

4.7.2 Each Contracting State shall ensure that operators providing service from that State include in their security programmes, measures and procedures to ensure safety on board their aircraft when passengers are to be carried who are obliged to travel because they have been the subject of judicial or administrative proceedings.

4.7.3 Each Contracting State shall ensure that the aircraft operator and the pilot-in-command are informed when passengers are obliged to travel because they have been the subject of judicial or administrative proceedings, in order that appropriate security controls can be applied.

4.7.4 Each Contracting State shall ensure that the carriage of weapons on board aircraft, by law enforcement officers and other authorized persons, acting in the performance of their duties, requires special authorization in accordance with the laws of the States involved.

4.7.5 Each Contracting State shall consider requests by any other State to allow the travel of armed personnel, including in-flight security officers, on board aircraft of operators of the requesting State. Only after agreement by all States involved shall such travel be allowed.

4.7.6 Each Contracting State shall ensure that the carriage of weapons in other cases is allowed only when an authorized and duly qualified person has determined that they are not loaded, if applicable, and then only if stowed in a place inaccessible to any person during flight time.

4.7.7 Each Contracting State that decides to deploy in- flight security officers shall ensure that they are government personnel who are specially selected and trained, taking into account the safety and security aspects on board an aircraft and deployed according to the threat assessment of the competent authority. The deployment of such officers shall be coordinated with concerned States and kept strictly confidential.

4.7.8 Each Contracting State shall ensure that the pilot-in-command is notified as to the number of armed persons and their seat location.

CHAPTER 5. MANAGEMENT OF RESPONSE TO ACTS OF UNLAWFUL INTERFERENCE

5.1 Prevention

5.1.1 Each Contracting State shall establish measures, when reliable information exists that an aircraft may be subjected to an act of unlawful interference, to safeguard the aircraft if it is still on the ground and to provide as much prior notification as possible of the arrival of such aircraft to relevant airport authorities and air traffic services of the States concerned if the aircraft has already departed.

5.1.2 Each Contracting State shall ensure, when reliable information exists that an aircraft may be subjected to an act of unlawful interference, that the aircraft is searched for concealed weapons, explosives or other dangerous devices, articles or substances. Prior notification of the search shall be provided to the operator concerned.

5.1.3 Each Contracting State shall ensure that arrangements are made to investigate, render safe and/or dispose of, if necessary, suspected dangerous devices or other potential hazards at airports.

5.1.4 Each Contracting State shall ensure that contingency plans are developed and resources made available to safeguard civil aviation against acts of unlawful interference. The contingency plans shall be tested on a regular basis.

5.1.5 Each Contracting State shall ensure that authorized and suitably trained personnel are readily available for deployment at its airports serving civil aviation to assist in dealing with suspected, or actual, cases of unlawful interference with civil aviation.

5.2 Response

5.2.1 Each Contracting State shall take appropriate measures for the safety of passengers and crew of an aircraft, which is subjected to an act of unlawful interference, while on the ground in the territory of the Contracting State, until their journey can be continued.

5.2.2 Each Contracting State responsible for providing air traffic services for an aircraft, which is the subject of an act of unlawful interference, shall collect all pertinent information on the flight of that aircraft and transmit that information to all other States responsible for the air traffic services units concerned, including those at the airport of known or presumed destination, so that timely and appropriate safeguarding action may be taken en route and at the aircraft's known, likely or possible destination.

5.2.3 Each Contracting State shall provide assistance to an aircraft subjected to an act of unlawful seizure, including the provision of navigation aids, air traffic services and per-mission to land as may be necessitated by the circumstances.

5.2.4 Each Contracting State shall take measures, as it may find practicable, to ensure that an aircraft subjected to an act of unlawful seizure which has landed in its territory is detained on the ground unless its departure is necessitated by the overriding duty to protect human life. However, these measures need to recognize the grave hazard attending further flight. States shall also recognize the importance of consultations, wherever practicable, between the State where that aircraft has landed and the State of the Operator of the aircraft, and notification by the State where the aircraft has landed to the States of assumed or stated destination.

5.2.5 Each Contracting State in which an aircraft subjected to an act of unlawful interference has landed shall notify by the most expeditious means the State of Registry of the aircraft and the State of the Operator of the landing and shall similarly transmit by the most expeditious means all other relevant information to:

a) the two abovementioned States;
b) each State whose citizens suffered fatalities or injuries;
c) each State whose citizens were detained as hostages;
d) each State whose citizens are known to be on board the aircraft; and
e) the International Civil Aviation Organization.

5.2.6 **Recommendation.** — *Each Contracting State should ensure that information received as a consequence of action taken in accordance with 5.2.2 is distributed locally to the air traffic services units concerned, the appropriate airport administrations, the operator and others concerned as soon as practicable.*

5.2.7 **Recommendation.** — *Each Contracting State should cooperate with other States for the purpose of providing a joint response in connection with an act of unlawful interference. When taking measures in their territory to free passengers and crew members of an aircraft subjected to an act of unlawful interference, each Contracting State should use, as necessary, the experience and capability of the State of the Operator, the State of manufacture and the State of Registry of that aircraft.*

5.3 Exchange of information and reporting

5.3.1 Each Contracting State concerned with an act of unlawful interference shall provide ICAO with all pertinent information concerning the security aspects of the act of unlawful interference as soon as practicable after the act is resolved.

5.3.2 **Recommendation.** — *Each Contracting State should exchange information with other Contracting States as considered appropriate on the management of response to an act of unlawful interference, at the same time supplying such information to ICAO.*

ATTACHMENT TO ANNEX 17

EXTRACTS FROM *ANNEX 2 — RULES OF THE AIR*

CHAPTER 3. GENERAL RULES

. . . . . .

3.7 Unlawful interference

An aircraft which is being subjected to unlawful interference shall endeavour to notify the appropriate ATS unit of this fact, any significant circumstances associated therewith and any deviation from the current flight plan necessitated by the circumstances, in order to enable the ATS unit to give priority to the aircraft and to minimize conflict with other aircraft.

Note 1. — Responsibility of ATS units in situations of unlawful interference is contained in Annex 11.

Note 2. — Guidance material for use when unlawful interference occurs and the aircraft is unable to notify an ATS unit of this fact is contained in Attachment B to this Annex.

Note 3. — Action to be taken by SSR-equipped aircraft which are being subjected to unlawful interference is contained in Annex 11, the PANS-ATM (Doc 4444) and the PANS-OPS (Doc 8168).

Note 4. — Action to be taken by CPDLC-equipped aircraft which are being subjected to unlawful interference is contained in Annex 11, the PANS-ATM (Doc 4444), and guidance material on the subject is contained in the Manual of Air Traffic Services Data Link Applications *(Doc 9694).*

. . . . . .

ATTACHMENT B. UNLAWFUL INTERFERENCE

1. General

The following procedures are intended as guidance for use by aircraft when unlawful interference occurs and the aircraft is unable to notify an ATS unit of this fact.

2. Procedures

2.1 Unless considerations aboard the aircraft dictate otherwise, the pilot-in-command should attempt to continue flying on the assigned track and at the assigned cruising level at least until able to notify an ATS unit or within radar coverage.

2.2 When an aircraft subjected to an act of unlawful interference must depart from its assigned track or its assigned cruising level without being able to make radiotelephony contact with ATS, the pilot-in-command should, whenever possible:

a) attempt to broadcast warnings on the VHF emergency frequency and other appropriate frequencies, unless considerations aboard the aircraft dictate otherwise. Other equipment such as on-board transponders and data links should also be used when it is advantageous to do so and circumstances permit; and
b) proceed in accordance with applicable special procedures for in-flight contingencies, where such procedures have been established and promulgated in the *Regional Supplementary Procedures (*Doc 7030); or
c) if no applicable regional procedures have been established, proceed at a level which differs from the cruising levels normally used for IFR flight by:
    1) 150 m (500 ft) in an area where a vertical separation minimum of 300 m (1 000 ft) is applied; or

2) 300 m (1 000 ft) in an area where a vertical separation minimum of 600 m (2 000 ft) is applied.

Note. — Action to be taken by an aircraft which is intercepted while being subject to an act of unlawful interference is prescribed in 3.8 of this Annex.

EXTRACTS FROM *ANNEX 6 — OPERATION OF AIRCRAFT* PART I — *INTERNATIONAL COMMERCIAL AIR TRANSPORT — AEROPLANES*

CHAPTER 13. SECURITY*

13.1 Domestic commercial operations

Recommendation. — *International Standards and Recommended Practices set forth in this Chapter should be applied by all Contracting States also in case of domestic commercial operations (air services).*

13.2 Security of the flight crew compartment

13.2.1 In all aeroplanes which are equipped with a flight crew compartment door, this door shall be capable of being locked, and means shall be provided by which cabin crew can discreetly notify the flight crew in the event of suspicious activity or security breaches in the cabin.

13.2.2 From 1 November 2003, all passenger-carrying aeroplanes of a maximum certificated takeoff mass in excess of 45 500 kg or with a passenger seating capacity greater than 60 shall be equipped with an approved flight crew compartment door that is designed to resist penetration by small arms fire and grenade shrapnel, and to resist forcible intrusions by unauthorized persons. This door shall be capable of being locked and unlocked from either pilot's station.

13.2.3 In all aeroplanes which are equipped with a flight crew compartment door in accordance with 13.2.2:

a) this door shall be closed and locked from the time all external doors are closed following embarkation until any such door is opened for disembarkation, except when necessary to permit access and egress by authorized persons; and
b) means shall be provided for monitoring from either pilot's station the entire door area outside the flight crew compartment to identify persons requesting entry and to detect suspicious behaviour or potential threat.

13.2.4 **Recommendation.** — *All passenger-carrying aeroplanes should be equipped with an approved flight crew compartment door, where practicable, that is designed to resist penetration by small arms fire and grenade shrapnel, and to resist forcible intrusions by unauthorized persons. This door should be capable of being locked and unlocked from either pilot's station.*

---

* In the context of this Chapter, the word "security" is used in the sense of prevention of illicit acts against civil aviation.

13.2.5 **Recommendation.** — *In all aeroplanes which are equipped with a flight crew compartment door in accordance with 13.2.4:*

a) *the door should be closed and locked from the time all external doors are closed following embarkation until any such door is opened for disembarkation, except when necessary to permit access and egress by authorized persons; and*
b) *means should be provided for monitoring from either pilot's station the entire door area outside the flight crew compartment to identify persons requesting entry and to detect suspicious behaviour or potential threat.*

13.3 Aeroplane search procedure checklist

An operator shall ensure that there is on board a checklist of the procedures to be followed in searching for a bomb in case of suspected sabotage and for inspecting aeroplanes for concealed weapons, explosives or other dangerous devices when a well-founded suspicion exists that the aeroplane may be the object of an act of unlawful interference. The checklist shall be supported by guidance on the appropriate course of action to be taken should a bomb or suspicious object be found and information on the least-risk bomb location specific to the aeroplane.

13.4 Training programmes

13.4.1 An operator shall establish and maintain an approved security training programme which ensures crew members act in the most appropriate manner to minimize the consequences of acts of unlawful interference. As a minimum, this programme shall include the following elements:

a) determination of the seriousness of any occurrence;
b) crew communication and coordination;
c) appropriate self-defense responses;
d) use of non-lethal protective devices assigned to crew members whose use is authorized by the State of the Operator;
e) understanding of behaviour of terrorists so as to facilitate the ability of crew members to cope with hijacker behaviour and passenger responses;
f) live situational training exercises regarding various threat conditions;
g) flight deck procedures to protect the aeroplane; and
h) aeroplane search procedures and guidance on least-risk bomb locations where practicable.

13.4.2 An operator shall also establish and maintain a training programme to acquaint appropriate employees with preventive measures and techniques in relation to passengers, baggage, cargo, mail, equipment, stores and supplies intended for carriage on an aeroplane so that they contribute to the prevention of acts of sabotage or other forms of unlawful interference.

13.5 Reporting acts of unlawful interference

Following an act of unlawful interference, the pilot-in-command shall submit, without delay, a report of such an act to the designated local authority.

13.6 Miscellaneous

13.6.1 **Recommendation. —** *Specialized means of attenuating and directing the blast should be provided for use at the least-risk bomb location.*

13.6.2 **Recommendation. —** *Where an operator accepts the carriage of weapons removed from passengers, the aeroplane should have provision for stowing such weapons in a place so that they are inaccessible to any person during flight time.*

EXTRACTS FROM *ANNEX 8 — AIRWORTHINESS OF AIRCRAFT*

CHAPTER 11. SECURITY

11.1 Aeroplanes used for domestic commercial operations

Recommendation. — *International Standards and Recommended Practices set forth in this chapter should be applied by all Contracting States for aeroplanes engaged in domestic commercial operations (air services).*

11.2 Least-risk bomb location

For aeroplanes of a maximum certificated take-off mass in excess of 45 500 kg or with a passenger seating capacity greater than 60 and for which the application for certification was submitted on or after 12 March 2000, consideration shall be given during the design of the aeroplane to the provision of a least-risk bomb location so as to minimize the effects of a bomb on the aeroplane and its occupants.

11.3 Protection of the flight crew compartment

Recommendation. — *In all aeroplanes, which are required by Annex 6, Part I, Chapter 13 to have an approved flight crew compartment door, and for which an application for amending the Type Certificate to include a derivative type design is submitted to the appropriate national authority, consideration should be given to reinforcing the flight crew compartment bulkheads, floors and ceilings so as to resist penetration by small arms fire and grenade shrapnel and to resist forcible intrusions, if these areas are accessible in flight to passengers and cabin crew.*

Note. — Standards and Recommended Practices concerning the requirements for the flight crew compartment door in all commercial passenger-carrying aeroplanes are contained in Annex 6, Part I, Chapter 13.

11.4 Interior design

For aeroplanes of a maximum certificated take-off mass in excess of 45 500 kg or with a passenger seating capacity greater than 60 and for which the application for certification was submitted on or after 12 March 2000, consideration shall be given to design features that will deter the easy concealment of weapons, explosives or other dangerous objects on board aircraft and that will facilitate search procedures for such objects.

EXTRACTS FROM *ANNEX 9 — FACILITATION*

CHAPTER 2. ENTRY AND DEPARTURE OF AIRCRAFT

A. General

. . . . . .

2.2 In developing procedures aimed at the efficient clearance of entering or departing aircraft, Contracting States shall take into account the application of aviation security and narcotics control measures, where appropriate.

. . . . . .

CHAPTER 3. ENTRY AND DEPARTURE OF PERSONS AND THEIR BAGGAGE

A. General

. . . . . .

3.2 In developing procedures aimed at the efficient application of border controls on passengers and crew, Contracting States shall take into account the application of aviation security, border integrity, narcotics control and immigration control measures, where appropriate.

. . . . . .

3.4 Contracting States shall not extend the validity of their machine readable travel documents.

Note 1. — Specifications for machine readable travel documents (Doc 9303, Series) do not permit alteration of the expiration date and other data in the machine readable zone.

Note 2. — States whose national legislation or regulations currently allow for the extension of the period of validity should undertake to amend the appropriate text in a reasonable period.

. . . . . .

C. Security of travel documents

. . . . . .

3.7 Contracting States shall regularly update security features in new versions of their travel documents, to guard against their misuse and to facilitate detection of cases where such documents have been unlawfully altered, replicated or issued.

3.8 Contracting States shall establish controls on the creation and issuance of travel documents in order to safeguard against the theft of their stocks and the misappropriation of newly issued travel documents.

3.9 **Recommended Practice.** — *Contracting States should incorporate biometric data in their machine readable passports, visas and other official travel documents, using one or more optional data storage technologies to supplement the machine readable zone, as specified in Doc 9303,* Machine Readable Travel

Documents. *The required data stored on the integrated circuit chip is the same as that printed on the data page, that is, the data contained in the machine-readable zone plus the digitized photographic image. Fingerprint image(s) and/or iris image(s) are optional biometrics for Contracting States wishing to supplement the facial image with another biometric in the passport. Contracting States incorporating biometric data in their Machine Readable Passports are to store the data in a contactless integrated circuit chip complying with ISO/IEC 14443 and programmed according to the Logical Data Structure as specified by ICAO.*

D. Travel documents

3.10 Contracting States shall begin issuing only Machine Readable Passports in accordance with the specifications of Doc 9303, Part 1, no later than 1 April 2010.

Note. — This provision does not intend to preclude the issuance of non-machine readable passports or temporary travel documents of limited validity in cases of emergency.

3.10.1 For passports issued after 24 November 2005 and which are not machine readable, Contracting States shall ensure the expiration date falls before 24 November 2015.

. . . . . .

I. Inspection of travel documents

3.31 Contracting States shall assist aircraft operators in the evaluation of travel documents presented by passengers, in order to deter fraud and abuse.

. . . . . .

3.33 Aircraft operators shall take necessary precautions at the point of embarkation to ensure that passengers are in possession of the documents prescribed by the States of transit and destination for control purposes as described in this chapter.

. . . . . .

K. Entry procedures and responsibilities

. . . . . .

3.46 The public authorities of each Contracting State shall seize fraudulent, falsified or counterfeit travel documents. The public authorities shall also seize the travel documents of a person impersonating the rightful holder of the travel document. Such documents shall be removed from circulation immediately and returned to the appropriate authorities of the State named as issuer or to the resident Diplomatic Mission of that State.

3.47 **Recommended Practice.** — *Where appropriate, Contracting States should introduce a system of advance passenger information which involves the capture of certain passport or visa details prior to departure, the transmission of the details by electronic means to their public authorities, and the analysis of such data for risk management purposes prior to arrival in order to expedite clearance. To minimize handling time during check-in, document reading devices should be used to capture the information in machine readable travel documents.*

. . . . . .

N. Identification and entry of crew and other aircraft operators' personnel

. . . . . .

3.70 Adequate controls shall be placed on the issuance of CMCs and other official crew identity documents to prevent fraud, for example, a background check and certification of employment status of an applicant prior to issuance, controls on blank card stock, and accountability requirements for issuing personnel.

. . . . . .

CHAPTER 4. ENTRY AND DEPARTURE OF CARGO AND OTHER ARTICLES

A. General

. . . . . .

4.6 Where practicable, in order to improve efficiency, modern screening or examination techniques shall be used to facilitate the physical examination of goods to be imported or exported.

. . . . . .

CHAPTER 5. INADMISSIBLE PERSONS AND DEPORTEES

. . . . . .

B. Inadmissible persons

. . . . . .

5.8 Contracting States that have reason to believe that an inadmissible person might offer resistance to his removal shall inform the aircraft operator concerned as far in advance as possible of scheduled departure so that the aircraft operator can take precautions to ensure the security of the flight.

. . . . . .

C. Deportees

. . . . . .

5.18 Contracting States removing deportees from their territories shall assume all obligations, responsibilities and costs associated with the removal.

EXTRACTS FROM *ANNEX 10 — AERONAUTICAL TELECOMMUNICATIONS*, VOLUME IV *(SURVEILLANCE RADAR AND COLLISION AVOIDANCE SYSTEMS)*

CHAPTER 2. GENERAL

. . . . . .

2.1 SECONDARY SURVEILLANCE RADAR (SSR)

. . . . . .

2.1.4 Mode A reply codes (information pulses)

. . . . . .

2.1.4.2.1 Code 7700 to provide recognition of an aircraft in an emergency.

. . . . . .

2.1.4.2.3 Code 7500 to provide recognition of an aircraft which is being subjected to unlawful interference.

2.1.4.3 Appropriate provisions shall be made in ground decoding equipment to ensure immediate recognition of Mode A codes 7500, 7600 and 7700.

EXTRACTS FROM *ANNEX 11 — AIR TRAFFIC SERVICES*

CHAPTER 2. GENERAL

. . . . . .

2.22 Service to aircraft in the event of an emergency

2.22.1 An aircraft known or believed to be in a state of emergency, including being subjected to unlawful interference, shall be given maximum consideration, assistance and priority over other aircraft as may be necessitated by the circumstances.

Note. — To indicate that it is in a state of emergency, an aircraft equipped with an appropriate data link capability and/or an SSR transponder might operate the equipment as follows:

a) *on Mode A, Code 7700; or*
b) *on Mode A, Code 7500, to indicate specifically that it is being subjected to unlawful interference; or*
c) *activate the appropriate emergency and/or urgency capability of ADS; or*
d) *transmit the appropriate emergency message via CPDLC.*

. . . . . .

2.22.2 When an occurrence of unlawful interference with an aircraft takes place or is suspected, ATS units shall attend promptly to requests by the aircraft. Information pertinent to the safe conduct of the flight shall continue to be transmitted and necessary action shall be taken to expedite the conduct of all phases of the flight, especially the safe landing of the aircraft.

. . . . . .

CHAPTER 5. ALERTING SERVICE

5.1 Application

5.1.1 Alerting service shall be provided:

. . . . . .

c) to any aircraft known or believed to be the subject of unlawful interference.

. . . . . .

5.2 Notification of rescue coordination centres

5.2.1 Without prejudice to any other circumstances that may render such notification advisable, air traffic services units shall, except as prescribed in 5.5.1, notify rescue coordination centres immediately an aircraft is considered to be in a state of emergency in accordance with the following:

. . . . . .

b) *Alert phase* when:

. . . . . .

except when evidence exists that would allay apprehension as to the safety of the aircraft and its occupants, or when

4) an aircraft is known or believed to be the subject of unlawful interference.

. . . . . .

5.5 Information to the operator

5.5.1 When an area control or a flight information centre decides that an aircraft is in the uncertainty or the alert phase, it shall, when practicable, advise the operator prior to notifying the rescue coordination centre.

Note. — If an aircraft is in the distress phase, the rescue coordination centre has to be notified immediately in accordance with 5.2.1.

5.5.2 All information notified to the rescue coordination centre by an area control or flight information centre shall, whenever practicable, also be communicated, without delay, to the operator.

5.6 Information to aircraft operating in the vicinity of an aircraft in a state of emergency

5.6.1 When it has been established by an air traffic services unit that an aircraft is in a state of emergency, other aircraft known to be in the vicinity of the aircraft involved shall, except as provided in 5.6.2, be informed of the nature of the emergency as soon as practicable.

5.6.2 When an air traffic services unit knows or believes that an aircraft is being subjected to unlawful interference, no reference shall be made in ATS air-ground communications to the nature of the emergency unless it has first been referred to in communications from the aircraft involved and it is certain that such reference will not aggravate the situation.

EXTRACTS FROM *ANNEX 13 — AIRCRAFT ACCIDENT AND INCIDENT INVESTIGATION*

CHAPTER 5. INVESTIGATION

. . . . . .

ORGANIZATION AND CONDUCT OF THE INVESTIGATION

. . . . . .

RESPONSIBILITY OF THE STATE CONDUCTING THE INVESTIGATION

. . . . . .

Informing aviation security authorities

5.11 If, in the course of an investigation it becomes known, or it is suspected, that an act of unlawful interference was involved, the investigator-in-charge shall immediately initiate action to ensure that the aviation security authorities of the State(s) concerned are so informed.

EXTRACTS FROM *ANNEX 14 — AERODROMES,* VOLUME I — *AERODROME DESIGN AND OPERATIONS*

CHAPTER 3. PHYSICAL CHARACTERISTICS

. . . . . .

3.14 Isolated aircraft parking position

3.14.1 An isolated aircraft parking position shall be designated or the aerodrome control tower shall be advised of an area or areas suitable for the parking of an aircraft which is known or believed to be the subject of unlawful interference, or which for other reasons needs isolation from normal aerodrome activities.

3.14.2 **Recommendation.** — *The isolated aircraft parking position should be located at the maximum distance practicable and in any case never less than 100 m from other parking positions, buildings or public areas, etc. Care should be taken to ensure that the position is not located over underground utilities such as gas and aviation fuel and, to the extent feasible, electrical or communication cables.*

. . . . . .

CHAPTER 5. VISUAL AIDS FOR NAVIGATION

. . . . . .

5.3 Lights

. . . . . .

5.3.23 Apron floodlighting *(see also 5.3.16.1 and 5.3.17.1)*

Application

5.3.23.1 **Recommendation.** — *Apron floodlighting should be provided on an apron, on a de-icing/anti-icing facility and on a designated isolated aircraft parking position intended to be used at night.*

Note 1. — Where a de-icing/anti-icing facility is located in close proximity to the runway and permanent floodlighting could be confusing to pilots, other means of illumination of the facility may be required.

Note 2. — The designation of an isolated aircraft parking position is specified in 3.14.

Note 3. — Guidance on apron floodlighting is given in the Aerodrome Design Manual, *Part 4.*

. . . . . .

CHAPTER 8. ELECTRICAL SYSTEMS

8.1 Electric power supply systems for air navigation facilities

. . . . . .

Application

. . . . . .

8.1.10 **Recommendation.** — *The following aerodrome facilities should be provided with a secondary power supply capable of supplying power when there is a failure of the primary power supply:*

. . . . . .

e) essential security lighting, if provided in accordance with 9.11;

. . . . . .

CHAPTER 9. AERODROME OPERATIONAL SERVICES, EQUIPMENT AND INSTALLATIONS

9.1 Aerodrome emergency planning

General

Introductory Note. — Aerodrome emergency planning is the process of preparing an aerodrome to cope with an emergency occurring at the aerodrome or in its vicinity. The objective of aerodrome emergency planning is to minimize the effects of an emergency, particularly in respect of saving lives and maintaining aircraft operations. The aerodrome emergency plan sets forth the procedures for coordinating the response of different aerodrome agencies (or services) and of those agencies in the surrounding community that could be of assistance in responding to the emergency. Guidance material to assist the appropriate authority in establishing aerodrome emergency planning is given in the Airport Services Manual, *Part 7.*

9.1.1 An aerodrome emergency plan shall be established at an aerodrome, commensurate with the aircraft operations and other activities conducted at the aerodrome.

9.1.2 The aerodrome emergency plan shall provide for the coordination of the actions to be taken in an emergency occurring at an aerodrome or in its vicinity.

Note. — Examples of emergencies are: aircraft emergencies, sabotage including bomb threats, unlawfully seized aircraft, dangerous goods occurrences, building fires and natural disasters.

9.1.3 The plan shall coordinate the response or participation of all existing agencies which, in the opinion of the appropriate authority, could be of assistance in responding to an emergency.

Note. — Examples of agencies are:

- *— on the aerodrome: air traffic control unit, rescue and fire fighting services, aerodrome administration, medical and ambulance services, aircraft operators, security services, and police;*
- *— off the aerodrome: fire departments, police, medical and ambulance services, hospitals, military, and harbour patrol or coast guard.*

9.1.4 **Recommendation.** — *The plan should provide for cooperation and coordination with the rescue coordination centre, as necessary.*

9.1.5 **Recommendation.** — *The aerodrome emergency plan document should include at least the following:*

a) *types of emergencies planned for;*
b) *agencies involved in the plan;*
c) *responsibility and role of each agency, the emergency operations centre and the command post, for each type of emergency;*
d) *information on names and telephone numbers of offices or people to be contacted in the case of a particular emergency; and*
e) *a grid map of the aerodrome and its immediate vicinity.*

. . . . . .

Emergency operations centre and command post

9.1.7 **Recommendation.** — *A fixed emergency operations centre and a mobile command post should be available for use during an emergency.*

9.1.8 **Recommendation.** — *The emergency operations centre should be a part of the aerodrome facilities and should be responsible for the overall coordination and general direction of the response to an emergency.*

9.1.9 **Recommendation.** — *The command post should be a facility capable of being moved rapidly to the site of an emergency, when required, and should undertake the local coordination of those agencies responding to the emergency.*

9.1.10 **Recommendation.** — *A person should be assigned to assume control of the emergency operations centre and, when appropriate, another person the command post.*

Communication system

9.1.11 **Recommendation.** — *Adequate communication systems linking the command post and the emergency operations centre with each other and with the participating agencies should be provided in accordance with the plan and consistent with the particular requirements of the aerodrome.*

Aerodrome emergency exercise

9.1.12 The plan shall contain procedures for periodic testing of the adequacy of the plan and for reviewing the results in order to improve its effectiveness.

Note. — The plan includes all participating agencies and associated equipment.

9.1.13 The plan shall be tested by conducting:

a) a full-scale aerodrome emergency exercise at intervals not exceeding two years; and
b) partial emergency exercises in the intervening year to ensure that any deficiencies found during the full-scale aerodrome emergency exercise have been corrected; and

reviewed thereafter, or after an actual emergency, so as to correct any deficiency found during such exercises or actual emergency.

Note. — The purpose of a full-scale exercise is to ensure the adequacy of the plan to cope with different types of emergencies. The purpose of a partial exercise is to ensure the adequacy of the response to individual participating agencies and components of the plan, such as the communications system.

. . . . . .

9.10 Fencing

Application

. . . . . .

9.10.3 **Recommendation.** — *A fence or other suitable barrier should be provided on an aerodrome to deter the inadvertent or premeditated access of an unauthorized person onto a non-public area of the aerodrome.*

Note 1. — This is intended to include the barring of sewers, ducts, tunnels, etc., where necessary to prevent access.

Note 2. — Special measures may be required to prevent the access of an unauthorized person to runways or taxiways which overpass public roads.

. . . . . .

9.10.5 **Recommendation.** — *Suitable means of protection should be provided to deter the inadvertent or premeditated access of unauthorized persons into ground installations and facilities essential for the safety of civil aviation located off the aerodrome.*

. . . . . .

Location

9.10.7 **Recommendation.** — *The fence or barrier should be located so as to separate the movement area and other facilities or zones on the aerodrome vital to the safe operation of aircraft from areas open to public access.*

. . . . . .

9.10.9 **Recommendation. —** *When greater security is thought necessary, a cleared area should be provided on both sides of the fence or barrier to facilitate the work of patrols and to make trespassing more difficult. Consideration should be given to the provision of a perimeter road inside the aerodrome fencing for the use of both maintenance personnel and security patrols.*

9.11 Security lighting

Recommendation. — *At an aerodrome where it is deemed desirable for security reasons, a fence or other barrier provided for the protection of international civil aviation and its facilities should be illuminated at a minimum essential level. Consideration should be given to locating lights so that the ground area on both sides of the fence or barrier, particularly at access points, is illuminated.*

EXTRACTS FROM *ANNEX 18 — THE SAFE TRANSPORT OF DANGEROUS GOODS BY AIR*

CHAPTER 2. APPLICABILITY

. . . . . .

2.2 Dangerous Goods Technical Instructions

2.2.1 Each Contracting State shall take the necessary measures to achieve compliance with the detailed provisions contained in the *Technical Instructions for the Safe Transport of Dangerous Goods by Air* (Doc 9284), approved and issued periodically in accordance with the procedure established by the ICAO Council. Each Contracting State shall also take the necessary measures to achieve compliance with any amendment to the Technical Instructions which may be published during the specified period of applicability of an edition of the Technical Instructions.

2.2.2 **Recommendation. —** *Each Contracting State should inform ICAO of difficulties encountered in the application of the Technical Instructions and of any amendments which it would be desirable to make to them.*

. . . . . .

CHAPTER 10. ESTABLISHMENT OF TRAINING PROGRAMMES

Dangerous goods training programmes shall be established and updated as provided for in the Technical Instructions.

EXTRACTS FROM DOC 9284 — *TECHNICAL INSTRUCTIONS FOR THE SAFE TRANSPORT OF DANGEROUS GOODS BY AIR*

Part 1. GENERAL

. . . . . .

CHAPTER 4 TRAINING

Parts of this Chapter are affected by State Variations AE 2, CA 18, HK 1, US 1; see Table A1

4.1 ESTABLISHMENT OF TRAINING PROGRAMMES

≠ 4.1.1 Initial and recurrent dangerous goods training programmes must be established and maintained by or on behalf of:

. . . . . .

g) agencies engaged in the security screening of passengers and their baggage and/or cargo.

EXTRACTS FROM THE PROCEDURES FOR AIR NAVIGATION SERVICES — *AIR TRAFFIC MANAGEMENT* (DOC 4444)

CHAPTER 5. SEPARATION METHODS AND MINIMA

. . . . . .

5.2 GENERAL PROVISIONS FOR THE SEPARATION OF CONTROLLED TRAFFIC

. . . . . .

5.2.1.2 Larger separations than the specified minima should be applied whenever exceptional circumstances such as unlawful interference or navigational difficulties call for extra precautions. This should be done with due regard to all relevant factors so as to avoid impeding the flow of air traffic by the application of excessive separations.

Note. — Unlawful interference with an aircraft constitutes a case of exceptional circumstances which might require the application of separations larger than the specified minima, between the aircraft being subjected to unlawful interference and other aircraft.

. . . . . .

CHAPTER 15. PROCEDURES RELATED TO EMERGENCIES, COMMUNICATION FAILURE AND CONTINGENCIES

15.1 EMERGENCY PROCEDURES

15.1.1 General

15.1.1.1 The various circumstances surrounding each emergency situation preclude the establishment of exact detailed procedures to be followed. The procedures outlined herein are intended as a general guide to air traffic services personnel. Air traffic control units shall maintain full and complete coordination, and personnel shall use their best judgement in handling emergency situations.

Note 1. — Additional radar procedures to be applied in relation to emergencies and contingencies are contained in Chapter 8, 8.8.1.

Note 2. — If the pilot of an aircraft encountering a state of emergency has previously been directed by ATC to operate the transponder on a specific code, that code will normally be maintained unless, in special circumstances, the pilot has decided or has been advised otherwise. Where ATC has not requested a code to be set, the pilot will set the transponder to Mode A Code 7700.

15.1.1.2 When an emergency is declared by an aircraft, the ATS unit should take appropriate and relevant action as follows:

a) unless clearly stated by the flight crew or otherwise known, take all necessary steps to ascertain aircraft identification and type, the type of emergency, the intentions of the flight crew as well as the position and level of the aircraft;
b) decide upon the most appropriate type of assistance which can be rendered;
c) enlist the aid of any other ATS unit or other services which may be able to provide assistance to the aircraft;
d) provide the flight crew with any information requested as well as any additional relevant information, such as details on suitable aerodromes, minimum safe altitudes, weather information;
e) obtain from the operator or the flight crew such of the following information as may be relevant: number of persons on board, amount of fuel remaining, possible presence of hazardous materials and the nature thereof; and
f) notify the appropriate ATS units and authorities as specified in local instructions.

15.1.1.3 Changes of radio frequency and SSR code should be avoided if possible and should normally be made only when or if an improved service can be provided to the aircraft concerned. Manoeuvring instructions to an aircraft experiencing engine failure should be limited to a minimum. When appropriate, other aircraft operating in the vicinity of the aircraft in emergency should be advised of the circumstances.

Note. — Requests to the flight crew for the information contained in 15.1.1.2 e) will be made only if the information is not available from the operator or from other sources and will be limited to essential information.

15.1.2 Priority

An aircraft known or believed to be in a state of emergency, including being subjected to unlawful interference, shall be given priority over other aircraft.

15.1.3 Unlawful interference and aircraft bomb threat

15.1.3.1 Air traffic services personnel shall be prepared to recognize any indication of the occurrence of unlawful interference with an aircraft.

15.1.3.2 Whenever unlawful interference with an aircraft is suspected, and where automatic distinct display of SSR Mode A Code 7500 and Code 7700 is not provided, the radar controller shall attempt to verify any suspicion by setting the SSR decoder to Mode A Code 7500 and thereafter to Code 7700.

Note. — An aircraft equipped with an SSR transponder is expected to operate the transponder on Mode A Code 7500 to indicate specifically that it is the subject of unlawful interference. The aircraft may operate the transponder on Mode A Code 7700, to indicate that it is threatened by grave and imminent danger and requires immediate assistance.

15.1.3.3 Whenever unlawful interference with an aircraft is known or suspected or a bomb threat warning has been received, ATS units shall promptly attend to requests by, or to anticipated needs of, the aircraft, including requests for relevant information relating to air navigation facilities, procedures and services along the route of flight and at any aerodrome of intended landing, and shall take such action as is necessary to expedite the conduct of all phases of the flight.

15.1.3.3.1 ATS units shall also:

a) transmit, and continue to transmit, information pertinent to the safe conduct of the flight, without expecting a reply from the aircraft;
b) monitor and plot the progress of the flight with the means available, and coordinate transfer of control with adjacent ATS units without requiring trans-missions or other responses from the aircraft, unless communication with the aircraft remains normal;
c) inform, and continue to keep informed, appropriate ATS units, including those in adjacent FIRs, which may be concerned with the progress of the flight;

   Note. — In applying this provision, account must be taken of all the factors which may affect the progress of the flight, including fuel endurance and the possibility of sudden changes in route and destination. The objective is to provide, as far in advance as is practicable in the circumstances, each ATS unit with appropriate information as to the expected or possible penetration of the aircraft into its area of responsibility.
d) notify:
   1) the operator or its designated representative;
   2) the appropriate rescue coordination centre in accordance with appropriate alerting procedures;
   3) the designated security authority;

   Note. — It is assumed that the designated security authority and/or the operator will in turn notify other parties concerned in accordance with pre-established procedures.
e) relay appropriate messages, relating to the circum-stances associated with the unlawful interference, between the aircraft and designated authorities.

15.1.3.4 The following additional procedures shall apply if a threat is received indicating that a bomb or other explosive device has been placed on board a known aircraft. The ATS unit receiving the threat information shall:

a) if in direct communication with the aircraft, advise the flight crew without delay of the threat and the circum-stances surrounding the threat; or
b) if not in direct communication with the aircraft, advise the flight crew by the most expeditious means through other ATS units or other channels.

15.1.3.5 The ATS unit in communication with the aircraft shall ascertain the intentions of the flight crew and report those intentions to other ATS units which may be concerned with the flight.

15.1.3.6 The aircraft shall be handled in the most expeditious manner whilst ensuring, to the extent possible, the safety of other aircraft and that personnel and ground installations are not put at risk.

15.1.3.7 Aircraft in flight shall be given re-clearance to a requested new destination without delay. Any request by the flight crew to climb or descend for the purpose of equalizing or reducing the differential between the outside air pressure and the cabin air pressure shall be approved as soon as possible.

15.1.3.8 An aircraft on the ground should be advised to remain as far away from other aircraft and installations as possible and, if appropriate, to vacate the runway. The aircraft should be instructed to taxi to a designated or isolated parking area in accordance with local instructions. Should the flight crew disembark passengers and crew immediately, other aircraft, vehicles and personnel should be kept at a safe distance from the threatened aircraft.

15.1.3.9 ATS units shall not provide any advice or suggestions concerning action to be taken by the flight crew in relation to an explosive device.

15.1.3.10 An aircraft known or believed to be the subject of unlawful interference or which for other reasons needs isolation from normal aerodrome activities shall be cleared to the designated isolated parking position. Where such an isolated parking position has not been designated, or if the designated position is not available, the aircraft shall be cleared to a position within the area or areas selected by prior agreement with the aerodrome authority. The taxi clearance shall specify the taxi route to be followed to the parking position. This route shall be selected with a view to minimizing any security risks to the public, other aircraft and installations at the aerodrome.

Note. — See Annex 14, Volume I, Chapter 3.

EXTRACTS FROM THE PROCEDURES FOR AIR NAVIGATION SERVICES — *AIRCRAFT OPERATIONS* (DOC 8168), VOLUME I — *FLIGHT PROCEDURES*

PART VIII. — SECONDARY SURVEILLANCE RADAR (SSR) TRANSPONDER OPERATING PROCEDURES

CHAPTER 1. OPERATION OF TRANSPONDERS

. . . . . .

1.4 EMERGENCY PROCEDURES

1.4.1 The pilot of an aircraft encountering a state of emergency shall set the transponder to Mode A Code 7700 except when previously directed by ATC to operate the transponder on a specified code. In the latter case the pilot shall maintain the specified code unless otherwise advised by ATC.

1.4.2 Notwithstanding the procedures at 1.4.1, a pilot may select Mode A Code 7700 whenever there is a specific reason to believe that this would be the best course of action.

. . . . . .

1.6 UNLAWFUL INTERFERENCE WITH AIRCRAFT IN FLIGHT

1.6.1 Should an aircraft in flight be subjected to unlawful interference, the pilot-in-command shall endeavour to set the transponder to Mode A Code 7500 to give indication of the situation unless circumstances warrant the use of Code 7700.

1.6.2 A pilot, having selected Mode A Code 7500 and subsequently requested to confirm this code by ATC in accordance with 1.1.5 shall, according to circumstances, either confirm this or not reply at all.

Note. — The absence of a reply from the pilot will be taken by ATC as an indication that the use of Code 7500 is not due to an inadvertent false code selection.

Appendix 14
ICAO Assembly Resolution A33-1

A33-1: Declaration on misuse of civil aircraft as weapons of destruction and other terrorist acts involving civil aviation

Witnessing the abhorrent terrorist acts which occurred in the United States on 11 September 2001 resulting in the loss of numerous innocent lives, human suffering and great destruction;

Expressing its deepest sympathy to the United States, to the more than seventy other States worldwide which lost nationals and to the families of the victims of such unprecedented criminal acts;

Recognizing that such terrorist acts are not only contrary to elementary considerations of humanity but constitute also use of civil aircraft for an armed attack on civilized society and are incompatible with international law;

Recognizing that the new type of threat posed by terrorist organizations requires new concerted efforts and policies of cooperation on the part of States;

Recalling its Resolutions A22-5, A27-9 and A32-22 on acts of unlawful interference and terrorism aimed at the destruction of civil aircraft in flight;

Recalling United Nations General Assembly Resolution 55/158 on *measures to eliminate international terrorism* and United Nations Security Council Resolutions 1368 and 1373 on *condemning and combatting international terrorism*;

The Assembly:

1. *Strongly condemns* these terrorist acts as contrary to elementary considerations of humanity, norms of conduct of society and as violations of international law;

Solemnly

2. *Declares* that such acts of using civil aircraft as weapons of destruction are contrary to the letter and spirit of the *Convention on International Civil Aviation*, in

particular its preamble and Articles 4 and 44, and that such acts and other terrorist acts involving civil aviation or civil aviation facilities constitute grave offences in violation of international law;

3. *Urges* all Contracting States to ensure, in accordance with Article 4 of the Convention, that civil aviation is not used for any purpose inconsistent with the aims of the *Convention on International Civil Aviation*, and to hold accountable and punish severely those who misuse civil aircraft as weapons of destruction, including those responsible for planning and organizing such acts or for aiding, supporting or harbouring the perpetrators;

4. *Urges* all Contracting States to strengthen cooperation in order to assist in the investigation of such acts and in the apprehension and prosecution of those responsible and to ensure that those who participated in these terrorist acts, whatever the nature of their participation, find no safe haven anywhere;

5. *Urges* all Contracting States to intensify their efforts in order to achieve the full implementation and enforcement of the multilateral conventions on aviation security, as well as of the ICAO Standards and Recommended Practices (SARPs) and Procedures relating to aviation security, to monitor such implementation, and to take within their territories appropriate additional security measures commensurate to the level of threat in order to prevent and eradicate terrorist acts involving civil aviation;

6. *Urges* all Contracting States to make contributions in the form of financial or human resources to ICAO's AVSEC mechanism to support and strengthen the combat against terrorism and unlawful interference in civil aviation; *calls on* Contracting States to agree on special funding for urgent action by ICAO in the field of aviation security referred to in paragraph 7 below; and *directs* the Council to develop proposals and take appropriate decisions for a more stable funding of ICAO action in the field of aviation security, including appropriate remedial action;

7. *Directs* the Council and the Secretary General to act urgently to address the new and emerging threats to civil aviation, in particular to review the -adequacy of the existing aviation security conventions; to review the ICAO aviation security programme, including a review of Annex 17 and other related Annexes to the Convention; to consider the establishment of an ICAO Universal Security Oversight Audit Programme relating to, *inter alia*, airport security arrangements and civil aviation security programmes; and to consider any other action which it may consider useful or necessary, including technical cooperation; and

8. *Directs* the Council to convene, at the earliest date, if possible, in the year 2001, an international high-level, ministerial conference on aviation security in Montreal with the objectives of preventing, combatting and eradicating acts of terrorism involving civil aviation; of strengthening ICAO's role in the adoption of SARPs in the field of security and the audit of their implementation; and of ensuring the necessary financial means as referred to in paragraph 6 above.

Appendix 15

Regulation (EC) No. 216/2008

REGULATION (EC) No 216/2008 OF THE EUROPEAN PARLIAMENT AND OF THE COUNCIL

of 20 February 2008

on common rules in the field of civil aviation and establishing a European Aviation Safety Agency, and repealing Council Directive 91/670/EEC, Regulation (EC) No 1592/2002 and Directive 2004/36/EC

(Text with EEA relevance)
(OJ No. L 79 of 19 March 2008, p. 1)

as amended by:

COMMISSION REGULATION (EC) No 690/2009
of 30 July 2009
amending Regulation (EC) No 216/2008 of the European Parliament and the Council on common rules in the field of civil aviation and establishing a European Aviation Safety Agency, and repealing Council Directive 91/670/EEC, Regulation (EC) No 1592/2002 and Directive 2004/36/EC
(Text with EEA relevance)
(OJ No. L 199 of 31 July 2009, p. 6)

and

REGULATION (EC) No 1108/2009 OF THE EUROPEAN PARLIAMENT AND OF THE COUNCIL
of 21 October 2009

amending Regulation (EC) No 216/2008 in the field of aerodromes, air traffic management and air navigation services and repealing Directive 2006/23/EC

(Text with EEA relevance)
(OJ No. L 309 of 24 November 2008, p. 51)

THE EUROPEAN PARLIAMENT AND THE COUNCIL OF THE EUROPEAN UNION,

Having regard to the Treaty establishing the European Community, and in particular Article 80(2) thereof,

Having regard to the proposal from the Commission,

Having regard to the Opinion of the Economic and Social Committee (1),

After consulting the Committee of the Regions,

Acting in accordance with the procedure laid down in Article 251 of the Treaty (2),

Whereas:

(1) A high and uniform level of protection of the European citizen should at all times be ensured in civil aviation, by the adoption of common safety rules and by measures ensuring that products, persons and organisations in the Community comply with such rules and with those adopted to protect the environment. This should contribute to facilitating the free movement of goods, persons and organisations in the internal market.

(2) In addition, third-country aircraft operated into, within or out of the territory where the Treaty applies should be subject to appropriate oversight at Community level within the limits set by the Convention on International Civil Aviation, signed in Chicago on 7 December 1944 (the Chicago Convention), to which all Member States are parties.

(3) The Chicago Convention already provides for minimum standards to ensure the safety of civil aviation and environmental protection relating thereto. Community essential requirements and rules adopted for their implementation should ensure that Member States fulfil the obligations created by the Chicago Convention, including those vis-à-vis third countries.

(4) The Community should lay down, in line with standards and recommended practices set by the Chicago Convention, essential requirements applicable to aeronautical products, parts and appliances, to persons and organisations involved in the operation of aircraft, and to persons and products involved in the training and medical examination of pilots. The Commission should be empowered to develop the necessary implementing rules.

(5) It would not be appropriate to subject all aircraft to common rules, in particular aircraft that are of simple design or operate mainly on a local basis, and those that are home-built or particularly rare or only exist in a small number; such aircraft should therefore remain under the regulatory control of the Member States, without any obligation under this Regulation on other Member States to recognise such national arrangements. However, proportionate measures should

be taken to increase generally the level of safety of recreational aviation. Consideration should in particular be given to aeroplanes and helicopters with a low maximum take-off mass and whose performance is increasing, which can circulate all over the Community and which are produced in an industrial manner. They therefore can be better regulated at Community level to provide for the necessary uniform level of safety and environmental protection.

(6) The scope of Community action should be clearly defined so that persons, organisations and products subject to this Regulation and its implementing rules can be identified without ambiguity. Such scope should be clearly defined by referring to a list of aircraft which are exempted from the application of this Regulation.

(7) Aeronautical products, parts and appliances, operators involved in commercial air transport, as well as pilots and persons, products and organisations involved in their training and medical examination, should be certified or licensed once they have been found to comply with essential requirements to be laid down by the Community in line with standards and recommended practices set by the Chicago Convention. The Commission should be empowered to develop the necessary implementing rules for establishing the conditions for the issue of the certificate or the conditions for its replacement by a declaration of capability, taking into account the risks associated with the different types of operations, such as certain types of aerial work and local flights with small aircraft.

(8) For non-commercial operations, the operational and licensing rules should be tailored to the complexity of the aircraft and a related definition should be set out.

(9) The privileges associated with the leisure pilot licence should be limited by the training received to obtain the related ratings, in accordance with the implementing rules.

(10) In order to achieve Community objectives as regards the freedom of movement of goods, persons and services, as well as those of the common transport policy, Member States should, without further requirements or evaluation, accept products, parts and appliances, organisations or persons certified in accordance with this Regulation and its implementing rules.

(11) Enough flexibility should be provided for addressing special circumstances such as urgent safety measures, unforeseen or limited operational needs. Provision should also be made for reaching an equivalent safety level by other means. Member States should be entitled to grant exemptions from the requirements of this Regulation and its implementing rules, provided that they are strictly limited in scope and subject to appropriate Community control.

(12) There is a need for better arrangements in all the fields covered by this Regulation so that certain tasks currently performed at Community or national level should be carried out by a single specialised expert body. There is, therefore, a need within the Community's existing institutional structure and balance of powers to establish a European Aviation Safety Agency (hereinafter referred to

as the Agency) which is independent in relation to technical matters and has legal, administrative and financial autonomy. To that end, it is necessary and appropriate that it should be a Community body having legal personality and exercising the implementing powers which are conferred on it by this Regulation.

(13) Under the Community institutional system, implementation of Community law is primarily the responsibility of the Member States. Certification tasks required by this Regulation and its implementing rules are therefore to be executed at national level. In certain clearly defined cases, however, the Agency should also be empowered to conduct certification tasks as specified in this Regulation. The Agency should, for the same reason, be allowed to take the necessary measures related to the operation of aircraft, the qualification of crew or the safety of third-country aircraft when this is the best means to ensure uniformity and facilitate the functioning of the internal market.

(14) Regulation (EC) No 2111/2005 (3) imposes a duty on the Agency to communicate all information that may be relevant for the updating of the Community list of air carriers which, for safety reasons, are subject to an operating ban in the Community. If the Agency refuses to grant an authorisation to an air carrier under the terms of this Regulation, it should pass on to the Commission all relevant information on which this refusal was based, so that the name of the air carrier may be entered, if necessary, on that list.

(15) The effective functioning of a Community civil aviation safety scheme in the fields covered by this Regulation requires strengthened cooperation between the Commission, the Member States and the Agency to detect unsafe conditions and take remedial measures as appropriate.

(16) The promotion of a 'culture of safety' and the proper functioning of a regulatory system in the fields covered by this Regulation require that incidents and occurrences be spontaneously reported by the witnesses thereto. Such reporting would be facilitated by the establishment of a non-punitive environment, and appropriate measures should be taken by Member States to provide for the protection of such information and of those who report it.

(17) Results of air accident investigations should be acted upon as a matter of urgency, in particular when they relate to defective aircraft design and/or operational matters, in order to ensure consumer confidence in air transport.

(18) To help achieve the safety objectives of this Regulation, the Community should be given powers to impose financial penalties on holders of certificates and approvals issued by the Agency. In accordance with the Community legal order, such financial penalties should be imposed by the Commission acting upon a recommendation of the Agency. It should be underlined that through the introduction of financial penalties the Commission will be able to give a more nuanced, flexible and graduated response to a breach of the rules, compared to the withdrawal of a certificate.

(19) Since all decisions taken by the Commission under this Regulation are subject to review by the Court of Justice of the European Communities in

accordance with the Treaty, the Court of Justice should, in accordance with Article 229 thereof, be given unlimited jurisdiction in respect of decisions by which the Commission imposes fines or periodic penalty payments.

(20) In order to respond to increasing concerns about the health and welfare of passengers during flights, it is necessary to develop aircraft designs which better protect the safety and health of passengers.

(21) The objectives of this Regulation may be efficiently achieved through cooperation with third countries. In such a case, the provisions of this Regulation and its implementing rules may be adapted through agreements concluded by the Community with these countries. In the absence of such agreements, Member States should nevertheless be allowed, subject to appropriate Community control, to recognise the approvals granted to foreign products, parts and appliances, organisations and personnel by a third country.

(22) In order to properly assist the Community, the Agency should be allowed to develop its expertise in all aspects of civil aviation safety and environmental protection covered by this Regulation. It should assist the Commission in the preparation of the necessary legislation and assist the Member States and industry in its implementation. It should be able to issue certification specifications and guidance material and to make technical findings and issue certificates as required, it should assist the Commission in monitoring the application of this Regulation and of its implementing rules, and it should be given the necessary authority to carry out its tasks.

(23) The Commission and the Member States should be represented within a Management Board in order to control effectively the functions of the Agency. This Board should be entrusted with the necessary powers to establish the budget, verify its execution, adopt the appropriate financial rules, establish transparent working procedures for decision making by the Agency and appoint the Executive Director. It is also appropriate that the Agency be allowed to conduct research and to organise appropriate coordination with the Commission and the Member States. It is desirable that the Agency assist the Community and its Member States in the field of international relations, including the harmonisation of rules, recognition of approvals and technical cooperation, and be entitled to establish the appropriate relations with the aeronautical authorities of third countries and international organisations competent in matters covered by this Regulation.

(24) In the interests of transparency, observers from interested parties should be represented within the Management Board of the Agency.

(25) Public interest requires the Agency to base its safety-related action solely on independent expertise, strictly applying this Regulation and the rules adopted by the Commission for its implementation. To that end, all safety-related decisions of the Agency should be made by its Executive Director, who should enjoy a high degree of flexibility to obtain advice and to organise the internal functioning of the Agency. When, however, the Agency has to develop draft rules of a general nature

to be implemented by national authorities, Member States should be involved in the process of decision.

(26) It is necessary to ensure that parties affected by decisions made by the Agency enjoy the necessary remedies in a manner which is suited to the special character of the field of aviation. An appropriate appeal mechanism should be set up so that decisions of the Executive Director can be subject to appeal to a specialised Board of Appeal, whose decisions are, in turn, open to action before the Court of Justice.

(27) In order to guarantee the full autonomy and independence of the Agency, it should be granted an autonomous budget whose revenue comes essentially from a contribution from the Community and from fees paid by the users of the system. Any financial contribution received by the Agency from Member States, third countries or other entities should not compromise its independence and impartiality. The Community budgetary procedure should be applicable as far as the Community contribution and any other subsidies chargeable to the general budget of the European Union are concerned. The auditing of accounts should be carried out by the Court of Auditors.

(28) Before any local offices of the Agency are set up, general rules should be established to clarify what requirements need to be met and what contribution the Member State concerned must provide.

(29) Since the objectives of this Regulation, namely the establishment and uniform application of common rules in the field of civil aviation safety and environmental protection, cannot be sufficiently achieved by the Member States and can therefore, by reason of the Europe-wide scope of this Regulation, be better achieved at Community level, the Community may adopt measures, in accordance with the principle of subsidiarity, as set out in Article 5 of the Treaty. In accordance with the principle of proportionality, as set out in that Article, this Regulation does not go beyond what is necessary in order to achieve those objectives.

(30) It has been recognised that the involvement of European countries not Members of the European Union should be pursued, so as to ensure a proper pan-European dimension in order to facilitate the improvement of civil aviation safety throughout Europe. European countries that have concluded agreements with the Community to adopt and apply the Community *acquis* in the field covered by this Regulation should be associated with its work in accordance with conditions to be agreed in the framework of those agreements.

(31) It is a general objective that the transfer of functions and tasks from the Member States, including those resulting from their cooperation through the Joint Aviation Authorities, to the Agency should be effected efficiently, without any reduction in the current high levels of safety, and without any negative impact on certification schedules. Appropriate measures should be adopted to provide for the necessary transition.

(32) This Regulation sets common rules in the field of civil aviation and establishes a European Aviation Safety Agency. Regulation (EC) No 1592/2002 of the

European Parliament and of the Council of 15 July 2002 on common rules in the field of civil aviation and establishing a European Aviation Safety Agency (4) should therefore be repealed.

(33) This Regulation establishes an appropriate and comprehensive framework for the definition and implementation of common technical requirements and administrative procedures in the field of civil aviation. Annex III to Council Regulation (EEC) No 3922/91 of 16 December 1991 on the harmonisation of technical requirements and administrative procedures in the field of civil aviation (5) and Council Directive 91/670/EEC of 16 December 1991 on mutual acceptance of personnel licences for the exercise of functions in civil aviation (6) should therefore be repealed in due course, without prejudice to the certification or licensing of products, persons and organisations already carried out in accordance with those acts.

(34) This Regulation establishes an appropriate and comprehensive framework for the safety of third-country aircraft using Community airports. Directive 2004/36/EC of the European Parliament and of the Council of 21 April 2004 on the safety of third-country aircraft using Community airports (7) should therefore be repealed in due course and without prejudice to the implementing measures on collection of information, ramp inspection and exchange of information.

(35) This Regulation will apply to any other area related to civil aviation safety on the basis of a future proposal in accordance with the Treaty.

(36) It is necessary to establish appropriate measures to ensure both the necessary protection of sensitive safety data and to provide the public with adequate information pertaining to the level of civil aviation safety and environmental protection relating thereto, taking into account Regulation (EC) No 1049/2001 of the European Parliament and of the Council of 30 May 2001 regarding public access to European Parliament, Council and Commission documents (8) and relevant national legislation. Decisions taken by the Agency pursuant to Article 8 of that Regulation should be capable of giving rise to the lodging of a complaint to the Ombudsman or should be capable of being the subject of an action before the Court of Justice, under Articles 195 and 230 of the Treaty respectively.

(37) The measures necessary for the implementation of this Regulation should be adopted in accordance with Council Decision 1999/468/EC of 28 June 1999 laying down the procedures for the exercise of implementing powers conferred on the Commission (9).

(38) In particular, power should be conferred on the Commission to adopt implementing rules for airworthiness, flight crew licensing and associated approvals, air operations, aircraft used by third-country operators, oversight and enforcement, as well as to adopt a regulation on the fees and charges of the Agency. Since those measures are of general scope and are designed to amend non-essential elements of this Regulation, *inter alia*, by supplementing it with new non-essential elements, they must be adopted in accordance with the regulatory procedure with scrutiny provided for in Article 5a of Decision 1999/468/EC.

(39) On grounds of efficiency, the normal time-limits for the regulatory procedure with scrutiny should be curtailed for the adaptation of the essential requirements for environmental protection and for the adoption of the implementing rules for environmental protection.

(40) On grounds of urgency it is necessary to apply the urgency procedure provided for in Article 5a(6) of Decision 1999/468/EC for the Commission to decide on the measures taken by Member States in immediate reaction to a safety problem, as well as on derogating approvals submitted by Member States,

HAVE ADOPTED THIS REGULATION:

CHAPTER I
PRINCIPLES

Article 1
Scope

1. This Regulation shall apply to:

(a) the design, production, maintenance and operation of aeronautical products, parts and appliances, as well as personnel and organisations involved in the design, production and maintenance of such products, parts and appliances;
(b) personnel and organisations involved in the operation of aircraft;
(c) the design, maintenance and operation of aerodromes, as well as personnel and organisations involved therein and, without prejudice to Community and national legislation on environment and land-use planning, the safeguarding of surroundings of aerodromes;
(d) the design, production and maintenance of aerodrome equipment, as well as personnel and organisations involved therein;
(e) the design, production and maintenance of systems and constituents for air traffic management and air navigation services (ATM/ANS), as well as personnel and organisations involved therein;
(f) ATM/ANS, as well as personnel and organisations involved therein.

2. This Regulation shall not apply to:

(a) products, parts, appliances, personnel and organisations referred to in paragraph 1(a) and (b) while carrying out military, customs, police, search and rescue, firefighting, coastguard or similar activities or services. The Member States shall undertake to ensure that such activities or services have due regard as far as practicable to the objectives of this Regulation;
(b) aerodromes or part thereof, as well as equipment, personnel and organisations, referred to in paragraph 1(c) and (d), that are controlled and operated by the military;
(c) ATM/ANS, including systems and constituents, personnel and organisations, referred to in paragraph 1(e) and (f), that are provided or made

available by the military. The Member States shall undertake to ensure that aircraft referred to in point (a) of this paragraph are separated, where appropriate, from other aircraft.

3. Member States shall, as far as practicable, ensure that any military facilities open to public use referred to in paragraph 2(b) or services provided by military personnel to the public referred to in paragraph 2(c), offer a level of safety that is at least as effective as that required by the essential requirements as defined in Annexes Va and Vb.

Article 2
Objectives

1. The principal objective of this Regulation is to establish and maintain a high uniform level of civil aviation safety in Europe.

2. Additional objectives are, in the fields covered by this Regulation, as follows:

(a) to ensure a high uniform level of environmental protection;
(b) to facilitate the free movement of goods, persons and services;
(c) to promote cost-efficiency in the regulatory and certification processes and to avoid duplication at national and European level;
(d) to assist Member States in fulfilling their obligations under the Chicago Convention, by providing a basis for a common interpretation and uniform implementation of its provisions, and by ensuring that its provisions are duly taken into account in this Regulation and in the rules drawn up for its implementation;
(e) to promote Community views regarding civil aviation safety standards and rules throughout the world by establishing appropriate cooperation with third countries and international organisations;
(f) to provide a level playing field for all actors in the internal aviation market.

3. The means of achieving the objectives set out in paragraphs 1 and 2 shall be:

(a) the preparation, adoption and uniform application of all necessary acts;
(b) the recognition, without additional requirements, of certificates, licences, approvals or other documents granted to products, personnel and organisations in accordance with this Regulation and its implementing rules;
(c) the establishment of an independent European Aviation Safety Agency (hereinafter referred to as the Agency);
(d) the uniform implementation of all necessary acts by the national aviation authorities and the Agency within their respective areas of responsibility.

Article 3
Definitions

For the purposes of this Regulation:

(a) 'continuing oversight' shall mean the tasks to be conducted to verify that the conditions under which a certificate has been granted continue to be fulfilled at any time during its period of validity, as well as the taking of any safeguard measure;

(b) 'Chicago Convention' shall mean the Convention on International Civil Aviation and its Annexes, signed in Chicago on 7 December 1944;

(c) 'product' shall mean an aircraft, engine or propeller;

(d) 'parts and appliances' shall mean any instrument, equipment, mechanism, part, apparatus, appurtenance, software or accessory, including communications equipment, that is used or intended to be used in operating or controlling an aircraft in flight; it shall include parts of an airframe, engine or propeller, or equipment used to manoeuvre the aircraft from the ground;

(da) 'ATM/ANS constituents' shall mean any constituent as defined in Article 2(19) of Regulation (EC) No 549/2004 of the European Parliament and of the Council of 10 March 2004 laying down the framework for the creation of the single European sky (the framework Regulation) (*);

(e) 'certification' shall mean any form of recognition that a product, part or appliance, organisation or person complies with the applicable requirements including the provisions of this Regulation and its implementing rules, as well as the issuance of the relevant certificate attesting such compliance;

(f) 'qualified entity' shall mean a body which may be allocated a specific certification task by, and under the control and the responsibility of, the Agency or a national aviation authority;

(g) 'certificate' shall mean any approval, licence or other document issued as the result of certification;

(h) 'operator' shall mean any legal or natural person, operating or proposing to operate one or more aircraft or one or more aerodromes;

(i) 'commercial operation' shall mean any operation of an aircraft, in return for remuneration or other valuable consideration, which is available to the public or, when not made available to the public, which is performed under a contract between an operator and a customer, where the latter has no control over the operator;

(j) 'complex motor-powered aircraft' shall mean:
  (i) an aeroplane:
    – with a maximum certificated take-off mass exceeding 5 700 kg, or
    – certificated for a maximum passenger seating configuration of more than nineteen, or
    – certificated for operation with a minimum crew of at least two pilots, or
    – equipped with (a) turbojet engine(s) or more than one turboprop engine, or
  (ii) a helicopter certificated:
    – for a maximum take-off mass exceeding 3 175 kg, or
    – for a maximum passenger seating configuration of more than nine, or
    – for operation with a minimum crew of at least two pilots, or
  (iii) a tilt rotor aircraft;

(k) 'flight simulation training device' shall mean any type of device in which flight conditions are simulated on the ground; they include flight simulators, flight training devices, flight and navigation procedures trainers and basic instrument training devices;
(l) 'rating' shall mean a statement entered on a licence, setting forth privileges, special conditions or limitations pertaining thereto.
(m) 'aerodrome' shall mean a defined area (including any buildings, installations and equipment) on land or water or on a fixed, fixed offshore or floating structure intended to be used either wholly or in part for the arrival, departure and surface movement of aircraft;
(n) 'aerodrome equipment' shall mean any equipment, apparatus, appurtenance, software or accessory, that is used or intended to be used to contribute to the operation of aircraft at an aerodrome;
(o) 'apron' shall mean a defined area intended to accommodate aircraft for purposes of loading or unloading passengers, mail or cargo, fuelling, parking or maintenance;
(p) 'apron management service' shall mean a service provided to manage the activities and the movement of aircraft and vehicles on an apron;
(q) 'ATM/ANS' shall mean the air traffic management functions as defined in Article 2(10) of Regulation (EC) No 549/2004, air navigation services defined in Article 2(4) of that Regulation, and services consisting in the origination and processing of data and formatting and delivering data to general air traffic for the purpose of safety-critical air navigation;
(r) 'ATM/ANS system' shall mean any combination of safety-related equipment and systems as defined in Article 2(39) of Regulation (EC) No 549/2004;
(s) 'flight information service' shall mean a service provided for the purpose of giving advice and information useful for the safe and efficient conduct of flights.

CHAPTER II
SUBSTANTIVE REQUIREMENTS

Article 4
Basic principles and applicability

1. Aircraft, including any installed product, part and appliance, which are:

(a) designed or manufactured by an organisation for which the Agency or a Member State ensures safety oversight; or
(b) registered in a Member State, unless their regulatory safety oversight has been delegated to a third country and they are not used by a Community operator; or
(c) registered in a third country and used by an operator for which any Member State ensures oversight of operations or used into, within or out of the Community by an operator established or residing in the Community; or

(d) registered in a third country, or registered in a Member State which has delegated their regulatory safety oversight to a third country, and used by a third-country operator into, within or out of the Community shall comply with this Regulation.

2. Personnel involved in the operations of aircraft referred to in paragraph 1(b), (c) or (d) shall comply with this Regulation.

3. Operations of aircraft referred to in paragraph 1(b), (c) or (d) shall comply with this Regulation.

3a. Aerodromes, including equipment, located in the territory subject to the provisions of the Treaty, open to public use and which serve commercial air transport and where operations using instrument approach or departure procedures are provided, and:

(a) have a paved runway of 800 metres or above; or
(b) exclusively serve helicopters;

shall comply with this Regulation. Personnel and organisations involved in the operation of these aerodromes shall comply with this Regulation.

3b. By way of derogation from paragraph 3a, Member States may decide to exempt from the provisions of this Regulation an aerodrome which:

– handles no more than 10 000 passengers per year, and
– handles no more than 850 movements related to cargo operations per year.

If such exemption by a Member State does not comply with the general safety objectives of this Regulation or any other rule of Community law, the Commission shall take a decision in accordance with the safeguard procedure referred to in Article 65(7) not to permit the exemption in question. In such a case, the Member State concerned shall revoke the exemption.

3c. ATM/ANS provided in the airspace of the territory to which the Treaty applies, as well as in any other airspace where Member States apply Regulation (EC) No 551/2004 of the European Parliament and of the Council of 10 March 2004 on the organisation and use of the airspace in the single European sky (the airspace Regulation) (**) in accordance with Article 1(3) of that Regulation, shall comply with this Regulation. Systems and constituents, personnel and organisations involved in the provision of these ATM/ANS shall comply with this Regulation.

4. Paragraph 1 shall not apply to aircraft referred to in Annex II.

5. Paragraphs 2 and 3 shall not apply to aircraft referred to in Annex II, with the exception of aircraft referred to in points (a)(ii), (d) and (h) thereof when used for commercial air transportation.

6. This Regulation shall not affect the rights of third countries as specified in international conventions, in particular the Chicago Convention.

Article 5
Airworthiness

1. Aircraft referred to in Article 4(1)(a), (b) and (c) shall comply with the essential requirements for airworthiness laid down in Annex I.

2. Compliance of aircraft referred to in Article 4(1)(b), and of products, parts and appliances mounted thereon shall be established in accordance with the following:

(a) products shall have a type-certificate. The type-certificate, and certification of changes to that type-certificate, including supplemental type-certificates, shall be issued when the applicant has shown that the product complies with a type-certification basis as specified in Article 20, established to ensure compliance with the essential requirements referred to in paragraph 1, and when it has no feature or characteristic making it unsafe for operation. The type-certificate shall cover the product, including all parts and appliances fitted thereon;

(b) the measures referred to in paragraph 5 may lay down a requirement for certification in respect of parts and appliances. The certificates for parts and appliances shall be issued when the applicant has shown that the parts and appliances comply with the detailed airworthiness specifications established to ensure compliance with the essential requirements referred to in paragraph 1;

(c) no aircraft shall be operated, unless it has a valid certificate of airworthiness. The certificate shall be issued when the applicant has shown that the aircraft conforms to the type design approved in its type-certificate and that relevant documentation, inspections and tests demonstrate that the aircraft is in condition for safe operation. This certificate of airworthiness shall remain valid as long as it is not suspended, revoked or terminated and as long as the aircraft is maintained in accordance with the essential requirements related to continuing airworthiness set out in point 1.d of Annex I and the measures adopted pursuant to paragraph 5;

(d) organisations responsible for the maintenance of products, parts and appliances shall demonstrate their capability and means to discharge the responsibilities associated with their privileges. Unless otherwise accepted these capabilities and means shall be recognised through the issuance of an organisation approval. The privileges granted to the approved organisation and the scope of the approval shall be specified in the terms of approval;

(e) organisations responsible for the design and manufacture of products, parts and appliances shall demonstrate their capability and means to discharge the responsibilities associated with their privileges. Unless otherwise accepted these capabilities and means shall be recognised through the issuance of an organisation approval. The privileges granted to the approved organisation and the scope of the approval shall be specified in the terms of approval;in addition:

(f) personnel responsible for the release of a product, part or appliance after maintenance may be required to hold an appropriate certificate (personnel certificate);
(g) the capability of maintenance training organisations to discharge the responsibilities associated with their privileges in relation to the issuance of the certificates referred to in point (f) may be recognised by the issuance of an approval.

3. Aircraft referred to in Article 4(1)(a) and products, parts and appliances mounted thereon shall comply with paragraph 2(a), (b) and (e) of this Article.

4. By way of derogation from paragraphs 1 and 2:

(a) a permit to fly may be issued when it is shown that the aircraft is capable of performing safely a basic flight. It shall be issued with appropriate limitations, in particular to protect third parties' safety;
(b) a restricted certificate of airworthiness may be issued to aircraft for which a type certificate has not been issued according to paragraph 2(a). In this case, the aircraft shall be shown to comply with specific airworthiness specifications and deviations from the essential requirements referred to in paragraph 1 shall nevertheless ensure adequate safety with regard to the purpose. Aircraft eligible for these restricted certificates, and limitations for use of these aircraft, shall be defined according to the measures referred to in paragraph 5;
(c) when the number of aircraft of the same type eligible for a restricted certificate of airworthiness so justifies, a restricted type certificate may be issued and an appropriate type certification basis shall be established.

5. The measures designed to amend non-essential elements of this Article, by supplementing it, shall be adopted in accordance with the regulatory procedure with scrutiny referred to in Article 65(4). Those measures shall specify in particular:

(a) conditions for establishing and notifying to an applicant the type-certification basis applicable to a product;
(b) conditions for establishing and notifying to an applicant the detailed airworthiness specifications applicable to parts and appliances;
(c) conditions for establishing and notifying to an applicant the specific airworthiness specifications applicable to aircraft eligible for a restricted certificate of airworthiness;
(d) conditions for issuing and disseminating mandatory information in order to ensure the continuing airworthiness of products;
(e) conditions for issuing, maintaining, amending, suspending or revoking type-certificates, restricted type-certificates, approval of changes to type-certificates, individual certificates of airworthiness, restricted certificates of airworthiness, permits to fly and certificates for products, parts or appliances, including:
   (i) conditions on the duration of these certificates, and conditions to renew certificates when a limited duration is fixed;

(ii) restrictions applicable to the issue of permits to fly. These restrictions should in particular concern the following:
- purpose of the flight,
- airspace used for the flight,
- qualification of flight crew,
- carriage of persons other than flight crew;

(iii) aircraft eligible for restricted certificates of airworthiness, and associated restrictions;

(iv) the minimum syllabus of maintenance certifying staff type rating training to ensure compliance with paragraph (2)(f);

(v) the minimum syllabus of pilot type rating and the qualification of associated simulators to ensure compliance with Article 7;

(vi) the master minimum equipment list as appropriate and additional airworthiness specifications for a given type of operation to ensure compliance with Article 8;

(f) conditions to issue, maintain, amend, suspend or revoke organisation approvals required in accordance with paragraph 2(d), (e) and (g) and conditions under which such approvals need not be requested;

(g) conditions to issue, maintain, amend, suspend or revoke personnel certificates required in accordance with paragraph 2(f);

(h) responsibilities of the holders of certificates;

(i) how aircraft referred to in paragraph 1 which are not covered by paragraphs 2 or 4 are to show compliance with the essential requirements;

(j) how aircraft referred to in Article 4(1)(c) are to show compliance with the essential requirements.

6. When adopting the measures referred to in paragraph 5, the Commission shall take specific care that they:

(a) reflect the state of the art and the best practices in the field of airworthiness;

(b) take into account worldwide aircraft experience in service, and scientific and technical progress;

(c) allow for immediate reaction to established causes of accidents and serious incidents;

(d) do not impose on aircraft referred to in Article 4(1)(c) requirements which would be incompatible with the International Civil Aviation Organization (ICAO) obligations of Member States.

Article 6
Essential requirements for environmental protection

1. Products, parts and appliances shall comply with the environmental protection requirements contained in Amendment 9 of Volume I and in Amendment 6 of Volume II of Annex 16 to the Chicago Convention as applicable on 20 November 2008, except for the Appendices to Annex 16.

2. The measures designed to amend non-essential elements of the requirements referred to in paragraph 1 in order to bring them into line with subsequent amendments to the Chicago Convention and its Annexes which enter into force after the adoption of this Regulation and which become applicable in all Member States, shall, in so far as such adaptations do not broaden the scope of this Regulation, be adopted in accordance with the regulatory procedure with scrutiny referred to in Article 65(5).

3. The measures designed to amend non-essential elements of the requirements referred to in paragraph 1, by supplementing them, shall, using as necessary the content of the Appendices referred to in paragraph 1, be adopted in accordance with the regulatory procedure with scrutiny referred to in Article 65(5).

Article 7
Pilots

1. Pilots involved in the operation of aircraft referred to in Article 4(1)(b) and (c), as well as flight simulation training devices, persons and organisations involved in the training, testing, checking or medical assessment of these pilots, shall comply with the relevant 'essential requirements' laid down in Annex III.

2. Except when under training, a person may only act as a pilot if he or she holds a licence and a medical certificate appropriate to the operation to be performed.

A person shall only be issued a licence when he or she complies with the rules established to ensure compliance with the essential requirements on theoretical knowledge, practical skill, language proficiency and experience as set out in Annex III.

A person shall only be issued a medical certificate when he or she complies with the rules established to ensure compliance with the essential requirements on medical fitness as set out in Annex III. This medical certificate may be issued by aero-medical examiners or by aero-medical centres.

Notwithstanding the third subparagraph, in the case of a leisure pilot licence a general medical practitioner who has sufficient detailed knowledge of the applicant's medical background may, if so permitted under national law, act as an aero-medical examiner, in accordance with detailed implementing rules adopted pursuant to the procedure referred to in Article 65(3); these implementing rules shall ensure that the level of safety is maintained.

The privileges granted to the pilot and the scope of the licence and the medical certificate shall be specified in such licence and certificate.

The requirements of the second and third subparagraphs may be satisfied by the acceptance of licences and medical certificates issued by or on behalf of a third country as far as pilots involved in the operation of aircraft referred to in Article 4(1)(c) are concerned.

3. The capability of pilot training organisations and of aeromedical centres to discharge the responsibilities associated with their privileges in relation to the issuance of licenses and medical certificates shall be recognised by the issuance of an approval.

Pilot training organisations or aero-medical centres shall be issued an approval when they comply with the rules established to ensure compliance with the relevant essential requirements as laid down in Annex III.

The privileges granted by the approvals shall be specified thereon.

4. A certificate shall be required in respect of each flight simulation training device used for the training of pilots. The certificate shall be issued when the applicant has shown that the device complies with the rules established to ensure compliance with the relevant essential requirements as set out in Annex III.

5. Persons responsible for providing flight training or flight simulation training, or for assessing pilots' skill, and aero-medical examiners shall hold an appropriate certificate. Such certificate shall be issued when it is shown that the person concerned complies with the rules established to ensure compliance with the relevant essential requirements as laid down in Annex III.

The privileges granted by the certificate shall be specified therein.

6. The measures designed to amend non-essential elements of this Article by supplementing it, shall be adopted in accordance with the regulatory procedure with scrutiny referred to in Article 65(4). Those measures shall specify in particular:

(a) the different ratings for pilots' licences and the medical certificates adequate for the different types of activities performed;
(b) the conditions for issuing, maintaining, amending, limiting, suspending or revoking licences, ratings for licences, medical certificates, approvals and certificates referred to in paragraphs 2, 3, 4 and 5, and the conditions under which such certificates and approvals need not be requested;
(c) the privileges and responsibilities of the holders of licences, ratings for licences, medical certificates, approvals and certificates referred to in paragraphs 2, 3, 4 and 5;
(d) the conditions for the conversion of existing national pilots' licences and of national flight engineers' licences into pilots' licences as well as the conditions for the conversion of national medical certificates into commonly recognised medical certificates;
(e) without prejudice to the provisions of bilateral agreements concluded in accordance with Article 12, the conditions for the acceptance of licences from third countries;
(f) how pilots of aircraft referred to in points (a)(ii), (d) and (f) of Annex II, when used for commercial air transportation, comply with the relevant essential requirements of Annex III.

7. When adopting the measures referred to in paragraph 6, the Commission shall take specific care that they reflect the state of the art, including best practices and scientific and technical progress, in the field of pilot training.

Such measures shall also include provisions for the issuance of all types of pilot licences and ratings required under the Chicago Convention, and of a leisure pilot licence covering non-commercial activities involving aircraft with a maximum certificated take off mass of 2 000 kg or less and which do not meet any of the criteria referred to in Article 3(j).

Article 8
Air operations

1. The operation of aircraft referred to in Article 4(1)(b) and (c) shall comply with the essential requirements set out in Annex IV and, if applicable, Annex Vb.

2. Unless otherwise determined in the implementing rules, operators engaged in commercial operations shall demonstrate their capability and means of discharging the responsibilities associated with their privileges. These capabilities and means shall be recognised through the issuance of a certificate. The privileges granted to the operator and the scope of the operations shall be specified in the certificate.

3. Unless otherwise determined in the implementing rules, operators engaged in the non-commercial operation of complex motor-powered aircraft shall declare their capability and means of discharging the responsibilities associated with the operation of that aircraft.

4. Cabin crew involved in the operation of aircraft referred to in Article 4(1)(b) and (c) shall comply with the essential requirements laid down in Annex IV. Those involved in commercial operations shall hold an attestation as initially set out in Annex III, Subpart O, point (d) of OPS 1 1005 as set out in Regulation (EC) No 1899/2006 of the European Parliament and of the Council of 12 December 2006 amending Council Regulation (EEC) No 3922/91 (10); at the discretion of the Member State, such attestation may be issued by approved operators or training organisations.

5. The measures designed to amend non-essential elements of this Article, by supplementing it, shall be adopted in accordance with the regulatory procedure with scrutiny referred to in Article 65(4). Those measures shall specify in particular:

- (a) conditions to operate an aircraft in compliance with the essential requirements set out in Annex IV and, if applicable, Annex Vb;
- (b) conditions for issuing, maintaining, amending, limiting, suspending or revoking the certificates referred to in paragraph 2 and the conditions under which a certificate shall be replaced by a declaration of the capability and means of the operator to discharge the responsibilities associated with the operation of the aircraft;
- (c) privileges and responsibilities of the holders of certificates;
- (d) conditions and procedures for the declaration by, and for the oversight of, operators referred to in paragraph 3 and the conditions under which a declaration shall be replaced by a demonstration of capability and means to discharge the responsibilities associated with the privileges of the operator recognised by the issuance of a certificate;
- (e) conditions for issuing, maintaining, amending, limiting, suspending or revoking the cabin crew attestation referred to in paragraph 4;

(f) conditions under which operations shall be prohibited, limited or subject to certain conditions in the interest of safety;
(g) how operations of aircraft referred to in point (a)(ii) and points (d) and (h) of Annex II, when used for commercial air transportation, comply with the relevant essential requirements set out in Annex IV and, if applicable, Annex Vb.

6. The measures referred to in paragraph 5 shall:

- reflect the state of the art and the best practices in the field of air operations,
- define different types of operations and allow for related requirements and compliance demonstrations proportionate to the complexity of operations and the risk involved,
- take into account worldwide aircraft experience in service, and scientific and technical progress,
- with regard to commercial transportation by aeroplane, and without prejudice to the previous indent, be developed initially on the basis of the common technical requirements and administrative procedures specified in Annex III to Regulation (EEC) No 3922/91,
- be based on a risk assessment and shall be proportional to the scale and scope of the operation,
- allow for immediate reaction to established causes of accidents and serious incidents,
- not impose on aircraft referred to in Article 4(1)(c) requirements which would be incompatible with the ICAO obligations of Member States,
- take into account the safety aspects related to ATM/ANS.

Article 8a
Aerodromes

1. Aerodromes and aerodrome equipment as well as the operation of aerodromes shall comply with the essential requirements set out in Annex Va and, if applicable, Annex Vb.

2. The compliance of aerodromes, aerodrome equipment and operation of aerodromes with the essential requirements shall be established in accordance with the following:

(a) a certificate shall be required in respect of each aerodrome. The certificate and certification of changes to that certificate shall be issued when the applicant has shown that the aerodrome complies with the aerodrome certification basis set out in point (b), and that the aerodrome has no feature or characteristic making it unsafe for operation. The certificate shall cover the aerodrome, its operation and its safety-related equipment;
(b) the certification basis for an aerodrome shall consist of the following:
   (i) the applicable certification specifications related to the type of aerodromes;

(ii) the provisions for which an equivalent level of safety has been accepted; and
(iii) the special detailed technical specifications necessary when the design features of a particular aerodrome or the experience in operation render any of the specifications referred to in point (i) inadequate or inappropriate to ensure conformity with the essential requirements set out in Annex Va;

(c) the measures referred to in paragraph 5 may lay down a requirement of certification in respect of safety-critical aerodrome equipment. The certificate for such equipment shall be issued when the applicant has shown that the equipment complies with the detailed specifications established to ensure compliance with the essential requirements referred to in paragraph 1;
(d) organisations responsible for the operation of aerodromes shall demonstrate their capability and means to discharge the responsibilities associated with their privileges. These capabilities and means shall be recognised through the issuance of the certificate referred to in point (a). They may also be recognised through the issuance of a separate certificate if the Member State where the aerodrome is located so decides. The privileges granted to the certified organisation and the scope of the certificate, including a list of aerodromes to be operated, shall be specified in the certificate;
(e) by way of derogation from point (d), Member States may decide that providers of apron management services shall be allowed to declare their capability and means of discharging the responsibilities associated with the services provided.

3. Member States shall ensure that provisions are in place to safeguard aerodromes against activities and developments in their surroundings which may cause unacceptable risks to aircraft using the aerodrome.

4. Aerodrome operators shall monitor activities and developments which may cause unacceptable safety risks to aviation in the aerodrome surroundings and take, within their competence, mitigating measures as appropriate.

5. The measures designed to amend non-essential elements of the requirements referred to in this Article, by supplementing it, shall be adopted in accordance with the regulatory procedure with scrutiny referred to in Article 65(4).

Those measures shall specify in particular:

(a) the conditions for establishing and notifying to an applicant the certification basis applicable to an aerodrome;
(b) the conditions for establishing and notifying to an applicant the detailed specifications applicable to aerodrome equipment;
(c) the conditions for issuing, maintaining, amending, suspending or revoking certificates for aerodromes and certificates for aerodrome equipment, including operating limitations related to the specific design of the aerodrome;

(d) the conditions for operating an aerodrome in compliance with the essential requirements set out in Annex Va and, if applicable, Annex Vb;
(e) the conditions for issuing, maintaining, amending, suspending or revoking the certificates referred to in paragraph 2(d);
(f) the responsibilities of the holders of certificates;
(g) the conditions for the acceptance and for the conversion of aerodrome certificates issued by Member States, including measures which are already authorised by the Member State concerned on the basis of notified deviations from Annex 14 of the Chicago Convention before the entry into force of this Regulation;
(h) the conditions for the decision not to permit exemptions referred to in Article 4(3b), including criteria for cargo aerodromes, the notification of exempted aerodromes and for the review of granted exemptions;
(i) the conditions under which operations shall be prohibited, limited or subject to certain conditions in the interest of safety;
(j) the conditions and procedures for the declaration by and for the oversight of service providers referred to in paragraph 2(e).

6. The measures referred to in paragraph 5 shall:

(a) reflect the state of the art and the best practices in the field of aerodromes and take into account the applicable ICAO Standards and Recommended Practices;
(b) be proportionate to the size, traffic, category and complexity of the aerodrome and nature and volume of operations thereon;
(c) take into account worldwide aerodrome operation experience, and scientific and technical progress;
(d) allow for immediate reaction to established causes of accidents and serious incidents;
(e) provide for the necessary flexibility for customised compliance.

Article 8b
ATM/ANS

1. Provision of ATM/ANS shall comply with the essential requirements set out in Annex Vb and, as far as practicable, Annex Va.

2. ATM/ANS providers shall be required to hold a certificate. The certificate shall be issued when the provider has demonstrated its capability and means of discharging the responsibilities associated with the provider's privileges. The privileges granted and the scope of the services provided shall be specified in the certificate.

3. By way of derogation from paragraph 2, Member States may decide that providers of flight information services shall be allowed to declare their capability and means of discharging the responsibilities associated with the services provided.

4. The measures referred to in paragraph 6 may lay down a requirement for certification in respect of organisations engaged in the design, manufacture and

maintenance of safety-critical ATM/ANS systems and constituents. The certificate for those organisations shall be issued when they have demonstrated their capability and means of discharging the responsibilities associated with their privileges. The privileges granted shall be specified in the certificate.

5. The measures referred to in paragraph 6 may lay down a requirement for certification, or alternatively, validation by the ATM/ANS provider, in respect of safety-critical ATM/ANS systems and constituents. The certificate for those systems and constituents shall be issued, or validation shall be given, when the applicant has shown that the systems and constituents comply with the detailed specifications established to ensure compliance with the essential requirements referred to in paragraph 1.

6. The measures necessary for the implementation of this Article shall be adopted in accordance with the regulatory procedure referred to in Article 5(3) of Regulation (EC) No 549/2004.

Those measures shall specify in particular:

(a) the conditions for the provision of ATM/ANS in compliance with the essential requirements set out in Annex Vb and, if applicable, in Annex Va;
(b) the conditions for establishing and notifying to an applicant the detailed specifications applicable to ATM/ANS systems and constituents;
(c) the conditions for issuing, maintaining, amending, suspending or revoking the certificates referred to in paragraphs 2 and 4;
(d) the responsibilities of the holders of certificates;
(e) the conditions and procedures for the declaration by, and for the oversight of service providers referred to in paragraph 3;
(f) the conditions under which operations shall be prohibited, limited or subject to certain conditions in the interest of safety.

7. The measures referred to in paragraph 6 shall:

(a) reflect the state of the art and the best practices in the field of ATM/ANS;
(b) be proportionate to the type and complexity of the services provided;
(c) take into account worldwide ATM/ANS experience, and scientific and technical progress;
(d) be developed using as far as practicable the relevant provisions of Regulation (EC) No 549/2004 and of Regulation (EC) No 550/2004 of the European Parliament and of the Council of 10 March 2004 on the provision of air navigation services in the single European sky (the service provision Regulation) (***), Regulation (EC) No 551/2004 and Regulation (EC) No 552/2004 of the European Parliament and of the Council of 10 March 2004 on the interoperability of the European Air Traffic Management network (the interoperability Regulation) (****) and provide for transitional mechanisms to ensure the continuity of certificates already granted under those Regulations; initially they shall include the safety provisions of those Regulations and, where appropriate, in case of future amendments, take into account latest scientific and technical progress;

(e) allow for immediate reaction to established causes of accidents and serious incidents.

Article 8c
Air traffic controllers

1. Air traffic controllers as well as persons and organisations involved in the training, testing, checking or medical assessment of air traffic controllers, shall comply with the relevant essential requirements set out in Annex Vb.

2. Air traffic controllers shall be required to hold a licence and a medical certificate appropriate to the service provided.

3. The licence referred to in paragraph 2 shall only be issued when the applicant for the licence demonstrates that he or she complies with the rules established to ensure compliance with the essential requirements regarding theoretical knowledge, practical skill, language proficiency and experience as set out in Annex Vb.

4. The medical certificate referred to in paragraph 2 shall only be issued when the air traffic controller complies with the rules established to ensure compliance with the essential requirements on medical fitness as set out in Annex Vb. The medical certificate may be issued by aero medical examiners or by aero medical centres.

5. The privileges granted to the air traffic controller and the scope of the licence and the medical certificate shall be specified in such licence and certificate.

6. The capability of air traffic controller training organisations, aero medical examiners and aero medical centres to discharge the responsibilities associated with their privileges in relation to the issuance of licences and medical certificates shall be recognised by the issuance of a certificate.

7. A certificate shall be issued to training organisations, aero medical examiners and aero medical centres for air traffic controllers that have demonstrated that they comply with the rules established to ensure compliance with the relevant essential requirements as set out in Annex Vb. The privileges granted by the certificate shall be specified therein.

8. Persons responsible for providing practical training or for assessing air traffic controllers' skill shall hold a certificate. The certificate shall be issued when the person concerned has demonstrated that he or she complies with the rules established to ensure compliance with the relevant essential requirements as set out in Annex Vb. The privileges granted by the certificate shall be specified therein.

9. Synthetic training devices shall comply with the relevant essential requirements set out in Annex Vb.

10. The measures designed to amend non-essential elements of this Article by supplementing it, shall be adopted in accordance with the regulatory procedure with scrutiny referred to in Article 65(4).

Those measures shall specify in particular:

(a) the different ratings and endorsements for air traffic controllers' licences;
(b) the conditions for issuing, maintaining, amending, limiting, suspending or revoking licences, ratings and endorsements for licences, medical certificates, approvals and certificates, and the conditions under which such certificates and approvals need not be requested, while providing for transitional mechanisms to ensure the continuity of approvals and certificates already granted;
(c) the privileges and responsibilities of the holders of licences, ratings and endorsements for licences, medical certificates, approvals and certificates;
(d) the conditions for the acceptance and for the conversion of air traffic controllers' licences as well as the conditions for the acceptance and for the conversion of national medical certificates into commonly recognised medical certificates.

11. The measures referred to in paragraph 10 shall reflect the state of the art, including best practices and scientific and technical progress, in the field of air traffic controller training. They shall initially be developed on the basis of the provisions of Directive 2006/23/EC of the European Parliament and of the Council of 5 April 2006 on a Community air traffic controller licence (*****).

Article 9
Aircraft used by a third-country operator into, within or out of the Community

1. Aircraft referred to in Article 4(1)(d), as well as their crew and their operations, shall comply with applicable ICAO standards. To the extent that there are no such standards, these aircraft and their operations shall comply with the requirements set out in Annexes I, III, IV and, if applicable, Annex Vb, provided these requirements are not in conflict with the rights of third countries under international conventions.

2. Operators engaged in commercial operations using aircraft referred to in paragraph 1 shall demonstrate their capability and means of complying with the requirements specified in paragraph 1.

The requirement referred to in the first subparagraph may be satisfied by acceptance of certificates issued by or on behalf of a third country.

The capabilities and means referred to in the first subparagraph shall be recognised through the issuance of an authorisation. The privileges granted to the operator and the scope of the operations shall be specified in that authorisation.

3. Operators engaged in non-commercial operations of complex motor-powered aircraft using aircraft referred to in paragraph 1 may be required to declare their capability and means of discharging the responsibilities associated with the operation of that aircraft.

4. The measures designed to amend non-essential elements of this Article, by supplementing it, shall be adopted in accordance with the regulatory procedure

with scrutiny referred to in Article 65(4). Those measures shall specify in particular:

(a) how aircraft referred to in Article 4(1)(d), or crew, which do not hold a standard ICAO certificate of airworthiness or licence, may be authorised to operate into, within or out of the Community;
(b) conditions to operate an aircraft in compliance with the provisions of paragraph 1;
(c) conditions for issuing, maintaining, amending, limiting, suspending or revoking the operator's authorisation referred to in paragraph 2, taking into account the certificates issued by the state of registry or the state of the operator, without prejudice to Regulation (EC) No 2111/2005 and its implementing rules;
(d) privileges and responsibilities of the holders of authorisations;
(e) conditions and procedures for the declaration by, and for the oversight of, operators referred to in paragraph 3;
(f) conditions under which operations shall be prohibited, limited or subject to certain conditions in the interest of safety in accordance with Article 22(1).

5. When adopting the measures referred to in paragraph 4, the Commission shall take specific care that:

(a) use is made, as appropriate, of ICAO recommended practices and guidance documents;
(b) no requirement exceeds what is required from aircraft referred to in Article 4(1)(b), and from the operators of such aircraft;
(c) use is made, where appropriate, of measures issued in accordance with Articles 5(5) and 8(5);
(d) the process by which authorisations are obtained is simple, proportionate, cost-effective and efficient in all cases, allowing for requirements and compliance demonstrations proportionate to the complexity of operations and the risk involved. The process shall in particular take account of:
   (i) results of the ICAO Universal Safety Oversight Audit Programme;
   (ii) information from ramp inspections and the Safety Assessment of Foreign Aircraft Programme records; and
   (iii) other recognised information on safety aspects with regard to the operator concerned;
(e) safety aspects related to ATM/ANS are taken into account.

Article 10
Oversight and enforcement

1. The Member States, the Commission and the Agency shall cooperate with a view to ensuring compliance with this Regulation and its implementing rules.

2. For the purposes of the implementation of paragraph 1, Member States shall, in addition to their oversight of certificates that they have issued, conduct

investigations, including ramp inspections, and shall take any measure, including the grounding of aircraft, to prevent the continuation of an infringement.

3. For the purposes of the implementation of paragraph 1, the Agency shall conduct investigations in accordance with Article 24(2) and Article 55.

4. In order to facilitate the taking of appropriate enforcement action by competent authorities, the Member States, the Commission and the Agency shall exchange information on identified infringements.

5. The measures designed to amend non-essential elements of this Article, by supplementing it, shall be adopted in accordance with the regulatory procedure with scrutiny referred to in Article 65(4). Those measures shall specify in particular:

(a) conditions for the collection, exchange and dissemination of information;
(b) conditions for conducting ramp inspections, including systematic ones;
(c) conditions for the grounding of aircraft that do not comply with the requirements of this Regulation or its implementing rules.

Article 11
Recognition of certificates

1. Member States shall, without further technical requirements or evaluation, recognise certificates issued in accordance with this Regulation. When the original recognition is for a particular purpose or purposes, any subsequent recognition shall cover only the same purpose or purposes.

2. The Commission, on its own initiative or at the request of a Member State or of the Agency, may initiate the procedure referred to in Article 65(7) to decide whether a certificate issued in accordance with this Regulation effectively complies with this Regulation and its implementing rules.

In case of non-compliance or ineffective compliance, the Commission shall require the issuer of a certificate to take appropriate corrective action and safeguard measures, such as limitation or suspension of the certificate. Moreover, the provisions of paragraph 1 shall cease to apply to the certificate from the date of the notification of the Commission's decision to the Member States.

3. When the Commission has sufficient evidence that appropriate corrective action has been taken by the issuer referred to in paragraph 2 to address the case of non-compliance or ineffective compliance and that the safeguard measures are no longer necessary, it shall decide that the provisions of paragraph 1 apply again to this certificate. These provisions shall apply as from the date of the notification of this decision to the Member States.

4. Pending the entry into effect of the measures referred to in Articles 5(5), 7(6) and 9(4) and the expiry of any transition periods provided for by those measures, and without prejudice to Article 69(4), certificates which cannot be issued in accordance with this Regulation may be issued on the basis of the applicable national regulations.

5. Pending the entry into effect of the measures referred to in Article 8(5) and the expiry of any transition periods provided for by those measures, and without prejudice to Article 69(4), certificates which cannot be issued in accordance with this Regulation may be issued on the basis of the applicable national regulations.

5a. Pending the entry into effect of the measures referred to in Articles 8a(5) and 8c(10) and the expiry of any transition periods provided for by those measures, and without prejudice to Article 69(4), certificates which cannot be issued in accordance with this Regulation may be issued on the basis of the applicable national regulations.

5b. Pending the entry into effect of the measures referred to in Article 8b(6) and the expiry of any transition periods provided for by those measures, and without prejudice to Article 69(4), certificates which cannot be issued in accordance with this Regulation may be issued on the basis of the applicable national regulations or, where applicable, on the basis of the relevant requirements of Commission Regulation (EC) No 2096/2005 of 20 December 2005 laying down common requirements for the provision of air navigation services (******).

6. The provisions of this Article shall be without prejudice to Regulation (EC) No 2111/2005 and its implementing rules.

Article 12
Acceptance of third-country certification

1. By way of derogation from the provisions of this Regulation and its implementing rules, the Agency or the aviation authorities in the Member State may issue certificates on the basis of certificates issued by aeronautical authorities of a third country, as provided for in recognition agreements between the Community and that third country.

2. (a) In the absence of an agreement concluded by the Community, a Member State or the Agency may issue certificates on the basis of certifications issued by the competent authorities of a third country in application of an agreement concluded by that Member State with the third country in question before the entry into force of the related provisions of this Regulation and notified to the Commission and the other Member States. The Agency may also issue such certificates on behalf of any Member State in application of an agreement concluded by one of the Member States with the third country in question.
   (b) If the Commission considers that:
   - the provisions of an agreement between a Member State and a third country would not provide for a level of safety equivalent to that specified by this Regulation and its implementing rules, and/or
   - such agreement would discriminate among Member States without compelling safety reasons or is contrary to Community foreign policy vis-à-vis a third country, it may, in accordance with the procedure laid

down in Article 65(2), require the Member State concerned to modify the agreement, to suspend its application or to renounce it, in accordance with Article 307 of the Treaty.

(c) Member States shall take the necessary measures to renounce agreements as soon as possible after the entry into force of an agreement between the Community and the third country in question, for those domains covered by that latter agreement.

Article 13
Qualified entities

When allocating a specific certification task to a qualified entity, the Agency or the national aviation authority concerned shall ensure that such entity comply with the criteria laid down in Annex V.

Qualified entities shall not issue certificates.

Article 14
Flexibility provisions

1. The provisions of this Regulation and of its implementing rules shall not prevent a Member State from reacting immediately to a safety problem which involves a product, person or organisation subject to the provisions of this Regulation.

The Member State shall immediately notify the Agency, the Commission and the other Member States of the measures taken and the reasons therefor.

2. (a) The Agency shall assess whether the safety problem can be addressed within the powers conferred on it in accordance with Article 18(d). In this case it shall, within one month of being notified pursuant to paragraph 1, take the appropriate decision.

(b) If the Agency concludes that the safety problem cannot be addressed in accordance with point (a), it shall, within the period referred to in that point, issue a recommendation in accordance with Article 18(b) as to whether this Regulation or its implementing rules should be amended and whether the notified measures should be withdrawn or maintained.

3. The measures designed to amend non-essential elements of this Regulation, *inter alia*, by supplementing it, and relating to whether an inadequate level of safety or a shortcoming in this Regulation or its implementing rules justify initiating their amendment and whether the measures adopted pursuant to paragraph 1 may be continued, shall be adopted in accordance with the regulatory procedure with scrutiny referred to in Article 65(6). In such a case the measures shall be implemented as appropriate by all Member States and the provisions of Article 11 shall apply to such measures. If the measures are found not to be justified, they shall be revoked by the Member State concerned.

4. Member States may grant exemptions from the substantive requirements laid down in this Regulation and its implementing rules in the event of unforeseen

urgent operational circumstances or operational needs of a limited duration, provided the level of safety is not adversely affected. The Agency, the Commission and the other Member States shall be notified of any such exemptions as soon as they become repetitive or where they are granted for periods of more than two months.

5. The Agency shall assess whether the exemptions notified by a Member State are less restrictive than the applicable Community provisions and, within one month of being notified thereof, shall issue a recommendation in accordance with Article 18(b) on whether these exemptions comply with the general safety objectives of this Regulation or any other rule of Community law.

If an exemption does not comply with the general safety objectives of this Regulation or any other rule of Community law, the Commission shall take a decision not to permit the exemption in accordance with the procedure referred to in Article 65(7). In such a case, the Member State concerned shall revoke the exemption.

6. Where an equivalent level of protection to that attained by the application of the rules implementing this Regulation can be achieved by other means, Member States may, without discrimination on grounds of nationality, grant an approval derogating from those implementing rules.

In such cases, the Member State concerned shall notify the Agency and the Commission that it intends to grant such an approval, and shall give reasons demonstrating the need to derogate from the rule concerned, as well as the conditions laid down to ensure that an equivalent level of protection is achieved.

7. Within two months of being notified in accordance with paragraph 6, the Agency shall issue a recommendation in accordance with Article 18(b) on whether an approval proposed in accordance with paragraph 6 fulfils the conditions laid downin that paragraph.

The measures designed to amend non-essential elements of this Regulation, by supplementing it, relating to whether a proposed approval may be granted shall be adopted in accordance with the regulatory procedure with scrutiny referred to in Article 65(6) within one month of receiving the Agency's recommendation. In such a case, the Commission shall notify its decision to all Member States, which shall also be entitled to apply that measure. The provisions of Article 15 shall apply to the measure in question.

Article 15
Information network

1. The Commission, the Agency and the national aviation authorities shall exchange any information available to them in the context of the application of this Regulation and its implementing rules. Entities entrusted with the investigation of civil aviation accidents and incidents, or with the analysis of occurrences, are entitled to access to that information.

2. Without prejudice to the public's right of access to the Commission's documents as laid down in Regulation (EC) No 1049/2001, the Commission shall adopt, in accordance with the procedure referred to in Article 65(3), measures for the dissemination to interested parties on its own initiative of the information referred to in paragraph 1 of this Article. These measures, which may be generic or individual, shall be based on the need:

(a) to provide persons and organisations with the information they need to improve aviation safety;
(b) to limit the dissemination of information to what is strictly required for the purpose of its users, in order to ensure appropriate confidentiality of that information.

3. The national aviation authorities shall, in accordance with their national legislation, take necessary measures to ensure appropriate confidentiality of the information received by them pursuant to paragraph 1.

4. In order to inform the public of the general safety level, a safety review shall be published annually by the Agency. From the entry into force of the measures referred to in Article 10(5), this safety review shall contain an analysis of all information received pursuant to Article 10. This analysis shall be simple and easy to understand and shall indicate whether there are increased safety risks. In this analysis, the sources of information shall not be revealed.

Article 16
Protection of the source of information

1. Where the information referred to in Article 15(1) is provided by a natural person on a voluntary basis to the Commission or the Agency, the source of such information shall not be revealed. When the information has been provided to a national authority, the source of such information shall be protected in accordance with national legislation.

2. Without prejudice to applicable rules of criminal law, Member States shall refrain from instituting proceedings in respect of unpremeditated or unintentional infringements of the law which come to their attention only because they have been reported pursuant to this Regulation and its implementing rules.

This rule shall not apply in cases of gross negligence.

3. Without prejudice to applicable rules of criminal law, and in accordance with the procedures set out in national law and practice, Member States shall ensure that employees who provide information in application of this Regulation and its implementing rules are not subject to any prejudice on the part of their employer.

This rule shall not apply in cases of gross negligence.

4. This Article shall apply without prejudice to national rules relating to access to information by judicial authorities.

CHAPTER III
THE EUROPEAN AVIATION SAFETY AGENCY

SECTION I
Tasks

Article 17
Establishment and functions of the Agency

1. For the purpose of the implementation of this Regulation, a European Aviation Safety Agency shall be established.

2. For the purposes of ensuring the proper functioning and development of civil aviation safety, the Agency shall:

(a) undertake any task and formulate opinions on all matters covered by Article 1(1);
(b) assist the Commission by preparing measures to be taken for the implementation of this Regulation. Where these comprise technical rules and in particular rules relating to construction, design and operational aspects, the Commission may not change their content without prior coordination with the Agency. The Agency shall also provide the Commission with the necessary technical, scientific and administrative support to carry out its tasks;
(c) take the necessary measures within the powers conferred on it by this Regulation or other Community legislation;
(d) conduct inspections and investigations as necessary to fulfil its tasks;
(e) in its fields of competence, carry out, on behalf of Member States, functions and tasks ascribed to them by applicable international conventions, in particular the Chicago Convention.

Article 18
Agency measures

The Agency shall, where appropriate:

(a) issue opinions addressed to the Commission;
(b) issue recommendations addressed to the Commission for the application of Article 14;
(c) issue certification specifications and acceptable means of compliance, as well as any guidance material for the application of this Regulation and its implementing rules;
(d) take the appropriate decisions for the application of Articles 20, 21, 22, 22a, 22b, 23, 54 and 55 including the granting of exemptions to holders of certificates it has issued, from the substantive requirements laid down in this Regulation and its implementing rules in the event of unforeseen urgent operational circumstances or operational needs of a limited duration, provided that the level of safety is not affected, that they are granted

for a period not exceeding two months, that they are notified to the Commission and that they are not renewed;
(e) issue the reports following standardisation inspections carried out pursuant to Articles 24(1) and 54.

Article 19
Opinions, certification specifications and guidance material

1. In order to assist the Commission in the preparation of proposals for basic principles, applicability and essential requirements to be presented to the European Parliament and to the Council and the adoption of the implementing rules, the Agency shall prepare drafts thereof. These drafts shall be submitted by the Agency as opinions to the Commission.

2. The Agency shall, in accordance with Article 52 and the implementing rules adopted by the Commission, develop:

(a) certification specifications and acceptable means of compliance; and';
(b) guidance material;

to be used in the certification process.

These documents shall reflect the state of the art and the best practices in the fields concerned and be updated taking into account worldwide aircraft experience in service, and scientific and technical progress.

Article 20
Airworthiness and environmental certification

1. With regard to the products, parts and appliances referred to in Article 4(1)(a) and (b), the Agency shall, where applicable and as specified in the Chicago Convention or its Annexes, carry out on behalf of Member States the functions and tasks of the state of design, manufacture or registry when related to design approval. To that end, it shall in particular:

(a) for each product for which a type-certificate or a change to a type-certificate is requested, establish and notify the type-certification basis. That certification basis consists of the applicable airworthiness code, the provisions for which an equivalent level of safety has been accepted and the special detailed technical specifications necessary when the design features of a particular product or the experience in operation render any of the airworthiness code provisions inadequate or inappropriate to ensure conformity with essential requirements;
(b) for each product for which a restricted certificate of airworthiness is requested, establish and notify the specific airworthiness specifications;
(c) for each part or appliance for which a certificate is requested, establish and notify the detailed airworthiness specifications;
(d) for each product for which environmental certification is required in accordance with Article 6, establish and notify the appropriate environmental requirements;

(e) conduct, itself or through national aviation authorities or qualified entities, investigations associated with products, parts and appliances certification;
(f) issue the appropriate type-certificates or associated changes;
(g) issue certificates for parts and appliances;
(h) issue the appropriate environmental certificates;
(i) amend, suspend or revoke the relevant certificate when the conditions according to which it was issued are no longer fulfilled or if the legal or natural person holding the certificate fails to fulfil the obligations imposed on it by this Regulation or its implementing rules;
(j) ensure the continuing airworthiness functions associated with the products, parts and appliances which are under its oversight, including reacting without undue delay to a safety problem and issuing and disseminating the applicable mandatory information;
(k) for aircraft for which a permit to fly is to be issued, establish airworthiness standards and procedures to comply with Article 5(4)(a);
(l) issue permits to fly to aircraft for the purpose of certification under the control of the Agency, in agreement with the Member State in which the aircraft is registered or is to be registered.

2. With regard to organisations, the Agency shall:

(a) conduct, itself or through national aviation authorities or qualified entities, inspections and audits of the organisations it certifies;
(b) issue and renew the certificates of:
  (i) design organisations; or
  (ii) production organisations located within the territory of the Member States, if requested by the Member State concerned; or
  (iii) production and maintenance organisations located outside the territory of the Member States;
(c) amend, suspend or revoke the relevant organisation certificate when the conditions according to which it was issued are no longer fulfilled, or if the organisation concerned fails to fulfil the obligations imposed on it by this Regulation or its implementing rules.

Article 21
Pilot certification

1. With regard to the personnel and organisations referred to in Article 7(1), the Agency shall:

(a) conduct, itself or through national aviation authorities or qualified entities, investigations and audits of the organisations it certifies and, where relevant, their personnel;
(b) issue and renew the certificates of pilot training organisations and aero-medical centres located outside the territory of the Member States and, where relevant, their personnel;

(c) amend, limit, suspend or revoke the relevant certificate when the conditions according to which it was issued by it are no longer fulfilled, or if the legal or natural person holding the certificate fails to fulfil the obligations imposed on it by this Regulation or its implementing rules.

2. With regard to the flight simulation training devices referred to in Article 7(1), the Agency shall:

(a) conduct, itself or through national aviation authorities or qualified entities, technical inspections of the devices it certifies;
(b) issue and renew the certificates of:
  (i) flight simulation training devices used by training organisations certified by the Agency; or
  (ii) flight simulation training devices located within the territory of the Member States, if requested by the Member State concerned;
  (iii) flight simulation training devices located outside the territory of the Member States;
(c) amend, limit, suspend or revoke the relevant certificate when the conditions according to which it was issued are no longer fulfilled, or if the legal or natural person holding the certificate fails to fulfil the obligations imposed on it by this Regulation or its implementing rules.

Article 22
Air operation certification

1. The Agency shall react without undue delay to a problem affecting the safety of air operations by determining corrective action and by disseminating related information, including to the Member States.

2. With regard to flight time limitation:

(a) the Agency shall issue the applicable certification specifications to ensure compliance with essential requirements and, as appropriate, the related implementing rules. Initially, the implementing rules shall include all substantive provisions of Subpart Q of Annex III to Regulation (EEC) No 3922/91, taking into account the latest scientific and technical evidence;
(b) a Member State may approve individual flight time specification schemes which deviate from the certification specifications referred to in point (a). In this case the Member State shall without delay notify the Agency, the Commission and the other Member States that it intends to grant approval for such an individual scheme;
(c) upon notification the Agency shall, within one month, assess the individual scheme on the basis of a scientific and medical evaluation. Thereafter the Member State concerned may grant the approval as notified, unless the Agency has discussed the scheme with that Member State and proposed changes thereto. Should the Member State agree with these changes, it may grant the approval accordingly;

(d) in the event of unforeseen urgent operational circumstances or operational needs of limited duration and non-repetitive nature, derogations to certification specifications may apply provisionally until the Agency expresses its opinion;
(e) should a Member State disagree with the Agency's conclusions concerning an individual scheme, it shall refer the issue to the Commission to decide whether that scheme complies with the safety objectives of this Regulation, in accordance with the procedure referred to in Article 65(3);
(f) the contents of individual schemes which are acceptable to the Agency, or on which the Commission has taken a positive decision in accordance with point (e), shall be published.

Article 22a
ATM/ANS

With regard to ATM/ANS referred to in Article 4(3c) the Agency shall:

(a) conduct, itself or through national aviation authorities or qualified entities, inspections, and audits of the organisations it certifies;
(b) issue and renew certificates of organisations located outside the territory subject to the provisions of the Treaty, responsible for providing services in the airspace of the territory to which the Treaty applies;
(c) issue and renew certificates of organisations providing pan-European services;
(d) amend, suspend or revoke the relevant certificate, when the conditions according to which it was issued are no longer fulfilled or if the holder of the certificate fails to fulfil the obligations imposed on it by this Regulation or by its implementing rules.

Article 22b
Air traffic controller certification

With regard to the persons and organisations referred to in Article 8c(1), the Agency shall:

(a) conduct, itself or through national aviation authorities or qualified entities, investigations and audits of the organisations it certifies and, where relevant, their personnel;
(b) issue and renew the certificates of air traffic controller training organisations located outside the territory of the Member States and, where relevant, their personnel;
(c) amend, suspend or revoke the relevant certificate when the conditions according to which it was issued by it are no longer fulfilled, or if the legal or natural person holding the certificate fails to fulfil the obligations imposed on it by this Regulation or its implementing rules.

Article 23
Third-country operators

1. With regard to operators of aircraft referred to in Article 4 (1)(d) engaged in commercial operations, the Agency shall:

(a) conduct, itself or through national aviation authorities or qualified entities, investigations and audits;
(b) issue and renew the authorisations referred to in Article 9 (2), unless a Member State carries out the functions and tasks of the state of operator in respect of these operators;
(c) amend, limit, suspend or revoke the relevant authorisation when the conditions according to which it was issued by it are no longer fulfilled, or if the organisation concerned fails to fulfil the obligations imposed on it by this Regulation or its implementing rules.

2. With regard to operators of aircraft referred to in Article 4 (1)(d) not engaged in commercial operations, the Agency shall:

(a) receive the declarations referred to in Article 9(3); and
(b) conduct, itself or through national aviation authorities or qualified entities, the oversight of operators from which it has received a declaration.

3. With regard to aircraft referred to in Article 4(1)(d), the Agency shall issue authorisations in accordance with Article 9(4) (a).

Article 24
Monitoring the application of the rules

1. The Agency shall conduct standardisation inspections in the fields covered by Article 1(1), in order to monitor the application by national competent authorities of this Regulation and of its implementing rules, and shall report to the Commission.

2. The Agency shall conduct investigations of undertakings to monitor the application of this Regulation and its implementing rules.

3. The Agency shall assess the impact of the implementation of this Regulation and its implementing rules, having regard to the objectives set out in Article 2.

4. The Agency shall be consulted on, and issue recommendations to the Commission for, the application of Article 14.

5. The working methods of the Agency for conducting the tasks referred to in paragraphs 1, 3 and 4 shall be subject to requirements to be adopted in accordance with the procedure referred to in Article 65(2), taking into account the principles laid down in Articles 52 and 53.

Article 25
Fines and periodic penalty payments

1. Without prejudice to Articles 20 and 55, at the Agency's request the Commission may:

(a) impose on the persons and the undertakings to which the Agency has issued a certificate, fines, where, intentionally or negligently, the provisions of this Regulation and its implementing rules have been breached;
(b) impose, on the persons and undertakings to which the Agency has issued a certificate, periodic penalty payments, calculated from the date set in the decision, in order to compel those persons and undertakings to comply with the provisions of this Regulation and its implementing rules.

2. The fines and periodic penalty payments referred to in paragraph 1 shall be dissuasive and proportionate to both the gravity of the case and the economic capacity of the certificate holder concerned, taking into particular account the extent to which safety has been compromised. The amount of the fines shall not exceed 4 % of the annual income or turnover of the certificate holder. The amount of the periodic penalty shall not exceed 2,5 % of the average daily income or turnover of the certificate holder.

3. The Commission shall adopt, in accordance with the procedure laid down in Article 65(3), the detailed rules for the implementation of this Article. In doing so, it shall specify in particular:

(a) detailed criteria for establishing the amount of the fine or periodic penalty payment; and
(b) procedures for enquiries, associated measures and reporting, as well as rules of procedure for decision-making, including provisions on rights of defence, access to file, legal representation, confidentiality and temporal provisions and the quantification and collection of fines and periodic penalty payments.

4. The Court of Justice of the European Communities shall have unlimited jurisdiction to review decisions whereby the Commission has fixed a fine or periodic penalty payment. It may cancel, reduce or increase the fine or periodic penalty payment imposed.

5. Decisions taken pursuant to paragraph 1 shall not be of a criminal law nature.

Article 26
Research

1. The Agency may develop and finance research in so far as is strictly related to the improvement of activities in its field of competence, without prejudice to Community law.

2. The Agency shall coordinate its research and development activities with those of the Commission and the Member States so as to ensure that policies and actions are mutually consistent.

3. The results of research funded by the Agency shall be published, provided the Agency does not classify them as confidential.

Article 27
International relations

1. The Agency shall assist the Community and the Member States in their relations with third countries in accordance with the relevant Community law. It shall, in particular, assist in the harmonising of rules and mutual recognition regarding approvals attesting the satisfactory application of rules.

2. The Agency may cooperate with the aeronautical authorities of third countries and the international organisations competent in matters covered by this Regulation in the framework of working arrangements concluded with those bodies, in accordance with the relevant provisions of the Treaty. Such arrangements shall have received the Commission's prior approval.

3. The Agency shall assist Member States to respect their international obligations, in particular those under the Chicago Convention.

SECTION II
Internal structure

Article 28
Legal status, location, local offices

1. The Agency shall be a body of the Community. It shall have legal personality.

2. In each of the Member States, the Agency shall enjoy the most extensive legal capacity accorded to legal persons under their laws. It may, in particular, acquire or dispose of movable and immovable property and may be a party to legal proceedings.

3. The Agency may establish its own local offices in the Member States, subject to their consent.

4. The Agency shall be represented by its Executive Director.

Article 29
Staff

1. The Staff Regulations of Officials of the European Communities, the Conditions of Employment of Other Servants of the European Communities and the rules adopted jointly by the institutions of the European Communities for purposes of the application of those Staff Regulations and Conditions of Employment shall apply to the staff of the Agency, without prejudice to the application of Article 39 of this Regulation to the members of the Board of Appeal.

2. Without prejudice to Article 42, the powers conferred on the appointing authority by the Staff Regulations and the Conditions of Employment shall be exercised by the Agency in respect of its own staff.

3. The Agency's staff shall consist of a strictly limited number of officials assigned or seconded by the Commission or Member States to carry out management duties. The remaining staff shall consist of other employees recruited by the Agency as necessary to carry out its tasks.

Article 30
Privileges and immunities

The Protocol on the Privileges and Immunities of the European Communities annexed to the Treaties establishing the European Community and the European Atomic Energy Community shall apply to the Agency.

Article 31
Liability

1. The contractual liability of the Agency shall be governed by the law applicable to the contract in question.

2. The Court of Justice of the European Communities shall have jurisdiction to give judgment pursuant to any arbitration clause contained in a contract concluded by the Agency.

3. In the case of non-contractual liability, the Agency shall, in accordance with the general principles common to the laws of the Member States, make good any damage caused by its services or by its servants in the performance of their duties.

4. The Court of Justice of the European Communities shall have jurisdiction in disputes relating to compensation for any damage as referred to in paragraph 3.

5. The personal liability of its servants towards the Agency shall be governed by the provisions laid down in the Staff Regulations or Conditions of Employment applicable to them.

Article 32
Publication of documents

1. Without prejudice to decisions taken on the basis of Article 290 of the Treaty, the following documents shall be produced in all official languages of the Community:

(a) the safety review referred to in Article 15(4);
(b) opinions addressed to the Commission pursuant to Article 19(1);
(c) the annual general report and programme of work referred to in Article 33(2)(b) and (c) respectively.

2. The translation services required for the functioning of the Agency shall be provided by the Translation Centre for bodies of the European Union.

Article 33
Powers of the Management Board

1. The Agency shall have a Management Board.

2. The Management Board shall:

(a) appoint the Executive Director, and the Directors on a proposal from the Executive Director, in accordance with Article 39;
(b) adopt the annual general report on the Agency's activities and forward it by 15 June at the latest to the European Parliament, the Council, the Commission, the Court of Auditors and the Member States; acting on behalf of the Agency, it shall forward annually to the European Parliament and the Council (hereinafter referred to as budgetary authority) any information relevant to the outcome of the evaluation procedures, in particular, information concerning the effects or consequences of changes in the tasks assigned to the Agency;
(c) before 30 November each year, and after receiving the opinion of the Commission, adopt the Agency's programme of work for the coming year and forward it to the European Parliament, the Council, the Commission and the Member States; this programme of work shall be adopted without prejudice to the annual Community budgetary procedure and the Community legislative programme in relevant areas of aviation safety; the opinion of the Commission shall be attached to the programme of work;
(d) adopt guidelines for the allocation of certification tasks to national aviation authorities and qualified entities in agreement with the Commission;
(e) establish procedures for making decisions by the Executive Director as referred to in Articles 52 and 53;
(f) carry out its functions relating to the Agency's budget pursuant to Articles 59, 60 and 63;
(g) appoint the members of the Board of Appeal pursuant to Article 41;
(h) exercise disciplinary authority over the Executive Director and over the Directors in agreement with the Executive Director;
(i) give its opinion on the measures relating to fees and charges as referred to in Article 64(1);
(j) establish its Rules of Procedure;
(k) decide on the linguistic arrangements for the Agency;
(l) complement, where appropriate, the list of documents referred to in Article 32(1);
(m) establish the organisational structure of the Agency and adopt the Agency's staffing policy.

3. The Management Board may advise the Executive Director on any matter strictly related to the strategic development of aviation safety, including research as defined in Article 26.

4. The Management Board shall establish an advisory body of interested parties, which it shall consult prior to making decisions in the fields referred to in paragraph 2(c), (e), (f) and (i). The Management Board may also decide to consult the advisory body on other issues referred to in paragraphs 2 and 3. The Management Board shall not be bound by the opinion of the advisory body.

5. The Management Board may establish working bodies to assist in carrying out its functions, including the preparation of its decisions and monitoring the implementation thereof.

Article 34
Composition of the Management Board

1. The Management Board shall be composed of one representative of each Member State and one representative of the Commission. Members shall be selected on the basis of their recognised experience and commitment in the field of civil aviation, their managerial capabilities and their expertise, which are to be used to further the objectives of this Regulation. The competent committee of the European Parliament shall be fully informed accordingly.

Each Member State shall appoint a member of the Management Board as well as an alternate who will represent the member in his/her absence. The Commission shall also designate its representative and alternate. The duration of the terms of office shall be five years. This term of office shall be renewable.

2. Where appropriate, the participation of representatives of European third countries and the conditions of such participation shall be established in the arrangements referred to in Article 66.

3. The advisory body referred to in Article 33(4) shall appoint four of its members to participate as observers in the Management Board. They shall represent, as broadly as possible, the different views represented in the advisory body. The duration of their term of office shall be 30 months, renewable once.

Article 35
Chairmanship of the Management Board

1. The Management Board shall elect a Chairperson and a Deputy Chairperson from among its members. The Deputy Chairperson shall ex officio replace the Chairperson in the event of his/her being prevented from attending to his/her duties.

2. The terms of office of the Chairperson and Deputy Chairperson shall expire when their membership of the Management Board ceases. Subject to this, the duration of the terms of office of the Chairperson and Deputy Chairperson shall be three years. These terms of office shall be renewable once.

Article 36
Meetings

1. Meetings of the Management Board shall be convened by its Chairperson.

2. The Executive Director of the Agency shall take part in the deliberations.

3. The Management Board shall hold at least two ordinary meetings a year. In addition it shall meet at the instance of the Chairperson or at the request of at least one third of its members.

4. The Management Board may invite any person whose opinion might be of interest to attend its meetings as an observer.

5. The members of the Management Board may, subject to the provisions of its Rules of Procedure, be assisted by advisers or experts.

6. The secretariat of the Management Board shall be provided by the Agency.

Article 37
Voting

1. Without prejudice to Article 39(1), the Management Board shall take its decisions by a two-thirds majority of its members. At the request of a member of the Management Board, the decision referred to in Article 33(2)(k) shall be taken by unanimity.

2. Each member designated pursuant to Article 34(1) shall have one vote. In the absence of a Member, his/her alternate shall be entitled to exercise his/her right to vote. Neither observers nor the Executive Director of the Agency shall vote.

3. The Rules of Procedure shall establish more detailed voting arrangements, in particular the conditions under which a member may act on behalf of another member as well as any quorum requirements, where appropriate.

Article 38
Functions and powers of the Executive Director

1. The Agency shall be managed by its Executive Director, who shall be completely independent in the performance of his/her duties. Without prejudice to the competencies of the Commission and the Management Board, the Executive Director shall neither seek nor take instructions from any government or from any other body.

2. The European Parliament or the Council may invite the Executive Director to report on the carrying out of his/her tasks.

3. The Executive Director shall have the following functions and powers:

(a) to approve the measures of the Agency as defined in Article 18 within the limits specified by this Regulation, its implementing rules and any applicable law;
(b) to decide on inspections and investigations as provided for in Articles 54 and 55;
(c) to allocate certification tasks to national aviation authorities or qualified entities according to guidelines set by the Management Board;
(d) to undertake any international functions and technical cooperation with third countries pursuant to Article 27;

(e) to take all necessary steps, including the adoption of internal administrative instructions and the publication of notices, to ensure the functioning of the Agency in accordance with the provisions of this Regulation;
(f) to prepare each year a draft general report and submit it to the Management Board;
(g) to exercise in respect of the Agency's staff the powers laid down in Article 29(2);
(h) to draw up estimates of the revenues and expenditure of the Agency pursuant to Article 59, and to implement the budget pursuant to Article 60;
(i) to delegate his/her powers to other members of the Agency's staff subject to rules to be adopted in accordance with the procedure referred to in Article 65(2);
(j) with the consent of the Management Board, to take decisions regarding the establishment of local offices in the Member States in accordance with Article 28(3);
(k) to prepare and to implement the annual programme of work;
(l) to respond to requests for assistance from the Commission.

Article 39
Appointment of senior officials

1. The Executive Director shall be appointed on grounds of merit and of documented competence and experience relevant for civil aviation. The Executive Director shall be appointed or dismissed by the Management Board on a proposal from the Commission. The Management Board shall take its decision by a three-quarters majority of its members. Before being appointed, the candidate selected by the Management Board may be asked to make a declaration before the competent committee or committees of the European Parliament and answer questions from its, or their, members.

2. The Executive Director may be assisted by one or more Directors. If the Executive Director is absent or indisposed, one of the Directors shall take his/her place.

3. The Directors of the Agency shall be appointed on grounds of professional competence relevant for civil aviation. The Directors shall be appointed or dismissed by the Management Board on a proposal from the Executive Director.

4. The terms of office of the Executive Director and the Directors shall be five years. The term of office of the Directors shall be renewable and the term of office of the Executive Director shall be renewable only once.

Article 40
Powers of the Boards of Appeal

1. One or more Boards of Appeal shall be established within the Agency.

2. The Board or Boards of Appeal shall be responsible for deciding on appeals against the decisions referred to in Article 44.

3. The Board or Boards of Appeal shall be convened as necessary. The number of boards of Appeal and the work allocated to it or them shall be determined by the Commission acting in accordance with the procedure referred to in Article 65 (3).

Article 41
Composition of the Boards of Appeal

1. A Board of Appeal shall consist of a Chairperson and two other members.

2. The Chairperson and the other members shall have alternates to represent them in their absence.

3. The Chairperson, the other members and their alternates shall be appointed by the Management Board from a list of qualified candidates adopted by the Commission.

4. Where the Board of Appeal considers that the nature of the appeal so requires, it may call up to two further members from the list referred to in paragraph 3.

5. The qualifications required for the members of each Board of Appeal, the powers of individual members in the preparatory phase of decisions and the voting conditions shall be determined by the Commission acting in accordance with the procedure referred to in Article 65(3).

Article 42
Members of the Board of Appeal

1. The term of office of the members of a Board of Appeal, including the Chairperson and any alternates, shall be five years. This term shall be renewable.

2. The members of a Board of Appeal shall be independent. In making their decisions they shall not be bound by any instructions.

3. The members of a Board of Appeal may not perform any other duties within the Agency. The members of a Board of Appeal may work on a part-time basis.

4. The members of a Board of Appeal may not be removed from office or from the list of qualified candidates during their term of office, unless there are serious grounds for such removal and the Commission, after obtaining the opinion of the Management Board, takes a decision to that effect.

Article 43
Exclusion and objection

1. The members of a Board of Appeal may not take part in any appeal proceedings if they have any personal interest therein, if they have previously been involved as representatives of one of the parties to the proceedings, or if they participated in the decision under appeal.

2. If, for one of the reasons listed in paragraph 1 or for any other reason, a member of a Board of Appeal considers that he/she should not take part in any appeal proceeding, he/she shall inform the Board of Appeal accordingly.

3. Members of a Board of Appeal may be objected to by any party to the appeal proceedings on any of the grounds given in paragraph 1, or if any such member is suspected of partiality. Any such objection shall not be admissible if, while being aware of a reason for objecting, the party to the appeal proceedings has taken a procedural step. No objection may be based on the nationality of members.

4. The Boards of Appeal shall decide as to the action to be taken in the cases specified in paragraphs 2 and 3 without the participation of the member concerned. For the purposes of taking this decision, the member concerned shall be replaced on the Board of Appeal by his/her alternate.

Article 44
Decisions subject to appeal

1. An appeal may be brought against decisions of the Agency taken pursuant to Articles 20, 21, 22, 22a, 22b, 23, 55 or 64.

2. An appeal lodged pursuant to paragraph 1 shall not have suspensory effect. The Agency may, however, if it considers that circumstances so permit, suspend the application of the decision appealed against.

3. An appeal against a decision which does not terminate proceedings as regards one of the parties may only be made in conjunction with an appeal against the final decision, unless the decision provides for separate appeal.

Article 45
Persons entitled to appeal

Any natural or legal person may appeal against a decision addressed to that person, or against a decision which, although in the form of a decision addressed to another person, is of direct and individual concern to the former. The parties to proceedings may be party to the appeal proceedings.

Article 46
Time limit and form

The appeal, together with the statement of grounds thereof, shall be filed in writing at the Agency within two months of the notification of the measure to the person concerned, or, in the absence thereof, of the day on which it came to the knowledge of the latter, as the case may be.

Article 47
Interlocutory revision

1. If the Executive Director considers the appeal to be admissible and well founded, he/she shall rectify the decision. This shall not apply where the appellant is opposed to another party to the appeal proceedings.

2. If the decision is not rectified within one month after receipt of the statement of grounds for the appeal, the Agency shall forthwith decide whether or not to

suspend the application of the decision pursuant to the second sentence of Article 44(2), and shall remit the appeal to the Board of Appeal.

Article 48
Examination of appeals

1. If the appeal is admissible, the Board of Appeal shall examine whether it is well founded.

2. When examining the appeal pursuant to paragraph 1, the Board of Appeal shall act expeditiously. It shall as often as necessary invite the parties to the appeal proceedings to file, within specified time limits, observations on notifications issued by itself or on communications from other parties to the appeal proceedings. Parties to the appeal proceedings shall be entitled to make oral presentations.

Article 49
Decisions on appeal

The Board of Appeal may exercise any power which lies within the competence of the Agency or may remit the case to the competent body of the Agency. The latter shall be bound by the decision of the Board of Appeal.

Article 50
Actions before the Court of Justice

1. Actions may be brought before the Court of Justice of the European Communities for the annulment of acts of the Agency which are legally binding on third parties, for failure to act and for damages caused by the Agency in the course of its activities.

2. Actions for the annulment of decisions of the Agency taken pursuant to Articles 20, 21, 22, 22a, 22b, 23, 55 or 64 may be brought before the Court of Justice of the European Communities only after all appeal procedures within the Agency have been exhausted.

3. The Agency shall take all necessary measures to comply with the judgment of the Court of Justice of the European Communities.

Article 51
Direct appeal

Member States and the Community institutions may lodge a direct appeal before the Court of Justice of the European Communities against decisions of the Agency.

SECTION III
Working methods

Article 52
Procedures for the development of opinions, certification specifications and guidance material

1. As soon as possible after the entry into force of this Regulation, the Management Board shall establish transparent procedures for issuing opinions,

certification specifications, acceptable means of compliance and guidance material referred to in Article 18(a) and(c).

Those procedures shall:

(a) draw on expertise available in the aviation regulatory authorities of Member States;
(b) whenever necessary, involve appropriate experts from relevant interested parties;
(c) ensure that the Agency publishes documents and consults widely with interested parties, according to a timetable and a procedure which includes an obligation on the Agency to make a written response to the consultation process.

2. When the Agency, pursuant to Article 19, develops opinions, certification specifications, acceptable means of compliance and guidance material to be applied by Member States, it shall establish a procedure for consulting the Member States. To this effect, it may create a working group in which each Member State is entitled to designate an expert.

3. Measures referred to in Article 18(a) and (c) and the procedures established pursuant to paragraph 1 of this Article shall be published in an official publication of the Agency.

4. Special procedures shall be established to address immediate action to be taken by the Agency to react to a safety problem and to inform the relevant interested parties of the action they are to take.

Article 53
Procedures for taking decisions

1. The Management Board shall establish transparent procedures for taking individual decisions as provided for in Article 18 (d).

Those procedures shall:

(a) ensure the hearing of the natural or legal person to be addressed in the decision and of any other party with a direct and individual concern;
(b) provide for notification of the decision to natural or legal persons and for its publication;
(c) provide for the natural or legal person to whom the decision is addressed, and any other parties to proceedings, to be informed of the legal remedies available to that person under this Regulation;
(d) ensure that the decision contains reasons.

2. The Management Board shall establish procedures specifying the conditions under which decisions are notified while taking due account of the appeal procedure.

3. Special procedures shall be established to address immediate action to be taken by the Agency to react to a safety problem and to inform the relevant interested parties of the action they are to take.

Article 54
Inspections of Member States

1. Without prejudice to the enforcement powers conferred by the Treaty on the Commission, the Agency shall assist the Commission in monitoring the application of this Regulation and its implementing rules by conducting standardisation inspections of Member States competent authorities as specified in Article 24(1). The officials authorised under this Regulation, and those seconded by the national authorities participating in such inspections, are thus empowered, in compliance with the legal provisions of the Member State concerned:

(a) to examine the relevant records, data, procedures and any other material relevant to the achievement of aviation safety levels in accordance with this Regulation;
(b) to take copies of or extracts from such records, data, procedures and other material;
(c) to ask for an oral explanation on the spot;
(d) to enter any relevant premises, land or means of transport.

2. The officials of the Agency authorised for the purpose of the inspections referred to in paragraph 1 shall exercise their powers upon production of an authorisation in writing specifying the subject matter, the purpose of the inspection and the date on which it is to begin. In good time before the inspection, the Agency shall inform the Member State concerned of the inspection and of the identity of the authorised officials.

3. The Member State concerned shall submit to the inspections and shall ensure that bodies or persons concerned also submit to them.

4. When an inspection carried out pursuant to this Article entails an inspection of an undertaking or an association of undertakings, the provisions of Article 55 shall apply. Where an undertaking opposes the inspection, the Member State concerned shall afford the necessary assistance to officials authorised by the Agency to enable them to carry out the inspection.

5. Reports drawn up in application of this Article shall be made available in the official language or languages of the Member State where the inspection took place.

Article 55
Investigation of undertakings

1. The Agency may itself conduct or assign to national aviation authorities or qualified entities all necessary investigations of undertakings in accordance with Articles 7, 20 21, 22, 22a, 22b 23 and 24(2). These investigations shall be carried out in compliance with the legal provisions of the Member States in which they are to be undertaken. To that end, the persons authorised under this Regulation are empowered:

(a) to examine the relevant records, data, procedures and any other material relevant to the execution of the tasks of the Agency;

(b) to take copies of or extracts from such records, data, procedures and other material;
(c) to ask for an oral explanation on site;
(d) to enter relevant premises, lands or means of transport of undertakings;
(e) to conduct inspections of aircraft in cooperation with Member States.

2. The persons authorised for the purpose of the investigations referred to in paragraph 1 shall exercise their powers upon production of an authorisation in writing specifying the subject matter and purpose of the investigation.

3. In good time before the investigation, the Agency shall inform the Member State in whose territory the investigation is to be carried out of the investigation and of the identity of the authorised persons. Officials of the Member State concerned shall, at the request of the Agency, assist those authorised persons to carry out their duties.

Article 56
Annual programme of work

The annual programme of work shall aim to promote the continuous improvement of European aviation safety and comply with the objectives, mandates and tasks of the Agency, as set out in this Regulation. It shall clearly indicate which of the mandates and tasks of the Agency have been added, changed or deleted in comparison with the previous year.

The presentation of the annual programme of work shall be based on the methodology used by the Commission as part of Activity-Based Management.

Article 57
Annual general report

The annual general report shall describe the way in which the Agency has implemented its annual programme of work. It shall clearly indicate which of the mandates and tasks of the Agency have been added, changed or deleted in comparison with the previous year.

The report shall outline the activities carried out by the Agency and evaluate the results thereof with respect to the objectives and timetable set, the risks associated with those activities, the use of resources and the general operations of the Agency.

Article 58
Transparency and communication

1. Regulation (EC) No 1049/2001 shall apply to documents held by the Agency.

2. The Agency may communicate on its own initiative in the fields within its mission. It shall ensure in particular that, in addition to the publication specified in Article 52(3), the public and any interested party are rapidly given objective, reliable and easily understandable information with regard to its work.

3. Any natural or legal person shall be entitled to address himself/herself in writing to the Agency in any of the languages referred to in Article 314 of the Treaty. That person shall have the right to receive an answer in the same language.

4. The information gathered by the Agency in accordance with this Regulation shall be subject to Regulation (EC) No 45/2001 of the European Parliament and of the Council of 18 December 2000 on the protection of individuals with regard to the processing of personal data by the Community institutions and bodies and on the free movement of such data (11).

SECTION IV
Financial requirements

Article 59
Budget

1. The revenues of the Agency shall consist of:

(a) a contribution from the Community;
(b) a contribution from any European third country with which the Community has concluded agreements as referred to in Article 66;
(c) the fees paid by applicants for, and holders of, certificates and approvals issued by the Agency;
(d) charges for publications, training and any other services provided by the Agency; and
(e) any voluntary financial contribution from Member States, third countries or other entities, provided such a contribution does not compromise the independence and impartiality of the Agency.

2. The expenditure of the Agency shall include staff, administrative, infrastructure and operational expenses.

3. Revenue and expenditure shall be in balance.

4. Regulatory budgets and the fees set and collected for certification activities shall be dealt with separately in the Agency's budget.

5. Each year the Management Board, on the basis of a draft statement of estimates of revenue and expenditure, shall produce a statement of estimates of revenue and expenditure of the Agency for the following financial year.

6. The statement of estimates referred to in paragraph 4, which shall include a draft establishment plan together with the provisional work programme, shall by 31 March at the latest be forwarded by the Management Board to the Commission and to the states with which the Community has concluded agreements as referred to in Article 66.

7. The statement of estimates shall be forwarded by the Commission to the budgetary authority together with the preliminary draft general budget of the European Union.

8. On the basis of the statement of estimates, the Commission shall enter in the preliminary draft general budget of the European Union the estimates it deems

necessary for the establishment plan and the amount of the subsidy to be charged to the general budget, which it shall place before the budgetary authority in accordance with Article 272 of the Treaty.

9. The budgetary authority shall authorise appropriations for the subsidy to the Agency. The budgetary authority shall adopt the establishment plan of the Agency.

10. The budget shall be adopted by the Management Board. It shall become final following final adoption of the general budget of the European Union. Where appropriate, it shall be adjusted accordingly.

11. The Management Board shall, as soon as possible, notify the budgetary authority of its intention to implement any project which may have significant financial implications for the funding of the budget, in particular any projects relating to property such as the rental or purchase of buildings. It shall inform the Commission thereof.

Where a branch of the budgetary authority has notified its intention to deliver an opinion, it shall forward its opinion to the Management Board within a period of six weeks from the date of notification of the project.

Article 60
Implementation and control of the budget

1. The Executive Director shall implement the budget of the Agency.

2. By 1 March at the latest following each financial year, the Agency's accounting officer shall communicate the provisional accounts to the Commission's accounting officer, together with a report on the budgetary and financial management for that financial year. The Commission's accounting officer shall consolidate the provisional accounts of the institutions and decentralised bodies in accordance with Article 128 of Council Regulation (EC, Euratom) No 1605/2002 of 25 June 2002 on the Financial Regulation applicable to the general budget of the European Communities (12).

3. By 31 March at the latest following each financial year, the Commission's accounting officer shall forward the Agency's provisional accounts to the Court of Auditors, together with a report on the budgetary and financial management for that financial year. The report on the budgetary and financial management for that financial year shall also be forwarded to the European Parliament and the Council.

4. Pursuant to Article 129 of Regulation (EC, Euratom) No 1605/2002, on receipt of the Court of Auditors' observations on the Agency's provisional accounts, the Executive Director shall draw up the Agency's final accounts under his own responsibility and submit them to the Management Board for an opinion.

5. The Management Board shall deliver an opinion on the Agency's final accounts.

6. The Executive Director shall, by 1 July at the latest following each financial year, forward the final accounts to the European Parliament, the Council, the Commission and the Court of Auditors, together with the Management Board's opinion.

7. The final accounts shall be published.

8. The Executive Director shall send the Court of Auditors a reply to its observations by 30 September at the latest. He shall also send this reply to the Management Board.

9. The Executive Director shall submit to the European Parliament, at the latter's request, any information necessary for the smooth application of the discharge procedure for the financial year in question, as provided for by Article 146(3) of Regulation (EC, Euratom) No 1605/2002.

10. The European Parliament, on a recommendation from the Council acting by a qualified majority, shall, before 30 April of year N + 2, give a discharge to the Executive Director in respect of the implementation of the budget for year N.

Article 61
Combating fraud

1. In order to combat fraud, corruption and other unlawful activities, the provisions of Regulation (EC) No 1073/1999 of the European Parliament and of the Council of 25 May 1999 concerning investigations conducted by the European Anti-Fraud Office (OLAF) (13) shall apply without restriction.

2. The Agency shall accede to the Interinstitutional Agreement of 25 May 1999 between the European Parliament, the Council of the European Union and the Commission of the European Communities concerning internal investigations by the European Anti-fraud Office (OLAF) (14) and shall issue, without delay, the appropriate provisions applicable to its staff.

3. Decisions concerning funding and the implementing agreements and instruments resulting therefrom shall explicitly state that the Court of Auditors and OLAF may carry out, if necessary, on-the-spot checks of the recipients of the Agency's funding and the agents responsible for its allocation.

Article 62
Evaluation

1. Within three years from the date of the Agency having taken up its duties, and every five years thereafter, the Management Board shall commission an independent external evaluation on the implementation of this Regulation.

2. The evaluation shall examine how effectively the Agency is fulfilling its mission. It shall also assess the impact of this Regulation, the Agency and its working practices in

establishing a high level of civil aviation safety. The evaluation shall take into account the views of stakeholders at both European and national level.

3. The Management Board shall receive the findings of the evaluation and issue recommendations regarding changes to this Regulation, the Agency and its working practices to the Commission, which may forward them, together with its own opinion as well as appropriate proposals, to the European Parliament and to the Council. An action plan with a timetable shall be included, if appropriate. Both the findings and the recommendations of the evaluation shall be made public.

Article 63
Financial provisions

The financial rules applicable to the Agency shall be adopted by the Management Board after consultation of the Commission. They may not depart from Commission Regulation (EC, Euratom) No 2343/2002 of 19 November 2002 on the framework Financial Regulation for the bodies referred to in Article 185 of Council Regulation (EC, Euratom) No 1605/2002 on the Financial Regulation applicable to the general budget of the European Communities (15) unless such departure is specifically required for the Agency's operation and the Commission has given its prior consent.

Article 64
Fees and charges regulation

1. The measures designed to amend non-essential elements of this Regulation, by supplementing it, relating to fees and charges shall be adopted in accordance with the regulatory procedure with scrutiny referred to in Article 65(4).

2. The Commission shall consult the Management Board on the draft of the measures referred to in paragraph 1.

3. The measures referred to in paragraph 1 shall determine in particular the matters for which fees and charges pursuant to Article 59(1)(c) and (d) are due, the amount of the fees and charges and the way in which they are to be paid.

4. Fees and charges shall be levied for:

(a) the issuing and renewal of certificates, as well as the related continuing oversight functions;
(b) the provision of services; they shall reflect the actual cost of each individual provision;
(c) the processing of appeals.

All fees and charges shall be expressed, and payable, in euro.

5. The amount of the fees and charges shall be fixed at such a level as to ensure that the revenue in respect thereof is in principle sufficient to cover the full cost of the

services delivered. These fees and charges, including those collected in 2007, shall be assigned revenues for the Agency.

CHAPTER IV
FINAL PROVISIONS

Article 65
Committee

1. The Commission shall be assisted by a committee.

2. Where reference is made to this paragraph, Articles 3 and 7 of Decision 1999/468/EC shall apply, having regard to the provisions of Article 8 thereof.

3. Where reference is made to this paragraph, Articles 5 and 7 of Decision 1999/468/EC shall apply, having regard to the provisions of Article 8 thereof.

The period laid down in Article 5(6) of Decision 1999/468/EC shall be set at one month.

4. Where reference is made to this paragraph, Article 5a(1) to (4), and Article 7 of Decision 1999/468/EC shall apply, having regard to the provisions of Article 8 thereof.

5. Where reference is made to this paragraph, Article 5a(1) to (4) and (5)(b), and Article 7 of Decision 1999/468/EC shall apply, having regard to the provisions of Article 8 thereof.

The time limits laid down in Article 5a(3)(c), (4)(b) and (4)(e) of Decision 1999/468/EC shall be set at 20 days.

6. Where reference is made to this paragraph, Article 5a(1), (2), (4), (5)(b) and (6), and Article 7 of Decision 1999/468/EC shall apply, having regard to the provisions of Article 8 thereof.

7. Where reference is made to this paragraph, Article 6 of Decision 1999/468/EC shall apply.

Before adopting its decision, the Commission shall consult the committee referred to in paragraph 1 of this Article.

The period provided for in Article 6(b) of Decision 1999/468/EC shall be set at three months.

When a Commission decision is referred to the Council by a Member State, the Council, acting by a qualified majority, may take a different decision within a period of three months.

Article 65a
Amendments

In accordance with the provisions of the Treaty, the Commission shall propose to amend Regulations (EC) No 549/2004, (EC) No 550/2004, (EC) No 551/2004 and (EC) No 552/2004 in order to take into account the requirements of this Regulation.

Article 66
Participation of European third countries

The Agency shall be open to the participation of European third countries which are contracting parties to the Chicago Convention and which have entered into agreements with the European Community whereby they adopted and apply Community law in the field covered by this Regulation and its implementing rules.

Under the relevant provisions of these agreements, arrangements will be developed which shall, *inter alia*, specify the nature and extent of, and the detailed rules for, the participation by these countries in the work of the Agency, including provisions on financial contributions and staff.

Article 67
Commencement of the Agency's operation

1. The Agency shall undertake the certification tasks incumbent upon it pursuant to Article 20 as from 28 September 2003. Until that date, Member States shall continue to implement applicable legislation and regulations.

2. During an additional transition period of 42 months from the date referred to in paragraph 1, Member States may continue to issue certificates and approvals by way of derogation from the provisions of Articles 5, 6, 12 and 20 under the conditions specified by the Commission in the measures adopted for their application. When in that context Member States issue certificates on the basis of certificates issued by third countries, the measures adopted by the Commission shall give due consideration to the principles laid down in Article 12(2)(b) and (c).

Article 68
Penalties

Member States shall lay down penalties for infringement of this Regulation and its implementing rules. The penalties shall be effective, proportionate and dissuasive.

Article 69
Repeals

1. Regulation (EC) No 1592/2002 is hereby repealed, without prejudice to the provisions of the second subparagraph.

References made to the repealed Regulation shall be construed as being made to this Regulation and should be read in accordance with the correlation table set out in Annex VI.

2. Council Directive 91/670/EEC is hereby repealed as from the entry into force of the measures referred to in Article 7(6).

3. Annex III to Regulation (EEC) No 3922/91 shall be deleted as from the entry into force of the corresponding measures referred to in Article 8(5).

4. The provisions of Article 11 shall apply to products, parts and appliances, organisations and persons whose certification has been performed, or recognised, in accordance with the provisions of the acts referred to in paragraph 1, 2 and 3 of this Article.

5. Directive 2004/36/EC is hereby repealed as from the entry into force of the measures referred to in Article 10(5) of this Regulation, and without prejudice to the implementing rules referred to in Article 8(2) of that Directive.

Article 70
Entry into force

This Regulation shall enter into force on the 20th day following its publication in the *Official Journal of the European Union.*

Articles 5, 6, 7, 8, 9 and 10 shall apply as from the dates specified in their respective implementing rules, but not later than 8 April 2012.

This Regulation shall be binding in its entirety and directly applicable in all Member States.

(1) OJ C 185, 8.8.2006, p. 106.

(2) Opinion of the European Parliament of 14 March 2007 (OJ C 301 E, 13.12.2007, p. 103), Council Common Position of 15 October 2007 (OJ C 277 E, 20.11.2007, p. 8) and Position of the European Parliament of 12 December 2007. Council Decision of 31 January 2008.

(3) Regulation (EC) No 2111/2005 of the European Parliament and of the Council of 14 December 2005 on the establishment of a Community list of air carriers subject to an operating ban within the Community and on informing air transport passengers of the identity of the operating air carrier (OJ L 344, 27.12.2005, p. 15).

(4) OJ L 240, 7.9.2002, p. 1. Regulation as last amended by Commission Regulation (EC) No 334/2007 (OJ L 88, 29.3.2007, p. 39).

(5) OJ L 373, 31.12.1991, p. 4. Regulation as last amended by Commission Regulation (EC) No 8/2008 (OJ L 10, 12.1.2008, p. 1).

(6) OJ L 373, 31.12.1991, p. 1.

(7) OJ L 143, 30.4.2004, p. 76. Directive as amended by Regulation (EC) No 2111/2005.

(8) OJ L 145, 31.5.2001, p. 43.

(9) OJ L 184, 17.7.1999, p. 23. Decision as amended by Decision 2006/512/EC (OJ L 200, 22.7.2006, p. 11).

(10) OJ L 377, 27.12.2006, p. 1.

(11) OJ L 8, 12.1.2001, p. 1.

(12) OJ L 248, 16.9.2002, p. 1. Regulation as amended by Regulation (EC) No 1525/2007(OJ L 343, 27.12.2007, p. 9).

(13) OJ L 136, 31.5.1999, p. 1.

(14) OJ L 136, 31.5.1999, p. 15.

(15) OJ L 357, 31.12.2002, p. 72.
(*) OJ L 96, 31.3.2004, p. 1.
(**) OJ L 96, 31.3.2004, p. 20.
(***) OJ L 96, 31.3.2004, p. 10.
(****) OJ L 96, 31.3.2004, p. 26.
(*****) OJ L 114, 27.4.2006, p. 22.
(******) OJ L 335, 21.12.2005, p. 13.

ANNEX I

Essential requirements for airworthiness referred to in Article 5

1. *Product integrity: product integrity must be assured for all anticipated flight conditions for the operational life of the aircraft. Compliance with all requirements must be shown by assessment or analysis, supported, where necessary, by tests.*

1.a. Structures and materials: the integrity of the structure must be ensured throughout, and sufficiently beyond, the operational envelope for the aircraft, including its propulsion system, and maintained for the operational life of the aircraft.

1.a.1. All parts of the aircraft, the failure of which could reduce the structural integrity, must comply with the following conditions without detrimental deformation or failure. This includes all items of significant mass and their means of restraint.

1.a.1.a. All combinations of load reasonably expected to occur within, and sufficiently beyond, the weights, centre of gravity range, operational envelope and life of the aircraft must be considered. This includes loads due to gusts, manoeuvres, pressurisation, movable surfaces, control and propulsion systems both in flight and on the ground.

1.a.1.b. Consideration must be given to the loads and likely failures induced by emergency landings either on land or water.

1.a.1.c. Dynamic effects must be covered in the structural response to these loads.

1.a.2. The aircraft must be free from any aeroelastic instability and excessive vibration.

1.a.3. The manufacturing processes and materials used in the construction of the aircraft must result in known and reproducible structural properties. Any changes in material performance related to the operational environment must be accounted for.

1.a.4. The effects of cyclic loading, environmental degradation, accidental and discrete source damage must not reduce the structural integrity below an acceptable residual strength level. All necessary instructions for ensuring continued airworthiness in this regard must be promulgated.

1.b. Propulsion: the integrity of the propulsion system (i.e. engine and, where appropriate, propeller) must be demonstrated throughout, and sufficiently beyond, the operational envelope of the propulsion system and must be maintained for the operational life of the propulsion system.

1.b.1. The propulsion system must produce, within its stated limits, the thrust or power demanded of it at all required flight conditions, taking into account environmental effects and conditions.

1.b.2. The fabrication process and materials used in the construction of the propulsion system must result in known and reproducible structural behaviour. Any changes in material performance related to the operational environment must be accounted for.

1.b.3. The effects of cyclic loading, environmental and operational degradation and likely subsequent part failures must not reduce the integrity of the propulsion system below acceptable levels. All necessary instructions for ensuring continued airworthiness in this regard must be promulgated.

1.b.4. All necessary instructions, information and requirements for the safe and correct interface between the propulsion system and the aircraft must be promulgated.

1.c. Systems and equipment

1.c.1. The aircraft must not have design features or details that experience has shown to be hazardous.

1.c.2. The aircraft, including those systems, equipment and appliances required for type-certification, or by operating rules, must function as intended under any foreseeable operating conditions, throughout, and sufficiently beyond, the operational envelope of the aircraft, taking due account of the system, equipment or appliance operating environment. Other systems, equipment and appliance not required for type-certification, or by operating rules, whether functioning properly or improperly, must not reduce safety and must not adversely affect the proper functioning of any other system, equipment or appliance. Systems, equipment and appliances must be operable without needing exceptional skill or strength.

1.c.3. The aircraft systems, equipment and associated appliances, considered separately and in relation to each other, must be designed such that any catastrophic failure condition does not result from a single failure not shown to be extremely improbable and an inverse relationship must exist between the probability of a failure condition and the severity of its effect on the aircraft and its occupants. With respect to the single failure criterion above, it is accepted that due allowance must be made for the size and broad configuration of the aircraft and that this may prevent this single failure criterion from being met for some parts and some systems on helicopters and small aeroplanes.

1.c.4. Information needed for the safe conduct of the flight and information concerning unsafe conditions must be provided to the crew, or maintenance personnel, as appropriate, in a clear, consistent and unambiguous manner. Systems, equipment and controls, including signs and announcements must be designed and located to minimise errors which could contribute to the creation of hazards.

1.c.5. Design precautions must be taken to minimise the hazards to the aircraft and occupants from reasonably probable threats, both inside and external to the aircraft, including protecting against the possibility of a significant failure in, or disruption of, any aircraft appliance.

1.d. Continuing airworthiness

1.d.1. Instructions for continuing airworthiness must be established to ensure that the aircraft type certification airworthiness standard is maintained throughout the operational life of the aircraft.

1.d.2. Means must be provided to allow inspection, adjustment, lubrication, removal or replacement of parts and appliances as necessary for continuing airworthiness.

1.d.3. The instructions for continuing airworthiness must be in the form of a manual, or manuals, as appropriate for the quantity of data to be provided. The manuals must cover maintenance and repair instructions, servicing information, trouble-shooting and inspection procedures, in a format that provides for a practical arrangement.

1.d.4. The instructions for continuing airworthiness must contain airworthiness limitations that set forth each mandatory replacement time, inspection interval and related inspection procedure.

2. *Airworthiness aspects of product operation*

2.a. The following must be shown to have been addressed to ensure a satisfactory level of safety for those onboard or on the ground during the operation of the product:

2.a.1. The kinds of operation for which the aircraft is approved must be established and limitations and information necessary for safe operation, including environmental limitations and performance, must be established.

2.a.2. The aircraft must be safely controllable and manoeuvrable under all anticipated operating conditions including following the failure of one or, if appropriate, more propulsion systems. Due account must be taken of pilot strength, flight deck environment, pilot workload and other human-factor considerations and of the phase of flight and its duration.

2.a.3. It must be possible to make a smooth transition from one flight phase to another without requiring exceptional piloting skill, alertness, strength or workload under any probable operating condition.

2.a.4. The aircraft must have such stability as to ensure that the demands made on the pilot are not excessive taking into account the phase of flight and its duration.

2.a.5. Procedures for normal operations, failure and emergency conditions must be established.

2.a.6. Warnings, or other deterrents intended to prevent exceedance of the normal flight envelope, must be provided, as appropriate to type.

2.a.7. The characteristics of the aircraft and its systems must allow a safe return from extremes of the flight envelope that may be encountered.

2.b. The operating limitations and other information necessary for safe operation must be made available to the crew members.

2.c. Product operations must be protected from hazards resulting from adverse external and internal conditions, including environmental conditions.

2.c.1. In particular, no unsafe condition must occur from exposure to phenomena such as, but not limited to, adverse weather, lightning, bird strike, high frequency radiated fields, ozone, etc., reasonably expected to occur during product operation.

2.c.2. Cabin compartments must provide passengers with suitable transport conditions and adequate protection from any expected hazard arising in flight operations or resulting in emergency situations, including fire, smoke, toxic gases and rapid decompression hazards. Provisions must be made to give occupants every reasonable chance of avoiding serious injury and quickly evacuating the aircraft and to protect them from the effect of the deceleration forces in the event of an emergency landing on land or water. Clear and unambiguous signs or announcements must be provided, as necessary, to instruct occupants in appropriate safe behaviour and the location and correct use of safety equipment. Required safety equipment must be readily accessible.

2.c.3. Crew compartments must be arranged in order to facilitate flight operations, including means providing situational awareness, and management of any expected situation and emergencies. The environment of crew compartments must not jeopardise the crew's ability to perform their tasks and its design must be such as to avoid interference during operation and misuse of the controls.

3. *Organisations (including natural persons undertaking design, manufacture or maintenance)*

3.a. Organisation approvals must be issued when the following conditions are met:

3.a.1. the organisation must have all the means necessary for the scope of work. These means comprise, but are not limited to, the following: facilities, personnel, equipment, tools and material, documentation of tasks, responsibilities and procedures, access to relevant data and record-keeping;

3.a.2. the organisation must implement and maintain a management system to ensure compliance with these essential requirements for airworthiness, and aim for continuous improvement of this system;

3.a.3. the organisation must establish arrangements with other relevant organisations, as necessary, to ensure continuing compliance with these essential requirements for airworthiness;

3.a.4. the organisation must establish an occurrence reporting and/or handling system, which must be used by the management system under point 3.a.2 and the arrangements under point 3.a.3, in order to contribute to the aim of continuous improvement of the safety of products.

3.b. In the case of maintenance training organisations, the conditions under points 3.a.3 and 3.a.4 do not apply.

ANNEX II

Aircraft referred to in Article 4(4)

Article 4(1), (2) and (3) do not apply to aircraft falling in one or more of the categories set out below:

(a) historic aircraft meeting the criteria below:
  (i) non-complex aircraft whose:
    – initial design was established before 1 January 1955, and
    – production has been stopped before 1 January 1975;or
  (ii) aircraft having a clear historical relevance, related to:
    – a participation in a noteworthy historical event, or
    – a major step in the development of aviation, or
    – a major role played into the armed forces of a Member State;

(b) aircraft specifically designed or modified for research, experimental or scientific purposes, and likely to be produced in very limited numbers;

(c) aircraft of which at least 51 % is built by an amateur, or a non-profit making association of amateurs, for their own purposes and without any commercial objective;

(d) aircraft that have been in the service of military forces, unless the aircraft is of a type for which a design standard has been adopted by the Agency;

(e) aeroplanes, helicopters and powered parachutes having no more than two seats, a maximum take-off mass (MTOM), as recorded by the Member States, of no more than:
  (i) 300 kg for a land plane/helicopter, single-seater; or
  (ii) 450 kg for a land plane/helicopter, two-seater; or
  (iii) 330 kg for an amphibian or floatplane/helicopter single-seater; or
  (iv) 495 kg for an amphibian or floatplane/helicopter two-seater, provided that, where operating both as a floatplane/helicopter and as a land plane/helicopter, it falls below both MTOM limits, as appropriate;
  (v) 472.5 kg for a land plane, two-seater equipped with an airframe mounted total recovery parachute system;
  (vi) 315 kg for a land plane single-seater equipped with an airframe mounted total recovery parachute system;

  and, for aeroplanes, having the stall speed or the minimum steady flight speed in landing configuration not exceeding 35 knots calibrated air speed (CAS);

(f) single and two-seater gyroplanes with a maximum take off mass not exceeding 560 kg;

(g) gliders with a maximum empty mass, of no more than 80 kg when single-seater or 100 kg when two-seater, including those which are foot launched;

(h) replicas of aircraft meeting the criteria of (a) or (d) above, for which the structural design is similar to the original aircraft;

(i) unmanned aircraft with an operating mass of no more than 150 kg;

(j) any other aircraft which has a maximum empty mass, including fuel, of no more than 70 kg.

ANNEX III

Essential requirements for pilot licensing referred to in Article 7

1.*Training*

1.a. General

1.a.1. A person undertaking training to fly an aircraft must be sufficiently mature educationally, physically and mentally to acquire, retain and demonstrate the relevant theoretical knowledge and practical skill.

1.b. Theoretical knowledge

1.b.1. A pilot must acquire and maintain a level of knowledge appropriate to the functions exercised on the aircraft and proportionate to the risks associated to the type of activity. Such knowledge must include at least the following:

(i) air law;
(ii) aircraft general knowledge;
(iii) technical matters related to the category of the aircraft;
(iv) flight performance and planning;
(v) human performance and limitations;
(vi) meteorology;
(vii) navigation;
(viii) operational procedures, including resource management;
(ix) principles of flight;
(x) communications; and
(xi) non-technical skills, including the recognition and management of threats and errors.

1.c. Demonstration and maintenance of theoretical knowledge

1.c.1. The acquisition and retention of theoretical knowledge must be demonstrated by continuous assessment during training, and where appropriate, by examinations.

1.c.2. An appropriate level of competence in theoretical knowledge must be maintained. Compliance must be demonstrated by regular assessments, examinations, tests or checks. The frequency of examinations, tests or checks must be proportionate to the level of risk associated with the activity.

1.d. Practical skill

1.d.1. A pilot must acquire and maintain the practical skills as appropriate to exercise his/her functions on the aircraft. Such skills must be proportionate to the risks associated to the type of activity and must cover, if appropriate to the functions exercised on the aircraft, the following:

(i) pre-flight and in-flight activities, including aircraft performance, mass and balance determination, aircraft inspection and servicing, fuel planning, weather appreciation, route planning, airspace restrictions and runway availability;
(ii) aerodrome and traffic-pattern operations;
(iii) collision avoidance precautions and procedures;

(iv) control of the aircraft by external visual reference;
(v) flight manoeuvres, including in critical situations, and associated 'upset' manoeuvres, as technically achievable;
(vi) normal and cross-wind take-offs and landings;
(vii) flight by reference solely to instruments, as appropriate to the type of activity;
(viii) operational procedures, including team skills and resource management, as appropriate to the type of operation, whether single or multi-crew;
(ix) navigation and implementation of rules of the air and related procedures, using as appropriate, visual reference or navigation aids;
(x) abnormal and emergency operations, including simulated aircraft equipment malfunctions;
(xi) compliance with air traffic services and communications procedures;
(xii) aircraft type or class specific aspects;
(xiii) additional practical skill training that may be required to mitigate risks associated with specific activities; and
(xiv) non-technical skills, including the recognition and management of threats and errors, using an adequate assessment methodology in conjunction with the technical skills assessment.

1.e. Demonstration and maintenance of practical skill

1.e.1. A pilot must demonstrate the ability to perform the procedures and manoeuvres with a degree of competence appropriate to the functions exercised on the aircraft, by:
(i) operating the aircraft within its limitations;
(ii) completing all manoeuvres with smoothness and accuracy;
(iii) exercising good judgement and airmanship;
(iv) applying aeronautical knowledge;
(v) maintaining control of the aircraft at all times in a manner such that the successful outcome of a procedure or manoeuvre is assured; and
(vi) non-technical skills, including the recognition and management of threats and errors, using an adequate assessment methodology in conjunction with the technical skills assessment.

1.e.2. An appropriate level of competence in practical skill must be maintained. Compliance must be demonstrated by regular assessments, examinations, tests or checks. The frequency of examinations, tests or checks must be proportionate to the level of risk associated with the activity.

1.f. Language Proficiency

A pilot must have demonstrated language proficiency to a degree appropriate to the functions exercised on the aircraft. Such demonstrated proficiency shall include:
(i) the ability to understand weather information documents;
(ii) the use of aeronautical en-route, departure and approach charts and associated aeronautical information documents; and

(iii) the ability to communicate with other flight crew and air navigation services during all phases of flight, including flight preparation.

1.g. Flight simulation training devices
When a flight simulation training device (FSTD) is used for training, or for demonstration that practical skill is acquired or maintained, this FSTD must be qualified to a given level of performance in those areas, which are relevant to completing the related task. In particular, the replication of configuration, handling qualities, aircraft performance, and systems behaviour must adequately represent the aircraft.

1.h. Training course
1.h.1. Training must be executed through a training course.
1.h.2. A training course must meet the following conditions:
(i) a syllabus must be developed for each type of course; and
(ii) the training course must comprise a breakdown of theoretical knowledge and practical flight instruction (including synthetic training), if applicable.

1.i. Instructors
1.i.1. Theoretical instruction
Theoretical instruction must be given by appropriately qualified instructors. They must:
(i) have appropriate knowledge in the field where instruction is to be given; and
(ii) be capable of using appropriate instructional techniques.
1.i.2. Flight and flight simulation instruction
Flight and flight simulation instruction must be given by appropriately qualified instructors, who have the following qualifications:
(i) meet the theoretical knowledge and the experience requirements appropriate for the instruction being given;
(ii) be capable of using appropriate instructional techniques;
(iii) have practised instructional techniques in those flight manoeuvres and procedures in which it is intended to provide flight instruction;
(iv) have demonstrated the ability to instruct in those areas in which flight instruction is to be given, including pre-flight, post-flight and ground instruction; and
(v) receive regular refresher training to ensure that the instructional standards are maintained up to date.
Flight instructors must also be entitled to act as pilot in command on the aircraft for which instruction is being given, except for training on new aircraft types.

1.j. Examiners
1.j.1. Persons responsible for assessing the skill of pilots must:
(i) meet the requirements for flight or flight simulation instructors;
(ii) be capable of assessing pilot performance and conducting flight tests and checks.

2. *Experience requirements*

2.a.1. A person acting as flight crew member, instructor or examiner must acquire and maintain sufficient experience for the functions being exercised, unless the implementing rules provide for competence to be demonstrated in accordance with point 1.e.

3. *Training organisations*

3.a. Training organisation requirements

3.a.1. A training organisation providing pilot training must meet the following requirements:

(i) have all the means necessary for the scope of responsibilities associated with their activity. These means comprise, but are not limited to, the following: facilities, personnel, equipment, tools and material, documentation of tasks, responsibilities and procedures, access to relevant data and record-keeping;

(ii) implement and maintain a management system relating to safety and the standard of training, and aim for continuous improvement of this system; and

(iii) establish arrangements with other relevant organisations, as necessary, to ensure continuing compliance with the above requirements.

4. *Medical fitness*

4.a. Medical criteria

4.a.1. All pilots must periodically demonstrate medical fitness to satisfactorily execute their functions, taking into account the type of activity. Compliance must be shown by appropriate assessment based on aero-medical best practice, taking into account the type of activity and the possible mental and physical degradation due to age.

Medical fitness, comprising physical and mental fitness, means not suffering from any disease or disability, which makes the pilot unable:

(i) to execute the tasks necessary to operate an aircraft; or

(ii) to perform assigned duties at any time; or

(iii) to perceive correctly his/her environment.

4.a.2. Where medical fitness cannot be fully demonstrated, mitigation measures that provide equivalent flight safety may be implemented.

4.b. Aero-medical examiners

4.b.1. An aero-medical examiner must:

(i) be qualified and licensed in the practice of medicine;

(ii) have received training in aviation medicine and regular refresher training in aviation medicine to ensure that assessment standards are maintained;

(iii) have acquired practical knowledge and experience of the conditions in which pilots carry out their duties.

4.c. Aero-medical centres

4.c.1. Aero-medical centres must meet the following conditions:

(i) have all the means necessary for the scope of responsibilities associated with their privileges. These means comprise, but are not limited to, the following: facilities, personnel, equipment, tools and material, documentation of tasks, responsibilities and procedures, access to relevant data and record-keeping;

(ii) implement and maintain a management system relating to safety and the standard of medical assessment, and aim for continuous improvement of this system;

(iii) establish arrangements with other relevant organisations, as necessary, to ensure continuing compliance with these requirements.

ANNEX IV

Essential requirements for air operations referred to in Article 8

1. *General*

1.a. A flight must not be performed if the crew members and, as appropriate, all other operations personnel involved in its preparation and execution are not familiar with applicable laws, regulations and procedures, pertinent to the performance of their duties, prescribed for the areas to be traversed, the aerodromes planned to be used and the air navigation facilities relating thereto.

1.b. A flight must be performed in such a way that the operating procedures specified in the Flight Manual or, where required the Operations Manual, for the preparation and execution of the flight are followed. To facilitate this, a checklist system must be available for use, as applicable, by crew members in all phases of operation of the aircraft under normal, abnormal and emergency conditions and situations. Procedures must be established for any reasonably foreseeable emergency situation.

1.c. Before every flight, the roles and duties of each crew member must be defined. The pilot in command must be responsible for the operation and safety of the aircraft and for the safety of all crew members, passengers and cargo on board.

1.d. Articles or substances, which are capable of posing a significant risk to health, safety, property or the environment, such as dangerous goods, weapons and ammunition, must not be carried on any aircraft, unless specific safety procedures and instructions are applied to mitigate the related risks.

1.e. All necessary data, documents, records and information to record the respect of the conditions specified in point 5.c must be retained for each flight and kept available for a minimum period of time compatible with the type of operation.

2. *Flight preparation*

2.a. A flight must not be commenced unless it has been ascertained by every reasonable means available that all the following conditions are complied with:

2.a.1. Adequate facilities directly required for the flight and for the safe operation of the aircraft, including communication facilities and navigation aids, are available for the execution of the flight, taking into account available Aeronautical Information Services documentation.

2.a.2. The crew must be familiar with and passengers informed of the location and use of relevant emergency equipment. Sufficient related information regarding emergency procedures and use of cabin safety equipment must be made available to crew and passengers using specified information.

2.a.3. The pilot in command must be satisfied that:

(i) the aircraft is airworthy as specified in point 6;

(ii) if required, the aircraft is duly registered and that appropriate certificates with respect thereto are aboard the aircraft;

(iii) instruments and equipment as specified in point 5 required for the execution of that flight are installed in the aircraft and are operative, unless waived by the applicable Minimum Equipment List (MEL) or equivalent document;

(iv) the mass of the aircraft and centre of gravity location are such that the flight can be conducted within limits prescribed in the airworthiness documentation;

(v) all cabin baggage, hold luggage and cargo is properly loaded and secured; and

(vi) the aircraft operating limitations as specified in point 4 will not be exceeded at any time during the flight.

2.a.4. Information regarding meteorological conditions for departure, destination and, where applicable, alternate aerodromes, as well as en-route conditions, must be available to the flight crew. Special attention must be given to potentially hazardous atmospheric conditions.

2.a.5. In case of flight into known or expected icing conditions, the aircraft must be certified, equipped and/or treated to operate safely in such conditions.

2.a.6. For a flight based on visual flight rules, meteorological conditions along the route to be flown must be such as to render compliance with these flight rules possible. For a flight based on instrument flight rules a destination and where applicable alternate aerodrome(s) where the aircraft can land must be selected, taking into account in particular the forecasted meteorological conditions, the availability of air navigation services, the availability of ground facilities and the instrument flight procedures approved by the State in which the destination and/or alternate aerodrome is located.

2.a.7. The amount of fuel and oil on board must be sufficient to ensure that the intended flight can be completed safely, taking into account the meteorological conditions, any element affecting the performance of the aircraft and any delays that are expected in flight. In addition, a fuel reserve must be carried to provide for contingencies. Procedures for in-flight fuel management must be established when relevant.

3. *Flight operations*

3.a. With regard to flight operations, all the following conditions must be complied with:

3.a.1. where relevant for the type of aircraft, during take-off and landing, and whenever deemed necessary by the pilot in command in the interest of safety, each crew member must be seated at their crew station and must use the provided restraint systems, taking into account the type of aircraft;

3.a.2. where relevant for the type of aircraft, all flight crew members required to be on flight deck duty must be and remain at their station, with their seatbelts fastened except en-route for physiological or operational needs;

3.a.3. where relevant for the type of aircraft and the type of operation, before take-off and landing, during taxiing and whenever deemed necessary in the interest of safety, the pilot in command must ensure that each passenger is properly seated and secured;

3.a.4. a flight must be performed in such a way that appropriate separation from other aircraft is maintained and that adequate obstacle clearance is ensured, during all phases of the flight. Such separation must at least be those required by the applicable rules of the air;

3.a.5. a flight must not be continued unless known conditions continue to be at least equivalent to those in point 2. Furthermore, for a flight based on instrument flight rules, an approach toward an aerodrome must not be continued below certain specified heights or beyond a certain position, if prescribed visibility criteria are not met;

3.a.6. in an emergency, the pilot in command must ensure that all passengers are instructed in such emergency action as may be appropriate to the circumstances;

3.a.7. a pilot in command must take all necessary measures so as to minimise the consequences on the flight of disruptive passenger behaviour;

3.a.8. an aircraft must not be taxied on the movement area of an aerodrome, or its rotor must not be turned under power, unless the person at the controls is appropriately competent;

3.a.9. the applicable in-flight fuel management procedures must be used, when relevant.

4. *Aircraft performance and operating limitations*

4.a. An aircraft must be operated in accordance with its airworthiness documentation and all related operating procedures and limitations as expressed in its approved flight manual or equivalent documentation, as the case may be. The flight manual or equivalent documentation must be available to the crew and kept up to date for each aircraft.

4.b. The aircraft must be operated in accordance with the applicable environmental documentation.

4.c. A flight must not be commenced or continued unless the aircraft's scheduled performance, considering all factors which significantly affect its performance level, allows all phases of flight to be executed within the applicable distances/areas and obstacle clearances at the planned operating mass. Performance factors which significantly affect take-off, en-route and approach/landing are, particularly:

(i) operating procedures;
(ii) pressure altitude of the aerodrome;
(iii) temperature;

(iv) wind;
(v) size, slope and condition of the take-off/landing area; and
(vi) the condition of the airframe, the power plant or the systems, taking into account possible deterioration.

4.c.1. Such factors must be taken into account directly as operational parameters or indirectly by means of allowances or margins, which may be provided in the scheduling of performance data, as appropriate to the type of operation.

5. *Instruments, data and equipment*

5.a. An aircraft must be equipped with all navigation, communication and other equipment necessary for the intended flight, taking account of air traffic regulations and rules of the air applicable during any phase of the flight.

5.b. When relevant, an aircraft must be equipped with all necessary safety, medical, evacuation and survival equipment, taking account of the risks associated to the areas of operation, the routes to be flown, the flight altitude and the duration of the flight.

5.c. All data necessary for the execution of the flight by the crew must be updated and available on board the aircraft taking account of applicable air traffic regulations, rules of the air, flight altitudes and areas of operation.

6. *Continuing airworthiness*

6.a. The aircraft must not be operated unless:
(i) the aircraft is in an airworthy condition;
(ii) the operational and emergency equipment necessary for the intended flight is serviceable;
(iii) the airworthiness document of the aircraft is valid; and
(iv) the maintenance of the aircraft is performed in accordance with its maintenance programme.

6.b. Before each flight or consistent series of consecutive flights, the aircraft must be inspected, through a pre-flight check, to determine whether it is fit for the intended flight.

6.c. The maintenance programme must contain in particular, maintenance tasks and intervals, especially those that have been specified as mandatory in the instructions for continuing airworthiness.

6.d. The aircraft must not be operated unless it is released to service by qualified persons or organisations, after maintenance. The signed release to service must contain in particular, the basic details of the maintenance carried out.

6.e. All records demonstrating the airworthiness of the aircraft must be kept until the information contained has been superseded by new information equivalent in scope and detail but not less than 24 months in the case of detailed maintenance records. When the aircraft is leased, all records demonstrating the airworthiness of the aircraft must be kept at least for the length of the lease.

6.f. All modifications and repairs must comply with the essential requirements for airworthiness. The substantiating data supporting compliance with the airworthiness requirements must be retained.

7. *Crew members*

7.a. The number and composition of the crew must be determined taking into account:
(i) the certification limitations of the aircraft, including if applicable, the relevant emergency evacuation demonstration;
(ii) the aircraft configuration; and
(iii) the type and duration of operations.

7.b. Cabin crew members must:
(i) be trained and checked on a regular basis to attain and maintain an adequate level of competency in order to perform their assigned safety duties; and
(ii) be periodically assessed for medical fitness to safely exercise their assigned safety duties. Compliance must be shown by appropriate assessment based on aero-medical best practice.

7.c. The pilot in command must have the authority to give all commands and take any appropriate actions for the purpose of securing the operation and the safety of the aircraft and of persons and/or property carried therein.

7.d. In an emergency situation, which endangers the operation or the safety of the aircraft and/or persons on board, the pilot in command must take any action he/she considers necessary in the interest of safety. When such action involves a violation of local regulations or procedures, the pilot in command must be responsible for notifying the appropriate local authority without delay.

7.e. Emergency abnormal situations must not be simulated when passengers or cargo are being carried.

7.f. No crew member must allow their task achievement/decision making to deteriorate to the extent that flight safety is endangered because of the effects of fatigue, taking into account, *inter alia*, fatigue accumulation, sleep deprivation, number of sectors flown, night duties or time zone changes. Rest periods must provide sufficient time to enable crew members to overcome the effects of the previous duties and to be well rested by the start of the following flight duty period.

7.g. A crew member must not perform allocated duties on board an aircraft when under the influence of psychoactive substances or alcohol or when unfit due to injury, fatigue, medication, sickness or other similar causes.

8. *Additional requirements for operation for commercial purposes and operation of complex motor-powered aircraft*

8.a. The operation for commercial purposes and the operation of complex motor-powered aircraft must not be undertaken unless the following conditions are met:

8.a.1. the operator must have directly or indirectly through contracts the means necessary for the scale and scope of the operations. These means comprise but are not limited to the following: aircraft, facilities, management structure, personnel, equipment, documentation of tasks, responsibilities and procedures, access to relevant data and record keeping;

8.a.2. the operator must use only suitably qualified and trained personnel and implement and maintain training and checking programmes for the crew members and other relevant personnel;

8.a.3. the operator must establish a MEL or equivalent document, taking account of the following:

(i) the document must provide for the operation of the aircraft, under specified conditions, with particular instruments, items of equipment or functions inoperative at the commencement of the flight;

(ii) the document must be prepared for each individual aircraft, taking account of the operator's relevant operational and maintenance conditions; and

(iii) the MEL must be based on the Master Minimum Equipment List (MMEL), if available, and must not be less restrictive than the MMEL;

8.a.4. the operator must implement and maintain a management system to ensure compliance with these essential requirements for operations and aim for continuous improvement of this system; and

8.a.5. the operator must establish and maintain an accident prevention and safety programme, including an occurrence reporting programme, which must be used by the management system in order to contribute to the aim of continuous improvement of the safety of operations.

8.b. The operation for commercial purposes and the operation of complex motor-powered aircraft must only be undertaken in accordance with an operator's operations manual. Such manual must contain all necessary instructions, information and procedures for all aircraft operated and for operations personnel to perform their duties. Limitations applicable to flight time, flight duty periods and rest periods for crew members must be specified. The operations manual and its revisions must be compliant with the approved flight manual and be amended as necessary.

8.c. The operator must establish procedures, as appropriate, so as to minimise the consequences to safe flight operations of disruptive passenger behaviour.

8.d. The operator must develop and maintain security programmes adapted to the aircraft and the type of operation including particularly:

(i) security of the flight crew compartment;
(ii) aircraft search procedure checklist;
(iii) training programmes;
(iv) protection of electronic and computer systems to prevent intentional system interference and corruption; and
(v) reporting acts of unlawful interference.

When security measures may adversely affect the safety of operations, the risks must be assessed and appropriate procedures developed to mitigate safety risks, this may necessitate the use of specialist equipment.

8.e. The operator must designate one pilot amongst the flight crew as the pilot in command.

8.f. The prevention of fatigue must be managed through a rostering system. For a flight, or series of flights, such a rostering system needs to address flight time, flight-duty periods, duty and adapted rest periods. Limitations established within the rostering system must take into account all relevant factors contributing to fatigue such as, in particular, number of sectors flown, time-zone crossing, sleep deprivation, disruption of circadian cycles, night hours, positioning, cumulative duty time for given periods of time, sharing of allocated tasks between crew members, and also the provision of augmented crews.

8.g. The tasks specified in point 6.a and those described in points 6.d and 6.e must be controlled by an organisation responsible for the continuing airworthiness management that must meet, in addition to those requirements of Annex I point 3.a, the following conditions:

(i) the organisation must be qualified for the maintenance of products, parts and appliances under its responsibility or have established a contract with such a qualified organisation for these products, parts and appliances; and
(ii) the organisation must establish an organisation manual providing, for use and guidance of personnel concerned, a description of all continuing airworthiness procedures of the organisation including when applicable a description of administrative arrangements between the organisation and the approved maintenance organisation.

ANNEX V

Criteria for qualified entities referred to in Article 13 ("qualified entity" or "entity")

1. The entity, its Director and the staff responsible for carrying out the checks, may not become involved, either directly or as authorised representatives, in the design, manufacture, marketing or maintenance of the products, parts, appliances, constituents or systems or in their operations, service provision or use. This does not exclude the possibility of an exchange of technical information between the involved organisations and the qualified entity.
2. The entity and the staff responsible for the certification tasks must carry out their duties with the greatest possible professional integrity and the greatest possible technical competence and must be free of any pressure and incentive, in particular of a financial type, which could affect their judgment or the results of their investigations, in particular from persons or groups of persons affected by the results of the certification tasks.
3. The entity must employ staff and possess the means required to perform adequately the technical and administrative tasks linked with the certification process; it should also have access to the equipment needed for exceptional checks.
4. The staff responsible for investigation must have:
   - sound technical and vocational training,
   - satisfactory knowledge of the requirements of the certification tasks they carry out and adequate experience of such processes,
   - the ability required to draw up the declarations, records and reports to demonstrate that the investigations have been carried out.
5. The impartiality of the investigation staff must be guaranteed. Their remuneration must not depend on the number of investigations carried out or on the results of such investigations.
6. The entity must take out liability insurance unless its liability is assumed by one Member State in accordance with its national law.
7. The staff of the entity must observe professional secrecy with regard to all information acquired in carrying out their tasks under this Regulation.

ANNEX Va

ESSENTIAL REQUIREMENTS FOR AERODROMES

A - Physical characteristics, infrastructure and equipment

1. *Movement area*

(a) Aerodromes shall have a designated area for the landing and take-off of aircraft, which satisfies the following conditions:
  (i) the landing and take-off area shall have dimensions and characteristics suitable for the aircraft intended to usethe facility;
  (ii) the landing and take-off area, where applicable, shall have a bearing strength sufficient to support repetitive operations of the intended aircraft. Those areas not intended for repetitive operations only need to be capable of supporting the aircraft;
  (iii) the landing and take-off area shall be designed to drain water and to prevent standing water becoming an unacceptable risk to aircraft operations;
  (iv) the slope and slope changes of the landing and take-off area shall not create an unacceptable risk to aircraft operations;
  (v) the surface characteristics of the landing and take-off area shall be adequate for use by the intended aircraft; and
  (vi) the landing and take-off area shall be free from objects which might create an unacceptable risk to aircraft operations.

(b) Where there are several designated landing and take-off areas, they shall be such that they do not create an unacceptable risk to aircraft operations.

(c) The designated landing and take-off area shall be surrounded by defined areas. These areas are intended to protect aircraft flying over them during take-off or landing operations or to mitigate the consequences of undershooting, running off the side or overrunning the take-off and landing area, and shall satisfy the following conditions:
  (i) these areas shall have dimensions appropriate to the aircraft operations anticipated;
  (ii) the slope and slope changes of these areas shall not create an unacceptable risk to aircraft operations;
  (iii) these areas shall be free from objects which might create an unacceptable risk to aircraft operations. This should not preclude frangible equipment to be located in those areas, if required to assist aircraft operations; and
  (iv) each of these areas shall have a bearing strength sufficient to serve its purpose.

(d) Those areas of an aerodrome, with their associated immediate surroundings, that are to be used for taxiing or parking aircraft, shall be designed to permit safe operation of the aircraft expected to use the particular facility under all the conditions planned for, and shall satisfy the following conditions:

(i) these areas shall have a bearing strength sufficient to support repetitive operations of the intended aircraft, except for areas which are expected for only occasional use which only need to be capable of supporting the aircraft;
(ii) these areas shall be designed to drain water and to prevent standing water becoming an unacceptable risk to aircraft operations;
(iii) the slope and slope changes of these areas shall not create an unacceptable risk to aircraft operations;
(iv) the surface characteristics of these areas shall be adequate for use by the intended aircraft; and
(v) these areas shall be free from objects which might create an unacceptable risk to aircraft. This should not preclude parking equipment required for that area in specifically identified positions or zones.

(e) Other infrastructure intended for use by aircraft shall be so designed that use of that infrastructure does not create an unacceptable risk to aircraft using it.
(f) Constructions, buildings, equipment or storage areas shall be located and designed so as not to create an unacceptable risk for aircraft operations.
(g) Suitable means shall be provided to prevent unauthorised persons, unauthorised vehicles or animals large enough to create an unacceptable risk to aircraft operations from entering the movement area, without prejudice to national and international animal protection provisions.

2. *Obstacle clearances*

(a) To protect aircraft proceeding to an aerodrome for landing, or for their departure from an aerodrome, arrival and departure routes or areas shall be established. Such routes or areas shall provide aircraft with the required clearance from obstacles located in the area surrounding the aerodrome taking due account of the local physical characteristics.
(b) Such obstacle clearance shall be appropriate to the phase of flight and type of operation being conducted. It shall also take into account the equipment being used for determining the position of the aircraft.

3. *Visual and non-visual aids and aerodrome equipment*

(a) AIDS shall be fit for purpose, recognisable and provide unambiguous information to users under all intended operational conditions.
(b) Aerodrome equipment shall function as intended under the foreseen operating conditions. Under operating conditions or in case of failure, aerodrome equipment shall not cause an unacceptable risk to aviation safety.
(c) The aids and their electrical power supply system shall be so designed that failures do not result in inappropriate, misleading or insufficient information being given to users or in interruption of an essential service.

(d) Suitable means of protection shall be provided to avoid damage or disturbance to such aids.
(e) Sources of radiation or the presence of moving or fixed objects shall not interfere with or adversely affect the performance of aeronautical communications, navigation and surveillance systems.
(f) Information on operation and use of aerodrome equipment shall be made available to relevant staff, including clear indications of the conditions which may create unacceptable risks to aviation safety.

4. *Aerodrome data*

(a) Data relevant to the aerodrome and the available services shall be established and kept up to date.
(b) The data shall be accurate, readable, complete and unambiguous. Appropriate integrity levels shall be maintained.
(c) The data shall be made available to the users and the relevant ANS providers in a timely manner, using a sufficiently secure and expeditious method of communication.

B - Operations and management

1. The aerodrome operator is responsible for operation of the aerodrome. The responsibilities of the aerodrome operator are as follows:

(a) the aerodrome operator shall have, directly or under contracts, all the means necessary to ensure safe operation of aircraft at the aerodrome. These means shall include, but are not limited to, facilities, personnel, equipment and material, documentation of tasks, responsibilities and procedures, access to relevant data and record-keeping;
(b) the aerodrome operator shall verify that the requirements of Section A are complied with at all times or take appropriate measures to mitigate the risks associated with non-compliance. Procedures shall be established and applied to make all users aware of such measures in a timely manner;
(c) the aerodrome operator shall establish and implement an appropriate aerodrome wildlife risk management programme;
(d) the aerodrome operator shall ensure that movements of vehicles and persons in the movement area and other operational areas are coordinated with movements of aircraft in order to avoid collisions and damage to aircraft;
(e) the aerodrome operator shall ensure that procedures to mitigate risks related to aerodrome operations in winter operation, adverse weather conditions, reduced visibility or at night, if applicable, are established and implemented;
(f) the aerodrome operator shall establish arrangements with other relevant organisations to ensure continuing compliance with these essential requirements for aerodromes. These organisations include, but are not limited to, aircraft operators, air navigation service providers, ground

handling service providers and other organisations whose activities or products may have an effect on aircraft safety;

(g) the aerodrome operator, either by itself or by means of contracts with third parties, shall ensure that procedures exist to provide aircraft with fuel which is uncontaminated and of the correct specification;

(h) manuals for maintenance of aerodrome equipment shall be available, applied in practice and cover maintenance and repair instructions, servicing information, troubleshooting and inspection procedures;

(i) the aerodrome operator shall establish and implement an aerodrome emergency plan, covering emergency scenarios that may occur at the aerodrome or in its surroundings. This plan shall be coordinated, as appropriate, with the local community emergency plan;

(j) the aerodrome operator shall ensure that adequate aerodrome rescue and firefighting services are provided. Such services shall respond to an incident or accident with due urgency and shall include at least equipment, extinguishing agents and a sufficient number of personnel;

(k) the aerodrome operator shall use only trained and qualified personnel for aerodrome operations and maintenance and shall implement and maintain training and check programmes to ensure the continuing competence of all relevant personnel;

(l) the aerodrome operator shall ensure that any person permitted unescorted access to the movement area or other operational areas is adequately trained and qualified for such access;

(m) the rescue and firefighting personnel shall be properly trained and qualified to operate in the aerodrome environment. The aerodrome operator shall implement and maintain training and check programmes to ensure the continuing competence of this personnel; and

(n) all rescue and firefighting personnel potentially required to act in aviation emergencies shall periodically demonstrate their medical fitness to execute their functions satisfactorily, taking into account the type of activity. In this context, medical fitness, comprising both physical and mental fitness, means not suffering from any disease or disability which could make this personnel unable:
   (i) to execute the tasks necessary to operate in aviation emergencies;
   (ii) to perform their assigned duties at any time; or
   (iii) to perceive their environment correctly.

2. *Management systems*

(a) The aerodrome operator shall implement and maintain a management system to ensure compliance with these essential requirements for aerodromes and to aim for continuous and proactive improvement of safety. The management system shall include organisational structures, accountability, responsibilities, policies and procedures.

(b) The management system shall include an accident and incident prevention programme, including an occurrence-reporting and analysis scheme.

The analysis shall involve the parties listed in point 1(f) above, as appropriate.

(c) The aerodrome operator shall develop an aerodrome manual and operate in accordance with that manual. Such manuals shall contain all necessary instructions, information and procedures for the aerodrome, the management system and for operations personnel to perform their duties.

C - Aerodrome surroundings

1. The airspace around aerodrome movement areas shall be safeguarded from obstacles so as to permit the intended aircraft operations at the aerodromes without creating an unacceptable risk caused by the development of obstacles around the aerodrome. Obstacle monitoring surfaces shall therefore be developed, implemented and continuously monitored to identify any infringing penetration.
   (a) Any infringement of these surfaces will require an assessment to identify whether or not the object creates an unacceptable risk. Any object posing an unacceptable risk shall be removed or appropriate mitigating action shall be taken to protect aircraft using the aerodrome.
   (b) Any remaining such obstacles shall be published and, depending on the need, shall be marked and, where necessary, made visible by means of lights.
2. Hazards related to human activities and land use, such as, but not limited to, items on the following list, shall be monitored. The risk caused by them shall be assessed and mitigated as appropriate:
   (a) any development or change in land use in the aerodrome area;
   (b) the possibility of obstacle-induced turbulence;
   (c) the use of hazardous, confusing and misleading lights;
   (d) the dazzling caused by large and highly reflective surfaces;
   (e) the creation of areas that might encourage wildlife activity in the surroundings of the aerodrome movement area;
   (f) sources of non-visible radiation or the presence of moving or fixed objects which may interfere with, or adversely affect, the performance of aeronautical communications, navigation and surveillance systems.
3. A local community emergency plan shall be established for aviation emergency situations occurring in the aerodrome local area.

D - Others

Except for aircraft emergency situations, when diverting to an alternate aerodrome, or under other conditions specified in each case, an aerodrome or parts thereof shall not be used by aircraft for which the aerodrome design and operatingprocedures are not normally intended.

ANNEX Vb

ESSENTIAL REQUIREMENTS FOR ATM/ANS AND AIR TRAFFIC CONTROLLERS

1. Use of the airspace

(a) All aircraft, excluding those engaged in the activities referred to in Article 1(2)(a), in all phases of flight or on the movement area of an aerodrome, shall be operated in accordance with common general operating rules and any applicable procedure specified for use of that airspace.

(b) All aircraft, excluding those engaged in the activities referred to in Article 1(2)(a), shall be equipped with the required constituents and operated accordingly. Constituents used in the ATM/ANS system shall also comply with the requirements in point 3.

2. Services

(a) Aeronautical information and data for airspace users for the purpose of air navigation

(i) The data used as a source for aeronautical information shall be of sufficient quality, complete, current and provided in a timely manner.

(ii) Aeronautical information shall be accurate, complete, current, unambiguous and be of adequate integrity in a suitable format for users.

(iii) The dissemination of such aeronautical information to airspace users shall be timely and use sufficiently reliable and expeditious means of communication protected from interference and corruption.

(b) Meteorological information

(i) The data used as a source for aeronautical meteorological information shall be of sufficient quality, complete and current.

(ii) To the extent possible, aeronautical meteorological information shall be precise, complete, current, be of adequate integrity and unambiguous in order to meet the needs of airspace users.

(iii) The dissemination of such aeronautical meteorological information to airspace users shall be timely and use sufficiently reliable and expeditious means of communication protected from interference and corruption.

(c) Air traffic services

(i) The data used as a source for the provision of air traffic services shall be correct, complete and current.

(ii) Air traffic services shall be sufficiently precise, complete, current, and unambiguous to meet the safety needs of users.

(iii) Automated tools providing information or advice to users shall be properly designed, manufactured and maintained to ensure that they are fit for their intended purpose.

(iv) Air traffic control services and related processes shall provide for adequate separation between aircraft and, where appropriate, assist in protection from obstacles and other airborne hazards and shall ensure prompt and timely coordination with all relevant users and adjacent volumes of airspace.

(v) Communication between air traffic services and aircraft and between relevant air traffic services units shall be timely, clear, correct and unambiguous, protected from interference and commonly understood and, if applicable, acknowledged by all actors involved.

(vi) Means shall be in place to detect possible emergencies and, when appropriate, to initiate effective search and rescue action. Such means shall, as a minimum, comprise appropriate alerting mechanisms, coordination measures and procedures, means and personnel to cover the area of responsibility efficiently.

(d) Communication services

Communication services shall achieve and maintain sufficient performance with regard to their availability, integrity, continuity and timeliness. They shall be expeditious and protected from corruption.

(e) Navigation service

Navigation services shall achieve and maintain a sufficient level of performance with regard to guidance, positioning and, when provided, timing information. The performance criteria include accuracy, integrity, availability and continuity of the service.

(f) Surveillance service

Surveillance services shall determine the respective position of aircraft in the air and of other aircraft and ground vehicles on the aerodrome surface, with sufficient performance with regard to their accuracy, integrity, continuity and probability of detection.

(g) Air traffic flow management

The tactical management of air traffic flows at Community level shall use and provide sufficiently precise and current information of the volume and nature of the planned air traffic affecting service provision and shall coordinate and negotiate re-routing or delaying traffic flows in order to reduce the risk of overloading situations occurring in the air or at the aerodromes.

(h) Airspace management

The designation of specific volumes of airspace for a certain use shall be monitored, coordinated and promulgated in a timely manner in order to reduce the risk of loss of separation between aircraft in all circumstances.

(i) Airspace design

Airspace structures and flight procedures shall be properly designed, surveyed and validated before they can be deployed and used by aircraft.

3. Systems and constituents

(a) General

ATM/ANS systems and constituents providing related information to and from the aircraft and on the ground shall be properly designed, manufactured, installed, maintained and operated to ensure that they are fit for their intended purpose.

(b) System and constituent integrity, performance and reliability

The integrity and safety-related performance of systems and constituents whether on aircraft, on the ground or in space, shall be fit for their intended purpose. They shall meet the required level of operational performance for all their foreseeable operating conditions and for their whole operational life.

(c) Design of systems and constituents

(i) Systems and constituents shall be designed to meet applicable safety requirements.

(ii) Systems and constituents, considered collectively, separately and in relation to each other, shall be designed in such a way that an inverse relationship exists between the probability that any failure can result in a total system failure and the severity of its effect on the safety of services.

(iii) Systems and constituents, considered individually and in combination with each other, shall be designed taking into account limitations related to human capabilities and performance.

(iv) Systems and constituents shall be designed in a manner that protects them from unintended harmful interactions with external elements.

(v) Information needed for manufacturing installation, operation and maintenance of the systems and constituents as well as information concerning unsafe conditions shall be provided to personnel in a clear, consistent and unambiguous manner.

(d) Continuing level of service

Safety levels of systems and constituents shall be maintained during service and any modifications to service.

4. Qualification of air traffic controllers

(a) General

A person undertaking training as an air traffic controller or as a student air traffic controller, shall be sufficiently mature educationally, physically and mentally to acquire, retain and demonstrate the relevant theoretical knowledge and practical skill.

(b) Theoretical knowledge

(i) An air traffic controller shall acquire and maintain a level of knowledge appropriate to the functions exercised and proportionate to the risks associated with the type of service.

(ii) Acquisition and retention of theoretical knowledge shall be demonstrated by continuous assessment during training, or by appropriate examinations.

(iii) An appropriate level of theoretical knowledge shall be maintained. Compliance shall be demonstrated by regular assessments or examinations. The frequency of examinations shall be proportionate to the level of risk associated with the type of service.

(c) Practical skill

(i) An air traffic controller shall acquire and maintain the practical skills appropriate to exercise his/her functions. Such skills shall be proportionate to the risks associated with the type of service and shall cover at least, if appropriate to the functions exercised, the following items:

i. operational procedures;
ii. task specific aspects;
iii. abnormal and emergency situations; and
iv. human factors.

(ii) An air traffic controller shall demonstrate the ability to perform the associated procedures and tasks with a level of competence appropriate to the functions exercised.

(iii) A satisfactory level of competence in practical skill shall be maintained. Compliance shall be verified by regular assessments. The frequency of these assessments shall be proportionate to the complexity and the level of risk associated with the type of service and the tasks performed.

(d) Language proficiency

(i) An air traffic controller shall demonstrate proficiency to speak and understand English to the extent he/she is able to communicate effectively in voice-only (telephone/radiotelephone) and in face-to-face situations on concrete and work-related topics, including in emergency situations.

(ii) Whenever necessary in a defined volume of airspace for ATS service provision purposes, an air traffic controller shall also have proficiency to speak and understand the national language(s) to the extent described above.

(e) Synthetic training devices (STD)

When an STD is used for practical training on situational awareness and human factors or to demonstrate that skills are acquired or maintained, it shall have a level of performance that allows adequate simulation of the working environment and operational situations appropriate to the training provided.

(f) Training course

(i) Training shall be given by a training course, which may comprise theoretical and practical instruction, including training on an STD, if applicable.

(ii) A course shall be defined and approved for each type of training.

(g) Instructors

(i) Theoretical instruction shall be given by appropriately qualified instructors. They shall:

i. have appropriate knowledge in the field where instruction is to be given; and
ii. have demonstrated the ability to use appropriate instructional techniques.

(ii) Instruction on practical skills shall be given by appropriately qualified instructors, who have the following qualifications:
   i. meet the theoretical knowledge and the experience requirements appropriate to the instruction being given;
   ii. have demonstrated the ability to instruct and to use appropriate instructional techniques;
   iii. have practised instructional techniques in those procedures in which it is intended to provide instruction; and
   iv. receive regular refresher training to ensure that the instructional competences are maintained.

(iii) Instructors on practical skills shall also be or have been entitled to act as an air traffic controller.

(h) Assessors
   (i) Persons responsible for assessing the skill of air traffic controllers shall:
      i. have demonstrated the ability to assess the performance of, and conduct tests and checks on air traffic controllers; and
      ii. receive regular refresher training to ensure that the assessment standards are maintained up to date.
   (ii) Assessors on practical skills shall also be or have been entitled to act as an air traffic controller in those areas in which assessment is to be made.

(i) Medical fitness of an air traffic controller
   (i) Medical criteria
      i. All air traffic controllers shall periodically demonstrate medical fitness to satisfactorily execute their functions. Compliance shall be shown by appropriate assessment taking into account the possible mental and physical degradation due to age;
      ii. Demonstration of medical fitness, comprising physical and mental fitness, shall include the demonstrated absence of any disease or disability, which makes the person providing an air traffic control (ATC) service unable:
         – to execute properly the tasks necessary to provide an ATC service,
         – to perform assigned duties at any time, or
         – to perceive correctly his/her environment.
   (ii) Where medical fitness cannot be fully demonstrated, mitigation measures that provide equivalent safety may be implemented.

5. Service providers and training organisations

(a) Service provision shall not be undertaken unless the following conditions are met:
   (i) the service provider shall have directly or indirectly through contracts the means necessary for the scale and scope of the service. These means shall comprise but are not limited to the following: systems,

facilities, including power supply, management structure, personnel, equipment and its maintenance, documentation of tasks, responsibilities and procedures, access to relevant data and record-keeping;

(ii) the service provider shall develop and keep up-to-date management and operations manuals relating to the provision of its services and operate in accordance with those manuals. Such manuals shall contain all necessary instructions, information and procedures for the operations, the management system and for operations personnel to perform their duties;

(iii) the service provider shall implement and maintain a risk-based management system to ensure compliance with the essential requirements in this Annex and aim for continuous proactive improvement of this system;

(iv) the service provider shall use only suitably qualified and trained personnel and implement and maintain training and checking programmes for the personnel;

(v) the service provider shall establish formal interfaces with all the other contributors to the service provision to ensure compliance with these essential requirements;

(vi) the service provider shall establish and implement a contingency plan covering emergency and abnormal situations that may occur in relation to its services;

(vii) the service provider shall establish and maintain an accident and incident prevention and safety programme including an occurrence reporting and analysis programme, which shall be used by the management system in order to contribute to the aim of continuous improvement of safety; and

(viii) the service provider shall make arrangements to verify that the safety performance requirements of any system and constituent they operate are met at any time.

(b) ATC service provision shall not be undertaken unless the following conditions are met:

(i) the prevention of fatigue of personnel providing an ATC service shall be managed through a rostering system. Such a rostering system needs to address duty periods, duty time and adapted rest periods. Limitations established within the rostering system shall take into account relevant factors contributing to fatigue such as, in particular, sleep deprivation, disruption of circadian cycles, night hours, cumulative duty time for given periods of time and also the sharing of allocated tasks between personnel;

(ii) the prevention of stress of personnel providing an ATC service shall be managed through education and prevention programmes;

(iii) the ATC service provider shall have in place procedures to verify that the cognitive judgement of personnel providing ATC services is not impaired or their medical fitness insufficient;

(iv) the ATC service provider shall take into account operational and technical constraints as well as human factor principles in its planning and operations.

(c) Communication, navigation and/or surveillance service provision shall not be undertaken unless the following condition is met:

The service provider shall keep relevant airspace users and ATS units informed on a timely basis of the operational status (and changes thereof) of their services provided for ATS purposes.

(d) Training organisations

A training organisation providing training for personnel providing an ATC service shall meet the following requirements:

(i) have all the means necessary for the scope of responsibilities associated with their activity. These means comprise, but are not limited to, the following: facilities, personnel, equipment, methodology, documentation of tasks, responsibilities and procedures, access to relevant data and record-keeping;

(ii) implement and maintain a management system relating to safety and the standard of training, and aim for continuous improvement of this system; and

(iii) establish arrangements with other relevant organisations, as necessary, to ensure continuing compliance with these essential requirements.

ANNEX VI

CORRELATION TABLE

Regulation (EC) No 1592/2002	*This Regulation*
Article 1	Article 1
Article 2(1)	Article 2(1)
Article 2(2)(a) to (e)	Article 2(2)(a) to (e)
-	Article 2(2)(f)
Article 2(3)	Article 2(3)
Article 3(a) to (g)	Article 3(a) to (g)
-	Article 3(h) to (l)
Article 4(1)(a) to (c)	Article 4(1)(a) to (c)
-	Article 4(1)(d)
-	Article 4(2) and (3)
Article 4(2)	Article 4(4)
-	Article 4(5)
Article 4(3)	Article 4(6)
Article 5(1)	Article 5(1)
Article 5(2), first subparagraph, introductory wording	Article 5(2), first subparagraph, introductory wording
Article 5(2), first subparagraph, points (a) to (c)	Article 5(2), first subparagraph, points (a) to (c)
Article 5(2), first subparagraph, point (d)	Article 5(2), first subparagraph, points (d) and (e)
Article 5(2), first subparagraph, points (e) and (f)	Article 5(2), first subparagraph, points (f) and (g)
-	Article 5(3)
Article 5(3)	Article 5(4)
Article 5(4), first subparagraph, introductory wording	Article 5(5), first subparagraph, introductory wording
Article 5(4), first subparagraph, points (a) to (d)	Article 5(5), first subparagraph, points (a) to (d)
Article 5(4), first subparagraph, point (e)(i) to (iii)	Article 5(5), first subparagraph, point(e)(i) to (iii)
-	Article 5(5), first subparagraph, point (e)(iv) to (vi)
Article 5(4), first subparagraph, points (f) to (i)	Article 5(5), first subparagraph, points (f) to (i)
-	Article 5(5), first subparagraph, point (j)
Article 5(5), first subparagraph, introductory wording	Article 5(6), first subparagraph, introductory wording

Regulation (EC) No 1592/2002	*This Regulation*
Article 5(5), first subparagraph, points (a), (b) and (c)	Article 5(6), first subparagraph, points (a), (b) and (c)
-	Article 5(6), first subparagraph, point (d)
Article 6	Article 6
-	Article 7
-	Article 8
-	Article 9
-	Article 10
Article 8(1)	Article 11(1)
-	Article 11(2) to (4)
Article 8(2)	Article 11(5)
-	Article 11(6)
Article 9	Article 12
-	Article 13
Article 10(1)	Article 14(1)
-	Article 14(2)
Article 10(2)	Article 14(3)
Article 10(3)	Article 14(4)
Article 10(4)	Article 14(5)
Article 10(5)	Article 14(6)
Article 10(6)	Article 14(7)
Article 11	Article 15
-	Article 16
Article 12	Article 17
Article 13, introductory wording	Article 18, introductory wording
Article 13(a)	Article 18(a)
-	Article 18(b)
Article 13(b)	Article 18(c)
Article 13(c)	Article 18(d)
-	Article 18(e)
Article 14	Article 19
Article 15(1), introductory wording	Article 20(1), introductory wording
Article 15(1)(a) to (j)	Article 20(1)(a) to (j)
-	Article 20(1)(k) and (l)
	Article 15(2) Article 20(2)
-	Article 21
-	Article 22
-	Article 23
Article 16(1) and (2)	Article 24(1) and (2)
-	Article 24(3)
Article 16(3)	Article 24(4)

Regulation (EC) No 1592/2002	*This Regulation*
Article 16(4)	Article 24(5)
-	Article 25
Article 17	Article 26
Article 18	Article 27
Article 19	Article 28
Article 20	Article 29
Article 21	Article 30
Article 22	Article 31
Article 23	Article 32
Article 24(1) to (4)	Article 33(1) to (4)
-	Article 33(5)
Article 25(1) and (2)	Article 34(1) and (2)
-	Article 34(3)
Article 26	Article 35
Article 27	Article 36
Article 28	Article 37
Article 29(1) and (2)	Article 38(1) and (2)
Article 29(3)(a) to (j)	Article 38(3)(a) to (j)
-	Article 38(3)(k) and (l)
Article 30	Article 39
Article 31	Article 40
Article 32	Article 41
Article 33	Article 42
Article 34	Article 43
Article 35	Article 44
Article 36	Article 45
Article 37	Article 46
Article 38	Article 47
Article 39	Article 48
Article 40	Article 49
Article 41	Article 50
Article 42	Article 51
Article 43	Article 52
Article 44	Article 53
Article 45	Article 54
Article 46(1), introductory wording	Article 55(1), introductory wording
Article 46(1)(a) to (d)	Article 55(1)(a) to (d)
-	Article 55(1)(e)
Article 46(2) and (3)	Article 55(2) and (3)
-	Article 56
-	Article 57
Article 47(1) and (2)	Article 58(1) and (2)

Regulation (EC) No 1592/2002	*This Regulation*
Article 47(3)	-
Article 47(4)	Article 58(3)
Article 47(5)	-
-	Article 58(4)
Article 48(1), introductory wording	Article 59(1), introductory wording
Article 48(1)(a)	Article 59(1)(a) and (b)
Article 48(1)(b) and (c)	Article 59(1)(c) and (d)
-	Article 59(1)(e)
Article 48(2) and (3)	Article 59(2) and (3)
	Article 59(4)
Article 48(4) to (10)	Article 59(5) to (11)
Article 49	Article 60
Article 50	Article 61
Article 51	Article 62
Article 52	Article 63
Article 53	Article 64
Article 54	Article 65
Article 55	Article 66
Article 56	Article 67
-	Article 68
Article 57	Article 69
Article 59	Article 70

Appendix 16

Regulation (EC) No. 300/2008 of the European Parliament and of the Council

of 11 March 2008

on common rules in the field of civil aviation security and repealing Regulation (EC) No 2320/2002

(Text with EEA relevance)

(OJ No. L 97 of 9 April 2008, p. 72)

as amended by:
COMMISSION REGULATION (EU) No 18/2010
of 8 January 2010

amending Regulation (EC) No 300/2008 of the European Parliament and of the Council as far as specifications for national quality control programmes in the field of civil aviation security are concerned (OJ No. L97 of 12 January 2010, p. 3)

THE EUROPEAN PARLIAMENT AND THE COUNCIL OF THE EUROPEAN UNION,

Having regard to the Treaty establishing the European Community, and in particular Article 80(2) thereof,

Having regard to the proposal from the Commission,

Having regard to the opinion of the European Economic and Social Committee (1),

Having consulted the Committee of the Regions, Acting in accordance with the procedure laid down in Article 251 of the Treaty (2), in the light of the joint text approved by the Conciliation Committee on 16 January 2008.

Whereas:

(1) In order to protect persons and goods within the European Union, acts of unlawful interference with civil aircraft that jeopardise the security of civil aviation should be prevented by establishing common rules for safeguarding civil aviation. This objective should be achieved by setting common rules and common basic standards on aviation security as well as mechanisms for monitoring compliance.

(2) It is desirable, in the interests of civil aviation security generally, to provide the basis for a common interpretation of Annex 17 to the Chicago Convention on International Civil Aviation of 7 December 1944.

(3) Regulation (EC) No 2320/2002 of the European Parliament and of the Council of 16 December 2002 establishing common rules in the field of civil aviation security (3) was adopted as a result of the events of 11 September 2001 in the United States. A common approach is needed in the field of civil aviation security and consideration should be given to the most effective means of offering assistance following terrorist acts that have a major impact in the transport field.

(4) The content of Regulation (EC) No 2320/2002 should be revised in the light of the experience gained, and the Regulation itself should be repealed and replaced by this Regulation seeking the simplification, harmonisation and clarification of the existing rules and the improvement of the levels of security.

(5) Given the need for more flexibility in adopting security measures and procedures in order to meet evolving risk assessments and to allow new technologies to be introduced, this Regulation should lay down the basic principles of what has to be done in order to safeguard civil aviation against acts of unlawful interference without going into the technical and procedural details of how they are to be implemented.

(6) This Regulation should apply to airports serving civil aviation located in the territory of a Member State, to operators providing services at such airports and to entities providing goods and/or services to or through such airports.

(7) Without prejudice to the Convention on offences and certain other acts committed on board aircraft, Tokyo, 1963, the Convention for the suppression of unlawful seizure of aircraft, The Hague, 1970, and the Convention for the suppression of unlawful acts against the safety of civil aviation, Montreal, 1971, this Regulation should also cover security measures that apply on board an aircraft, or during a flight, of Community air carriers.

(8) Each Member State retains the competence to decide whether to deploy in-flight security officers on aircraft registered in that Member State and on flights of air carriers licensed by it as well as to ensure, in accordance with paragraph 4.7.7 of Annex 17 to the Chicago Convention on International Civil Aviation and under the terms of that Convention, that such officers are government personnel who are specially selected and trained, taking into account the required security and safety aspects on board an aircraft.

(9) The various types of civil aviation do not necessarily present the same level of threat. In setting common basic standards on aviation security, the size of the aircraft, the nature of the operation and/or the frequency of operations at airports should be taken into account with a view to permitting the grant of derogations.

(10) Member States should also be allowed, on the basis of a risk assessment, to apply more stringent measures than those laid down in this Regulation.

(11) Third countries may require the application of measures that differ from those laid down in this Regulation in respect of flights from an airport in a Member State to, or over, that third country. However, without prejudice to any bilateral agreements to which the Community is a party, it should be possible for the Commission to examine the measures required by the third country.

(12) Even though, within a single Member State, there may be two or more bodies involved in aviation security, each Member State should designate a single authority responsible for the coordination and monitoring of the implementation of security standards.

(13) In order to define responsibilities for the implementation of the common basic standards on aviation security and to describe what measures are required by operators and other entities for this purpose, each Member State should draw up a national civil aviation security programme. Furthermore, each airport operator, air carrier and entity implementing aviation security standards should draw up, apply and maintain a security programme in order to comply both with this Regulation and with whichever national civil aviation security programme is applicable.

(14) In order to monitor compliance with this Regulation and with the national civil aviation security programme, each Member State should draw up and ensure the implementation of a national programme to check the level and quality of civil aviation security.

(15) In order to monitor the application by Member States of this Regulation, and also to make recommendations to improve aviation security, the Commission should conduct inspections, including unannounced inspections.

(16) As a general rule, the Commission should publish measures that have a direct impact on passengers. Implementing acts setting out common measures and procedures for the implementation of the common basic standards on aviation security which contain sensitive security information, together with Commission inspection reports and the answers of the appropriate authorities should be regarded as EU classified information within the meaning of Commission Decision 2001/844/EC, ECSC, Euratom of 29 November 2001 amending its internal rules of procedure (4). Those items should not be published and should be made available only to those operators and entities with a legitimate interest.

(17) The measures necessary for the implementation of this Regulation should be adopted in accordance with Council Decision 1999/468/EC of 28 June 1999 laying

down the procedures for the exercise of implementing powers conferred on the Commission (5).

(18) In particular, the Commission should be empowered to adopt general measures amending non-essential elements of the common basic standards by supplementing them, set criteria allowing Member States both to derogate from the common basic standards and to adopt alternative security measures, and adopt specifications for national quality control programmes. Since those measures are of general scope and are designed to amend non-essential elements of this Regulation by supplementing it with new non-essential elements, they must be adopted in accordance with the regulatory procedure with scrutiny provided for in Article 5a of Decision 1999/468/EC.

(19) When, on imperative grounds of urgency, the normal time-limits for the regulatory procedure with scrutiny cannot be complied with, the Commission should be able to apply the urgency procedure provided for in Article 5a(6) of Decision 1999/468/EC for the adoption of common rules for safeguarding civil aviation.

(20) The goal of 'one-stop security' for all flights within the European Union should be advanced.

(21) Furthermore, it should not be necessary to rescreen passengers or their baggage arriving on flights from third countries that have aviation security standards equivalent to those laid down by this Regulation. Therefore, without prejudice to the right of each Member State to apply more stringent measures, or to the respective competences of the Community and Member States, decisions of the Commission, and, where necessary, agreements between the Community and third countries, which recognise that the security standards applied in the third country are equivalent to the common standards, should be encouraged since these further one-stop security.

(22) This Regulation is without prejudice to the application of rules on aviation safety, including those relating to the transport of dangerous goods.

(23) Penalties should be provided for infringements of the provisions of this Regulation. Those penalties, which may be of a civil or administrative nature, should be effective, proportionate and dissuasive.

(24) The Ministerial Statement on Gibraltar Airport, agreed in Cordoba on 18 September 2006 during the first Ministerial meeting of the Forum of Dialogue on Gibraltar, will replace the Joint Declaration on Gibraltar Airport made in London on 2 December 1987, and full compliance with it will be deemed to constitute compliance with the 1987 Declaration.

(25) Since the objectives of this Regulation, namely to safeguard civil aviation against acts of unlawful interference and to provide a basis for a common interpretation of Annex 17 to the Chicago Convention on International Civil Aviation, cannot be sufficiently achieved by the Member States and can therefore, by reason

of the scale and effects of this Regulation, be better achieved at Community level, the Community may adopt measures, in accordance with the principle of subsidiarity as set out in Article 5 of the Treaty. In accordance with the principle of proportionality, as set out in that Article, this Regulation does not go beyond what is necessary in order to achieve those objectives,
HAVE ADOPTED THIS REGULATION:

Article 1
Objectives

1. This Regulation establishes common rules to protect civil aviation against acts of unlawful interference that jeopardise the security of civil aviation.
It also provides the basis for a common interpretation of Annex 17 to the Chicago Convention on International Civil Aviation.

2. The means of achieving the objectives set out in paragraph 1 shall be:

(a) the setting of common rules and common basic standards on aviation security;
(b) mechanisms for monitoring compliance.

Article 2
Scope

1. This Regulation shall apply to the following:

(a) all airports or parts of airports located in the territory of a Member State that are not exclusively used for military purposes;
(b) all operators, including air carriers, providing services at airports referred to in point (a);
(c) all entities applying aviation security standards that operate from premises located inside or outside airport premises and provide goods and/or services to or through airports referred to in point (a).

2. The application of this Regulation to the airport of Gibraltar is understood to be without prejudice to the respective legal positions of the Kingdom of Spain and the United Kingdom with regard to the dispute over sovereignty over the territory in which the airport is situated.

Article 3
Definitions

For the purposes of this Regulation:

1. 'civil aviation' means any air operation carried out by civil aircraft, excluding operations carried out by State aircraft referred to in Article 3 of the Chicago Convention on International Civil Aviation;
2. 'aviation security' means the combination of measures and human and material resources intended to safeguard civil aviation against acts of unlawful interference that jeopardise the security of civil aviation;

3. 'operator' means a person, organisation or enterprise engaged, or offering to engage, in an air transport operation;
4. 'air carrier' means an air transport undertaking holding a valid operating licence or equivalent;
5. 'Community air carrier' means an air carrier holding a valid operating licence granted by a Member State in accordance with Council Regulation (EEC) No 2407/92 of 23 July 1992 on licensing of air carriers (6);
6. 'entity' means a person, organisation or enterprise, other than an operator;
7. 'prohibited articles' means weapons, explosives or other dangerous devices, articles or substances that may be used to commit an act of unlawful interference that jeopardises the security of civil aviation;
8. 'screening' means the application of technical or other means which are intended to identify and/or detect prohibited articles;
9. 'security control' means the application of means by which the introduction of prohibited articles may be prevented;
10. 'access control' means the application of means by which the entry of unauthorised persons or unauthorised vehicles, or both, may be prevented;
11. 'airside' means the movement area of an airport, adjacent terrain and buildings or portions thereof, access to which is restricted;
12. 'landside' means those parts of an airport, adjacent terrain and buildings or portions thereof that are not airside;
13. 'security restricted area' means that area of airside where, in addition to access being restricted, other aviation security standards are applied;
14. 'demarcated area' means an area that is separated by means of access control either from security restricted areas, or, if the demarcated area itself is a security restricted area, from other security restricted areas of an airport;
15. 'background check' means a recorded check of a person's identity, including any criminal history, as part of the assessment of an individual's suitability for unescorted access to security restricted areas;
16. 'transfer passengers, baggage, cargo or mail' means passengers, baggage, cargo or mail departing on an aircraft other than that on which they arrived;
17. 'transit passengers, baggage, cargo or mail' means passengers, baggage, cargo or mail departing on the same aircraft as that on which they arrived;
18. 'potentially disruptive passenger' means a passenger who is either a deportee, a person deemed to be inadmissible for immigration reasons or a person in lawful custody;
19. 'cabin baggage' means baggage intended for carriage in the cabin of an aircraft;
20. 'hold baggage' means baggage intended for carriage in the hold of an aircraft;

21. 'accompanied hold baggage' means baggage, carried in the hold of an aircraft, which has been checked in for a flight by a passenger travelling on that same flight;
22. 'air carrier mail' means mail whose origin and destination are both an air carrier;
23. 'air carrier materials' means materials either whose origin and destination are both an air carrier or that are used by an air carrier;
24. 'mail' means dispatches of correspondence and other items, other than air carrier mail, tendered by and intended for delivery to postal services in accordance with the rules of the Universal Postal Union;
25. 'cargo' means any property intended for carriage on an aircraft, other than baggage, mail, air carrier mail, air carrier materials and in-flight supplies;
26. 'regulated agent' means an air carrier, agent, freight forwarder or any other entity who ensures security controls in respect of cargo or mail;
27. 'known consignor' means a consignor who originates cargo or mail for its own account and whose procedures meet common security rules and standards sufficient to allow carriage of cargo or mail on any aircraft;
28. 'account consignor' means a consignor who originates cargo or mail for its own account and whose procedures meet common security rules and standards sufficient to allow carriage of that cargo on all-cargo aircraft or mail on all-mail aircraft;
29. 'aircraft security check' means an inspection of those parts of the interior of the aircraft to which passengers may have had access, together with an inspection of the hold of the aircraft in order to detect prohibited articles and unlawful interferences with the aircraft;
30. 'aircraft security search' means an inspection of the interior and accessible exterior of the aircraft in order to detect prohibited articles and unlawful interferences that jeopardise the security of the aircraft;
31. 'in-flight security officer' means a person who is employed by a state to travel on an aircraft of an air carrier licensed by it with the purpose of protecting that aircraft and its occupants against acts of unlawful interference that jeopardise the security of the flight.

Article 4
Common basic standards

1. The common basic standards for safeguarding civil aviation against acts of unlawful interference that jeopardise the security of civil aviation shall be as laid down in the Annex.

Additional common basic standards not foreseen at the entry into force of this Regulation should be added to the Annex in accordance with the procedure referred to in Article 251 of the Treaty.

2. General measures, designed to amend non-essential elements of the common basic standards referred to in paragraph 1 by supplementing them, shall be adopted

in accordance with the regulatory procedure with scrutiny referred to in Article 19(3).

These general measures shall concern:

(a) methods of screening allowed;
(b) categories of articles that may be prohibited;
(c) as regards access control, grounds for granting access to airside and security restricted areas;
(d) methods allowed for the examination of vehicles, aircraft security checks and aircraft security searches;
(e) criteria for recognising the equivalence of security standards of third countries;
(f) conditions under which cargo and mail shall be screened or subjected to other security controls, as well as the process for the approval or designation of regulated agents, known consignors and account consignors;
(g) conditions under which air carrier mail and air carrier materials shall be screened or subjected to other security controls;
(h) conditions under which in-flight supplies and airport supplies shall be screened or subjected to other security controls, as well as the process for the approval or designation of regulated suppliers and known suppliers;
(i) criteria for defining critical parts of security restricted areas;
(j) criteria for staff recruitment and methods of training;
(k) conditions under which special security procedures or exemptions from security controls may be applied; and
(l) any general measures designed to amend non-essential elements of the common basic standards referred to in paragraph 1 by supplementing them not foreseen at the date of entry into force of this Regulation.

On imperative grounds of urgency, the Commission may use the urgency procedure referred to in Article 19(4).

3. Detailed measures for the implementation of the common basic standards referred to in paragraph 1 and the general measures referred to in paragraph 2 shall be laid down in accordance with the regulatory procedure referred to in Article 19(2).

These shall include:

(a) requirements and procedures for screening;
(b) a list of prohibited articles;
(c) requirements and procedures for access control;
(d) requirements and procedures for the examination of vehicles, aircraft security checks and aircraft security searches;
(e) decisions to recognise the equivalence of security standards applied in a third country;

(f) as regards cargo and mail, procedures for the approval or designation of, and the obligations to be fulfilled by, regulated agents, known consignors and account consignors;
(g) requirements and procedures for security controls of air carrier mail and air carrier materials;
(h) as regards in-flight supplies and airport supplies, procedures for the approval or designation of, and the obligations to be fulfilled by, regulated suppliers and known suppliers;
(i) definition of critical parts of security restricted areas;
(j) staff recruitment and training requirements;
(k) special security procedures or exemptions from security controls;
(l) technical specifications and procedures for approval and use of security equipment; and
(m) requirements and procedures concerning potentially disruptive passengers.

4. The Commission shall, by amending this Regulation through a decision in accordance with the regulatory procedure with scrutiny referred to in Article 19(3), set criteria to allow Member States to derogate from the common basic standards referred to in paragraph 1 and to adopt alternative security measures that provide an adequate level of protection on the basis of a local risk assessment. Such alternative measures shall be justified by reasons relating to the size of the aircraft, or by reasons relating to the nature, scale or frequency of operations or of other relevant activities.

On imperative grounds of urgency, the Commission may use the urgency procedure referred to in Article 19(4).

The Member States shall inform the Commission of such measures.

5. Member States shall ensure the application in their territory of the common basic standards referred to in paragraph 1. Where a Member State has reason to believe that the level of aviation security has been compromised through a security breach, it shall ensure that appropriate and prompt action is taken to rectify that breach and ensure the continuing security of civil aviation.

Article 5
Security costs

Subject to the relevant rules of Community law, each Member State may determine in which circumstances, and the extent to which, the costs of security measures taken under this Regulation to protect civil aviation against acts of unlawful interference should be borne by the State, the airport entities, air carriers, other responsible agencies, or users. If appropriate, and in conformity with Community law, Member States may contribute with users to the costs of more stringent security measures taken under this Regulation. As far as may be practicable, any charges or transfers of security costs shall be directly related to the costs of providing the security services concerned and shall be designed to recover no more than the relevant costs involved.

Article 6
More stringent measures applied by Member States

1. Member States may apply more stringent measures than the common basic standards referred to in Article 4. In doing so, they shall act on the basis of a risk assessment and in compliance with Community law. Those measures shall be relevant, objective, non-discriminatory and proportional to the risk that is being addressed.

2. Member States shall inform the Commission of such measures as soon as possible after their application. Upon reception of such information, the Commission shall transmit this information to the other Member States.

3. Member States are not required to inform the Commission where the measures concerned are limited to a given flight on a specific date.

Article 7
Security measures required by third countries

1. Without prejudice to any bilateral agreements to which the Community is a party, a Member State shall notify the Commission of measures required by a third country if they differ from the common basic standards referred to in Article 4 in respect of flights from an airport in a Member State to, or over, that third country.

2. At the request of the Member State concerned or on its own initiative, the Commission shall examine the application of any measures notified under paragraph 1 and may, in accordance with the regulatory procedure referred to in Article 19(2), draw up an appropriate response to the third country concerned.

3. Paragraphs 1 and 2 shall not apply if:

(a) the Member State concerned applies the measures concerned in accordance with Article 6; or
(b) the requirement of the third country is limited to a given flight on a specific date.

Article 8
Cooperation with the International Civil Aviation Organisation

Without prejudice to Article 300 of the Treaty, the Commission may conclude a Memorandum of Understanding concerning audits with the International Civil Aviation Organisation (ICAO) in order to avoid duplicate monitoring of Member States' compliance with Annex 17 to the Chicago Convention on International Civil Aviation.

Article 9
Appropriate authority

Where, within a single Member State, two or more bodies are involved in civil aviation security, that Member State shall designate a single authority (hereinafter referred to as the appropriate authority) to be responsible for the coordination and monitoring of the implementation of the common basic standards referred to in Article 4.

Article 10
National civil aviation security programme

1. Every Member State shall draw up, apply and maintain a national civil aviation security programme.

That programme shall define responsibilities for the implementation of the common basic standards referred to in Article 4 and shall describe the measures required by operators and entities for this purpose.

2. The appropriate authority shall make available in writing on a 'need to know' basis the appropriate parts of its national civil aviation security programme to operators and entities which it deems to have a legitimate interest.

Article 11
National quality control programme

1. Every Member State shall draw up, apply and maintain a national quality control programme.

That programme shall enable the Member State to check the quality of civil aviation security in order to monitor compliance both with this Regulation and with its national civil aviation security programme.

2. The specifications for the national quality control programme shall be adopted by amending this Regulation through the addition of an annex in accordance with the regulatory procedure with scrutiny referred to in Article 19(3).

On imperative grounds of urgency, the Commission may use the urgency procedure referred to in Article 19(4).

The programme shall allow for the swift detection and correction of deficiencies. It shall also provide that all airports, operators and entities responsible for the implementation of aviation security standards that are located in the territory of the Member State concerned shall be regularly monitored directly by, or under the supervision of, the appropriate authority.

Article 12
Airport security programme

1. Every airport operator shall draw up, apply and maintain an airport security programme.

That programme shall describe the methods and procedures which are to be followed by the airport operator in order to comply both with this Regulation and with the national civil aviation security programme of the Member State in which the airport is located.

The programme shall include internal quality control provisions describing how compliance with these methods and procedures is to be monitored by the airport operator.

2. The airport security programme shall be submitted to the appropriate authority, which may take further action if appropriate.

Article 13
Air carrier security programme

1. Every air carrier shall draw up, apply and maintain an air carrier security programme.

That programme shall describe the methods and procedures which are to be followed by the air carrier in order to comply both with this Regulation and with the national civil aviation security programme of the Member State from which it provides services.

The programme shall include internal quality control provisions describing how compliance with these methods and procedures is to be monitored by the air carrier.

2. Upon request, the air carrier security programme shall be submitted to the appropriate authority, which may take further action if appropriate.

3. Where a Community air carrier security programme has been validated by the appropriate authority of the Member State granting the operating licence, the air carrier shall be recognised by all other Member States as having fulfilled the requirements of paragraph 1. This is without prejudice to a Member State's right to request from any air carrier details of its implementation of:

(a) the security measures applied by that Member State under Article 6; and/or
(b) local procedures that are applicable at the airports served.

Article 14
Entity security programme

1. Every entity required under the national civil aviation security programme referred to in Article 10 to apply aviation security standards shall draw up, apply and maintain a security programme.

That programme shall describe the methods and procedures which are to be followed by the entity in order to comply with the national civil aviation security programme of the Member State in respect of its operations in that Member State.

The programme shall include internal quality control provisions describing how compliance with these methods and procedures is to be monitored by the entity itself.

2. Upon request, the security programme of the entity applying aviation security standards shall be submitted to the appropriate authority, which may take further action if appropriate.

Article 15
Commission inspections

1. The Commission, acting in cooperation with the appropriate authority of the Member State concerned, shall conduct inspections, including inspections of airports, operators and entities applying aviation security standards, in order to monitor the application by Member States of this Regulation and, as appropriate, to make recommendations to improve aviation security. For this purpose, the

appropriate authority shall inform the Commission in writing of all airports in its territory serving civil aviation other than those covered by Article 4(4).

The procedures for conducting Commission inspections shall be adopted in accordance with the regulatory procedure referred to in Article 19(2).

2. Commission inspections of airports, operators and entities applying aviation security standards shall be unannounced. The Commission shall in good time before an inspection inform the Member State concerned thereof.

3. Each Commission inspection report shall be communicated to the appropriate authority of the Member State concerned, which shall, in its answer, set out the measures taken to remedy any identified deficiencies.

The report, together with the answer of the appropriate authority, shall subsequently be communicated to the appropriate authority of the other Member States.

Article 16
Annual report

Every year the Commission shall present a report to the European Parliament, the Council and the Member States informing them of the application of this Regulation and of its impact on improving aviation security.

Article 17
Stakeholders' Advisory Group

Without prejudice to the role of the Committee referred to in Article 19, the Commission shall establish a Stakeholders' Advisory Group on Aviation Security, composed of European representative organisations engaged in, or directly affected by, aviation security. The role of this group shall be solely to advise the Commission. The Committee referred to in Article 19 shall keep the Stakeholders' Advisory Group informed during the entire regulatory process.

Article 18
Dissemination of information

As a general rule, the Commission shall publish measures that have a direct impact on passengers. However, the following documents shall be regarded as EU classified information within the meaning of Decision 2001/844/EC, ECSC, Euratom:

(a) measures and procedures as referred to in Articles 4(3), 4(4), 6(1) and 7(1), if containing sensitive security information;
(b) the Commission inspection reports and the answers of the appropriate authorities referred to in Article 15(3).

Article 19
Committee procedure

1. The Commission shall be assisted by a Committee.

2. Where reference is made to this paragraph, Articles 5 and 7 of Decision 1999/468/EC shall apply, having regard to the provisions of Article 8 thereof.

The period laid down in Article 5(6) of Decision 1999/468/EC shall be set at one month.

3. Where reference is made to this paragraph, Article 5a(1) to (4) and Article 7 of Decision 1999/468/EC shall apply, having regard to the provisions of Article 8 thereof.

4. Where reference is made to this paragraph, Article 5a(1), (2), (4), and (6) and Article 7 of Decision 1999/468/EC shall apply, having regard to the provisions of Article 8 thereof.

Article 20
Agreements between the Community and third countries

When appropriate, and in conformity with Community law, agreements recognising that the security standards applied in a third country are equivalent to Community standards could be envisaged in aviation agreements between the Community and a third country in accordance with Article 300 of the Treaty, in order to advance the goal of 'one-stop security' for all flights between the European Union and third countries.

Article 21
Penalties

Member States shall lay down the rules on penalties applicable to infringements of the provisions of this Regulation and shall take all measures necessary to ensure that they are implemented. The penalties provided for must be effective, proportionate and dissuasive.

Article 22
Commission report on financing

The Commission will report, no later than 31 December 2008, on the principles of the financing of the costs of civil aviation security measures. That report will consider what steps need to be taken in order to ensure that security charges are used exclusively to meet security costs, and to improve the transparency of such charges. The report will also address the principles necessary to safeguard undistorted competition between airports and between air carriers, and the different methods to ensure consumer protection as regards the distribution of the costs of security measures between taxpayers and users. The Commission report will be accompanied, if appropriate, by a legislative proposal.

Article 23
Repeal

Regulation (EC) No 2320/2002 is hereby repealed.

Article 24
Entry into force

1. This Regulation shall enter into force on the 20th day following its publication in the *Official Journal of the European Union*.

2. It shall apply as from the date specified in the implementing rules adopted in accordance with the procedures referred to in Article 4(2) and (3), but not later than 24 months after the entry into force of this Regulation.

3. By way of exception to paragraph 2, Articles 4(2), 4(3), 4(4), 8, 11(2), 15(1) second subparagraph, 17, 19 and 22 shall apply from the date of entry into force of this Regulation.

This Regulation shall be binding in its entirety and directly applicable in all Member States.

(1) OJ C 185, 8.8.2006, p. 17.

(2) Opinion of the European Parliament of 15 June 2006 (OJ C 300 E, 9.12.2006, p. 463), Council Common Position of 11 December 2006 (OJ C 70 E, 27.3.2007, p. 21) and Position of the European Parliament of 25 April 2007 (not yet published in the Official Journal), Legislative Resolution of the European Parliament of 11 March 2008 (not yet published in the Official Journal) and Council Decision of 4 March 2008.

(3) OJ L 355, 30.12.2002, p. 1. Regulation as amended by Regulation (EC) No 849/2004 (OJ L 158, 30.4.2004, p. 1, corrected by OJ L 229, 29.6.2004, p. 3).

(4) OJ L 317, 3.12.2001, p. 1. Decision as last amended by Decision 2006/548/EC, Euratom (OJ L 215, 5.8.2006, p. 38).

(5) OJ L 184, 17.7.1999, p. 23. Decision as amended by Decision 2006/512/EC (OJ L 200, 22.7.2006, p. 11).

(6) OJ L 240, 24.8.1992, p. 1.

ANNEX I

COMMON BASIC STANDARDS FOR SAFEGUARDING CIVIL AVIATION AGAINST ACTS OF UNLAWFUL INTERFERENCE (ARTICLE 4)

1. AIRPORT SECURITY

1.1 **Airport planning requirements**

1. When designing and constructing new airport facilities or altering existing airport facilities, requirements for the implementation of the common basic standards set out in this Annex and its implementing acts shall be fully taken into account.
2. At airports the following areas shall be established:
   (a) landside;
   (b) airside;
   (c) security restricted areas; and
   (d) critical parts of security restricted areas.

1.2. **Access control**

1. Access to airside shall be restricted in order to prevent unauthorised persons and vehicles from entering these areas.
2. Access to security restricted areas shall be controlled in order to ensure that no unauthorised persons and vehicles enter these areas.
3. Persons and vehicles may be granted access to airside and security restricted areas only if they fulfil the required security conditions.
4. Persons, including flight crew members, shall have successfully completed a background check before either a crew identification card or an airport identification card authorising unescorted access to security restricted areas is issued to them.

1.3. **Screening of persons other than passengers and items carried**

1. Persons other than passengers, together with items carried, shall be screened on a continuous random basis upon entering security restricted areas in order to prevent prohibited articles from being introduced into these areas.
2. All persons other than passengers, together with items carried, shall be screened upon entering critical parts of security restricted areas in order to prevent prohibited articles from being introduced into these parts.

1.4. **Examination of vehicles**
Vehicles entering a security restricted area shall be examined in order to prevent prohibited articles from being introduced into these areas.

1.5. **Surveillance, patrols and other physical controls**
There shall be surveillance, patrols and other physical controls at airports and, where appropriate, in adjacent areas with public access, in order to identify

suspicious behaviour of persons, to identify vulnerabilities which could be exploited to carry out an act of unlawful interference and to deter persons from committing such acts.

2. DEMARCATED AREAS OF AIRPORTS
Aircraft parked in demarcated areas of airports to which alternative measures referred to in Article 4(4) apply, shall be separated from aircraft to which the common basic standards apply in full, in order to ensure that security standards applied to aircraft, passengers, baggage, cargo and mail of the latter are not compromised.

3. AIRCRAFT SECURITY

1. Before departure, an aircraft shall be subjected to an aircraft security check or aircraft security search in order to ensure that no prohibited articles are present on board. An aircraft in transit may be subjected to other appropriate measures.
2. Every aircraft shall be protected from unauthorised interference.

4. PASSENGERS AND CABIN BAGGAGE

4.1. **Screening of passengers and cabin baggage**

1. All originating, transfer and transit passengers and their cabin baggage shall be screened in order to prevent prohibited articles from being introduced into security restricted areas and on board an aircraft.
2. Transfer passengers and their cabin baggage may be exempted from screening, if:
   (a) they arrive from a Member State, unless the Commission or that Member State has provided information that those passengers and their cabin baggage cannot be considered as having been screened to the common basic standards; or
   (b) they arrive from a third country where the security standards applied are recognised as equivalent to the common basic standards in accordance with the regulatory procedure referred to in Article 19(2).
3. Transit passengers and their cabin baggage may be exempted from screening, if:
   (a) they remain on board the aircraft; or
   (b) they do not mix with screened departing passengers other than those who board the same aircraft; or
   (c) they arrive from a Member State, unless the Commission or that Member State has provided information that those passengers and their cabin baggage cannot be considered as having been screened to the common basic standards; or
   (d) they arrive from a third country where the security standards applied are recognised as equivalent to the common basic standards in accordance with the regulatory procedure referred to in Article 19(2).

4.2. **Protection of passengers and cabin baggage**

1. Passengers and their cabin baggage shall be protected from unauthorised interference from the point at which they are screened until departure of the aircraft on which they are carried.
2. Screened departing passengers shall not mix with arriving passengers, unless:
   (a) the passengers arrive from a Member State, provided that the Commission or that Member State has not provided information that those arriving passengers and their cabin baggage cannot be considered as having been screened to the common basic standards; or
   (b) the passengers arrive from a third country where the security standards applied are recognised as equivalent to the common basic standards in accordance with the regulatory procedure referred to in Article 19(2).

4.3. **Potentially disruptive passengers**
Before departure potentially disruptive passengers shall be subjected to appropriate security measures.

5. HOLD BAGGAGE

5.1. **Screening of hold baggage**

1. All hold baggage shall be screened prior to being loaded onto an aircraft in order to prevent prohibited articles from being introduced into security restricted areas and on board aircraft.
2. Transfer hold baggage may be exempted from screening, if:
   (a) it arrives from a Member State, unless the Commission or that Member State has provided information that this hold baggage cannot be considered as having been screened to the common basic standards; or
   (b) it arrives from a third country where the security standards applied are recognised as equivalent to the common basic standards in accordance with the regulatory procedure referred to in Article 19(2).
3. Transit hold baggage may be exempted from screening if it remains on board the aircraft.

5.2. **Protection of hold baggage**
Hold baggage to be carried on an aircraft shall be protected from unauthorised interference from the point at which it is screened or accepted into the care of the air carrier, whichever is earlier, until the departure of the aircraft on which it is to be carried.

5.3. **Baggage reconciliation**

1. Each item of hold baggage shall be identified as accompanied or unaccompanied.
2. Unaccompanied hold baggage shall not be transported, unless that baggage has been either separated due to factors beyond the passenger's control or subjected to appropriate security controls.

6. CARGO AND MAIL

6.1. **Security controls for cargo and mail**

1. All cargo and mail shall be subjected to security controls prior to being loaded on an aircraft. An air carrier shall not accept cargo or mail for carriage on an aircraft unless it has applied such controls itself or their application has been confirmed and accounted for by a regulated agent, a known consignor or an account consignor.
2. Transfer cargo and transfer mail may be subjected to alternative security controls to be detailed in an implementing act.
3. Transit cargo and transit mail may be exempted from security controls if it remains on board the aircraft.

6.2. **Protection of cargo and mail**

1. Cargo and mail to be carried on an aircraft shall be protected from unauthorised interference from the point at which security controls are applied until the departure of the aircraft on which it is to be carried.
2. Cargo and mail that are not adequately protected from unauthorised interference after security controls have been applied shall be screened.

7. AIR CARRIER MAIL AND AIR CARRIER MATERIALS

Air carrier mail and air carrier materials shall be subjected to security controls and thereafter protected until loaded onto the aircraft in order to prevent prohibited articles from being introduced on board an aircraft.

8. IN-FLIGHT SUPPLIES

In-flight supplies, including catering, intended for carriage or use on board an aircraft shall be subjected to security controls and thereafter protected until loaded onto the aircraft in order to prevent prohibited articles from being introduced on board an aircraft.

9. AIRPORT SUPPLIES

Supplies intended to be sold or used in security restricted areas of airports, including supplies for duty-free shops and restaurants, shall be subjected to security controls in order to prevent prohibited articles from being introduced into these areas.

10. IN-FLIGHT SECURITY MEASURES

1. Without prejudice to the applicable aviation safety rules:
   (a) unauthorised persons shall be prevented from entering the flight crew compartment during a flight;
   (b) potentially disruptive passengers shall be subjected to appropriate security measures during a flight.
2. Appropriate security measures such as training of flight crew and cabin staff shall be taken to prevent acts of unlawful interference during a flight.
3. Weapons, with the exception of those carried in the hold, shall not be carried on board an aircraft, unless the required security conditions in

accordance with national laws have been fulfilled and authorisation has been given by the states involved.

4. Paragraph 3 shall also apply to in-flight security officers if they carry weapons.

11. STAFF RECRUITMENT AND TRAINING

1. Persons implementing, or responsible for implementing, screening, access control or other security controls shall be recruited, trained and, where appropriate, certified so as to ensure that they are suitable for employment and competent to undertake the duties to which they are assigned.
2. Persons other than passengers requiring access to security restricted areas shall receive security training, before either an airport identification card or crew identification card is issued.
3. Training as mentioned in paragraphs 1 and 2 shall be conducted on initial and recurrent basis.
4. Instructors engaged in the training of the persons mentioned in paragraphs 1 and 2 shall have the necessary qualifications.

12. SECURITY EQUIPMENT

Equipment used for screening, access control and other security controls shall comply with the defined specifications and be capable of performing the security controls concerned.

ANNEX II

Common specifications for the national quality control programme to be implemented by each Member State inthe field of civil aviation security

1. DEFINITIONS

1.1. For the purposes of this Annex, the following definitions shall apply:

(1) 'annual traffic volume' means the total number of passengers arriving, departing and in transit (countedonce);
(2) 'appropriate authority' means the national authority designated by a Member State pursuant to Article 9 tobe responsible for the coordination and monitoring of the implementation of its national civil aviationsecurity programme;
(3) 'auditor' means any person conducting national compliance monitoring activities on behalf of the appropriate authority;
(4) 'certification' means a formal evaluation and confirmation by or on behalf of the appropriate authority that aperson possesses the necessary competencies to perform the functions of an auditor to an acceptable level asdefined by the appropriate authority;
(5) 'compliance monitoring activities' means any procedure or process used for assessing the implementation ofthis Regulation and the national aviation security programme;
(6) 'deficiency' means a failure to comply with an aviation security requirement;
(7) 'inspection' means an examination of the implementation of security measures and procedures in order todetermine whether they are being carried out effectively and to the required standard and to identify anydeficiencies;
(8) 'interview' means an oral check by an auditor to establish whether specific security measures or proceduresare implemented;
(9) 'observation' means a visual check by an auditor that a security measure or procedure is implemented;
(10) 'representative sample' means a selection made from amongst possible options for monitoring which issufficient in number and range to provide a basis for general conclusions on implementing standards;
(11) 'security audit' means an in-depth examination of security measures and procedures in order to determine ifthey are being fully implemented on a continual basis;
(12) 'test' means a trial of aviation security measures, where the appropriate authority simulates intent to commitan act of unlawful interference for the purpose of examining the effectiveness of the implementation ofexisting security measures;
(13) 'verification' means an action taken by an auditor to establish whether a specific security measure is actuallyin place;

(14) 'vulnerability' means any weakness in the implemented measures and procedures which could be exploited tocarry out an act of unlawful interference.

2. POWERS OF THE APPROPRIATE AUTHORITY

2.1. Member States shall provide the appropriate authority with the necessary powers for monitoring and enforcing allrequirements of this Regulation and its implementing acts, including the power to impose penalties in accordancewith Article 21.

2.2. The appropriate authority shall perform compliance monitoring activities and have the powers necessary to requireany identified deficiency to be rectified within set timeframes.

2.3. A graduated and proportionate approach shall be established regarding deficiency correction activities andenforcement measures. This approach shall consist of progressive steps to be followed until correction isachieved, including:

(a) advice and recommendations;
(b) formal warning;
(c) enforcement notice;
(d) administrative sanctions and legal proceedings.

The appropriate authority may omit one or more of these steps, especially where the deficiency is serious orrecurring.

3. OBJECTIVES AND CONTENT OF THE NATIONAL QUALITY CONTROL PROGRAMME

3.1. The objectives of the national quality control programme are to verify that aviation security measures areeffectively and properly implemented and to determine the level of compliance with the provisions of thisRegulation and the national civil aviation security programme, by means of compliance monitoring activities.

3.2. The national quality control programme shall include the following elements:

(a) organisational structure, responsibilities and resources;
(b) job descriptions of, and qualifications required for auditors;
(c) compliance monitoring activities, including scope of security audits, inspections, tests and, following an actualor potential breach of security, investigations, frequencies for security audits and inspections and also classification of compliance;
(d) surveys, where there is cause to reassess security needs;
(e) deficiency correction activities providing details concerning deficiency reporting, follow-up and correction inorder to ensure compliance with aviation security requirements;

(f) enforcement measures and, where appropriate, penalties, as specified in points 2.1 and 2.3 of this Annex;
(g) reporting of compliance monitoring activities carried out including, where appropriate, information exchangebetween national bodies on compliance levels;
(h) monitoring process of the airport, operator and entity internal quality control measures;
(i) a process to record and analyse the results of the national quality control programme to identify trends andsteer future policy development.

4. COMPLIANCE MONITORING

4.1. All airports, operators and other entities with aviation security responsibilities shall be regularly monitored toensure the swift detection and correction of failures.

4.2. Monitoring shall be undertaken in accordance with the national quality control programme, taking intoconsideration the threat level, type and nature of the operations, standard of implementation, results of internalquality control of airports, operators and entities and other factors and assessments which will affect the frequencyof monitoring.

4.3. Monitoring shall include the implementation and effectiveness of the internal quality control measures of airports, operators and other entities.

4.4. Monitoring at each individual airport shall be made up of a suitable mixture of compliance monitoring activitiesand provide a comprehensive overview of the implementation of security measures in the field.

4.5. The management, setting of priorities and organisation of the quality control programme shall be undertakenindependently from the operational implementation of the measures taken under the national civil aviation securityprogramme.

4.6. Compliance monitoring activities shall include security audits, inspections and tests.

5. METHODOLOGY

5.1. The methodology for conducting monitoring activities shall conform to a standardised approach, which includestasking, planning, preparation, on-site activity, the classification of findings, the completion of the report and thecorrection process.

5.2. Compliance monitoring activities shall be based on the systematic gathering of information by means of observations, interviews, examination of documents and verifications.

5.3. Compliance monitoring shall include both announced and unannounced activities.

6. SECURITY AUDITS

6.1. A security audit shall cover:

(a) all security measures at an airport; or
(b) all security measures implemented by an individual airport, terminal of an airport, operator or entity; or
(c) a particular part of the National Civil Aviation Security Programme.

6.2. The methodology for conducting a security audit shall take into consideration the following elements:

(a) announcement of the security audit and communication of a pre-audit questionnaire, if appropriate;
(b) preparation phase including examination of the completed pre-audit questionnaire and other relevant documentation;
(c) entry briefing with airport/operator/entity representatives prior to beginning the monitoring activity on-site;
(d) on-site activity;
(e) debriefing and reporting;
(f) where deficiencies are identified, the correction process and the associated monitoring of that process.

6.3. In order to confirm that security measures are implemented, the conduct of a security audit shall be based on asystematic gathering of information by one or more of the following techniques:

(a) examination of documents;
(b) observations;
(c) interviews;
(d) verifications.

6.4. Airports with an annual traffic volume of more than 10 million passengers shall be subject to a security auditcovering all aviation security standards at least every 4 years. The examination shall include a representative sample of information.

7. INSPECTIONS

7.1. The scope of an inspection shall cover at least one set of directly linked security measures of Annex I to thisRegulation and the corresponding implementing acts monitored as a single activity or within a reasonable timeframe, not normally exceeding three months. The examination shall include a representative sample ofinformation.

7.2. A set of directly linked security measures is a set of two or more requirements as referred to in Annex I to thisRegulation and the corresponding implementing acts which impact on each other so closely that achievement ofthe objective cannot be adequately assessed unless they are considered together. These sets shall include those listedin Appendix I to this Annex.

7.3. Inspections shall be unannounced. Where the appropriate authority considers that this is not practicable,inspections may be announced. The methodology for conducting an inspection shall take into consideration the following elements:
(a) preparation phase;
(b) on-site activity;
(c) a debrief, depending on the frequency and the results of the monitoring activities;
(d) reporting/recording;
(e) correction process and its monitoring.

7.4. In order to confirm that security measures are effective, the conduct of the inspection shall be based on thesystematic gathering of information by one or more of the following techniques:

(a) examination of documents;
(b) observations;
(c) interviews;
(d) verifications.

7.5. At airports with an annual traffic volume of more than 2 million passengers the minimum frequency forinspecting all sets of directly linked security measures set out in chapters 1 to 6 of Annex I to this Regulationshall be at least every 12 months, unless an audit has been carried out at the airport during that time. Thefrequency for inspecting all security measures covered by chapters 7 to 12 of Annex I shall be determined by theappropriate authority based on a risk assessment.

7.6. Where a Member State has no airport with an annual traffic volume exceeding 2 million passengers, therequirements of point 7.5 shall apply to the airport on its territory with the greatest annual traffic volume.

8. TESTS

8.1. Tests shall be carried out to examine the effectiveness of the implementation of at least the following securitymeasures:
(a) access control to security restricted areas;
(b) aircraft protection;
(c) screening of passengers and cabin baggage;
(d) screening of staff and items carried;
(e) protection of hold baggage;
(f) screening of cargo or mail;
(g) protection of cargo and mail.

8.2. A test protocol including the methodology shall be developed taking into consideration the legal, safety andoperational requirements. The methodology shall address the following elements:

(a) preparation phase;
(b) on-site activity;

(c) a debrief, depending on the frequency and the results of the monitoring activities;
(d) reporting/recording;
(e) correction process and the associated monitoring.

9. SURVEYS

9.1. Surveys shall be carried out whenever the appropriate authority recognises a need to re-evaluate operations inorder to identify and address any vulnerabilities. Where a vulnerability is identified, the appropriate authority shall-require the implementation of protective measures commensurate with the threat.

10. REPORTING

10.1. Compliance monitoring activities shall be reported or recorded in a standardised format which allows for an on-going analysis of trends.

10.2. The following elements shall be included:

(a) type of activity;
(b) airport, operator or entity monitored;
(c) date and time of the activity;
(d) name of the auditors conducting the activity;
(e) scope of the activity;
(f) findings with the corresponding provisions of the National Civil Aviation Security Programme;
(g) classification of compliance;
(h) recommendations for remedial actions, where appropriate;
(i) time frame for correction, where appropriate.

10.3. Where deficiencies are identified, the appropriate authority shall report the relevant findings to the airport,operators or entities subjected to monitoring.

11. COMMON CLASSIFICATION OF COMPLIANCE

11.1. Compliance monitoring activities shall assess the implementation of the national civil aviation security programmeusing the harmonised classification system of compliance set out in Appendix II.

12. CORRECTION OF DEFICIENCIES

12.1. The correction of identified deficiencies shall be implemented promptly. Where the correction cannot take placepromptly, compensatory measures shall be implemented.

12.2. The appropriate authority shall require airports, operators or entities subjected to compliance monitoring activitiesto submit for agreement an action plan addressing any deficiencies outlined in the reports together with atimeframe for implementation of the remedial actions and to provide confirmation when the correction process has been completed.

13. FOLLOW-UP ACTIVITIES RELATED TO THE VERIFICATION OF THE CORRECTION

13.1. Following confirmation by the airport, operator or entity subjected to monitoring that any required remedialactions have been taken, the appropriate authority shall verify the implementation of the remedial actions.

13.2. Follow-up activities shall use the most relevant monitoring method.

14. AVAILABILITY OF AUDITORS

14.1. Each Member State shall ensure that a sufficient number of auditors are available to the appropriate authoritydirectly or under its supervision for performing all compliance monitoring activities.

15. QUALIFICATION CRITERIA FOR AUDITORS

15.1. Each Member State shall ensure that auditors performing functions on behalf of the appropriate authority:

(a) are free from any contractual or pecuniary obligation to the airport, operator or entity to be monitored; and
(b) have the appropriate competencies, which include sufficient theoretical and practical experience in the relevantfield.
Auditors shall be subject to certification or equivalent approval by the appropriate authority.

15.2. The auditors shall have the following competencies:

(a) an understanding of current applicable security measures and how they are applied to the operations beingexamined including:
—an understanding of security principles,
—an understanding of supervisory tasks,
—an understanding of factors affecting human performance,
(b) a working knowledge of security technologies and techniques;
(c) a knowledge of compliance monitoring principles, procedures and techniques;
(d) a working knowledge of the operations being examined;
(e) an understanding of the role and powers of the auditor.

15.3. Auditors shall undergo recurrent training at a frequency sufficient to ensure that existing competencies aremaintained and new competencies are acquired to take account of developments in the field of security.

16. POWERS OF AUDITORS

16.1. Auditors carrying out monitoring activities shall be provided with sufficient authority to obtain the informationnecessary to carry out their tasks.

16.2. Auditors shall carry a proof of identity authorising compliance monitoring activities on behalf of the appropriateauthority and allowing access to all areas required.

16.3. Auditors shall be entitled to:

(a) obtain immediate access to all relevant areas including aircraft and buildings for monitoring purposes; and
(b) require the correct implementation or repetition of the security measures.

16.4. As a consequence of the powers conferred on auditors, the appropriate authority shall act in accordance with point2.3 in the following cases:

(a) intentional obstruction or impediment of an auditor;
(b) failure or refusal to supply information requested by an auditor;
(c) when false or misleading information is supplied to an auditor with intent to deceive; and
(d) impersonation of an auditor with intent to deceive.

17. BEST PRACTICES

17.1. Member States shall inform the Commission of best practices with regard to quality control programmes, auditmethodologies and auditors. The Commission shall share this information with the Member States.

18. REPORTING TO THE COMMISSION

18.1. Member States shall annually submit a report to the Commission on the measures taken to fulfil their obligationsunder this Regulation and on the aviation security situation at the airports located in their territory. The referenceperiod for the report shall be 1 January – 31 December. The report shall be due three months after completion ofthe reference period.

18.2. The content of the report shall be in accordance with Appendix III using a template provided by the Commission.

18.3. The Commission shall share the main conclusions drawn from these reports with Member States.

Appendix I

Elements to be included in the set of directly linked security measures

The sets of directly linked security measures as referred to in point 7.1 of Annex II shall include the following elements ofAnnex I to this Regulation and the corresponding provisions in its implementing acts:

For point 1 — Airport security:

(i) point 1.1; or
(ii) point 1.2 (except provisions relating to identification cards and vehicle passes); or
(iii) point 1.2 (provisions relating to identification cards); or

(iv) point 1.2 (provisions relating to vehicle passes); or
(v) point 1.3 and the relevant elements of point 12; or
(vi) point 1.4; or
(vii) point 1.5.

For point 2 — Demarcated areas of airports:

the whole point

For point 3 — Aircraft security:

(i) point 3.1; or
(ii) point 3.2.

For point 4 — Passengers and cabin baggage:

(i) point 4.1 and the relevant elements of point 12: or
(ii) point 4.2; or
(iii) point 4.3.

For point 5 — Hold baggage:

(i) point 5.1 and the relevant elements of point 12; or
(ii) point 5.2; or
(iii) point 5.3.

For point 6 — Cargo and mail:

(i) all provisions relating to screening and security controls applied by a regulated agent, except as detailed in points (ii)to (v) below; or
(ii) all provisions relating to security controls applied by known consignors; or
(iii) all provisions relating to account consignors; or
(iv) all provisions relating to the transportation of cargo and mail; or
(v) all provisions relating to the protection of cargo and mail at airports.

For point 7 — Air carrier mail and air carrier materials:

the whole point

For point 8 — In-flight supplies:
the whole point

For point 9 — Airport supplies:
the whole point

For point 10 — In-flight security measures:
the whole point

For point 11 — Staff recruitment and training:

(i) all provisions relating to staff recruitment at airport, air carrier or entity; or
(ii) all provisions relating to staff training at an airport, air carrier or entity.

Appendix II

Harmonised classification system of compliance

The following classification of compliance shall apply to assess the implementation of the national civil aviation securityprogramme.

	Security audit	*Inspection*	*Test*
Fully compliant	√	√	√
Compliant, but improvement desirable	√	√	√
Not compliant	√	√	√
Not compliant, with serious deficiencies	√	√	√
Not applicable	√	√	
Not confirmed	√	√	√

Appendix III

CONTENT OF REPORT TO THE COMMISSION

1. Organisational structure, responsibilities and resources

(a) Structure of the quality control organisation, responsibilities and resources, including planned future amendments (see point 3.2(a)).
(b) Number of auditors – present and planned (see point 14).
(c) Training completed by auditors (see point 15.2).

2. Operational monitoring activities

All monitoring activities carried out, specifying:

(a) type (security audit, initial inspection, follow up inspection, test, other);
(b) airports, operators and entities monitored;
(c) scope;
(d) frequency; and
(e) total man-days spent in the field.

3. Deficiency correction activities

(a) Status of the implementation of the deficiency correction activities.
(b) Main activities undertaken or planned (e.g. new posts created, equipment purchased, construction work) andprogress achieved towards correction.
(c) Enforcement measures used (see point 3.2(f)).

4. General data and trends

(a) Total national annual passenger and freight traffic and number of aircraft movements.
(b) List of airports by category.
(c) Number of air carriers operating from the territory by category (national, EU, third country).
(d) Number of regulated agents.
(e) Number of catering companies.
(f) Number of cleaning companies.
(g) Approximate number of other entities with aviation security responsibilities (known consignors, ground handlingcompanies).

5. Aviation security situation at airports

General context of the aviation security situation in the Member State.

Appendix 17

Regulation (EC) No. 1008/2008 of the European Parliament and of the Council

of 24 September 2008

on common rules for the operation of air services in the Community (Recast)

(Text with EEA relevance)

(OJ No. L 293 of 31 October 2008, p. 3)

THE EUROPEAN PARLIAMENT AND THE COUNCIL OF THE EUROPEAN UNION,

Having regard to the Treaty establishing the European Community, and in particular Article 80(2) thereof,

Having regard to the proposal from the Commission,

Having regard to the opinion of the European Economic and Social Committee,[1]

Having regard to the opinion of the Committee of the Regions,[2]

Acting in accordance with the procedure laid down in Article 251 of the Treaty,[3]

---

1. OJ C 175, 27.7.2007, p. 85.
2. OJ C 305, 15.12.2007, p. 11.
3. Opinion of European Parliament of 11 July 2007 (OJ C 175 E, 10.7.2008, p. 371), Council Common Position of 18 April 2008 (OJ C 129 E, 27.5.2008, p. 1) and Position of the European Parliament of 9 July 2008 (not yet published in the Official Journal).

Whereas:

(1) A number of substantial changes are to be made to Council Regulations (EEC) No 2407/92 of 23 July 1992 on licensing of air carriers,[4] (EEC) No 2408/92 of 23 July 1992 on access of Community air carriers to intra-Community air routes,[5] and (EEC) No 2409/92 of 23 July 1992 on fares and rates for air services.[6] In the interests of clarity, these Regulations should be recast and consolidated into one single Regulation.

(2) In order to ensure a more efficient and consistent application of Community legislation for the internal aviation market a series of adjustments to the current legal framework is required.

(3) Recognising the potential link between the financial health of an air carrier and safety, more stringent monitoring of the financial situation of air carriers should be established.

(4) Given the growing importance of air carriers with operational bases in several Member States and the need to ensure the efficient supervision of these air carriers, the same Member State should be responsible for the oversight of the air operator certificate and of the operating licence.

(5) To ensure consistent monitoring of the compliance with the requirements of the operating licences of all Community air carriers, licensing authorities should carry out regular assessments of the air carriers' financial situation. Therefore, the latter should provide sufficient information on their financial situation, especially in the first two years of their existence as these are particularly critical for the survival of an air carrier on the market. In order to avoid a distortion of competition arising from the different application of the rules at national level, it is necessary to reinforce the financial oversight of all Community air carriers by Member States.

(6) To reduce risks to passengers, Community air carriers failing to fulfil the requirements for maintaining a valid operating licence should not be allowed to continue operations. In such cases, the competent licensing authority should revoke or suspend the operating licence.

(7) According to Regulation (EC) No 785/2004 of the European Parliament and of the Council of 21 April 2004 on insurance requirements for air carriers and aircraft operators[7] an air carrier should be insured to cover liability in case of accidents with respect to passengers, cargo and third parties. Obligations should also be placed upon air carriers for insurance to cover liability in case of accidents with respect to mail.

(8) In order to avoid excessive recourse to lease agreements of aircraft registered in third countries, especially wet lease, these possibilities should only be allowed in exceptional circumstances, such as a lack of adequate aircraft on the Community

4. OJ L 240, 24.8.1992, p. 1.
5. OJ L 240, 24.8.1992, p. 8.
6. OJ L 240, 24.8.1992, p. 15.
7. OJ L 138, 30.4.2004, p. 1.

market, and they should be strictly limited in time and fulfil safety standards equivalent to the safety rules of Community and national legislation.

(9) With respect to employees of a Community air carrier operating air services from an operational base outside the territory of the Member State where that Community air carrier has its principal place of business, Member States should ensure the proper application of Community and national social legislation.

(10) In order to complete the internal aviation market, still existing restrictions applied between Member States, such as restrictions on the code sharing on routes to third countries or on the price setting on routes to third countries with an intermediate stop in another Member State (sixth freedom flights) should be lifted.

(11) To take into account the special characteristics and constraints of the outermost regions, in particular their remoteness, insularity and small size, and the need to properly link them with the central regions of the Community, special arrangements may be justified regarding the rules on the period of validity of the contracts for public service obligations covering routes to such regions.

(12) The conditions under which public service obligations may be imposed should be defined clearly in an unambiguous way, while the associated tender procedures should allow a sufficient number of competitors to take part in the tenders. The Commission should be able to obtain as much information as necessary to be able to assess the economic justifications for public service obligations in individual cases.

(13) The rules in force with regard to traffic distribution between airports serving the same city or conurbation should be clarified and simplified.

(14) It is appropriate to ensure that Member States have the possibility to react to sudden problems resulting from unforeseeable and unavoidable circumstances, which make it technically or practically very difficult to carry out air services.

(15) Customers should have access to all air fares and air rates irrespective of their place of residence within the Community or their nationality and irrespective of the place of establishment of the travel agents within the Community.

(16) Customers should be able to compare effectively the prices for air services of different airlines. Therefore the final price to be paid by the customer for air services originating in the Community should at all times be indicated, inclusive of all taxes, charges and fees. Community air carriers are also encouraged to indicate the final price for their air services from third countries to the Community.

(17) The measures necessary for the implementation of this Regulation should be adopted in accordance with Council Decision 1999/468/EC of 28 June 1999 laying down the procedures for the exercise of implementing powers conferred on the Commission.[8]

8. OJ L 184, 17.7.1999, p. 23.

(18) Since the objective of this Regulation, namely more homogeneous application of Community legislation with regard to the internal aviation market cannot be sufficiently achieved by the Member States because of the international character of air transport, and can therefore be better achieved at Community level, the Community may adopt measures, in accordance with the principle of subsidiarity as set out in Article 5 of the Treaty. In accordance with the principle of proportionality, as set out in that Article, this Regulation does not go beyond what is necessary in order to achieve that objective.

(19) The Ministerial Statement on Gibraltar Airport, agreed in Cordoba on 18 September 2006, during the first ministerial meeting of the Forum of Dialogue on Gibraltar, will replace the Joint Declaration on the airport made in London on 2 December 1987, and full compliance with it will be deemed to constitute compliance with the 1987 declaration.

(20) It is therefore necessary to repeal Regulations (EEC) No 2407/92, (EEC) No 2408/92 and (EEC) No 2409/92,

HAVE ADOPTED THIS REGULATION:

CHAPTER I
GENERAL PROVISIONS

Article 1
Subject matter

1. This Regulation regulates the licensing of Community air carriers, the right of Community air carriers to operate intra-Community air services and the pricing of intra-Community air services.

2. The application of Chapter III of this Regulation to the airport of Gibraltar is understood to be without prejudice to the respective legal positions of the Kingdom of Spain and the United Kingdom with regard to the dispute over sovereignty over the territory in which the airport is situated.

Article 2
Definitions

For the purposes of this Regulation:

1. ‘operating licence’ means an authorisation granted by the competent licensing authority to an undertaking, permitting it to provide air services as stated in the operating licence;
2. ‘competent licensing authority’ means an authority of a Member State entitled to grant, refuse, revoke or suspend an operating licence in accordance with Chapter II;
3. ‘undertaking’ means any natural or legal person, whether profit-making or not, or any official body whether having its own legal personality or not;
4. ‘air service’ means a flight or a series of flights carrying passengers, cargo and/or mail for remuneration and/or hire;

5. 'flight' means a departure from a specified airport towards a specified destination airport;
6. 'local flight' means a flight not involving carriage of passengers, mail and/or cargo between different airports or other authorised landing points;
7. 'airport' means any area in a Member State especially adapted for air services;
8. 'air operator certificate (AOC)' means a certificate delivered to an undertaking confirming that the operator has the professional ability and organisation to ensure the safety of operations specified in the certificate, as provided in the relevant provisions of Community or national law, as applicable;
9. 'effective control' means a relationship constituted by rights, contracts or any other means which, either separately or jointly and having regard to the considerations of fact or law involved, confer the possibility of directly or indirectly exercising a decisive influence on an undertaking, in particular by:
   (a) the right to use all or part of the assets of an undertaking;
   (b) rights or contracts which confer a decisive influence on the composition, voting or decisions of the bodies of an undertaking or otherwise confer a decisive influence on the running of the business of the undertaking;
10. 'air carrier' means an undertaking with a valid operating licence or equivalent;
11. 'Community air carrier' means an air carrier with a valid operating licence granted by a competent licensing authority in accordance with Chapter II;
12. 'business plan' means a detailed description of the air carrier's intended commercial activities for the period in question, in particular in relation to the expected market development and the investments to be carried out, including the financial and economic implications of these activities;
13. 'intra-Community air service' means an air service operated within the Community;
14. 'traffic right' means the right to operate an air service between two Community airports;
15. 'seat-only sales' means the sale of seats, without any other service bundled, such as accommodation, directly to the public by the air carrier or its authorised agent or a charterer;
16. 'scheduled air service' means a series of flights possessing all the following characteristics:
    (a) on each flight seats and/or capacity to transport cargo and/or mail are available for individual purchase by the public (either directly from the air carrier or from its authorised agents);
    (b) it is operated so as to serve traffic between the same two or more airports, either:
    —according to a published timetable, or
    —with flights so regular or frequent that they constitute a recognisably systematic series;

17. 'capacity' means the number of seats or the payload offered to the general public on a scheduled air service over a given period;
18. 'air fares' means the prices expressed in euro or in local currency to be paid to air carriers or their agents or other ticket sellers for the carriage of passengers on air services and any conditions under which those prices apply, including remuneration and conditions offered to agency and other auxiliary services;
19. 'air rates' means the prices expressed in euro or in local currency to be paid for the carriage of cargo and the conditions under which those prices apply, including remuneration and conditions offered to agency and other auxiliary services;
20. 'Member State(s) concerned' means the Member State(s) between or within which an air service is operated;
21. 'Member State(s) involved' means the Member State(s) concerned and the Member State(s) where the air carrier(s) operating the air service is (are) licensed;
22. 'conurbation' means an urban area comprising a number of cities or towns which, through population growth and expansion, have physically merged to form one continuous built up area;
23. 'management account' means a detailed statement of income and costs of an air carrier for the period in question including a breakdown between air-transport-related and other activities as well as between pecuniary and non-pecuniary elements;
24. 'dry lease agreement' means an agreement between undertakings pursuant to which the aircraft is operated under the AOC of the lessee;
25. 'wet lease agreement' means an agreement between air carriers pursuant to which the aircraft is operated under the AOC of the lessor;
26. 'principal place of business' means the head office or registered office of a Community air carrier in the Member State within which the principal financial functions and operational control, including continued airworthiness management, of the Community air carrier are exercised.

CHAPTER II
OPERATING LICENCE

Article 3
Operating licence

1. No undertaking established in the Community shall be permitted to carry by air passengers, mail and/or cargo for remuneration and/or hire unless it has been granted the appropriate operating licence.

An undertaking meeting the requirements of this Chapter shall be entitled to receive an operating licence.

2. The competent licensing authority shall not grant operating licences or maintain them in force where any of the requirements of this Chapter are not complied with.

3. Without prejudice to any other applicable provisions of Community, national, or international law, the following categories of air services shall not be subject to the requirement to hold a valid operating licence:

(a) air services performed by non-power-driven aircraft and/or ultralight power-driven aircraft; and
(b) local flights.

Article 4
Conditions for granting an operating licence

An undertaking shall be granted an operating licence by the competent licensing authority of a Member State provided that:

(a) its principal place of business is located in that Member State;
(b) it holds a valid AOC issued by a national authority of the same Member State whose competent licensing authority is responsible for granting, refusing, revoking or suspending the operating licence of the Community air carrier;
(c) it has one or more aircraft at its disposal through ownership or a dry lease agreement;
(d) its main occupation is to operate air services in isolation or combined with any other commercial operation of aircraft or the repair and maintenance of aircraft;
(e) its company structure allows the competent licensing authority to implement the provisions of this Chapter;
(f) Member States and/or nationals of Member States own more than 50 % of the undertaking and effectively control it, whether directly or indirectly through one or more intermediate undertakings, except as provided for in an agreement with a third country to which the Community is a party;
(g) it meets the financial conditions specified in Article 5;
(h) it complies with the insurance requirements specified in Article 11 and in Regulation (EC) No 785/2004; and
(i) it complies with the provisions on good repute as specified in Article 7.

Article 5
Financial conditions for granting an operating licence

1. The competent licensing authority shall closely assess whether an undertaking applying for the first time for an operating licence can demonstrate that:

(a) it can meet at any time its actual and potential obligations established under realistic assumptions, for a period of 24 months from the start of operations; and
(b) it can meet its fixed and operational costs incurred by operations according to its business plan and established under realistic assumptions, for a period of three months from the start of operations, without taking into account any income from its operations.

2. For the purposes of the assessment referred to in paragraph 1, each applicant shall submit a business plan for, at least, the first three years of operation. The business plan shall also detail the applicant's financial links with any other commercial activities in which the applicant is engaged either directly or through related undertakings. The applicant shall also provide all relevant information, in particular the data referred to in point 1 of Annex I.

3. Paragraphs 1 and 2 shall not apply to an undertaking applying for an operating licence intended to cover operations with aircraft of less than 10 tonnes maximum take-off mass (MTOM) and/or less than 20 seats. Such undertakings shall demonstrate that their net capital is at least EUR 100 000 or provide, when required by the competent licensing authority, all relevant information for the purposes of the assessment referred to in paragraph 1, in particular the data referred to in point 1 of Annex I.

The competent licensing authority may nevertheless apply paragraphs 1 and 2 to an undertaking applying for an operating licence under the provisions of the previous subparagraph that intends to operate scheduled air services or whose turnover exceeds EUR 3 million per year.

Article 6
Air operator certificate

1. The granting and validity of an operating licence shall at any time be dependent upon the possession of a valid AOC specifying the activities covered by the operating licence.

2. Any modification in the AOC of a Community air carrier shall be reflected, where appropriate, in its operating licence.

Article 7
Proof of good repute

1. Where, for the purpose of issuing an operating licence, proof is required that the persons who will continuously and effectively manage the operations of the undertaking are of good repute or that they have not been declared bankrupt, the competent licensing authority shall accept as sufficient evidence in respect of nationals of Member States the production of documents issued by the competent authorities in the Member State of origin or the Member State where the person has his/her permanent residence showing that those requirements are met.

2. Where the Member State of origin or the Member State where the person has his/her permanent residence does not issue the documents referred to in paragraph 1, such documents shall be replaced by a declaration on oath or—in Member States where there is no provision for declaration on oath—by a solemn declaration made by the person concerned before a competent judicial or administrative authority or, where appropriate, a notary or qualified professional body of the Member State of origin or the Member State where the person has his/her permanent residence. Such authority, notary or qualified professional body shall issue a certificate attesting the authenticity of the declaration on oath or solemn declaration.

3. The competent licensing authority may require that the documents and certificates referred to in paragraphs 1 and 2 be presented no more than three months after their date of issue.

Article 8
Validity of an operating licence

1. An operating licence shall be valid as long as the Community air carrier complies with the requirements of this Chapter.

A Community air carrier shall at all times be able on request to demonstrate to the competent licensing authority that it meets all the requirements of this Chapter.

2. The competent licensing authority shall closely monitor compliance with the requirements of this Chapter. It shall in any case review compliance with these requirements in the following cases:

(a) two years after a new operating licence has been granted;
(b) when a potential problem has been suspected; or
(c) at the request of the Commission.

In case the competent licensing authority suspects that financial problems of a Community air carrier might affect the safety of its operations, it shall immediately inform the authority competent for the AOC.

3. The operating licence shall be resubmitted for approval when a Community air carrier:

(a) has not started operations within six months of the granting of an operating licence;
(b) has ceased its operations for more than six months; or
(c) which has been licensed on the basis of the first subparagraph of Article 5(3) intends to engage in operations with aircraft above the size threshold specified in Article 5(3) or no longer complies with the financial conditions set out therein.

4. A Community air carrier shall provide to the competent licensing authority its audited accounts no later than six months following the last day of the respective financial year, unless otherwise provided for in national law. During the first two years of operation of a Community air carrier, the data as referred to in point 3 of Annex I shall be made available to the competent licensing authority upon request.

The competent licensing authority may at any time assess the financial performance of a Community air carrier to which it has granted an operating licence by requesting the relevant information. As part of such an assessment, the Community air carrier in question shall update the data referred to in point 3 of Annex I and provide it to the competent licensing authority upon request.

5. A Community air carrier shall notify the competent licensing authority:

(a) in advance of any plans for the operation of a new air service to a continent or a world region not previously served, or any other substantial change in the scale of its activities, including, but not limited to, changes in the type or number of aircraft used;

(b) in advance of any intended mergers or acquisitions; and

(c) within 14 days of any change in the ownership of any single shareholding which represents 10 % or more of the total shareholding of the Community air carrier or of its parent or ultimate holding company.

6. If the competent licensing authority deems the changes notified under paragraph 5 to have a significant bearing on the finances of the Community air carrier, it shall require the submission of a revised business plan incorporating the changes in question and covering, at least, a period of 12 months from its date of implementation as well as the data referred to in point 2 of Annex I, in addition to the information to be provided under paragraph 4.

The competent licensing authority shall take a decision on the revised business plan as to whether the Community air carrier can meet its existing and potential obligations during that period of 12 months. Such a decision shall be taken not later than three months after all the necessary information has been submitted to it.

7. In relation to Community air carriers licensed by it the competent licensing authority shall decide whether the operating licence shall be resubmitted for approval in case of change in one or more elements affecting the legal situation of a Community air carrier and, in particular, in the case of a merger or takeover.

8. Paragraphs 4, 5 and 6 shall not apply to Community air carriers exclusively engaged in operations with aircraft of less than 10 tonnes MTOM and/or less than 20 seats. Such Community air carriers shall at all times be able to demonstrate that their net capital is at least EUR 100 000 or to provide when required by the competent licensing authority the information relevant for the purposes of the assessment referred to in Article 9(2).

The competent licensing authority may nevertheless apply paragraphs 4, 5 and 6 to Community air carriers licensed by it that operate scheduled air services or whose turnover exceeds EUR 3 million per year.

Article 9
Suspension and revocation of an operating licence

1. The competent licensing authority may at any time assess the financial performance of a Community air carrier which it has licensed. Based upon its assessment, the authority shall suspend or revoke the operating licence if it is no longer satisfied that this Community air carrier can meet its actual and potential obligations for a 12-month period. Nevertheless, the competent licensing authority may grant a temporary licence, not exceeding 12 months pending financial reorganisation of a Community air carrier provided that safety is not at risk, that this temporary licence reflects, when appropriate, any changes to the AOC, and that there is a realistic prospect of a satisfactory financial reconstruction within that time period.

2. Whenever there are clear indications that financial problems exist or when insolvency or similar proceedings are opened against a Community air carrier licensed by it the competent licensing authority shall without delay make an in-depth assessment of the financial situation and on the basis of its findings review the status of the operating licence in compliance with this Article within a time period of three months.

The competent licensing authority shall inform the Commission of its decisions, relating to the status of the operating licence.

3. When the audited accounts referred to in Article 8(4) have not been communicated within the deadline indicated in that Article, the competent licensing authority shall, without undue delay, request the Community air carrier to communicate these audited accounts.

If the audited accounts are not communicated within one month, the operating licence may be revoked or suspended.

4. The competent licensing authority shall suspend or revoke the operating licence if the Community air carrier knowingly or recklessly furnishes the competent licensing authority with false information on an important point.

5. In case a Community air carrier's AOC is suspended or withdrawn, the competent licensing authority shall immediately suspend or revoke that air carrier's operating licence.

6. The competent licensing authority may suspend or revoke the operating licence of a Community air carrier if such a carrier no longer satisfies the requirements relating to good repute set out in Article 7.

Article 10
Decisions on operating licences

1. The competent licensing authority shall take a decision on an application as soon as possible, and not later than three months after all the necessary information has been submitted, taking into account all available evidence. The decision shall be communicated to the applicant. A refusal shall indicate the reasons therefor.

2. Procedures for granting, suspending and revoking operating licences shall be made public by the competent licensing authorities, which shall inform the Commission thereof.

3. A list of decisions of the competent licensing authorities to grant, suspend or revoke operating licences shall be published annually in the *Official Journal of the European Union*.

Article 11
Insurance requirements

Notwithstanding Regulation (EC) No 785/2004, an air carrier shall be insured to cover liability in case of accidents with respect to mail.

Article 12
Registration

1. Without prejudice to Article 13(3), aircraft used by a Community air carrier shall be registered, at the option of the Member State whose competent authority issues the operating licence, in its national register or within the Community.

2. In accordance with paragraph 1, the competent authority shall, subject to applicable laws and regulations, accept on its national register, without any discriminatory fee and without delay, aircraft owned by nationals of other Member States and transfers from aircraft registers of other Member States. No fee shall be applied to transfers of aircraft in addition to the normal registration fee.

Article 13
Leasing

1. Without prejudice to Article 4(c), a Community air carrier may have one or more aircraft at its disposal through dry or wet lease agreement. Community air carriers may freely operate wet-leased aircraft registered within the Community except where this would lead to endangering safety. The Commission shall ensure that the implementation of such a provision is reasonable and proportionate and based on safety considerations.

2. A dry lease agreement to which a Community air carrier is a party or a wet lease agreement under which the Community air carrier is the lessee of the wet-leased aircraft shall be subject to prior approval in accordance with applicable Community or national law on aviation safety.

3. A Community air carrier wet leasing aircraft registered in a third country from another undertaking shall obtain prior approval for the operation from the competent licensing authority. The competent authority may grant an approval if:

(a) the Community air carrier demonstrates to the satisfaction of the competent authority that all safety standards equivalent to those imposed by Community or national law are met; and
(b) one of the following conditions is fulfilled:
   (i) the Community air carrier justifies such leasing on the basis of exceptional needs, in which case an approval may be granted for a period of up to seven months that may be renewed once for a further period of up to seven months;
   (ii) the Community air carrier demonstrates that the leasing is necessary to satisfy seasonal capacity needs, which cannot reasonably be satisfied through leasing aircraft registered within the Community, in which case the approval may be renewed; or
   (iii) the Community air carrier demonstrates that the leasing is necessary to overcome operational difficulties and it is not possible or reasonable to lease aircraft registered within the Community, in which case the approval shall be of limited duration strictly necessary for overcoming the difficulties.

4. The competent authority may attach conditions to the approval. Such conditions shall form part of the wet lease agreement.

The competent authority may refuse to grant an approval if there is no reciprocity as regards wet leasing between the Member State concerned or the Community and the third country where the wet-leased aircraft is registered.

The competent authority shall inform the Member States concerned about an approval it has granted for wet leasing aircraft registered in a third country.

Article 14
Right to be heard

The competent licensing authority shall ensure that, when adopting a decision to suspend or revoke the operating licence of a Community air carrier, the Community air carrier concerned is given the opportunity of being heard, taking into account the need, in some cases, for an urgency procedure.

CHAPTER III
ACCESS TO ROUTES

Article 15
Provision of intra-Community air services

1. Community air carriers shall be entitled to operate intra-Community air services.

2. Member States shall not subject the operation of intra-Community air services by a Community air carrier to any permit or authorisation. Member States shall not require Community air carriers to provide any documents or information which they have already supplied to the competent licensing authority, provided that the relevant information may be obtained from the competent licensing authority in due time.

3. If the Commission, on the basis of information obtained under Article 26(2), finds that the operating licence granted to a Community air carrier is not in compliance with the requirements of this Regulation it shall forward its findings to the competent licensing authority which shall send its comments to the Commission within 15 working days.

If the Commission, after examining the comments of the competent licensing authority, maintains that the operating licence is not compliant, or no comments have been received from the competent licensing authority it shall, in accordance with the procedure referred to in Article 25(2), take a decision to request the competent licensing authority to take the appropriate corrective measures or to suspend or revoke the operating licence.

The decision shall set a date by which the corrective measures or actions by the competent licensing authority shall be implemented. If the corrective measures or actions have not been implemented by that date the Community air carrier shall not be entitled to exercise its rights under paragraph 1.

The Community air carrier may resume exercising its rights under paragraph 1 upon notification to the Commission by the competent licensing authority that the corrective measures have been implemented and that the competent licensing authority has verified the implementation.

4. When operating intra-Community air services, a Community air carrier shall be permitted to combine air services and to enter into code share arrangements, without prejudice to the Community competition rules applicable to undertakings.

Any restrictions on the freedom of Community air carriers to operate intra-Community air services arising from bilateral agreements between Member States are hereby superseded.

5. Notwithstanding the provisions of bilateral agreements between Member States, and subject to the Community competition rules applicable to undertakings, Community air carriers shall be permitted by the Member State(s) concerned to combine air services and to enter into code share arrangements with any air carrier on air services to, from or via any airport in their territory from or to any point(s) in third countries.

A Member State may, in the framework of the bilateral air service agreement with the third country concerned, impose restrictions on code share arrangements between Community air carriers and air carriers of a third country, in particular if the third country concerned does not allow similar commercial opportunities to Community air carriers operating from the Member State concerned. In doing so, Member States shall ensure that restrictions imposed under such agreements do not restrict competition and are non-discriminatory between Community air carriers and that they are not more restrictive than necessary.

Article 16
General principles for public service obligations

1. A Member State, following consultations with the other Member States concerned and after having informed the Commission, the airports concerned and air carriers operating on the route, may impose a public service obligation in respect of scheduled air services between an airport in the Community and an airport serving a peripheral or development region in its territory or on a thin route to any airport on its territory any such route being considered vital for the economic and social development of the region which the airport serves. That obligation shall be imposed only to the extent necessary to ensure on that route the minimum provision of scheduled air services satisfying fixed standards of continuity, regularity, pricing or minimum capacity, which air carriers would not assume if they were solely considering their commercial interest.

The fixed standards imposed on the route subject to that public service obligation shall be set in a transparent and non-discriminatory way.

2. In instances where other modes of transport cannot ensure an uninterrupted service with at least two daily frequencies, the Member States concerned may include in the public service obligation the requirement that any Community air carrier intending to operate the route gives a guarantee that it will operate the route for a certain period, to be specified, in accordance with the other terms of the public service obligation.

3. The necessity and the adequacy of an envisaged public service obligation shall be assessed by the Member State(s) having regard to:

(a) the proportionality between the envisaged obligation and the economic development needs of the region concerned;
(b) the possibility of having recourse to other modes of transport and the ability of such modes to meet the transport needs under consideration, in particular when existing rail services serve the envisaged route with a travel time of less than three hours and with sufficient frequencies, connections and suitable timings;
(c) the air fares and conditions which can be quoted to users;
(d) the combined effect of all air carriers operating or intending to operate on the route.

4. When a Member State wishes to impose a public service obligation, it shall communicate the text of the envisaged imposition of the public service obligation to the Commission, to the other Member States concerned, to the airports concerned and to the air carriers operating the route in question.

The Commission shall publish an information notice in the *Official Journal of the European Union*:

(a) identifying the two airports connected by the route concerned and possible intermediate stop-over point(s);
(b) mentioning the date of entry into force of the public service obligation; and
(c) indicating the complete address where the text and any relevant information and/or documentation related to the public service obligation shall be made available without delay and free of charge by the Member State concerned.

5. Notwithstanding the provisions of paragraph 4, with respect to routes where the number of passengers expected to use the air service is less than 10 000 per annum, the information notice on a public service obligation shall be published either in the *Official Journal of the European Union* or in the national official journal of the Member State concerned.

6. The date of entry into force of a public service obligation shall not be earlier than the date of publication of the information notice referred to in the second subparagraph of paragraph 4.

7. When a public service obligation has been imposed in accordance with paragraphs 1 and 2 the Community air carrier shall be able to offer seat-only sales provided that the air service in question meets all the requirements of the public service obligation. Consequently that air service shall be considered as a scheduled air service.

8. When a public service obligation has been imposed in accordance with paragraphs 1 and 2, any other Community air carrier shall at any time be allowed to commence scheduled air services meeting all the requirements of the public service obligation, including the period of operation that may be required in accordance with paragraph 2.

9. Notwithstanding paragraph 8, if no Community air carrier has commenced or can demonstrate that it is about to commence sustainable scheduled air services on a route in accordance with the public service obligation which has been imposed on that route, the Member State concerned may limit access to the scheduled air services on that route to only one Community air carrier for a period of up to four years, after which the situation shall be reviewed.

This period may be up to five years if the public service obligation is imposed on a route to an airport serving an outermost region, referred to in Article 299(2) of the Treaty.

10. The right to operate the services referred to in paragraph 9 shall be offered by public tender in accordance with Article 17, either singly or, in cases where justified for reasons of operational efficiency, for a group of such routes to any Community air carrier entitled to operate such air services. For reasons of administrative efficiency, a Member State may issue a single invitation to tender covering different routes.

11. A public service obligation shall be deemed to have expired if no scheduled air service has been operated during a period of 12 months on the route subject to such obligation.

12. In case of sudden interruption of service by the Community air carrier selected in accordance with Article 17, the Member State concerned may, in case of emergency, select by mutual agreement a different Community air carrier to operate the public service obligation for a period up to seven months, not renewable, under the following conditions:

(a) any compensation paid by the Member State shall be made in compliance with Article 17(8);
(b) the selection shall be made among Community air carriers in compliance with the principles of transparency and non-discrimination;
(c) a new call for tender shall be launched.

The Commission and the Member State(s) concerned shall be informed without delay of the emergency procedure and of its reasons. At the request of a Member State, or on its own initiative, the Commission may, in accordance with the procedure referred to in Article 25(2) suspend the procedure if it considers after its assessment that it does not meet the requirements of this paragraph or is otherwise contrary to Community law.

Article 17
Public tender procedure for public service obligation

1. The public tender required in Article 16(10) shall be conducted according to the procedure set out in paragraphs 2 to 10 of this Article.

2. The Member State concerned shall communicate the entire text of the invitation to tender to the Commission except where, in accordance with Article 16(5), it has made the public service obligation known through the publication of a notice in its

national official journal. In such case the tender shall also be published in the national official journal.

3. The invitation to tender and the subsequent contract shall cover, inter alia, the following points:

(a) the standards required by the public service obligation;
(b) rules concerning amendment and termination of the contract, in particular to take account of unforeseeable changes;
(c) the period of validity of the contract;
(d) penalties in the event of failure to comply with the contract;
(e) objective and transparent parameters on the basis of which compensation, if any, for the discharging of the public service obligations shall be calculated.

4. The Commission shall make the invitation to tender known through an information notice published in the *Official Journal of the European Union*. The deadline for submission of tenders shall not be earlier than two months after the day of publication of such an information notice. In case the tender concerns a route to which the access had already been limited to one carrier in accordance with Article 16(9), the invitation to tender will be published at least six months before the start of the new concession in order to assess the continued necessity of the restricted access.

5. The information notice shall provide the following information:

(a) Member State(s) concerned;
(b) air route concerned;
(c) period of validity of the contract;
(d) complete address where the text of the invitation to tender and any relevant information and/or documentation related to the public tender and the public service obligation shall be made available by the Member State concerned;
(e) deadline for submission of tenders.

6. The Member State(s) concerned shall communicate without delay and free of charge any relevant information and documents requested by a party interested in the public tender.

7. The selection among the submissions shall be made as soon as possible taking into consideration the adequacy of the service, including the prices and conditions which can be quoted to users, and the cost of the compensation required from the Member State(s) concerned, if any.

8. The Member State concerned may compensate an air carrier, which has been selected under paragraph 7, for adhering to the standards required by a public service obligation imposed under Article 16. Such compensation may not exceed the amount required to cover the net costs incurred in discharging each public service obligation, taking account of revenue relating thereto kept by the air carrier and a reasonable profit.

9. The Commission shall be informed in writing and without delay of the results of the public tender and of the selection by the Member State including the following information:

(a) numbers, names and corporate information of tenderers;
(b) operational elements contained in the offers;
(c) compensation requested in the offers;
(d) name of the selected tenderer.

10. At a request of a Member State or on its own initiative, the Commission may request Member States to communicate, within one month, all relevant documents relating to the selection of an air carrier for the operation of a public service obligation. In case the requested documents are not communicated within the deadline, the Commission may decide to suspend the invitation to tender in accordance with the procedure referred to in Article 25(2).

Article 18
Examination of public service obligations

1. Member States shall take all necessary measures to ensure that any decision taken under Articles 16 and 17 can be reviewed effectively and, in particular, as soon as possible on the grounds that such decisions have infringed Community law or national rules implementing Community law.

In particular, at a request of a Member State or on its own initiative, the Commission may request Member States to communicate, within two months:

(a) a document justifying the need for the public service obligation and its compliance with the criteria mentioned in Article 16;
(b) an analysis of the economy of the region;
(c) an analysis of the proportionality between the envisaged obligations and the economic development objectives;
(d) an analysis of the existing air services, if any, and of the other modes of transport available which could be considered a substitute for the envisaged imposition.

2. At the request of a Member State which considers that the development of a route is being unduly restricted by the terms of Articles 16 and 17, or on its own initiative, the Commission shall carry out an investigation and, within six months of receipt of the request and in accordance with the procedure referred to in Article 25(2), shall take a decision on the basis of all relevant factors on whether Articles 16 and 17 shall continue to apply in respect of the route concerned.

Article 19
Traffic distribution between airports and exercise of traffic rights

1. The exercise of traffic rights shall be subject to published Community, national, regional and local operational rules relating to safety, security, the protection of the environment and the allocation of slots.

2. A Member State, after consultation with interested parties including the air carriers and airports concerned, may regulate, without discrimination among destinations inside the Community or on grounds of nationality or identity of air carriers, the distribution of air traffic between airports satisfying the following conditions:

(a) the airports serve the same city or conurbation;
(b) the airports are served by adequate transport infrastructure providing, to the extent possible, a direct connection making it possible to arrive at the airport within 90 minutes including, where necessary, on a cross-border basis;
(c) the airports are linked to one another and to the city or conurbation they serve by frequent, reliable and efficient public transport services; and
(d) the airports offer necessary services to air carriers, and do not unduly prejudice their commercial opportunities. Any decision to regulate the distribution of air traffic between the airports concerned shall respect the principles of proportionality and transparency, and shall be based on objective criteria.

3. A Member State concerned shall inform the Commission of its intention to regulate the distribution of air traffic or to change an existing traffic distribution rule.

The Commission shall examine the application of paragraphs 1 and 2 of this Article and, within six months of receipt of the information from the Member State, and in accordance with the procedure referred to in Article 25(2), shall decide whether the Member State may apply the measures.

The Commission shall publish its decision in the *Official Journal of the European Union* and the measures shall not be applied before the publication of the Commission's approval.

4. With respect to traffic distribution rules existing at the time of the entry into force of this Regulation, the Commission shall at the request of a Member State and may on its own initiative examine the application of paragraphs 1 and 2 and, in accordance with the procedure referred to in Article 25(2), shall decide whether the Member State may continue to apply the measure.

5. The Commission shall publish its decisions made under this Article in the *Official Journal of the European Union*.

Article 20
Environmental measures

1. When serious environmental problems exist, the Member State responsible may limit or refuse the exercise of traffic rights, in particular when other modes of transport provide appropriate levels of service. The measure shall be non-discriminatory, shall not distort competition between air carriers, shall not be more restrictive than necessary to relieve the problems, and shall have a limited period of validity, not exceeding three years, after which it shall be reviewed.

2. When a Member State considers that action under paragraph 1 is necessary it shall, at least three months before the entry into force of the action, inform the

other Member States and the Commission, providing adequate justification for the action. The action may be implemented unless within one month of receipt of the information a Member State concerned contests the action or the Commission, in accordance with paragraph 3, takes it up for further examination.

3. At the request of another Member State or on its own initiative, the Commission may, in accordance with the procedure referred to in Article 25(2), suspend the measures if they do not meet the requirements of paragraph 1 or are otherwise contrary to Community law.

Article 21
Emergency measures

1. A Member State may refuse, limit or impose conditions on the exercise of traffic rights to deal with sudden problems of short duration resulting from unforeseeable and unavoidable circumstances. Such action shall respect the principles of proportionality and transparency and shall be based on objective and non-discriminatory criteria.

The Commission and the other Member States shall be informed without delay of such action with its adequate justification. If the problems necessitating such action continue to exist for more than 14 days, the Member State shall inform the Commission and the other Member States accordingly and may, with the agreement of the Commission, prolong the action for further periods of up to 14 days.

2. At the request of the Member State(s) involved or on its own initiative, the Commission may suspend this action if it does not meet the requirements of paragraph 1 or is otherwise contrary to Community law.

CHAPTER IV
PROVISIONS ON PRICING

Article 22
Pricing freedom

1. Without prejudice to Article 16(1), Community air carriers and, on the basis of reciprocity, air carriers of third countries shall freely set air fares and air rates for intra-Community air services.

2. Notwithstanding the provisions of bilateral agreements between Member States, Member States may not discriminate on grounds of nationality or identity of air carriers in allowing Community air carriers to set fares and rates for air services between their territory and a third country. Any remaining restrictions on pricing, including with respect to routes to third countries, arising from bilateral agreements between Member States are hereby superseded.

Article 23
Information and non-discrimination

1. Air fares and air rates available to the general public shall include the applicable conditions when offered or published in any form, including on the Internet, for air

services from an airport located in the territory of a Member State to which the Treaty applies. The final price to be paid shall at all times be indicated and shall include the applicable air fare or air rate as well as all applicable taxes, and charges, surcharges and fees which are unavoidable and foreseeable at the time of publication. In addition to the indication of the final price, at least the following shall be specified:

(a) air fare or air rate;
(b) taxes;
(c) airport charges; and
(d) other charges, surcharges or fees, such as those related to security or fuel;where the items listed under (b), (c) and (d) have been added to the air fare or air rate. Optional price supplements shall be communicated in a clear, transparent and unambiguous way at the start of any booking process and their acceptance by the customer shall be on an 'opt-in' basis.

2. Without prejudice to Article 16(1), access to air fares and air rates for air services from an airport located in the territory of a Member State to which the Treaty applies, available to the general public shall be granted without any discrimination based on the nationality or the place of residence of the customer or on the place of establishment of the air carrier's agent or other ticket seller within the Community.

Article 24
Penalties

Member States shall ensure compliance with the rules set out in this Chapter and shall lay down penalties for infringements thereof. Those penalties shall be effective, proportionate and dissuasive.

CHAPTER V
FINAL PROVISIONS

Article 25
Committee

1. The Commission shall be assisted by a committee.

2. Where reference is made to this paragraph, Articles 3 and 7 of Decision 1999/468/EC shall apply, having regard to the provisions of Article 8 thereof.

Article 26
Cooperation and right to obtain information

1. Member States and the Commission shall cooperate in applying and in monitoring the application of this Regulation.

2. In order to carry out its duties under this Regulation the Commission may obtain all necessary information from Member States, which shall also facilitate the

provision of information by air carriers licensed by their competent licensing authorities.

3. Member States shall, according to their national legislation, take the necessary measures to ensure appropriate confidentiality of the information received by them pursuant to this Regulation.

Article 27
Repeal

Regulations (EEC) No 2407/92, (EEC) No 2408/92 and (EEC) No 2409/92 shall be repealed.

References to the repealed Regulations shall be construed as references to this Regulation and shall be read in accordance with the correlation table in Annex II.

Article 28
Entry into force

This Regulation shall enter into force on the day following its publication in the *Official Journal of the European Union*.

This Regulation shall be binding in its entirety and directly applicable in all Member States.

ANNEX I

INFORMATION TO BE PROVIDED PURSUANT TO ARTICLES 5 AND 8

1. Information to be provided by a first-time applicant from a financial fitness point of view
1.1. The most recent internal management accounts and, if available, audited accounts for the previous financial year.
1.2. A projected balance sheet, including profit-and-loss account, for the following three years.
1.3. The basis for projected expenditure and income figures on such items as fuel, fares and rates, salaries, maintenance, depreciation, exchange rate fluctuations, airport charges, air navigation charges, ground handling costs, insurance, etc. Traffic/revenue forecasts.
1.4. Details of the start-up costs incurred in the period from submission of an application to the commencement of operations and an explanation of how it is proposed to finance these costs.
1.5. Details of existing and projected sources of finance.
1.6. Details of shareholders, including nationality and type of shares to be held, and the Articles of Association. If part of a group of undertakings, information on the relationship between them.
1.7. Projected cash-flow statements and liquidity plans for the first three years of operation.
1.8. Details of the financing of aircraft purchase/leasing including, in the case of leasing, the terms and conditions of contract.

2. Information to be provided for assessment of the continuing financial fitness of existing licence holders planning a change in their structures or in their activities with a significant bearing on their finances
2.1. If necessary, the most recent internal management balance sheet and audited accounts for the previous financial year.
2.2. Precise details of all proposed changes e.g. change of type of service, proposed takeover or merger, modifications in share capital, changes in shareholders, etc.
2.3. A projected balance sheet, with a profit-and-loss account, for the current financial year, including all proposed changes in structure or activities with a significant bearing on finances.
2.4. Past and projected expenditure and income figures on such items as fuel, fares and rates, salaries, maintenance, depreciation, exchange rate fluctuations, airport charges, air navigation charges, ground handling costs, insurance, etc. Traffic/revenue forecasts.
2.5. Cash-flow statements and liquidity plans for the following year, including all proposed changes in structure or activities with a significant bearing on finances.
2.6. Details of the financing of aircraft purchase/leasing including, in the case of leasing, the terms and conditions of contract.

3. Information to be provided for assessment of the continuing financial fitness of existing licence holders
3.1. Audited accounts no later than six months following the last day of the relevant financial year, unless otherwise provided for in national law and, if necessary, the most recent internal management balance sheet.
3.2. A projected balance sheet, including profit-and-loss account, for the forthcoming year.
3.3. Past and projected expenditure and income figures on such items as fuel, fares and rates, salaries, maintenance, depreciation, exchange rate fluctuations, airport charges, air navigation charges, ground handling costs, insurance, etc. Traffic/revenue forecasts.
3.4. Cash-flow statements and liquidity plans for the following year.

ANNEX II

CORRELATION TABLE
(Referred to in Article 27)

Regulation (EEC) No 2407/92	*This Regulation*
Article 1(1)	Article 1
Article 1(2)	Article 3(3)
Article 2	Article 2
Article 3(1)	Article 3(2)
Article 3(2)	the second subparagraph of Article 3(1)
Article 3(3)	the first subparagraph of Article 3(1)
Article 4(1)	Article 4
Article 4(2)	Article 4(f)
Article 4(3)	—
Article 4(4)	Article 4(f)
Article 4(5)	the second subparagraph of Article 8(1)
Article 5(1)	Article 5(1)
Article 5(2)	Article 5(2)
Article 5(3)	Article 8(5)
Article 5(4)	Article 8(6)
Article 5(5)	Article 9(1)
Article 5(6)	Article 8(4)
Article 5(7)	Article 5(3) and Article 8(8)
Article 6	Article 7
Article 7	Article 11
Article 8(1)	Article 4(c)
Article 8(2)	Article 12(1)
Article 8(3)	Article 13(2) and (3)
Article 8(4)	Article 12(2)
Article 9	Article 6
Article 10(1)	Article 13(2) and (3)
Article 10(2)	Article 13(2) and (3)
Article 11(1)	Article 8(1)
Article 11(2)	Article 8(3)
Article 11(3)	Article 8(7)
Article 12	Articles 9(2) to (6)
Article 13(1)	Article 10(2)
Article 13(2)	Article 10(1)
Article 13(3)	—
Article 13(4)	Article 10(3)
Article 14	—
Article 15	—
Article 16	—

Regulation (EEC) No 2407/92	*This Regulation*
Article 17	—
Article 18(1)	Article 26(1)
Article 18(2)	Article 26(3)
Article 19	—
ANNEX	ANNEX I

Regulation (EEC) No 2408/92	*This Regulation*
Article 1(1)	Article 1
Article 1(2)	Article 1(2)
Article 1(3)	—
Article 1(4)	—
Article 2	Article 2
Article 3(1)	Article 15(1) and (2)
Article 3(2)	—
Article 3(3)	—
Article 3(4)	—
Article 4(1)(a)	Article 16(1)
Article 4(1)(b)	Article 16(3)
Article 4(1)(c)	Article 16(2)
Article 4(1)(d)	Article 16(9)
—	Article 17(1)
—	Article 17(2)
—	Article 17(4)
—	Article 17(5)
—	Article 17(6)
Article 4(1)(e)	Article 17(3)
Article 4(1)(f)	Article 17(7)
Article 4(1)(g)	—
Article 4(1)(h)	Article 17(8)
—	Article 17(9)
—	Article 17(10)
Article 4(1)(i)	Article 18(1)
Article 4(1)(j)	Article 16(7)
Article 4(1)(k)	—
Article 4(2)	—
Article 4(3)	Article 18(2)
Article 4(4)	—
Article 5	—
Article 6(1) and (2)	—

Regulation (EEC) No 2408/92	*This Regulation*
Article 7	Article 15(4) and (5)
Article 8(1)	Article 19(2)
Article 8(2) Article 19(1)	
Article 8(3)	Article 19(3)
Article 8(4)	—
Article 8(5)	—
Article 9(1)	Article 20(1)
Article 9(2)	Article 20(1)
Article 9(3)	Article 20(2)
Article 9(4)	Article 20(3)
Article 9(5)	Article 22(1)
Article 9(6)	Article 22(2)
Article 9(7)	—
Article 9(8)	—
Article 10	—
Article 11	Article 25
Article 12(1)	Article 26(2)
Article 12(2)	—
Article 13	—
Article 14(1)	Article 26(1)
Article 14(2)	Article 26(3)
Article 15	—
Article 16	—
ANNEX I	—
ANNEX II	—
ANNEX III	—
—	ANNEX II

Regulation (EEC) No 2409/92	*This Regulation*
Article 1(1)	Article 1
Article 1(2)	Article 21(1)
Article 1(3)	—
Article 2	Article 2
Article 3	—
Article 4	Article 23
Article 5(1)	Article 22
Article 5(2)	—
Article 5(3)	—
Article 5(4)	—

Regulation (EEC) No 2409/92	*This Regulation*
Article 6	—
Article 7	—
Article 8	—
Article 9	—
Article 10(1)	Article 26(1)
Article 10(2)	Article 26(3)
Article 11	—
Article 12	—
—	Article 27
—	Article 28

Index

B

D

R

V

W

Y